Latin American Foreign Policies

Latin American Foreign Policies
An Analysis

Harold Eugene Davis
and Larman C. Wilson

with coauthors Victor Alba, G. Pope Atkins, David Bushnell, Orville G. Cope, Edith B. Couturier, Thomas J. Dodd, W. Raymond Duncan, John J. Finan, Roy Arthur Glasgow, E. James Holland, Hans J. Hoyer, Thomas L. Karnes, Sheldon B. Liss, Mary Jeanne Reid Martz, Alberto M. Piedra, and Brady B. Tyson

THE JOHNS HOPKINS UNIVERSITY PRESS
Baltimore and London

The Johns Hopkins University Press, Baltimore, Maryland 21218
The Johns Hopkins University Press Ltd., London

Library of Congress Catalog Card Number 74-24386
ISBN 0-8018-1694-7 (clothbound)
ISBN 0-8018-1695-5 (paperbound)

Library of Congress Cataloging in Publication data
will be found on the last printed page of this book.

This book is gratefully dedicated
to the students
who contributed so largely
to its creation

Contents

Preface

The authors' purpose in this study is to examine Latin American international and foreign policy, country by country, analyzing the problems the nations confront, their policies for dealing with these problems, and the positions they assume in their relations with one another, with other countries of the world, and with international organizations. We believe that this work is original in approach and that its equivalent is not found in English, Spanish, or Portuguese.

The authors were moved to undertake this project by the realization, after years of teaching courses on Latin American foreign policy and international relations, that little useful material is available on the subject and, in particular, that no suitable manuals or reference works exist—not even a comprehensive bibliographical guide. It is true that the foreign relations of the Latin American nations have been studied in the United States since the 1920s, but usually from the standpoint of U.S. foreign policy or within the context of U.S.-Latin American relations, rather than from the policy perspective of the Latin American nations.

The scholars who contributed to this book were selected because of their known interest in the subjects they were asked to write upon. A nuclear group of five is from The American University; the other authors are from institutions across the country. Some are younger scholars, others are senior scholars in the field. This generation span gives the work the points of view of two generations of scholarship. The authorship is also diverse in the sense of including historians, political scientists, and an economist and in representing different intellectual and theoretical perspectives. We believe that this interdisciplinary and theoretical diversity is an asset to our book. We have not sought to impose uniformity of policy views upon the authors but have asked only that they address themselves to the same questions.

The chapters in this book have been used experimentally a number of times, in Xerox form, as the major text in a course on the international relations of Latin America at The American University—a course for advanced undergraduates and beginning graduate students. In this class the collection has been tested and criticized several times with a view toward its improvement. Its use convinced us that it fills a definite gap in the literature and provides a useful teaching resource—one that students have responded to in a positive way. On the basis of this use and the valuable student criticisms herewith gratefully acknowledged, the book was expanded, updated, and completely rewritten. Bibliographical notes have been added to remedy in part the lack of a comprehensive bibliographical guide to the field.

Our debts to colleagues and peers for their assistance are too numerous to mention individually, but we are particularly grateful to Dr. Robert W. Gregg, dean of the School of International Service of The American University, for his encouragement and support of this project when it was originally proposed for classroom use. We also thank the two anonymous readers selected by the Johns Hopkins University Press for their helpful suggestions for improving the manuscript. Finally, we thank our coauthors for their fine cooperation and patience in bearing with us through two revisions of the text.

Harold Eugene Davis
Larman C. Wilson

Contributors

Harold Eugene Davis, University Professor Emeritus of Latin American Studies at The American University, has written numerous books on Latin American history and government and on inter-American relations. He headed the Division of Education in the Office of the Coordinator of Inter-American Affairs (1943–46), has been a Fulbright lecturer in Chile (1958–59) and India (1965–66), and has lectured at the National University of Mexico (1962). Among his many books on Latin America are *History of Latin America* (1968), *Government and Politics in Latin America* (1958), and *Latin American Thought: A Historical Introduction* (1973 and 1974).

Larman C. Wilson, professor of international relations at the School of International Service, The American University, specializes in international law and organization and in inter-American relations. He has done research in the Dominican Republic and Mexico and has traveled extensively in Latin America and Europe. His publications include articles on inter-American relations, and he is the coauthor of *The United States and the Trujillo Regime* (1972).

Victor Alba, professor of political science at Kent State University, is an internationally known writer and lecturer. Born in Spain and long a resident of Mexico, he directed the *Revista Panoramas* in Mexico City and has lectured in every Latin American country. Among his many books are *Politics and the Labor Movement in Latin America* (1969), *The Latin Americans* (1970), and *Catalonia* (1974).

G. Pope Atkins is professor of political science at the U.S. Naval Academy. He lived in Argentina and Ecuador for three years. He is the coauthor of *The United States and the Trujillo Regime* (1972) and "The Armed Forces in Latin American Politics" in *Civil-Military Relations*, ed. Charles L. Cochran (1974).

David Bushnell is professor of history at the University of Florida. He has specialized in the history of Colombia and is the author of *The Santander Regime in Gran Colombia* (1954). He has translated from the Spanish *Eduardo Santos and the Good Neighbor* (1967).

Orville G. Cope is chairman of the Department of Political Science at the College of Idaho. He conducted research in Argentina, Brazil, and Chile in the 1960s. In addition to his articles on Chile, he has written *Coalition Formation, Christian Democracy, and the 1970 Presidential Election in Chile* (1972).

Edith B. Couturier, holder of a doctorate in Latin American history from Columbia University, has offered courses on Latin American diplomatic history at The American University. She was awarded a Doherty Foundation Grant for research in Mexico (1956-58) and has traveled in Central America. The product of her research on Mexican social history has appeared in *Historia Mexicana* and in the *Encyclopedia of Latin American History*.

Thomas J. Dodd is a professor in the School of Foreign Service, Georgetown University. His teaching has included courses in Mexican history at the Institute for Advanced Studies, Guadalajara, Mexico. He has advised the Agency for International Development on library resources in Central America and has traveled throughout Latin America. His research has been on Mexico and early Colombian-Panamanian relations.

W. Raymond Duncan is professor of political science at the State University of New York (Brockport). He has conducted research in Mexico and several South American countries. In addition to articles on Cuba and on Soviet policy in Latin America, he has edited *Soviet Policy in Developing Countries* (1970) and coedited *The Quest for Change in Latin America* (1970).

John J. Finan is professor of Latin American studies at the School of International Service, The American University. He has served as political officer in the U.S. embassy in Colombia (1958-61). His special areas of research are Latin American diplomatic history and the history of Latin American land systems, particularly in Argentina and Mexico.

Roy Arthur Glasgow is professor of history at Boston University. He has traveled in the Caribbean, Mexico, and South America and has specialized in the study of Guyana. He is the author of *Guyana: Race and Politics Among Africans and East Indians* (1970).

E. James Holland is a dean and a professor in the Department of Government, Angelo State University (Texas). He has been the recipient of an OAS Fellowship for research in Bolivia (1966). His research has centered on the foreign relations of Bolivia in the Chaco War.

Hans J. Hoyer, who teaches Latin American history at George Mason University, was in the Peace Corps in Chile (1966-68) and was awarded an OAS Fellowship for research in the Plate countries (1974). He has contributed to the *Area Handbook for Bolivia* (1974) and the *Area Handbook for Argentina* (1975).

Thomas L. Karnes is professor of history at the Arizona State University and has specialized in the study of Central America. Two of his major books are *The Failure of Union, Central America, 1824-1960* (1961) and *The Latin American Policy of the United States* (1972).

Sheldon B. Liss, professor of history at the University of Akron, has done research on several Latin American countries and has traveled widely in Latin America. He has written *A Century of Disagreement: The Chamizal Conflict, 1864-1964* (1965) and *The Canal: Aspects of United States-Panamanian Relations* (1967) and is coauthor of *Man, State, and Society in Latin American History* (1972).

Mary Jeanne Reid Martz teaches in the Department of Political Science at Clemson University. Her doctoral dissertation at Duke University was on "The Pacific Settlement of Controversies in the Inter-American System, 1948-1970" (1971), and she has done research in the Andean countries.

Alberto M. Piedra is professor of economics at The Catholic University of America. Born in Cuba, he has been an economist at the Organization of American States and a consultant for the Inter-American Development Bank. He has written on Latin American economic topics and has edited *Socio-Economic Change in Latin America* (1970).

Brady B. Tyson, professor of Latin American studies at the School of International Service, The American University, spent four years working among university students in Brazil (1961-66). His writings, which are mainly on Brazil, include "The Emerging Role of the Military as National Modernizers and Managers in Latin America: The Cases of Brazil and Peru" in *Latin American Prospects for the 1970s: What Kinds of Revolutions?* ed. David H. Pollock and Arch R. M. Ritter (1973).

General and Background Aspects

I/Harold Eugene Davis

The Analysis of Latin American Foreign Policies

PURPOSE OF THIS BOOK

This volume presents a view of the international relations and the foreign policies of the nations that lie to the south of the United States, which are commonly, though inaccurately, known as Latin America. The authors have attempted to look at these policy questions from the standpoint of the individual Latin American nations. Since the task seemed too great for a single scholar to carry out, given the lack of suitable monographic material to draw upon, a total of sixteen specialists have agreed to treat the countries (or groups of countries) of their speciality. These authors are political scientists, historians, and economists.

Although the literature on Latin American relations is abundant (much of it in English), little of it is devoted to serious analysis of the foreign policies of the individual nations. Works in English have tended to emphasize the problems of U.S. policy in these hemispheric relations, frequently treating the area as a unit. A large proportion of the studies have been historical, treating such general topics as British, French, or U.S. policy toward Hispanic-American independence or the relations of the United States (occasionally of other countries) toward individual nations. These latter studies, such as those of James M. Callahan, Arthur P. Whitaker, J. Fred Rippy, Frederick B. Pike, Lawrence F. Hill, Henry Clay Evans, Rayford Logan, E. Taylor Parks, Thomas F. McGann, Harold F. Peterson, and Howard F. Cline, are useful for the authors' purposes, but they are only too obviously oriented toward U.S. policy.[1]

Nor have Latin American scholars provided much guidance in the form of policy studies of their own countries; with a few notable

---

1. Such works as the following: James M. Callahan, *American Foreign Policy in Mexican Relations* (New York: Macmillan Co., 1932); Howard F. Cline, *The United States and Mexico*, rev. ed. (Cambridge: Harvard University Press, 1963); Henry Clay Evans, *Chile and the United States* (Durham, N.C.: Duke University Press, 1927); Charles C. Griffin, *The United States and the Disruption of the Spanish Empire, 1810–1822* (New York: Columbia University Press, 1937); Lawrence F. Hill, *Diplomatic Relations between the United States and Brazil* (Durham, N.C.: Duke University Press, 1932); Rayford Logan, *Diplomatic Relations of the United States and Haiti, 1776–1891* (Chapel Hill: University of North Carolina Press, 1941); Thomas F. McGann, *Argentina, the United States, and the Inter-American System, 1890–1914* (Cambridge: Harvard University Press, 1957); E. Taylor Parks, *Colombia and the United States, 1765–1934* (Durham, N.C.: Duke University Press, 1935); Frederick B. Pike, *Chile and the United States* (Notre Dame, Ind.: Notre Dame University

3

exceptions, their works have been merely historical (or polemical, as is the rather extensive literature directed against the "imperialism" of the United States). A few scholars, notably Mexican, Argentine, and Brazilian, have attempted policy analyses, and in recent years some well-considered statements have been made by Latin American presidents in annual messages to Congress. With such materials our authors have had to work, and given the fragmentary character of these sources, they have had to work with caution.[2]

Two major preoccupations of the United States account in part for a distorted U.S. concept of Latin America in international affairs. One, dating from the time of independence, is a fear that the area south of the border might fall under the control of a hostile power or powers and threaten the United States in a military sense. Thus, today, we have the Inter-American Treaty of Reciprocal Assistance, the Inter-American Defense Board, and the Inter-American Defense College. Thus, too, the umbrella of U.S. nuclear defense has made possible a treaty agreement among the Latin American nations barring nuclear weapons. Yet, even in the area of military defense, the most significant agreements in terms of concrete power are binational—U.S. agreements with individual nations under which military assistance is provided. Nor has a threat to security been conceived by the United States merely as a military threat. Political threats supported from outside America—monarchism, renewed European colonialism in the nineteenth century, fascism and various forms of revolutionary communism in the twentieth century—have also contributed to the unrealistic U.S. consideration of Latin America as a unity. New economic inroads made by rising industrial powers have had a similar effect.

The second preoccupation of U.S. policy that has led to thinking of Latin America as a global whole may be described as a kind of subsuming of the end sought. Since the days of Blaine and Garfield, but more particularly since World War I, some U.S. leaders, in and out of government, have been obsessed with the idea that Latin America should be unified in friendly relations to the United States, thus becoming a source of strength to the United States rather than a threat to her security. But in this respect, too, the concept of a wholistic Latin America lacks reality; it has been realistic only in so far as the Latin American nations have elected to act as a unit. This they have done infrequently.

Press, 1963); Harold F. Peterson, *Argentina and the United States, 1810–1960* (Albany: State University of New York Press, 1964); J. Fred Rippy, *The United States and Mexico* (New York: Alfred A. Knopf, 1926); Robert F. Smith, *The United States and Cuba: Business and Diplomacy, 1917–1960* (New York: Bookman Associates, 1960); Arthur P. Whitaker, *The United States and Argentina* (Cambridge: Harvard University Press, 1954).

2. A scanty but increasing literature deals with the comparative analysis of foreign policies. See, for example, Richard L. Merrit, *Systematic Approaches to Comparative Politics* (Chicago: Rand McNally, 1970), esp. chaps. 1 and 7.

THE "LATIN" AND "FAMILY
OF NATIONS" STEREOTYPES

Even to suggest the value of a comparative analysis of Latin American foreign policies raises this basic question: do the nations that occupy the area south of the United States have enough in common to justify studying them together, let alone calling them "Latin"? It is well to begin by noting that the idea of a "Latin" America is a great overgeneralization, if not a meaningless stereotype, for Latin America is far from being consistently Latin in ethnic origin, in language, or in culture. Nor are the nations enough alike in the state of their economic development or in the style of their political life to justify the assumption that they will pursue the same policy objectives.

The native tongues of millions of Latin Americans include such non-Latin languages as English, Dutch, Quechua, Aymará, Guaraní, Otomie, and Maya. In Mexico, Guatemala, Ecuador, Peru, Paraguay, and Bolivia, persons of indigenous or mixed Amerindian-European ancestry, many of whom speak indigenous languages, outnumber those of unmixed European ancestry. In northeastern Brazil, Haiti, Jamaica, Trinidad, parts of Cuba, and other areas of the Caribbean, persons of African ancestry predominate. In Guyana and Trinidad, East Indians (from India) vie with Afro-Americans for numerical predominance, while Amerindians (the indígenes) and Europeans constitute small minorities. Manuel González Prada, one of Peru's most noted intellectuals, once composed this humorous imaginary epitaph to illustrate the irony of calling his country Latin:

Aquí descansa Manongo
De pura raza latina.
Su madre vino del Congo
Su abuelo emigró de China.[3]

(Here lies Manongo
Of pure Latin race.
His mother came from the Congo,
His grandfather hailed from China).

Some nations of this "Latin" America have extremely low levels of per capita national product, while others have levels that compare not unfavorably with those of developed Western nations. Some are highly urbanized, others are predominantly rural. Constitutional representative government has operated successfully in some countries, while authori-

---

3. Quoted in Luis Alberto Sánchez, *Perú, retrato de un país adolescente* (Lima: Universidad Nacional de San Marcos, 1963).

tarian rule of various types has been more characteristic of others, even over long periods of time.

Another stereotypic concept in the thinking about the area is that the nations of Latin America constitute a "family." In one sense this is true, for eighteen of the twenty-five nations come from what was once the Spanish empire in America (nineteen, if Puerto Rico is included). These nations, moreover, have two-thirds of the population and the territory. In this family sense, Brazil, the largest nation, is a cousin once or twice removed, while French-speaking Haiti is more like an outcast from the essentially Spanish circle. The new English-speaking nations of the Caribbean area are probably closer to Haiti in an ethnic and sociological (but not a linguistic) sense than to Spanish America. But they differ markedly from Haiti, the oldest "Latin" nation, in language, politics, and economy. On the whole, the concept of the family must therefore be regarded at least partly as a myth, especially insofar as it concerns the relationship with the United States. It is a useful myth, however, and true in the sense that it helps to give meaning to a kind of marriage of convenience or necessity between the United States and the nations to the south in the Organization of American States (OAS). In the OAS, the nations take on the semblance of a family, psychologically speaking, by sharing an ambivalent relationship of attraction and repulsion toward their powerful northern neighbor.

The distorted and unrealistic U.S. view of Latin American foreign relations has been increased, if anything, by much of the current criticism of the Latin American policy of the United States—criticism which, while justified to a degree, lacks realism because it all too often overlooks facts of Latin American history and politics. Again, the tendency to present Latin America as a whole (or merely as part of the developing world) has distorted reality.

To rectify this distortion, the authors of this book propose that students approach the international relations of the area by analyzing the problems presented to each nation in its relations with other nations and the policies that evolve from confronting these problems. But, in view of the authors' individual approaches and diverse disciplinary backgrounds, the editors have tried to give some uniformity to the work by asking each author to deal with certain basic questions. Accordingly, the authors have been asked to examine along four lines the foreign policies pursued by Latin American nations and the OAS. Although they are distinguishable, these are four closely interrelated lines of analysis. Formulated as questions, they are as follows:

1. What are the major international problems confronted by the nation?
2. What are the historical antecedents—the major problems confronted in the past that have produced settled doctrine or policy positions?

3. How do the forces of domestic politics, including those of interest groups, affect the formulation of foreign policy, and what is the process of formulation in the nation studied?
4. How does the nation view her position today in relations with other nations, regions, and international organizations?

The collaborating authors agreed to follow the foregoing outline, but the critical reader will quickly discover considerable differences in the way the outline has been developed. In part, the differences reflect the varied academic backgrounds of the authors. Although all have broad interdisciplinary interests, differences in emphasis and treatment of historical and economic aspects of policy are a natural result of disciplinary specializations. Other differences result from the distinct theoretical and methodological approaches used, which involve differing views of the nature and dynamics of politics and policy formulation and distinct perspectives and concerns in policy analysis.

DEFINING THE PROBLEMS

In pursuing the first line of analysis, that of discovering and defining the problems confronted by a given country in its external relations, the problems have been analyzed in a variety of ways in order to understand the preoccupations that govern each nation's international behavior and the ends its policies seek to achieve. In the present-day world of almost instantaneous communication, these foreign relations range, in varying degrees of tension and importance, from those with immediate neighbors; to those with more remote powers, great and small; to those with international organizations. The gamut of the problems to be confronted and the decisions to be made would make the eyes of Prince Metternich, or even Lord Salisbury, pop with amazement were he to come alive in this amazingly tragic late twentieth century. The brief treatment imposed by limitations of space makes it difficult for this book to do much more than enumerate and define some of the major problems. They range from complicated border controversies to questions that affect all the cultural, social, political, military, and economic activities of the times. The difficulty of even modest success in definition is complicated, and the definitions themselves are obscured, by the widely differing conditions in and objectives of the countries with which relations are conducted.

Many of these problems (as will become apparent in subsequent chapters), if not actually shared in the sense of bringing a multilateral confrontation, are shared in a general sense by many of the countries. They all, for example, except for the island republics of Cuba, Jamaica, and Trinidad and Tobago, have had serious boundary problems with their neighbors. Although few of these boundary issues are serious today, most of the nations have difficulty controlling immigration and trade across their borders. All, in varying degrees, have policy problems affecting foreign capital investment and loans—both public and private— the regulation of foreign corporations, and currency exchange. These problems vary from country to country, depending on the nation's state of economic development, the state of her credit, the nature of her exports, and the extent to which she has nationalized her economy and carried out extensive programs of land redistribution. All, again in varying degrees, suffer from real or imagined dependency on the more industrialized nations, particularly the United States, even though they occasionally manage to maintain a united stance. As in the past, most of the nations today find subversive elements, often with links outside their borders, working to effect (or prevent) revolutionary change.

In recent years, the control of fishing and offshore drilling for petroleum in coastal waters and the extension of this control far beyond the traditional territorial waters have become important questions for many of the nations. For Spanish-, Portuguese-, and French-speaking nations, questions of church policy toward the Vatican have special importance. The authoritarian regimes existing in Spain and Portugal have posed special problems for Spanish America and Brazil. Haiti's policy of emphasizing *négritude* in her relations with the new nations of Africa has had significant implications for the other nations with large Afro-American polulations.

HISTORICAL ANTECEDENTS

The second line of analysis is historical. One of the distinctive historical experiences that gave a "family" character to the Spanish-American nations was their position as "orphans" within the larger family of nations at the time of independence. Both Spain and the Vatican withheld formal recognition of them for ten to twenty-five years, and in some cases much longer, while first the United States and then Great Britain moved to recognize them promptly—in a sense, to "adopt" them. France withheld recognition of Haiti for many years and then granted it only on harsh economic terms. Portugal, however, recognized the independence of Brazil promptly. But the fact that Spanish America was isolated even from Spain during much of the Napoleonic period contributed further to making the new nations appear like international orphans. Partly as a result of this isolation, the Latin American nations, even after 1835, were generally considered by Europe to have little importance as states. In fact, the first effective appearance of Latin American states in a general international conference came more than three-quarters of a century after independence, in the Second Hague Peace Conference (1907).

The European attitude was not one of benign neglect, however. Hence, the relations of the emerging Latin American nations with the nations of Europe during and immediately following independence were a fundamental factor in shaping the basic lines of their national policies. Latin Americans learned early the game of playing these powers one against the other, and they did so with varying degrees of success during the age of Metternich. During the nineteenth century, political weakness and civil strife invited armed intervention by Britain, France, and Spain, often with the object of establishing colonies or protectorates. Few of the nations escaped the need to ward off such threats. Occasionally, they were able to draw the United States in to support them and occasionally, as in Mexico in the 1830s and 40s and in Central America during the 1850s, intervention came *from* the United States.

After the overthrow of the French-supported empire of Maximilian in Mexico (1867), overt threats of recolonization ceased, giving way to the more indirect forms of economic penetration. By the time of the First World War, Britain had achieved a predominant place in Latin American economic life through a capital investment of some $5,000 million. Already, however, the growing power of the United States, both political and economic, was bringing changes in Latin American policy toward Europe, signaled by Brazil's raising her diplomatic mission to the United States to ambassadorial status and assigning Joaquim Nabuco as the first ambassador. The role of Nabuco in strengthening the U.S. position in Latin America was paralleled by that of Porfirian Mexico in urging the United States to mediate in South American controversies and to play a larger role in Central America.

From the war of 1898 until the Second World War, the Latin American nations confronted an informal entente of Britain and the United States on Latin American matters. After the First World War, however, this Anglo-American power was challenged from two quarters—the growing economic and Fascist nationalism of Germany and Italy (with support from Franco's Spain and Salazar's Portugal) and the increasing international influence of the Communist Soviet Union, as expressed in the growth of Latin American Communist and other Marxist-oriented parties. After 1935 the Comintern policy of encouraging Communist party participation in Popular Front governments gave the Soviet relationship greater importance, for a time, in Chile, Cuba, Spain, and even in Mexico. But it brought no major shift in national policies. On the one hand, the increasing threat of communism and other movements from the Left tended to bring together the old Liberals and the Conservative Catholics who wanted to delay or prevent relations with the Soviet Union. On the other hand, the questions presented by the Fascist powers' trade and propaganda drives pitted Conservatives against Liberals, except insofar as anti-Yankee propaganda could bring them together in a kind of fanatical xenophobia.

In the years immediately following World War II, the preponderant power of the United States and the issues of the cold war seemed at times to reduce the nations to the status of satellites. Moreover, because of their preoccupation with international aspects of economic development and because international agencies were playing a larger role, the nations confronted new and complex issues of policy, calling for decisions difficult to make and carry out without U.S. support. At the same time, revolutionary political forces and movements, erupting from both ends of the political spectrum, often seemed able to dictate foreign policy decisions or at least to impose a veto on them. Frequently, these changes seemed merely to create tensions between the Latin American nations and the United States, while doing little or nothing to formulate policies to improve the relations of one Latin American nation with another or with nations in other parts of the world.

Until World War I, the nations of Europe claimed a right to intervene in the Latin American nations to defend the rights of their nationals and to enforce the payment of debts owed by the Latin American governments. Britain, Germany, and Italy were the chief actors, although other nations claimed the right under international law and participated in an intervention in Venezuela in the winter of 1902-3. The United States also claimed this right and, under the Monroe Doctrine, did not oppose such interventions unless they threatened to lead to permanent control of the intervened country. By the late nineteenth century, however, Argentina had proposed the multilateral adoption of the principle of international law, formulated by her foreign minister, Luis María Drago, that the public debt did not allow the right of intervention. Argentina openly expressed support of the Drago principle at the time of the Venezuelan claims controversy, and the American states came gradually to adopt it, broadening it into a general proscription of intervention. After World War I, the nations of Europe rarely asserted the old right of intervention, while the interventionist policy of the United States in the Caribbean area made interventionism largely an issue of United States–Latin American relations. The outcome of the controversy over U.S. intervention was a broad prohibition of intervention, written into the Inter-American Convention on the Rights and Duties of States in 1933, making antiintervention a basic principle of the policies of all the American nations and thus constituting a basic principle of the evolving inter-American system.

During the early years of their national life, boundary problems held high priority in the foreign relations of all the nations except Cuba, Jamaica, and Trinidad, producing wars and resulting in problems of irredenta and revanche, some of which still trouble their relations. In South America, Brazilian expansionism at the expense of Spanish America accounted for a number of these boundary controversies. The Paraguayan War was one result. Chilean expansionism ranked second only to that of Brazil as a source of such conflicts, notably the War of the Pacific. The expansionism of the United States led to Mexico's loss of Texas and the U.S. Southwest. Mexico, on the other hand, created a comparable issue in her relations with Guatemala, while British claims to Belize troubled both Mexico and Guatemala. The international legal principle of *uti possidetis* guided the Spanish-American and Brazilian approaches to the settlement of these early boundary problems, but Brazil gave the principle a meaning quite different from that given it by the Spanish-American nations. For the latter, it meant acceptance of provincial boundaries defined by the Spanish crown in the year 1810. For Brazil, it meant something closer to the right of adverse possession, as developed in Anglo-American law.

FOREIGN POLICY FORMULATION

The third line of analysis proposed is that of policy formulation. Although foreign policy, or at least some parts of it, is usually formulated with less open discussion than that given to domestic policy, the authors of this book have been asked to assume that foreign policy formulation is neither more mysterious than, nor essentially different as a political process from, the formulation of domestic policy. Analysis may therefore follow patterns similar to those employed in studying decision making on domestic issues. As a caveat against oversimplification, however, it must be added that since the elements to be analyzed, the issues involved, and the aggregates of demand often differ significantly from the international to the national scene, it can not be assumed that foreign and domestic policy formulation will always follow the same process or involve the same forces in the same proportions in the same country. Differences are to be expected, even though in the long run foreign policy tends to be an outward projection of domestic politics.

When foreign policy formulation is analyzed from the standpoint of such formative forces as the national power structure and the value systems and biases implanted in national psychology, at least three major kinds of facts emerge for consideration: (1) psychological residues from past international experiences, and doctrinal positions derived from them; (2) pressures exerted by other countries or groups of countries (allies, enemies, or neither), touching on real or imaginary interests; and (3) political pressures exerted from within a country by national forces. When the analysis is made from the standpoint of process it is harder to generalize, despite constitutional similarities. The process differs from country to country because of differences in political climate and patterns of political behavior, in the strength or weakness of government, in preoccupations derived from past experience, in the political style of leadership, and in the extent to which foreign policy in general, or a given question in particular, becomes a vital issue in national politics. Some nations are more successful than others in separating foreign policy from national politics. All nations are able to do so on some issues that generate little political heat.

The prevailing pattern of government in Latin America—with rare exceptions, even under authoritarian regimes—is that of the unipersonal presidential system, which combines the positions of head of state and head of government in one person. Constitutions generally charge the president with responsibility for the conduct of foreign relations. This function is of course assumed by a provisional executive under dictatorial systems, whether within or without the formal constitution. The president invariably acts through a foreign minister, and this minister is usually the voice of the president on all major questions. Yet, some countries have had ministers whose personal influence has been a major factor in formulating basic policy. The list of such ministers would in fact be rather long and would include, among others, such notable figures as the Baron de Rio Branco of Brazil, Luis Drago of Argentina, and Baltasar Brum of Uruguay. Although this strong leadership has been much less common in most countries, few nations, if any, have failed to produce at least one foreign minister who gave distinction to this office. In recent years, the increased complexity and enlarged volume of international relations, together with professionalization in the diplomatic corps, has tended to give ministers more autonomy in some of the major countries, so that more matters are now handled routinely, without reference to the president, than was previously the case.

All member nations of the OAS are committed by its Charter to representative government. But the popular role in politics varies considerably from nation to nation and from time to time. In all countries a power elite, varying somewhat in composition from nation to nation, comprises military leaders, business entrepreneurs, large landowners, cattlemen, clergymen, politicians of various kinds (including members of Congress and state legislators), bureaucrats, and labor leaders. In one way or another they exercise considerable influence upon the formulation of both domestic and foreign policy.

Congresses participate in policy formation, their actual influence varying considerably according to the degree of presidential power—and the degree of this power varies not only from country to country but also from one period to another in the same country. Congresses control appropriations, often more than some foreign observers have thought. Congressional approval is commonly required for the appointment of foreign ministers and ambassadors. The approval of one or both houses of Congress is necessary for the ratification of treaties, and treaties have often failed to win this approval. The record of the Argentine Congress in refusing approval of treaties is particularly notable.

Although interest groups in Latin America have generally lacked the organization and strength of those in the United States, they make their influence felt in various ways—through direct contact with the president or the foreign minister, through speeches and personal contacts with their representatives in Congress, and through the press, radio, and television. Church officials also make their views known in many ways. Papal nuncios occasionally convey policy views of the Vatican on other than church matters; these papal views may also come through Latin American diplomatic representatives in Rome. The armed services, through spokesmen in the cabinets, have exercised increasing influence on foreign policy formation in recent years. Army pressure, for example, forced President Arturo Frondizi of Argentina to reverse Argentina's position on the expulsion of Cuba from the OAS in 1962. The *golpe* that drove Peruvian President Fernando Belaunde Terry from office in 1968 was directed in part against the course he was following in the settlement of a major international problem in relation to a foreign-owned petroleum company (International Petroleum Company).

POLICY RELATING TO VARIOUS COUNTRIES AND REGIONS

The fourth line of analysis pursued in this book examines the policies followed by a given nation in its relations with other nations and regions in respect to major specific issues that confront it. This examination, though carried out differently by each author, attempts, first of all, to identify and define policy positions, separating tactics from the broader, long-range strategies and separating the rhetoric of public discussion from the courses actually pursued. It then analyzes the positions so defined in relation to the ends of policy; the influences that affected the formulation of the positions, including the doctrine derived from historical experience; the power available for maintaining these positions; and the several priorities assigned to them. If the treatment of this fourth line of analysis is less complete than the reader would wish, it is because of the limitations of space imposed on each author and because the authors have usually concentrated on the first two lines of analysis.[4]

BOUNDARY PROBLEMS

Today, the most important boundary problems are questions of irredenta, such as Ecuador's claim against Peru, Bolivia's claims against Chile, Paraguay's claim against Argentina and Brazil, Venezuela's claim against

4. J. Fred Rippy, *British Capital Investments in Latin America, 1822–1949* (Minneapolis: University of Minnesota Press, 1959).

Guyana, and Guatemala's claim to Belize. Some of the most difficult of
these irredenta questions, such as those of Ecuador and Venezuela just
mentioned, arise from questioning the validity of treaty settlements
previously ratified by both parties to the conflicts. Other questions relate
to unmarked boundaries for which treaties do not provide a clear
definition, as in portions of the mountain boundary between Chile and
Argentina. Probably the most troublesome of the irredenta problems, the
Tacna-Arica controversy that troubled the relations of Chile and Peru
(and so those of the rest of America) for three decades, was a holdover from
the War of the Pacific (1879–83). Happily, it was settled in 1929 by a
compromise agreement between the two countries.

RELATIONS WITH THE UNITED STATES

A complex of problems concerning the relations of the Latin American
nations with their powerful northern neighbor has emerged as their
greatest international preoccupation of the twentieth century. These
relations cover a wide range of political, cultural, and economic questions. They include hemisphere defense, the issues raised by the cold war
and by the Cuban Revolution, the problem of establishing a hemisphere
court of human rights, questions connected with the existence of such
military-naval bases as Guantánamo in Cuba, and the special problems of
the existing and proposed Panama canals. Economic problems embrace
all aspects of the Alliance for Progress and affect the Central American
Common Market and other subregional arrangements—the Andean
Group, the Latin American Free Trade Association (LAFTA), the proposed Latin American Common Market, the Caribbean Free Trade
Association (CARIFTA). A central issue in all these arrangements, at least
in the past, has been U.S. capital investment. When the flow of British
capital investment into Latin America diminished in the early years of
this century, the United States became the principal supplier of investment capital and, therefore, the inescapable focus of economic policy
issues.

RELATIONS WITH THE OAS

As Larman Wilson's essay (chapter 3) demonstrates, the Inter-American
system is the core of a cluster of political and international legal problems
that involve the relations of the Latin American nations with one
another, with the United States, and with the rest of the world. At the
center of the Inter-American system is the Organization of American
States, which, as James G. Blaine formulated it almost a century ago,
brought the nations of *Spanish* America together in a union that they

were unable to achieve for themselves, in order to promote the peaceful settlement of their international disputes and to encourage their international trade.[5] These problems—too many, too complex, and too interrelated to be set forth here in any detail—include financial support of the OAS and its specialized organizations and their relationships to UN agencies. Other issues (which will be developed) include the role, scope, and authority of the organization and particularly its structure for dealing with multilateral programs for economic development and for protecting regional economic interests in relations with the United States and the evolving European Common Market.

Policy questions related to the OAS also concern multilateral (regional) measures for dealing with external threats of subversion; measures for maintaining the system of representative constitutional government, to which all are pledged by the OAS Charter; the highly controversial issue of joint intervention for this purpose, which various nations have urged in the past; and problems of the protection of human rights in accordance with the American Declaration of the Rights and Duties of Man and the Statute of the Inter-American Commission on Human Rights. OAS policy problems also include the application of a complicated network of treaties for the peaceful settlement of international disputes, a special aspect of which concerns issues connected with the right of diplomatic asylum under the inter-American treaties. Recognition policy, both as it relates to membership in the OAS and to codification of a regional policy in respect to recognizing new governments has been a recurrent policy problem within the organization. Other problems have included cold war policy measures such as the Caracas Declaration of Solidarity (1954), which defined the establishment of a Communist government in an American state as a threat to the peace of the hemisphere within the scope of the Rio Treaty; the united stand against the Soviet Union in the Cuban missile crisis (1962); and the adoption of sanctions against Cuba and the Dominican Republic in the 1960s.

ECONOMIC POLICY PROBLEMS

A separate chapter by Alberto M. Piedra, immediately following this one, discusses international economic policies; but a few of the major policy issues may appropriately be mentioned here. It is characteristic of the state of economic foreign policy that these issues tend to be unsettled, rather than agreed, common, policy positions. These problems of policy are

5. See A. Curtis Wilgus, "Blaine and the Pan American Movement," *Hispanic American Historical Review* 5 (November 1932): 663; Samuel Flagg Bemis, *The Latin American Policy of the United States* (New York: Harcourt, Brace & Co., 1943); Alice Felt Tyler, *The Foreign Policy of James G. Blaine* (Minneapolis: University of Minnesota Press, 1927), pp. 109–305; and McGann, *Argentina, the United States, and the Inter-American System.*

both multilateral and bilateral, embracing such questions as the extent to which economic action should be carried on through OAS-related (or UN) agencies or through bilateral arrangements. Should the American nations close ranks in a large common market, as agreed to in principle by the American presidents at Punta del Este in 1967? Should the purpose be to bargain for better terms of trade with the European Common Market? Or should the major objective of any such union be to bargain for better terms with the United States, with whom so large a part of their foreign trade is conducted? Would it be better, as Raúl Prebisch has urged, to join with other Third World nations and work through the United Nations Conference on Trade and Development (UNCTAD) to achieve this end? Is it preferable to work with smaller regions, such as Central America, a group of Caribbean countries (CARIFTA), the Plate River region, or the Andean Group? Or, in the final analysis, is it better for each nation to pursue its national interest mainly through binational arrangements, as Mexico has done so successfully?

After World War II, the Latin Americans were disillusioned with private foreign capital for a number of reasons and insisted upon their need for more public capital from the United States. From the Chapultepec Conference of 1945 to the Buenos Aires Economic Conference of 1957, they engaged in a sterile policy debate with the United States on this and related issues, one result of which was a compromise in the Alliance for Progress that provided for both public and private foreign capital to total $2,000 million from all sources each year for ten years. But today, the Latin American nations are almost as disillusioned with respect to the public capital provided under the Alliance, except, perhaps, for what comes through the Inter-American Development Bank and other international agencies. The real problem, as they now see it, is how Latin Americans together can best bargain for more favorable terms of trade and investment (or loans) with the United States (and other nations providing capital), so that they, rather than the capital source, will derive the economic benefit from the resulting development.

Since the 1957 Buenos Aires Economic Conference it has been possible to see the emergence of certain common principles of international economic policy. These include such matters as support for commodity agreements on export staples, support for the Inter-American Development Bank, and a broadened area of free trade in the Americas. The policy of preferring public to private foreign capital investment seems to have dominated Latin American national policies (with some exceptions, to be sure) during most of the years since World War II. More recently, however, the Andean countries have shown signs of relying much more heavily upon foreign capital provided through international agencies only. Increasingly, too, the nations agree upon policies requiring that enterprises employing foreign capital have a majority of national stockholders and that provision be made for some reinvestment of profits. Foreign ownership of extractive industries is forbidden more and more. Many such businesses already in existence have been nationalized, and provision is increasingly being made for their reversion, together with the communication, transportation, power, and banking industries, to national ownership.

NATIONAL AND HEMISPHERIC DEFENSE

By the Inter-American Treaty of Reciprocal Assistance of 1947, pursuant to the World War II agreement of the American nations at Chapultepec in 1945, defense against any external attack from inside or outside the hemisphere (including Canada) was made the joint responsibility of all nations of America. An Inter-American Defense Board has been charged with the coordination of strategic plans, although it has no command responsibilities. The board also sponsors an Inter-American Defense College in which senior officers from the armed forces and from ministries of external relations pursue studies of various hemispheric and national policy issues.

During the Korean War, a consultation of foreign ministers in Washington (1951) endorsed the UN stand supporting South Korea but decided against any multilateral military action. Opposing the establishment of U.S. bases (as during World War II), the conference agreed that each nation should maintain the armed forces essential to its own defense and also such army, air, and naval bases as might be necessary for hemispheric defense. The Latin American multilateral treaty banning nuclear armaments from the area shows clearly the desire of the nations to avoid involvement in the great power armaments race. It also shows, as did the Cuban missile crisis of 1962, that the nations relied basically for their defense upon the nuclear power of the United States. The implication for national and hemispheric defense of any decline in the credibility of the U.S. nuclear umbrella remains yet to be seen.

LATIN AMERICAN POLICY
AND INTERNATIONAL LAW

A concern for international law has marked the foreign policy thinking of the Latin American nations. These nations have not only relied upon international law (in the customary manner) in defining national policy positions in disputes with other countries; they have also persistently sought, as an objective of national policy, to extend the application of international law. This emphasis on international law was a natural enough product of the era in which the nations achieved independence, a response to the need of new nations born of revolution to justify their sovereign existence in a generally hostile world. It also derived in part from the nations' Iberian heritage, which included a tradition of international law based upon the Christian theory of natural law as the law of God. This tradition emphasized that international law was the law of peaceful intercourse among states, rather than the law of war and peace as presented by Hugo Grotius and Samuel von Pufendorf. Because the Spanish-American nations had been part of a single, closely knit empire, and because Brazil had inherited something of the close historical relationships between Spain and Portugal, the new nations held from the beginning certain legal concepts of interdependence and solidarity with their neighbors rather than of rigid sovereign independence. The concept of national sovereignty tended to be limited by international (natural) law. One of the more obvious results of this importance that Latin Americans attached to international law was a dedication to the settlement of international disputes by arbitration. Another result, somewhat less obvious, was a willingness of the nations to enter into treaties with their neighbors and with Spain, extending virtually full rights of citizenship to one anothers' nationals.

It is worthy of special note that a major treatise on international law, the first important work by an American author, came from the pen of Andrés Bello, the Venezuelan scholar who was an advisor to the Chilean ministry of foreign relations in the early years of independence. Other scholars and statesmen have followed Bello's example, producing an important Latin American literature on international law. In the following chapters, the student will see a concrete expression of this interest in the general acceptance of the principle (first formulated by Thomas Jefferson as U.S. secretary of state and later incorporated in the Monroe Doctrine) of recognizing the government de facto as the legitimate government. But he will also see it in such interesting Latin American theories for dealing with the recognition of governments that owe their existence to revolution as the Ecuadoran (Carlos R. Tobar) theory of withholding recognition from a government that has overthrown its predecessor by a military *golpe*. This is the complete opposite of the Mexican (Genaro Estrada) principle that no nation has the right to withhold such recognition, and it is opposed in principle to the Uruguayan (Eduardo Rodríguez Larreta) principle of inter-American consultation prior to recognition.

Some students would say that two major Latin American contributions to international law are the closely related Calvo and Drago principles, both Argentine, the first rejecting the right of foreign investors to appeal to their home governments for protection until they had exhausted the resources of local justice, the second rejecting the long established right of intervention to enforce the payment of foreign debts and claims. As chapter 3 points out, a number of basic principles of public international law, produced in some respects by the Latin American international experience, have been incorporated in such multilateral treaties as the Montevideo Convention on the Rights and Duties of States, the Charter of the Organization of American States, and the Inter-American Treaty of Reciprocal Assistance. These include among others the following principles, or norms, of the public international law of the Americas:

1. Maintaining the system of representative constitutional government is a multilateral obligation.
2. Conquest gives no right to territory.
3. No nation has a right to intervene by force in another nation.
4. An act of aggression against one American state is an act of aggression against all.
5. The nations of America shall consult when confronted with a threat to the peace of the hemisphere.
6. All international disputes shall be settled by arbitration or other peaceful means.
7. Regional organizations are useful for defense and other purposes and are not incompatible with universal international organization.[6]

Finally, all the nations of the area who are members of the OAS (except Cuba) have a commitment to utilize that organization as a major channel for their relations with one another and in some degree with the outside world. In general, however, there is little positive agreement about the scope of this commitment to use the OAS. Nor is there much Latin American agreement about what the OAS should become; areas of particular sensitivity are the relationship of the OAS with the United States, the use of the OAS as a vehicle for Latin American integration and development, and the issue of political pluralism.

INDEPENDENCE IN FOREIGN POLICY

In recent years, as later chapters show, scholars have frequently written of a Latin American dependency status, while Latin American writers and statesmen have called for more independent national foreign policies for their countries. One of the most notable recent examples of this demand for independence was a statement of Jânio Quadros during his short-lived presidency of Brazil. With much less fanfare Mexico has managed to achieve increasing independence in her international actions, even to the point of maintaining nearly normal relations with the Cuba of Fidel Castro, which the United States and the other American states have boycotted because of Cuban-sponsored revolutionary activities in Ameri-

6. See part 1, arts. 1 20, of the Charter.

can countries. In fact, some of the nations, such as Mexico and Argentina, asserted an independent position early in their history. Thus, Argentina withdrew support of the ambitious plans of José de San Martín and refused to participate in Simón Bolívar's Congress in 1826. Under President Juan Manuel de Rosas, Argentina also sought to follow an independent policy. Mexico hoped to follow an independent policy in the 1830s but later fell under the influence of foreign pressures. The critical reader will note, however, that no Latin American nation managed in the nineteenth century to achieve the degree of independence in its foreign relations that Monroe and Adams achieved for the United States in the 1820s.

It must be pointed out that the meaning of an independent (or a dependent) policy is far from clear in the Latin American scene. The most common meaning (which is highly conceptualized) has concerned dependence upon the United States, especially in relation to the bipolarity of the post–World War II power structure and the issues of the cold war. In this connection, an independent foreign policy has not meant complete independence—and certainly not isolation—as much as solidarity for the purpose of bargaining more effectively with the United States and the European Common Market group of nations.

Sometimes the independent policy is expressed in terms of nonalignment. But as a position statement, this formulation involves a contradiction when nations seek to join with other Third World countries, yet reject the idea of forming anything like a bloc. Argentina under Juan Perón and, in a more striking fashion, Cuba under Fidel Castro, provide examples. As Enrique Suárez Gaona of Mexico has recently pointed out, "a very clear notion among the neutralists is that a transnational solidarity exists among the exploited."[7] But this idea of a kind of class stratification of nations contradicts the existing reality of the solidarity, however limited by national diversity, among the Latin American nations. Spanning categories from the poorest (Haiti, Bolivia) to the richest (Argentina, Venezuela), this solidarity, because of historical, cultural, and religious ties, in some respects embraces Spain, Portugal, and France. It finds concrete expression in such developments as the Central American Common Market, the Andean Group, and the Latin American Free Trade Association. That these organizations stand in the way of any theoretical concept of complete independence in foreign policy or even a consistent policy of a nonalignment association with the Third World was evident in the general failure of Latin American nations in the New Delhi and Santiago conferences of the United Nations Conference on Trade and Development to support Raúl Prebisch's thesis that the developing nations should join together to bargain with the developed nations on terms of trade.

7. "Lázaro Cárdenas y el Neutralismo Actual," *Revista de la Universidad de México* 25, no. 5 (May 1971): 18–24.

Mexico may well provide the best illustration of the nature and possibilities, the positive aspects as well as the limitations, of independence in foreign policy. In the years since World War II, Mexico has pursued a consistent and generally successful policy of guarding her independence by pursuing a low-key policy, adhering carefully to positions that she can justify in international law and that conform to her treaty commitments, while enabling her to keep international issues to a minimum in her internal politics. Several Latin American nations undoubtedly have the power to pursue such independent policies if they wish to take the risks and pay the price Mexico has been willing to pay. In fact, Brazil, Mexico, and Argentina are as able to pursue such a policy as most nations in the world. Colombia, Venezuela, Chile, Peru, and Cuba could come near doing so. Speaking to the Atlanta General Assembly of the OAS in 1974, the Brazilian foreign minister, for example, stated the view that the era of automatic alignments had passed. But real independence requires more than a political decision; it requires enough economic strength and enough internal psychological unity for the definition and support of an independent stance.

Even those Latin American nations that have the potential power seem little inclined, on the whole, to risk so radical a departure from past policy. The peril of such a fundamental change from traditional and OAS ties with the United States was brought home by the Cuban missile crisis, and the unanimous reaction of the Latin American states (other than Cuba) to the threat it presented. The more realistic policy of Chile under the Salvador Allende regime appeared for a time to be a more likely course for the other nations to follow. Chile sought independence by seeking, both directly and through the OAS and the United Nations, ties with all other parts of the world. The disastrous outcome of the Chilean experiment, however, suggests that it should not be taken as a model. Still, it is inconceivable that even Cuba, tied as she is to the Soviet power sphere, should reject the power advantages of acting in concert with the other nations of Latin America—one of the near world powers, if properly organized—when she again has the chance to do so.

BIBLIOGRAPHICAL NOTE

In addition to works cited in footnotes, the student may profitably consult such works as Samuel Shapiro, ed., *Cultural Factors in Inter-American Relations* (Notre Dame, Ind.: University of Notre Dame Press, 1968); Victor Alba, *The Latin Americans* (New York: Frederick A. Praeger, 1969), chap. 7; Richard Gray, ed., *Latin America and the United States in the 1970s* (Itasca, Ill.: F. E. Peacock Publishers, 1971); Edward J. Williams, *The Political Themes of Inter-American Relations* (Belmont, Calif.: Duxbury Press, 1971); Earl T. Glauert and Lester D. Langley, eds., *The United States and Latin America* (Reading, Mass.: Addison Wesley Publishing Co., 1971); Federico G. Gil, *Latin American–United*

States Relations (New York: Harcourt Brace Jovanovich, 1971); and Santiago Dantas, *Política externa independente* (Rio de Janeiro: Editora Civilizacão Brasileira, 1962).

On "dependency," see John Johnson, "Independencia and the Future of United States–Latin American Relations," in *New Horizons for the United States in World Affairs*, ed. Sydney Nettleton Fisher (Columbus: Ohio State University Press, 1966), and María del Rosario Green, "Las relaciones de Estados Unidos y América Latina en el marco de la dependencia," *Foro Internacional* 13, no. 3 (January–March 1973): 327–47.

Latin America: A Catalog of Dissertations, published in 1974 by University Microfilms in Ann Arbor, Michigan, includes numerous studies of questions relating to Latin American foreign relations.

2/Alberto M. Piedra

Problems of Foreign Economic Relations

Latin America has several options in the area of foreign economic relations. These options vary from country to country, but there is often a definite tendency for certain countries with given characteristics to group together and follow a common foreign economic policy. The underlying reason for the creation of such groups varies, depending on the natural endowments of the countries concerned and the ideological objectives of the ruling elites. Thus, countries may be grouped together either as producers of raw material goods or as producers of processed or semi-processed manufactured goods. Among the raw material producers a distinction can also be made between petroleum- and nonpetroleum-producing countries. These distinct groups tend to follow different foreign economic policies.

Latin American countries may also be grouped according to the political and ideological objectives of their ruling classes. Governments with definite socialistic inclinations have specific objectives that almost always clash with the goals of governments that are more committed to the Western type of economy and that rely heavily on the free interplay of market forces. As a result, their foreign economic policies are far from being the same.

Perhaps the most realistic approach to the problem of Latin America's foreign economic relations lies within the area of this second option: an analysis of the different policies of the various groups of governments in the light of their prevailing ideological objectives. Such an analysis would tend to classify Latin America into three basically distinct groups of countries. The socialist group, led by Cuba and followed to a certain extent by Peru—until recently also by Chile—postulate policies that foster close ties with the socialist nations. As a result, this group of countries is dependent on the Soviet bloc nations, with all the limitations and constraints that such a dependence implies in terms of political and economic freedom.

A point that is often overlooked when discussing the dependence of the socialized Latin American countries upon the resources of the Soviet Union is the serious burden that such a dependence entails for the USSR. Although statistics are not available, there seems to be ample evidence to support the notion that the economic burden is becoming unbearable for the Soviet Union, given its limited capital resources. Sooner or later these dependent nations must attempt to diversify their economic and trade policies so as to loosen their ties with the Soviet Union. The Eastern European countries provide the best example of such a phenomenon.

Another group of countries, led by Brazil, still fosters policies that are more closely linked with the traditional markets of Latin America, especially with the United States. It is interesting to note that Brazil, which relies heavily on private initiative for its economic development, is rapidly becoming a major industrial power. Given time, it may well become the rival of Japan in the Western Hemisphere.

A third group of countries has not yet set its path toward development in a clear and distinct manner. The situation is uncertain, and it is still too early to determine whether this group has chosen the road to socialism, with its greater dependence on the Soviet Union and the countries of Eastern Europe, or whether it will continue to foster policies more akin to those of Western economies, which emphasize individual initiative and entrepreneurship. The best example of this group is Argentina; the restored regime of Juan Perón, continued after his death by his wife, the vice-president, still (1975) lacks a well-defined foreign economic policy.

However, in spite of the various alternatives open to Latin America in the area of foreign economic relations, many points of agreement can be found. Apart from the general desire to foster economic development and raise the standard of living of the population, the Latin American countries tend to agree on certain points that can be traced to common economic problems. This paper will stress these points of agreement and not the major differences of, or possible alternatives to, Latin American foreign economic policies.

Trade, because it constitutes one of the major sources of foreign exchange, can be considered the focal point of Latin America's economic development. Most Latin American countries would agree that the slow growth of the value of Latin America's exports has been largely responsible for the area's not having reached the level of economic development visualized by the Alliance for Progress.

The inadequacy of investments, both domestic and foreign, and the poor utilization of existing resources have also been blamed for the slow economic growth of Latin America. In the early stages of Latin America's economic development, a flow of foreign capital was considered sufficient to meet the investment needs of the region. However, it was soon realized that this capital flow did not, by itself, constitute the solution to Latin America's economic ills. The area was not able to absorb the foreign capital, and all sorts of bottlenecks resulted. Technical assistance was then considered indispensable, but here again, difficulties arose when it was realized that the countries in the process of development very often lacked the preparation and the technical know-how so important for the successful application of transferred technology.

The proceedings of the several United Nations Conferences on Trade and Development (UNCTAD), such as the 1972 meeting in Santiago, Chile, indicate that general agreement on the need to adopt certain international policies beneficial to the underdeveloped nations does exist (the report of the sixth session of the Committee for Development Planning of the United Nations [Tinbergen Report] and the recommendations that have come out of two major meetings of the Special Latin American Coordinating Committee [CECLA], the Latin American Consensus of Viña del Mar, and the Declaration of Buenos Aires support this indication.)[1] The export earnings of the developing countries must be increased and the flow of financial assistance and know-how from the developed countries must be expanded. These general objectives have also been brought out by the United Nations Special Committee for Development, especially by the Economic Commission for Latin America (ECLA), and by many prominent Latin American leaders who have more than once indicated the dangers of a widening economic gap between the developed and underdeveloped areas of the world unless proper measures are taken to remedy the situation. Raúl Prebisch must be given a prominent place among these leaders. His theories, although not always received sympathetically, have nevertheless become the cornerstone of the demands not only of many Latin Americans but also of the whole underdeveloped world.[2]

Thus, an appropriate flow of financial resources and an adequate adaptation of technical and scientific methods to the needs of the Latin American countries have become, along with trade, the rallying point of all Latin American countries. With regard to what measures the industrialized nations must take in order to help accelerate the rate of economic growth in the developing countries, the Latin American countries seem at least to have agreed upon what should be done in three major areas of foreign economic policy: trade, finance, and technical cooperation. A brief review of the major objectives in these areas is necessary.

1. The Special Latin American Coordinating Committee (CECLA) is an international consultative body that is exclusively Latin American. It was established at an Inter-American Economic and Social Council (IA-ECOSOC) conference in São Paulo, in November 1963, with the purpose of presenting a unified Latin American position at the first United Nations Conference on Trade and Development (UNCTAD), which took place in Geneva in 1964. The first CECLA meeting actually took place in Alta Gracia, Argentina, in 1964. It established the basis for Latin America's future commercial policies with the developed nations. The Latin American Consensus of Viña del Mar, an outgrowth of CECLA, presents the position of the Latin American countries vis-à-vis the United States with regard to economic and social cooperation. The Declaration of Buenos Aires, a document published as a result of the sixth CECLA meeting at the ministerial level, which took place in Buenos Aires in July 1970, discusses Latin America's trade relations with the European Economic Community (EEC).

2. Raúl Prebisch, *Change and Development: Latin America's Great Tasks: Report Submitted to the Inter-American Development Bank* (New York: Praeger Publishers, 1971).

TRADE

According to recent statistics, the share in total world exports of the countries in the process of development decreased between 1950 and 1970 from 32 to 18 percent.[3] Between 1961 and 1968, the average annual rate of growth of the value of total world exports was 8.7 percent. This average annual rate increased to 13.7 percent between 1967 and 1970.[4] Exports of underdeveloped countries, excluding petroleum, increased at a much lower rate.

The average yearly rate of growth of the value of Latin American exports during the period 1961–70 amounted to 5.7 percent.[5] Between 1967 and 1970, the yearly average increased to 8.6 percent.[6] However, Latin America's share in world trade decreased from 7.2 percent in 1961 to 6.7 percent in 1968.[7]

During the same period (1961–70) the value of Latin American imports followed a similar pattern, although the rate of expansion was somewhat greater. The average annual increase was 11.3 percent between 1967 and 1970 and approximately 14.0 percent in 1970. In the future it would be advantageous for Latin America to adjust its increase in imports to the long run trend in exports.

Overall, Latin America had a favorable balance of payments during the period 1967–70. However, during this period the current account showed an increasing negative balance, mainly as a result of the large deficit in the service sector. The trade balance, though positive, began to deteriorate in 1970, and in 1971 a substantial deficit was recorded. This deficit was caused mainly by a slackening rate of expansion in the industrialized countries.[8] The increased value of oil exports from Latin America was unable to compensate for the overall decline in the export value of the area's principal agricultural products and primary metals.

In the decade of the 1960s, the prices of imports increased less rapidly than in the previous decade. This tendency, together with more favorable prices for exports, contributed to an improvement in Latin America's terms of trade during the period 1961–70. Nevertheless, in the longer term between 1950 and 1970 an overall deterioration took place in terms of

3. International Bank for Reconstruction and Development, *Trends in Developing Countries* (Washington, D.C., 1971).

4. International Monetary Fund, *Annual Report, 1972* (Washington, D.C., 1972), p. 9.

5. International Monetary Fund, *International Financial Statistics* (Washington, D.C., 1972). See also Lester B. Pearson, *Partners in Development: Report of the Commission on International Development* (New York: Frederick A. Praeger, 1969), p. 45.

6. Inter-American Development Bank, Social Progress Trust Fund, *Socio-Economic Progress in Latin America, Annual Report, 1971* (Washington, D.C., 1971), p. 37.

7. Inter-American Development Bank, Social Progress Trust Fund, *Socio-Economic Progress in Latin America, Annual Report, 1970* (Washington, D.C., 1970).

8. International Monetary Fund, *Balance of Payments Yearbook* (Washington, D.C., 1957–), vols. 22(1965–69), 23(1966–70), and 24(1967–71).

trade. Such a trend may very well be accentuated in the future as a result of the Smithsonian Agreement of 18 December 1971, which devalued the dollar and initiated a series of international monetary adjustments.[9] This will probably be the case in the less developed countries, which export basic products other than petroleum. The demand for imports will remain relatively inelastic in these countries, even though the prices of imported goods, expressed in dollars, will probably rise as a result of the realignment. On the other hand, export unit values, with the exception of petroleum, will not, for the most part, rise as rapidly. It is also possible that in the longer run "the price changes stemming from the realignment may lead to an expansion of 1 1/2 to 2 percent in the volume of their imports."[10] These volume changes could very well compensate for the price changes and bring about an eventual improvement in the collective trade balance of the less developed countries.

However, with the exception of Venezuela and, to a lesser extent, Ecuador and Trinidad and Tobago, the recent energy crisis will affect the trade balance of most Latin American countries adversely, thus worsening the area's balance of payments situation. These countries will now have to pay much higher prices for their oil imports, and as the costs of production will most certainly increase in the industrialized nations, they will also have to pay higher prices for the capital equipment and raw materials they must import in order to carry out their development programs. In addition, freight charges will rise, and the countries bordering the Pacific will have the added expense of increasing costs connected with the use of the Panama Canal.

Thus, in the longer run, the increase in the price of oil and its derivatives will have a tremendous impact on Latin America. A few countries, such as Venezuela, will benefit from increasing foreign exchange and will experience further improvements in their terms of trade. But for the majority of the other countries, the energy crisis will most certainly have negative effects in proportion to the degree of a country's dependence on oil imports. In certain cases it is highly possible that as much as one-third of the export earnings of a given country will have to be used for the purchase of the much-needed petroleum.

The United States is still the largest market for Latin American products. However, the share of total Latin American exports sent to the United States decreased considerably during the 1960s. This trend can be seen in table 2.1.

Table 2.1 clearly indicates that the share of Latin American exports to the United States decreased substantially between 1960 and 1970. On the other hand, the European Economic Community (EEC) and Japan

9. The United States again devalued the dollar on 12 February 1973, bringing about a new wave of currency readjustments.
10. International Monetary Fund, *Annual Report, 1972*, p. 12.

Table 2.1 Export Markets of Latin America: Value and Percent of Total Exports
for 1960, 1965, and 1970

(millions of $U.S.)

Export Markets	Total Exports					
	1960		1965		1970	
	Value	%	Value	%	Value	%
United States	3417.6	40.2	3749.7	33.6	4784.0	31.5
Canada	176.4	2.1	402.1	3.6	497.9	3.3
Japan	196.5	2.3	428.3	3.8	964.9	6.4
Great Britain	884.3	10.4	813.1	7.3	780.4	5.1
EEC	1514.6	17.8	2215.3	19.8	3193.8	21.0
Latin America	739.7	8.7	1236.6	11.2	1982.3	13.0
Other	1570.2	18.5	2319.2	20.7	2986.0	19.7
Total	8499.3	100.0	11174.3	100.0	15189.3	100.0

Source: Data provided by the Inter-American Development Bank, Washington, D.C., 1972.

significantly increased their importance as markets for Latin American products. The table definitely seems to corroborate the theory that Latin America is looking for and finding new markets for its export trade.

The Latin American countries have always been aware of the need to expand their export markets, especially in the area of basic products. Only during the last decade or so has greater emphasis been placed on developing export markets for their manufactured and semimanufactured goods. That is why the Latin American countries have become increasingly concerned over the adoption by the industrialized nations of unilateral measures that could interfere with the free flow of goods.

Insofar as imports are concerned, Japan increased substantially her share of Latin America's total imports. Something similar can be said of Canada, although to a lesser extent. Table 2.2 indicates these trends.

Special attention was given at the UNCTAD meetings to Latin America's foreign trade problems. UNCTAD recommendations called on the developed countries to lower all barriers to trade, whether tariff or nontariff, that impede the entry of goods from both tropical and temperate zones into the markets of the industrialized countries.[11] Temporary, and at least partial, reimbursement should also be given to the underdeveloped countries in order to compensate them for the fiscal and tariff charges imposed on their goods when they enter the more developed countries of the world.

In respect to manufactured and semimanufactured goods, UNCTAD has recommended a principle of general preference to replace the principle of reciprocity. Free access, without restrictions of any type, should be

11. The Charter of Algiers was adopted in Algiers in 1967. *Group of 77, Ministerial Meeting, Algiers, 1967.* UN Doc. No. A/C.2/L.980.

Table 2.2 Import Markets of Latin America: Value and Percent of Total Imports
for 1960, 1965, and 1970

(millions of $U.S.)

Import Markets	1960 Value	1960 %	1965 Value	1965 %	1970 Value	1970 %
United States	3507.2	43.3	3897.7	41.1	5993.4	40.3
Canada	199.9	2.5	318.7	3.3	524.5	3.6
Japan	212.7	2.6	390.7	4.2	884.1	5.9
Great Britain	623.2	7.7	583.2	6.2	835.8	5.7
EEC	1581.0	19.5	1661.1	17.4	2670.5	17.9
Latin America	849.2	10.5	1432.9	14.2	2093.3	13.4
Other	1134.0	13.9	1216.5	12.9	1834.6	12.5
Total	8107.2	100.0	9500.8	100.0	14836.2	100.0

Source: Data provided by the Inter-American Development Bank, Washington, D.C., 1972.

given to all manufactured and semimanufactured goods going from underdeveloped into developed countries.

Furthermore, it was recommended that the developed countries immediately grant to the underdeveloped countries all concessions granted during the Kennedy Round that might be of interest to the less developed countries.[12] These concessions would apply to all countries in the process of development, whether they are or are not members of the General Agreement on Trade and Tariffs (GATT).

Similar conclusions were reached in the 1970 report of the Committee for Development Planning of the United Nations (Tinbergen Report), in which guidelines and proposals for the Second United Nations Development Decade were put forward. The report states that "each developed country should undertake further liberalization of imports, concentrating this time on the goods obtained mostly from developing countries."[13]

It is further recommended in the Tinbergen Report that the industrialized nations should review their trade policies during the decade of the 1970s in order to remove impediments to trade. Obviously, this may entail structural changes in the economies of the developed nations, because resources may have to be shifted from one area of production to another. The application of such a policy would be painful in the short run, as in the case of some farmers in the south of the United States and in France who would no longer be able to compete favorably with the cheaper

12. The so-called Kennedy Round owes its name to President John F. Kennedy and refers to a series of formal GATT negotiations on tariff reductions that began in November 1964.
13. United Nations Economic and Social Council, 49th Session, Committee for Development Planning, 6th Session, *Towards Accelerated Development. Proposals for the Second UN Development Decade, 1970* (Tinbergen Report), Doc. No. ST ECA 128. 5–15 Jan. 1970, pp. 20–21.

agricultural products imported from abroad. In the long run, however, it
would be advantageous to the developed nations because the improved
overall level of efficiency would benefit the consumer.[14] It is particularly
stressed in the Tinbergen Report that the developed countries should
reduce their output of high-cost agricultural products by a small percentage each year. Discrimination against imports of manufactured
goods from underdeveloped countries should be eliminated—in particular, tariffs against imports of manufactured goods made from raw materials produced in underdeveloped nations. Thus, the report clearly
agrees with the recommendations of UNCTAD when it says that "the
system of preferences proposed by UNCTAD constitutes an appropriate contribution to the elimination of impediment to trade."[15]

Market regulation of basic products is recommended in certain cases to
avoid such excessive fluctuations in world prices as have often played
havoc with the economies of the underdeveloped countries. Thus, commodity arrangements are considered not only normal but even necessary
for establishing a stable price level that is remunerative for the producers
and equitable for the consumers, one which in the long run balances
market forces of supply and demand. The report recommends that
commodity agreements not be limited to such basic products as wheat,
tin, coffee, and sugar. For example, "agreement on cocoa and tea should
be concluded no later than the end of 1971," and "the scope of the sugar
agreement should be enlarged through the participation of the European
Economic Community (EEC) and the United States of America."[16] In
addition, the developed nations should lend their support to commodity
agreements by contributing to the financing of buffer stocks.[17]

The proposals recommended by the Latin American countries in the
Consensus of Viña del Mar (1969) are in many ways similar to those made
by UNCTAD and by the Committee for Development Planning of the
United Nations. Although the Consensus of Viña del Mar appeared a few
months earlier than the Tinbergen Report, it is mentioned later here
because it expresses the view of the Latin American countries exclusively
and is directed primarily at the United States. It stresses the need "to
negotiate with the United States timetables for the elimination of these

14. See *The Rockefeller Report on the Americas* (Chicago: Quadrangle Books, 1969). See
also Milton Friedman, *Capitalism and Freedom* (Chicago: University of Chicago Press,
1962).

15. Tinbergen Report, p. 21.

16. Ibid., p. 22. Thus far no agreement has been reached on cacao. In December 1971
and in early 1972 several consultation meetings were held in Geneva, but without any
apparent success. Resumption of the discussions is scheduled for the near future.

17. A buffer stocks plan is often called an ever-normal granary and refers to a method of
stabilization in agriculture. The plan is supposed to stabilize prices and consumption and
also the income of the farmer.

market restrictions (tariff and non-tariff obstacles, as for example, quotas, safety and health regulations, etc.) on Latin American products of a special interest, jointly identifying the obstacles in question."[18]

As a result of the recommendations expressed in the Consensus of Viña del Mar, the Special Committee for Consultation and Negotiation (CECON)[19] began to hold meetings in Washington, D.C. in 1970, but with little apparent success. At these meetings the Latin American countries presented to the United States a more detailed list of their demands. However, because of the trend toward a new type of protectionism in the United States, the outcome of these requests is doubtful.

The consensus pointed out the need to observe the timetable on commodity agreements fixed at the second UNCTAD meeting held in New Delhi in 1968. It stressed the need to eliminate all discriminatory measures against the sale of Latin American basic products in the industrialized countries and to adopt a general nonreciprocal and nondiscriminatory system of preferences in order to increase Latin America's exports of manufactured and semimanufactured goods to the United States and the rest of the world. The consensus also stressed the need to respect certain generally accepted principles in the area of surplus sales and to prevent the inconveniences and distortions of trade brought about by loans "tied" to purchases in the country of origin.

The Declaration of Buenos Aires (1970), approved by all Latin American countries except Cuba, emphasized the need for the European Economic Community to facilitate the access of Latin American manufactured and semimanufactured goods into the European Common Market area. It specifically requested that the EEC countries endorse the quick establishment of a system of general preferences, nonreciprocal and nondiscriminatory, vis-à-vis manufactured and semimanufactured products originating in Latin America.[20]

The recommendations made at the several UNCTAD conferences have been partially accepted by the industrialized nations. Seventeen member countries of the Organization for Economic Cooperation and Development (OECD) have agreed to a "Generalized System of Preferences for Manufactured and Semi-manufactured Goods Exported from the Developing Countries." The United Kingdom put similar systems into

18. Special Latin American Coordinating Committee, *The Latin American Consensus of Viña del Mar, Viña del Mar, Chile, May 1969.* This document appears in many places, including *Inter-American Relations*, a committee print of the U.S. Senate Committee on Foreign Affairs, 93rd Cong., 1st sess., 1973-74 (Washington, D.C.: Government Printing Office, 1973), pp. 262-72.

19. A special committee created within the OAS as a result of the Latin American Consensus of Viña del Mar.

20. Special Latin American Coordinating Committee, *Declaration of Buenos Aires*, Buenos Aires, 30 July 1970. See *Comercio Exterior* (Mexico) 20, no. 8 (August 1970): 617-19.

effect on 1 January 1972. The United States has not yet approved legislation granting such generalized preferences.[21]

FINANCE

The Latin American nations have frequently stressed the need for a greater and more generous transfer of real resources from the more developed to the less developed countries. It is argued that the industrialized nations must see to it that a continuous flow of capital is channeled into countries in the earlier stages of economic growth. The financing of such funds would help them acquire the capital equipment and know-how so necessary for development purposes.

The inadequacy of the savings ratio has been considered by many economists to be one of the major factors responsible for the slow economic development of Latin America. Nevertheless, between 1967 and 1970 gross investments as a percentage of the Gross Domestic Product (GDP) increased from 18.1 to 19.3 percent, according to the Inter-American Development Bank. During the same period domestic savings increased from 16.6 percent in 1967 to 17.2 percent in 1970. Approximately 10 percent of all investments were financed from external sources.[22] Savings still fall short of the investment coefficient of 26.5 percent recommended by Prebisch for the year 1980.

According to UNCTAD, the industrialized nations of the world should annually provide the developing countries with a net amount equal to one percent of their Gross National Product (GNP). The General Assembly of the United Nations, in its resolution 2415 (XXIII) concerning aid values, recommended that the more developed countries of the world set 1972 as a deadline for the attainment of the objectives established at the Second UNCTAD conference. The Tinbergen Report corroborates these objectives by declaring that within the mentioned one percent and within the time limit described, "developed countries should consider providing a minimum of 0.75 percent of their Gross National Product by way of net official financial resource transfers as defined in UNCTAD decision 27 (II)."[23]

The fact that this public sector component of net transfer of financial resources should be at least 0.75 percent of the GNP does not, however, set a limit to the flow of private resources. On the contrary, according to

21. Inter-American Development Bank, Social Progress Trust Fund, *Socio-Economic Progress in Latin America: Annual Report, 1971*, p. 37.
22. Inter-American Development Bank, Social Progress Trust Fund, *Socio-Economic Progress in Latin America: Annual Report, 1972*, p. 36. See also Organization of American States, *Latin American Development and the Alliance for Progress* (Washington, D.C., 1972), pp. 288–89.
23. Tinbergen Report, p. 25.

UNCTAD the flow should increase and, whenever possible, the developed countries should, through proper fiscal policies, encourage private investments in those types of activities that are considered especially socially beneficial. Unfortunately, some of the policies followed by certain less developed countries have not been very propitious to foreign private investments.[24] Nevertheless, it is estimated that since the Alliance for Progress came into existence, U.S. firms "have invested an additional $3,200 million in the Caribbean area, Central America, and the South American continent."[25] However, during the same period (1961–68) the net capital outflow *to* the United States amounted to approximately $4,000 million.[26]

At the third UNCTAD meeting, in Santiago, Chile, in the spring of 1972, the Latin American countries stressed the need to reform the international monetary system. It is imperative, they claimed, that the countries in the process of development participate in the preparation and negotiation of reform proposals and in all discussions concerning international monetary affairs. This third UNCTAD meeting recommended that there should be a link between the creation of reserves and development financing. The linkage between the Special Drawing Rights (SDR) and international financial assistance should, it was insisted, be given high priority.[27]

The Tinbergen Report stresses the need for the developed countries to provide at least 70 percent of their total official development assistance in the form of grants. These grants should be concentrated in the poorer countries. The report also points out the need for a continuous and uninterrupted flow of funds from the developed to the underdeveloped countries. The industrialized countries should establish special funds on a national level to help the developing countries. In order to avoid the inconveniences of certain budgetary rules, financial aid should be handled on a fixed program and revolving basis.[28]

The Tinbergen Report also emphasizes the need to channel financial funds into the developing countries through multilateral institutions.

24. The Overseas Private Insurance Corporation (OPIC) is a U.S. government insurance agency having as its main function the underwriting of business investments abroad. As a result of Chile's nationalization policies, OPIC awarded Kennecott Copper Corporation $66.9 million to cover most of its losses. Anaconda Company also received payment from OPIC to cover the loss of its equity investment.

25. U.S., Congress, House of Representatives, *Hearings before the Sub-Committee on Inter-American Affairs. Part I: Towards a Strategy for Inter-American Affairs* (Washington, D.C.: Government Printing Office, 1969).

26. Ibid. See also Council for Latin America, *The Effects of United States and Other Foreign Investments in Latin America* (New York, January 1970).

27. The Special Drawing Rights (SDRs) are an international currency created by the International Monetary Fund to supplement and eventually replace gold and the dollar as a monetary reserve. The SDRs are destined to play a leading role in the world monetary system.

28. Tinbergen Report, p. 29.

These disbursements should be made in accordance with the needs and requirements of the particular developing country. Another important point brought out by this report is that the developed countries should make available part of their increased monetary reserves, not necessarily in the form of SDRs, to the developing countries. This could be done in the form of "direct contributions by developed countries of some proportion of their annual allocations of SDRs to the International Development Association (IDA) and regional development banks, while another method would require contributions of national currency to IDA in some proportion to the annual allocation of SDRs to developed countries."[29]

According to the Consensus of Viña del Mar, in all aid programs inter-American financial cooperation requires that a real transfer of resources take place and that these resources be granted in accordance with national development policies and plans, always respecting the freedom of the underdeveloped countries to set their own priorities. The policy of "tied" loans, which is often practiced by developed nations, should be abolished because of its adverse effects on the Latin American economies. Effective mechanisms should be created to liberalize external credits, reduce interest rates, and lengthen the time for repayment. Contributions to IDA should be renewed, and any discriminatory practice against Latin America in the area of external financing should be eliminated.

Two more points made by the Consensus of Viña del Mar deserve to be mentioned. The first is the demand that the U.S. capital market be made more accessible to the Latin American countries and their regional bodies. The second is that more funds be made available by the United States to help finance Latin American exports. These measures, it was held, would improve the competitive position of Latin America's products in the world markets.

Finally, the Consensus of Viña del Mar recommended that "private foreign investment should not be considered as aid or calculated as part of financial cooperation for development purposes."[30] It should act as a complement to national investment decisions. Otherwise, there is a real danger that the foreign flow of investments might distort competitive conditions and create serious dislocations in the economy of Latin America. In the area of international monetary relations, the member states of CECLA, at their meeting in Viña del Mar, prepared the way for the recommendations made by UNCTAD in Santiago in 1972. They recommended that Latin America play a larger role "in the discussions on the reform of the international monetary system, including those which

29. Ibid., p. 30. See also Alexandre Kafka, "Some Aspects of Latin America's Financial Relations with the International Monetary Fund," in *Socio-Economic Change in Latin America*, ed. Alberto M. Piedra (Washington, D.C.: Catholic University of America Press, 1970).
30. The Latin American Consensus of Viña del Mar.

take place outside the sphere of the International Monetary Fund (IMF) and particularly within the so-called Group of Ten."[31]

In response to the need for a reform of the international monetary system, the Committee of Governors of the International Monetary Fund (IMF), the Committee of Twenty (C20), was created. This committee quickly initiated the preparatory work necessary to bring about the desired monetary reforms. The developing countries, especially those in Latin America, have given this committee wide support. They believe that the pressure exerted by C20 on the industrialized countries will bring increased recognition of their demands in the field of international monetary relations.

An important point requiring further study is related to Latin America's repayment of its external public debt. According to the Inter-American Development Bank, the net external financing received by Latin America in 1971 amounted to $2,742 million, a decline of 7 percent from 1970. In 1967 the amount received equaled $1,871.4 million. Approximately 42 percent of the amount received in 1971 was in the form of net public financing and the remaining 58 percent came from private sources.[32]

At the end of 1971 the area's external public debt amounted to $21,555 million. That same year the service burden of this external public debt, both in terms of interest payments and amortization, reached a total of $2,651 million. During the period 1960–70 the service burden of Latin America's external public debt averaged 13.6 percent of the area's export earnings.[33]

As stated earlier, the total inflow of long-term capital resources averaged slightly over 10 percent of required domestic gross investment between 1967 and 1970. However, external financing represented 2.4 percent of GDP in 1970 and 3.1 percent in 1971. In 1960 it represented only 1.8 percent.[34]

Overall, the financial terms of credit from external sources have not changed significantly between 1968 and 1971. In spite of the increased cost of money in the money markets of the developed countries, no hardening of financial credits has taken place. In fact, on the average, the rate of interest to be paid by Latin America for the financial resources received

31. Ibid. See also Kafka, "Some Aspects of Latin America's Financial Relations with the International Monetary Fund."

32. Inter-American Development Bank, Social Progress Trust Fund, Socio-Economic Progress in Latin America, Annual Report, 1972, p. 406.

33. Ibid., p. 57. According to a study made by the OAS, the service burden of the external public debt amounted to 8.1 percent in 1961 and 14.9 percent in 1969, and was expected to be approximately 16 percent in 1973. See Organización de los Estados Americanos, El Financiamiento Externo Oficial en la Estrategía del Desarrollo de América Latina: Implicaciones para los Setenta (Washington, D.C., 1972), p. 12.

34. Ibid., p. 390.

from abroad remained relatively constant between 1968 and 1971. The average for the period 1968–70 was 6.62 percent, and in 1971 it had decreased to 6.60 percent.

Negotiations are under way to relieve the present service burden of the external public debt, especially in the case of such countries as Argentina, Chile, and Uruguay, where it represents about 20 percent of export earnings. As a result of the energy crisis, the situation will probably deteriorate even more unless drastic steps are taken immediately to remedy the situation.

It is sometimes said that the Soviet Union gives better credit facilities than the Western economies when transferring capital resources to the less developed countries. Thus, it is argued, it would be beneficial for Latin America and the other less developed countries to rely more heavily on the Soviet bloc countries for their development needs. Apart from the fact that the whole problem of Soviet transfer of capital resources and technology requires a much deeper analysis than this paper will permit, a few pertinent comments may clarify certain misconceptions. Although it may be true that the USSR very often offers mild service charges for the transfer of capital resources to the less developed countries, it is also true that such a policy constitutes a heavy burden for the Soviet Union, which must somehow be offset by other benefits. Part of the loss from lower interest payments can be compensated for by delivering lower quality goods or by charging higher prices for capital equipment. Besides, the Soviet government is desirous of penetrating the markets of the less developed countries in order to make them more dependent economically. In this way, the Soviets are better prepared to compete effectively at a later date with the domestic industries. Economic dependence can easily become the first step towards political control. Such a policy can also have favorable repercussions on the Communist parties of the countries that receive Soviet aid.

Thus, given these conditions and Russia's limited capital resources, it is doubtful whether Soviet economic aid can replace and prove more beneficial to Latin America than aid given by the industrial societies of Western Europe, Japan, and the United States. Experience in Cuba and, more recently, in Chile, tend to corroborate this point.

TECHNICAL COOPERATION

A special place in the area of assistance should be given to technical and scientific cooperation. On this particular point there seems to be general agreement among the underdeveloped countries, especially the Latin American nations, that skills should be channeled from where they are relatively abundant to where they are scarce. For this purpose, technical assistance will have to be increased significantly.

Undoubtedly, the world is experiencing a scientific and technological revolution that has seen no equal in history. However, in this as in other respects, the gap between the developed and the underdeveloped countries of the world is enormous. Approximately 6 percent of the total active population of the more developed nations are scientists and technicians. In the underdeveloped world, this figure falls to less than 1 percent. According to Felipe Herrera, the former president of the Inter-American Development Bank, 75 percent of the annual increase in the GNP of the industrialized nations is the result of technological development and only 25 percent is the result of increase in population. In the underdeveloped countries it is just the opposite.[35] Herrera claims, in addition, that fifteen nations do 95 percent of the world's scientific research. The remaining 5 percent is done by the other nations of the world, which constitute over 65 percent of the world's population and which lack human resources that are geared toward scientific and technological development.

The United States spends approximately $112 per capita for research purposes, an amount which represents twice the sum of total per capita expenditures in Latin America, for both economic and social purposes. This is, in part, the reason why average productivity per active person in Latin America is between six to three times less than in countries where technology is used in a more intensive way.

The chiefs of state in Punta del Este (1967) agreed to create a Regional Program for Scientific and Technological Development.[36] Multinational scientific and technological research institutes were planned, and it was decided to create an Inter-American Fund for Scientific and Technological Development. The idea of the fund was to prepare personnel of high academic standing to meet the scientific and technical needs of Latin America. Unfortunately, for the program to succeed the so-called brain drain must stop and, as some Latin Americans have said, a "relief operation" be initiated. Incentives should be offered, the Punta del Este statement went on, not only to stop the brain drain but also to encourage the return of many professional men to their native countries.

According to UNCTAD, the developed countries must do everything in their power to transmit their level of knowledge and technology to the countries in the process of development. A significant part of the research and development expenditures of the developed nations should be dedicated to projects that are of interest to the developing countries. Private

35. Instituto para la Integración de América Latina (INTAL), *Boletín de la Integración*, no. 21 (August 1967), p. 444; speech given by Felipe Herrera at the Universidad Técnica del Estado in Santiago, Chile, 26 June 1967.

36. This was the summit meeting of presidents, which took place in Punta del Este, Uruguay, in April 1967. A Specialized Conference on the Application of Science and Technology for the Development of Latin America (CACTAL) met in Brasilia from 12 to 19 May 1972. It was generally agreed there that a greater effort should be made to apply science and technology to the development of Latin America.

foundations and institutions should be invited to do likewise. Underdeveloped countries should be given access to the industrial patents of the more industrialized nations. Such a policy would make it easier for the manufactured goods of the underdeveloped countries to compete efficiently in world markets with the products of the technically more advanced nations.

UNCTAD also stresses the need for the developed countries to try to eliminate all types of restrictions related to market distribution and price fixing that are practiced by firms in the industrialized nations. Furthermore, the entrepreneurs in the more advanced countries should be encouraged to invest in the exporting industries of the underdeveloped countries. Thus, they should be given realistic information about the economic and political conditions of those countries.

According to the Tinbergen Report, there is great need for international cooperation in the field of scientific research. More attention should be devoted to fostering technologies appropriate for underdeveloped regions and care should be taken that certain types of technology are not forced upon countries in the process of development simply because they are favored by the aid and investment policies of the more advanced countries.

The Tinbergen Report suggests the transfer of 0.05 percent of the GNP of the industrialized countries in order to support science and technology in the developing countries. It also suggests, finally, that by 1980 approximately 5 percent of the research and development expenditures of the industrialized countries should be dedicated to specific problems related to countries in the process of development.[37]

In Viña del Mar the Latin American leaders brought out in a special way the role of the United States in programs of scientific and technological cooperation. Special funds, they said, should be granted for such programs—funds that would not require repayment. They endorsed most of the recommendations made by UNCTAD, at least implicitly, and stressed the need for the United States to intensify its financial support to Latin America in order to speed up the development of the scientific and technological infrastructure of the region. These Latin American leaders also urged the United States to respect the wishes of its neighbors to the south in matters related to economic planning, as stipulated by the appropriate regional or national bodies.

Finally, a word or two should be said on import substitution as a means for industrialization and regional economic integration. Both objectives have rated high on the list of Latin American priorities. The attainment of political and economic integration of the continent would also fulfill a long-desired dream in Latin America.

37. Tinbergen Report, p. 33.

IMPORT SUBSTITUTION

During the years immediately preceding and following World War II, industrialization through import substitution played a leading role in the policy decisions of most Latin American countries. Industrialization was considered an important factor in the development of Latin America and, thus, an important basis for its expansion.[38] National policies were geared toward the creation of domestic industries that would meet the demand of consumers at home. Such policies required the application of all sorts of restrictive measures in the area of international trade and relied heavily on development from within.

The policy of import substitution, however, came under fire when it was realized, in the 1960s, that Latin America could not isolate herself from the outside world. The policy was blamed for the proliferation of industries without due regard for economic efficiency. Costs of production and tariffs had reached unbelievably high levels. The Latin American consumer was deprived of the benefits derived from specialization and economies of scale. As Prebisch very clearly stated, "a healthy form of internal competition [had] failed to develop, to the detriment of efficient production."[39]

The position that import-substituting industrilization was the result of official development policy has been challenged by Professor Stefan H. Robock of Columbia University, who claims that the Latin American experience shows that few countries have formulated "coherent industrial development plans, until quite recently."[40] He believes that import-substitution measures were applied mainly to resolve balance of payments problems and not to promote industrialization. "Thus, a more accurate interpretation of recent history is that the strategy of industrialization alleged to have been tried and found wanting [has] in fact rarely, if ever, been adapted as a strategy of industrialization."[41]

Albert Hirschman also rejects the idea that import-substituting industrialization was exclusively the result of official development policy. He emphasizes the role of "wars, balance of payments difficulties, growth of the domestic market (as a result of export growth),"[42] together with official development policy, as important factors contributing to the process of industrialization.

38. United Nations, *The Economic Development of Latin America* (New York, 1950).

39. United Nations, *Towards a Dynamic Development Policy for Latin America* (New York, 1963), p. 71.

40. Stefan H. Robock, "Industrialization through Import Substitution or Export Industries: A False Dichotomy," in *Industrial Organization and Economic Development*, ed. J. W. Markham and G. F. Papanck (Boston: Houghton Mifflin Co., 1970), p. 354.

41. Ibid., p. 355.

42. Albert Hirschman, *A Bias for Hope: Essays on Development and Latin America* (New Haven: Yale University Press, 1971), p. 90.

Independently of the view taken in relation to import substitution as a strategy for industrialization, it nevertheless seems true that the process of import substitution has tended to slow down and can no longer be considered a propelling force behind industrial development.[43] As many consumer goods that were previously imported came increasingly to be produced at home, import substitution declined in importance. The Latin American countries were thus forced to look for new and enlarged markets outside their own limited frontiers.

REGIONAL ECONOMIC INTEGRATION

The Latin American Free Trade Association (LAFTA)

Created with great enthusiasm in February 1960 as a result of the Treaty of Montevideo, LAFTA, in the opinion of many experts, has not lived up to expectations. It was supposed to permit the Latin American nations to benefit from a larger market and take advantage of economies of scale. In this way, it was believed, trade between the various Latin American countries could increase substantially and the process of industrialization could continue. However, in spite of the gains made in intrazonal trade, LAFTA has had to face increasing difficulties.

As a result of the many problems arising from the need to comply with the agreed-upon annual tariff reductions, the Agreement of Cartagena was signed in 1969. The agreement extended from 1973 to 1980, the period for completing the free trade area. It also called for further studies to help the member countries approve new measures tending toward the fulfillment of the treaty objectives. The Protocol of Cartagena and the newly formed Andean Group have renewed the faith in the integration movement.

The Andean Group

The Cartagena Agreement was signed in May 1969 by five Andean nations—Bolivia, Chile, Columbia, Ecuador, and Peru—in order to accelerate the process of achieving the integration of Latin America. Venezuela joined the group in February 1973. The Andean Group, as this subregional integration movement is called, is attempting to enlarge and strengthen the markets of several of the economically less advanced countries of LAFTA so that they may be able to compete on an equal footing with the member countries that are at a more advanced stage of economic development. In this way the less developed countries hope to have greater leverage to negotiate on a joint basis with their partners within LAFTA.

43. United Nations, *Economic Survey of Latin America, 1964* (New York, 1966).

One of the most talked-about achievements of the Andean Group was the signing of an agreement in Lima, in December 1970, on the treatment of foreign capital and on a common policy relating to patents, licenses, and royalties. This well known Decision 24 undoubtedly put strains on foreign investments, and the wisdom of the decision can only be measured in terms of how it will affect the flow of private foreign capital into the area.

The Central American Common Market (CACM)

The CACM was established as a result of the Treaty of Managua, signed in December 1960 by Costa Rica, El Salvador, Guatemala, Honduras, and Nicaragua. The treaty included not only the commitments made in a multilateral treaty of 1958 but also various bilateral agreements which had existed previously in the region. Although for a number of years CACM appeared to be the most successful of all integration movements in the underdeveloped world, serious doubts about its very survival have since arisen. All the countries involved in the original signing of the treaty are in deep political and economic crisis. Honduras, for political and economic reasons, withdrew from the treaty in 1970.

The Caribbean Free Trade Association (CARIFTA)

The Treaty of St. John, signed in 1968, brought about the creation of CARIFTA. Its purpose is to foster trade expansion and diversification within the Caribbean area. In July 1973, as a result of the signing of the Treaty of Chaguaramas, between the governments of Barbados, Guyana, Jamaica, and Trinidad and Tobago, the Caribbean Community (CARICOM) was established. It is expected that the remaining members of CARIFTA will join.

PROBLEMS OF POLICY

Drastic and deep-rooted changes are rapidly occurring in Latin America. Although not all of these changes have necessarily been for the better, overall Latin America has made substantial progress in its long and difficult path toward development. Certain development goals set by the Latin American countries have already been attained, but it is still too early to determine whether the long-run objectives will also be achieved. In spite of the efforts made through LAFTA and the other regional mechanisms, Latin America has come to realize that its industrialization process cannot continue unless it takes an outward look at the area of foreign trade. Latin America must no longer look exclusively for markets for its traditional basic products, no matter how important they may be. New outlets must be found for its manufactured goods; otherwise, industrialization will not advance at a pace rapid enough to meet the demands of development.

LAFTA has not been able to promote industrialization in any significant manner. In spite of the gains achieved, most of the tariff reductions have taken place in the area of agriculture; thus, tariff reductions have not helped the process of industrialization in any large measure. In fact, there are still tariffs on manufactured goods that have never been negotiated among LAFTA countries. It might be added that the more developed countries of LAFTA are less worried about competition than their less developed neighbors. Consequently, the high-cost countries are less inclined to submit to tariff reductions and liberalization programs. On the other hand, the more developed countries of Latin America are more interested in expanding their markets outside the area than in making concessions to their less privileged partners. All these factors, together with the disastrous effects of runaway inflation (so characteristic of some Latin American countries) have slowed down the positive effects of economic integration and made some people skeptical about the success of LAFTA and the proposed Latin American Common Market. The creation of the Andean Group within LAFTA is one attempt to remedy this situation.

Whether the Andean Group will succeed or not remains a moot point. It must not be forgotten that when the Cartagena accord was signed, in May 1969, the socioeconomic systems prevailing in the five member countries were rather similar. However, after the advent of the government of Salvador Allende in Chile and with the new economic directives of the Peruvian government, the original equilibrium has been altered. Chile, in a very marked way, took the path toward socialism, reducing her strong dynamic private sector. The large industries and the banking system were nationalized, along with most of the foreign trade sector. These new trends obviously had an impact on the future of the Andean Group, if only because tariffs do not operate the same way in a free market economy as they do in the so-called state-operated economies. Tariffs play a decisive role in the former but not in the latter. Although the Allende regime was overthrown in 1973, these changing conditions raise serious doubts about the future of the treaty arrangement as conceived by its signatories and about the economic relations of the member states.

The new emphasis on international trade as a leverage for industrialization requires that Latin America take steps to make its manufactured goods competitive in the world markets. First and foremost, industrial plants must be used at optimum capacity so that production costs can be reduced to a minimum—something which unfortunately is not common in Latin America. Many of the protected industries in Latin America are operating at less than full capacity and, because of their small market, cannot benefit from economies of scale. In other cases, the long-run viability of the industry was overlooked, and serious shortcomings developed, the industry simply managing to survive under the protection of high tariff walls. Many industries do not have the potential to become efficient. Thus, plants often have to be modernized and the level of productivity increased. This requires large new investments, which must be financed either with private or public funds. Often the Latin American countries are neither financially nor technically prepared to meet these demands but depend on financial and technical assistance from the more developed countries of the world.

In respect to private foreign investments, it is only fair to point out that although the Latin American countries desire to receive the benefits of large capital inflows, they have not yet established the rules of the game insofar as investment guarantees are concerned. It must not be forgotten that Latin America is living in a critical period of history and unless the climate is propitious for foreign capital, capital will not flow into the area. Capital looks for profits, but it also requires a minimum of guarantees. Otherwise, it will search for new horizons. Very often the political climate is totally inappropriate for capital investments and, unless it changes, investments will not be forthcoming. Political stability is a *sine qua non* for foreign investment. Latin America must be prepared to receive foreign capital, public or private, and establish the rules of the game, however radically the existing rules may need to be changed. Mexico is a case in point. Although she has strict rules concerning foreign capital, she is the Latin American country that attracts the most foreign capital. At least the investor knows where he stands and what he can expect. Nothing is more devastating to foreign capital movements than total uncertainty about the future.

Certain commercial policies of the more developed countries of the world make it difficult for Latin America to sell its products in the protected markets of Europe and North America. Governments in these regions often limit imports through such restrictive measures as tariffs, import quotas, consumption taxes, and similar regulations. Under these conditions it is almost impossible for Latin America to introduce the products of newly established industries into the European and North American markets.

Latin America must, therefore, define and strengthen its policies in the areas of trade, financial assistance, and technical cooperation. As already indicated, industrialization has been a key factor in the process of development during the past years. Notwithstanding the great importance of agriculture to Latin America, it is imperative that this process of industrialization continue. But to do this, Latin America needs the help and assistance of the more developed nations of the world, those which can provide financial and technical assistance and can open their markets to Latin American exports. Thus, for many years Latin America will continue to depend on the financial and economic resources of the United States and the industrialized countries of Western Europe and Japan. Soviet economic aid, as already indicated, offers a poor and not very reliable substitute for the assistance provided by the Western countries on either a bilateral or a multilateral basis.

There is no doubt that external financial aid contributed to the high rates of economic growth that characterized most Latin American countries during the 1960s. Without these external capital resources it is difficult to visualize how Latin America could have reached its present level of development. However, the servicing of the public external debt—which, as already indicated, is costing some countries as much as 20 percent of their export earnings per year—is a point of great concern. New solutions to these pressing problems must be found; otherwise, the short-run benefits of external assistance may very well become an unbearable burden in the longer run. The countries receiving the financial assistance must measure very carefully the potential benefits of the resources received against their future costs, especially in terms of the service burden.

More emphasis must be placed on the use of resources for the development of new export industries geared toward the international market and less on the typical import-substituting industries that characterized the Latin American development model of past years.

The United States and the other industrial countries of Western Europe and Japan must find new ways of coordinating their own development plans with the needs of the less developed countries. The implementation of such a policy is even more important and urgent today, when the energy crisis threatens to bring to a standstill the development plans of many of the less developed countries that are not exporters of oil. Resources previously used for economic development will now have to be spent on petroleum imports. The possibility also exists that, as a result of the energy crisis, the industrialized societies will want to become more self-sufficient with regard to basic products that they previously imported from the less developed countries. Technological progress may make it possible for the economically more advanced countries to develop new techniques that will lead to the discovery of substitutes for some of these previously imported raw materials. All this will require greater cooperation between the more and the less developed countries if the world is not to experience a widening of the gap between both groups of countries and greater and more drastic economic and political upheavals.

These goals, which seem to be shared by the various countries of Latin America, could very well serve as the basis for a future unified Latin American foreign economic policy. Today we live in a world of power blocs in which, to a large degree, decisions are made on the basis of strength. It seems ironical that the Latin American countries still present to the world the image of a house divided within itself, one in which antagonisms between its members have yet to be overcome. In this light,

Latin America appears a poor rival to other powerful world blocs. Creation of the Latin American Common Market may yet turn out to be a major step toward the integration of the continent and the fulfillment of Bolívar's dream. LAFTA may not have fulfilled the expectations of many, but it still may prove to be the main instrument through which Latin American integration is attained and a common united foreign economic policy is achieved.

BIBLIOGRAPHICAL NOTE

In addition to the works cited in footnotes, the following publications are also recommended:

Baer, Werner. "Import Substitution Industrialization in Latin America: Experiences and Interpretations." *Latin American Research Review* 7 (Spring 1972): 95–122.

Balassa, Bela, and Associates. *The Structure of Protection in Development Countries.* Baltimore: Johns Hopkins University Press, 1971.
An excellent study dealing with the problems of protection in the developing countries.

Bauer, P. T. *Dissent and Development: Studies and Debates in Development Economics.* Cambridge: Harvard University Press, 1972.
An interesting critique of the traditional theories and policies of development.

Bruno, M. "The Optional Selection of Export-promoting and Import Substitution Projects," pp. 88–135. In *Planning the External Sector: Techniques, Problems and Policies.* New York: United Nations, 1967.

Bruton, Henry. "Productivity Growth in Latin America." *American Economic Review* 57 (December 1967): 1099–1116.

ECIEL (Programa de Estudios Conjunctos sobre Integración Económica Latinoamericana). *Industrialization in a Latin American Common Market.* Washington, D.C.: Brookings Institution, 1972.

Frank, Isaiah. *Assisting Development of Low-Income Countries: Priorities for U.S. Government Policy.* Committee for Economic Development. Washington, D.C., September 1969.
A scholarly and competent analysis for the projection of economic priorities.

Handbook of Latin American Studies. Prepared in the Library of Congress and published at Gainesville: University of Florida Press, 1936–.
An annotated annual bibliography of the most important current publications in Latin America relating to all fields of research, including economics and international relations.

Hirschman, Albert. "The Political Economy of Import-Substituting Industrialization in Latin America." *Quarterly Journal of Economics* 87 (February 1968): 1–32.
An excellent analysis of the policies of import substitution in Latin America.

Johnson, H. G. "The Costs of Protection and Self-Sufficiency." *Quarterly Journal of Economics* 79 (August 1965): 356–72.

Krieger-Vasena, Adelbert, and Pazos, Javier. *Latin America: A Broader World Role*. London: Ernest Benn, 1973.
The authors are critical of Latin America's traditional policy of import substitution and stress the need to adopt new technologies to promote the export of manufactured goods.

Little, I. M. D., Scitovsky, T., and Scott, M. *Industry and Trade in Some Developing Countries*. London: Oxford University Press, 1970.
The authors conclude that emphasis should be placed on the development of exports and administrative controls should be replaced by a better use of the price mechanism.

Streeten, Paul, ed. *Grand Strategies for Development*. Papers of the 9th Cambridge Conference on Development Problems, September 1972. London: Macmillan Press, 1973.
Of special interest is the excellent article written by Felipe Pazos, "Regional Integration of Trade among Less Developed Countries."

3/Larman C. Wilson

Multilateral Policy and the Organization of American States: Latin American-U.S. Convergence and Divergence

Professor Gordon Connell-Smith has rightly observed that the Inter-American system serves as "a form of multilateral diplomacy through which the American states conduct a part of their international relations." He goes on to add:

Although representing only a fraction of inter-American diplomacy, the inter-American system affects—at times significantly—bilateral relations between the American states. It has frequently provided a convenient, sometimes even necessary, framework within which bilateral agreements (mainly between the United States and individual Latin American countries) have been concluded, . . .[1]

In recent years interest has increased in the role of the Organization of American States (OAS) in multilateral policy. For example, it has been asked whether the multilateral policy role of the OAS was increasing or decreasing; whether the OAS was becoming a major multilateral instrument in the various areas of inter-American concern (economic, military, political, and social); whether the OAS was facilitating the convergence, or unity, of Latin American policy vis-à-vis the United States, and if this was true, whether it was producing greater convergence or divergence between Latin American and U.S. policies. The Latin Americans also pose another question, which involves the role of the United States inside and outside the OAS: has U.S. policy served as a catalyst to increase convergence with Latin American policy or to increase divergence from it?

These concerns and questions are relevant in view of the 1967 Protocol of Buenos Aires amendments (in effect in 1970) to the OAS Charter, to the resultant debate about their cause and effect,[2] to the increasing awareness

NOTE: Personal appreciation is extended to the following scholars and experts on inter-American relations whose comments improved this chapter: Gordon Connell-Smith, John C. Dreier, F. V. García-Amador, William Manger, and César Sepúlveda.

1. Gordon Connell-Smith, *The Inter-American System* (London and New York: Oxford University Press, 1966), p. xv.

2. John C. Dreier, "New Wine and Old Bottles: The Changing Inter-American System," *International Organization* 22 (Spring 1968): 477–93; and William Manger, "Reform of the OAS," *Journal of Inter-American Studies* 10 (January 1968): 1–14. See also Jerome Slater, "The Decline of the OAS," *International Journal* 24 (Summer 1969): 497–506.

that the inter-American system is in "transition,"[3] and to increasing Latin American criticism of the OAS and the United States, which has prompted an effort to restructure both the OAS and the inter-American system.

Before discussing the questions posed, I should indicate my frame of reference. First, I believe that U.S. policy has been a major determinant in the development of multilateral policy and Latin American–U.S. interaction. But the Latin American nations' response to U.S. policy, particularly when their own policies converged and became more unified, had the effect of altering and moderating U.S. policy. This response indicates a major dilemma confronting the nations of Latin America in their interdependent relationship with North America, which may be stated as follows. Latin America needs U.S. assistance and cooperation, but at the same time it recognizes U.S. predominance over inter-American relations—a predominance that has led Latin America to try to constrain the United States in the hemisphere. Each side, therefore, having different needs and perceptions of its own interests, has interacted by bargaining and engaging in a series of economic and political trade-offs. (In fact, this dilemma, or ambivalence, in Latin American–U.S. relations, plus the major power status of the United States in the hemisphere and in the world, may give this chapter, unintentionally, the appearance of centering upon the role of the United States in the inter-American system, especially in the OAS.)

Second, U.S.–Latin American policy from the formulation of the Monroe Doctrine to the present has consistently pursued two principal strategic goals: preventing foreign influence and control and maintaining political stability.[4] In pursuing these goals, the United States has employed a variety of tactics. For example, to combat the influences of Spain, France, England, Germany and Italy (fascism), and the Soviet Union (communism), such means have been used as customs receiverships, banking consortia, armed intervention during World War I, blocked accounts, trade embargoes, and cooperation with dictators, to the sponsoring of an "invasion" (Bay of Pigs) and the landing of troops (the Dominican Republic in 1965). In maintaining political stability, the tactics have included, *inter alia*, military occupation of a country and supervision of its

3. M. Margaret Ball, *The OAS in Transition* (Durham, N.C.: Duke University Press, 1969). Professor Dreier's distinction between the inter-American system and the OAS will be used, in which the former refers to "the broad complex of juridical principles, political policies, and administrative arrangements that has grown up among the American republics over the years" and the latter to "the principal multilateral organizational through which the system operates" (John C. Dreier, *The Organization of American States and the Hemisphere Crisis* [New York: Frederick A. Praeger, 1962], p. 11).

4. Connell-Smith, *The Inter-American System*; Jerome Slater, *The OAS and United States Foreign Policy* (Columbus: Ohio State University Press, 1967); and Howard J. Wiarda, "The Context of United States Policy toward the Dominican Republic: Background to the Revolution of 1965," mimeographed (Cambridge: Center for International Affairs, Harvard University, 8 Dec. 1966).

elections, the withholding or granting of recognition, the furnishing of military aid, and assistance in economic development. It is worth noting that within the context of the cold war and the triumph of Castro, the two goals have tended to merge. For example, since it was assumed that foreign influence is prevented by assuring political stability, certain tactics were developed to facilitate stability: economic development and social reform (Alliance for Progress), training in counterinsurgency, and civic action.[5]

LATIN AMERICAN-U.S. POLICY CONVERGENCE AND DIVERGENCE THROUGH WORLD WAR II

Convergence: Independence, Trade, and Peaceful Settlement

Recently independent, the Latin American republics were interested in protection and self-defense. They therefore welcomed President Monroe's proclamation in 1823 and its implication of protection. Although several Latin American-initiated conferences were held, it was the First International Conference of American States (Washington, 1889-90) that demonstrated mutual Latin American-U.S. interests in certain fields. There was agreement over the encouragement of commerce, which the United States stressed since she wanted to export manufactures, and over the peaceful settlement of disputes. The agenda even included an unsuccessful U.S. proposal for a Pan American customs union. (Subsequently, however, a Commerce Bureau was set up.) (The initial efforts concerning peaceful settlement were significant because of the fear of European intervention, persistent boundary conflicts, and the appearance in the late nineteenth century of such large-scale power conflicts as the War of the Triple Alliance and the War of the Pacific.)

Divergence: Political-Military

Although mutual interest in expanding trade and peaceful settlement continued, for the first quarter of the twentieth century the United States frequently intervened in Latin America in pursuit of her goals of preventing foreign intervention and maintaining stability. This sometimes included landing troops, especially in the Caribbean and Central America, in the name of various corollaries to the Monroe Doctrine. As a result, the Latin American countries tended to unite against the United States, using the regular International Conferences of American States as a forum for pressuring the United States to cease her Monroe Doctrine-sanctioned interventions. After World War I, Latin American

5. Slater, *The OAS and United States Foreign Policy*; and Wiarda, "The Context of United States Policy toward the Dominican Republic."

spokesmen attacked the practice that made the U.S. secretary of state the president ex officio of the Governing Board and the U.S. policy of keeping such "political topics" as intervention off the agendas of the conferences.

In their challenge to U.S. policy during the first three decades of the century and in their efforts to change it, the Latin American states stressed principles of international law and organization and developed and applied their own legal doctrines.[6] The Calvo and Drago doctrines, which had first been directed against European intervention, were now directed against North America. Chile's Alejandro Alvarez wrote that a regional school of American international law existed, a major rule of which was nonintervention. After World War I, the United States was being pressured to accept certain legal principles, and the Latin American nations tried to go outside the Pan-American regional system and use the League of Nations as a counterpoise to U.S. intervention. This approach failed because article 21 of the League Covenant accepted as valid "regional understandings like the Monroe Doctrine."

Convergence: Political-Military

Near the end of the Hoover administration the United States started to respond and began lessening her political divergence with Latin America. This change initiated the Good Neighbor Policy, including U.S. acceptance of the nonintervention principle at the 1933 Montevideo Conference when she became a party to the Convention on the Rights and Duties of States. Three years later in Buenos Aires, she withdrew her reservations to the 1933 treaty and accepted the Additional Protocol Relative to Non-Intervention. By this time, with nonintervention accepted as the cornerstone of the inter-American system, a number of legal rules had been accepted by the system: nonintervention, sovereign equality, equal treatment of nationals and aliens, peaceful settlement, consultation, and de facto recognition.[7]

By the time of the 1938 Lima Conference the solution of the problems of the codification of international law and (especially) of the peaceful settlement of disputes were fairly well advanced. Two important conventions on peaceful settlement had been accepted by a number of states: the 1923 Treaty to Avoid or Prevent Conflicts Between the American States (Gondra Treaty) and the 1933 Anti-War Treaty of Non-Agression and Conciliation (Saavedra Lamas Treaty.) The development of a

6. H. B. Jacobini, *A Study of the Philosophy of International Law as Seen in Works of Latin American Writers* (The Hague: Martinus Nijhoff, 1954); and C. Neale Ronning, *Law and Politics in Inter-American Diplomacy* (New York: John Wiley & Sons, 1963).

7. Pan American Union, Inter-American Juridical Committee, *Contribution of the American Continent to the Principles of International Law That Govern the Responsibility of the State* . . . (Washington, D.C., 1958).

multilateral policy under the impetus of the Good Neighbor Policy was advanced at the Lima Conference in the Declaration of the Principles of the Solidarity of America (Declaration of Lima), which, from the Latin American viewpoint, had the effect of "multilateralizing" and "continentalizing" the Monroe Doctrine.

The three Meetings of Consultation of Ministers of Foreign Affairs in Panama (1939), Havana (1940), and Rio de Janeiro (1942) were prompted by the outbreak of World War II and early U.S. involvement in it. The meetings were important for their creation of regional machinery and for their development of concepts that were to be important in inter-American relations following the war. Agreements were reached at these meetings upon collective security, upon severing relations with the Axis, and upon various measures of economic and military cooperation; but several specific provisions of these agreements are interesting in retrospect. While the Panama meeting created what soon became known as the Inter-American Juridicial Committee, the Havana meeting borrowed an idea from the Mexico City Pan American conference of 1901–2 and proposed an Inter-American bank. The plan was approved by eight Latin American states but never went into effect, largely because the U.S. Senate withheld approval in the face of Argentine objections. (Not until nineteen years later did the United States finally accept such a bank, then upon a unified demand by the nations of Latin America.) At the Rio meeting the United States proposed suspending for the duration of the war all tariffs and trade barriers (exactly what the Latin American countries began requesting and bargaining for in the late 1960s!). The conference also agreed to create the Inter-American Defense Board to study and recommend strategies of hemispheric defense.

There was disagreement in the United States about the role of the Inter-American Defense Board. The War Department favored a minimal role, one that was consultative and multilateral in name only. The State Department, however, supported by the Latin American governments, preferred a more active role, one that was advisory and multilateral. In practice, during the war, the U.S. Army and the U.S. Navy limited the Defense Board to the consideration of matters they felt could not be handled in bilateral relations with Latin American governments.

As the war progressed and plans were being made for a new postwar international organization, the Latin American states supported retaining and strengthening the regional (inter-American) approach while the United States favored the global (UN) plans. The Latin American governments resented their exclusion from the 1944 Dumbarton Oaks Conference and were critical of its proposals, which seemed to exclude the small nations. The stage was thus set for the last wartime hemispheric conference before that of San Francisco to establish the United Nations.

The 1945 Conference on the Problems of War and Peace in Mexico City (Chapultepec Conference) strengthened the regional approach when it was decided to base the inter-American system on three treaties:

1. a treaty of reciprocal assistance;
2. a charter of the organization of American states; and
3. a comprehensive treaty on pacific settlement.[8]

While these three commitments were to be worked out formally in the postwar period, an Economic Charter of the Americas was approved—a harbinger of the Alliance for Progress in its statement of principles relating to the economic development of Latin America. Most important was the Act of Chapultepec, which provided that an attack against one nation of America was an attack against all. It provided for consultation in cases of attack and for agreement about measures of collective self-defense and the imposing of sanctions, including the use of armed force. The Declaration of Lima (1938) had provided for consultation in the case of an exterior threat to the peace of the hemisphere, but this was the first time that an attack by one American state against another was provided for. It was also the first time the use of armed force was agreed to as a sanction against a threat to hemispheric peace.

At San Francisco a few months later, the Latin American bloc, its regional approach now joined to and partly accepted by the United States, held out for coordinating the regional and universal approaches and for maintaining the autonomy of the inter-American system. Because it constituted 40 percent of the votes, the Latin American bloc was in a good bargaining position. The success of its bargaining appeared in the addition of article 51 and articles 52–54 (the latter comprising chapter 8, "Regional Arrangements") to the UN Charter. Article 51, the Vandenburg Resolution, provided for the "inherent right of individual or collective self-defense . . . until the Security Council" could take action in a dispute. Article 52 specified the relationship between the United Nations and regional organizations, stating that members of the latter "shall make every effort to achieve pacific settlement of local disputes through such regional arrangements . . . *before* referring them to the Security Council" (italics added).

In late 1945 the foreign minister of Uruguay, Eduardo Rodríguez Larreta, made a case for collective action against such dictators as Juan Perón in Argentina, in the name of promoting democracy and peace.[9] The Rodríguez Larreta proposal appeared to violate the nonintervention principle in the interest of protecting representative government. The

8. J. Lloyd Mecham, *A Survey of United States–Latin American Relations* (Boston: Houghton Mifflin Co., 1965), p. 167.
9. Ronning, *Law and Politics in Inter-American Diplomacy*, pp. 68–69.

discussions that resulted were revived in the 1950s and 1960s when the United States attempted to convert the OAS into an "anti-Communist alliance." Even though the United States readily accepted the proposal as a means of toppling Perón, most of the Latin American states were suspicious of U.S. acceptance and were unwilling to compromise the hard-won nonintervention concept.

LATIN AMERICAN–U.S. POLICY DIVERGENCE AND CONVERGENCE: THE COLD WAR

Divergence: Economic Assistance

Soon after the end of World War II, the wartime alliance broke down, especially between the United States and the Soviet Union. The United States became preoccupied with the problems of protecting and rebuilding Europe, of containing the Soviet bloc by economic (European Recovery Program, or Marshall Plan) and military (North Atlantic Treaty Organization, or NATO) means. The United States, having come to regard Latin America as a low priority area, was chiefly interested in maintaining the status quo there; her concern, as demonstrated by President Truman at the 1951 Fourth Meeting of Consultation of Foreign Ministers in Washington (which was prompted by the Korean War), was to prevent Communist influence. Consequently, she greatly reduced economic and financial aid and pursued her wartime policy of assuming the responsibility for hemispheric defense, helping certain of the larger Latin American countries to make a contribution by providing military aid. The Latin Americans believed that they were being "neglected" and that their cooperation during World War II had been forgotten.

The permanent bases for the inter-American system were laid, in keeping with the Mexico City conference's commitments, in the early cold war period. The first basic document, the Inter-American Treaty of Reciprocal Assistance (Rio Treaty, or Rio Pact) was drawn up at the 1947 Rio conference, in which Latin America and the United States exhibited differing priorities. While Latin America was interested in strengthening the regional system in coordination with the United Nations and with improving economic cooperation with the United States, the United States was primarily interested in cold war collective security. The United States was able to confine the conference to the preparation of a security treaty (the major agenda item), postponing the date of the conference on economic cooperation desired by the Latin American nations. The Rio Treaty, which went into effect in 1948, had two particularly important articles, especially in view of such subsequent events as the invocation against Castro's Cuba in 1962. Article 6 provided for a meeting of the Organ of Consultation to decide upon collective measures if any American state was "affected by an aggression which is *not an armed* attack or by an extra-continental or intra-continental conflict, or by *any other fact or situation that might endanger the peace* of America." Article 8 indicated the range of "measures" or sanctions to be applied, ranging from "recall of chiefs of diplomatic missions" to the *"use of armed forces"* (italics added).

The 1948 Bogotá conference, continuing the considerable noneconomic convergence, drew up the other two treaties pledged at the Mexico City (Chapultepec) conference. The first treaty, the OAS Charter, set up a juridicially complete and integrated regional system. The principles enunciated earlier, such as nonintervention, sovereign equality, and peaceful settlement of disputes, were reaffirmed, and the machinery was created for increasing the effectiveness of the regional system. Article 15 (article 18 under the amended Charter) contained an absolute ban on intervention. But article 19 (now article 22) provided an exception to the nonintervention principle, for "measures adopted for the maintenance of peace and security in accordance with existing treaties." Brief chapters on economic, social, and cultural standards were included in the charter. The following machinery was created: (1) the Inter-American Conference, the supreme organ; (2) Meetings of Consultation of Foreign Ministers, for urgent problems; (3) the Council of the OAS, with three subsidiary organs—an Economic and Social Council, a Council of Jurists (with its Juridical Committee from the 1940 Havana meeting), and a Cultural Council; and (4) the Pan American Union, now to be the secretariat. The Charter became effective in 1951.

The second convention drawn up at Bogotá was the Inter-American Treaty of Pacific Settlement (Pact of Botoá), which was to supersede and bring together into one document all earlier conciliation treaties. Unfortunately, this proposed treaty, now partly antiquated and unaccept-able to the United States from the start, has become only partially an inter-American document, for only thirteen states have ratified it. This means that those states that have not ratified the Pact of Bogotá are still governed by the earlier conciliation treaties of the 1920s and 30s.

A major disagreement developed at Bogotá between Latin America and the United States over the nature of economic cooperation, the subject of a conference agreed upon at Chapultepec but postponed after the Rio conference of 1947. The Latin Americans wanted greater economic aid, with an emphasis upon public capital. Favoring a multilateral approach, they now proposed that an Inter-American bank (requested in 1940) be set up. The United States opposed this multilateral economic policy, favoring a bilateral and private capital approach. As a result, a weak economic agreement was signed at Bogotá in 1948, and the Latin American desire for more consideration of the topic was incorporated in a resolution calling for a Specialized Inter-American Economic Conference of Ministers of Finance (this economic conference was delayed by the United States until 1957; it was held in that year in Buenos Aires).

The Bogotá conference of 1948 also dealt with human rights, a topic of long-standing concern, in the American Declaration of the Rights and Duties of Man. This declaration began by stating: "The international protection of the rights of man should be the principal guide of an evolving American law." Two other resolutions were enacted. One proposed an Inter-American Court to Protect the Rights of Man (the OAS Juridical Committee was charged with drawing up a draft). The second dealt with The Preservation and Defense of Democracy in America. The latter was the first inter-American resolution to mention "communism."

Divergence: "Communism" and Economic Assistance

The increasing preoccupation of the United States with communism and Latin America's growing dissatisfaction with U.S. economic policy had been readily apparent by the mid-1950s. At the Fourth Meeting of Consultation of Foreign Ministers (Washington, 1951) and at the Caracas conference (1954), it was obvious that the United States was trying to convert the OAS into an "anti-Communist alliance."[10] The Latin Americans, on the other hand, were countering with proposals for economic and social development. In addition to this bargaining with the United States, the Latin American governments were also turning to the United Nations for economic aid, through the Economic and Social Council (ECOSOC), the International Bank for Reconstruction and Development (IBRD), and the International Monetary Fund (IMF). It is worth noting, however, that despite their increasing criticisms of the United States, they still voted with the United States in the General Assembly of the United Nations on cold war issues.[11]

The Fourth Meeting of Consultation of Foreign Ministers was called by President Truman in 1951 to consider the Korean situation. The resultant Declaration of Washington stressed the importance of American military cooperation and readiness in case of a crisis, of the need for economic cooperation and for the elimination of economic conditions conducive to communism, and of the necessity for increasing internal measures to suppress Communist subversive activities. And the Inter-American Defense Board was assigned the responsibility of preparing military plans for the collective defense of the hemisphere.

By the time of the Tenth Inter-American Conference at Caracas in 1954, most of the Latin American governments were benefiting in the area of technical assistance from President Truman's Point Four program as well as from increased military aid under the 1951 Mutual Security Act. However, they believed that their economic assistance needs were being

10. Slater, *The OAS and United States Foreign Policy*, chaps. 3 and 4.
11. John A. Houston, *Latin America in the United Nations* (New York: Carnegie Endowment for International Peace, 1956); and Thomas Hovet, Jr., *Bloc Politics in the United Nations* (Cambridge: Harvard University Press, 1960).

neglected, and they viewed the Caracas conference as an opportunity to
bargain for more economic aid. The United States wanted a commitment
to collective action against the "international communist conspiracy" that
she believed had gained control in Guatemala. Secretary of State Dulles
submitted a proposal, the Declaration of Solidarity for the Preservation of
the Political Integrity of the American States Against the Intervention of
International Communism, designed to lay the basis for the OAS as an
anti-Communist alliance. It provided that the establishment of a
Communist-controlled government in an American nation was a threat to
hemispheric peace under the Rio Treaty. The resolution was passed after
considerable debate (Argentina and Mexico abstained) and after certain
economic and political trade-offs had been made.

The resolution of the "Communist" problem in Guatemala was
interesting in terms of OAS–U.S. relations and of Guatemala's appeal to
the United Nations. The arrival of a shipment of arms in Guatemala from
Eastern Europe shortly after the Caracas conference prompted the United
States to sign mutual defense pacts with, and to airlift arms to, Honduras
and Nicaragua. On 18 June 1954, an armed band of insurgents (the "Army
of Liberation"), equipped indirectly by the United States in Honduras,
entered Guatemala. Guatemala invoked the services of the Inter-American
Peace Committee and thus involved the OAS for the first time in the
controversy with the United States. By the time the committee was ready to
send an investigating team to Guatemala, Guatemala had appealed to the
UN Security Council. At this time Guatemala had not ratified the Rio Pact
or the OAS Charter. She brought her case before the Security Council twice
and was turned down twice; each time a debate ensued between the United
States and the USSR in which the former urged the "primacy" of the OAS
and the latter argued the "primacy" of the United Nations.[12] The U.S.
position prevailed in the Council. After Guatemala was turned down for
the second time in the United Nations, the OAS Council met and set a
date for a meeting of the Organ of Consultation, preferring not to act
provisionally itself in that capacity. Guatemala then also approved a
visit of the Inter-American Peace Committee's investigating team. But
before the team arrived the Arbenz Government had collapsed and
been replaced by an anti-Communist junta.

This outcome indicated both the major role played by the United States
in overturning the Arbenz government and her reluctance to use the OAS in
the controversy. Secretary of State Dulles's view was that the solution
was a "triumph for the system of balance between regional organization and world organization," but this was a judgment of doubtful
validity; his opinion that the Communist threat in Guatemala was "a

12. Inis L. Claude, Jr., "The OAS, the UN, and the United States," *International
Conciliation*, no. 547 (March 1964), pp. 21–46.

direct challenge to our Monroe Doctrine, the first and most fundamental of our foreign policies," was presumptuous, to say the least.[13]

Many Latin American governments viewed the role of the United States
in this case as an intervention in the domestic affairs of Guatemala,
contrary to the Treaty of Montevideo and the OAS Charter.

The United States Responds to
Economic Policy Divergence

It took a while for the United States to respond to Dr. Milton Eisenhower's
enlightened report after his 1953 trip to Latin America, in which he
recommended the need for economic cooperation. His brother, President
Dwight D. Eisenhower, merely said in his 1954 message to Congress that
"military assistance must be continued. Technical assistance must be
maintained. Economic assistance can be reduced."[14] The need for change
was being increasingly realized, but the United States was slow to respond
to Latin American economic initiatives. The uncompromising stance of
the United States at the 1954 economic conference in Rio de Janeiro
assured the meeting's failure. The United States was also resistant
particularly to Latin American requests for an Inter-American bank and
for commodity agreements, at the 1957 Buenos Aires Economic Conference. However, after having been strongly rebuffed by the Latin Americans
for her position, and being aware of the united front against her, the United
States reversed her position a few months after the conference and complied
with the Latin American consensus for creating an Inter-American bank
(which was established in 1959) and signing commodity agreements.

The major catalyst for change was the treatment of Vice-President
Nixon in Lima and Caracas during his South American trip in May 1958.
Congress and the executive branch were shocked out of their peripheral
concern for Latin America; even the Vice-President admitted that "Caracas
was a much-needed shock treatment which jolted us out of dangerous
complacency."[15] Nixon's reception prompted a congressional investigation of Latin American–U.S. relations[16] and another trip by Dr. Milton
Eisenhower.

Other Latin American developments that also had an impact upon
United States policy were (1) the Brazilian proposal for an Operation Pan
America, (2) regional integration movements, and (3) the rise to power of
Castro in Cuba. In the 1950s, the Latin American countries had responded
to the findings and recommendations of the United Nations Economic

13. (U.S.) *Department of State Bulletin* 30 (25 June 1954): 43–44.
14. Quoted in Connell-Smith, *The Inter-American System*, p. 160.
15. Richard M. Nixon, *Six Crises* (New York: Doubleday & Co., 1962), p. 229.
16. The U.S. Senate authorized funds to finance a series of independent studies:
Committee on Foreign Relations, *United States–Latin American Relations: Compilation of
Studies*, 86th Cong., 2d sess., 1960.

Commission for Latin America (ECLA), especially the ideas of its executive secretary, Raúl Prebisch, which embraced plans for regional integration, commodity agreements, and the formation of common markets as approaches to economic development.[17] The United States was regularly outvoted in the Latin American–dominated ECLA, whose creation the Latin Americans had supported in the United Nations Economic and Social Council in 1948. There finally resulted the Treaty Establishing a Free-Trade Area and Instituting the Latin American Free-Trade Association (Treaty of Montevideo) creating LAFTA in 1960. Limited at first to Argentina, Brazil, Chile, Uruguay, Paraguay, Peru, and Mexico, LAFTA later comprised all the South American nations. In 1958, the Multilateral Treaty on Central American Free Trade and Economic Integration (Tegucigalpa Treaty) had brought together all the Central American countries except Panama in the Central American Common Market (CACM). In 1958, President Juscelino Kubitschek of Brazil made several proposals to President Eisenhower for improving economic relations, which culminated in his proposal of Operation Pan America. The same year the American foreign ministers, meeting informally in Washington, created the Committee of Twenty-One to "study the formulation of new measures for economic operation," and an OAS committee drafted proposals for the Inter-American Development Bank that were approved in 1959.[18] In August 1960, President Eisenhower requested congressional authorization for $500 million to complement the plans for Operation Pan America, and the next month the Act of Bogotá (Measures for Social Improvement and Economic Development Within the Framework of Operation Pan America), resulting from a meeting of the Committee of Twenty-One, was signed. These changes in U.S. economic policy during the last year of the Eisenhower Administration made possible a developing convergence, laying the foundation for the Alliance for Progress.

The Alliance for Progress, built upon these earlier foundations, was in part the Kennedy administration's response to the rise of Fidel Castro and to new Latin American exigencies. It was in effect a new economic and policy measure that merged the two strategic goals of preventing—and counteracting—foreign (Communist) influence and subversion, and maintaining stability.[19] President Kennedy formally proposed what he called an "alliance for progress" at a White House reception for the American ambassadors two months after his inauguration. He recom-

17. Two affiliates of the World Bank (IBRD) were created that provided much more favorable terms for loans for underdeveloped countries: the International Finance Corporation (IFC) in 1956 and the International Development Association (IDA) in 1960.

18. Around this time Castro proposed that the United States undertake Latin America's economic development for a ten-year period to the amount of $300–$400 million. The United States rejected the proposal.

19. Slater, *The OAS and United States Foreign Policy*; and Wiarda, "The Context of United States Policy toward the Dominican Republic."

mended support of economic integration and announced that he had requested the Congress to appropriate $500 million (following up the Eisenhower proposal) as the first step by the United States toward fulfilling the promise of the Act of Bogotá.

A few months later, following a trip by UN Ambassador Adlai Stevenson to South America, the American economic ministers met in Punta del Este, Uruguay. This 1961 meeting gave the Alliance for Progress a basis in an inter-American document, the Charter of Punta del Este, and launched a ten-year, $1,000 million development program.[20] It was agreed that the $1,000 million for economic and social investment would be raised on an annual basis as follows: 80 percent from Latin American capital, public and private; 10 percent from U.S. government loans and grants; 4 percent from private U.S. capital; and 6 percent from other foreign private capital and international lending agencies. The parties also committed themselves, *inter alia*, to peaceful political change, agrarian, fiscal, and social reform and to development in a variety of fields, thereby achieving a new inter-American policy convergence.

Convergence over Trujillo and Divergence over Castro

The Trujillo dictatorship was a challenge to the inter-American system— and the United States—not only because of its long and oppressive rule but especially because of the instability and tension it provoked by its interventions in the Caribbean and because it was a target for a revolution analogous to the overthrow of Fulgencio Batista and the triumph of Castro in Cuba. Recurring tensions in the Caribbean, such as the attempted invasions of the Dominican Republic by exiles, prompted the 1959 Fifth Meeting of Consultation of Foreign Ministers in Santiago, Chile. After considering a report of the Inter-American Peace Committee on democracy, human rights, and political tension,[21] the ministers debated the desirability of the OAS taking collective action against dictatorial regimes in fulfilling the inter-American system's commitment to representative democracy and the protection of human rights. The Latin American consensus was against taking such action on the ground that it would violate the nonintervention principle, although two neighbors of the Dominican Republic, Cuba and Venezuela, favored taking action, arguing that nonintervention was a "shield" behind which dictators were hiding and that collective action was not contrary to the OAS Charter. The United States, then preferring the stability tactic, joined the Latin American consensus. Although the resulting Declaration of Santiago strongly con-

20. Harvey S. Perloff, *Alliance for Progress: A Social Invention in the Making* (Baltimore: Johns Hopkins University Press, 1969).

21. Pan American Union, *Special Report on the Relationship Between Violations of Human Rights or the Non-Exercise of Representative Democracy and the Political Tensions That Affect the Peace of the Hemisphere* (Washington, D.C., 1960).

demned dictatorial regimes, the debate over nonintervention had indicated the importançe attached to international law in Latin America,
indicating that the nonintervention principle was considered a legal obligation whereas the commitment to democracy and human rights was
viewed as only a moral duty. This meeting also authorized the creation of the Inter-American Commission on Human Rights, but gave it
very limited power.

In June 1960, agents of the Dominican government attempted to kill
President Rómulo Betancourt of Venezuela. The assassination attempt
prompted the Sixth Meeting of Ministers of Foreign Affairs called under
the Rio Treaty, meeting in San José, Costa Rica. After an OAS Council
committee report established the complicity of the Dominican government
in the assassination attempt, the meeting considered the measures to be
taken. The majority of the Latin American delegates favored the
application of collective sanctions, whereas the United States at the outset
opposed sanctions and advocated instead OAS supervision of free elections
in the Dominican Republic. A resolution was finally adopted condemning
the Dominican Republic for its "aggression" and "attack" and providing
for diplomatic, economic, and trade sanctions. This *first* example of
collective sanctions imposed by the OAS gave the United States an
opportunity to work through the OAS as a means of pressuring Trujillo to
make democratic reforms and to adopt the reforms demanded by the
Alliance for Progress. The sanctions, which were expanded as a bargaining
device to get a commitment to hold free elections (and were even continued
after Trujillo's assassination in May 1961), were in effect until January
1962.[22] Although OAS-observed elections were held in December 1962,
subsequent events demonstrated the failure of this major effort to carry out
the Alliance for Progress reforms through the overthrow of the elected
government. That the Trujillo legacy was too strong to overcome in such a
short time was soon to appear.

Efforts by the United States to oppose "Communist" governments in the
Caribbean (mainly in Cuba but also in the Dominican Republic in 1965)
led her to continue the policy of regarding the OAS as an anti-Communist
alliance,[23] resorting to unilateral intervention, and developing new tactics
directed toward strengthening internal security in such countries as the
Dominican Republic. These efforts, particularly unilateral intervention,
as in the Dominican Republic, caused an increasing trend toward Latin

22. The USSR wanted the Security Council to approve the OAS sanctions against Trujillo
as an "enforcement action" under article 53 of the UN Charter. Instead, the Security Council
voted to "take note" of the OAS action. Claude, "The OAS, the UN, and the United States,"
pp. 48–50.

23. In 1957 President Prado of Peru proposed linking the OAS and NATO. The United
States favored this, but Latin America was opposed.

American-U.S. divergence, with the exception of the brief convergence during the Cuban missile crisis in 1962. These actions also accelerated two related trends in Latin American national policies. The first was an increased Latin American tendency to turn to the United Nations; the second, a drive to amend the OAS Charter.

The approach of the United States in the Cuban case after 1959, together with the earlier Guatemalan and later Dominican cases, indicated that the United States, as Bryce Wood and Minerva Morales have observed, "had become more regional than the original regionalists" at the San Francisco conference.[24] Not only did she continue her policy of "trying the OAS first" apropos of Cuba, but she argued for the application of article 6 of the Rio Treaty, whereas most of the Latin Americans preferred the application of the milder article 39 of the OAS Charter.[25]

Worsening Cuban-U.S. relations and the threat of Soviet intervention—particularly after Castro's charge, in July 1960, that the United States was planning an invasion and Chairman Nikita Khrushchev's response that the Sovet Union would come to Cuba's aid by using intercontinental misssiles[26]—resulted in the Seventh Meeting of Consultation of Foreign Ministers. Meeting also in San José immediately after the sixth meeting had ended, this seventh meeting focused upon "threats of extraconti- nental intervention." The Peace Committee of the OAS submitted a report on Caribbean tensions, which it held had been increasing on account of Soviet-sponsored activities in the area. After considerable discussion of the extent of Soviet influence and after exchanges be- tween the Cuban and the U.S. representatives, the ministers approved the Declaration of San José, condemning "extracontinental interven- tion." This document fell short of what the United States had advocated, since it only condemned communism and made no mention of Cuba.

Cuba was an important issue in the 1960 U.S. presidential campaign, and the Democratic challenger, Senator John F. Kennedy, took the offensive, placing the Republican nominee, Vice-President Richard M. Nixon, on the defensive. Senator Kennedy criticized the Eisenhower Administration's Cuban policy, arguing that an all-out quarantine should be applied, that U.S. intervention might be necessary, and that the numerous Cuban exiles in the United States should be given aid. Vice- President Nixon countered, in the fourth TV debate with his opponent, by stressing inter-American treaties in which the United States had agreed not

    24. Bryce Wood and Minerva M. Morales, "Latin America and the United Nations," in Norman J. Padelford and Leland M. Goodrich, eds., *The United Nations in the Balance* (New York: Frederick A. Praeger, 1965), p. 358.
    25. (Now article 59): "The Meeting of Consultation . . . shall be held in order to consider problems of an urgent nature and of common interest to the American States. . . ."
    26. *New York Times*, 10 July 1960.

to intervene in Latin America, arguing that the United States "would lose all of [her] friends in Latin America" if it intervened in Cuba.[27] This was an interesting statement, for by this time it was an open secret that the United States was supporting a Cuban-exile invasion. After less than three months in office, President Kennedy approved the invasion plan of Cuban exiles, recruited and trained by the United States in Guatemala, which he had inherited from his predecessor. The U.S.-sponsored invasion at the Bay of Pigs in mid-April failed; the members of the Cuban Brigade were defeated, and most of them were captured. In refusing to dispatch U.S. military units to assure the invasion's success, President Kennedy adhered to his 12 April press conference statement that "there will not be under any conditions, an intervention in Cuba by the United States armed forces."[28]

After the Bay of Pigs fiasco, the debate in Latin America and the United States about intervention and nonintervention was resumed. Most of the Latin American nations considered the invasion to be an illegal U.S. intervention. President Kennedy responded to the defeat in an address to the American Society of Newspaper Editors on 20 April entitled "The Lesson of Cuba." In it appeared a statement that has been called the Kennedy Corollary to the Monroe Doctrine:

. . . Should it ever appear that the inter-American doctrine of non-intervention merely conceals or excuses a policy of nonaction—if the nations of this Hemisphere should fail to meet their commitments against outside Communist penetration— then I want it clearly understood that this Government will not hesitate in meeting its primary obligations which are to the security of our nation.[29]

In May 1961, the UN Special Fund made a decision that conflicted with U.S. Cuban policy and illustrated the difference between bilateral and multilateral aid. It was decided, despite the fact that the United States contributed around 40 percent of the Special Fund's budget, to make funds available to the Cuban government to promote crop diversification. The United States protested strongly and tried to hold up the aid, forbidding the use of dollars and U.S. equipment and technicians. The aid was ultimately made available to Cuba, but not until early 1963.

The increasing economic dependence of Cuba upon the Soviet Union and charges of subversion in Latin America emanating from Cuba resulted in the Eighth Meeting of Consultation of Foreign Ministers (Punta del

27. See Larman C. Wilson, "Law and Intervention in the Cuban 'Invasion' of 1961," *Revue de Droit International*, no. 4 (October–December 1965), pp. 347–55.
28. *New York Times*, 13 Apr. 1961.
29. (U.S.) *Department of State Bulletin* 44 (8 May 1961): 659–61. In the General Assembly Mexico introduced a resolution condemning the United States and calling for peaceful settlement of disputes, which did not mention the OAS. Although defeated, six other Latin American states voted for it.

Este, Uruguay) in January 1962, initiated by Colombia and called by Peru to consider the charges. Although the United States felt that the consultation was premature in terms of getting a firm commitment against Cuba, she made a major effort in support of such action. The Inter-American Peace Committee presented a report supporting the "hard line" group that wanted sanctions, in which it attempted to document the "transformation" of Cuba and concluded that the close ties between Cuba and the Soviet bloc were "evidently incompatible with the principles and standards that govern the regional system."[30] The resultant debate between the "hard line," led by the United States, and the "soft line" (or "legalists"), led by Mexico, revolved around the applicability of article 6 of the Rio Treaty, what measures could be taken, the nature of the Cuban government, and the question of excluding Cuba from the organization— especially since there is no exclusion provision in the OAS Charter. Even though the Final Act was signed by all states except Cuba, the most controversial part, titled Exclusion of the Present Government of Cuba from Participation in the Inter-American System, received just the required two-thirds majority in plenary session. Cuba voted against it and six states abstained.[31] Haiti's shift from the "soft line" to the "hard line" assured the necessary fourteenth vote. As a consequence of this resolution, the Cuban government, because it had "identified itself as a Marxist-Leninist government," was excluded from participation in the OAS. Cuba was also excluded from the Inter-American Defense Board, and an economic sanction was imposed—"to suspend immediately trade with Cuba in arms and implements of war of every kind." Finally, a resolution was adopted calling for "broadening and strengthening" the Human Rights Commission.

Following the decision that Cuba had excluded herself from the OAS, Castro appealed to the UN Security Council a few months later to request an advisory opinion of the International Court of Justice concerning the legality of OAS regional action and Cuba's "exclusion." The Soviet Union supported the appeal, but it was rejected by the Security Council, Chile and Venezuela voting with the United States. It should be noted that Mexico, consistent in her view of international law, considered the Punta del Este action against Cuba to be illegal, since the Charter does not provide for expulsion of a member, and favored Cuba and the United States submitting their major problems to the World Court. The so-called exclusion of Cuba raises an interesting point about the U.S. approach of keeping the United Nations out of inter-American disputes. How can the "primacy" of the

---

30. Pan American Union, *Report of the Inter-American Peace Committee to the Eighth Meeting of Ministers of Foreign Affairs, 1962* (Washington, D.C., 1962).
31. Argentina, Bolivia, Brazil, Chile, Ecuador, and Mexico.

OAS be argued in dealing with Cuba, when Cuba is not permitted to participate in that organization?

Convergence: Cuban Missiles

The major event of 1962 was the Cuban missile crisis, which brought a unified Latin American reaction against the threat of Soviet missiles in Cuba and support for multilateral action to force their withdrawal.[32] In mid-October, President Kennedy was informed that missiles with an "offensive" capability were being established, ready for launching in Cuba. Six days later, in an evening address to the nation, the president revealed the new military threat posed by Cuba and announced the actions that were going to be taken. After stating that the United States would institute a "strict quarantine on all offensive military equipment under shipment to Cuba," President Kennedy warned the Soviet Union that it would be subject to retaliation if any missiles were launched from Cuba. He further stated that the United States was calling an immediate meeting of the OAS Organ of Consultation (under articles 6 and 8 of the Rio Treaty) and an emergency session of the UN Security Council. The next day the OAS Council, acting provisionally as the Organ of Consultation, met to consider the U.S. case. The conclusive proof of the presence of Soviet missiles in Cuba, constituting external intervention in Latin America, was sufficient to gain Latin American approval of the U.S.-sponsored resolution, although Bolivia, Brazil, and Mexico attached reservations. In the UN Security Council, the United States submitted a resolution calling for the withdrawal of the missiles, and the Soviet Union countered with one condemning the "blockade." Neither resolution was voted upon, for the sake of facilitating bilateral negotiations between the two major powers. The U.S. "quarantine" of Cuba produced no incidents, and near its end naval units of Argentina and Venezuela joined those of the United States.

One point should be noted about the role of Castro. During the process of the U.S.-Soviet negotiations, Castro vetoed a plan agreed upon by the two major protagonists and supported by the secretary-general to have the United Nations oversee the missile withdrawal. Castro stood firm against considerable Soviet pressure and UN urging; he could not prevent the withdrawal of missiles but he did prevent inspection by the United Nations. A major commitment of the United States to the Soviet Union for the missile withdrawal was that she would not invade Cuba.

On account of the missile crisis and the negotiations between the United States and the Soviet Union for an agreement banning the testing of nuclear weapons, some of the Latin American nations began taking steps

32. See Larman C. Wilson, "International Law and the United States Cuban Quarantine of 1962," *Journal of Inter-American Studies* 7 (October 1965): 485–92.

toward making their area a nuclear-free zone. In April 1963, before the U.S.-Soviet Nuclear Test Ban Treaty was signed, five Latin American presidents issued a joint declaration calling for the denuclearization of Latin America. Late that year the UN General Assembly approved a resolution on the denuclearization of Latin America.[33] Four years later the Treaty for the Prohibition of Nuclear Weapons in Latin America (Treaty of Tlatelolco) was signed. All the Latin American nations except Argentina and Cuba, which did not sign it, have ratified this treaty.

Divergence: Political-Security

The Johnson administration had its first international crisis in early 1964, with Panama. The flag riots were provoked by U.S. high school students in the Canal Zone when they violated a Panama–U.S. agreement of 1963 between President John F. Kennedy and President Robert Chiari of Panama that the Panamanian flag could be flown in the Canal Zone where the United States flag was flown by civilian authorities. The students' refusal to permit the flying of the Panamanian flag resulted in mob action, destruction of property, sniping, and loss of life. Panama accused the United States of "aggression" and an "unprovoked armed attack," announced that she was severing diplomatic ties with the United States, appealed to the OAS for a meeting of the Organ of Consultation under the Rio Treaty, and requested a meeting of the United Nations Security Council.

The United States was shocked by Panama's actions, because it was the first time that the Rio Treaty had been invoked against the United States by an OAS member. After preliminary discussions between the two countries, Panama agreed to defer her request for invoking the Rio Treaty until the Inter-American Peace Committee had had an opportunity to attempt conciliation. The Security Council, with the Soviet Union dissenting, also deferred action. The Peace Committee played a useful role but was not able to bridge the gap between Panama's insistence upon "negotiating" a new canal treaty and the U.S. stress upon "discussing" it. The Peace Committee withdrew from the controversy when Panama announced that she was going to request invocation of the Rio Treaty. Panama's request was discussed at length by the OAS Council and approved by sixteen votes. Only Chile voted against the request; Panama and the United States were not eligible to vote. The Council, acting provisionally as the Organ of Consultation, set up a General Committee to attempt to bring about an agreement between the disputants. The impasse was finally broken when

33. A Preparatory Commission drew up a treaty, which was signed in 1967. In 1970 the Agency for Proscription of Nuclear Arms in Latin America was formed with headquarters in Mexico to enforce the 1967 treaty, and in 1971 the United States ratified a protocol to support and respect the treaty. Although twenty countries have ratified the Treaty of Tlatelolco, the

the two countries agreed to enter into negotiations to "review" and "revise" (the two meanings of *"revisar"*) the existing canal treaty.[34]

In 1964, a new economic channel for Latin American (and Afro-Asian) bargaining was opened by the United Nations—the United Nations Conference on Trade and Development (UNCTAD). The Latin American countries prepared for UNCTAD I by meeting under the auspices of the Special Committee on Latin American Coordination (CECLA) (created in 1963) in Argentina, in March 1964 to discuss common problems and to prepare a set of proposals. These proposals were supported at UNCTAD. UNCTAD I was chaired by Raúl Prebisch of ECLA, who became the secretary-general when UNCTAD achieved official status. At this conference the Afro-Asian countries supported the Latin American position on trade. As a result, there was formed a Third World bloc of developing countries for pressuring the developed countries, which has been described as a North-South split, partly transcending the East-West split.

Convergence: Political-Security

Also in 1964, the OAS met again on Cuba and approved a number of sanctions. This meeting resulted from Cuban-supported subversive activities in Venezuela in 1963 evidenced by that government's finding a cache of arms and plans for revolution. Venezuela requested a meeting of ministers under the Rio Treaty "to consider measures that must be taken to deal with the acts of intervention and aggression . . . affecting the territorial integrity and the sovereignty of Venezuela."[35] The OAS Council convoked the meeting and, acting provisionally, appointed an investigating committee. After a thorough investigation, the committee presented a report to the council in early 1964, corroborating Venezuela's charges. The Ninth Meeting of Consultation of Foreign Ministers was called in July to decide upon the action to be taken. Cuba was condemned for its "acts of aggression and of intervention" against Venezuela, and sanctions were voted in compliance with the Rio Treaty. These included the severance of consular and diplomatic relations and the suspension of all trade and sea transportation. The vote for sanctions was fifteen to four; the four Latin American countries that still had official and economic relations with

---

United States became a party to the second protocol in 1971 but not to the first, which would ban nuclear weapons in Puerto Rico and the Virgin Islands.

34. Subsequent negotiations resulted in a new treaty, which was not made final and released because of elections in both countries in 1968 but was passed on to new administrations.

35. Pan American Union, *Ninth Meeting of Consultation of Ministers of Foreign Affairs . . .: Final Act* (Washington, D.C., 1964), p. 1.

Cuba—Bolivia, Chile, Mexico, and Uruguay—voted against them. All of the dissenters, except Mexico, subsequently severed relations.

Divergence Political-Security

It was U.S. intervention in the Dominican civil war in 1965 that exacerbated inter-American relations and accelerated the trend of the Latin American states to turn to the United Nations and to amend the OAS Charter. Juan Bosch had been elected in OAS-observed elections in late 1962, but he was overthrown by the military the following year. Thereafter, Donald Reid Cabral soon came to the fore as the head of the triumvirate that emerged out of the military-created civilian junta. On 24 April 1965, a golpe took place, led by a few pro-Bosch army units with popular civilian support. Reid Cabral was overthrown by this "constitutional" group that wanted to recall Bosch to power. This prompted a counter-golpe supported by the bulk of the military with the national police (the "loyalist" group), which violently opposed Bosch. The resultant struggle for power provoked a civil war.[36]

A junta speaking for the "loyalist" side requested the United States to intervene in order to restore law and order. The United States responded by landing four hundred Marines on 28 April. Thus began the first phase of the two-phase unilateral military intervention of the United States. Although the official justifications for the two phases were separately advanced, they soon merged, the second becoming a continuation of the first. The initial landing of Marines was one of "humanitarian intervention"—protecting lives—and the United States justified it, without OAS approval, on the basis of the need for quick action. The second phase, the rapid buildup of troops (they soon totaled around twenty-three thousand), was to prevent a "second Cuba" (probably the motivation behind the first phase as well). President Johnson's justification was presented in his speech to the nation on 2 May in which he said that the revolution had been joined by "Communist leaders, many of them trained in Cuba, . . . [and that it] had been taken over . . . and placed into the hands of a band of Communist conspirators." He also said: ". . . as long as I am President . . . we are going to defend ourselves. . . . We will honor our treaties. We will keep our commitments."[37] The foreign minister of Uruguay referred to the 2 May speech as the Johnson Corollary to the Monroe Doctrine, by which he meant that once again a U.S. president was

36. Jerome Slater, *Intervention and Negotiation: The United States and the Dominican Revolution* (New York: Harper & Row, 1970), chap. 2. See also Larman C. Wilson, "Estados Unidos y La Guerra Civil Dominicana: el reto a las relaciones interamericanas," *Foro Internacional* 8, no. 2 (October–December 1967): 155–78.
37. *New York Times*, 3 May 1965.

justifying his country's right of unilateral intervention.[38] Despite the claim
of neutrality in the civil war, it is clear that the real reason for U.S.
intervention was to prevent the victory of the pro-Bosch side.

The reaction in Latin America to the Dominican intervention was
particularly negative, and protest was made at home, in the OAS, and in the
United Nations. Critical resolutions were introduced in both organizations, many of which were not passed. Chile, Mexico, Uruguay, and
Venezuela were the most critical nations. Chile requested the OAS Council
to convoke the Organ of Consultation under the Charter (the Tenth
Meeting of Consultation of Foreign Ministers began its first session on 1
May). The four states stressed the nonintervention principle and U.S.
violation of it and introduced resolutions requesting the United States to
withdraw from the Dominican Republic.

After landing troops, the United States directed its efforts toward
obtaining OAS endorsement of the action, concentrating upon the creation
of an Inter-American Peace Force to occupy the nation. The resolution for
creating such a force, introduced in the Tenth Meeting of Consultation of
Foreign Ministers on 6 May 1965, produced great debate. The resolution
was adopted by a vote of fourteen to five, Chile, Ecuador, Mexico, Peru, and
Uruguay voting against it; Venezuela abstained.[39] The Inter-American
Defense Board was requested to prepare a technical-military study on a
unified command for the peace force. The unified command was set up
with a Brazilian General in command (the U.S. commander in the
Dominican Republic became his deputy), and in late May military
contingents from Latin America began to arrive, almost all from nations
with military governments, such as Brazil, Honduras, Nicaragua, and
Paraguay. These forces soon added some 1,750 troops to the large U.S.
contingent, which still numbered approximately 23,000.

In the UN Security Council, despite major efforts by U.S. Ambassador
Adlai Stevenson, the United States was unable to keep the Security Council
out of the Dominican crisis and thus maintain the OAS monopoly.
Whereas the United Nations had formerly done no more than debate such
hemispheric crises as those of Guatemala in 1954, the Dominican Republic
in 1960, and Cuba in 1961 and 1962, this time the Security Council held
twenty-eight meetings on the Dominican Republic, permitted a Cuban
representative and one from each warring side in the Dominican civil war
to participate, and passed a resolution empowering the secretary-general to
send "a representative to the Dominican Republic for the purpose of

38. *Washington Post*, 5 May 1965. See also Larman C. Wilson, "The Monroe Doctrine,
Cold War Anachronism: Cuba and the Dominican Republic," *Journal of Politics* 28 (May
1966): 322-46.

39. Included among the fourteen votes, the required two-thirds majority, was that of the
Dominican Representative whose government (Reid Cabral) had been overthrown.

reporting to the Security Council on the present situation."[40] The secretary-general also sent a military adviser. The United States was particularly unhappy when the secretary-general's representative, a Latin American (José Antonio Mayobre), sent back reports that were critical of the U.S. military's lack of "impartiality."[41]

A provisional Dominican government was agreed upon in August to prepare for elections. The OAS-observed elections were then held in July 1966; this time, Joaquín Balaguer defeated Juan Bosch for the presidency, and the Inter-American Peace Force was withdrawn two months later. A settlement had finally been reached after a number of parties had played varying roles—parties that included the papal Nuncio, the OAS, various commissions, the secretary-general and an ad hoc committee of the OAS, the United Nations, and the United States. The U.S. role was the major one, but the United States had clearly paid a high political price for her unilateral intervention, in terms of inter-American relations and the relation between the OAS and United Nations. This was apparent at the Second Special Inter-American Conference (Rio, November 1965) when the United States tried to get approval for a permanent peace force. Although Brazil introduced such a resolution and made a case for "counterintervention," there was overwhelming Latin American opposition.[42]

LATIN AMERICAN-U.S. POLICY
CONVERGENCE AND DIVERGENCE: 1967-74

Several conferences, two of them in 1967, resulted from the development of trends that reflected "the growing influence of the new wine of contemporary nationalism" in Latin America.[43] The first, the Third Special Inter-American Conference, held in February, was the culmination of a Latin American drive to amend the OAS Charter by incorporating the Alliance for Progress commitments, thus making the OAS a more useful instrument for economic and social development. What emerged was the Protocol of Buenos Aires amendments to the OAS Charter. The background to this successful movement is interesting, for it appears on the

---

40. (U.S.) *Department of State Bulletin* 53 (31 May 1965): 885.

41. U.S., Congress, Senate, Committee on Foreign Relations, *Background Information Relating to the Dominican Republic*, 89th Cong., 1st sess., 1965, p. 30.

42. Six states—Chile, Colombia, Mexico, Peru, the Dominican Republic and Uruguay—added a resolution to the Final Act stressing that no additional powers had been given to the Council for the maintenance of peace. See James R. Jose, *An Inter-American Peace Force within the Framework of the Organization of American States: Advantages, Impediments, and Implications* (Metuchen, N.J.: Scarecrow Press, 1970).

43. Dreier, "New Wine and Old Bottles," p. 477.

surface, at least, that the amendments represent a convergence mainly beneficial to Latin America. The increasing Latin American concern had been to strengthen the economic and social side of the OAS—and its machinery—so that the organization could better serve the needs of economic development. The goal, therefore, was to incorporate the Alliance for Progress commitments into the OAS Charter and thus expand the multilateral activities of the OAS by getting the United States to agree to specific long-term commitments and to accept additional financial obligations. At the same time, many Latin American governments, cognizant of U.S. predominance in the OAS, wanted to limit the expanding political role of the Council.

The draft amendment proposals of the American chiefs of states and the special committees were scheduled for consideration at the Second Special Inter-American Conference, which was postponed from June until November 1965 on account of the Dominican crisis. The conference passed two acts, the Act of Rio de Janeiro and the Economic and Social Act of Rio, committing its members to Charter revision and setting up guidelines for preparing the revisions, which were to be submitted to a conference the following year. The American chiefs of state met in Panama in 1966, and the United States was expected to accept specific commitments concerning economic and social "standards." However, to the Latin American's chagrin, the Johnson administration, which had earlier tentatively agreed to accept such commitments, responded to the expressed opposition of the Senate Foreign Relations Committee and indicated a willingness to support general obligations only. The Latin Americans believed that the United States had reneged. After bargaining at subsequent meetings in Washington and Punta del Este, Uruguay, a series of amendments were approved. They were submitted to the Third Special Inter-American Conference, held in early 1967 in Buenos Aires and were approved as the Protocol of Buenos Aires.

The amendments went into effect in 1970, after ratification by two-thirds of the nations, and it is worthwhile summarizing their major provisions.[44] There was a substantial increase in commitment in the areas of economic and social standards. The number of articles concerning the former was expanded from two to fourteen; a few of them were very extensive. The number of articles on the latter was not increased, but each article was made much more comprehensive. New sections were added on educational and scientific standards. In general, the economic and social side of the OAS—the Inter-American Economic and Social Council (IA-ECOSOC) and the CIAP—was strengthened and upgraded. (CIAP, the Spanish initials for the Inter-American Committee on the Alliance for

44. See articles by Dreier and Manger cited in n 2.

Progress, had been created in 1963 on the basis of the recommendations of former Presidents Alberto Lleras Camargo of Colombia and Juscelino Kubitschek of Brazil for the purpose of providing a permanent, multilateral body that would increase the effectiveness of the Alliance.) The political side was weakened, for example, the powers of the Council, although the peace-keeping area was enhanced by strengthening the Peace Committee (renamed the Committee on Peaceful Settlement) and the Commission on Human Rights.

A part of the new allocation of priorities and powers is indicated by certain structural changes (see p. 54 for the original structure). A new General Assembly, to meet annually, replaced the former Inter-American Conference, which last met in 1954. The former Council became the Permanent Council and was placed on a par with the IA-ECOSOC and Inter-American Council for Education, Science, and Culture ("Education" and "Science" were added). These changes exemplify a shift in OAS emphasis from political-security to economic-social affairs, and also a shift to the primacy of Latin American over U.S. interests.[45]

A second meeting of the American presidents was held in April 1967. It was agreed at this meeting that a Latin American Common Market (LACM) should be achieved in 1985 by merging the present CACM and LAFTA. It was also agreed to stress trade and increase Latin America's export earnings by seeking agreement for trade preferences with the developed countries. The Johnson administration pledged support for the development of LACM and agreed to continue aiding various agencies in CACM and LAFTA. This aid has continued with the Nixon and Ford administrations.

During the late 1960s additional efforts were made to develop other regional integration arrangements. In September 1968, LAFTA approved the creation of the Andean Subregional Group (ASG) consisting of Bolivia, Chile, Colombia, Ecuador, and Peru (Venezuela joined in 1973). In 1968 the Andean Development Corporation was set up, and the ASG became effective in 1970. Also in 1968, the Caribbean Free Trade Association (CARIFTA)—Trinidad and Tobago, Barbados, Guyana, Jamaica, and the British-associated states of the Leeward and Windward Islands—went into effect. Early the next year a development treaty was signed by Argentina, Brazil, Bolivia, Paraguay, and Uruguay—the Cuenca de La Plata Group— for the mutual development of the Plate River Basin.

In 1969 the Latin Americans increased their pressure upon the United States outside of the OAS by two means: (1) the Peruvian government's nationalization of the International Petroleum Company (IPC); and (2) the Latin American Consensus of Viña del Mar, to be noted later.

45. Dreier, "New Wine and Old Bottles," p. 491.

A new U.S. administration, that of President Nixon, began to work out its policy of response; and the OAS machinery for peace keeping was severely challenged by the so-called Soccer War between Honduras and El Salvador, which dealt a stunning blow to CACM.

U.S. Responses: Economic Convergence

President Nixon responded to the October 1968 coup and the IPC nationalization by the government of General Juan Velasco Alvarado by cutting off military aid to Peru; but the application of the Hickenlooper Amendment was avoided by entering into continuing discussions.[46] Military aid was later resumed but the discussions continued. In 1969 President Nixon sent New York Governor Nelson A. Rockefeller to Latin America on a presidential fact-finding mission. The governor's mission (Secretary-General Galo Plaza of the OAS had recommended to President Nixon that Governor Rockefeller head the mission) visited twenty Latin American countries. Visits to Chile, Peru, and Venezuela in the spring and summer had to be canceled because of stormy protests.

A new high in Latin American economic policy convergence and unity was achieved at the meeting of the Special Latin American Coordinating Committee (CECLA) in Viña del Mar, Chile. Meeting from March to May 1969, the committee formulated a common Latin American position on economic policy for bargaining within UNCTAD in general and with the United States in particular. This common policy was presented in a document known as the Consensus of Viña del Mar. The consensus stated that development programs should be based upon national needs and priorities, stressed the importance of a fairer international division of labor, and requested the end of nontariff trade barriers, a lessening of conditions imposed on outside aid, more flexible terms on international loans, more multilateral as opposed to bilateral aid, and the provision of trade preferences for Latin American imports into the United States.[47] The consensus was presented personally to President Nixon by the foreign minister of Chile, in the company of a group of Latin American ambassadors. Shortly thereafter it was the major topic of discussion at an IA-ECOSOC meeting in Trinidad. It was agreed to create a Special Committee for Consultation and Negotiation (CECON) between Latin America and the United States on economic cooperation and trade.

President Nixon responded to the Consensus of Viña del Mar at the end of October in a Latin American policy speech before the annual meeting of

46. This amendment requires the suspension of economic aid if just compensation for nationalized property is not paid within six months (the six-month period expired in April 1969). In 1974 Peru agreed to pay the U.S. government $76 million for distribution to expropriated U.S. companies. IPC was awarded $22 million.

47. *Washington Post*, 12 June 1969; and *Alliance for Progress Weekly Newsletter*, 22 Dec. 1969, pp. 1–2.

the Inter-American Press Association in Washington. He stressed "a new kind of partnership" in accord with the consensus and, drawing upon portions of the Rockefeller Report, emphasized economic development, regional integration, the multilateral aid approach, and trade expansion. He promised his support in reducing nontariff trade barriers, generalized trade preferences, and the untying of aid and loans.[48] In November, when he released the Rockefeller Report,[49] the president reaffirmed several points of this speech, stressing both economic and military aid. He accepted the report's view, which had been that of the Johnson administration as well, that there was a "new military" in Latin America, one that was "professional" and a major catalyst for economic and social development and reform. He also accepted the report's recommendations of support in the form of military aid and its recognition of the need for helping the Latin American military maintain "internal security."

In July 1969, hostilities broke out between two CACM members, El Salvador and Honduras, as previously noted. CACM progress came to a standstill; stopping this conflict was a major challenge to the OAS. Although it came to be called the Soccer War because of the nationalist riots growing out of three soccer games, particularly riots in Honduras directed against Salvadoran emigrants, the real causes were the demand for land reform and Salvadoran migration. Over the years, approximately 300,000 nationals from densely populated El Salvador had migrated to sparsely populated Honduras, where they found jobs and remained. However, in May 1969, the director of the Honduras Agrarian Reform Institute evicted a number of these Salvadorans from their land and their homes in order to make room for Hondurans. Dissension and pressure that had been building up came to a boil in connection with soccer games between teams of Honduras and El Salvador. Salvadorans thus became the scapegoats for a number of internal problems. They were attacked, and their property was damaged.

The OAS first became involved in late June and early July when El Salvador appealed to the Commission of Human Rights, charging Honduras with "genocide," Honduras presenting countercharges. The commission sent a subcommittee to visit both countries in order to verify the charges. In early July, Honduras requested a convocation of the Organ of Consultation under the Rio Treaty, which was done with the Permanent Council acting provisionally the day after Salvadoran troops moved into Honduras. The council appointed a Special Committee to conduct an on-the-spot study of the situation. The Thirteenth Meeting of Consultation of Foreign Ministers that ensued adopted resolutions calling for the suspension of hostilities and the withdrawal of troops, the creation of a

48. *New York Times*, 31 Oct. 1969.
49. *The Rockefeller Report on the Americas* (Chicago: Quadrangle Books, 1969).

vigilance system, an agreement upon guarantees to protect the human rights of nonnationals in each country, and an end to mass media propaganda by both sides.[50]

For a time, El Salvador refused to withdraw her troops, pending guarantees for the protection of her nationals in Honduras. Consequently, the foreign ministers came close to applying sanctions against El Salvador; twelve OAS members sponsored a resolution branding El Salvador an aggressor and recommending economic sanctions. Finally, El Salvador agreed to withdraw her troops, making an agreement possible. Thus, the OAS was again instrumental in bringing about peace, at least temporarily, pending final agreements between the two countries.

Human rights, an issue in the "Soccer War" and one of long-standing American interest, although subordinated to the nonintervention principle, was the subject of a Special Inter-American Conference on Human Rights held in Costa Rica in late 1969, which worked out an American Convention on Human Rights.[51] The convention defined a variety of civil and political, as well as economic, social, and cultural rights; it strengthened the Commission on Human Rights, and provided for the creation of an Inter-American Court of Human Rights—an idea nurtured since the days of the Central American Court of Justice (1907–18) and assisted by the example of the European Court of Human Rights. There is little optimism about the acceptance of this convention, for only twelve states have been willing to sign it and only one (Costa Rica) has ratified it.

Convergence to Divergence: Terrorism and the Tuna War

Two major problems came before the OAS in 1970 and 1971, both having important legal, political, and economic dimensions. Neither problem was resolved; both will pose major future challenges to inter-American relations and to the OAS. The first problem, that of terrorism and political kidnapping, produced a divergence both within Latin America and between some Latin American nations and the United States. The second, the claim of Ecuador (and many others) to a 200-mile offshore zone for fishing, has produced a major divergence between Latin America and the United States.

The topic of terrorism, which also involves questions of political asylum and extradition, was suggested to the Permanent Council as an agenda item for the First Special General Assembly (1970) by Argentina and Uruguay. Before the General Assembly convened in June, the Permanent Council had already approved a resolution condemning terrorism, kidnapping, and extortion as crimes against humanity. After

---

50. *OAS Chronicle* 4 (July-September 1969): 1–2.

51. The 1948 Bogotá conference had approved a "Declaration" on human rights and had directed the Juridical Committee to draw up a draft for an Inter-American Court.

discussing the problem, during which those Latin American countries having a terrorism problem were the most vocal and desirous of strong action, the Inter-American Council of Jurists (IACJ) was requested to present a legal opinion and prepare a draft convention. While the IACJ legal opinion on terrorism was unanimous, its broad draft convention produced a division within the council. Chile voted against it and two other members abstained.[52] The convention classed terrorism, kidnapping, and extortion as common crimes when they had "international significance," and their perpetrators were therefore not eligible for political asylum.

The work of the IACJ was considered at the Third Special General Assembly in early 1971. Here a major debate occurred between those wanting a broad convention (the "hard line") that would provide for international action against persons threatening public order and those preferring a limited convention (the "soft line") that would apply only to the kidnappers of foreign officials. A part of the debate related to whether terrorists were entitled to political asylum and whether a state has an obligation either to extradite a terrorist or to try him in its own courts. The Chilean delegate argued that the United Nations was the proper place for working out a convention on terrorism, since it was a global problem. He argued that the draft convention compromised both the nonintervention principle and the institution of political asylum.[53] Finally, the "hard line" states, Argentina, Ecuador, Guatemala, Haiti, and Paraguay, led by Brazil, walked out. The more limited convention was then approved, receiving thirteen votes. (Chile voted against it and two states—Bolivia and Peru—abstained.) The convention provided that murder, kidnapping, assault and extortion were "common crimes of international significance" and that those committing them should be denied political asylum; the perpetrator was either to be extradited or tried where apprehended.[54]

During the 1970s, Ecuador and Peru have given the United States (and other nations) serious difficulties over fishing, because they claim a 200-mile limit to their territorial waters. In this regard it should be noted that the overwhelming majority of the Latin American countries now claim 200 miles as a territorial sea, patrimonial sea, or maritime zone.[55] These countries, and many in Africa and Asia, consider that fish within 200 miles of their shores are part of their natural resources. While the United States sees the problem in legal and security terms and has opposed the 200-mile claims, the Latin American countries see it in economic terms, as part of

52. Organization of American States, *Documents Prepared by the Inter-American Juridical Committee on Acts of Terrorism . . . 13 January 1971* (Washington, D.C., 1971).

53. I am indebted to Mr. Eugenio Castro, M.A., former member of my seminar on the OAS, for this information.

54. *Washington Post*, 2 Feb. 1971.

55. Francisco V. García-Amador, "The Latin American Contribution to the Development of the Law of the Sea," *American Journal of International Law* 68 (January 1974): 33–50.

their economic development. In preparation for the first plenary of the Third United Nations Law of the Sea Conference, which was held at Caracas, Venezuela, the summer of 1974, they worked through the United Nations General Assembly, Seabed Committee, and UNCTAD to establish their claims. At the Caracas conference the Latin American nations maintained their position, and the consensus that emerged, to be finalized in treaty form at the Geneva session in 1975, involved a 12-mile territorial sea limit and a 200-mile economic zone.

Even though the United States has opposed these claims, during 1972 and 1973 she moved toward a regional accommodation in anticipation of the 1974 conference. Evidence of the changing U.S. position (she still insists, however, upon the free right of navigation in these waters) was provided in the 1972 bilateral shrimp agreement with Brazil. By this agreement, a specified number of U.S. private fishing boats are permitted to fish for shrimp during specified seasons within Brazil's 200-mile limit.

Starting in late 1970 and continuing into 1973, Ecuador seized and fined an increasing number of private U.S. fishing boats within her claimed 200-mile limit. (In 1973, Peru took her place as the major seizer of U.S. private fishing boats.) As a result, in January 1971 the United States invoked the Pelly Amendment, empowering the president to cut off U.S. aid and military-credit sales to a country that seizes U.S. private fishing vessels within 200 miles of its shores. Ecuador responded by accusing the United States of "coercion" and "aggression," charging that she had violated article 19 of the OAS Charter,[56] and requesting a meeting of the Organ of Consultation.[57] The Permanent Council approved Ecuador's request overwhelmingly; the United States abstained. Subsequently, the United States tried to head off the meeting by proposing that the dispute be referred to the OAS Committee on Peaceful Settlement or the International Court of Justice. Ecuador and the United States presented their cases before the Fourteenth Meeting of Consultation of Foreign Ministers in Washington in 1971, which adopted a resolution urging the two nations to resume negotiations and calling upon all members of the OAS to observe the Charter provisions. The United States, looking to an agreement, resumed talks with Ecuador, Chile, and Peru.

Convergence to Divergence: Relations with Cuba and the Nature of the OAS

In the 1970s, several international meetings occurred in which U.S. policies were criticized and which evidenced a growing divergence. In 1972 these

56. "No State may use or encourage the use of coercive measures of an economic or political character in order to force the sovereign will of another State and obtain from it advantages of any kind."
57. *Washington Post*, 27 Jan. 1971.

included the Second General Assembly of the OAS in Washington; in 1973, the meetings of IA-ECOSOC in Bogotá, ECLA in Quito, the UN Security Council in Panama City, and the Third General Assembly in Washington; and in 1974, the Fourth General Assembly in Atlanta. Panama initiated the Security Council session held in Panama, and then used it to attack the United States over the Panama Canal. The United States vetoed a Security Council resolution calling for a treaty granting Panama "effective sovereignty" over the canal. With the exception of the UN Security Council session, these meetings focused criticism upon presumed U.S. domination of the OAS and, more specifically, U.S. opposition to an OAS conference to reconsider the Cuban question,[58] and upon the U.S. role in the field of economic aid and cooperation.

Over the years, since the 1962 OAS decision to prohibit Cuba's participation in the OAS and the 1964 imposition of diplomatic and economic sanctions, an increasing number of Latin American countries, including a number that still observe the 1964 sanctions, had come to favor calling an OAS conference to reconsider Cuban participation in the organization. Also during these years several Latin American states had renewed, contrary to the 1964 sanction decision, diplomatic and economic relations with Cuba. These states, which originally complied with the sanction decision (Mexico alone did not), included Peru, Chile (this action of the Allende government was rescinded by the Chilean military after it overthrew Allende in September 1973), Panama, and Argentina, where the resumption of relations with Cuba was one of the first acts of the Cámpora government in 1973. Added to this number were those countries that became members of the OAS after 1964 and therefore were not bound by the sanction decision—Barbados, Jamaica, and Trinidad and Tobago. (Guyana, which became independent in 1966 and is not an OAS member, also has ties with Cuba.) Ironically, Venezuela, the catalyst for the 1964 sanctions, reestablished relations with Cuba in December 1974.

The question of an OAS conference to reconsider Cuban participation in the OAS was strongly supported at both the second and third OAS General Assembly sessions in 1972 and 1973. At the former, the United States strongly opposed and blocked the proposal that had the support of at least a developing Latin American plurality, taking the legal position that such an action required a two-thirds vote of the entire OAS membership. At the 1973 session there was more Latin American support for the proposal and the United States indicated a willingness to start preparing for what seemed to be the inevitable. A resolution was adopted from this meeting accepting the concept of a "plurality of ideologies" in the hemisphere.[59]

58. Barry Sklar, *U.S. Policy Toward Cuba: A Pro-Con Discussion on the Resumption of Relations*, Library of Congress, Congressional Research Service, 72-43 F (Washington, D.C., 9 Feb. 1972).
59. *Alliance for Progress Weekly Newsletter*, 23 Apr. 1973, p. 2.

This resolution paved the way for the subsequent OAS decision, at the initiative of Colombia, Costa Rica, and Venezuela, to call a Meeting of Ministers of Foreign Affairs to consider lifting the Cuban sanctions, which would then make legal the resumption of normal relations with Cuba and permit Cuban participation in the OAS. The foreign ministers met at Quito, Ecuador, in November 1974, and the resolution for reversing the OAS position received only twelve votes—two short of the required two-thirds. Chile, Paraguay, and Uruguay voted against the resolution, and six states—Bolivia, Brazil, Guatemala, Haiti, Nicaragua, and the United States—abstained. Four states voting for the change—Colombia, Ecuador, Honduras, and Venezuela—indicated that they would go ahead anyway and establish normal relations with Cuba.[60] The question of Cuban participation in the OAS is interesting in view of Castro's attitude, inasmuch as he has reviled the OAS, charging that the organization is completely controlled by the United States.

In view of Castro's opinion of the OAS and certain other considerations, a good case can be made that the question of renewed Cuban participation in the OAS has become moot and that an OAS meeting to consider the proposition becomes increasingly unlikely with the passage of time. Supporting this view is the expanding number of Latin American countries that have resumed diplomatic and economic relations with Cuba, which will soon place the United States among a shrinking minority of states that have not renewed these relations. There is a similar trend outside the OAS, as more and more states increase their trade relations with Cuba—including, in addition to the Soviet bloc, Canada, England, the members of the European Economic Community, and Japan. Not only do these trends render U.S. Cuban policy ineffective, at least in economic terms, but it appears that the United States compromised its Cuban position when it reluctantly approved in April 1974 the sale to Cuba by Argentina of automobiles manufactured by U.S. private subsidiaries in Argentina. Other governments will soon follow suit. In fact, at the same meeting of American foreign ministers in Washington (prior to the Fourth OAS General Assembly) at which the United States announced her decision on the export of Argentine automobiles, another major step was taken against U.S. Cuban policy. A consensus was reached, strongly opposed by Chile, that Cuba be invited to attend the next meeting of foreign ministers, scheduled to be held in Argentina in 1975. (This meeting, to be held outside the OAS, like the Bogotá and Mexico City meetings in 1973 and 1974, was postponed indefinitely by Argentina in early 1975.)

At the other conferences mentioned above (ECLA, IA-ECOSOC, OAS General Assemblies), the United States was criticized for both her neglect of

60. *Washington Post*, 13 Nov. 1974.

and her intervention in Latin America; the focus was upon alleged U.S. domination of the OAS. Again, comparable to the debates preceding the 1967 Protocol of Buenos Aires, there was stress upon the need to get the United States to adopt clearer commitments in the economic aid field and to restrict her political use of the OAS. As a prescription, it was argued by many Latin Americans that Latin America needed an alternative to the OAS, perhaps in the form of a revitalized ECLA or an institutionalized CECLA. Some even argued that the Latin American countries should form their own OAS, with its headquarters somewhere in Latin America.[61] It was at the Third OAS General Assembly in 1973 that these criticisms were directly presented to the United States. As a result, a resolution was passed providing for the creation of a committee to study the entire inter-American system and to prepare recommendations for its reform. The Special Committee was subsequently appointed for this purpose, holding its first session in Lima in May. After three sessions in 1973, the committee prepared its report of recommendations, which was approved in December and then circulated to the American nations; it was also put on the agenda of the 1974 OAS General Assembly. Another resolution that was approved, the United States abstaining, criticized multinational corporations; the resolution urged the adoption of measures to prevent such corporations from engaging "in acts of intervention in the internal or external affairs of the states."[62] The Fourth General Assembly also had an agenda item on the same topic, but under the label "transnational enterprises."

Following the Third General Assembly session in Washington in April 1973, Secretary of State William Rogers made a trip to Latin America to clarify and defend U.S. policies. In one speech he told his audience that President Nixon would ask the Congress for authority to give tariff preferences to developing countries.

Dr. Henry A. Kissinger, appointed secretary of state in January 1974, continued his efforts, initiated in late 1973 (as assistant to the president for National Security Affairs), to develop a new dialogue with Latin America, as a possible means for reducing the growing policy divergence between Latin America and the United States. After his speech to the United Nations in October 1973, he had met in New York with the Latin American foreign ministers and ambassadors to the United Nations and had asked for their cooperation in starting a new dialogue. This meeting was followed by the convening in Bogotá in November of the Latin American foreign ministers for the purpose of drawing up a list of problem areas and preparing a plan of action for presentation to the United States. Their list of proposals for a "new relationship with the United States" included eight

61. See, by a former deputy coordinator for the Alliance for Progress, William D. Rogers, "Adiós, OAS: A U.S. Pullout Would Help," *Washington Post*, 8 Apr. 1973.
62. *Alliance for Progress Weekly Newsletter*, 23 Apr. 1973, p. 2.

major points, some of them quite critical, such as U.S. control of the
Panama Canal, the role of U.S. private multinational corporations in
Latin America, and the problems of access for Latin American goods and
products to the U.S. market. These points were readied for presentation to
Secretary Kissinger at a meeting of foreign ministers to be held in Mexico
City in February 1974.

Prior to the opening of the conference in Mexico, Secretary Kissinger
visited Panama and signed a preliminary accord with the Panamanian
government in which the United States agreed to enter into negotiations
for a modernized Panama Canal Treaty, one that would provide for the
eventual relinquishing of jurisdiction and sovereignty by the United
States. This agreement was hailed by the Latin American foreign ministers
in Mexico. The Mexico City meeting produced the conciliatory, but
problem-oriented, Declaration of Tlatelolco. The declaration committed
the American states to continue their talks about mutual interests and
problems at the Fourth General Assembly of the OAS, which would meet
in Atlanta in the spring, and welcomed the Panama agreement between the
United States and Panama. (The Latin American acclaim concerning the
agreement was soon dissipated, however, when thirty-one U.S. Senators
endorsed a resolution in late March calling upon the United States to retain
full jurisdiction and sovereignty over the canal.) In the declaration the U.S.
government pledged to support legislation providing for generalized trade
preferences, to avoid the implementation of any new restrictions on Latin
American trade, and to maintain the present aid levels.[63]

In late April 1974 the Fourth General Assembly convened in Atlanta,
and on its agenda were certain of the problem topics identified at the
Bogotá meeting—the "Restructuring of the Inter-American System"
and "Analysis and Evaluation of the Activities of Transnational Enterprises." In addition, there were items on the "Strengthening of the Inter-
American System for the Maintenance of Peace" and "Consideration of
the Draft Convention on Extradition." Secretary Kissinger, after men-
tioning the usual concepts of equality, cooperation, nonintervention,
respect, etc., in his address to the Assembly, reiterated the commitments
of the United States concerning trade and aid. He stressed the energy
and food shortages and pledged his nation's help. He also observed that
the Rio Treaty and the OAS needed to be "adjusted to new conditions."[64]

CONCLUSION

The OAS has developed primarily upon the bases of Latin American–U.S.
interactions over their respective interests, and it has become an important

63. *OAS Chronicle* 9 (April–June 1974): 4–5.
64. U.S., Department of State, "'Good Partner' Policy for Americas," News Release, 20
Apr. 1974, p. 7.

mechanism for multilateral policy in certain fields. This interaction has changed in time as (1) the United States employed a variety of means to pursue its two goals of preventing foreign influence and maintaining stability in Latin America, and (2) the Latin American nations responded by placing restraints upon U.S. power in the OAS and reducing their economic dependence upon their northern neighbor. The inter-American system has been a bargaining arena for Latin American nations themselves and for the alteration of Latin American–U.S. policy convergence and divergence. Since World War II, the Latin American nations have increasingly worked outside the OAS to help their bargaining within. Throughout its evolution, the inter-American system has exhibited the ability to transcend Latin American–U.S. policy convergence in one field: the peaceful settlement of disputes. There has also been one field of constant divergence: U.S. interference in Latin American affairs. This explains why the machinery for peace keeping has been quite successful and has developed to a high level, as in the Inter-American Committee on Peaceful Settlement and the Organ of Consultation. The divergence caused by U.S. interventions has sometimes impaired the settlement of American disputes. In particular, her cold war efforts to transform the OAS into an anti-Communist alliance and her preoccupation with Cuba have made the United States reluctant to use the regular dispute-settling organs whenever the issue of communism was involved.

The Latin American response to this cold war divergence over both economic-social and political-security matters has been to go outside the OAS and the inter-American system to the United Nations in two ways: (1) for multilateral economic assistance she has turned to ECOSOC, ECLA, and UNCTAD, and also to the developed countries in Europe and Asia; and (2) she has turned to the United Nations to offset the U.S. practice of "trying the OAS first" in American disputes involving communism. At the same time, the Latin American republics have worked to strengthen the inter-American system by organizing new economic institutions (the Inter-American Development Bank), by stressing economic development and integration, by forming new regional groupings (CACM, LAFTA, ASG, and CARIFTA) as bargaining units, and by amending the OAS Charter to enhance the economic and social side of the OAS structure (IA-ECOSOC and CIAP). As a result, some of these agencies, such as the Development Bank, have become powerful catalysts for unifying Latin American economic policy.

The Latin American drive to amend and reform the OAS Charter reflects the accumulating frustration arising from the complex and slow process of economic development. It is also part of the increasing economic nationalism and sensitivity about economic intervention, which includes, for many Latin Americans, almost anything that presumably impedes the development process. A major thrust of this criticism is directed against those believed to be responsible for Latin America's economic dependency.

As a result, the view of dependency as a major obstacle to development has included major criticism of the capitalistic system; of private investment, both foreign and domestic; of multinational firms; of bilateral aid, and of the role of the United States in international financial organizations, including the Inter-American Development Bank, the World Bank, and the International Monetary Fund. Thus, the forthcoming restructuring of the OAS is an instrumental aspect of the Latin American criticisms. Despite the sharply critical tone of the debate and the rhetoric about the OAS, which will doubtless be changed both formally and informally in response, it appears likely that the OAS, because of its usefulness to both sides, will continue to function as an important multilateral channel for the inter-American system with both Latin American and U.S. support.

BIBLIOGRAPHICAL NOTE

Official Sources. For the United Nations, in addition to the *Official Records* of the major organs, which include the complete deliberations, the *UN Monthly Chronicle* provides a summary of activities in political and security, economic and social, and legal fields, etc. For the Organization of American States, besides the official minutes of the major organs, there is the *OAS Chronicle*, a bimonthly summary of actions and activities. See also the *Annual Report of the Secretary General*, the annual *Decisions of the Council*, and the *Final Act* of the Meetings of Consultation of Ministers of Foreign Affairs. Another useful publication is *Applications of the Inter-American Treaty of Reciprocal Assistance*, 3 volumes, which summarizes the conciliation activities of the Organ of Consultation in inter-American disputes. There are two important publications of the Inter-American Development Bank: the *Annual Report*, which summarizes its financial and technical activities and provides statistical totals; and the annual reports of the Social Progress Trust Fund, *Socio-Economic Progress in Latin America*, which presents a profile on each Latin American country. And for the United States, see the weekly *Department of State Bulletin* for policy statements, summaries of treaty developments, etc.; and congressional hearings before the House Foreign Affairs Committee's Subcommittee on Inter-American Affairs and the Senate Foreign Relations Committee's Sub-Committee on American Republics' Affairs. An invaluable collection of documents, prepared for the Committee on Foreign Affairs by the Congressional Research Service, Library of Congress, is *Inter-American Relations: A Collection of Documents, Legislation, Descriptions of Inter-American Organizations, and Other Material Pertaining to Inter-American Affairs* (93rd Cong., 1st sess., 1973–74) (Washington, D.C.: Government Printing Office, 1973).

　　Books. Most of the works are on inter-American and U.S.–Latin American relations, mainly histories of the latter; unfortunately, there are few studies of Latin American foreign policy and international relations, particularly from the Latin American viewpoint. One such work by an Argentinian, a professor of political science in the United States, is Carlos A. Astiz, ed., *Latin American International*

Politics: Ambitions, Capabilities, and the National Interest of Mexico, Brazil, and Argentina (Notre Dame, Ind.: University of Notre Dame Press, 1969); another is C. Neale Ronning, *Law and Politics in Inter-American Diplomacy* (New York: John Wiley & Sons, 1963), in which a political scientist presents the Latin American approach to and view of law and politics. Another useful book from the viewpoint of the major powers is Herbert Goldhamer, *The Foreign Powers in Latin America* (Princeton: Princeton University Press, 1972), by a Rand Corporation social scientist who examines the "interests" and "instruments" of the powers in Asia, Europe, and North America vis-à-vis Latin America.

The leading works on inter-American and U.S.–Latin American relations are the following: Norman A. Bailey, *Latin America in World Politics* (New York: Walker & Co., 1967), by a political scientist who applies a framework of "paramounts," "sub-paramounts," "clients," and "floaters"; Robert N. Burr, *Our Troubled Hemisphere: Perspectives on United States–Latin American Relations* (Washington, D.C.: Brookings Institution, 1967), a critical study of U.S. policy by a historian; Luigi R. Einaudi, ed., *Beyond Cuba: Latin America Takes Charge of Its Future* (New York: Crane, Russak & Co., 1974), a collection by economists and political scientists with sections on "Economics" and "International Relationships"; Yale H. Ferguson, ed., *Contemporary Inter-American Relations: A Reader in Theory and Issues* (Englewood Cliffs, N.J.: Prentice-Hall, 1972), an excellent collection on "analytical perspectives" and "patterns and problems" by a political scientist; Jerome Slater, *The OAS and United States Foreign Policy* (Columbus: Ohio State University Press, 1967), a political scientist's study of U.S. use of the OAS as an anti-Communist and antidictatorial alliance; and Edward J. Williams, *The Political Themes of Inter-American Relations* (Belmont, Calif.: Duxbury Press, 1971), a study of imperialism, communism, intervention, aid to dictators, etc., by a political scientist.

The major books on the OAS or on regionalism are: M. Margaret Ball, *The OAS in Transition* (Durham, N.C.: Duke University Press, 1969), a comprehensive study (with the exception of the cultural and legal areas) by a political scientist; Gordon Connell-Smith, *The Inter-American System* (London: Oxford University Press, 1966), a British historian's incisive study; John C. Dreier, *The Organization of American States and the Hemisphere Crisis* (New York: Frederick A. Praeger, 1962), a concise analysis by a former U.S. Ambassador to the OAS for ten years and later a professor; Francisco V. García-Amador, *The Inter-American System: Its Development and Strengthening* (Dobbs Ferry, N.Y.: Oceana Publications, 1966), a factual summary with all of the basic instruments by the director of the OAS Department of Legal Affairs; Robert W. Gregg, ed., *International Organization in the Western Hemisphere* (Syracuse, N.Y.: Syracuse University Press, 1968), with chapters by Dreier, Connell-Smith, Miguel S. Wionczek (economist on integration), and Michael K. O'Leary (political scientist); William Manger, *Pan America in Crisis: The Future of the OAS* (Washington, D.C.: Public Affairs Press, 1961), a critical study by a career OAS civil servant and deputy secretary-general, later a professor; Joseph S. Nye, Jr., ed., *International Regionalism: Readings* (Boston: Little, Brown & Co., 1968), with chapters by economists, historians, and political scientists on world order, security, supranationalism, and economic integration in both developed and underdeveloped areas; Nye, *Peace in Parts: Integration and Conflict in Regional Organization* (Boston: Little, Brown & Co., 1971), which examines the contribution of the OAS (and the Organization of African Unity) to integration and the peaceful settlement of disputes; and A. J. Thomas, Jr., and Ann van Wynen Thomas, *The OAS* (Dallas: Southern Methodist University Press, 1963), a comprehensive analytical and legal study by two lawyers and international law professors. Another legal study written by a lawyer, which is far less technical, is that of William Everett Kane, *Civil Strife in Latin America: A Legal History of United States Involvement* (Baltimore: Johns Hopkins University Press, 1972).

Professional Journals. Two leading Latin American journals are *Estudios Internacionales* at the University of Santiago (Chile) and *Foro Internacional* at the Colegio de México. In the United States, there is *Current History*, a monthly journal that devotes two or three entire issues to Latin America each year; *Inter-American Economic Affairs*; the *Journal of Inter-American Studies*; *Latin American Research Review*; and *International Organization*.

4/Victor Alba

Spanish Diplomacy in Latin America and a Note on Portuguese Diplomacy

Spain has always regarded Spanish America as a source of power. During the colonial period, this power was related mainly to the gold and silver from Latin American mines. After the loss of the colonies, Spain tried to gain influence among the Latin American population and governments, not only to protect Spanish material interests but also, and especially, to enhance her prestige and her possible role in world politics—even if it was a minor role. This was especially evident in the League of Nations and has also appeared in the United Nations.

FOUR HISTORICAL PHASES

Spain's foreign policy toward Latin America has passed through four distinct phases. In the first, it was not properly speaking a foreign policy, because Spanish America formed part of Spain. In the second, after having opposed the independence of her colonies, Spain had no relations with them and even tried to recapture some of them as colonies. In the third phase, Spain recognized the existence of her former colonies as sovereign countries and established relations with them that fluctuated between correct and tense, interrupted on some occasions by acts of violence. Finally, after the loss of the last colonies (Cuba and Puerto Rico) in 1898, Spain tried to recover her former influence in Latin America, especially her cultural and diplomatic influence.

An analysis of these four stages—the theme of this chapter—is not in itself sufficient for an understanding of the complexity of the relations between the former mother country and her ex-colonies. The political events in Spain, for example, although they are not reflected in Spanish-Hispano-American diplomatic relations, do influence Latin America and, indirectly, Latin American relations with Spain. For example, the influence of Spanish Liberals was manifested in the Liberal military *golpe* of Rafael del Riego in 1820, which aided the victory of the insurgent Latin American army; later, the Spanish Civil War and its subsequent wave of political emigration influenced Latin American culture. In similar fashion, Spanish America—as a colony, as a group of independent countries, and as an international system within the general system of the United Nations—has influenced Spain, and events in Spanish America have often been related to Spanish history. This can be seen in the consequences to Spain's economy and politics of the loss of the colonies between 1810 and 1823 and in the loss of Cuba and Puerto Rico in 1898.

As in other countries, there have been some constants in Spain's foreign policy during the past centuries, despite changes in her political regimes. Prior to Spanish-American independence, these policy constants relate to North Africa and Western Europe, to the Mediterranean, and to Great Britain. Spanish America was marginal in this context, since Spain initiated few wars for her colonies. Rather, her colonies suffered the consequences of the wars that Spain initiated for reasons that had nothing to do with them—wars fought for federal power in Europe, or in defense of Catholicism, or as expressions of rivalry with England and France.

Thus, even after independence, Spanish policy toward Latin America could change from time to time without affecting the constants of Spanish diplomacy. It would seem that Spain's international relations and Spain's relations with her former colonies were two different systems that could not be placed in the same category. In fact, it might be said that Spain's relations with Latin America, despite the community of language, religion, culture (in part), and history (also in part), have been more a cultural hobby than a vital factor in Spanish diplomacy, despite all the talk about the mother country and the intimate ties between Spain and Latin America in the rhetoric of banquets and ceremonies attended by diplomats from both sides of the Atlantic. The truth, however, is that the fundamental line of Spanish diplomacy would scarcely have changed had Latin America never been discovered.

The discovery and conquest of the New World posed problems of international law for Spain in connection with questions of Indian policy. The questions were not raised by governors or conquerors, however, so much as by church leaders. The Dominican Francisco de Vitoria and the Jesuit Francisco Suárez (true founders of the law of nations) espoused views of the equality of nations and peoples, even those that were savage, and defended the concept that sovereignty derived from the people. A contrary view was held, however, by the great Spanish scholar Juan Gines de Sepúlveda, in a famous debate with Father Bartolomé de las Casas, the famous defender of the Indians. Sepúlveda argued, citing Aristotle, that the Indians were fit only for slavery, while Las Casas held that the Indians of America met all of Aristotle's tests for culture and civilization and were not fit subjects for slavery.

Views such as those of Las Casas were not unique; friars frequently held that the Indians were human beings and that as such they were free before and after conversion and that their paganism was no reason for making war on them. The Dominican canonist Matías Paz and the lay jurist Palacios Rubios affirmed such views in contravention of both crown interests and current prejudice.

The First Phase: Colonial Relationship

Despite such views of international and natural law, the relation of Spain with the Indies cannot be included in the category of foreign relations. For the court, once the Indies were conquered, they became part of the crown patrimony. Just as the Council of Castile governed the kingdom of Castile and the Council of Aragon governed Aragon, Valencia, and Catalonia, so too, from the time of the conquest, the Council of the Indies governed this new appendage of the crown. The crown saw it as one more kingdom in the totality of countries that formed a kind of community of kingdoms within one empire. Hence, the representatives of the monarch in America were called viceroys, as were his representatives in Catalonia and Naples.

The Bourbon dynasty, much more centralist than that of the Hapsburgs, did not abandon this older point of view, although it put it to one side in respect to the peninsular kingdoms. Bourbon counselors even entertained a project, which was never realized, of making new kingdoms of the American viceroyalties and giving them to the sons of Charles III; together they would form an imperial community united by dynastic ties.

The Spanish possession of the Indies, nevertheless, raised some diplomatic problems that went beyond international law. What relations should the Indies have with other countries? Spain answered by applying the doctrine of *mare clausum*, whereby she closed her colonies and her seas to all powers except Portugal. This policy did not, however, prevent the Spanish kings from granting concessions to some foreign creditors in payment or guarantee of their loans, such as those granted the German Fugger family in Venezuela. The doctrine of *mare clausum*, scholastic and medieval in origin, was rejected by England and other powers who believed in the freedom of the high seas and in the principle of effective occupation as the legal basis of territorial rights and who therefore tried to occupy as much Latin American territory as they could.

Spain was so desirous of keeping her colonies isolated that she tried at various times to arrive at agreement with her enemies to prevent wars with them from spreading to the Indies. Sometimes she achieved this objective, but at other times she had to stave off filibusters and the pirates who obliged her to unite her ships in a single fleet and protect her colonies with forts and garrisons.

But this discussion of colonial policy is marginal to our main theme. Spain really had to take diplomatic positions regarding Latin America when her former colonies achieved independence.

The Second Phase: Independence

The idea that America belonged to the Spanish crown was confirmed at the Cortes of Cádiz (1810–14), to which the Spanish criollos (but not the blacks or the Indians) sent representatives. When Ferdinand VII returned to the throne, Spanish diplomacy tried to isolate the insurgent Americans. In 1815, 1823, and 1824 the Spanish ministers to the European courts received instructions to seek European support for Spain in its war with the colonies. They might have had some success had not the Monroe Doctrine and the policy of Canning restrained the interventionist impulses of some courts. Spain could not prevent the colonists from receiving some help in their independence movements from the United States and Great Britain. Her one success was gained with Pope Pius VII, who exhorted the Latin Americans to obey their king.

Until 1835 Spain refused to recognize her ex-colonies as independent countries. She promoted some expeditions to recover New Spain; the first consequence was the expulsion from Mexico of Spanish officials and the military, and the second was a move to expel all Spaniards during the administrations of Guadalupe Victoria and Vicente Guerrero. After the death of Ferdinand in 1833, the Spanish court began to relinquish its dream of recovering the lost colonies or conferring Bourbon monarchs on them, and the process of recognition began.

The Spanish court's dreams of reconquest were not supported by well-informed Spanish public opinion. The Spanish press, in general, showed little inclination toward such dreams. However, it seems that the true character of the American insurgence was not understood in Spain, and many persons believed it was possible to reach some kind of accommodation. During the three years of the constitutional regime, from 1820 to 1823, the Spanish press made repeated appeals to reason and called for an understanding of the Americans. However, the recognition of independence was never mentioned, not even by the most liberal elements. During the absolutist periods, the press—not very free, as may be supposed—followed the official line and asked systematically for the use of force to quell the rebellion. America was a minor, it was said, and Spain ought to exercise a paternal guardianship, for if she did not do so chaos and disintegration would ensue. Nevertheless, it should be pointed out that the information published on the wars of independence was objective and generally true, considering the limited sources available.

When the Liberals came to power after the death of Ferdinand VII, they abandoned what was by then an impossible hope of reconciliation, recognizing that the only possible conciliation lay in the acceptance of normal relations with the ex-colonies. The first logical step was to recognize the former colonies' independence, their existence as juridical entities. Mexico was the first to be recognized, in 1836. Other recognitions followed upon the discreet negotiations between Spanish and Spanish-American representatives in the European capitals. In some cases, Spain obtained indemnification for the damages sustained by her nationals during the wars of independence and the internal struggles that followed.

To understand Spanish policy toward Latin America from that moment onward it is necessary to understand the struggles between traditionalists and Liberals in the peninsula. The preponderance of the Liberals made possible the agreement of the former mother country with her ex-colonies, aided by the similar struggle that was taking place in the ex-colonies, in which the Liberals generally had the advantage. Aside from diplomatic and economic interests, a certain similarity of ideological positions (in Spain and America) also facilitated the change of Spanish policy.

The negotiation of recognition treaties was begun through London. In these negotiations the independence of the new countries was not under dispute; only concrete questions were debated. These questions, although not always of basic importance, did not lack symbolic meaning. For example, there were questions of the public debt and its payment, tariff questions, and questions arising from the imprisonment of and injury to Spaniards. No great obstacles arose to the solution of these problems.

The question of the debt was not so simple. The ex-colonial countries agreed only to accept responsibility for debts contracted since the wars of independence; but Spain, exhausted by the cost of its own civil war, refused to assume the responsibility of preindependence debts incurred for the colonies. Despite the Spanish position, the American point of view finally prevailed in almost all cases.

The problem of nationality was very sensitive and no less serious. Should the Spaniards in the new countries continue to be Spaniards or become nationals of the new countries? Should Spanish immigrants keep their nationality or adopt that of the country that received them? If one accepted the Spanish point of view that all persons born in Spain, and their children, were Spanish, the American countries would find themselves populated largely by Indians and foreigners. If one accepted the American point of view that every resident should adopt the nationality of the country in which he lived, Spain would have fewer citizens, since all her emigrants would cease to be Spaniards. And, since emigration had continued despite the lack of diplomatic relations, it would surely increase when those relations were established. Moreover, the fact that the immigrants sought Spanish protection when faced with legal problems sometimes gave rise to resentment against them, but it also strengthened the American view that they should become citizens of their adopted nations.

The Third Phase: Independence to 1930

The problem of nationality found no quick or easy solution. In many cases, it remained unresolved at the time of recognition, leaving an inexhaustible source of conflict. For the immigrants, the situation seemed ideal. They did not pay taxes in their country of origin nor in their host country; they felt they had obligations toward neither country but rights in both. This was not just a Spanish problem, for Spanish America received large numbers of emigrants from other European countries. It was more serious for Spain, however, because the volume of emigrants was so great.

The question of nationality was aggravated by the internal struggles in the American countries. The immigrants tended to be conservative politically and to support the Conservative parties, above all when they had made money in America and owned businesses or lands. Hence, the Liberals, when they won office, treated the Spaniards as they did the other Conservatives; but when the Spaniards called for the protection of their consul, there was conflict. In some countries this unresolved situation continued until as late as 1860. In an Argentine case, for example, Domingo Faustino Sarmiento intervened on behalf of the Buenos Aires government to argue that a Spanish printer who published a Conservative newspaper was subject to the same risks as any other Argentine printer—including the risk of seeing his print shop assaulted by the Liberals. He could have recourse to local justice but not to consular protection. The American governments, Sarmiento said, should imitate the example of the United States, even though U.S. consuls defended North Americans in Latin America much as the Europeans defended their own nationals.

Finally, in 1864, the Spanish government recognized by law that the sons of Spaniards born in American lands should have the nationality of their country of birth. Only then did some countries, such as Argentina, achieve full diplomatic recognition—countries which until then had had only consular relations with Spain. Much later, the problem was definitively resolved by dual citizenship agreements signed by Spain and the majority of the American countries. Under these agreements, nationals of Spain and the American signatory enjoy full citizenship rights in each country, according to the place of residence. Thus, a Cuban became governor of a Spanish province in 1932, and a Mexican has directed a political newspaper in Madrid. The reverse case, however, of Spaniards entering Latin American politics and holding political office, is practically nonexistent. Argentina, despite Sarmiento's views of 1860, abandoned her earlier position in 1904 when she promulgated the so-called law of residence, making it possible to deport any immigrant who harbored "subversive ideas."

While these negotiations in respect to recognition and nationality were continuing with some countries, satisfactory outcomes having been reached with others, the dream of reconquest had not been completely abandoned. It was as though the desire for empire continued in the subconscious, rising to consciousness from time to time in unforeseen circumstances, producing situations that smacked more of the grotesque than of the dramatic. Thus, in 1864, Spain carried on an absurd war in the Pacific when a small Spanish squadron attacked Peru; when Chile came to the aid of her northern neighbor, the Spanish ships bombarded Valparaiso.

On another occasion, in 1861, Spain took advantage of Dominican internal disorder to foment an intrigue and get the former colony to ask the "mother country" to accept its annexation. This relationship lasted until the Dominicans, weary of Spanish domination, rebelled in 1865 and regained their independence with very little struggle.

Another attempt at intervention ended quite differently. A squadron of English, French, and Spanish ships sailed to Mexico in 1861 to exact payment of debts to their nationals. The chief of the Spanish expedition, General Juan Prim, discovered that the French intended to implant an empire and subsequently convinced the English to leave with the Spaniards. These senseless attempts took place after the end of the Spanish civil wars (the Carlist wars), and one of their purposes, doubtless, was to provide an outlet for the desires of the military for action.

Spain continued to be oriented fundamentally toward Europe, with Latin America a somewhat marginal diplomatic concern. Probably it could not have been otherwise, given the resentment that still remained from the negotiations for recognition and the ill-feeling that had been aroused by the adventures of the 1860s. Nevertheless, her former colonies retained a strong sympathy for Spain. Spanish-American Conservatives openly considered themselves pro-Hispanic or Hispanophile, while the Liberals (who in this era were usually pro–North American) were Hispanophobe, though not bitterly so. It will be recalled that in Latin America, all cities (except in Mexico) display statues of the conquistadors, and the streets bear the names of viceroys.

Dazzled by her European policies, Spain wasted this reservoir of good will in Spanish America at the time of her brief war with the United States, in 1898. For three years, the Spanish army had sustained a bloody struggle for independence against the Cuban Warriors, who were now nearing victory. Naturally, the cause of the Cuban patriots had the sympathy of a large segment of Latin American public opinion. Spain could have changed this feeling when the United States intervened in the conflict by presenting herself more clearly as a bulwark against the expansionism of Washington, which was then disturbing the Spanish-American chanceries much more than was Spanish colonialism. She could have done this by granting Cuban independence before U.S. intervention.

But Madrid preferred to confide in the completely inefficacious good offices of Paris rather than turn to the Latin American chanceries. Although it is doubtful that the latter course, if taken, would have had any substantial result, it would at least have established certain ties between Madrid and the capitals of the former Indies. But Madrid could not think in these terms, for the only ties she saw with Spanish America were the immigrants and the savings they sent home. No one was then speaking of a community of culture, of *hispanidad*, or of any special relationship beyond that which was expressed—but not felt—in such rhetorical phrases as the "mother country" and the "nations, daughters of Spain." Nor was anyone in the academic realm then attempting to combat the black legend that the Anglo-Saxon historians had created around Spain's historical role in America.

During the earlier Ten Years War (1868–78) for Cuban independence, and even for many years before that time, Liberals in Spain had protested the continuation of slavery in Cuba and Puerto Rico and had presented proposals to abolish it; once the war started, they opposed sending Spanish forces to Cuba. In the rebellion of 1895–98, some groups favored the Cuban cause. These groups consisted of intellectuals without a defined ideology but with a liberal vision of things, as well as republicans, socialists, and anarchists. Once the war in the Caribbean was ended, there arose out of these groups, particularly the first group, the initial attempts to establish cultural contacts with Spanish America and create a community—not diplomatic and formal, but sentimental and intellectual.

The historian Rafael Altamira is the most outstanding personality of this group. Altamira, Miguel de Unamuno, José Ortega y Gasset, Ramón de Valle Inclán, Adolfo González Posada, and others of this "Generation of 1898" kept up a continuous correspondence with Latin American intellectuals. Some, such as Altamira, Valle Inclán, and Ortega, came to Latin America to give lectures. Just as modernism in literature received a decisive impulse through the work of Rubén Darío (much of it written in Spain), so the influence of the "Generation of 1898," as a reaction to the colonial disaster, inspired many Spanish-American intellectuals to seek ways of modernizing their own societies.

The Hispano-American Congress held in Spain in 1900 was the first extradiplomatic contact between the former colonies and the mother country, meeting now on a footing of equality. The congress was organized by the University of Oviedo (the North of Spain provided the greater part of the Spanish emigrants to America). Francisco Posada is said to have remarked that the Pan-Hispanism that developed out of this congress, in addition to cultural interpenetration, was intended to achieve a strong economic alliance, a kind of "Zollverein." Spain, he thought, would thus realize her true mission in Spanish America.

Spain had not lost her characteristic air of superiority. With modest subsidies and some resounding declarations, the government tried to capitalize on this private initiative of the intellectuals. Thus, an official proclamation by a minister of state declared on 16 April 1900 that Spain would cultivate bonds of sympathy with Spanish America. But such a movement, based more on the past than on the future, could not lead to anything concrete. Spain was not a country that exported either capital or technicians. And the ideas she exported were of little practical use to the Latin Americans. The whole matter was confined to contacts between intellectuals.

During his dictatorship in the 1920s, General Miguel Primo de Rivera tried to give official sanction to this Hispano-Americanism. But his efforts were limited to two symbolic gestures: the transatlantic flight of the plane "Plus Ultra" (piloted by Captain Ramón Franco), the first flight over the South Atlantic; and the Hispano-American fair in Seville in 1929.

This Hispano-American movement did achieve one not unimportant result, however. It created an atmosphere of reconciliation, erasing bitterness and making Spain once more acceptable in America. The scanty official action contributed nothing to this change. It was attributable to personal contacts at the intellectual level, reflecting the millions of personal contacts between Spaniards and Spanish Americans at the level of daily Latin American life. Official action was limited to police collaboration in the pursuit of anarchists who went from one country to another and to appeals to the good offices of the king of Spain (actually, to one of his diplomats) to arbitrate certain border conflicts between Latin American countries.

At the same time that Altamira and others were undertaking their paternalistic movement, another movement arose, also one of intellectuals, but with political implications. This was Ibero-Americanism. Created by Portuguese and Spanish writers, it proposed to affirm the cultural community of Spain, Portugal, Spanish America, and Brazil. Its most outstanding figures were Camilo Barcia, Juan del Nido, and Emilio Zurano. It found some echo in Argentina, none in Brazil, and very little in Portugal. In Madrid it led to the founding of the Ibero-American Union, which later joined the Latin Union created by some Frenchmen for the purpose of affirming the Latin character of Latin America, France, Portugal, and Spain. These movements consisted merely of intellectual speculations, conferences, and pamphlets; they never had any influence on diplomacy.

The Fourth Phase: Since 1930

In the 1930s the Spanish republic tried to change Spanish relations with Spanish America. Strictly speaking, the republic had no foreign policy except to maintain its adhesion to the League of Nations and make the charter of the League part of the national constitution. It rejected an alliance proposed by France and continued monarchical politics in Morocco, now "pacified." But it managed to give a certain luster to the cultural community with Spanish America. In 1931, at Geneva, the republic's minister of labor, the Socialist Francisco Largo Caballero, gathered together the Latin American delegates to the meeting of the International Labor Organization (ILO) and told them that the establishment of the Republic was for Spaniards what independence had been for Spanish Americans. The new republican Spain, he declared, proposed to liquidate historical resentments. Hispano-Americanism should be based not on the past, but on the future.

The republic, by treaties, extended dual citizenship to residents of almost all Latin American countries and did not object to various Latin Americans becoming deputies or governors, as mentioned earlier. The postal rates between the Latin American countries and Spain were made the same as for domestic mail. The number of scholarships for Latin American students was increased, and a scientific expedition to the Amazon (which the Spanish Civil War had prevented), was underwritten. But in the five years that the republic lasted, little more was done. One must remember that when the republic was established in Spain, there were military dictatorships in the majority of Latin American countries. The climate was not propitious for a diplomacy that looked to the future.

Nor did the period of civil war in which the republic ended favor cooperation. The Spanish struggle divided public opinion in Latin America, as it did in the rest of the world, even within families and in most political parties. The republican government made an effort to attract the sympathy of the Latin American governments, especially with an eye to gaining their votes in the League of Nations. But with the exception of a few countries, notably Mexico, it achieved little support, because either authoritarian parties or the military governed in most countries. The republic did manage to maintain diplomatic relations during the civil war with most of the small Latin American nations that in 1937 recognized the junta of General Francisco Franco. But at Geneva the Latin American votes, except Mexico's, were not on the side of the republic. Mexico not only supported the republic but also sold it arms (bought in the United States). This it did not so much for ideological motives as to follow its traditional antiinterventionist diplomacy; the Mexican government considered the Italian, German, and Portuguese intervention on the side of the Spanish rebels sufficient reason to justify its support of the Republic, that is to say, the legitimate government. One exception was the government of Fulgencio Batista in Cuba; because Communists supported it and because it was good for his image, Batista verbally supported the Spanish republic. (This support was continued, with small financial contributions to the Spanish republican government in exile, after the World War II, by the Grau and Prío governments and also by Batista after he had returned to power in 1952).

The Latin American embassies in Madrid and their consulates in various cities became refuges for numerous politicians, businessmen, and other Spaniards who feared the republic and its worker-allies; the embassies rented entire buildings to house them. The republican government always granted such persons safe-conduct, even though it knew that many of them would fight on the rebel side. It thus respected the right of Latin Americans to diplomatic asylum, despite the fact that Spain had never recognized this right officially. It should be pointed out that the Latin American consulates in the rebel-zone cities did not grant asylum to the republicans later when they were pursued by enemy forces. Thus, properly speaking, there was no consistent Spanish policy toward Latin America during the civil war, but only a Latin American policy toward Spain.

The end of the Spanish Civil War and the beginning of World War II posed a new situation, unprecedented in diplomatic history. All the Latin American governments, except that of Mexico, recognized the government of General Francisco Franco in 1939. And they maintained relations with his government during World War II. During that epoch, it was difficult for Spain to carry out any action that was not strictly diplomatic. Certain Falangist organizations (adherents to the only official Spanish party, the Spanish Falange) tried to propagate their ideology and maintained contact with groups of German Nazis and Italian Fascists in Argentina, Chile, and Brazil. The Argentine Congress undertook an investigation of the activities of these groups of citizens of Spanish, German, and Italian origin, assuming that they followed the instructions of foreign governments. But in other countries these activities found the support of the authorities, the Falangists and, almost always, the church. The Brazilian bishop C. Duarte Costa was excommunicated in 1944 for denouncing (Spanish) Falange activity in Brazil.

Because Getulio Vargas showed such sympathy for the Falange (although later Brazil was on the Allied side and sent an expeditionary force to Europe), the Spanish government used Rio de Janeiro as the center of its propaganda activity in Latin America. Its ambassador there, Raimundo Fernández Cuesta, coordinated the activity of Falangists in all the Spanish embassies of the New World. In Madrid, an Institute of Hispanic Studies had been created to give a cultural veneer to this ideological expansion. But the war limited its activity because of the difficulty of communication between the New World and the Old and the near impossibility of travel between the two.

Only after World War II was Madrid able to accentuate its policy of ideological expansion. Then there was talk of reconstituting the empire, and many Latin American rightist elements adopted the Falangist philosophy as their own, after having supported Franco with money and propaganda during the Spanish Civil War.

This ideological expansionism was called *hispanidad*. For Ramiro de Maeztú (1875–1936), who formulated the concept before the civil war, it was a question of vindicating the role of Spain in America and of making a kind of Spanish-American bloc based on Catholicism, traditionalist political organization, and Spanish cultural values. But in practice the politics of *hispanidad* consisted of inviting Conservative politicians and intellectuals (whose books were published in Madrid) to visit Spain, giving scholarships to students of like ideology, and trying to promote Falangist ideals in the ex-colonies. The objective of these actions was something more than merely increasing Spain's cultural influence.

The founding Assembly of the United Nations had refused Spain entry until she had a democratic government. The Latin American countries voted in favor of this exclusion. Spain wanted to be accepted by the United Nations and, through *hispanidad*, she exercised pressure to this end on influential groups and on governments. Little by little, in successive UN assemblies, the number of Latin American votes favorable to the admission of Spain increased until finally only Mexico (still faithful to her antiintervention principle) was opposed. In January of 1956, when Spain was admitted to the United Nations (with favorable votes from the United States and the USSR in addition to those of the Latin American countries and others), relations between Spain and her former colonies were normalized. It must be added that various countries had never withdrawn their ambassadors from Spain, despite the UN resolution to that effect. In 1950 Colombia, Peru, Argentina (three dictatorships), and Brazil had proposed that the UN General Assembly rescind the withdrawal resolution; the Assembly agreed, with sixteen of the nineteen Latin American countries voting for the proposal.

During this period, Spain had established close ties with the Juan Perón government in Argentina, although these ties were later weakened for commercial reasons. Eva Perón was received in Madrid by the chief of state, who invited her to dine with him. Later, Spain discreetly helped the Conservative government of Laureano Gómez of Colombia (1950–53) during the civil war (*La Violencia*) in that country.

This policy of *hispanidad* paralleled (with less intensity) the Spanish policy of friendship with the Arab countries, who also voted for Spain in the United Nations. Spain once more obtained Arab and Latin American votes there in the 1960s, when she raised the question of Gibraltar, demanding its return from Great Britain.

From the years following the Spanish Civil War, until the present, some sixty to seventy thousand republican exiles who emigrated to Spanish America from France also carried out in their intellectual and business activities what could properly be called a policy of *hispani-dad*—if this be understood not as an identification with traditional values but as a contribution to the cultural and material progress of America. There is no doubt that the technical and cultural contribution of the exiled Spaniards was both superior to and more constant and lasting than any that Spain could make with her politically conservative form of *hispanidad*, which never went beyond official spheres. These groups of Spanish exiles exercised pressure on the governments and public opinion of the Latin American countries, and while international conditions were favorable, secured recognition from a dozen Latin American governments of the republican government in exile established in 1946 in Mexico. But as the cold war intensified and the international situation changed, the Latin American governments turned to the side of the official Spanish regime. The new wave of dictatorships in Latin America after 1948 also contributed to this trend.

Since Spain's entry into the United Nations, the importance to Madrid of a Latin American bloc to support its position has declined. The only question Spain has pending today which might some day require a UN decision is that of Gibraltar. Spain's pretension to make herself a bridge between the Western world and the Arab world and between the West and Latin America has also lost ground; Madrid's diplomatic power was never equal to such a role in the first place. Since the entrance in 1956 into the Spanish government of leaders who were members of the lay religious order *Opus Dei*, Spain has turned more and more toward Western Europe, hoping some day to be accepted into the European Common Market. Madrid continues, however, to pay a certain amount of attention to Latin America, no longer so much ideological as commercial and cultural, even though the presence for several years of *Opus Dei* members in the Spanish government (until 1974) favors the extension of this lay group to Latin America and its penetration into Latin American political spheres.

In accordance with this new Spanish policy line, certain symbolic gestures have been accentuated. For example, a Congress of Hispanic Institutions was celebrated in Madrid in 1963, attended by delegates from thirty-seven countries. In this congress it was pointed out that by the end of the century 700 million people will speak Spanish and that it is therefore necessary to prepare the instruments for giving them a common culture. In 1965, the Spanish government put at the disposition of the Inter-American Development Bank (IADB) $20 million in credits for the purchase of Spanish products necessary for Latin American development. In 1971, another $50 million was offered to the IADB for the same purpose.

Spain has also aided Spanish America in the religious field. In 1966 more than sixteen thousand Spanish religious, including nine thousand women, were working in Spanish America. The number of religious has since declined somewhat, because of the split between progressives and traditionalists in the Spanish church. The Spanish hierarchies want to send to Latin America the young priests who might cause trouble in Spain, whereas the Latin American governments prefer more moderate priests.

Spain has sometimes taken advantage of her diplomatic relations to oppose anti-Franco propaganda. In 1965, for example, she got the Argentine government to prohibit the showing of *To Die in Madrid*, a film about the Spanish Civil War. But in general, these attempts have not met with success. Even in the dictatorships, anti-Franco books and reviews are circulated and published.

Spain's diplomatic policy now aspires to be more relevant to the present day. A press release from the Spanish ministry of foreign affairs in April 1971 said that Spain would go beyond her traditional cultural emphasis in her relations with Ibero-America, taking into account all the development needs of the area. The minister called on Spanish society to join in creating an Ibero-American mentality. Madrid evidently realizes that her influence in Latin America must be based on new realities. Thus, she is endeavoring to show her interest in Latin American social concerns and to stimulate investment and business ties with Latin America. In both respects she is helped by never having responded to U.S. pressure on Cuba; Spain maintains good relations and extensive trade with the country of Fidel Castro.

But all this is peripheral to the realities of Spanish-American international relations. The specific weight of Spanish economy and power is too light to have an effect in Latin America. Hence, in the final analysis, Spain's role in the international life of Latin America today is secondary.

A NOTE ON PORTUGAL

The international policy of Portugal has differed from that of Spain basically in that, because of her small size and geographic position, Portugal has been much less involved in European conflicts. Yet these conflicts could not help but affect her policy tangentially, because of her continuing alliance with England. This was especially evident in the invasion of Portugal by the forces of Napoleon (1807), which forced the flight of the court to Brazil and the subsequent establishment of the Brazilian empire, making Brazil the monarchical exception in republican Ibero-America.

Portugal, engrossed in early modern times in very profitable commerce with her Asiatic colonies, and hence with the establishment of colonies in Africa as way stations along the route to Asia, paid relatively little attention to Brazil. The Portuguese presence in Brazil, although powerful from a cultural point of view, was less evident than that of Spain in the Spanish colonies. Moreover, when the French and the Dutch occupied parts of Brazil, it was the natives of Brazil rather than the forces sent from Lisbon who fought against the invaders. The diplomacy of Lisbon did little—could do little—to aid in the recovery of the Brazilian territories that had been temporarily occupied.

After the independence of Brazil, there were no conflicts between the courts in Rio and Lisbon because of dynastic ties. The Luso-Britannic alliance protected British capital investments in Brazil and attracted to the country the familiar attention of Lisbon investors.

After the early 1930s the authoritarian regime of Antonio de Oliveira Salazar (1889-1974) provided ideological and political support for the Franco movement in Spain and, at least indirectly, for the authoritarian tendencies of the Vargas regime in Brazil. In recent times Portugal has usually been able to count on the vote of Brazil in the United Nations (except at times during the presidencies of Quadros and Goulart). Under the present regime (1974), and for almost a decade, Brazil has supported Portugal on her colonial policies. Brasilia shows a growing interest in achieving some kind of hegemony between Portugal and her African colonies. This policy began to change in January 1974, when Brazil publicly condemned colonialism for the first time in a joint declaration by Brazilian and Nigerian foreign ministries. In exchange, Brazil was promised an association with the Nigerian National Oil Company. (English translation by Alicia B. Edwards)

BIBLIOGRAPHICAL NOTE ON SPAIN

Bollo Cabrios, Palmira. "Prolegómenos a la ley de nacionalidad y de reconocimiento de la independencia argentina por España." In *Trabajos y comunicaciones*. La Plata: Departamento de Historia, Universidad Nacional de la Plata, 1970.

Delgado, Jaime. *La independencia de América en la prensa española*. Madrid: Seminario de Problemas Hispanoamericanos, 1959.

Estrada, Santiago de. *Nuestras relaciones con la Iglesia*. Buenos Aires: Ediciones Teoría, 1963.

Fernández Artucio, Hugo. *The Nazi Underground in South America*. New York & Toronto: Farrar & Rinehart, 1942.

Hanke, Lewis. *El prejuicio racial en el Nuevo Mundo*. Santiago: Editorial Universitaria, 1958.

Maeztú, Ramiro de. *Defensa de la Hispanidad*, 3d ed. Valladolid: n.p., 1938.

Mesa, Roberto. *El colonialismo en la crisis del XIX español*. Madrid: Editorial Ciencia Nueva, 1967.

Moch, Jules y Germaine. *L'ouvre d'une révolution: L'Espagne Républicaine.* Paris: Rieder, 1933.

Mousset, Albert. *La política exterior de España, 1873-1918.* Madrid: Biblioteca Nueva, 1918.

Normano, J. F. *The Struggle for South America.* Boston: Houghton Mifflin Co., 1931.

Parry, J. H. *The Spanish Theory of Empire in the Sixteenth Century.* Cambridge: At the University Press, 1940.

Rio Cisneros, Agustín del. *Viraje político español durante la segunda guerra mundial y réplica al cerco internacional.* Madrid: Ediciones del Movimiento, 1965.

Rodríguez Castillo, Gonzalo. *Communist World Offensive Against Spain.* Madrid: n.p., 1949.

Whitaker, Arthur P. *Spain and the Defense of the West.* New York: Harper & Bros., 1962.

BIBLIOGRAPHICAL NOTE ON PORTUGAL

Andrade, Theófilo. "Fundamentos da Comunidade Luso-Brasileira." *Sociedade de Geografía de Lisboa. Boletim,* Series 87, nos. 1-3 (January–March 1969) and 4-6 (April–June 1969).

Bastos, João Pereira. *Angola e Brasil, duas terras lusídadas do Atlântico.* Lourenço Marques: n.p., 1964.

Carvalho, Henrique de Miranda Vasconcelos Martins de. *Missão de Portugal e do Brasil no mundo de amanha.* Lisbon: Academia Internacional de Cultura Portuguesa, 1966.

——. *Política externa portuguesa.* Lisbon: Junta de Investigações do Ultramar, 1964.

——. *Política externa portuguesa relacionada com o Atlântico.* Lisbon: Instituto Superior de Ciencias Sociais e Política Ultramarina, n.d.

Fragoso, José Manuel de Magalhaes Pessoa e. *Coordenadas de política externa.* Lisbon: Edições Panorama, 1966.

Malan, Alfredo Souto. "Comunidade luso-brasileira." *Revista Militar,* no. 7 (July 1969), pp. 375-86.

Nobueira, Alberto Marciano Gorjao Franco. *Debate singular.* Lisbon: n.p., 1970.

Rego, Antonio da Silva. *Relações luso-brasileiras (1822-1953).* Lisbon: n.p., 1966.

Rodrigues, Betencourt. *Uma Confederação lusa-brasileira.* Lisbon: n.p., 1923.

5/Victor Alba

Vatican Diplomacy in Latin America

It is very difficult to speak of Vatican diplomacy because it involves both political and religious policies. One can not say precisely how the Vatican influences the Catholic church in each country and how the church in each country influences the Vatican. It becomes more difficult when present Vatican diplomacy is considered, since there are diverse, opposing tendencies within the church. For example, how is the archbishop of Recife, Hélder Câmara, being supported by the Vatican in his denunciations of the Brazilian political regime, and how does the Vatican's Brazilian policy differ from the position taken by Dom Hélder?

POLICY OBJECTIVES

In spite of variations, some constants do exist—at least they did until the time of Pope John XXIII—that permit us to speak of a Vatican diplomacy in Latin America. Since these constants also appear within the churches of all Latin American countries, we may affirm that there is some agreement among them. These constants may be summarized as follows:

1. Vatican diplomacy tries to maintain normal relations with all types of political regimes, separating religious and political issues.
2. Vatican diplomacy strives basically to defend the interests of the Catholic church in the realms of property and education.
3. Vatican diplomacy is less sharp and intransigent than the local church in the defense of these latter interests, but it does not disavow (at least publicly) the intransigent attitude of the local churches.

Only by the decisions of Vatican Council II has the systematic coincidence of attitudes between Vatican policy and that of any one of the local churches weakened.

THE CATHOLIC CHURCH TODAY

In order to understand the historical situation we must first sketch briefly the Catholic church's position in Latin American society.

Some countries have both missionary zones and dioceses; but a majority have only dioceses. There are forty-three thousand priests, thirty-two thousand of whom are in Argentina, Brazil, Chile, Colombia, and Mexico. Nineteen thousand are diocesan priests and the rest are members of religious orders or are engaged in nonparochial activities. Some twelve thousand five hundred priests are foreign (seven thousand being Spanish).

A very large percentage of the population is Catholic. In no country do Protestants or other religious groups exceed 5 percent—with the exception of Brazil and Chile, where the percentage of Protestants is higher. There is a large Jewish community in Argentina, and there are a number of "pagans" in the regions with a "savage" Indian population—the Amazonia, for example. But the culturally active population is mostly Catholic. Outside the most cultured classes (the middle and upper classes), the Catholicism in much of Latin America is of a syncretic type with pre-Colombian and African survivals, depending on whether the countries considered have a large Indian or Negro population. Many parishes are so large that the majority of the parishioners have little if any opportunity to attend mass. In the countryside, especially, pastoral activity is scattered, reaching only a very small proportion of the population. There is a growing religious indifference or apathy in large segments of the middle classes (especially among professional people), but not in the working class (with a few exceptions); this is contrary to what happens, for instance, in Western Europe, notably in Spain.

The majority of the Latin American countries maintain diplomatic relations with the Holy See and receive papal nuncios. The most notable exception in this respect is Mexico, for reasons that will appear later.

VATICAN POLICY DURING THE COLONIAL ERA

Vatican diplomacy did not exercise any influence in the Portuguese and Spanish colonies, nor in the conquest itself. This was due above all to the institution of the *patronato real* ("royal patronage"), established at the time of the conquest and evangelization of the Canary Islands (1418) and reinforced at the time of the conquest of Granada, the last land of the Peninsula ruled by the Arabs (1492). Under the *patronato real* the Spanish sovereigns had the right to present bishops (in fact, to name them) and to intervene in the management of the benefices and tithes of the church. When the expeditions of discovery began, Pope Alexander VI (of Spanish origin) issued two bulls, *Inter caetera divinae* (3 May 1493) and *Eximiae devotionis* (4 May 1493), which gave the Spanish and Portuguese monarchs the same rights in the New World. The first of these bulls divided the zones of discovery between Spain and Portugal; but soon these zones were revised in the treaty between the two countries signed at Tordesillas in 1494. These bulls not only were opposed by many countries (upon learning of them, Francis I of France asked where Adam's testament that gave half the world to the Spanish and Portuguese was); they were challenged by numerous theologians, especially by the Spaniards Francisco de Victoria and Francisco Suárez, who denied that the Holy See and the Spanish crown had the right to dispose of the lands of infidel monarchs.

With these bulls, the Vatican renounced all authority to intervene in the life of the American colonies. The Spanish crown, through its Council of Indies, named the bishops, delimited the dioceses and, in reality, governed the church from the viceroyalities. The Portuguese crown did likewise. (For a time the two crowns were united.) Hence, frequent clashes occurred between the viceroys and the civil authorities, on one side, and the missionaries and bishops, on the other. At first, in the sixteenth century, these conflicts arose from the desire of the priests to protect the Indians and create the proper conditions for their conversion. In the seventeenth century the clashes occurred over questions of precedence, since the church had almost completely abandoned the functions of missionary and protector and had become a large proprietor; its concern was to protect its material interests. In the eighteenth century the conflict was frankly defensive, opposing the reform efforts of Ferdinand VI and Charles III of Spain and the Portuguese minister, Manquês de Pombal. As part of this nationalist reform, Pombal expelled the Jesuits from Brazil in 1759; eight years later the Spanish crown also expelled them from its territories.

Two illustrations will give an idea of how far the Vatican had to keep itself from the life of the colonies. When Rome organized the Congregation for the Propagation of the Faith, the Council of the Indies forbade any representative of the institution to enter the colonies. Rome could only react by putting the books of the theologian Juan de Solórzano, who justified the council's decision, on the Index. A century later, however, when Charles III issued a Royal Order (1765) in which he proclaimed himself "Vicar and Delegate of the Sovereign Pontiff" and by which he attributed to himself functions of the Pope with respect to the Spanish and colonial church, the Vatican took no action.

In these disputes the Holy See did not intervene, just as it had not intervened in the sixteenth-century polemics concerning the protection of Indians. Thus, we see that the campaigns of Father Bartolomé de las Casas were not supported by the Vatican but developed completely apart from it, practically ignored by the pontiff. In the same way, when the colonial church was being transformed into a temporal power, the Vatican neither benefited from it nor tried to stop it. By the *patronato real* and the bulls of 1492 the pope had renounced his power over the colonial church.

THE VATICAN AND INDEPENDENCE

After independence the Holy See encountered difficulties in reestablishing control over the churches of the old colonies, now converted into independent countries. This difficulty was increased by the attitude adopted by the Vatican during the wars for independence between 1808 and 1823, wars in which many of the clergy actively participated on the patriot side. In these struggles a profound division arose between the lower clergy, generally criollo, who were born in America and favored independence, and the high clergy, mostly from the Peninsula, who generally favored the Royalists and the maintenance of Spanish rule.

Since the church was legally subject to Spanish authority, the hierarchies systematically condemned the attempts at independence. Miguel Hidalgo and José M. Morelos, the two priests who initiated the struggle for Mexican independence, were captured by the Royalist forces, condemned by the Inquisition, and then handed over to the secular arm for execution.

After the restoration of Ferdinand VII the situation in the colonies was so desperate for the crown that Ferdinand in 1816 requested from the pope a condemnation of the independence leaders. For the first time in more than three centuries the king of Spain was willing to recognize that the Vatican had a role in the colonies, even if it was only admonitory. On 30 January 1816, Pope Pius VII issued an encyclical in which he exhorted "the faithful with the greatest energy to maintain the obedience and fidelity that they owe to their Monarch."

But in 1820 a military coup of the Liberals forced Ferdinand VII to abandon for three years his absolutist policy. Rome then became alarmed and changed its attitude with respect to the independence of the Hispanic-American colonies, thinking it was better to see them independent than subject to the Spanish Liberals. The Pope then wrote to the bishops in the colonies, asking them to inform him of the needs of the church in the fledgling nations. The bishops, fearful of the influence of the Spanish Liberals, now supported for a time the very independence movements that until then they had condemned.

But this was for a very short period. When the army of the Holy Alliance restored the absolutist regime in Spain (1823), the Vatican reverted to its previous policy and the Catholic church in America again opposed independence. This time the Vatican policy was followed with less unanimity, many priests and even some bishops remaining on the side of the *independentistas*. Only after Ferdinand VII had died, in 1835, did the Vatican officially abandon its opposition to independence—at a time when the church in Latin America had in practice already accepted it.

The majority of the rulers of the new countries were Liberals, but they were firmly attached to the Catholic religion. They sought to establish direct relations with Rome, but Rome was tied to Madrid and the Holy Alliance. The Latin American governments pursued two objectives: the recognition by the Holy See of their independence and the continuation of the *patronato* system. In many countries, although they did not have this formal recognition, the governments arrogated to themselves the privileges of the *patronato*; they named bishops, collected the tithes, and often suspended or expelled Spanish priests. In some places measures for the secularization of temples and convents were adopted. This alarmed the Vatican.

Were the new countries to conserve the *patronato real* system or would achieving independence put an end to it? Latin American and Vatican diplomats argued over this question for almost a dozen years. Should the expropriated religious foundations be restored? Should the Jesuit order be readmitted? Should the *fueros* of the clergy be maintained?

The first country to which the Holy See yielded was Brazil, where there had been no fight over church policy and where the monarch was legitimate. In 1829 Brazil had a papal nuncio. Five years later the government of the emperor named an ambassador to the Holy See. For Spanish America it was more difficult. Rome was controlled by Spanish pressure exercised in different ways. For example, in the conclave of 1831, Spain, using her *exclusivium*, vetoed the suggestion of Cardinal Guistiniani, which had been made to the deceased Pope Leo XII (1823–29), that he name bishops in New Granada in spite of Spanish opposition. Spain, in effect, still considered that she had a right to the *patronato real* system and, therefore, that she and not the "rebel" governments should name the new bishops. She hoped that if they were not named, the people would become angry with the governments and would ask to return to their "legitimate sovereign." The Vatican was more realistic than Madrid and understood that this would never happen; but it did not dare to be deaf to the Spanish exhortations. The death of Ferdinand VII in 1835 eased things, since Spain began to adopt a more realistic policy in respect to her old colonies and to recognize their independence. In 1836 there was a nuncio in New Granada, and in 1837 Mexico named a minister plenipotentiary to the Vatican.

Pope Gregory XVI, in the encyclical *Sollicitudo eclesiarum* of 1831, found the formula, stating that upon establishing relations with *de facto* regimes for ecclesiastical questions, the Holy See would not prejudge in respect to pending claims in relations with such regimes.

VATICAN RELATIONS AFTER INDEPENDENCE

For almost half a century after the appearance of *Sollicitudo eclesiarum*, relations between the Holy See and the Latin American countries were superficial and intermittent. No country, except Brazil, named ambassadors; only plenipotentiary ministers or chargés d'affaires were appointed, and these positions were often vacant. This situation reflected the internal tensions of the countries themselves, in which the struggles between

Liberals and Conservatives were carried on largely around the question of relations between church and state. When the Liberals predominated in a government, they usually left the post at the Holy See vacant.

The Vatican did not have at its command much influence to impede the expropriation and the secularization that the Liberal governments in many countries (Mexico, Venezuela, Guatemala, Argentina) dictated, so it left the task of opposition to the local churches, giving support with declarations and encyclicals, but not dictating their conduct. On various occasions the Vatican apparently tried to use its influence to soften the attitude of a (local) church when it appeared that a hardening of the attitude of the Liberals might thereby be avoided. But this outcome was rarely achieved.

In 1870, when the acute period of Latin American Liberal anticlericalism may be said to have ended, the diplomatic situation was as follows. Bolivia, Guatemala, and El Salvador had plenipotentiary ministers at the Holy See. Costa Rica and Ecuador had chargés d'affaires. Brazil had a resident minister. The other countries did not maintain relations with the Holy See or, if they had them, did not name diplomatic representatives. Pontifical representation was also uncertain. Although there were nuncios in various countries, it was only after 1870, with the end of the Papal State, that the Vatican organized its diplomacy in Latin America. In 1877 two papal envoys were sent to Spanish American countries: one to Bolivia, Chile, Ecuador, and Peru; the other to Argentina, Paraguay, and Uruguay. In 1881 a third envoy was accredited to Santo Domingo, Haiti, and Venezuela. They were not called nuncios, but Apostolic Delegates and Extraordinary Envoys. Sometimes, the representative of the Holy See was expelled, as occurred, for example, in Argentina in 1888, when he energetically opposed the establishment of lay education.

In addition to the threat of expropriation, the Catholic church had to face another danger: the tendency of some governments to create national churches, separated from Rome, as had occurred early in the nineteenth century in Paraguay under Dr. José Gaspar Francia and in El Salvador in the epoch of José Matías Delgado. Similar but unsuccessful attempts occurred in Venezuela, Brazil, and Mexico. Even the Ecuadoran theocrat García Moreno gave orders to the clergy without consulting Rome.

It was Pope Pius IX (1846–78) who undertook the task of regularizing relations with Latin America. In 1858 he founded the Colegio Pio Latinoamericano in Rome, and his diplomats negotiated concordats with Bolivia in 1851, with Guatemala and Costa Rica in 1860, with Honduras and Nicaragua in 1861, and with Venezuela and Ecuador in 1862. At this same time Catholic missionary work was begun in several Latin American countries. Now it no longer happened, as before, that an entire country might sometimes find itself without bishops because of the quarrels concerning the *patronato*.

By the beginning of the twentieth century, the long and generally quiet efforts of papal diplomacy had succeeded in normalizing relations with all the Latin American countries. Sometimes the relations were strictly formal, at other times they were tendentious. But almost everywhere, through constitutional provisions or laws, there was a clear norm of separation of church and state, contrary to the predictions of many Conservatives; the separation of church and state and the normalization of the legal situation of the church favored the church over the pretensions of the state. Some exceptions need to be noted: in Argentina, for instance, the president has to be a Catholic; in Venezuela, until 1960, the *patronato* was still the norm. In many countries where the separation of church and state was established in the constitution, in practice the church had an almost controlling influence over education and the religious policies of the government, while in other countries where the separation did not exist in the constitution, the church had lost power and in practice could not influence the decisions of the government. The general tendency, though, was toward an increasing de facto separation. The eleven countries in which the Catholic church is constitutionally separated from state today are Brazil, Chile, Cuba, Ecuador, El Salvador, Guatemala, Honduras, Mexico, Nicaragua, and Uruguay.

In general, a renaissance in the Latin American church has occurred since the First World War. Although the ecclesiastical hierarchies have collaborated closely with the governments, especially when they were Conservative or military, Catholic groups have arisen that interested themselves in the workers and sponsored Catholic labor unions. Catholic lay groups went on to form Christian Democratic parties in many countries. Those in Chile and Venezuela became strong enough to gain political control in their nations. On only two occasions in this century has the church clashed sharply with the legal powers. In Mexico around 1921 the bishops criticized the government and brought the country to the edge of civil war, decreeing a strike of priests that lasted three years. Finally, seeing that the people were not giving their support, the church yielded and established a relation of mutual respect with the government. But the government did not renew relations with the Vatican. In this case, the Vatican had basically supported the bishops. It did the same in another conflict, that of the Argentine church with the government of General Juan Perón in 1954–55. This conflict provoked some burning of churches by the Peronists and determined that the church would cease its support of Perón and support the military groups that finally overthrew him. In other cases, when a dictatorship was tottering, the church tried to mediate and avoid bloody conflicts, as in Colombia (1957), Costa Rica (1948), and Venezuela (1958). It did the same thing in a case of foreign intervention in the Dominican Republic in 1965, when the nuncio tried to mediate.

CONTEMPORARY POLICY

In general, the Vatican plays a role of restraining the impetuosity of local churches and Catholic lay groups. There are no longer any persecutions of priests; the only exception was that of Haiti under François Duvalier, for a time. Today Rome realizes that it can not maintain the monopoly on education that it had in so many nations during the nineteenth century. The last serious attempt at conserving this near monopoly occurred in the Mexican conflict under President Plutarco Elías Calles, in 1924, when the priests abandoned the churches and there was an uprising of Catholic peasants (*cristeros*). Finally, it should be noted that the church has sometimes offered opposition when it considered that the civil power was going too far. This has been the case in its relations with the military since 1964 and especially since 1969, and with Paraguay under President Alfredo Stroessner since 1969.

The moderating influence of the Vatican appears clearly in the case of Cuba under Castro. The majority of the Catholic church was anti-Castro, reflecting the sentiments of its most faithful adherents in the middle and upper classes and of many of their priests, half of whom were Spanish and many of whom were banished. But this sentiment was also related to Castro's suppression of many church privileges, especially that of maintaining church schools. But Cuban relations with the Vatican were not broken, and little by little the priests who had not been exiled adapted themselves to the new circumstances, under the influence of successive pontifical nuncios. Today, relations between Castro and the church are cordial, and the chief liberty that exists on the island is religious.

This normality of the Catholic church's situation in Latin America has permitted both an expansion of church activity and a better organization of its institutions. This way was already indicated by the Latin American Plenary Council (Rome, 1899) and by the formation, around 1930, of Catholic Action in the majority of the Latin American countries. It appeared also in the plenary conference of the Latin American Episcopate in Rio de Janerio (1953) and culminated in the foundation of CELAM (Consejo Episcopal Latinoamericano) in a meeting at Rio de Janerio in 1958.

These efforts to coordinate the episcopate on the continent, which are actively encouraged by the Vatican, are (among other things) attempts to act at a level where there is no *patronato*, a level on which the church can feel entirely independent of the civil power. In this sense, CELAM, which assembles periodically as a consequence of the Rio Conference, gives the church an effective instrument. In it the Vatican undoubtedly exercises influence, through the bishops who are cardinals, through the nuncios, and especially through the theologians who collaborate in the work of the conference.

In its first years CELAM was chiefly concerned with the problems of organization and propagation of the faith. But in more recent years, especially since 1965, it has preferred to concern itself with social questions. In this respect it has yielded not only to a general tendency in the church, to which the older bishops are grudgingly giving in, but also to the pressures of a good part of the younger clergy. Mention should be made here of the CELAM conference of 1969, with its clear statement in favor of social reforms, political freedom, and economic independence. Although the action of the church in these directions has been limited, the CELAM statements have provided many "progressive" priests with theoretical ammunition for their preaching. This has been especially visible in Brazil, where the government, after the military coup of 1964, has consistently been opposed by large segments of the church, including many bishops and archbishops, and has persecuted and jailed many priests.

Other continental organisms exist, such as the Inter-American Conference for Catholic Education, the Inter-American Union of Family Fathers (*Padres de Familia*), the organization of Latin American Catholic Universities, and the American Union of Christian Educators. These titles suggest the degree to which the church concentrates its efforts in education. And this emphasis has in great part been the result of Vatican influence that has tried to move the Latin American church away from its habit of intervening in politics.

A parallel to the Latin American church organization exists in Rome, in an organization in the Vatican concerned with Latin American Affairs. Pope Pius XII created it in 1955 as a simple committee to prepare the Rio Conference. In 1958 it became a Pontifical Commission for Latin America. In it are grouped the eight Vatican institutions related to Latin America. This commission doubtless influences CELAM and in general the Latin American Church.

Although the activity of these organizations displays itself chiefly in theological and ecclesiastical matters, there are other fields in which the Holy See intervenes in a subtle way and with different degrees of success. A few examples will illustrate these other types of Vatican activity.

In 1936 Eugenio Cardinal Pacelli (later Pius XII) visited President Franklin D. Roosevelt. Apparently, Roosevelt had sought the help of the Vatican in carrying out the Good Neighbor Policy with the Latin American countries. Two years before, the same cardinal had traveled through the countries of South America.

During the Spanish Civil War, the papal nuncios exercised discreet pressure on the Latin American governments to break relations with the government of the Spanish Republic or not to support it with their votes in the League of Nations. Once the civil war had ended, the Vatican discreetly backed Spanish efforts to support authoritarian movements in Latin America. A Brazilian bishop, Monsignor C. Duarte Costa, who opposed this policy in his country, was excommunicated in 1944 when he denounced this Vatican policy.

Today an active sympathy for the Christian Democratic movements and parties exists in Rome. The Chilean party, for example, has had the open support of the Jesuits, who would not have acted against Vatican wishes. Father Roger Vekemens, a noted Jesuit sociologist, has trained many Christian Democratic workers and has greatly influenced the policy of the Chilean party. Furthermore, it is generally known that the German Christian Democracy and the West German bishops give financial support to the Latin American Christian Democrats. This would not occur without Vatican approval. Much more hesitant is the support to CLASC, the union of Christian labor unions, whose radical activities alarm many Catholic leaders. In 1972, CLASC changed its name to CLAT (Confederación Latinoamericana de Trabajadores), following a similar decision by the International Christian Workers Confederation.

The present-day profound division in the Catholic church does not affect the relations between the Vatican and the different countries. Nor are these relations affected by the activities enthusiastically adopted by priests like Father Camilo Torres of Colombia, who died as a participant in guerrilla warfare. But the schism does restrict the activity of certain organizations openly supported by the Vatican, especially those supported financially by the North American church, whose ties with Rome are close. This schism explains, for example, why the Vatican disapproved the activities of Father Grégoire Lemercier of Cuernavaca, Mexico, who was psychoanalyzing priests, and the activities of the Inter-American Center for Documentation (CIDOC), also in Cuernavaca. In this center priests were preparing for missionary labor of a social character under the direction of Father Ivan Illich, who left the priesthood in 1968 after appearing before several Vatican organizations.

These reactions against activities of the progressive sector of the church followed the visit of Pope Paul VI to Bogotá in 1968. In his discourses in the Colombian capital at this time the pope, after urging the leaders of society to effect reforms, said to the Colombian peasants: "We exhort you not to put your confidence in violence and revolution, since this is contrary to Christian spirit."[1] Thus, the Vatican has taken the side of moderate forces in the Latin American church, rejecting both the progressive, or radical, as well as the traditional sectors. This position was further indicated in 1971 by representatives of Rome to the Brazilian government, who spoke of the tortures suffered by various priests accused of opposing the ruling regime.

It is difficult to say to what extent Vatican diplomacy determines church attitudes. It can not even be affirmed completely that the policies

1. The discourse of 23 Aug. 1968 was published at Paris, under the title "A las pobres," in *Informaciones Católicas Internacionales*, no. 320 (2 Sept. 1968).

followed by ecclesiastical organizations for international aid reflect the thinking of the Vatican, since these organizations do not depend directly on Rome but on some specific national or regional church organization or nonpontifical institution.

This national character of attitudes toward foreign aid to the church has even led to accusations that the church is a party to "North American diplomatic imperialism," since a great part of such aid comes from dioceses in the United States. And when, following the decisions of the Vatican in the case of Father Illich, the aid he had been receiving from North American churches was suspended, it was because the United States had pressured Rome to end an activity that was not favorable to U.S. policy. Thus, on this question, at least in the minds of many people, the interests of U.S. and Vatican diplomacy appeared mixed.

Foreign Catholic aid to religious and extrareligious activities in Latin America is diverse and, probably, less important than is believed. The reason is simple. For some decades Latin America has been a mission land; the missions have been supported by voluntary contributions. However, the people who contribute to sustaining the missions do not feel inclined to contribute funds for labors of a social character. The backers of missions are customarily traditional Catholics who view with a jaundiced eye other than traditional church activities. Mission activities have to be supported, then, with institutional funds, either from Vatican congregations or from dioceses of other countries (Germany, the United States). But when the aid comes not from private individuals but from institutions, there is a tendency for control to be exerted on the funds given, thus arousing resentment and distrust. The church is not an exception to this general rule.

The principal present sources of aid are the following: Papal Volunteers for Apostolic Work, an organization created by the Pontifical Commission in 1960, a kind of Catholic peace corps; the CICOP (Catholic Inter-American Cooperation Program), created through the initiative of some North American cardinals in 1964, in collaboration with several Latin American cardinals; the Missionary Society of St. James the Apostle, founded by the North American Cardinal Cushing, which has sent some five thousand priests, monks, and nuns to Latin America; the Office for Latin American Affairs in Ottawa and the Latin American Bureau of the Catholic Welfare Conference in Washington, created as a consequence of a conference celebrated in 1959 at Georgetown University (Washington, D.C.); the Adventist Fund (German) for the apostolate in Latin America; the Iuvate Fund (German), which collects a percentage of the salaries of the clergy and dedicates it to social projects in Latin America and other areas; the Seminary Scholarship Fund (German) for Latin American seminarians; the German Central Church-State Organization of the different German churches and the government, for social projects; the Holland Fund for the Church in Peril; and various other funds, mostly Dutch, Belgian and French, which dedicate an important part of their resources to Latin America.

This simple list indicates the scope of the Vatican's interest in Latin America, since all these organizations, although autonomous, are closely related to Rome. This interest is basically apostolic. But it undoubtedly has diplomatic implications and indirectly influences the foreign policy of the Latin American countries.

It would be erroneous to believe, however, that Vatican diplomacy is a decisive factor in the contemporary international politics of Latin America. Because it tries to stay on the periphery (outside) of the internal quarrels of the church in those countries, except in very serious cases, the governments do not see in the Vatican a means for intervening in the church or for avoiding the radicalization of parts of it; this removes, for the time being, any threat of pressure from the pontifical diplomats.

The church is not threatened by national forces today as it was in earlier periods of Latin American history. In any case, the threats that now hang over her come from within more than from governments and political movements. And this threat of division is what the Vatican tries to avoid, not so much through her diplomacy as through her internal organisms.

On the other side, although there is a renewal of the faith in certain Latin American groups, it is certainly true that the moral influence of the Latin American church has diminished and that the church has, therefore, less influence in elections and military coups. This fact, in turn, deprives Vatican diplomacy of instruments of pressure.

In summary, it may be said that relations between the Holy See and the Latin American countries have had more importance in recent years for the internal policy of the nations than for their foreign policy. Today this importance is diminishing in both areas. (English Translation by Keith Miceli)

BIBLIOGRAPHICAL NOTE

Accioly, Hildebrando. *Os primeiros nuncios no Brasil.* São Paolo: Instituto Progresso Editorial, 1949.

Coleman, W. J. *The First Apostolic Delegation in Rio de Janeiro and Its Influence in Spanish America.* Washington, D.C.: Catholic University of America Press, 1950.

Considine, John J. "Aid to the Latin American Church." *America*, 30 Sept. 1967.

────── . *The Church in the New Latin America.* Notre Dame, Ind.: Notre Dame University Press, 1964.

Detroyat, Leone. *La corte de Roma y el emperador Maximiliano.* México: L. Elizagi, 1870.

Dussêl, Enrique. *Hipótesis para una historia de la Iglesia en América Latina.* Barcelona: Editorial Estela, 1967.

Graham, Robert A. *Vatican Diplomacy: A Study of Church and State on the International Plane.* Princeton: Princeton University Press, 1959.

Houtart, F., and E. Pin. *The Church and the Latin American Revolution.* New York: Sheed & Ward, 1965.

Leturia, Pedro. *Bolívar y Teón XII.* Caracas: Parra León Hermanos, 1931.

———— . *La Emancipación hispanoaméricana en los informes episocopales a Pío VII.* Buenos Aires: Imprenta de la Universidad, 1935.

———— . *Relaciones entre la Santa Sede e Hispanoamérica.* Caracas: Sociedad Bolivariana de Venezuela, 1959–60.

———— . *El ocaso del Patronato Real en la América Española.* Madrid: "Razón y Fe," 1925.

Manhattan, Avro. *The Vatican in World Politics.* New York: Smithers & Bonellie, 1949.

Oviedo Cavada, Carlos. *La Misión Irarrázabal en Roma, 1947–50.* Santiago: Universidad Católica de Chile, 1962.

Paz, Carlos. *Bolivia en Roma.* La Paz: n.p., 1923.

Rama, Carlos M. "La política vaticanista en América Latina." *Cuadernos Americanos* (México, D.F.), Yr. 19, no. 5 (September-October 1960).

Samuel, Albert. *Castrisme, Communisme, Democratie Chretienne en Amerique Latine.* Lyon: Chronique Social de France, 1965.

Sanguinetti, M. J. *La representación diplomática del Vaticano en los países del Plata.* Buenos Aires: n.p., 1954.

Vallier, Ivan. *Catholicism, Social Control, and Modernization.* Englewood Cliffs, N.J.: Prentice-Hall, 1970.

II

Mexico and Central America

6/Edith B. Couturier
Mexico

INTRODUCTION

Mexico's geographic position on the U.S. border is the primary influence on her foreign policy. Decisions have had to be measured by their impact on her relations with her northern neighbor. Because of her proximity to the United States, Mexico has received foreign investments, tourist dollars, employment for her citizens, and emigration opportunities not readily available to other Latin American countries. Hence the United States dominates her economic life.

Mexico's closeness to the United States has created vulnerabilities. She often has reckoned with the possibility of armed invasion, and this possibility limits options in foreign relations. A virulent anti-U.S. position, such as that pursued intermittently by Argentina, would have been dangerous for Mexico. Hence, most Mexican governments steer a difficult course between friendship with, but independence from, the United States in matters of foreign policy.

A realistic assessment of her international position combined with capable management of her foreign policy has led to Mexico's ascent to a position of international prestige. On the whole, this policy has reflected the possibilities available to a second-ranking power. Mexico has earned a place of special respect among the nations of the world by pursuing a foreign policy that stresses legal consistency and a careful understanding of world politics.

Realization of her relative ranking in the international community was the first step in the development of Mexico's foreign policy. On achieving independence from Spain in 1821, Mexico had hoped to become one of the major world powers, but Spain and the Vatican, traditionally the most important states for Mexico, both refused to recognize her independence.[1] Spain, moreover, spent fifteen years devising plans for the reconquest of Mexico.[2] Although Great Britain and the United States did recognize Mexico, the meddling of their envoys in the internal affairs of the new republic revealed Mexico's weaknesses. Mexico's rapid and frightening defeat by the United States in 1846–47, before European aid could even be considered, dramatized her debility.

Less than twenty years later, the French army occupied Mexico—albeit at the request of some Mexican politicians—and proved that Mexico

1. Francisco Cuevas Cancino, "The Foreign Policy of Mexico," in *Foreign Policies in a World of Change*, ed. Joseph Black (New York: Harper & Row, 1963), p. 644.
2. Jaime Delgado, *España y México en el siglo xix*, 3 vols. (Madrid: Consejo Superior de Investigaciones Científicas, 1950–54), 2: 11.

117

could easily be invaded and occupied. But the difficulties experienced by the French army and their inability to complete the pacification of the country also proved that permanent foreign conquest was impossible.[3]

Mexico's experiences between 1821, when she achieved independence, and 1867, when the French occupation ended, schooled her diplomats to evolve techniques of negotiation with more powerful nations. Mexico separated her foreign ministry from internal affairs in order to facilitate the conduct of diplomacy. In fact, it became a proverb among Texans "that when a Texan fights a Mexican, he can win, but when he parleys, he is doomed."[4] Mexico's relations with Europe were those of a former colony that was a weak nation unable to rely on allies. Mexico placed little emphasis on her relations with other Latin American nations in these early years.[5] Thus, she had to deal alone with the great northern neighbor with which she shared two thousand miles of common boundary.

MEXICAN FOREIGN POLICY ISSUES

Three issues have dominated Mexico's foreign policy in the past and continue to concern her policy makers in the present: boundary disputes; economic questions, such as trade, public debt, and foreign investment; and finally, the legal questions of recognition and nonintervention.

Territorial Issues and Boundary Conflicts

Mexico stands between the United States, the most powerful nation in the hemisphere, and the Central American nations, the weakest group in continental Latin America. Forceful military settlement of boundary disputes has not been a practical alternative for Mexico, either in relation to Guatemala or the United States. Her geographic position, therefore, helped to determine her peaceful tradition in foreign policy.

U.S. envoys to Mexico in the years before 1846 frequently tried to purchase Texas and California. Mexico persistently refused to sell any part of the territory to which she had legal claim as the heir to the Spanish

3. For a description of Mexican foreign policy before 1867, see the following: Carlos Bosch García, *Historia de las relaciones entre México y los Estados Unidos* (México: Escuela Nacional de Ciencias Políticas y Sociales, 1957); and Bosch García, *Problemas diplomáticas del México independiente* (México: Colegio de México, 1947). The major documents have been collected in a series published by the Secretaría de Relaciones Exteriores called *Archivo histórico diplomático mexicano*, which began publication in 1923. Of special value for the French intervention is Luis Weckmann, ed., *Las Relaciones Franco-Mexicanas (1823-67)*, 2 vols. (México: Secretaría de Relaciones Exteriores, 1962).

4. Walter Prescott Webb, as quoted in Daniel Cosió Villegas, *The United States against Porfirio Díaz* (Lincoln: University of Nebraska Press, 1964).

5. Richard B. McCornack, "Relaciones de México con Hispano-América: 1821-1855," *Historia Mexicana* 8 (1953): 352-71.

empire in North America. Spain had only partially occupied and colonized this area before Mexican independence. Beginning in 1822, enterprising and aggressive U.S. citizens settled Mexican territories, especially Texas. This rapidly growing "Anglo" population in Texas sought autonomy within the Mexican Federation. When they came into conflict with a Centralist Conservative government in 1836, the Texans established an independent republic. Nine years later, the United States annexed Texas, and a border dispute brought U.S. invasion and the occupation of most of Mexico. The 1848 peace treaty allowed the United States to settle the boundary to its own satisfaction, taking nearly half of Mexico's national territory. In the Gadsden Purchase of 1853, the United States bought a small additional area from Mexico, comprising the southern sections of the states of Arizona and New Mexico.

Border incidents plagued relations between the United States and Mexico during the last half of the nineteenth century. Cattle rustlers and Indians battled in the huge desert no man's land between the settled regions of the United States and Mexico. Frequent claims and counterclaims of damages to property and livestock exacerbated relations. In a treaty made in 1882, armed units of either country were permitted to cross the border in pursuit of malefactors. Only the gradual settlement of permanent populations along the borders and the pacification of the Indians eliminated the disputes.[6]

Two serious boundary disputes between Mexico and the United States have carried over into the twentieth century. One involves the winding Rio Grande and the other concerns scarce water from the Colorado River.

The Rio Grande forms the international boundary between the cities of El Paso, Texas, and Juárez, Mexico. Its shifting course transferred the Chamizal territory to the U.S. side of the river, creating another boundary issue between the United States and Mexico. The question was arbitrated in 1911, giving Mexico the land; but the United States refused to accept the decision. The matter dragged on in alternate negotiations and recriminations for years.[7] Finally, in 1962, the United States accepted the terms of the 1911 award. Mexico had clearly become a power to be reckoned with, one whose friendship was to be valued in the dangerous days of concern over the spread of Castro's communism, even at the cost of domestic political interests and pressures in the United States. Despite favorable settlement of the U.S. boundary, Mexico did not break ties with Cuba in 1962. Alone among the Latin American nations, she has continuously maintained diplomatic relations with Castro in defiance of

6. Daniel Cosío Villegas, *Historia Moderna de México: La Vida Política Exterior*, 6 vols. (México: Editorial Hermes, 1963), 5, pt. 2: 34–46, 77–250; Cosío Villegas, *The United States against Porfirio Díaz*.
7. Sheldon B. Liss, *A Century of Disagreement: The Chamizal Conflict, 1854–1964* (Washington: University Press of Washington, D.C., 1965).

the policy of the Organization of American States and in opposition to
the United States.

Settlement of the final boundary dispute between Mexico and the
United States occurred only in September 1973. Water from the Colorado
River, an international river, has been divided between the two nations in
order to irrigate the desert. In 1961, Mexican farmers in the Mexicali
valley noticed that the water reaching their farms had an excessively high
saline content, the result of the completion of the Wellton-Mohawk
irrigation works. Mexican farmers received water that had a salinity
rating of 4,000 parts per million; while U.S. farmers' irrigation water
measured only 1,300 parts per million. Mexico viewed this as a violation
of the spirit of the agreements "dividing the waters."[8]

When President Luis Echeverría visited the United States in June 1972,
he exacted an agreement that would guarantee to Mexican farmers the
same quality of water that U.S. farmers enjoyed. Secretary of State Henry
Kissinger implemented this agreement in September 1973 when he
allocated funds to lower the salt content of the water Mexico used for
irrigation. Although the United States negotiated this issue, it was
difficult to make her own citizens conform. The temporary ruin of some
Mexicali farmland remained as one last sign of one hundred and fifty
years of boundary disputes and of the ability of the United States, as the
stronger power, to ultimately decide the outcome of conflict between the
two countries.

Three issues stemming from their common boundary dominated the
relations between Mexico and the United States in the 1960s and early
1970s. One was the network for illegal importation of drugs that operated
out of Mexico, supplying U.S. users. U.S. insistence on aggressive action
brought about close cooperation between the Mexican and American
police, who together burned poppy fields, raided storage depots, and
destroyed private airfields in the desert regions of northern Mexico. These
measures have so far failed to halt the drug traffic and have at times been
resented by Mexico as violations of her sovereignty.

A second recent boundary issue arose in 1965, when U.S. manufacturers began the practice of building twin factories—one in the United States
for manufacturing parts and the other in Mexico for assembling the parts
into finished commodities. The parts enter Mexico duty free and pay only
a 10 percent tax when reentering the United States. The Mexican factories
provide needed employment, while the U.S. firms, which produce commodities such as electronics, can compete effectively with Italy, Spain,

8. For events up to 1966, see Norris Hundley, *Dividing the Waters: A Century of Conflict between the United States and Mexico* (Berkeley: University of California Press, 1966). For an especially useful brief summary of the issues, see Donald F. Campbell, "The Colorado River: Dividing the Waters," *Southeast Latin Americanist*, September 1972, pp. 4-11; and Marvin Alisky, "U.S.-Mexican Border Conflicts and Compromises," ibid., September 1973, pp. 1-4.

and Japan in the U.S. market. Although the program got off to a slow start, the annual value of commodities produced under this arrangement between 1968 and 1971 jumped from seven million to $350 million annually. Predictably, trade unions resented competition from Mexicans who earned 75 percent less than U.S. workers.[9]

The wage differential lies at the root of the third boundary problem—the migration of Mexican workers. Between 1942 and 1964, a limited number of Mexican workers entered the United States under the *bracero* program. Even though these workers received lower pay than U.S. laborers, this opportunity provided many Mexicans with the chance to buy farms or to start their own businesses. It has been considered one of the most effective U.S. foreign aid programs, although this was not its intention. When the program ended in 1964, it appeared to precipitate an enormous tide of illegal migration. It was estimated that in 1972 alone, 1,350,000 workers entered the United States illegally—in the trunks of cars, crowded into trailer rigs, or by such old-fashioned methods as walking or swimming the Rio Grande. Each year the U.S. government deports hundreds of thousands of illegal immigrants, who search for jobs as far north as Chicago and Racine, Wisconsin.

Neither Mexicans nor North Americans nor Chicanos can agree on a policy to restrict immigration. Many Chicanos view the 1848 border as artifical and advocate unrestricted passage across it. Spanish Americans inhabited the Southwest long before the Anglos, and they have been arriving in large waves of immigration since the turn of the century.

Many North Americans, including unions of Chicano workers, advocate strict enforcement of immigration laws because their struggle for better wages and working conditions is threatened by illegal immigrants who act as strikebreakers. The abundance of illegal laborers lowers the living standards for Chicano workers. Proposals for preventing immigration range from making employers who hire illegal workers subject to heavy fines and jail,[10] to constructing a two thousand mile-long electronic fence similar to the one used in Vietnam.

Mexican policy can hardly be consistent on this issue. It is a source of concern that more than half a century after the revolution, which was to give land to the peasants and rights to the workers, so many people need to leave Mexico to find a decent job. If present population trends continue, Mexico will have 135 million people by the year 2000, and there is little prospect of finding employment for them under present programs. Mexican acquiescence in the matter of migration is inevitable. Some Mexicans view the *pochos* (Mexicans who ape U.S. ways) with contempt, because their Spanish is corrupted by English and because they are neither Mexican nor American. Other Mexicans envy their opportuni-

9. Alisky, "U.S.–Mexican Border Conflicts and Compromises."
10. William Chapman, "Mexican 'Illegals' Now Seek U.S. Cities," *Washington Post*, 9 Dec. 1973.

ties. As in all the problems arising from Mexico's proximity to the United States, the issue of immigration is a sword that cuts two ways, by its very nature defying easy solution.

Mexico, as the "colossus of the North" for her southern neighbor, Guatemala, has resolved the boundary issues between them to her own advantage, always with peaceful means. Shortly after independence, the Central American states, including Guatemala, separated from Mexico, but the district of Chiapas remained in dispute. Chiapas elected to join Mexico, but adjusting the boundary proved difficult. Negotiations, strengthened by the presence of a secure and stable government, resulted in cession of the disputed area to Mexico in 1882 and final treaty confirmation in 1899.

The section of Central America called Belize, or British Honduras, which borders on Mexico and Guatemala, remains an unresolved issue between the two nations. Mexico opposes the return of Belize to Guatemala, claiming certain historical rights over the area based on colonial possession. When Britain relinquishes her sovereignty over Belize, Mexico will oppose annexation to Guatemala in favor of self-determination for her population. Guatemala's hopes of ever regaining Belize, in the light of Mexico's opposition, seem indeed very dim.

Economic Issues

Far more persistent in Mexico's foreign policy have been the economic issues that confront any capital-poor nation. Throughout much of her history, Mexico's political instability has compounded her economic problems.

After independence, Mexico eagerly sought foreign investment, commodities, and loans but failed to produce enough silver or other exports to create a favorable exchange balance. Changes of government and frequent civil wars raised the public debt. Foreign residents of Mexico, their property damaged in civil disorder, claimed further indemnities against Mexico. Failure to pay the ever mounting public debt caused foreign intervention, leading not only to the occasional occupation of the port city of Vera Cruz but also to the full-scale invasion of the nation in 1862 by the French army. The defeat of the French-sponsored empire took nearly five years and left an additional burden of foreign debt. The Mexican Revolution of 1910 again made it impossible for Mexico to meet her debt service and created new foreign claims against the government. Once more the threats of intervention rumbled in the United States.[11]

Mexico's experiences have prompted her firm adherence to the Drago doctrine, which states that the public debt should never give cause for

11. The history of the Mexican foreign debt can be found in Jan Bazant, *Historia de la deuda exterior de México* (México: Colegio de México, 1964).

armed intervention by other nations. Her consistency in support of this principle, while scrupulously meeting her own obligations—except in brief moments of severe civil stress—constitutes another principle of Mexican foreign policy.

In 1918, Mexico proposed another tenet of inter-American law, the Carranza doctrine, providing for equality of treatment for foreigners and her own citizens and stating that diplomacy should not serve private business interests.[12] Despite Mexico's advocacy of the Carranza doctrine, foreigners have, in fact, received preference in payment of claims. When Mexico was expropriating and dividing up the large haciendas, her own citizens received nonredeemable treasury bonds, while alien landowners got cash. The realities of international relations and Mexico's need for investment and trading credits, combined with her inability and unwillingness to pay for expropriated land, necessitated a policy of discrimination against her own citizens.[13]

Another critical economic issue in Mexico's relations with the industrialized countries of the world was the expropriation or nationalization of mines, oil, or industry. Mexico's 1917 constitution revived an old Spanish law asserting the government's right to nationalize the "subsoil," i. e., any mineral found under the layer of top soil.

In 1920, when Alvaro Obregón became President of Mexico by revolution, the United States refused to recognize his government until it received assurances that U.S. mines and oil wells would not be expropriated. Negotiations continued for three years, and Mexico finally promised that nationalization would not apply to property exploited before 1917.[14] Despite this promise, which Mexicans felt was made under the duress of nonrecognition, Mexico expropriated the foreign oil companies in 1938.

Mexico had good reason again to fear armed intervention. These fears proved ungrounded, however, for no U.S. armies massed at the border, no threatening ultimata came from the North. The United States sent no armies, because of the Good Neighbor Policy, the need for Mexican cooperation in the pending conflagration of World War II, and the presence of Josephus Daniels, a sympathetic U.S. ambassador. This successful assertion of national economic self-determination had an

12. The Carranza doctrine is in part a restatement of the Calvo principle, but it also includes provisions for the repudiation of the Monroe Doctrine. Robert F. Smith, *The United States and Revolutionary Nationalism in Mexico, 1916–1932* (Chicago: University of Chicago Press, 1972), pp. 81–82; Modesto Seara Vázquez, *La Política exterior de México* (México: Editorial Esfinge, S.A., 1969), p. 165.

13. Jorge Castañeda, "Revolution and Foreign Policy: Mexico's Experience," *Political Science Quarterly* 78, no. 3 (September 1963): 402.

14. The convention that ended in U.S. recognition of the Obregón government produced the Bucareli agreements. Antonio Gómez Robledo, "Los Convenios de Bucareli ante el derecho internacional," in *Trabajos jurídicos de homenaje a la Escuela Libre de Derecho en su xxv aniversario* (México: Editorial Polis, 1938), pp. xiv–238; Howard F. Cline, *The United States and Mexico* (New York: Atheneum, 1963), pp. 209–11.

enormous psychological impact on Mexico. The "colossus of the north" had been challenged; Mexico had braved the storm and survived.[15]

In 1961, when the opportunity occurred to nationalize the electrical industry, long subsidized by the Mexican government, Mexico paid a steep price for the foreign-owned shares. Critics opined that Mexico had received no more tangible profit than a change in title, so great was the prestige attached to national ownership of basic industry. Adequate compensation for nationalized property was a price that rapidly growing Mexico could easily afford.[16]

In 1971, the government purchased 51 percent of the stock in the copper-producing Cananea Mining Company for $48 million, thus completely "Mexicanizing" the mining industry.[17]

Since the mid-1930s, Mexico has consistently asserted control over investment. Laws requiring from 51 to 75 percent Mexican ownership of any corporation are asserted (on the books) as a concession to public opinion. But investors have connived to circumvent them by placing "straw men" as owners of the dominant national shares. Greater insistence on Mexican middle- and upper-level management, limitations or prohibitions on imports, and demands for increased manufacturing in Mexico have reflected popular interest in creating a national industrial base, providing jobs for Mexicans, and lessening the use of foreign skills and products. Mexico's economic policy during the 1960s continued to emphasize import substitution, i.e., making commodities rather than importing them. In order to sell in the Mexican market, manufacturers had to change their assembly plants to full-scale manufacturing enterprises.

Luis Echeverría, when he became president in December of 1970, launched Mexico on an ambitious policy of international leadership among developing nations. First he acted as an advocate of the Third World powers by introducing measures in international organizations which would aid the underdeveloped world. He proposed and propagandized for international programs designed to aid raw-material-producing nations through such devices as stabilizing their prices at a high level, lowering customs barriers in the advanced countries, and making international lending agencies completely apolitical. This new Mexican leader-

15. Cline, *The United States and Mexico*, pp. 239–47; Frank Tannenbaum, *Mexico: The Struggle for Peace and Bread* (New York: Alfred A. Knopf, 1950), pp. 278–81; Bryce Wood, *The Making of the Good Neighbor Policy* (New York: Columbia University Press, 1961), pp. 203–23.

16. Miguel S. Wionczek, "Electric Power: The Uneasy Partnership," in *Public Policy and Private Enterprise in Mexico*, ed. Raymond Vernon (Cambridge: Harvard University Press, 1964), pp. 91–110. As a historical parallel, it might be noted that Mexico had nationalized some of her railroads in 1908 during the last years of the dictatorship of Porfirio Díaz.

17. Martin C. Needler, "A Critical Time for Mexico," *Current History* 56 (February 1972): 85.

ship of the Third World has aimed to alter their unfavorable economic balance of trade.

The second part of Echeverría's foreign economic policy has aggressively promoted Mexican exports. Trade experts have replaced scholars and diplomats in the most important posts in the foreign relations corps; commercial missions have been sent to Europe, Canada, and Japan; increased contacts with eastern Europe have been made in order to diversify markets.[18] In April 1973, Echeverría visited China and signed a reciprocal trade pact with her, arranging for commercial exchange in hard currencies.[19] Economic cooperation with Central America includes provision for Mexican credits for joint enterprises, thus facilitating Mexico's penetration of that area. This Central American cooperation expands the 1966 overtures of President Gustavo Díaz Ordaz.[20]

Mexico joined the Latin American Free Trade Association (LAFTA) with some reluctance, since her traditional economic ties were with Europe and the United States. Mexico's participation in LAFTA occurred at a time when her intellectuals were displaying increased interest in their Latin American tradition. Passing rapidly from a theoretical interest to business, she arranged for marketing industrial products for which she had surplus capacity. Mexico utilized the LAFTA machinery to reach bilateral trade agreements and to enter the South American market in a significant way.[21]

Mexico has placed special emphasis on her relations with the Andean Pact nations, encouraged by her favorable balance of trade and its increasing volume between 1967 and 1972. All of the Andean nations shared a common commitment to regional integration and flexibility in economic forms. In October 1972, a mixed Andean-Mexican commission was formed. This was followed in August 1973 by a seminar of high government officials that agreed to finance an investment bank, create multinational enterprises operating within the two regions, adopt similar rules towards foreign companies and the transfer of technology, coordinate their industrial development, and facilitate trade. Mexico has displayed particular enthusiasm for these measures, but she still needs to

18. For descriptions of Mexico's trade with Japan and Eastern Europe, see Blanca Torres, "México en la estructura del comercio y la cooperación internacional de los países socialistas," *Foro Internacional* 13, no. 2 (October–December 1972): 178–210; and Luis Medina Peña, "La Política exterior japonesa," ibid., pp. 211–34.

19. *New York Times*, 12 Apr. 1973.

20. Weston H. Agor and Andrés Suárez, "The Latin American Political Sub-System," in Douglas A. Chalmers, ed., *Changing Latin America: New Interpretations of its Politics and Society. Proceedings of the Academy of Political Science* 30, no. 4 (1972): 164; Ramón Luna, "Proyección de México sobre Centroamérica," *Foro Internacional* 14, no. 4 (April–June 1974): 465.

21. Phillippe C. Schmitter and Ernst B. Haas, *Mexico and Latin American Economic Integration*, Institute of International Studies, Research Series no. 5 (Berkeley: University of California, 1964).

train and employ technicians and administrators on the middle levels to carry out such plans.[22]

Certainly Mexico's impressive economic growth has given her increased status within Latin America and has accorded her a leading place among the second-ranking nations of the world. She has achieved this wealth without participating in the U.S. foreign aid program. Programs ranging from the construction of a highway network to the development of a variety of export industries grew solely with Mexican initiative and capital. Benefits from access to LAFTA have been shared by the multinational corporations with local factories and by Mexicans who received jobs and income that came from increased investment. Mexico's economic progress exemplifies some of the possibilities for other developing nations. The 1974 discovery of a large new oil field in the state of Chiapas may well enhance Mexico's potential role in hermispheric and world trade relations.

On the other hand, despite her rapidly increasing industrial base, Mexico still depends upon the United States for 70 percent of her foreign trade and continues to need foreign private capital investment for economic progress.[23] The cost of creating new industrial jobs increases annually; the impact of rising inflation on living standards and Mexico's 3.5 percent annual population growth—the fourth highest in the world —continue to erode the benefits of her economic progress.

Legal Issues: Recognition and Nonintervention

In Latin America, the peaceful transition of presidents in office, a commonly respected electoral procedure, and other aspects of a representative constitutional tradition have frequently been absent. In the recent past, this political instability has given U.S. diplomacy a powerful tool—that of delaying recognition of a new government until any outstanding differences between it and the United States had been resolved or until a government more palatable to the United States had gained power. Failure to obtain U.S. recognition in the past could cause the downfall of governments.[24]

Mexico was particularly susceptible to the action of nonrecognition, which could be considered a form of intervention in her internal politics. Having developed a stable political system since the 1930s, Mexico has evolved a consistent policy towards recognition, embodied in the Estrada Doctrine, a major Mexican contribution to inter-American law. This

22. Romeo Flores Caballero, "México y el Pacto Andino," *Foro Internacional* 14, no. 4 (April–June 1974): 608–10.

23. Lorenzo Meyer, "Cambio político y dependencia: México en el siglo XX," *Foro Internacional* 13, no. 2 (October–December 1972); see especially p. 137 which contains a chart detailing the continued importance of U.S. investment in the Mexican market.

24. See, for example, Wood, *The Making of the Good Neighbor Policy*, pp. 81–104.

doctrine derives from an agonizing history of difficulties over delayed recognition by other countries. During the time of Iturbide's empire in 1821, Joel Poinsett, the North American envoy, cautioned against recognizing a monarchy; but the United States did establish diplomatic relations. At the time of the Civil Wars of the Reform and the empire of Maximilian (1857-67), recognition was a key to both Liberal and Conservative protagonists. The government of Porfirio Díaz in 1876 was denied recognition for months until Mexico made a substantial payment meeting claims of private citizens. Mexico's twentieth-century experiences with the issue of U.S. recognition have been even more painful. U.S. recognition of one of the competing generals vying for control of Mexico between 1913-17 was a necessary preliminary to reaching the presidency. A three-year delay in the recognition of Obregón threatened Mexico's stability between 1920 and 1923.

In 1930, in the wake of the depression, both military and democratic governments fell throughout Latin America. The foreign minister, Genaro Estrada, proposed that Mexico not withhold recognition of existing governments. The consistency of this policy in relation to Latin America has been remarkable. Mexico urged the recognition of the radical Grau San Martín government in Cuba in 1933 but failed to obtain U.S. agreement. In splendid political impartiality, Mexico in 1945 worked for adherence by the alleged proto-Fascist nationalist Argentine government to the inter-American and world organizations.

Mexico's position on recognition is part of an uncompromising diplomatic policy of nonintervention. Mexico worked for the Additional Protocol on Non-Intervention at the Inter-American Congress in Buenos Aires in 1936, in which all signatories agreed to repudiate armed intervention. Mexico opposed U.S. intervention in Guatemala in 1954, in the Dominican Republic in 1965, and in Cuba since 1959.

The independence of Mexico's foreign policy has been tested in the case of Castro's Cuba because the Castro government has clearly maintained control of Cuba in the face of U.S. hostility, invasion, and the sanctions imposed by the Organization of American States. Mexico has consistently adhered to legal principle in maintaining diplomatic relations with Cuba, whether during the liberal government of López Mateos (1958-64) or during the more conservative regime of Díaz Ordaz (1964-70).

Franco's Spain still constitutes one exception to the policy of automatic recognition. Mexico refuses to recognize Franco, who has controlled Spain for more than three decades. Instead, she maintains formal relations with the shadowy Spanish republican government in exile. The Mexican government claims that it has no reason to have diplomatic relations with Franco, because his government is the product of German and Italian Fascist intervention in the Spanish Civil War of 1936-39. It

128   6 / EDITH B. COUTURIER

might be speculated that Mexico's continued support of the republicans is
traceable to three sources: Mexico's military support during the civil war
years; the number of refugee republicans who contributed so substantially
to the cultural and educational life of Mexico after 1939; and the fact that
Mexican assistance to the Spanish Republic occurred during the period of
the Mexican Revolution (1934–49), when President Cárdenas carried out
large-scale land reform and nationalized foreign-owned oil. But this
policy toward Franco's Spain is an aberration in Mexico's foreign policy.
Yet even in this case, it should be noted that Mexico pursues a policy
totally independent of the United States. The United States has recognized Franco Spain; Mexico, for her own reasons, refuses to do so. With
this one exception, for forty years Mexico has invariably followed a policy
of recognition of existing governments.

THE CONDUCT OF MEXICAN FOREIGN POLICY

The president of Mexico determines her foreign policy stance. He makes
the important decisions and major appointments. But each president
exercises his prerogative differently. Some presidents have pursued an
active and assertive foreign policy. Four such leaders were Venustiano
Carranza (1918–20), Lázaro Cárdenas (1934–40), Miguel Alemán
(1946–52), and Adolfo López Mateos (1958–64). Each had sought the
peaceful aggrandizement of Mexico in the eyes of other nations, whether
juridically (through aid to anti-Fascists and expropriation of the foreign
oil industry), economically (through aggressive business, tourist, and
cultural developments), or diplomatically (through constant contacts
with other heads of state by traveling and receiving visits). On the other
hand, the presidential administrations of Adolfo Ruiz Cortines (1952–58)
and Gustavo Díaz Ordaz (1964–70) were characterized by periods of
consolidation, in domestic as well as foreign policy.[25]

The president leads; the legislature accepts; the bureaucracy implements. The daily decisions and the administration of Mexican foreign
policy are carried out by the Department of External Relations. Even
though its budget has been small, it is one of the two most prestigious
departments in the government. In the past, the Mexican secretary of
foreign relations has been an outstanding civil servant or a notable
intellectual. Mexico's ambassadors to international organizations or to
other nations were frequently selected from the ranks of scholars, artists,
or writers in order to emphasize Mexico's cultural interests and to give
these figures an opportunity to spend extensive periods of time abroad.

Until the administration of Luis Echeverría, foreign economic matters
were the responsibility of the Treasury Department (*Hacienda*) and the

25. David A. White, *Mexico in World Affairs, 1928–1968* (Ph.D. diss., University of
California [Los Angeles], 1969), pp. 340–42.

national industrial development bank (Financiera Nacional), which determined questions of foreign investment. Both departments worked according to the policies laid down by the president. But as part of the concerted economic drive of the 1970s, foreign relations and foreign economic policy have been centralized under the Department of Foreign Relations.

Public opinion and domestic politics have historically been a minor influence on the making of foreign policy. Although newspapers have always commented on foreign policy matters, criticism of the government has been rare. In the past, career bureaucrats of the foreign ministry have exercised their own judgment without much pressure from public opinion. These functionaries, however, had to take into consideration the latent anti-U.S. sentiments, such as were manifested when the United States gave aid to the Guatemalan rebels in 1954.

But during 1962 and 1963, public opinion in Mexico was actively brought to bear on the government in relation to its policy toward Cuba. From that time on, public opinion has been a more important factor in foreign policy matters. In 1962–63, Conservatives and industrialists tried openly to convince the government to break off diplomatic relations with Castro's Cuba and join the majority in the OAS in imposing sanctions. They feared economic disaster from the leftward trend of the López Mateos government, from public expressions of radicalism, from the nationalization of the electrical industry, and from the withdrawal of some foreign capital. Also in the early 1960s, proleftist groups sought a more aggressively pro-Castro policy. Ex-President Cárdenas convoked a Latin American Congress for National Sovereignty, Economic Emancipation, and Peace, in March 1961. These groups tried to mobilize public support for a more leftist foreign policy.

Despite public statements critical of the government by the Right and by the Left, both failed to sway the official government policy. Mexico refused to break relations with Cuba or to vote sanctions against her in the OAS; she maintained her traditional nationalist stance, rather than appear to submit to specific domestic pressures.[26]

By the time of the 1965 crisis over U.S. intervention in the Dominican Republic, all groups, including the most conservative, supported the stand of the Mexican government, thereby indicating a return to the official public support usually accorded the president.

The Party of the Institutionalized Revolution (PRI), the Mexican political party whose candidate becomes the president of Mexico, alternates between the Right and the Left in its policy positions. In 1964, a Conservative candidate, Gustavo Díaz Ordaz, was chosen by the PRI to replace Adolfo López Mateos because of the party elite's fears of in-

26. For this analysis of public opinion and foreign policy, I have utilized Olga Pellicer de Brody, "Grupos patronales y política exterior," *Foro Internacional* 10, no. 1 (January-

creasing radicalism in both foreign and domestic policies. Luis Echeverría, whose presidential term began in December 1970, utilized leftist rhetoric and programs in foreign policy. He has tried to change his reputation as the initiator of the Tlatelolco student massacre in the fall of 1968, when he was secretary of the interior, by becoming a spokesman for radical foreign and domestic policies. In May 1971, a Conservative group called *Los Halcones* ("the hawks") seriously challenged his regime by killing thirteen students who were part of a demonstration that was to meet with the president in the main plaza. This challenge was overcome only with the support of the army.[27]

Echeverría's relations with the Socialist governments in Latin America have been cordial. He strengthened ties with Castro's Cuba and the radical military regime in Peru, and he gave Chilean Socialist President Salvador Allende financial credits and moral and material assistance. When the military overthrew Allende in September 1973, the Mexican ambassador gave refuge to hundreds of people, and Mexico welcomed and cared for a number of political exiles.

Mexican leadership of the Third World has been stressed by her advocacy of a Charter of Economic Rights and Duties, which insists on high prices for commodities produced by underdeveloped countries, the right of expropriation, and preferential trade treatment without reciprocity. However, at the Lima meeting of the "group of 77", Mexico moderated the anti–U.S. policies of the other delegates from the Third World. In pursuing a more active pro-Third World policy, Echeverría has exerted pressure on the United States for trade concessions and achieved settlement of the Colorado River dispute.

Whether these shifts in foreign policy from one presidential administration to the next are a function of public pressure, personal choice, or concern over economic problems and the balance of payments, or are merely the swing of the pendulum, is impossible to determine.[28] But the shifts have occurred, and they are examples of Mexico's independence from the United States in matters of diplomacy.

MEXICO'S WORLD POSITION

Mexico in the 1970s has moved to a position of international prominence. Since 1940, her record of political stability, consistent economic growth, and pursuit of an independent foreign policy have given her a position of

---

March 1972): 1–27; and *México y la revolución cubana* (México: Colegio de México, 1972), pp. 90–110.

27. Needler, "A Critical Time for Mexico," p. 83.

28. Ibid., p. 85. It is Needler's view that these shifts were caused by the swing of the pendulum. Lorenzo Meyer notes that the Mexican system shifts to the Left when there is need for a change, and makes concessions to the disaffected.

.

leadership whenever she chooses to exercise it among the nations of the world and in international organizations.

Ecumenism (universalism), regionalism, the equality of nations, the juridical bases of Mexican foreign policy, the peaceful tradition, the international politics of the Mexican Revolution—these are only some of the principles enunciated as part of her foreign policy. But in choosing the emphasis to be placed on any particular principle or in resolving the contradictions among them, Mexican policy makers have been pragmatic and realistic in assessing their relations to the nations concerned.

While ties with the United States must dominate Mexico's foreign policy, more intimate relations with the other nations of the world have come to be an important part of Mexico's present-day tactics.

In her relations with Western Europe, Mexico emphasizes cultural matters and industrial investment. She has welcomed large numbers of European tourists, conducted art exchanges, and participated in international cultural events, in addition to sponsoring the 1968 Olympics. These have been important factors in policy toward Europe since the end of World War II. Many Mexicans study in France, and French language and literature influence sectors of the Mexican middle class without challenging the importance of the English language and U.S. educational institutions. Mexico encourages European trade and investment: Italy, Germany, France, and England have all established industrial facilities in Mexico, thus further lessening her dependence upon the United States.

In May of 1972, President Echeverría visited Japan with the expectation of increasing trade and investment with the third-richest nation in the world and of obtaining technical know-how. Mexican intellectuals and planners hoped that this visit would be extended to include more than a bilateral trade agreement. A possibility of Mexican participation in a block of nations, including Canada, Australia, and New Zealand, as well as Japan, has been presented as the kind of initiative that Mexico must assume if she is to be a serious contender for world power.[29]

Until 1970, in regard to Eastern Europe, the Soviet Union, and Communist China, Mexico tended to follow the lead of the United States, maintaining formally correct, but distant, relations. In the fall of 1971, when the United States still proposed recognition of both Chinese governments, the Mexican president made a speech in the United Nations advocating the admission of the Peking government and the expulsion of Taiwan. Mexico recognized Peking very soon thereafter and has actively promoted trade with all of these Communist countries—another sign of increasing independence and self-assertiveness in foreign policy.

Mexico's attitude toward Latin America reflects the vicissitudes of her foreign policy in the other areas. Only in 1958 did Mexico seek peaceful

29. Luis Medina Peña, "La política exterior japonesa," *Foro Internacional* 13, no. 2 (October–December 1972): 229–31.

leadership within Latin America. During the administration of Díaz
Ordaz (1964–70), Mexico withdrew from this effort. The chief Latin
American initiative Díaz Ordaz displayed was a trip to Central America.
Mexico's policy in the Echeverría administration has strengthened economic ties, and she has utilized her respected position within Latin
America, as the principal stable democratic power, to enhance her claims
to Third World leadership. Unlike Brazil, Mexico does not have a
military dictatorship; she has achieved a formula for stability that eludes
Argentina. Like other Latin American countries, Mexico is extremely
nationalist, often oratorically against the United States. But it is an
introverted nationalism that seeks little external aggrandizement.[30] Mexico has rarely tried to export her revolution and has given other Latin
American countries little guidance on issues of land reform and the
nationalization of industries, although she had been an innovator in these
areas herself.

Mexico's attitude toward international organizations has tended to
follow the vicissitudes of her relations with the United States. From 1889
to the time of the Mexican Revolution of 1910, she was a supporter of
Pan-Americanism, urging Latin American and U.S. cooperation on
judicial and economic matters of common interest. During the years of
the revolution, between 1910 and 1925, Mexico withdrew from inter-
American political affairs. She was not represented at the 1923 Santiago
Conference of the American States, for example, because only envoys
accredited to Washington could be delegates, and the United States
refused to recognize the Mexican government.[31]

Beginning in 1928, Mexico actively participated in Pan-American
congresses, leading the battles for nonintervention. She also participated
in the League of Nations. She was an enthusiastic supporter of the United
Nations, marshaling the Latin American nations on its behalf. She
especially worked with the United Nations Commission on Trade and
Development. She worked vigorously to obtain agreement on a treaty for
the denuclearization of Latin America.

When cold war politics began to dominate the United Nations after
1948, Mexico refused to hold leadership positions. She would not serve on
the Security Council and did not actively participate in debates on
controversial political issues. This Mexican silence expressed her old
realistic tradition. She often disagreed with U.S. policy, but the disagree-

30. Arthur B. Whitaker, "Nationalism and Social Change in Latin America," in *Politics
of Change in Latin America*, ed. Joseph Maier and Richard W. Weatherhead (New York:
Frederick A. Praeger, 1964), as quoted in Frederick Turner, *The Dynamics of Mexican
Nationalism* (Chapel Hill: University of North Carolina Press, 1968), p. 8.
31. At the 1923 Santiago Conference, the most influential person was the Mexican
ambassador to Chile, who could not attend the meetings (S. G. Inman, *Inter-American
Conferences, 1826–1954: History and Problems* [Washington: University Press of Washington, D.C., 1954], p. 101).

ments were on issues peripheral to Mexico's central concerns. Thus, her noninvolvement reflected her determination to pursue other interests, while neither alienating nor being subservient to the United States.

Mexico has consistently opposed the majority in the Organization of American States on issues of recognition and on strengthening the organization by providing for permanent peacekeeping machinery. Mexico feels that giving more power to the OAS would permit U.S. intervention in the internal affairs of the member states. Moreover, Mexico has often been isolated in the voting on political matters in inter-American organizations. In 1954, only Mexico and Argentina refused to vote for the condemnation of the Guatemalan government, which the United States claimed was pro-Communist. In the eighth meeting of foreign ministers in Punta del Este in Uruguay, in January 1962, Mexico refused to vote for the expulsion of Cuba from the OAS; she continued to trade with Cuba and carried on diplomatic relations with her. She opposed the 1964 sanctions against Cuba and the U.S. intervention in the Dominican Republic in 1965. As long as the United States dominates the OAS, she continues to advocate a limited and nonpolitical role for that organization.

CONCLUSION

Because of Mexico's commitment to economic development, which requires international investment and markets, she has only limited choices in the field of foreign policy. She has succeeded in expressing her independence in matters of juridical interpretation. But her international position remains precarious. Tourist dollars supply the deficit in her balance of payments; any sharp decline in tourist income threatens her economic stability. For a variety of her products, the United States is still the only market.

Although Mexico enjoys the respect of most members of the world community and is a power to be reckoned with in Latin American affairs, she has not reached the rank of the great powers. As the largest Spanish-speaking nation in a world in which Spanish has become a major international language, Mexico occupies a position of special importance today, rivaling Brazil for leadership of the whole Luso-Hispanic world, which now has a population approaching 300 million. How she will exercise that leadership role is still uncertain. As recently as the Tlateloco conference of February 1974, Mexico displayed an ambivalent vision of her part in hemispheric affairs. To assume Third World leadership; to conduct a dialogue with the United States leading to economic and political concessions; or to act as a spokesman for hemispheric unity, conciliating the differences among the Latin American nations and between Latin America and the United States—all are viable options for

Mexico at present. The path that her foreign policy will pursue depends, now more than at any time in the past, on domestic events and public opinion.[32]

BIBLIOGRAPHICAL NOTE

There are several interesting brief statements available in English on Mexican foreign policy. See George Blanksten, "The Foreign Policy of Mexico," in *Foreign Policy in World Politics*, ed. Roy C. Macridis (Englewood Cliffs, N.J.: Prentice-Hall, 1962); Francisco Cuevas Cancino, "The Foreign Policy of Mexico," in *Foreign Policies in a World of Change*, ed. Joseph Black (New York: Harper & Row, 1963); and Jorge Castañeda, "Revolution and Foreign Policy, Mexico's Experience," *Political Science Quarterly* 78, no. 3 (September 1963): 391–417. See also *Current History* 66 (May 1973), which is devoted to Mexico and has articles on "Mexico in the World Economy" and "Mexico's Foreign Policy: Disguised Dependency."

Two books on Mexico contain interesting variations on the theory and conduct of Mexican foreign policy; the earlier statement is by Frank Tannenbaum, *Mexico: The Struggle for Peace and Bread* (New York: Alfred A. Knopf, 1950), chap. 14; the later statement is by Frank R. Brandenburg, *The Making of Modern Mexico* (Englewood Cliffs, N.J.: Prentice-Hall, 1964), chap. 12. Brandenburg discusses the operation and formulation of Mexico's policy critically but sympathetically.

Modesto Seara Vázquez, *La Política exterior de México: La práctica de México en el derecho international* (México: Editorial Esfinge, 1969), deals with the major issues in Mexican foreign policy, its formulation, organization, and practice. The book contains an excellent bibliography and the texts of twenty-five major documents in Mexican foreign policy.

The annual *Informes*, or state of the union messages, delivered by the Mexican president to Congress on 1 September, provide a clue to the dominant concerns and issues of Mexican foreign policy from year to year.

From a whole group of books dealing with U.S. and Mexican relations, both special aspects and general problems, Howard F. Cline, *The United States and Mexico* (Cambridge: Harvard University Press, 1963), has an excellent bibliographical guide and the most readable account of twentieth-century Mexico in her relations with the United States.

For the nineteenth-century history of Mexican foreign policy, Daniel Cosío Villegas, ed., *Historia Moderna de México: La Vida Política Exterior*, 6 vols. (México: Editorial Hermes, 1963), has volumes devoted exclusively to Mexico's foreign policy from 1867 to 1910.

Foro Internacional, published by the Colegio de México, has a relevant series of articles on Mexican and Latin American foreign policy. See especially vols. 6, 13, and 14, which contain a number of interesting articles on Mexico's foreign

32. Olga Pellicer de Brody, "Comentario sobre la conferencia de cancilleres americanos y la política de México hacia la América Latina," *Foro Internacional* 14, no. 4 (April–June 1974): 630.

policy. For the history of Mexico's foreign policy, *Historia Mexicana* and the *Hispanic-American Historical Review* both contain articles on special aspects of Mexican policy.

There are a number of dissertations written for U.S. universities that deal with various aspects of the problems of Mexico and the United States; for example, see David A. White's "Mexico in World Affairs: 1928-68," a University of California (Los Angeles) dissertation (1968) that has an interesting formulation of the modern period.

7/Thomas L. Karnes
The Central American Republics

The reader of a study on Latin American foreign policies must recognize immediately the necessity of giving Central America a different treatment than that accorded the larger states. However small, Central America is nevertheless a region, and its components function both jointly and separately. Each of the small nations discussed in this chapter—Guatemala, El Salvador, Honduras, Nicaragua, Costa Rica, and Panama (which is included for convenience, although it is not historically part of Central America)—has its own foreign policy. Boundaries, immigration, transportation, exiles, and trade constitute continuing factors in the region's bilateral and multilateral relations. Geographical proximity counts; Costa Rica watches Nicaragua more than she does El Salvador. Size matters; Guatemala usually leads. But like a family, Central America pulls together when threatened from without. For a century this meant fear of political absorption by Great Britain or the United States. Today, the Central American reacts against the Saxon's cultural invasion and, more importantly, against excessive reliance upon the United States as Central America's chief supplier and market. Not necessarily an evil, this costly relationship places the Central Americans at risk, and the economic advantages all accrue to the superpower. For the past two decades much Central American energy has been spent on breaking that tie, and the end of that story has yet to be told.

Table 7.1 gives some pertinent statistics on Central America that may prove handy.

HISTORICAL BACKGROUND

The Spanish conquest of Central America began with Columbus's fourth visit to the New World in 1502. While the strategic value of this American bridge was soon apparent to the conquistadores, they found little else of value and moved only slowly into the region—from the south by way of Panama between 1509 and 1522 and from the north by way of Mexico around 1522. In 1525 the Spanish crown concluded that Honduras had developed sufficiently to be called a province, and within the next decade that same title was extended to most of the other major Central American districts. For many years jurisdictional changes were the rule on the isthmus, but by 1570 Central America was something of a political entity, ruled by an *audiencia* headquartered in Antigua, Guatemala.

For two hundred fifty years a handful of Spaniards controlled the economy and the local political destiny of a million or so people, most of whom were all or part Indian. Spain demanded little from, and gave less

136

Table 7.1 Selected Statistics on Central America

Nation	Population (1971 est.)	Area (sq. mi.)	Annual population growth rates, 1960–72 (%)	Life expectancy (yrs.)	Literacy (% of total population)	Per capita gross domestic product (U.S. $)
Costa Rica	1,843,000	19,653	3.3	68.6	85.7	553.40
El Salvador	3,662,000	8,083	3.4	58.5	59.6	303.60
Guatemala	5,604,000	42,040	3.3	52	37.9	376.00
Honduras	2,761,000	43,277	3.4	55	47.3	278.10
Nicaragua	1,972,000	53,668	2.8	52.5	57	467.00
Panama	1,524,000	29,208	3.1	66.9	79.4	779.00

Source: Inter-American Development Bank, Economic and Social Progress in Latin America (Washington, D.C., 1973).

to, the dozing kingdom, as it was popularly called, but wealth came to a few colonials from silver and gold mines and substantial indigo and cacao exports; subsistence came from the sale of tobacco, corn, beans, baskets, and pots, chiefly in local markets. Amid this benevolent or, at least, amiable neglect, a modest elite emerged around the larger towns, and their interests, not necessarily inconsistent with those of the surrounding natives, produced a determined provincialism.

In theory this Guatemalan *audiencia* was subordinate to the viceroyalty of New Spain located in Mexico City, but Central America's backwardness and the difficulty of communications kept the offices separate and encouraged Central Americans to avoid most of their political obligations. Thus, decades of daily practice vied with old but weak governmental ties for the Central Americans' loyalty when in 1808 Napoleon invaded Spain, drove the Bourbon rulers into exile, and forced a series of significant political decisions upon the untrained Central American people. For the next dozen years the future of the Bourbon authority in America remained much in doubt; Central American colonials, unconcerned with and unready for independence, gradually realized that it was being thrust upon them.

But even to the declining Spanish power the Central Americans did not react as a unit—nor did the provinces. Instead, village by village they held their open cabildos and, often in the wake of Mexican troops, voted to adhere to the newly independent Mexico, which in 1822 called itself an empire. A shady opportunist named Agustín Iturbide served briefly as emperor, but after his short rule the Central American villages again had to make a choice. This time they joined hands, creating on paper a Federal Republic of the five states of Central America, while Panama, reflecting its closer ties, remained a part of the republic of Colombia.

The Federal Republic of Central America, proclaimed in 1824, officially lasted only until 1842. Probably reflecting accurately the political innocence of the electorate, the constitution gave little authority to the national government, and in the words of one critic, united the provinces with saliva. The republic failed most of its practical tests; localism, foreignism, liberalism, and clericalism chased one another around until civil war and bankruptcy drove each of the states back to the natural protection of the village. These conditions were modified slightly by such purely external forces as European investors and a handful of immigrants, plus the occasionally heroic efforts of native despots like Guatemala's Justo Rufino Barrios, who was killed in 1885 attempting to impose a new federation by arms; meanwhile, the Central Americans grew their crops and at least once a decade held conferences, which were unsuccessful, designed to restore the Federal Republic.[1]

1. See Franklin D. Parker, *The Central American Republics* (London: Oxford University Press, 1964), and Mario Rodríguez, *Central America* (Englewood Cliffs, N.J.: Prentice-Hall, 1965), for the best accounts of the growth of the five Central American States.

The twentieth century brought some change, as the North American replaced the European investor and merchant, and his government in Washington reacted firmly to fiscal or political misconduct that might threaten the security of the Panama Canal or precipitate European intervention. More realistic today, the modern Central American nations continue to hold assemblies and sign conventions on unity, but they are now designed more for economic growth than for political unity.

REGIONAL INTEGRATION: ECONOMIC AND POLITICAL

Economic Integration

Without question Central America's most important problem today is to make viable the organization known as the Central American Common Market (CACM). While the centripetal and centrifugal forces in Central America have continued to conflict with each other since 1824, the struggle achieved a new dimension as a result of the Second World War. Although the war and its aftermath brought some prosperity to certain sectors, Central American leaders anticipated stagnation for the future and concluded that the region's problems were primarily economic. Statesmen cast the primary blame on Central America's dependence upon agricultural exports, which amounted to perhaps one-fourth of the region's income; four exports—coffee, bananas, cotton, and cocoa—produced some 90 percent of that one-fourth. This was traditional colonial economy, with benefits and faults, supporters and opponents. But by the 1950s most economists in the region concluded that the mold had to be broken.[2] New competitors with the same products were arising; terms of trade were steadily worsening, even in years when coffee sales increased; per capita income scarcely kept abreast of the birth rate; and the vulnerability of the economy to outside forces could not long be tolerated by people imbued with new concepts and expectations.

In short, Central America's modest gains were beginning to appear illusory in a world of increasing agricultural efficiency, increasing industrialization, and increasing economic centralization.

Specific solutions to the predicament came from the United Nations Economic Commission for Latin America (ECLA) in the 1950s. ECLA's analysis, fundamentally accepted by Central America, was that the region was facing a critical deficiency of demand; for presumably sound and provable reasons, world demand for the agricultural production of

2. Roger D. Hansen, *Central America: Regional Integration and Economic Development* (Washington, D.C.: National Planning Association, 1967), p. 5; Carlos M. Castillo, *Growth and Integration in Central America* (New York: Frederick A. Praeger, 1966), pp. 53–56. Panama has been invited to participate in the market discussions, but no agreement has yet been reached on her status.

underdeveloped areas was too inelastic for economic growth. ECLA's chief solution was import substitution, thereby reducing the region's reliance upon the more sophisticated economies of the world for costly, processed goods.[3]

Obviously Central American states could operate independently in the direction ECLA pointed, but their history of aspirations for unity and the markedly slow progress of some bilateral steps taken in the 1950s dictated a regional approach. In 1952 the Central American Economic Cooperation Committee was established, with a permanent secretariat and staff to promote development through integration of the states' economies. Aided by ECLA, this committee completed a number of background studies leading to the creation of various regional institutes and, in 1958, the Multilateral Treaty of Central American Free Trade and Economic Integration. A somewhat tighter General Treaty on Central American Integration superseded this and was ratified by the five states by 1963.

Within four years CACM had virtually achieved its immediate goals— about 95 percent (by value) of intraregional trade moved freely across national lines, and uniform tariff rates were being applied to some 75 to 80 percent (also by value) of Central America's imports.[4]

To push beyond these preliminary accomplishments, several special agencies were created, the most important initially being the Central American Bank for Economic Integration, the Central American Clearing House, the System of Central American Integration Industries, and the Central American Institute for Industrial Technology Research.[5]

In its youth CACM grew lustily. Intrazonal trade increased from $32 million in 1960 to $250 million in 1968; as desired by the five governments, expansion in industrial production completely outstripped all the other elements measured in that growth. New manufacturing grew almost as rapidly, and domestic and foreign private investment was regularly augmented at a rate in excess of 10 percent. Nevertheless, the regional economic problems were not solved. In 1968 Costa Rica and Nicaragua made significant unilateral departures in tariff policy, and in 1969 the tragic Soccer War occurred.

The Soccer War

This brief, bitter struggle between Honduras and El Salvador broke out in June 1969 when wild supernationalists of each state began abusing the visiting soccer teams during the course of World Cup preliminaries. But that match (the finals of which had to be moved to neutral Mexico) merely

3. Hansen, *Central America*, pp. 18–19.
4. Ibid., pp. 25–27; U.S., Department of State, *The Central American Common Market*, by Joseph Pincus (Washington, D.C.: Government Printing Office, 1962), p. 75.
5. Inter-American Development Bank, Social Progress Trust Fund, *Socio-Economic Progress in Latin America, Annual Report, 1971* (Washington, D.C., 1971).

excited into open warfare ill-feelings a generation old, the result of the migration of an estimated 200,000 Salvadorans into the relatively vacant Honduran lands. Many farmed or worked for the fruit companies; others went into business with enough success to create sharp animosities and attempts to boycott Salvadoran commercial firms throughout Honduras.

Border towns were damaged when Salvadoran forces invaded Honduras, and thousands of the emigrants returned "home." (Some of these had spent their entire adulthood in Honduras.) The Organization of American States arranged a truce, but some of the common market enthusiasm was gone. The two nations' relations were not only severed; Honduras withdrew from the market and cut off much regional intercourse by closing the Inter-American highway.

The market (CACM) is not dead, and the results of the "Soccer War" cannot yet be assessed. Even though Honduras and El Salvador do not trade with one another, intrazonal trade in 1970 was unsurpassed, totaling nearly $300 million, some 20 percent greater than in 1969. Recent figures indicate that Honduras may be returning to old patterns of exporting outside the zone while local trade deteriorates.[6]

One can conclude with guarded optimism that stubborn nationalistic and also technical obstacles to full integration still abound, but Central America's economy is finally growing, with reasonable direction.

Political Integration

If economic viability is Central America's most important problem today, just as surely was her past dominated by the chronic question of political unification. While substantial ethnic and cultural differences exist among the states (Costa Rica's being the most obvious), the peoples nevertheless have much in common, including a long colonial history and important Spanish traditions. For these reasons the combination of the states into some form of a single government has seemed beyond argument for a century and a half, and that same logic assumes that such a merger would be entirely beneficial to all parties. This theory has in fact often been advanced as a solution to any problem facing a particular generation of Central Americans.

The usual model is a modified copy of the Federal Republic of 1824, whose failure is based on a handful of pet theories, perhaps the most eclectic and acceptable of which is the unreadiness in Central America at that time for a complex form of government. Between twenty-five and thirty times, two or more Central American states have attempted to join one another politically. Some of these efforts were very simple, often the expression of personalist politics; others were more complex and buttressed with treaties, some of which even obtained scattered diplomatic

6. Ibid., p. 56.

recognition.[7] Without exception the unions failed, sometimes before the proverbial ink had dried on treaty ratifications. The reasons, again, are many and often applicable to only some single failure. Clearly, proximity and similarity of institutions are not cement enough. Political union is a worthwhile goal, and when it is attained it will be because the people of Central America are ready to contribute something to it, not just because they feel that union might do something for them.

Federal union has been described in this essay as a problem of the past and, by implication, not of the future. I do not have the temerity to suggest that the question will not rise again. Many Central Americans believe in the inevitability of a *gran patria*, and that in itself might bring it about. But the successes, so far, of CACM—especially the modest progress in the integration of some industries, in banking, and in investment—may lash the five (six) states together in a form not now foreseen. In the 1820s the president of the Federal Republic, Francisco Morazán, attempted to govern through an unfamiliar instrument resembling the U.S. constitution. Now the horse of economics is pulling the wagon of politics—or perhaps a better metaphor would be that the tractor is pulling the trailer—and this is the way it should be. Central America may thus be moving unobtrusively toward closer political union.

HISTORY OF RELATIONS WITH OUTSIDE POWERS: GREAT BRITAIN AND THE UNITED STATES

Great Britain

Second to their diplomatic relations with one another, the Central American states and Panama have been most concerned with Great Britain and—since the 1890s—the United States. Britain won the first skirmishes in the investment and marketing war with the United States, engaging in profitable lending procedures from the early 1820s, the same decade that her merchants moved into Guatemala. This second South Sea Bubble popped with the failure of the Federal Republic, and British bondholders became more wary, although many a financial house profited in the handling of defaults. More important than Central America's bonds or raw materials, however, was the British strategic concern with the isthmus. Steered by diplomat Frederick Chatfield ("eternal agent" and "publick evil" to many Central Americans) into the channels of active interventionism, Great Britain nearly acquired another dominion.[8]

7. Ibid., pp. 54-55, 206, 234; Hansen, *Central America*, p. 34.
8. See Thomas L. Karnes, *The Failure of Union: Central America, 1824-1960* (Chapel Hill: University of North Carolina Press, 1961), for an analysis of the attempts to unite

By mid-century the United States had awakened, startled by Chatfield's gains. American diplomatists Elijah Hise and Ephraim Squier were the first representatives to recognize the dangers of British hegemony; their signals to Washington resulted in an accommodation. The Clayton-Bulwer Treaty was signed in 1850 and, though deliberately confusing in its terms, saved Central America from its British partners. This treaty, contrary to the interpretation given it by some Americans, did not mean that the English had to depart from the Caribbean. It marked, instead, the beginning of the end: the British gave the Bay Islands back to Honduras in 1859 and the unlikely "mosquito kingdom" to Honduras and Nicaragua over a three-decade period beginning in the 1860s. British influence lingered elsewhere, especially in Costa Rica and Guatemala for many years, but it was commercial in nature and lacked much of the more ominous financial and political restraint of the near past.[9]

Today Great Britain retains on the isthmus only her crown colony of British Honduras. This tiny exception occasionally exacerbates Central American peace, however, for both Guatemala and Mexico have at times laid claim to Belize, as its citizens prefer to call it. The British base their ownership on occupation since the days of the seventeenth-century woodcutters who held off the Spanish and forced a series of treaties recognizing certain British rights. Mexico seems less concerned today about the question, but Guatemalan politicians often make it an issue of great moment when other problems suggest the need of a distraction. At the heart of the dispute is a complex and unconsummated treaty of 1859 between Guatemala and Great Britain. Referral to the International Court of Justice has been suggested, but too many conditions have been attached to make it likely that the parties will soon seek such a hearing.[10] The preference of the citizens of the region has been spoken in soft voices; they are racially, linguistically, and nationally mixed; many who are tied emotionally to Guatemala work for the great British plantations and perhaps behave cautiously. Present plans provide for early independence within the British sphere.

Central America. The Organization of Central American States (ODECA), created in 1951 but not functioning until 1955, can be classified as the latest attempt at union because its charter says that this is what it is. Politically it has done little, but it works closely with, and is of some help to, the Central American Common Market.

9. See Mario Rodríguez, *A Palmerstonian Diplomat in Central America: Frederick Chatfield, Esq.* (Tucson: University of Arizona Press, 1964), for an engrossing study of this unusual diplomat.

10. British Honduras has around 100,000 people and an area of some 9,000 square miles. D. A. G. Waddell, *British Honduras* (London: Oxford University Press, 1961); R. A. Humphreys, *The Diplomatic History of British Honduras, 1638–1901* (London: Oxford University Press, 1961); and Wayne Clegern, *British Honduras, Colonial Dead End, 1859–1900* (Baton Rouge: Louisiana State University Press, 1967) make up the leading works on this colony.

The United States

As Britain's interests called her elsewhere in the late nineteenth century, she could observe with some comfort that the young United States was replacing her as chief exporter to, and importer from, the Caribbean, as chief supplier of investment funds and as sole guardian. That the Central Americans were aware of the United States long before the 1890s is clear enough; the 1824 constitution of the Federal Republic includes some obvious copying of both the U.S. Declaration of Independence and the 1787 Constitution. Even a bit earlier a Salvadoran assembly had announced the annexation of El Salvador to the United States in the hopeless assumption that the act would prevent an invasion by Mexico. The United States ignored this bit of manifest destiny and the invasion took place; the offer was withdrawn when Iturbide fell. In 1825 Central America received diplomatic recognition from the United States, the first non-Latin American nation to make this overture. A Guatemalan minister in 1825 told the Central American congress that it was his hope that the recently enunciated doctrine of President James Monroe would protect Central America from reannexation by Spain, and Central America urged Simón Bolívar to invite the United States to the 1826 Congress of Panama.[11]

The United States did not take advantage of this residue of good will, however, and in the 1830s and 1840s, when Great Britain was expanding her Central American influence so rapidly, the Yankee was exploiting his vast frontier at home and exhibiting little concern for Central America.

The major exception to this generalization was the lamentable activity of William Walker of Tennessee, epitome of the fruitless, destructive filibuster, who for his own vague reasons sought a private empire in Central America. Taking advantage of traditional Nicaraguan partisanship, Walker linked himself to an out-of-office faction and launched four campaigns between 1855 and 1860 for control of Nicaragua and, conceivably, the entire isthmus. That Walker's wars were complicated by a struggle among U.S. financial giants for a transisthmian route proved the more frightening to the Central Americans. Firmly uniting for the first time in history, they finally succeeded in destroying Walker and developed in the process the first feelings of Yankeephobia.

In the last half of the nineteenth century U.S. interest in Central America grew very slowly. State Department policy was to encourage the union of Central America, going as far as to grant diplomatic recognition to the "Greater Republic of Central America" (composed of Honduras, Nicaragua, and El Salvador), which from 1896 until its dissolution in 1898 never elected its first president and congress.

11. See Joseph B. Lockey, "Diplomatic Futility," *Hispanic American Historical Review* 10 (August 1930): 265–94, for some of these episodes.

To Central America, official U.S. policy had much less immediate significance than the arrival of big business during the same decade. The first serious economic penetration was led by the North American Minor Keith, who completed a railway from Puerto Limón to the central plateau of Costa Rica. He made it pay by introducing large-scale banana culture and establishing a regular shipping service with various U.S. ports. By 1899 a group of small growers managed by Keith merged with another group led by the Boston Fruit Company, and the United Fruit Company came into being. Never the large octopus described by Latin Americans and fairly modest by U.S. standards, the company wielded substantial local power in the small banana-producing states, and it was to make United Fruit the most hated corporation in Central America for the next generation. Since there were no great protests to the contrary, many observers concluded that United Fruit was an agent of the United States and the example writ large of many corporations to come.[12]

By the turn of the century Central Americans found it increasingly difficult to separate the aims of U.S. defense and finance and did in fact often conclude that they were identical. Some investment houses and a few corporations made inordinate profits; although they were not agents of the U.S. government, they had one important aim in common: the maintenance of Central America's stability. Conceivably this could be obtained by overthrowing uncooperative regimes; more often, however, they learned that cheaper protection would be purchased through the predictable conditions that hired politicians could provide.

Probably one-half of the private investment in Central America in the early twentieth century went into the development of export agriculture, the chief market for which was the United States. Even as late as the 1950s (before CACM had its impact) more than three-fourths of the value of exports from Central America came from the three crops of coffee, bananas, and cotton, and well over half of these sales were made in the United States. Imports from the United States usually exceeded these sales in small degree. The results in Central America were numerous, but the most obvious were: (1) a regularly unfavorable balance of trade and a scarcity of dollars; (2) a dangerous vulnerability to world prices, which could not be set in Central America; (3) susceptibility to the shifting tastes of the Yankee consumer; (4) the possibility of complete disaster from the forces of nature; and (5) great losses from even a temporary shortage of shipping. On the other hand, this foreign capital did mean better wages and working conditions and expedited Central American development greatly.

12. Important portions of this story are recorded in Watt Stewart, *Keith and Costa Rica* (Albuquerque: University of New Mexico Press, 1964) and Stacy May and Galo Plaza, *The United Fruit Company in Latin America* (New York: National Planning Association, 1958).

The Panama Canal

By World War I U.S. concern for her canal at Panama became intertwined with the vague aims of defense and investment. Construction of a canal somewhere through the isthmus had been a dream from the time of Balboa and Cortés, and its story needs no retelling here. The inordinate task was made possible in 1903 when President Theodore Roosevelt permitted New York investment houses to finance a handful of ever-available Panamanian revolutionists against the Colombian Congress, which was stalling for a greater share of the canal's future profits. Roosevelt, in the name of world progress, prevented Colombia from suppressing the revolt, recognized Panama's independence, and concluded a highly favorable treaty with the infant republic. The canal followed.

The canal is bordered by a narrow strip of land, the Canal Zone, piercing the isthmus from Atlantic to Pacific. The 1903 treaty between Panama and the United States provided for U.S. control of the zone "in perpetuity," a most unusual feature. A later generation of Panamanians, less impressed with the financial blessings of the canal, insisted upon greater equality between Panamanian and American workers, merchants, and flags. While many minor irritations were adjudicated and the annuity paid to Panama was regularly augmented, the issues of ownership and sovereignty were clearly not solved to Panama's satisfaction.

The question of changing total U.S. jurisdiction over the Canal Zone has been under frequent discussion since the mid-1960s, and the proposals are evidently so touchy to the pride of both states that much negotiation remains secret. U.S. Secretary of State Henry A. Kissinger visited Panama in February 1974 and agreed "in principle" with the administration of President Omar Torrijos that future treaties would gradually phase out U.S. control over the Panama Canal. Undoubtedly, much congressional and military opposition from Washington still stands in the way of drafting and ratification.[13]

The second canal is also old business; engineers and scientists have studied alternative routes intensively for a decade. Until 1971 the United States seemed to have an easy answer in the Bryan-Chamorro Treaty, which permitted a canal through Nicaragua. But in that year the two nations agreed to abrogate the treaty, leaving the route question wide open. Panama takes the interesting stand that a new canal will be detrimental to her and that she must therefore be compensated when it commences operation.

Central America's relationship with the United States is, then, for good or for evil, a special thing, and nothing demonstrates this more clearly

13. *Phoenix Gazette*, 8 Feb. 1974.

than the subject of intervention. For the purposes of this chapter, *intervention* will be restricted to the narrowest of interpretations, that is, the use of, or the threat of the use of, military force in another nation's internal affairs. Sometimes U.S. Marines were landed briefly to protect lives and property; sometimes they stayed for months, or years, as in Nicaragua for most of the two decades preceding 1933; and sometimes they had to fight natives in wars as unpopular at home as they were in Central America. A warship in a harbor could be a sufficient threat. Once, the five Central American foreign ministers were isolated on a storm-tossed American cruiser long enough to agree to a peace conference. Central American statesmen have been called to Washington—to sign treaties or to create the world's first International Court of Justice or to receive medals that might intimidate restless rivals. For most of the 1920s the United States applied an exceptional policy in Central America (and in a sense also in Mexico), which these nations thought might reduce barracks revolts: the withholding of recognition from regimes headed by the leader of an armed uprising. When the Central Americans themselves found this procedure too restrictive, the United States agreeably returned to the traditional practice of recognizing responsible governments irrespective of how they acquired office.

The relationship thus described has been viewed from Washington as generally paternalistic; Central Americans have considered it colonial and therefore detrimental to their growth. While it can be declared that neither U.S. commerce nor U.S. military might has brought much political and economic democracy to Central America, it must also be recognized that there was little sign, except in Costa Rica, of this phenomenon before the United States appeared on the stage. The relationship is probably a three-step-forward, two-step-backward kind of thing; an undoubtedly more enlightened North American businessman and an increasingly informed North American public are at least doing their share to make the U.S. impact on Central America less suffocating and more profitable to the region. If, as so often is said, democracy is a luxury, perhaps Central America can soon afford to go shopping.

INDIVIDUAL FOREIGN POLICIES

To generalize about the foreign policies of the individual isthmian nations is more difficult than one might guess. Paramount, of course, are the relations the nations have with one another. Inevitably there have been boundary disputes, some festering for decades—Panama versus Costa Rica; Costa Rica versus Nicaragua, Nicaragua versus Honduras, and so on. The record for acceptance of outside settlement is reasonably good.

Panama

As indicated at the beginning of this chapter, Panama is not historically a part of Central America. She was invited to participate in CACM primarily because of her unique economic relationship with the United States and because her economy is more healthy than Central America's, but she has not joined, although she participates regularly in some market activities. Colombia, the nation of which Panama was once a province, can do little for Panama because of her own prolonged distresses and the very poor communications between the two nations. The major concern in Panama's foreign policy remains the United States. A tiny, powerful oligarch is committed to a program of pestering the United States for more and more concessions, some but not all of which are related to the canal; the program is made more successful by a vigorous nationalism. This oligarchy does little flirting with the rivals of the United States. Panama's per capita gross domestic product is so far beyond the Central American average as to indicate real short-run success in her foreign policy.

Costa Rica

Costa Rica is not so free of latifundia and dictatorships as reputation would have it, but her people and most of her rulers have a high concern for social and political welfare. Costa Rica works hard to prove that she is not dependent on anyone, and she is as strongly isolationist as a nation could be, given her location. Isolationist is perhaps an unfair description, however, for Costa Rica likes to play an active role in world problems that do not too closely touch her. Historically, this isolationism takes the form of separation from Central America. Always the most reluctant of the five to participate in federation movements, Costa Rica did not even send representatives to two-thirds of the conferences called to discuss the subject. The reasons—a feeling of social, racial, and political superiority over her neighbors—may be unpopular elsewhere, but they are real. Costa Rica was the last to join CACM and, in fact, delayed some elements of it for a matter of years. The "Ticos" have at last joined Central America, but with much caution and reluctance.[14]

Nicaragua

More than any other Central American state, Nicaragua has been influenced by extraisthmian forces. Her unusually vital location, combined with a chronic internal weakness brought on by a mindless liberal-versus-conservative struggle in the early nineteenth century, invited foreign

14. Thomas L. Karnes, "La Norma de conducta de Costa Rica," *Revista de los Archivos Nacionales de Costa Rica* 17 (July–December 1953): 266–72.

intervention. The British early availed themselves of this situation through their "mosquito kingdom" and at San Juan del Sur athwart the strategic San Juan River. The Clayton-Bulwer Treaty, the activities of William Walker, and increasing diplomatic negotiations for a canal reflected Britain's replacement by the United States in the latter half of the century.

American interest in Nicaragua did not decline after the Theodore Roosevelt administration suddenly reversed itself in 1902 and selected Panama as the proper canal route. Even before the canal was finished, U.S. determination to protect the whole isthmian region prompted full-scale intervention into unhappy Nicaragua. Early during that intervention the two states consummated the Bryan-Chamorro Treaty (1914), giving the United States various islands for future naval bases along Nicaragua's shores, plus exclusive and perpetual right to build an interoceanic canal through Nicaragua. It was a tempting route because so much of it was a natural waterway; but it was never used, in part because of questions of diplomacy raised by Nicaragua's neighbors. The San Juan River serves as part of the border between Nicaragua and Costa Rica, while the most likely location for a naval base under terms of the Bryan-Chamorro Treaty was within the Gulf of Fonseca, bounded not only by Nicaragua but by Honduras and El Salvador as well. In 1916 all three of these Central American neighbors brought suit against Nicaragua in the Central American Court of Justice, denouncing this treaty for its purported infringement of their rights. The court, a unique venture into the compulsory arbitration of international disputes, had originally been sponsored by the United States, in 1907. Yet, ten years later, when the court ruled for the plaintiffs (although recognizing its inability to nullify the Bryan-Chamorro Treaty), the United States directed Nicaragua to ignore the verdicts and remove itself from the court. The court died the next year.

Since the 1930s the government of Nicaragua has been organized around the Samoza family, completely dependable in its support of U.S. interests and policies and strong enough to end the turbulence of an earlier day. Quietly and surprisingly the Nixon administration agreed with Nicaragua to terminate the Bryan-Chamorro Treaty in April 1971.[15]

Honduras

Honduras's foreign policy, at least in important matters, has been determined by her location and her agriculture. Lightly populated and underdeveloped, Honduras is in the middle of Central America. She was often the highway for invaders passing through or the staging area for exiles planning a coup. Delegates to the Central American Peace Confer-

15. (U.S.) *Department of State Bulletin* 63 (10 Aug. 1970).

ence held in Washington in 1907 secured a promise of the five treaty signatories to preserve the neutrality of Honduras. Never completely enforced, the stipulation helped end the old possibility of a general Central American war. Traditionally, Honduras, together with El Salvador, has been most active in the federation movement; one can hope that the 1969 "Soccer War" was an aberration. In CACM, Honduras's role has been to purchase fabricated goods from her more advanced neighbors and sell them her agricultural products. Honduras and the Alliance for Progress are aware of this regressiveness and work to correct it. The banana companies—United Fruit Company and a growing rival, Standard Fruit Company—operate with an efficiency that keeps Honduras very high on the list of fruit exporters. Neither company seems anxious to be labeled imperialistic; both are finding ways to create small native businessmen and turn them into partners. Nevertheless, the Yankee dollar will have a long run in Honduras.

El Salvador

The smallest nation in Latin America, El Salvador has been fiercely unionistic. She has lived by export—of her unionism, her coffee, her surplus peasants to Honduras, and most recently, her manufactured goods to CACM countries. As early as 1948 El Salvador presented an example of military-sponsored reform, apparently ending the long tradition there and in Guatemala of meddling with the other's administration when it was not of the same Liberal or Conservative party stripe.

El Salvador is probably the only Central American state that is crowded, at least in a statistical sense. There is considerable latifundia, but there is also simply not enough farm land. Until industry can absorb many more workers, this will be so; dangerously, it would seem, relief has come from extralegal migration into Honduras, whose flow was checked by the 1969 war. Foreign policy has thus been aimed at balancing Guatemalan power (from colonial times) and at exploiting Honduras's backwardness.

Guatemala

The most populous and the strongest state of Central America has been Guatemala, but her powerful leaders—Rafael Carrera and Justo Rufino Barrios in the nineteenth century, Manuel Estrada Cabrera and Jorge Ubico in the twentieth—did little to advance the cause of unionism. Their legacy was despotism, and a fertile field for reform opened after World War II. In modern Guatemala international policy has meant relations with the United States. Progressive labor and social security legislation was passed in the 1940s but not enforced. The subsequent administration of Jacobo Arbenz was too blatantly Communist and anti-American for the

Eisenhower government, so in 1954 Arbenz's overthrow was arranged. Swinging back to the right, Guatemala became a staging area in 1961 for part of the Bay of Pigs invasion of Cuba to eliminate Castro—a procedure (irrespective of the target) anathema to most Latin American states. Guatemala today is subject to much selective violence, some but not all of it obviously anti-Yankee. Belize is still coveted, and El Salvador must be watched; radicalism and reaction make government most difficult, but the United States continues to buy three-fourths of Guatemala's coffee and provides a great deal of additional subsidy. That is the key to Guatemala's foreign policy.

CONCLUSION

Since Central America is small and gives an appearance of unity, most treatises on the subject rather logically oversimplify the history and present development of these states. They *are* very similar, sharing a common history, race, language, and religion—even their climate, export products, and stage of economic development are alike. But a single fact overrides all of these similarities; the states are not and never have been one nation. Predictions are fruitless, but it should be remembered that while time may solve some problems, it also strengthens the growing feelings of particularism in each of the Central American republics.

One should not, therefore, expect a single Central American foreign policy—and there is none. Under certain sets of circumstances, some or all of the states may behave alike; just as predictably, in other circumstances they will follow separate goals and policies. In short, they act like sovereign states of any size. (Considered as a part of, or apart from, Central America, Panama demonstrates even more individualism than the five and is surprisingly resourceful in negotiating with the United States.)

Central America teaches the concerned student that appearances are often deceiving. The Soccer War did not destroy the Central American Common Market, as some observers too quickly predicted. The war for the moment has literally and figuratively detoured it; but the greatest year in the market's history was 1970, the first complete year after the war's close. The only sensible conclusion is that CACM's future is unclear.

A continually rediscovered banality is that continuity and change accompany one another in our world. Central America offers no exception to that judgment. Waves of superficial change break constantly over the region, yet underneath, and only slightly altered, the problems of underdeveloped economies and underdeveloped governments remain. While these problems retain their grip on Central America, she can never move far from the power of the United States.

BIBLIOGRAPHICAL NOTE

Readers seeking more literature on Central America should begin with the standard guide, William J. Griffith, "The Historiography of Central America since 1830," *Hispanic American Historical Review* 40 (November 1960): 548–69. Huge gaps in that field of learning were pointed out by Griffith; many remain unfilled, but the publication dates cited in this bibliography demonstrate that Central Americanists have been increasingly active in the past decade. There is still no single study that might be said to deal with foreign policy, however. Space limitations force only a sketchy listing here, but in general information for this chapter was drawn from the following works.

The best background discussions in English are Franklin D. Parker, *The Central American Republics* (London: Oxford University Press, 1964) and Mario Rodríguez, *Central America* (Englewood Cliffs, N.J.: Prentice-Hall, 1965). Parker's work is encyclopedic in nature; Rodríguez's is briefer and more interpretive. Neither stresses foreign policy. John D. Martz, *Central America* (Chapel Hill: University of North Carolina Press, 1959) emphasizes the 1940s and 1950s.

Specialized studies are more abundant. For the Central American Common Market and related economic matters, recommended works are: Committee for Economic Development, *Desarollo Económico de Centroamérica* (New York, 1964), for policy recommendations; Roger D. Hansen, *Central America: Regional Integration and Economic Development* (Washington, D.C.: National Planning Association, 1967), for the best analysis of CACM in terms of aims, organization, and problems; U.S., Department of State, *The Central American Common Market*, by Joseph Pincus (Washington, D.C.: Government Printing Office, 1962), for the origins and detailed framework of the market. See also Carlos M. Castillo, *Growth and Integration in Central America* (New York: Frederick A. Praeger, 1966); Thomas L. Karnes, *The Failure of Union: Central America, 1824–1960* (Chapel Hill: University of North Carolina Press, 1961); Joseph B. Lockey, "Diplomatic Futility," *Hispanic American Historical Review* 10 (August 1930): 265–94; Laudelino Moreno, *Historia de las relaciones interestatuales de Centro América* (Madrid: Compañía Iberoamericana de Publicaciones, 1928); Dana G. Munro, *Intervention and Dollar Diplomacy in the Caribbean, 1900–1921* (Princeton: Princeton University Press, 1964); Mario Rodríguez, *A Palmerstonian Diplomat in Central America: Frederick Chatfield, Esq.* (Tucson: University of Arizona Press, 1964); and Richard Salisbury, "Costa Rican Relations with Central America," in *Graduate Studies on Latin America at the University of Kansas*, ed. Charles Stansifer (Lawrence: University of Kansas Press, 1973), pp. 12–25.

III

The Caribbean Area

8/W. Raymond Duncan

Cuba

PROBLEMS OF CUBAN FOREIGN POLICY

One of the most fascinating aspects of Cuban foreign policy is its contradictory responses to the outside world. Admittedly, most foreign policies appear enigmatic at times. But contemporary Cuba exhibits a unique case of apparent schizophrenia. To be sure, its external relations operate under unusual conditions. As of 1975, diplomatic ostracism is still imposed by the Organization of American States (OAS). The inter-American community also exercises a trade embargo against Cuba. But even within this context of hemispheric isolation, Havana's diplomacy is strikingly contradictory. It reflects a search for maximum independence, although it is highly dependent upon the Soviet Union. It maintains a radical nationalist posture while adhering to the internationalist ideology of Marxism-Leninism. Moreover, Fidel Castro Ruz, first secretary of the Cuban Communist party and prime minister of the revolutionary government, has shown himself capable of more than attacking the United States for its policies in Vietnam and Latin America. In the past he has attacked the traditional pro-Soviet Latin American Communist parties and even Soviet policy in Latin America. He continually condemns hemispheric oligarchies and supports more participatory forms of government. Yet, Cuba is itself governed by a highly centralized and militarized authority, a single party system, under Castro's own personalist direction.

While these contradictory responses are understandable in light of Cuban history and Castro's revolutionary goals, they reflect a number of international problems posed for the island. Finding the right combination of policies to pursue internal socialist development and political independence has been a delicate task of balancing potential long-range gains against short-term costs. For example, trade and economic ties with Moscow risked either alienating Cuban support by arousing excessive nationalism or allowing the development of Soviet dominance. Defining relations with Latin American states became difficult, given the natural ties of Spanish culture, but there were wide differences among the nations on how to effect social change. Hostility toward the United States ensured a common external enemy against which to mobilize internal commitments, but it led to severed relations with a close and important trading partner. Future problems ultimately may focus on possible détente with Washington and the OAS, which are both perceived in the average Cuban mind as natural "enemies" of the Cuban people.

The Historical Antecedents

Like that of all states, Cuban foreign policy is conditioned by its legacy
from the past. This heritage, a result of geography, unresolved domestic
problems, and experiences with foreign countries, is the consciousness of
shared events extending backward in history and tending to project
forward into the future. It helps to create the "national image" of
memories, beliefs, and assumptions through which the leaders' perceptions of the outside world are filtered. It influences the basic choices of
decision makers in formulating foreign policy and conducting external
relations within the prevailing international power structure.

This historical inheritance shapes the answers to the questions revolutionary leaders face in their search for national development. How do we
change? What priorities do we emphasize in economic, political, and
social life? What kind of identity with, and commitment to, the nation
should we encourage? Historical memories provide answers to many of
these questions and to the interaction between foreign policy and evolving national self-perceptions and expectations. These historical memories are a key to some of the contradictions in Cuba's contemporary
foreign policy.

While it would be inaccurate to pose geographical determinism as the
major element shaping the views of past leaders, geography is a permanent conditioning factor. Like other states that had been traditionally
exposed, often subjugated, to the diplomatic pressures of foreign powers
before undergoing a major revolution (Mexico in 1910; China in 1911),
Cuba was frequently the subject of another state's control in matters of
foreign policy, not having full control of her own.

Cuba's island position has strategic importance at the entrance to the
Caribbean. Only ninety miles off the North American coast and blessed
with a topography and a climate favorable for the cultivation of sugar
cane, her development has been caught up in the web of international
power politics since the sixteenth century. The basic configuration of
Cuban hemispheric affairs is well known: the island's importance to
Spain as an outpost against threatening French, Dutch, and British
interests in the Caribbean; growing U.S. interest in Cuba as a key link in
its hemispheric and Caribbean interests, including the Panama Canal; the
Cuban-Spanish struggles from 1868 to 1878 (known as the Ten Years'
War) and from 1895 to 1898, in the latter of which the United States
joined; the "right" of U.S. intervention in Cuban affairs through the
Platt Amendment, not abolished until 1934.[1] Cuba's (strategic) im-

---

1. Among other things, the Platt Amendment provided that the government of Cuba
(1) could not enter into any treaty or other compact with any foreign power that would impair
the independence of Cuba; (2) could not assume or contract any public debt it could not
service out of its current income; (3) consented to the right of U.S. intervention in order to

portance to both Russia and the United States appears in recent events, including the extensive Soviet aid to Cuba, the severity of U.S. reactions to Cuban Marxism-Leninism, the ill-fated Bay of Pigs invasion of April 1961, and the missile crisis of October 1962.

What is critical to understanding Cuban foreign policy is not so much the direct geographic importance of Cuba to various foreign states as the indirect impact this has had on the perceptions of Cuban intellectuals. What did many of them "see" in Cuban history? Toward the end of the nineteenth century, long after other Spanish colonies had gained their independence, the struggle for Cuban sovereignty finally erupted in the bloody Ten Years' War (1868–78). Ironically, the eventual Cuban victory over Spain in 1898 entailed U.S. intervention; the *patria* had not won its true independence alone, nor had it achieved complete freedom. Precisely at the time of separation from Spain in 1898, Cuba became locked into U.S. power politics for an era of interventions under the Platt Amendment that extended over three decades.

When the Platt Amendment was formally repealed in 1934, large American investments in the sugar industry were retained, as was U.S. control over extensive latifundia (large land holdings); American influence in the corporate and financial life of Cuba was extensive. This lack of control over natural economic resources, coupled with the legacy of foreign involvement in Cuban affairs, accentuated what many educated Cubans have seen as a general Cuban sentiment that their country lacked true national independence and moral integrity.[2]

In 1898, the United States replaced Spain in the minds of many Cuban intellectuals as the major external impediment to full nationhood. It is not surprising, in the context of the anti-Yankee feeling to which this relationship led, that the Cuban Revolution has been distinctly anti–U.S. since 1959. Nor is it strange that Fidel Castro has carefully identified the revolution as a continuation of the national struggle begun in 1868, citing past Cuban heroes, for example, José Martí, as his forerunners.

Years of Spanish and North American influence helped shape the basic characteristics of the Cuban polity and economy and the reactions to this situation on the part of many Cuban patriots. Spain's authoritarian, Hispano-Catholic rule in Cuba had not prepared the island for self-government. Nor was effective self-government achieved during the Platt

preserve Cuban independence; (4) would sell or lease to the United States lands necessary for coaling or for naval stations to enable the United States to maintain the independence of Cuba. This amendment was named after Senator Platt, chairman of the Senate Committee on Foreign Relations.

2. The Cuban historian Herminio Portell-Vilá often argued that a colonial sugar industry impeded the historic quest for true independence. See *Historia de Cuba en sus relaciones con los Estados Unidos y España*, 4 vols. (Havana, Jesús Montero, 1938–41). For excellent background reading to this subject, see Ramón Eduardo Ruiz, *Cuba: The Making of a Revolution* (Amherst: University of Massachusetts Press, 1968).

Amendment years. Politics after 1898 was characterized by irresponsibility, corruption, waste of public funds, and intimidation of the electorate by the army. Moreover, since business and commerce were dominated by Spaniards and Americans, many educated Cubans moved into governmental positions; they turned to politics, as one historian wrote in 1924, in order to earn a living.[3]

By the time the Platt Amendment was revoked in 1934, the Cuban government had become the largest employer of workers in the Cuban middle sectors, and the government budget had become fair game for politicians who disposed of public posts irresponsibly.[4] Political parties and elections had only marginal utility for achieving political and economic reforms. To be sure, political reforms had been attempted, and promises had been made to improve economic conditions. But the initial efforts and promises of Ramón Grau San Martín and Carlos Prío Socarrás largely ended in continued corruption, although the Prio government did begin some basic changes, such as establishing the National Bank, a Cuban currency, a national development bank, and a pilot agrarian reform program. By the time Fidel Castro began his organized guerrilla movement in the Sierra Maestra in the late 1950s, much had been written and discussed in Cuba about the effects of Spanish and North American influence. The range of this debate included Cuba's sugar-based economy, with its seasonal characteristics and its yearly unemployment effects; the poor living conditions it meant for large numbers of Cubans in rural areas; the centralized land-holding system it involved, dominated by a small number of owners; and U.S. influence in these and other domestic areas.

The 1950s were years of increasing popular frustration with Cuban life as it was, with old politicans, including Fulgencio Batista, and with cynicism concerning the promised but unimplemented reforms, many of them embodied in the constitution of 1940. These frustrations were evidenced by the rise of revolutionary action-oriented groups during the 1940s and 1950s. More conservative interests, led by Batista after his 1952 coup, reacted with increased repression and violence. Among the groups advocating a radical overhaul of Cuban life, a reform more in line with what José Martí had earlier exposed, was that led by Fidel Castro.[5] And because so much of Cuba's domestic setting was enmeshed in U.S.

3. See Charles E. Chapman, "The Cuban Election Problem," *American Review of Reviews* 70 (October 1924): 413–19. An expanded governmental bureaucracy as the main dispenser of goods, services, and employment in developing countries is not unusual. See James C. Scott, *Comparative Political Corruption* (Englewood Cliffs, N.J.: Prentice-Hall, 1972), chap. one.

4. *Problems of the New Cuba*, Report of the Commission on Cuban Affairs (New York: Foreign Policy Association, 1935), p. 5.

5. An exremely useful and important documentary and analytic account of the setting inside Cuba that led to Castro's movement is provided by Rolando E. Bonachea and Nelson P.

interests, reform of the system could only mean some kind of restructuring of Cuban–U.S. relations, if Batista were toppled from power.

But more than geography, popular frustration and U.S. involvement in Cuba lies at the base of the Cuban Revolution. There is the general question of Cuban political culture and its effects upon political rule. With some exceptions, it can be argued that the basic political styles adopted on the continent also developed in Cuba after 1898: powerful leaders (Gerardo Machado and Fulgencio Batista), the key role of the military as a power base for these leaders, an ineffective parliamentary system, and an inefficient electoral system marred by corruption. Politics rapidly became firmly based on personalities and personalist loyalty patterns rather than upon national institutions capable of peaceful transfers of political power, although it is true that political parties such as the *Partido Auténtico, the Partido Ortodoxo,* and the Communist party did enjoy substantial, loyal followings before the Batista coup of 1952. After Batista's coup, coercion, "spoils," patronage, favors, and corruption were very much the rule of the political game.

To these dimensions of prerevolutionary Cuba must be added another. Circulating among educated Cubans was the idealized image of a Cuba independent of foreign control in which human dignity and social justice for all people would exist. This image was clearly derived from the struggles of 1868–78 and 1895–98 against Spain. It was reinforced by the writings and actions of José Martí, whose works, personal life, and eventual death in the struggle for independence laid the basis for a Martí cult that legitimized armed revolutionary action. Castro has defined himself as a product of this legacy.

The factionalism, violence, and armed struggle that escalated after Batista's 1952 coup accentuates a final key point. The political legitimacy of Cuba's state institutions—presidency, legislature, electoral system, and political parties—never completely captured the loyalty of either Cuba's leaders or their followers. Neither accountability of leadership to the led, nor responsibility of followers to participate actively in state political institutions seemed firmly based, although the period between 1940 and 1952 appeared stronger in these aspects than other periods. This "legitimacy vacuum," or absence of a spirit of citizenship, may in turn have been spawned by a weak notion of common nationality in Cuba, which left the island's population highly fragmented. To be sure, there had been nationalist movements, but there is a real question as to how strong and how deeply felt national feeling in Cuba was. A number of Cuban intellectuals—Jorge Mañach, León Aguilar, Ramiro Guerra y Sánchez,

Valdes in their book of selected works of Fidel Castro, *Revolutionary Struggle*, vol. 1 of *The Selected Works of Fidel Castro* (Cambridge, Mass.: M.I.T. Press, 1972), especially their excellent introductory essay.

Alberto Lamar Schweyer, Rafael Estenger, Mercedes García Tuduri, Fernando Ortiz—have raised this question over the years.[6]

New Forces After 1959

Castro gave Cuba new goals of revolutionary proportions, justified by past social and economic goals and by the ideology of Marxism-Leninism. Caught in cold war politics at a time of national revolutionary change, he opted for support by the Soviet Union, using Marxism-Leninism and the Cuban Communist party as a base from which to enter the Soviet orbit. He built a national power structure around the Cuban Communist party, his own charismatic leadership, and a new national military organization. The new features of Cuban social and political life resulting from this structure affected the formation and substance of Cuban foreign policy. Similarly, foreign policy decisions had a direct bearing upon the process of national integration inside Cuba.

The Marxist-Leninist interpretation of Cuba's revolution accentuated the historic quest for independence from the United States. It provided an ideological rationale for reinforcing the hostility between Cuba and North America generated years before. It also provided the new leadership, headed by Castro, with a ready set of symbols with which to mobilize Cubans against their outside enemy—now labeled as the leader of the "imperialist" and "capitalist" powers—uniting them in a common cause to build the new Cuba. In turn, U.S. foreign policy, including support of the Bay of Pigs invasion, sponsorship of the embargo against trade with Cuba, and exhortations against the Castro regime within the OAS, seemed to confirm the "devil theory" of U.S. policy and attitudes toward Cuba that Castro and his followers espoused.

Revolutionary Ideology and National Interest in Cuban Diplomacy

In analyzing the foreign policy of a state, one source of information includes published documents, speeches, and interviews. Analyzing Cuban diplomacy on the basis of this kind of information would give unjustified weight to purely "rational" factors; speeches and documents do not always reflect the effects of fortuitous events or the irrational

6. See Jorge Mañach, "El Proceso Cubano y Su Perspectiva," *Bohemia* (Havana), 31 Oct. 1954, p. 52; León Aguilar, *Pasado y ambiente en el proceso cubano* (Havana. Ediciones Insula, 1957); Ramiro Guerra y Sánchez, *Historia de Cuba* (Havana: Librería Cervantes de R. Veloso, 1922); Alberto Lamar Schweyer, *La Crisis del Patriotismo* (Havana, 1929); Rafael Estenger, "Cubanidad y Derrotismo," *Revista Bimestre Cubana* 46 (1940): 369-89; Marcedes García Tuduri, "Personalidad y Nacionalidad en Heredia," *Revista Bimestre Cubana* 43 (1939): 421-27; and Fernando Ortiz, "La Decadencia Cubana," *Revista Bimestre Cubana* 19 (1924): 35 (where Ortiz remarks that "the worst thing about Cuba is that it is not a Cuban people").

inputs into foreign policy decisions. Another kind of information is found in the ideological pronouncements of foreign policy makers. An evaluation based exclusively on these ideological tracts, however, tends to emphasize militant, irrational, and often expansionist priorities. It underestimates the force of power and security considerations; moreover, it obscures the impact of personalities in day-to-day foreign policy decisions or in tactical and strategic planning.

Foreign Policy Formulation

Diplomacy is not automatic and impersonal; nor is it determined by purely ideological perspectives. It is part of the human drama and cannot, therefore, be separated from the character of its central decision makers or the cultures of the societies they represent. In Cuban foreign policy we must add to available documents, speeches, interviews, and ideological pronouncements such other vital ingredients as the idiosyncracies of the decision makers who determine and implement foreign policies, the structure of government that affects foreign policy decisions, the major values of the society that influence its external behavior, and the ideological or geographic challenges posed to the society under study.[7] These basic variables are in a constant state of flux; they are relative and not mutually exclusive. The student of diplomacy is faced by a complex and challenging setting, one not susceptible to easy analysis.

These preliminary remarks suggest that Cuban foreign policy, with its militant Marxist-Leninist dimension, is by no means purely ideological. Yet, the ideological element cannot be written off simply by arguing that only national interest or Fidel Castro's personality determines foreign policy decisions. To state the more obvious importance of ideology in Cuban diplomacy, Marxism-Leninism became a key link in Cuban-Soviet relations after 1959.[8] Moscow demonstrated great interest in Cuba after 1959, particularly when Fidel began to state his commitment to Marxism-Leninism in December 1961. Moscow undoubtedly would have been interested in any radical nationalist and anti–U.S. trends in Cuba, since reducing U.S. power had long been a Soviet goal in the developing countries of Africa, Asia, and Latin America and since U.S. power in the Caribbean seemed beyond challenge. As Cuba turned toward Marxism-Leninism, so Moscow turned toward Cuba and Latin America with an

7. For additional reading on these points see James N. Rosenau, "Pre-Theories and Theories of Foreign Policy," in *Approaches to Comparative and International Politics*, ed. R. Barry Farrell (Evanston: Northwestern University Press, 1966), pp. 27–92. See also Vernon V. Aspaturian, "Soviet Foreign Policy," in *Foreign Policy and World Politics*, ed. Roy C. Macridis (Englewood Cliffs, N.J.: Prentice-Hall, 1962), pp. 137–41.
8. On central benefits to the USSR in supporting Cuba, see my own essay, "Moscow and Cuban Radical Nationalism," in *Soviet Policy in Developing Countries*, ed. W. Raymond Duncan (Boston: Ginn-Blaisdell, 1970), pp. 107–33.

enthusiasm not seen before in the region. Adoption of a Marxist-Leninist ideology also helped to insure aid to a developing Cuba greatly in need of technical assistance, military aid, and outlets for its sugar production (after losing the U.S. market) at a time when its revolutionary domestic and foreign policies challenged U.S. interests throughout the hemisphere.

Moreover, the adoption of Marxism-Leninism gave Fidel Castro not only a modern instrument for national integration (see below) but also an ideological base from which to become the outstanding Latin American critic of U.S. policy and a notable leader in the Latin American modernization process.

A more subtle link between ideology and national interest and power is concealed within these overt relationships between Marxism-Leninism and Cuban diplomacy. Cuba's Marxist-Leninist ideology makes the foreign-policy-making elite acutely aware of the importance of power and security in world politics. The ideological world of Marxism-Leninism is one of bipolarity, divided between the world socialist system and the Western "captalist-imperialistic" powers. It is one of tension, conflict, and competition between these two worlds. According to the script, the Western enemies, led by the United States, will seek to maximize power at all costs. Thus, to build countervailing Cuban power is paramount, as is defense of national security, political independence, and the country's cultural legacy.

While such basic foreign policy goals have remained constant throughout Castro's era, the strategy of attaining them has changed. A Cuban-Soviet relationship replaced Cuban–U.S. ties, as Castro sought to maximize power and security while restructuring the Cuban polity, economy, and society.[9] But this relationship itself went through several phases of crisis, confrontation, and accommodation reflecting Castro's ability to promote Cuban independence even when isolated in the hemisphere and in need of outside aid. By the early 1970s, Cuban-Soviet harmony was at an all-time high; yet Castro's domestic and foreign postures showed the imprint of an independent *Cuban* style.

Secondly, Cuba's relationship with the other Latin American states has reflected strategic shifts. Castro's early emphasis on rural guerrilla warfare against established regimes and his consequent isolation within the inter-American system by U.S. and OAS sanctions reached a new

---

9. See the excellent essay on Cuba's relations with the Soviet Union by Edward González, "Relationship with the Soviet Union," in *Revolutionary Change in Cuba*, ed. Carmelo Mesa-Lago (Pittsburgh: University of Pittsburgh Press, 1971), pp. 81–104; see also Jaime Suchlicki, "An Assessment of Castroism," *Orbis* 16 (Spring 1971): 35–57; and Leon Gouré and Julian Weinkle, "Cuba's New Dependency," *Problems of Communism* 21 (March–April 1972): 68–79. The many internal changes in Cuba since 1959 are explored in Mesa-Lago's *Revolutionary Change in Cuba*, a well documented and up-to-date analysis of key trends.

phase by the early 1970s.[10] By this time Castroite diplomacy had evolved toward a policy of normalized state-to-state relations, accepting the notion of different paths to socialism; at the same time some members of the OAS were proposing that Cuba be brought back into the inter-American system. Castro's support of Salvadore Allende's peaceful, united front and of Marxist change in Chile, of Peru's military-led reforms after 1968, and of Panama's canal struggle with the United States indicated his evolving diplomacy. Corresponding new attitudes among Latin American countries appeared in Peru's resolution in an OAS meeting in April 1972, calling for an end to the collective sanctions imposed on Cuba, and in the establishment of diplomatic relations with Cuba by Barbados, Guyana, Jamaica, and Trinidad and Tobago in October 1972.[11] These actions matched the diplomatic and trade ties of Chile, Mexico, Peru, and Argentina. Significantly, and in contrast to earlier assumptions that rural guerrilla warfare could sweep out of the hemisphere those governments opposed to Cuba and isolating its revolutionary change, Castro announced that Cuban diplomatic relations with OAS members (all recent except those with Mexico) had frustrated North America's attempts to "isolate" the island.[12] Here was the birth of new policy prescriptions to improve Cuba's inter-American position.

As if to symbolize and strengthen the ending of isolation, Castro began to travel extensively outside the island in the 1970s. He toured Chile and visited Peru and Ecuador in November and December 1971. This was followed by a trip to ten states in Africa, eastern europe, and the USSR in May, June, and July 1972, all of which put the new Cuban diplomacy in sharp relief. In addition, the recent tours seem to indicate, as the Cuban press agency, *Prensa Latina*, has repeatedly stressed, that Cuba could make decisions not totally those of a one-man show (Fidel). It could be added that they accentuated a show of independence from the diplomatic and trade restraints imposed by the OAS and the United States, although how independent Cuba was from the USSR remained in question, given Cuba's growing economic indebtedness to the Soviet Union.

10. For solid background reading on Cuba's growing isolation in the Western Hemisphere, see Gordon Connel-Smith's *The Inter-American System* (London and New York: Oxford University Press, 1966). Castro has persistently emphasized the point of Cuba's isolation as a goal of U.S. diplomacy.

11. The readmission of Cuba failed to pass, with Secretary of State William P. Rogers arguing for continued sanctions, saying that "Cuba's continued interventionist behavior and its support for revolution—even though on a different scale than in the past—still constitute a threat to the peace and security of the Hemisphere." *Facts on File*, 23–29 April 1972, p. 301. But debate on the issue indicated that attitudes in the hemisphere were changing.

12. Radio Broadcast, Havana, in Spanish to the Americas, 15 Dec. 1972.

CUBAN IDEOLOGY AND FOREIGN POLICY

The precise impact of ideology upon foreign policy is the subject of much controversy. Some scholars believe that it is highly irrelevant; others see it as the key to basic decisions. An analysis of Cuba's revolutionary ideology—Marxism-Leninism with a heavy nationalist bias—suggests that it plays a basic role in the foreign policy formulation process.[13] This role is similar to that of Marxism-Leninism in the Soviet Union and China or to that of non-Communist ideologies elsewhere, for example, Mexico's more ad hoc "revolutionary" ideology. Cuba's revolutionary ideology is, or consists of a set of ideas, values, and beliefs that unite the people behind the decisions of the leaders. The ideology operates as a legitimization of those decisions. It symbolizes hope for a change in the existing conditions to Cubans dissatisfied with the prevailing socio-economic order and provides a basis for communication between the leaders and the led. Finally, the ideology provides a plan of action to change present Cuban society and also underdeveloped societies outside Cuba.

As interpreted by Castro, this ideology is vital to contemporary Cuba, which is engaged in total revolution; it is a means of stimulating national integration and maximum participation in development programs. It helped to build a Cuban national conscience after 1959, serving as a basic communication system through which to mobilize Cubans for new national commitments. Fidel Castro, Ernesto "Che" Guevara, and other members of the revolutionary elite have linked the themes of antiimperialism, class struggle, socialist unity, and economic determinism to the creation of a "New Man" possessed of the technical and cultural skills required to forge a new Cuba. Cuban Marxism-Leninism neatly spelled out the central values of the "New Man"—work, unity, struggle, dignity, and commitment to development and change. Cuba went on a wartime footing after 1959, with a spirit of combat aimed at changing traditional attitudes of subservience, apathy, political alienation, and frustration.

The ideology of Marxism-Leninism linked the politics of internal mobilization to foreign policy. The achievement of internal security was linked to the external North American threat. The struggle against underdevelopment in Cuba was joined to the struggle to overcome poverty elsewhere in Latin America and in the underdeveloped countries of Africa and Asia. Cubans began to promote their new goals throughout Latin America. As the leader of a new wave in the Western Hemisphere, Fidel Castro and other Cuban revolutionary leaders deemed the experi-

---

13. For an interpretation of ideology opposed to this view, see Andrés Suárez, "Leadership, Ideology, and Political Party," in Mesa-Lago, *Revolutionary Change in Cuba*, pp. 3-21.

ences of Cuba to be not only relevant but mandatory for her neighbors. The Cuban Revolution thus acquired a universal dimension not attained in such other Latin American revolutions as those of Mexico in 1910 and Bolivia in 1952.

The relationship of Cuba's revolutionary ideology and domestic mobilization to her foreign policy does not mean that Cuba's Marxism-Leninism evolved in a form similar to the Soviet variety. Indeed, significant differences emerged to produce deep fissures in the Soviet-Cuban bonds as the revolution wore on. These differences were no doubt to be expected, given a variety of factors—Castro's strong personality, the violence inside Cuba during Castro's early revolutionary years, the independent origin of the Cuban Revolution vis-à-vis Moscow, Cuba's isolated position in the Western Hemisphere after 1959, the absence of *strong* active participation by the pro-Soviet Communist party in its initial stages, and the development of a revolutionary ideology *after* the overthrow of the government rather than *before* the attainment of power.[14]

Characteristics of Cuba's Revolutionary Ideology

What were the specific characteristics of Cuba's revolutionary ideology that made it so different from Soviet Marxism-Leninism? First, Fidel Castro replaced the old guard, pro-Soviet Communists with his own men after 1962. Loyalty to Fidel rather than doctrinal orthodoxy became the criterion for election to leadership positions in the Communist party, and Castro's charismatic personality rather than doctrinaire adherence to Marxism-Leninism came to dominate the revolutionary process. Marxism-Leninism came to mean in large measure what Fidel said it meant.

Secondly, Che Guevara provided much of the doctrinal inspiration on which Fidel drew. Guevara's doctrinal principles, pulled together from the experiences in the Sierra Maestra, emphasized the central thesis of guerrilla warfare as the basic means for social revolution in Latin America.[15] This proposition ran directly counter to the key role that Marxist-Leninist doctrine assigned to Communist parties and to the stages of economic development that must be reached before basic political transitions might occur. Moreover, it ran counter to Moscow's support of Latin America's traditional Communist parties which were

14. On these points, see Daniel Tretiak, "Sino-Soviet Rivalry in Latin America," *Problems of Communism* 12 (January–February 1963): 26–34; Boris Goldenberg, "The Cuban Revolution: An Analysis," ibid. 12 (September–October 1963): 1–9.
15. See Guevara's book, *La guerra de guerrillas* (Havana: Ediciones Minfar, 1960); and John D. Martz, "Doctrine and Dilemmas of the Latin American 'New Left,'" *World Politics* 22, no. 2 (January 1970): 17–196.

oriented, in Moscow's image, toward peaceful parliamentary tactics and toward "forming the broadest possible front of democratic and anti-imperialist forces."[16]

A third difference between Cuban and Soviet Marxism-Leninism was the more voluntarist (human will) element in Havana. Owing much to Guevara's writings, Castro's revolutionary ideology stressed the need to use subjective elements to precipitate basic change rather than wait for other, "objective" conditions to ripen for revolution, as in traditional Marxism-Leninism. This placed an emphasis on armed struggle that is contrary to the Soviet position.

EVOLUTION OF CUBA'S REVOLUTIONARY IDEOLOGY AND FOREIGN CUBAN POLICY

The development of these ideological positions in Cuban foreign policy have been roughly divided into major periods. The key periods suggested are: (1) January 1959 to February 1960; (2) February 1960 to late 1963; (3) late 1963 to January 1966; (4) January 1966 to August 1968; (5) August 1969 to the present.[17]

The first phase was between January 1959, when Castro came to power, and February 1960, when the then first deputy premier of the Soviet Union, Anastas Mikoyan, visited Cuba. This phase was marked by the transition from "democratic," "humanist" principles to a "national-liberationist" revolution with pronounced Marxist and pro-Communist affiliations.[18] Mikoyan's visit and the ensuing economic ties between Cuba and the USSR indicated the termination of Moscow's ambivalence toward the Cuban Revolution and a new willingness to support Havana. This did not mean, however, that Castro had been admitted completely into the Soviet camp.

Events between Mikoyan's visit and late 1963 constituted the second phase. It was highlighted by Fidel's more complete adoption of Marxism-Leninism as the official ideology of the revolution, coupled with a strong assertion of armed insurrection as the fundamental path toward real change in the "objective" conditions of Latin America, as defined by Che Guevara—the latifundia systems, the reactionary oligarchies, the alliances between the middle sectors and the landowners, and the basic

16. Articles by Latin American Communist party leaders affirmed this position throughout the 1960s, viz. Pedro Motta Lima (Brazilian Communist), "The Revolutionary Process and Democracy in Latin America," *World Marxist Review* 8 (August 1965). See also the essays in Mesa-Lago, *Revolutionary Change in Cuba*, sect. 2, "The Economy."

17. An additional period might be added, from the missile crisis to Fidel and Raúl Castro's visits to Moscow in late 1963. Tense relations between Cuba and the USSR marked this era, owing to the missile crisis of October 1962.

18. See Edward González, "Castro's Revolution, Cuban Communist Appeals, and the Soviet Response," *World Politics* 21, no. 1 (October 1968): 39–68.

supportive force of U.S. "imperialism." During this period, Fidel declared that the revolution was in fact "socialist" and that he was a Marxist-Leninist and would be one until he died.[19]

This transition period seems to have dispelled any lingering Soviet doubts about Fidel's real ideological position, for the Russians agreed to establish strategic missiles in Cuba, leading to the missile crisis of October 1962.[20] And by the end of 1963, despite public disagreements between Havana and Moscow over the outcome of the missile crisis, Castro's "socialism" was formally accepted by the USSR in a joint Cuban-Soviet communique.[21] Nevertheless, Cuba's *líder máximo* continued to press the issue of armed struggle in the hemisphere, openly expressing his displeasure at the rejection of this policy by most of the Latin American Communist parties.[22]

The third phase, between late 1963 and January 1966, was one of clear moderation of Castro's armed struggle position and his opposition against U.S. imperialism.[23] It was accompanied by a reduction in U.S. threats after the missile crisis, by the destruction in Cuba caused by hurricane 'Flora,' by Soviet affirmations of solidarity with Havana—missile removals notwithstanding—and by a trade crisis due to domestic economic problems in Cuba (see below). During this phase, Che Guevara—who had been the principal advocate of guerrilla warfare tactics—disappeared from the Cuban scene. Fidel even declared that he was ready to consider compensation for nationalized U.S. property, providing trade might be restored. Additionally, the November 1964 Havana conference of twenty-two Latin American Communist parties produced a joint communique that showed signs of a Cuban rapprochement with traditional Latin American communism. The communique paid homage to the Cuban position, supporting guerrilla warfare in countries where Communist support had not been previously forthcoming, such as Guatemala, Honduras, Colombia, Paraguay, and Haiti. But the communique also emphasized the right of each national party to determine its own "correct line," thus moderating Cuba's previous claim that armed violence was the only path to change. This moderate phase

19. For background reading on this point, see Andrés Suárez, *Cuba: Castroism and Communism, 1959-1966* (Cambridge, Mass.; M.I.T. Press, 1967), pp. 131-42.

20. An in-depth account of the missile crisis is to be found in Graham T. Allison, *Essence of Decision* (Boston: Little, Brown & Co., 1971). See also Arnold Horelick, "The Cuban Missile Crisis: An Analysis of Soviet Calculations and Behavior," in *Soviet Policy in Developing Countries,* ed. W. Raymond Duncan (Boston: Ginn-Blaisdell, 1970), pp. 142-65.

21. This communique, dated 23 May 1963, was distributed by the news agencies TASS and *Prensa Latina.*

22. See Castro's speech to the Havana congress of American women on 16 Jan. 1963; translated from the *Prensa Latina* version, as published by *El Siglo* (Santiago de Chile); also in Ernst Halperin, "Castroism: Challenge to the Latin American Communists," *Problems of Communism* 12 (September-October 1963): 17-18.

23. See Suárez, *Cuba,* pp. 191-95.

ended with the Tricontinental Conference, held in Havana in January 1966.

Castro again intensified his stress on armed struggle after the Tricontinental Conference. Havana Radio broadcast a series of interviews with Latin American guerrilla leaders from Guatemala, Colombia, Venezuela, and the Dominican Republic, stressing in each interview that the predominant struggle for national liberation must be armed struggle. These programs resumed Cuba's sharp attacks on Latin America's Communist parties, with particular emphasis on those of Chile and Venezuela. Castro singled out the reform-oriented governments of Chile and Venezuela for specific polemic condemnation. And when the Latin American Solidarity Organization (LASO) first convened in Havana in July and August 1967, the principal points developed were that "armed struggle is the fundamental line of revolution in Latin America," that "Latin American revolutionaries will battle against imperialism, bourgeoise oligarchies and latifundistas," and that "armed struggle is inevitable."[24] Possible reasons for Fidel's shift back to a "hard line" at this time include his sensitivity to charges that he had sold out his revolutionary principles in exchange for continued Soviet support and that his 1964 agreement with Latin American Communist parties had been a onesided affair.[25] But this fourth period—one of intensified strain with both the USSR and the United States—evolved into a new era of moderation, visible in the events after the summer of 1968.

This new, fifth phase in the evolution of Cuba's revolutionary ideology and foreign policy began after Havana, surprisingly, had supported the Soviet invasion of Czechoslovakia in August 1968. Given the intense friction that marked Cuban-Soviet relations after the Tricontinental Conference, owing to Castro's insistence on the armed struggle thesis, Havana's reaction to the invasion was a clear turning point in policy. Fidel thereafter began to moderate his advocacy of guerrilla warfare and armed struggle in the hemisphere, showing increased flexibility in his approach to reform governments, which he had formerly chastised. Like the period of moderation between late 1963 and the Tricontinental Conference, the major emphasis at home was now on strengthening the party organization and developing the Cuban economy, in this case with specific attention to the projected ten million ton sugar-harvest goal of 1970. Havana ceased its daily radio broadcasts debunking the reform efforts of Chile and Venezuela and began to speak

24. See *La Nación* (Santiago), 11 Aug. 1967.

25. For background reading to this period, see D. Bruce Jackson, *Castro, the Kremlin, and Communism in Latin America* (Baltimore: Johns Hopkins Press, 1969); and W. Raymond Duncan, "Moscow and Cuban Radical Nationalism," in Duncan, ed., *Soviet Policy in Developing Countries*. It could be argued that this period marked an attempt by Havana to set up Cuba as a third center of world communism, distinct from Russia and China, especially given the two major conferences held in Havana in 1966 and 1967.

of possible resumption of diplomatic relations with those governments of Latin America that were willing to "rid themselves of United States political control."[26] On the key question of armed struggle, Havana acknowledged that there might even be cases where armed struggle would not be indispensable.[27]

FORCES BEHIND THE LATEST PHASE

The forces behind this latest phase had both domestic and international dimensions. Domestically, Castro faced severe economic and social strains. Partly as a result of a drought in eastern Cuba, the 1968 sugar harvest by mid-March was almost a million tons below the mid-March total of 1967.[28] Certainly it was a gloomy picture that faced Castro relative to the eight-million-ton goal he had set for 1968. Moreover, as reported in 1969, Cuba was plagued by a number of social problems that were closely tied to economic difficulties. Worker apathy bordering on passive resistance, absenteeism, indiscipline, shoddy work, low labor productivity, disorganization, and carelessness with equipment were reportedly widespread.[29] Other difficulties included growing juvenile delinquency, crime, and truancy. Castro admitted in March 1968 that "the situation in Cuba is not easy" with popular discontent rife. These economic and social distresses help to account for the renewed strengthening of the party upon such base organizations as the Committees for the Defense of the Revolution (CDRs) and for increased militarization to combat the crime, indifference, and absenteeism that already affected production. Given these problems, and in light of the goal to produce a ten-million-ton sugar harvest in 1970, it is not unlikely that Castro toned down Cuban antagonism with Moscow in an effort to assure continued economic aid from socialist states.

The international setting of mid-1968 was also favorable to a moderation of the revolutionary ideology. Castro's theory of armed struggle in the hemisphere did not look impressive in practice. Che Guevara's effort to establish a revolutionary *foco* in Bolivia had failed, illustrating his misinterpretation of the objective and subjective conditions for revolution in that country. Bolivian peasants did not respond well to Che's plans, and support from the Bolivian Communist party was lukewarm at best.[30] Che's death in October 1967 helped reaffirm

26. Press Conference held by Carlos Rafael Rodríguez, member of Cuban Politburo, in Lima, Perú, April 1969. See *Granma Weekly Review* 15 June 1969.

27. Ibid.

28. Speech by Fidel Castro at Havana University, 13 Mar. 1968, Havana Radio.

29. *New York Times*, 12 Oct. 1969.

30. Moscow was not particularly enamoured of guerrilla activities in Bolivia. *Pravda* reported guerrilla clashes in June 1967 and quoted Jorge Kolle, secretary to the Bolivian Communist party (PCB), as saying that the party "supported" the guerrillas but had its own

Moscow's and the Latin American Communist parties' argument that power could best be attained through peaceful "united fronts." Meanwhile, other guerrilla movements in Latin America were not doing well. The guerrillas in Venezuela were less numerous and active than they had been earlier.[31] The Rebel Armed Forces of the Edgar Ibarra Front in Guatemala, led by César Montes, were on the defensive, as were the Colombian guerrillas. And the highly publicized Latin American Solidarity Organization, founded at the conclusion of the Tricontinental Conference of January 1966, was noticeably ineffective. Castro might well have concluded from these events that further ideological shifts were in order.

CONTEMPORARY CUBAN FOREIGN POLICY

Three key trends in Cuban foreign policy can be identified in the early 1970s, reflecting Castro's continued attempts to maximize Cuba's long-range power (ability and resources to influence the behavior of other state leaders) in the pursuit of Cuban security, political independence, and revolutionary objectives. They are (1) increasing economic dependency on the Soviet Union, which is essential to long-term growth in power; (2) realism in relations with Latin American states; and (3) new possibilities of change in U.S.–Cuban relations.

Increasing Economic Dependence on the USSR

One major trend in Cuba is growing economic indebtedness to the USSR, together with more coordinated economic decision making and increasing similarity of ideological line by Cuba vis-à-vis the USSR. According to a *New York Times* report, Cuba's debt to the Soviet Union is now over $400 million, military aid excluded.[32] Moreover, the doubling of Soviet economic aid (to about $2 million per day), the admittance of the island to

line of broad mass struggle and that armed struggle was not the only definitive form of struggle (*Pravda*, 15 June 1967). See also "The Castroite Bolivian Debacle in Perspective," *Communist Affairs* 6, no. 2 (March–April 1968): 3–10; and "The Challenge of Castroism in Chile," *PEC* (Política Económica de Cultura) (Santiago) 1 Mar. 1968, pp. 10–11; Joint Publications Research Service, no. 44, *Translations on Latin America*, p. 876, where PEC argues that Bolivian Communists deliberately undermined the activities of Guevara's group. For a study of the doctrine and the problems of left-wing movements in Latin America, see Martz, "Doctrine and Dilemmas of the Latin American 'New Left,'"

31. See "Discord Grows Between Castro and the Communists," *Este y Oeste* (Caracas /Paris), March 1968, pp. 10–17; Joint Publications Research Service, no. 45, *Translations on Latin America*, p. 497.

32. *New York Times*, 5 Jan. 1973. Of course Cuba also receives large amounts of military aid, e.g., Soviet missile-carrying launches that doubled Cuban missile and antiaircraft equipment in 1972, MIG-23's, and help from Soviet military experts. See *Granma Weekly Review*, 18 Apr. 1972 and 13 Aug. 1972.

the Council of Mutual Economic Assistance (COMECON) in 1972, and the establishment of an intergovernmental coordinating committee presumably increased Moscow's leverage on Cuban economic policy making. Moreover, the increase in the number of Soviet military and economic advisers in Cuba since 1971, coupled with government reshuffles to put Cuban military men in positions of managerial dominance, indicates additional Soviet influence.[33]

Undoubtedly, Castro must have viewed these costs as less than the benefits derived for his domestic needs, particularly in view of the continuing OAS embargo. The cost—servicing a growing national debt, the lack of economic independence, and the continuation of an essentially sugar-based economy, despite the replacement of the United States by the USSR in Cuban economic life—is reduced by other features of the Cuban-Soviet relationship. Castro needs continued support for the development of his socialist objectives, which should in the long run augment Cuba's power. Technical aid will help mechanize the sugar harvest and expand electricity, oil refining, and textile, metallurgic, and electronic computation installations; moreover, the Soviets have pledged to help Cuba search for oil.[34] Capital formation of this type must come from the outside, since Castro's Cuba cannot easily produce it domestically. Meanwhile, in reference to Havana's indebtedness to the USSR, Castro maintains that "there is not one single Cuban working for a Soviet-owned enterprise," noting the difference in aid from the Soviets as contrasted with the period of U.S. influence in pre-Castro times.[35] Indeed, his speech to the Fourth Conference of Non-Aligned Nations, in Algiers September 1973, not only stressed Havana's very close relations with Moscow (so different from the 1966–68 period) but insisted that such a relationship by no means implied a dominant-submissive ("imperialist") tie:

How can the Soviet Union be labelled imperialist? Where are its monopoly corporations? Where is its participation in the multinational companies? What factories, what mines, what oilfields does it own in the underdeveloped world? What worker is exploited in any country of Asia, Africa, or Latin America by Soviet capital?[36]

The new Soviet-Cuban economic agreements of 1973 entailed still other positive benefits for Cuba. Payments on Cuban debts to the USSR are to be

33. See Suchlicki, "An Assessment of Castroism," pp. 35–38; *Latin America* (London), 19 May 1972, pp. 154–55; and Carmelo Mesa-Lago, "The Sovietization of the Cuban Revolution," *World Affairs* 136 (Summer 1973): 3–35.
34. *Granma Weekly Review*, 14 Jan. 1973, pp. 2–3, where Castro reported to the people on the economic agreements signed with the USSR. For a brief but sound discussion of Soviet problems with Cuba, see Leon Gouré's review of two Soviet books on Cuba in *Problems of Communism* 21 (November–December 1972): 87–89.
35. Havana Domestic Radio/Television Services in Spanish, 29 Jan. 1974.
36. *Granma Weekly Review*, 16 Sept. 1973.

deferred until 1986, followed by repayment over a twenty-five year period. The new Soviet credits were extended to cover Cuba's 1973, 1974, and 1975 trade deficits. The Soviets also agreed to purchase Cuban sugar at eleven cents per pound. In addition, Moscow committed herself to continue purchasing Cuban nickel and cobalt.[37] All this suggests that Castro's own political resources—leadership of a Communist government in the Americas, reduction of U.S. power in the Caribbean, and advocacy of radical nationalist policies—are not insignificant in Soviet perceptions and should not be discounted in assessing the mutual benefits in Soviet-Cuban relations. That both Cuba and the USSR had much to gain from their affair was symbolized by the visit to Cuba of Leonid I. Brezhnev, general secretary of the Communist party of the Soviet Union, in January and February 1974.

While much can be said about Cuban dependence on economic aid, it should also be stressed that Castro's own perceptions of the situation, and those drilled home everyday to students, workers, and the military, are that Cuba is freer and more independent today than at any time in her history. As Castro stated in his speech of 31 December 1973, commemorating the fifteenth anniversary of the Cuban Revolution of 30 December 1958:

... And you, combatants, are the firm guardians, the custodians, the defenders of this opportunity created by our people, because never before in our history have we enjoyed such unity, such strength, such peace; never before have we had equal opportunities for work; never was the fatherland so much the master of its destiny! And for this sovereign fatherland, for this fatherland that is master of its destiny, for this country where justice prevails, much blood has been shed on this land.[38]

Relations with the Latin American States

A second trend in Cuban foreign relations is discernible. Cuba's foreign policies in the 1970s demonstrate an increasingly realistic attitude toward the Latin American states. Cuba continues to widen its diplomatic and trade ties in Latin America, even while the de jure OAS embargo exists. By moderating the stand on armed struggle (the emphasis during 1966–68), by endorsing the "many paths to socialism" approach, by stressing the similarity of underdevelopment problems facing the Latin American states, and by emphasizing a "Latin American" identity of interests, Cuba has developed a posture that coincides more favorably with the tides of nationalism running through Latin America (e.g., Peru's expropriation of foreign enterprises, Chile under Allende, Panama's renegotiated Canal

---

37. *New York Times*, 5 Jan. 1973. It should be pointed out, however, that the 1973 agreements also increased Soviet control over the Cuban economy by setting up twenty-nine joint Soviet-Cuban committees to run various sectors of the economy and society.
38. Havana Radio Broadcast in Spanish to the Americas, 31 Dec. 1973.

treaty with the United States, and the Andean Pact).[39] To be sure, this realignment of her foreign policy conforms with the Soviet Union, suggesting Soviet influence over Castro's policy. But it should be remembered that Cuba also stands to gain from this realism; dividends could be forthcoming in more viable trade and economic ties within the hemisphere, with Peru, Panama, Argentina, Mexico, Barbados, Guyana, Jamaica, and Trinidad and Tobago—and perhaps even the United States. As Castro stressed in a speech of 13 May 1973 condemning the OAS: "In the coming years forms of cooperation between the Cuban Revolution and other Latin American governments—even though they may not be socialist—can develop."[40]

Castro continued relations with such non-Communist states outside the Western Hemisphere as Japan, Canada, Spain, France, Britain, and Italy. The British extended a $7 million credit line to Cuba in March 1972; the Japanese are now trading; the European Economic Community has extended trade preferences to the island.[41] Given Moscow's distance from Havana, these trends, coupled with those in Latin America, suggest attempts to modify some of the problems associated with Soviet trade, such as freight costs, low quality goods, and higher prices paid for Soviet imports.

U.S.-Cuban Relations

Unpredictable U.S.-Cuban relations seemed to be entering a new phase in 1974. To be sure, many of Castro's statements continued to be extremely hostile to Yankee "imperialism," and special conditions for a possible rapprochement with Washington remained in his policy statements. In the USSR during July 1972, Castro reiterated the familiar themes of resolving the Vietnam war, shutting down the U.S. naval base at Guantánamo, and ending the economic and political blockade of Cuba. In July of that year he stated that Cuba was prepared to live for "five, fifteen, or even thirty years without relations with the United States."[42]

39. The leftward trends are offset by specific rightist forces. These include the defeat of the Tupamaros guerrillas in Uruguay and the rise of military power there during the early 1970s; the military overthrow of Chile's Communist government, headed by President Salvadore Allende in September 1973; and Perón's curbs on terrorism in Argentina during 1973.

40. *Granma Weekly Review*, 13 May 1973, p. 3.

41. Havana has broadcast its view that Japanese trade has helped to break the blockade. The Japanese extended commercial credits for the purchase of buses, bulldozers, and equipment for the sugar industry. It also sells Cuba batteries, fertilizers, medical supplies, tin, tires, toys, and fishing equipment. In return, Cuba exports sugar and sea food (Havana Radio Broadcast in Spanish to the Americas, 30 Nov. 1972).

42. *Facts on File*, 27 Aug.-2 Sept. 1972, p. 686. See also Mesa-Lago, "The Sovietization of the Cuban Revolution," pp. 22-35.

Yet the possibilities for a rapprochement seem to exist. One key condition for renewed relations with the United States, that of a Vietnam settlement, has been met. During Salvadore Allende's visit to Cuba in December 1972, Castro stated that only one condition had still to be met if talks were to be opened with Washington: ending the economic blockade.[43] Given Soviet pressure in Havana and Moscow's relaxed relations with Washington, it is conceivable that the Soviets would like to see relations reestablished as a possible means to reinforce the Soviet-American détente and to lessen Soviet economic support of the Cuban government. From the U.S. viewpoint, it is a favorable factor that revolutionary propaganda and support for guerrilla movements has subsided, bringing guerrilla complaints against this trend.[44]

Indeed, that Cuba was no longer completely off-limits for Washington was illustrated by the attendance of U.S. scientists at the Havana Oceanographic Conference in June 1972, a conference called by the United Nations to study currents and plankton drift in the Caribbean and its effects on fish. Cuba's agreement in 1972 to cooperate in the control of airline highjacking problems also suggested a new turn, despite Castro's oratory. But it remains to be seen how and to what extent these events might result in a Cuba–U.S. rapprochement.

Castro can be, as he has been in the past, unpredictable. Even in the 1970s, with growing accomodation vis-à-vis the Latin American governments and the Soviet Union, the signs of *fidelista* independence of thought are there. Cuba's reaction to the overthrow of the Chilean president, Salvadore Allende, in September 1973 was sharp, with Castro stating that "Cuban revolutionaries know that now there's no alternative other than revolutionary armed struggle."[45] And at a time of great speculation about restored U.S.–Cuban relations, shortly after Brezhnev's 1974 visit to Cuba, Castro stated that he was not "in any hurry" to improve relations with Washington.[46]

In the early 1970s a movement developed in Latin America to remove the sanctions against Cuba. Argentina took the initiative, supported by Mexico and other nations. The United States responded, indicating that action by the OAS must precede U.S. action. Pat M. Holt, of the staff of the Senate Foreign Relations Committee, was sent to Cuba to report on the

43. Paris Radio Broadcast, 14 Dec. 1972.
44. Castro undoubtedly changed his ideological line on the paramount necessity of violent, rural guerilla struggle over more peaceful, united-front tactics as a result of weighing the costs of such a posture against the benefits of modifying it. With Che Guevara dead, serious economic difficulties at home, pressure from the Soviets, opposition to the violent stand by Latin America's governments, and a poor showing by other guerrilla leaders in Latin America, it was rational to change gears. By the 1970s the gains in this modified policy were clearly visible.
45. *Granma Weekly Review*, 7 Oct. 1973.
46. *New York Times*, 17 Feb. 1974.

situation. His visit was followed by that of two Senators, Jacob K. Javits (Republican) of New York, and Claiborne Pell (Democrat) of Rhode Island, both members of the committee. As this book goes to press it appears likely that a Meeting of Consultation of the Foreign Ministers of the OAS will recommend removal of the sanctions.

If this is done, a thorny problem will still exist from the Cuban standpoint—that of return to participation in the OAS, with possible obligations like those under the Inter-American Treaty of Reciprocal Assistance, which Cuba has renounced. Both Castro and Cuban Foreign Minister Raúl Roa García have advocated an organization that would exclude the United States. This position, if continued, will complicate the restoration of normal relations between Cuba and the other Latin American nations and will present a serious obstacle to completely friendly relations between Cuba and the United States.

BIBLIOGRAPHICAL NOTE

Numerous sources on contemporary Cuban foreign policy are available. Excellent collections of materials are found in Harvard's Widener Library, in the Library of Congress, at the University of Florida (Gainesville) and at the University of Miami (Coral Gables). First rate bibliographies include one published by the Library of Congress, entitled *Cuban Acquisitions and Bibliography*, compiled and edited by Earl J. Pariseau (April 1970) and another edited by Jaime Suchliki of the University of Miami, entitled *The Cuban Revolution: A Documentary Bibliography, 1952–1968*.

Additional useful sources are the *Radio Free Europe Reports* and the translated materials of the Joint Publications Research Service. The weekly edition of *Granma Weekly Review*, official organ of the Central Committee of the Communist Party of Cuba (in English), carries the major speeches of Castro and other leading members of the Cuban communist party. Numerous articles on Castro's foreign policy have been published in *Problems of Communism*, a well-known bimonthly publication of the U.S. Information Agency.

Books

Bonachea, Rolando E., and Valdes, Nelson P. *Revolutionary Struggle*, vol. 1 of *The Selected Works of Fidel Castro*. Cambridge, Mass.: M.I.T. Press, 1972. A first rate collection of the selected works of Fidel Castro, documented, edited, with an extremely penetrating introductory essay. It provides an excellent study of the setting out of which Fidel Castro emerged inside Cuba, giving a clue to his personalist direction of foreign policy after 1959. The selections center around six phases as suggested by the chapter titles: "University years," "Toward the Moncada," "Imprisonment," "Organizing in Cuba," "Exile," and "Guerrilla War."

Duncan, W. Raymond, and Goodsell, James Nelson. *The Quest for Change in Latin America*. New York: Oxford University Press, 1970. Section 5 of this work deals with the connections between domestic and foreign policy in Cuba since 1959. Section 7 provides documents and commentary on the great debate of revolution versus reform, initiated sharply by Castro's insistence on violent revolution, particularly after the Tricontinental Conference.

Jackson, D. Bruce. *Castro, the Kremlin, and Communism in Latin America.* Baltimore: Johns Hopkins Press, 1969. While including the foreign policy configurations since 1962, this work is particularly useful for the study of events shortly before and after the Tricontinental Conference of January 1966—a major turning point in Moscow-Havana relations. It also highlights Castro's frictions with other Latin American Communists after January 1966.

Lockwood, Lee. *Castro's Cuba, Cuba's Fidel.* New York: Vintage Books, 1969. This book probes Castro's perceptions and expectations about revolutionary change and foreign policy. It is based upon an American journalist's interviews with Cuba's *líder máximo.*

MacGaffey Wyatt, and Barnett, Clifford R. *Twentieth Century Cuba.* Garden City, N.Y.: Doubleday & Co., 1965. Particularly good on the social and economic setting out of which Castro's revolution evolved. Less comprehensive than Hugh Thomas's book, it is succinct, focussing on the events through approximately April 1961.

González, Edward. *Cuba under Castro: The Limits of Charisma.* Boston: Houghton Mifflin Co., 1974. A thorough, well-balanced, and well-documented study of the evolution of Castro's revolutionary movement. Essential reading for understanding the linkages between domestic and foreign policy after 1959.

Mesa-Lago, Carmelo, ed. *Revolutionary Change in Cuba.* Pittsburgh: University of Pittsburgh Press, 1971. An authoritative, up-to-date study of Cuba's revolution, containing a number of important essays on foreign relations (by Andrés Suárez, Edward González, and Ernesto F. Betancourt). In addition, the book examines in individual essays important corollary issues in the polity, economy, and society, which are related to foreign policy.

Plank, John, ed. *Cuba and the United States.* Washington, D.C.: Brookings Institution, 1967. Includes ten essays on Cuban–U.S. relations from various perspectives. A useful addition for study of Castro's foreign policy.

Eduardo Ruiz, Ramón. *Cuba: The Making of a Revolution.* Amherst: University of Massachusetts Press, 1968. Solid reading for Cuba's perspective of the outside world. Contains a very helpful bibliography.

Suárez, Andrés. *Cuba: Castroism and Communism, 1959–1966.* Cambridge, Mass.: M.I.T. Press, 1967. A very thorough analysis of the intricate forces operating on Castro's foreign policy decisions, emphasizing Castro as a consummate politician. It focuses upon domestic as well as foreign interrelationships, e.g., Castroism, communism, Russia, and China, and concludes with a discussion of the Tricontinental Conference of January 1966. An epilogue to subsequent events is included.

Suchlicki, Jaime. *Cuba, Castro, and Revolution.* Coral Gables: University of Miami Press, 1972. An important contribution to the growing studies of the Cuban revolution, with essays on foreign relations by Foy D. Kohler, Leon Gouré and Julian Weinkle, and M. Michael Kline. Excellent reading for students and professionals.

Thomas, Hugh. *Cuba: The Pursuit of Freedom.* New York: Harper & Row, 1971. A comprehensive history of Cuba, beginning with the English expedition to capture Havana in 1762 and ending with the ten-million-ton sugar harvest of 1970. An excellent reference book for the beginning and serious student wishing to probe the historic background to post-1959 events.

Articles

Dinerstein, Herbert. "Soviet Policy in Latin America." *American Political Science Review* 61, no. 1 (March 1967): 80–90.

Fagen, Richard. "The Cuban Revolution: Enemies and Friends." In *Enemies in Politics,* pp. 184–231. Edited by David J. Finlay, Ole R. Holsti, and Richard R. Fagen. Chicago: Rand McNally & Co., 1967.

González, Edward. "Castro's Revolution, Cuban Communist Appeals, and the Soviet Response." *World Politics* 21, no. 1 (October 1968): 36–68.

Gouré, Leon, and Weinkle, Julian. "Cuba's New Dependency." *Problems of Communism* 21 (March–April 1972): 68–79.

Mesa-Lago, Carmelo. "Castro's Domestic Course." *Problems of Communism* 22 (September–October 1973): 27–38.

———. "The Sovietization of the Cuban Revolution: Its Consequences for the Western Hemisphere." *World Affairs* 36 (Summer 1973): 3–35.

9/Roy Arthur Glasgow
The Commonwealth Caribbean Countries

INTERNATIONAL PROBLEMS OF THE REGION

In a recent edition of his *Politics Among Nations*, Hans J. Morgenthau stated that the traditional distinctions between foreign and domestic policies were no longer valid. The main reason is the close correlation between internal events, their external repercussions, and the manner in which these are evaluated. This statement is particularly true of the Commonwealth Caribbean countries since independence,[1] because their foreign policies have so clearly been extensions of their domestic policies. A. N. Robinson, former minister of external affairs of Trinidad and Tobago, has stated the relationship thus:

Insofar as foreign policy aims are concerned, our objectives are essentially an extension of our domestic policies which are principally concerned with raising living standards and improving generally the quality of life of the broad masses of our population.[2]

Without carrying the generalization too far we may say that this has been the principal goal of the Commonwealth Caribbean governments of Barbados, Guyana, Jamaica, Trinidad and Tobago, and the other Leeward and Windward Island states. In this chapter our aim is to examine the foreign policies of the Commonwealth Caribbean countries since independence, particularly the big four—Jamaica, Guyana, Barbados and Trinidad and Tobago. Our approach will define the international problems confronting these states, their motivations and strategies within the Western Hemisphere, taking into account the historical background and the cultural-ethnic identity within which their policy is oriented.[3] Finally, the main part of the chapter will analyse the influence of domestic conditions on foreign policy, the aims and rationale of the foreign policies of the Commonwealth Caribbean countries, and the methods they pursue in their new thrust toward regional cooperation.

Because they are one-crop economies with high rates of unemployment and underemployment (15 to 20 percent of the labor force), inadequate

1. The governments of the English-speaking territories have adopted this term to designate the future economic and, it is hoped, political entity that will also embrace non-English-speaking and nonindependent territories of the Caribbean.
2. *Express Independent Magazine*, 31 Aug. 1969.
3. Charles O. Lerche, Jr., and Abdul A. Said, *Concepts of International Politics* (Englewood Cliffs, N.J.: Prentice-Hall, 1964), pp. 1-2.

income distribution, low rates of domestic savings, and substantial population growth rates and inflation, the Commonwealth Caribbean countries face serious internal economic problems. (See table 9.1 for the population of the Commonwealth Caribbean countries in 1970.) Since most of the islands are major exporters of one or more of such crops as sugar, citrus, bananas, coffee, or rice, a penny or two decrease in the world market price may mean the difference between economic survival and economic disaster. To the groups of anxious and nervous market watchers, life is risky, a gigantic game of chance determined largely by external forces beyond the control of the region. This is, in part, largely responsible for the picaroon attitude so prevalent in the area.

Thus, the international economic policies of the region seek to eliminate or modify these forces through the achievement of a high growth rate, improved living standards, and the reduction of unemployment. This is a formidable, perhaps Sisyphean, undertaking, since economic conditions depend on the goodwill and vagaries of other nations. Cogent examples of this dependence of the Commonwealth Caribbean countries are their persistent quest for the protection of Commonwealth preferential markets and for new markets, their encouragement of tourism, their need for aid for infrastructural projects, and their formation into regional groupings.

HISTORICAL ANTECEDENTS

The external relations of Barbados, Guyana, Jamaica, and Trinidad and Tobago, and also those of the other Caribbean islands, have historically been determined by geopolitical, economic, and demographic considerations largely shaped and controlled by European and North American forces. Spain, convinced that by the will of God she was destined to

Table 9.1 Population of Commonwealth Caribbean Countries in 1970

(in thousands)

Country	Number
Jamaica	1,972
Trinidad and Tobago	1,040
Barbados	253
Leeward Islands	143
Belize	120
St. Lucia	110
Grenada	105
St. Vincent	95
Dominica	74
Guyana	742

Source: *1970 United Nations Yearbook* (New York, 1970).

possess and rule over the Caribbean Sea, and perceiving it as a *mare nostrum*, engaged in a series of bitter clashes in the area with Britain, France, Holland, and later on, the United States. The Spaniards introduced the slave plantation economy in Hispaniola, creating a new social and economic order—a sugar economy—in the New World. This system more than any other single factor has conditioned the life style and patterns of behavior of the area. For these Caribbean economies were developed and exploited to supply raw materials to Europe; in return they imported food, capital goods, and the reprocessed products of their exports. *Las Siete Partidas*, the thirteenty-century Spanish code, accepted slavery as a valid part of the economic and social order. Spain, and subsequently other European countries, disillusioned with the work performance of the Indian on plantations and in mines in America, turned to the African for the solution to the labor problem. In spite of the tremendous profits made from sugar, the islands became progressively poorer as their wealth was exported to Europe and dissipated in the rival wars that convulsed that area. The changing world economy and the scarcity of capital produced nightmarish moments for the one-crop island producers who, between the seventeenth and nineteenth centuries, moved from the center of the world's economic stage to its obscure periphery. As the twentieth century dawned in the Caribbean, the region displayed a number of small islands that were poor and backward, with undiversified economies. But this century has also seen the beginning of a realization that there is a need for closer cooperation among the islands.

Historically, the Caribbean has looked outward, expanding its trade relationship at one time or another with Britain, France, Spain, the Netherlands, and to some extent, the United States. Since the islands developed as colonies of certain metropolitan countries, receiving trade preferences and some economic aid, a rigid bilateral relationship developed, opening few commercial and economic options outside the Commonwealth and fostering the opinion that the Caribbean would profit little from trading with Latin America. Consequently, West Indians became familiar figures in London and later in Toronto and Ottawa. As the twentieth century dawned large numbers of West Indians, unable to find employment at home, departed for Britain, Canada, and the United States. This migration reached its peak during the late 1950s and early 1960s, when Britain placed restrictions on Commonwealth immigration into that country.

In frustration, West Indians turned to Canada and the United States, not only as outlets for their surplus population but as sources of technological assistance, foreign aid, and private investment and as markets for their exports. As a buyer of sugar and a supplier of foreign aid, Canada made an economic contribution exceeding that of the United States, presumably because of her long established Caribbean ties and membership in the Commonwealth. The Canadian Government, through the Canadian International Development Agency (CIDA), sponsors aid programs, grants, and teachers in the Caribbean, particularly in the Leeward and Windward Islands. Other aid institutions are the Canadian Overseas Book Corporation (COBC) and the Canadian University Services Overseas (CUSO).

In spite of some gains, a general disenchantment has developed in the West Indies concerning the long-term efficacy of private foreign investment, which has led to black power disturbances. When one reviews the external orientation of the Caribbean, only Belize (formerly British Honduras) had ties with the Latin Americans before the middle 1960s. Belize's territorial dispute with Guatemala has forced her, as a matter of strategy, to seek closer relations with Mexico and Jamaica.

Thus, in considering the external politics of the Commonwealth Caribbean countries since independence, we note that the social values of the leaders and their conceptions of what is "good" for the "well-being" of their people are rooted in their historical consciousness. These countries have shared cultural experiences such as slavery, the development of a heterogeneous population, foreign intervention, foreign imposed cultures and languages, and a one-crop trading economy. Seldom confronted with issues that permitted a choice, leaders are accustomed to having their fate determined elsewhere. The absence of any Caribbean central authority has allowed external economic forces to shape supply and demand and, consequently, the prices of their major primary products.[4]

It is not surprising, therefore, that having inherited such obstacles in their social structure, the leaders of the newly emerging island states have been cautious, defensive, ambiguous, and uncertain in their pronouncements and actions.[5] Consequently, within four to seven years after the demise of the West Indian Federation in 1962—a demise brought about by Caribbean leaders—we observe two movements for regional economic cooperation developing. The first, the Caribbean Free Trade Association (CARIFTA), was formed in 1965 by Barbados, Antigua, and Guyana; the second, the Eastern Caribbean Common Market, was formed in 1968 to include the Leeward and Windward Islands. Several days later, on 30 April, 1968, the political leaders of Trinidad and Tobago joined Antigua, Barbados, and Guyana to become a member of the two and a half-year-old CARIFTA.

4. Mary Proudfoot, *Britain and the United States in the Caribbean* (London: Faber & Faber, 1954), p. 154; and Sir Harold Mitchell, *Europe in the Caribbean* (London: W. G. R. Chambers, 1963), pp. 6-7.
5. For an analysis of this type of behavior on the part of Caribbean leaders, see Roy Arthur Glasgow, *Guyana: Race and Politics among Africans and East Indians* (The Hague: Martinus Nijhoff, 1970), pp. 115-17.

REGIONAL INTEGRATION: A SEARCH FOR
SECURITY AND WELL-BEING

The realities of independence, the disenchantment of the developed world with the marginal efforts of the developing countries, and Britain's courting of and entry into the European Economic Community (EEC) created a growing sense of insecurity on the part of Commonwealth Caribbean governments and the realization that no single island state could hope to satisfy its own present and future needs. They began to realize, furthermore, that their traditional dependence on Britain had to be replaced with a new dependence—first, on themselves and second, on their region.

Historians can identify at least two currents in the external relations of these countries. The first is a search for security and well-being that brought recognition and a new awareness of one another. This awareness prompted the first efforts to form some type of association to confront the economic realities of the age. In the opinion of Caribbean leaders, regional integration could increase the standard of living in their own countries as it had in Europe, increasing efficiency by optimizing trade and maximizing production.[6] Integration, or the creation of a larger market, facilitates the diversification of an economy by providing stimuli for industrialization—and diversification presumably enhances the bargaining power of a group. It is doubtful, however, whether the island states could develop sufficient economic muscle through diversification to significantly influence economic or political events elsewhere.

The second important current in the external relations of these island states is the diversification of trade relations, increasing those with Latin America and the United States and lessening those with their traditional and preferential trading partner, the United Kingdom. The Commonwealth Caribbean countries, as small territories with small populations, have most of the disadvantages of being small; they are heavily dependent on foreign trade, they have limited markets, and the range of their primary products is not diversified.[7] The argument in favor of increasing their Latin American contacts might be convincing if we accepted the premise that a solution to many of their problems lay in a judicious combination of regional and extraregional trading arrangements that could facilitate the optimization of resources. The traditional inhibiting

6. Rolf Sannwald and Jacques Stohler, *Economic Integration: Theoretical Assumptions and Consequences of European Unification* (Princeton: Princeton University Press, 1959), p. 21.

7. A. D. Knox, "Some Economic Problems of Small Countries," in *Problems of Smaller Territories*, ed. Burton Benedict (London: Athlone Press, 1967), pp. 36–37.

factor of political union need not arise, as it is believed that a substantial degree of economic integration can be encouraged, attained, and combined with the political autonomy that each unit treasures.[8] Present indications are that many heads of governments of Commonwealth Caribbean countries understand this principle and see that they can have their economic gains without sacrificing their political prestige. This has been one of the main reasons why the leaders have, for the most part, been enthusiastic in their pronouncements on CARIFTA.

The formation of CARIFTA, under the leadership of Guyanese Prime Minister Forbes Burnham and Errol Barrow, prime minister of Barbados, may be viewed as the first painful postindependence step toward the formation of a specific Caribbean identity, at least in terms of economic values. A commitment to Caribbean unity has been one of the main planks in Guyana's foreign policy.[9] Thus, a few weeks after assuming office in 1964, Burnham made the first attempts at establishing closer links with Caribbean territories. Both Guyana and Barbados had new leaders who had not been actively involved in the demise of the West Indian Federation; so they approached the task of closer Caribbean unity with consciences unburdened by a historical sense of guilt.

A combination of motives was probably instrumental in initiating and fostering the establishment of CARIFTA by Guyana and Barbados. In Guyana, serious internal problems caused by the acute cultural divisions between Africans and East Indians and by the border problems with Venezuela and Surinam created an obvious need for cooperation with the other Commonwealth Caribbean states. Prime Minister Barrow, a vigorous exponent and supporter of Pan-Caribbean movements,[10] saw little future for either sugar or the Commonwealth. A similar view was held by Prime Minister Eric Williams of Trinidad and Tobago, who at Punta del Este in 1967 declared that "the fact of the matter is that Commonwealth trade insofar as it exists today is rapidly declining."[11] He pointed out that Trinidad and Tobago had actually been losing under the "so-called trade preferences." Presumably, such arguments could also be advanced for the other Commonwealth Caribbean territories.

The case of Barbados was different. Sugar is her main export, and the bulk of it was covered by the Commonwealth Agreement of 1951 under which the United Kingdom purchased a certain tonnage. Barbados's allocation for 1968 under this agreement was 141,627 tons, out of which

8. Political and economic fragmentation have been an integral part of the region's history, although as early as 1905 the British claimed that their ultimate policy was the establishment of a federal government in the area. See William Sanders, "The Confederal System in the Caribbean," in *The Caribbean: Current United States Relations*, ed. A. Curtis Wilgus (Gainesville: University of Florida Press, 1966), p. 205.

9. *Guyana Journal* 1, no. 1 (April 1968): 15.

10. *New York Times*, 1 Dec. 1966.

11. *New York Times*, 18 June 1967.

local consumption was 12,000 tons.[12] Like other area governments, she was interested in preserving the preferential price structure paid by the United Kingdom, which was fixed at $104.40 (U.S.) per ton, or more than triple the price of sugar ($29.40 per ton) on the world market. The cost of production in the West Indies, incidentally, is above the world market price.[13] The same preferential pricing is true for other area exports such as bananas and citrus fruits. The 1973 entry of the United Kingdom into the EEC is certain to affect the trading positions of these territories, damaging if not wrecking their economies.

With a view to preserving these preferences in order to provide full employment and an improved standard of living, while simultaneously reorienting their trading partners, Barbados, Guyana, and Antigua established CARIFTA in December 1965. Some intellectuals and politicians argue that this regional grouping was merely an initial step toward the attainment of a viable economic community, or common market, and possibly a political union. In any case, it appears that the foreign policies of these Commonwealth Caribbean countries have evolved with the single purpose of preserving, expanding, and improving their trade with both traditional and new trading partners. The signatory countries agreed among other things to the "liberalization" of trade, the removal of barriers among member countries, and the erection of a common external tariff leading to regional integration.

Whether the present actions and policies of the Commonwealth Caribbean governments have produced or will produce the sustained momentum necessary to carry an integrationist movement to its logical end—either a viable economic community or a political entity—is questionable. There are, however, a number of promising signs. Since the experiment received its main impetus from within the Caribbean rather than from Europe or North America, it has been easier to generate enthusiasm among its members, especially since their nationalist feelings could not be piqued by charges that CARIFTA, or any successor to it, was a neocolonialist venture. The abortive West Indies Federation suffered from this psychological handicap, because early in this century successive British governments had pushed the federal idea in the West Indies.[14] The

12. *West Indies and Caribbean Yearbook, 1970* (London: Thomas Skinner, 1969), p. 105.
13. Roy Preiswerk, "The New Regional Dimensions of the Foreign Policies of Commonwealth Caribbean States," in *Regionalism and the Commonwealth Caribbean*, Institute of International Relations, Special Lecture Series no. 2, ed. Roy Preiswerk (Trinidad, 1969), pp. 6 7.
14. Eric Williams, "The Failure of a Federation," *Round Table* 207 (June 1962): 273. In 1958, ten British Caribbean territories—Jamaica, Trinidad and Tobago, Grenada, Barbados, St. Vincent, St. Lucia, Dominica, Montserrat, Antigua, and St. Kitts-Nevis—formed a loose federation and agreed to create a viable state out of separate islands that vary enormously "in size, ethnicity, economic development, resources, population and political development." One of the first controversies was over a federal capital. After much acrimony, Port of Spain,

developing nationalist consciousness of the leaders and the masses, fueled by events in Africa and Asia and by their historical insularity, may have been additional factors. However, *pari passu* with the above are other social factors that might work against the momentum.[15]

As early as 1956 the functional approach had been suggested as an effective tool in uniting the territories, since it was argued that "political union can be effectively approached through the development of cooperative action in handling specific problems of an economic or technical nature."[16] Functionalism is seen by its advocates as a major theoretical basis for the solution of political conflicts and for the development of economic and social cooperation between states.[17]

An outstanding example of the earnest efforts of the states to promote free trade is the action of members to remove all but sixteen exceptions on the trading list.[18] This means that from CARIFTA's inception on 1 May 1968, all trade among member states, with minor exceptions, has been free.[19] The dynamism of this step augurs well for the association and for future efforts along these lines, as it signals a commitment and a sense of sacrifice, customs duties forming a significant part of national revenue.

CARIFTA was originally founded on the pragmatic and appealing principles of functional cooperation and economic unity; it subsequently attracted Dominica, Grenada, St. Kitts-Nevis-Anguilla, St. Lucia, St. Vincent, a hesitant Jamaica, and Montserrat. CARIFTA members meeting in Guyana gave the green light to Belize, which subsequently became a

---

Trinidad, was selected. In March and April 1958, the first federal elections took place, and a prime minister, a cabinet, and a senate were appointed and a parliament opened. But, as internal controversy engulfed the fragile federation, the insular instincts of the member states triumphed, leading to the death of the federation in 1962, after Jamaicans voted against unity.

15. See below for a discussion of internal social factors and their effect on foreign policy.

16. Jesse Harris Proctor, Jr., "The Functional Approach to Political Union: Lessons from the Effort to Federate the British Caribbean Territories," *International Organization* 10, no. 1 (February 1956): 35.

17. Inis L. Claude, Jr., *Swords into Plowshares: The Problems and Progress of International Organization*, 3d ed. (New York: Random House, 1964), pp. 345–46. The Caribbean has a history of organizational cooperation, as the West Indies Bar Association, the West Indian Teachers Association, the Federation of Civil Servants of the West Indies, and the West Indian Court of Appeals (to name just a few) demonstrate. The last named has been replaced recently by the Regional Court of Appeals (1970). Regional cooperation on tourism and in university education are operational. The faculty at the Institute of Social and Economic Studies of the University of the West Indies have clarified many common Caribbean problems, for example, the CARIFTA machinery. Finally, the Heads of Governments of CARICOM Countries Conference is the major regional policy making body.

18. Havelock Brewster and Clive Y. Thomas, *The Dynamics of West Indian Economic Integration* (Mona, Jamaica: Institute of Social and Economic Research, 1967), pp. 47–52. In assessing the future viability of CARIFTA—a hazardous undertaking indeed—Brewster and Thomas enumerated the many commodities that could be the basis of expanded regional trade.

19. Frank Rampersad, "Caribbean Cooperation and Integration: The Caribbean Free Trade Association," in *Regionalism and the Commonwealth Caribbean*, p. 73.

member.[20] The Bahamas, Haiti, and the Dominican Republic have been
reported to be interested in joining. Some Commonwealth Caribbean
leaders, particularly Prime Minister Williams of Trinidad and Tobago,
have long conceived of a Caribbean economic community that embraced
the entire region.[21] In effect, this means that French, Dutch, and U.S.
possessions, as well as the Caribbean associated states, would also be
eligible for membership. The rationale is that a viable community cannot
be attained without the full participation of *all* countries in the region.

Jung-Gun Kim, in a study of nonmember participation, has argued that
ideals of international organization could not be attained without "the
participation or cooperation of non-members."[22] It would appear, then,
that such countries as Cuba, Haiti, Surinam, and French Guiana could
qualify for membership. But formal membership for many of these non-
Commonwealth territories might produce new problems. While countries
like Surinam and French Guiana are sparsely populated and could provide
an emigration outlet for overpopulated Caribbean territories, their
metropolitan economic ties and special relationships with the EEC might
be obstacles. Additional questions arise, for example, whether it would be
strategically preferable to delay their admittance to the association until
there is a stronger West Indian consciousness within and among
CARIFTA members. Assuming that this consciousness develops, what
type of policy or what institution should be created to facilitate non-
Commonwealth Caribbean participation, in view of the often repeated
statement that in an interdependent world countries cannot be pariahs for
long?

Mr. Kamaluddin Mohammed, former minister for West Indian affairs in
the government of Trinidad and Tobago, advocated Cuba's membership in
CARIFTA.[23] And Prime Minister Eric Williams, at the sixth meeting of the
Inter-American Economic and Social Council (IA-ECOSOC), declared
that Cuba should be readmitted to membership in the Organization of
American States (OAS). In an act that declared their independence in
external relations and reflected a level of consultation between them,
Guyana, Trinidad and Tobago, Jamaica, and Barbados agreed to establish
diplomatic relations with Cuba in December 1972.

Although Venezuela has joined the Andean Common Market, she has
also enquired about receiving observer status at future CARIFTA talks,
indicating that member countries may have to make arrangements for the
possible accession of a non-Commonwealth Caribbean state. According to

20. *Caribbean Business Week*, July 1970.
21. Eric Williams, *From Columbus to Castro: The History of the Caribbean, 1492–1969*
(London: Andre Deutsch, 1970), p. 497.
22. Jung-Gun Kim, "Non-member Participation in the Organization of American
States," *Journal of Inter-American Studies* 10 (April 1968): 194.
23. *Trinidad Guardian*, 22 Apr. 1969.

Dr. Jatar Dotti of Venezuela, his country views "closer relations with CARIFTA countries, not only politically, but economically."[24] Recently, the Papelera Industrial de Venezuela, in collaboration with St. Lucia, Dominica, St. Vincent, and Grenada, agreed to establish the first regional manufacturing plant in the Caribbean. The plant, which will be located at Vieux Fort, St. Lucia, will produce banana boxes initially but will later expand into packaging different goods for other CARIFTA members.[25] This plant development, therefore, is one of the first steps toward a rational system based on the development of regional integrated industries.

Most of the CARIFTA countries were apparently so satisfied with the economic and psychic gains realized up to 1972 that at the meeting of heads of government at Port of Spain, Trinidad, on 9 October 1972,[26] they agreed that the Caribbean Community (CARICOM) should be formed on 1 May 1973, providing for a common market with a common external tariff. This new step in regional integration may give rise to further investigatory studies directed, for example, toward the formulation of a broad, long-term regional perspective plan based on the identification of regional natural resources; another such study might include projections of indirect demand for agricultural, industrial, and mineral products in the region.

The charters of CARIFTA and CARICOM make a distinction between their more developed members—Guyana, Jamaica, Trinidad and Tobago, and Barbados—and the other, less developed countries, by granting less tariff protection for the former, the "big four." But this arrangement has failed to satisfy the small countries, particularly Montserrat, who opted not to join CARICOM. The small states that benefit under the Agricultural Marketing Protocol, which created minimum prices and export quotas for agricultural exports, have formed an Eastern Caribbean Common Market (ECCM) to defend their interests.

It thus appears that the survival of regional unity depends on patience and understanding in allaying the fears and suspicions of the small states. As indicated earlier, intra-Caribbean trade has picked up momentum. A glance at table 9.2 shows that imports to and between the big four, and between the smaller islands, have increased. Note that the data refer to trade movements between a big-four member and the other three members. Similarly, ECCM reflects the increase, as well as some of the problems, of this intra-Caribbean trade.

24. *Trinidad Guardian*, 21 Apr. 1970.
25. *Times of the Americas* (Washington, D.C.), 12 Aug. 1970.
26. *Trinidad Guardian*, 1 May 1970. See also *OAS Information Service*, E119/69, 7 Oct. 1969; and United Nations Economic Commission for Latin America, *Economic Survey of Latin America, 1970* (New York, 1972). Trade among CARIFTA members in locally manufactured products was largely duty-free. The larger countries fulfilled their commitments by reducing tariffs by 20 percent each year; the other states adopted measures to cut tariffs by 50 percent on 1 May 1973.

Table 9.2 CARIFTA: Intra-Area Imports of the Big Four and the Eastern Caribbean
Common Market, 1967–69

(millions of $ East Caribbean)

Country	1967	1968	1969
Barbados	13.2	16.8	21.1
Guyana	25.6	29.4	32.4
Jamaica	7.7	7.6	11.7
Trinidad and Tobago	16.4	16.0	23.2
Subtotal	62.9	69.8	88.4
ECCM	26.8	(30.0)[a]	(37.0)[a]
TOTAL	89.7	(99.8)[a]	(125.4)[a]

Source: Economic Survey of Latin America (New York: United Nations, 1970), p. 137.
[a]Estimates based on incomplete data.

POLITICAL ISSUES AND CONFLICT RESOLUTION

While Montserrat has opted against CARICOM, citing economic hardship
and lack of protection for her interests, some enquiries have been made by
other island states (the Dominican Republic and Haiti) about the prospects
of joining the market. What are the prospects of this new economic
community? It is tempting, but perilous, to predict an optimistic outcome
at this stage. According to Eric Williams we are "now proceeding towards
more meaningful integration."[27] Whether CARICOM can maintain
momentum on this course by attracting new members—for example, the
Dominican Republic, Surinam, and Venezuela—and carry this momentum over into the more political CARICOM in spite of the serious border
problems between a foundation member, an intended member, and other
interested members, is problematical. Even CARICOM members currently
involved in matters of an economic nature may eventually find themselves
involved in apparently miniscule political problems of an intraregional or
even a broader international nature. These matters may have important
regional dimensions. A final resolution of the Guyana-Venezuela border
problem has been tactfully postponed, presumably for both political and
economic considerations. Since Belize is in CARICOM, it is inevitable that
members would become involved in its territorial dispute with Guatemala.
So far, little attention has been paid to, or provision made for, this aspect of
community business in terms of providing machinery for conflict
resolution.

The Anguilla issue is a clear illustration of the problem of the
Commonwealth Caribbean states; the member states were caught unawares

27. Williams, From Columbus to Castro, p. 497.

by Anguilla's secession and thus had no contingency plans for arbitrating the dispute. Although the leaders, particularly Mr. Kamaluddin Mohammed of Trinidad and Tobago, Mr. Shridath Ramphal, attorney general of Guyana, Mr. Milton Cato, chief minister of St. Vincent, and Mr. Cameron Tudor, Barbadian minister of Caribbean and Latin American affairs, all played important roles in resolving the conflict, it appears that they were galvanized after the fact of British intervention.[28] The refusal of Jamaica, Barbados, Guyana, and Trinidad and Tobago to provide a peacekeeping force on "independent" Anguilla was consistent with their stated position one year earlier (October 1968), in which they called upon Great Britain to take all necessary steps to end the secession.[29] Their lack of action may be viewed as another serious shirking of their regional responsibilities. Their leaders had not made the psychological transition, the metamorphosis, from the colonial state of dependency, indifference, and lethargy, to independence, commitment, and foresight in thought and action. Equally important in this connection, however, is the divided position taken at that time by the big-four members of CARIFTA on the "independent" course pursued by Anguilla.

The leaders of Trinidad and Tobago and Jamaica had denounced the invasion, while their counterparts in Guyana and Barbados had endorsed it. A thorough examination of the political considerations that determined these stands is beyond the scope of this chapter; but a lingering suspicion persists in the minds of some leaders of the smaller islands—suspicion born of their experiences in dealing with Jamaica and Trinidad and Tobago during the ill-fated federation[30]—that the two largest states, irrespective of their official pronouncements, are at heart lukewarm toward any type of association that would compromise their sovereignty. Since some political

28. The British invasion of Anguilla was accomplished by two Royal Navy frigates and four helicopters (*New York Times*, 24 Mar. 1969). *Le Figaro*, 19 Mar. 1969, commenting on the British action, remarked: "The old British Lion has opened an eye. One thought he had gone to sleep for all eternity in his kennel behind the Prime Minister's desk."

29. *Fifth Conference of Heads of Government of Commonwealth Caribbean Countries*, Press Release no. 4, 6 Feb. 1969, pp. 2-5. At the constitutional talks in London, in 1966, the Anguillans opposed the introduction of associated statehood unless satisfactory constitutional provisions could be made for local government. On 27 February 1967, they rejected statehood and expelled the police force, subsequently nominating a caretaker government. This secession was approved by referendum, and new political instutions were created. Ronald Webster emerged as the leader of the secessionist state, attempting to agree upon a conciliatory path with his rival, Mr. Bradshaw. After several extensive efforts at reconciling the parties had failed, the island was invaded by British troops (see Yves Collart, "Regional Conflict Resolution and the Integration Process in the Commonwealth Caribbean" in Preiswerk, ed., *Regionalism and the Commonwealth*, p. 171; *Report of the Commonwealth Conference on Anguilla Presented to Parliament by the Secretary of State for Commonwealth Affairs by Command of Her Majesty, October 1967* [London]).

30. See the various proceedings of the Federal Legislature as recorded in *Parliamentary Debates: Proceedings and debates of the Second Session, 1959-61* (Port of Spain, Trinidad: Government Printing Office, 1959-61).

compromise is a *sine qua non* of any progressive association of states, and since the Anguilla problem was in the first instance political in the sense of being a quest for independence, it is possible that the political posture of these two states in this confusing crisis betrayed their true feelings toward Caribbean unity.

The border problem between Guyana and Venezuela had more far-reaching effects than the family quarrel among the two Commonwealth Caribbean member states of Anguilla and St. Kitts. Among the effects of the conflict were the use of force by Venezuela, her sponsoring of a secessionist movement in the Rupununi region of Guyana, the legal and other barriers she placed in the path of both Guyana's participation in international conferences and also the entry of investment capital into Guyana, and her objection to Guyana's membership in the OAS. A discussion of this Venezuela-Guyana conflict in relation to wider aspects of Latin American affairs is attempted below. In this section mention will be made only of the response of the former CARIFTA members to a peaceful settlement of this boundary dispute.

At first the dispute presented a serious challenge to the leaders of Trinidad and Tobago, who historically had cultivated Venezuela's friendship. While condemning the use of force as a means of solving the dispute, the prime minister of Trinidad and Tobago remained scrupulously impartial to avoid jeopardizing relations with either country. Presumably, he was also mindful of the fact that Venezuela has an historic claim to Trinidad and Tobago and that his island state is an integral part of that nation in the Venezuelan constitution.[31] Intensive behind-the-scenes activity by the Trinidadians was successful in procuring an agreement between the two nations that was signed by their foreign ministers in Port of Spain, on 18 June 1970. This agreement, which shelves the dispute for at least twelve years, will be extended automatically unless either nation exercises the option to end it at the conclusion of the above period.[32]

Prime Minister Burnham informed his Parliament of the accord, in terms characteristic of his country's foreign policy, noting that the agreement "imposes on Guyana the obligation of exploring new ways and means of improving relations with Venezuela, of promoting mutual confidence and friendly intercourse between Guyana and Venezuela as befitting neighboring and peace-loving nations."[33] To all appearances, the solution to this problem was regionally induced, particularly as the United States had "washed her hands of it" in an attempt to avoid alienating two of her hemispheric allies.

31. The author was apprised of this claim in a conversation with Dr. Harry Major, first secretary of the embassy of Trinidad and Tobago in Rio de Janeiro, Brazil, on 11 August 1970. Dr. Major formerly represented Trinidad and Tobago in Venezuela.
32. *Christian Science Monitor*, 23 June 1970.
33. *New York Times*, 10 June 1970.

INTERNAL POLICIES AND FOREIGN POLICY

Any serious consideration of Commonwealth Caribbean foreign policies must address itself to the role of the masses, to their self-perceptions and their effect on both internal affairs and foreign policy. Throughout the history of associational movements in the Caribbean, no serious attempt had ever been made by the brown, middle-class leaders to enlist the cooperation of the black masses in forging unity. This is not to suggest that such an attempt, if it had taken place, would have succeeded in commanding their loyalties. What we suggest, however, is that efforts directed at closer unity are fruitless unless they receive mass moral support. The level of consciousness and conscience of the masses must be heightened so that they can consolidate their power along functional lines. In the present Caribbean social milieu certain cultural biases create a crippling and distorted social attitude and have traditionally emasculated mass cooperative efforts.

The social order in the Caribbean is based on many gradations of color, from white at the top, through yellow and brown, to black at the bottom. Social attitudes and values place a premium on whiteness and lightness that has encouraged disharmony and weakened solidarity.[34] It is not surprising, therefore, that the whites and browns who rule these states are viewed with increasing distrust by the black masses and that they have been unable to generate the needed political and moral support among the latter, for either the ill-fated federation or for CARICOM. When one considers that in the federation referendum, held in Jamaica to determine its future federal role, it was mainly the middle class (some 51 percent voted for federation) who voted for federation, while the masses opposed it, the grotesqueness of the social attitudes becomes clearer. CARICOM may well suffer from the same crippling legacy, since the masses associate it with the political and economic ascendancy of the middle class.

The failure of the middle class to solve the chronic problems of inflation, unemployment, underemployment, and discrimination have further contributed to the alienation that recently manifested itself in black power riots and in the growth of black power organizations. Under existing conditions it would be extremely difficult to mobilize the masses to support any Caribbean cooperative enterprise. Eric Williams, in his recent book, *From Columbus To Castro*, alludes to this chronic Caribbean problem when he mentions that Cuba under Fidel Castro is the only Caribbean country that has been able to surmount these divisions by uniting the masses.[35]

34. Lewis E. Bobb, "The Federal Principle in the British West Indies: An Appraisal of Its Use," *Social and Economic Studies* 15, no. 1 (March 1966): 257.
35. Williams, *From Columbus to Castro*, p. 497.

An important aspect of the black power movement, one which will influence foreign policy, is its bitter opposition to the "right-wing essentially capitalist governments" that have sold out to the "neo-colonialists who come mostly from North America, but also from Britain and Europe."[36] This cry is gaining momentum from Jamaica to Trinidad; it has exploded in demonstrator's attacks on Canadian banks, in the firebombing of the home of U.S. Vice Consul Frank W. Hagen on 8 March 1970, and in an alleged attempt to topple the Trinidadian government. One consequence of these actions was a movement centered in Trinidad and Tobago and dedicated to assuming more national operational control over the economy. In this respect, Williams admitted that "we have already gone further than any other Caribbean territory except Cuba."[37] National participation in the economies of these island states will increasingly extend to include the commanding heights of industry, which is largely foreign owned and controlled.[38] Efforts at *localizing* (nationalizing) these foreign enterprises will affect the foreign policies of the Commonwealth and of the Caribbean states, particularly those affecting relations with the capital-exporting countries of North America and Europe.

RELATIONS WITH LATIN AMERICA

Ever since 1961, when the short-lived West Indies Federation became concerned about Patrice Lumumba's death, the search has gone on for closer ties with Africa and Israel.[39] In the United Nations, representatives of West Indian governments allied themselves with the Afro-Asian countries against racialism and colonialism, particularly on the South-West Africa issue. At various times they attended nonaligned conferences as observers; they established diplomatic missions in Africa and exchanged state visits with African and Asian leaders.

But the major extraterritorial thrust of the Caribbean states since independence has been toward Latin America. Historically, their attitude toward the Caribbean area was an uninformed one, marred by indifference and, sometimes, hostility. To Latin Americans, the Caribbean meant economic and political domination and exploitation by the United States, so in many cases they adopted a hands-off attitude. When, for example, Cheddi Jagan and Forbes Burnham, protesting the suspension of the Guyanese constitution, appealed to the delegates at the Tenth Inter-

36. *Washington Post*, 25 Dec. 1969.
37. *Nationwide Broadcast*, delivered by Dr., The Right Honorable Eric Williams, on 30th June 1970 (Port of Spain, Trinidad: Government Printing Office, 1970), p. 6.
38. See the proposals of Lloyd Best, in *Black Power & National Reconstruction: Proposals following the February Revolution* ([Trinidad?], 1970).
39. *Parliamentary Debates: Proceedings and Debates of the Second Session, 1959–61*, 49th sitting, 23 March 1961.

American Conference in Caracas in 1954, they were not even admitted to speak to this body. Only the Guatemalan Congress expressed concern by condemning "British imperialistic aggression."[40] In contrast, the intervention of Castillo Armas to execute a *golpe* in Guatemala elicited a vociferous uproar. The attitude of the Latin Americans toward the Caribbean has subsequently changed; there is a growing feeling of Third World solidarity and partnership against the developed countries. Thus, the first contacts between Trinidad and Tobago and Venezuela dealt with the surtax on Trinidadian imports and increasing involvement in cooperative ventures, particularly with respect to petroleum, tourism, and education.[41]

During the Third Special Inter-American Conference, held in Buenos Aires in February 1967, the government of Trinidad and Tobago applied for membership in the OAS. According to the 1964 Act of Washington, any independent American state, by directing a note to the secretary general indicating its disposition to ratify the OAS Charter and accept the obligations of membership, especially with reference to collective security, was entitled to membership. A special commission of the OAS, comprising Argentina, Colombia, Guatemala, Venezuela, and Uruguay studied the request presented and supported by Venezuela and verified the fact that Trinidad and Tobago had fulfilled the requirements for membership.[42] Trinidad and Tobago was admitted to the OAS at a special session on 23 February 1967, creating for the Latin American nations what Dr. José A. Mora, then OAS secretary-general, referred to as "a new stage in hemisphere relations, one in which the Inter-American System is broadened, not merely in membership, but in outlook."[43]

At this conference Eric Williams made his firm pledge to the Latin American countries to set up a common market by 1970. Since independence, Williams has been enunciating and pursuing a foreign policy that places less emphasis on Europe and more on the Western Hemisphere. Speaking on the British Broadcasting Corporation's "Panorama" in 1964, he reiterated his view of the unimportance of the Commonwealth and of the need for the Commonwealth Caribbean nations to develop relations with the United States and Latin America.[44]

Diplomatic missions have since been exchanged with Brazil, Mexico, and Venezuela. A Brazilian trade mission visited Trinidad in August 1970

40. Robert D. Tomasek, "British Guiana: A Case Study of British Colonial Policy," *Political Science Quarterly* 74, no. 3 (September 1959): 440.

41. Roy Preiswerk, "The Relevance of Latin America to the Foreign Policy of Commonwealth Caribbean States," *Journal of Inter-American Studies* 11 (April 1969): 248. See also Eric Williams, *History of the People of Trinidad and Tobago* (Port of Spain: P. N. M. Publishing Co., 1960).

42. Organization of American States, *Report of the Special Commission with reference to the request for admission by Trinidad and Tobago*, OAS/SER.G/IV, 23/2/1967.

43. *OAS Information Service*, E 21/67, 13 Mar. 1967.

44. *Trinidad Guardian*, 4 July 1964.

to discuss trade, tourism, and joint cooperation on petroleum.[45] The two countries have since abolished visas, signed a cultural exchange program, and exchanged (unilaterally on Trinidad's part) engineers. Cruzeiro do Sul, the Brazilian airline, has introduced twice-weekly flights from Port of Spain to Belem.

Jamaica's foreign policy, while expressing support for the United Nations, the West, the Commonwealth, Caribbean cooperation, and Afro-Asian aspirations, has been oriented principally toward gaining the North European market. Her position toward Caribbean economic unity and relations with Latin America has been hesitant and ambiguous. This may be why Bolivia opposed her admission to the OAS on 25 June 1969, declaring that she was not truly independent of Great Britain.[46] This view is also held by a large segment of the Jamaican population. Speaking to a citizen's association in 1969, Willis O. Isaacs, member of Parliament for St. Ann's, declared that "Jamaica is a colonial State in spite of all our talk of independence."[47] Since the Peoples' National party won the elections in 1971, there has been a change in Jamaica's Caribbean posture, a movement somewhat away from the United Kingdom and more toward support of the Caribbean area, Latin America, and Asia.

Whatever the truth of these charges, Jamaica has been moving quietly to encourage new ties with Latin America. She was the second hemispheric country to announce that she would maintain diplomatic contact with Cuba, though at the consular level and in spite of OAS pronouncements. In 1966 she established an embassy in Mexico, and she has an ambassador to Trinidad and Tobago who is also accredited to Venezuela. Jamaica and Venezuela, inspired by the history of Bolívar's sojourn in Jamaica, have decided to "strengthen and deepen the fraternal bonds of friendship between them."[48] Joint committees have been established to determine ways and means of effecting technical cooperation in tourism, community development, trade, livestock and other farming, fishing, and agrarian reform.

Since attaining independence, Barbados and Guyana have promoted a more aggressive foreign policy. The former immediately sought membership in the OAS, declaring that "our community of interests now resides with the members of the OAS."[49] Guyana is barred from OAS membership because of her territorial dispute with Venezuela. Prime Minister Barrow of Barbados, with characteristic bluntness, has described the chief attraction of the OAS as its development funds.[50] Essentially, this is the motivation of

45. "Brasil procura ganhar um mercado em Trinidad," *Correio da Manhã* (Rio de Janeiro), 15 Aug. 1970.
46. *OAS Information Service*, E 75/69, 25 June 1969.
47. *Daily Gleaner* (Jamaica), 19 May 1970.
48. *Daily Gleaner*, 16 May 1970.
49. Preiswerk, "The Relevance of Latin America to the Foreign Policy of CC States," in Preiswerk, ed., *Regionalism and the Commonwealth*, p. 249.
50. *New York Times*, 1 Dec. 1966.

the Commonwealth Caribbean governments that foster closer ties with Latin America by joining the OAS.

Commonwealth Caribbean countries are seeing that their national interests lie more and more within the hemisphere and are accordingly devising appropriate foreign policies. They see that at the end of the present century Latin America will have a population of 600 million, and that Brazil alone will have 200 million inhabitants.[51] This is an enormous market, with great potential for these trading island states.

Guyana has been involved more closely with her South American neighbors, because she shares a common frontier with Brazil, Venezuela, and Surinam. In 1968, Brazilian troops were airlifted to the Guyanese frontier because of the possibility of disturbances arising from the forthcoming Guyanese elections, and presumably because of her sensitivities concerning the territory of Amazonas.[52] Since that time, friendly Guyanese-Brazilian relations have developed, the two countries exchanging diplomatic and trade missions and Brazil establishing an economic and technical aid mission. Guyana is now building a 273 mile cooperative highway linking Georgetown with Boa Vista, Brazil. The Brazilian airline, Cruzeiro do Sul, has increased its flights to Georgetown to two per week. The most outstanding act of friendliness by the Brazilian government to Guyana was its detention in Boa Vista of the secessionist terrorists who had sought refuge within her borders in 1969.[53]

The most serious foreign disputes facing the newly independent nation of Guyana have been her border problems with Venezuela, which claims 58,000 square miles—five-eighths of Guyana's territory—and with Surinam, which claims a 6,000 square mile area. Both disputes have led to armed clashes. The dispute with Venezuela was the more serious, inasmuch as the Venezuelan government embarked on a policy of economic aggression against those investors who contributed to Guyana's economic development.[54] Venezuela blocked Guyana's membership in the Inter-American Development Bank and sought unsuccessfully to prevent her from signing the treaty to ban nuclear weapons in Latin America, the Treaty of Tlatelolco.[55] In 1966, Venezuelan diplomatic personnel in Guyana were discovered in a clandestine attempt to interfere in Guyanan internal affairs by subverting members of her Amerindian community. In

51. In *O Brasil, A Africa e O Futuro* (Rio de Janeiro: Laemmert, 1969), Amilcar Alencastre develops the interesting argument that Venezuela and Brazil need to abandon Latin American integration efforts and seek friends elsewhere.

52. "Em direção a Guiana," *Correio de Manhã*, 18 Aug. 1968.

53. C. A. Nascimento and R. A. Burrowes, *Forbes Burnham, A Destiny to Mould: Selected Discourses by the Prime Minister of Guyana* (London: Longman Caribbean, 1970), p. 171. Courses in Brazilian Portuguese were introduced in Guyana, and students were taken on a visit to Manaus by Professor Paulo De Paulo. The University of Guyana has approved a Chair of Portuguese Studies.

54. See, for example, Venezuela's full page advertisement in the *Times* (London), 15 June 1968.

55. *Excelsior* (Mexico), 10 Sept. 1968.

1969, Guyana faced a secessionist movement in the Rupununi area that she claimed was aided and abetted by the Venezuelan authorities. Both disputes were eventually left "hanging fire," as temporary arrangements were made with the help of Trinidad and Tobago.

The increasing proliferation of small Caribbean states joining the OAS could seriously affect Latin American voting power within the Organization and thus create new problems. In January 1973 the secretary-general of the OAS, Galo Plaza, sought inclusion of this item on the OAS agenda. The measure was defeated in the OAS Council, and some members stated that the eventual emergence of some twenty-four small Caribbean nations, with a total population of only 13 million, would adversely affect the voting power of the organization. The increasing tendency of the Latin American delegations to caucus together, instead of relying on the OAS, might signal a general "loosening" of OAS ties and indicate the decreasing political importance of this organization.[56]

Insofar as economic cooperation and integration is concerned, CARICOM may ultimately merge with one of the Latin American regional groups.[57] No one can say what the prospects of such a merger would be, since only Trinidad and Barbados are firmly committed to future Latin American integration efforts. Guyana is excluded and will therefore have to seek her future with the Commonwealth Caribbean countries, unless Venezuela, in particular, and Latin America, in general, can be persuaded to accept Guyana and the Commonwealth Caribbean organizations as part of the region.

If anything is clear in this murky sea of regionalism, it is that the differences of size, the insularity, and the varying levels of ethnicity and of political and economic development of these states present formidable difficulties. The incontrovertible fact is that separation and insularity were institutionalized by historical realities and have to some extent been confirmed by present-day realities. Geographical separation has bred a form of self-sufficiency and a trend toward hedging, rather than a desire to pool resources. This condition has been reinforced by the failure of the West Indies Federation and the fears about the future of CARICOM. But by making regional association a *fait accompli*, the island states have indicated that their problems are soluble.

In the immediate future, a sense of nationhood may emerge forcefully, creating a united nation. This reality depends on the diplomacy of the large countries and the extent to which they can convince the smaller and less

56. Jerome Slater, "Decline of the OAS," *International Journal* 24 (1968-69): 505.
57. Sir Harold Mitchell, "Conflict and Cooperation in Tomorrow's Caribbean," *International Journal* 24 (1969): 559. It has been suggested that Mexico, Central America, and the Commonwealth Caribbean countries might form a subregional unit of one million square miles and a population (1970) of 84 million (see Helio Jaguaribe, *Political Development* [New York: Harper & Row, 1973], p. 468).

developed states that their interests will be more effectively served in a larger unit. Surely, in a world in which the larger countries are forming regional groupings, there is little or no place for small states with nonviable economies.

BIBLIOGRAPHICAL NOTE

The bibliographic material on the postindependence (early 1960s) foreign policies of the Commonwealth Caribbean countries is understandably meagre. My assessment of their external relations for this chapter was structured from conversations with public officials and the man on the street, and I have made use of scholarly articles, particularly those in Caribbean journals and Caribbean, Brazilian, Venezuelan, and some North American (the *New York Times*, the *Washington Post*) newspapers. It should be noted that the data are somewhat skewed toward the Caribbean countries that are geographically closer to South America (Barbados, Guyana, and Trinidad and Tobago). These countries have adopted more aggressive intraregional and extraregional foreign policies. Some of the main sources are listed below.

Main Primary Sources. An important source is the *Fifth Conference of Heads of Government of Commonwealth Caribbean Countries*, Press Release no. 4, 6 Feb. 1969, which gives a synthesis of different political viewpoints of the Caribbean governments. Various issues of the *Guyana Journal*, a periodical publication of the Guyanese government, are valuable for identifying national foreign relations trends. Published documents of the Organization of American States, notably the *OAS Information Service*, are also helpful. I made extensive use of the prolific literary efforts of the prime minister of Trinidad and Tobago, Eric Williams, notably his *History of the People of Trinidad and Tobago*. Much valuable information was obtained in an interview with Dr. Harry Major of the embassy of Trinidad and Tobago on 10 August 1970, in Rio de Janeiro. Dr. Major's previous position was in Caracas, Venezuela, and he was therefore in a unique position to analyze the foreign policy trends of the Caribbean countries.

Some Secondary Sources. Several studies dealing with various aspects of the foreign policies of the West Indies are also invaluable. Excellent studies on the subject are Roy Preiswerk, ed. *Regionalism of the Commonwealth Caribbean*, Special Lecture Series no. 2, (Trinidad: Institute of International Relations, 1969); and Preiswerk, *Documents on International Relations in the Caribbean* (Institute of Caribbean Studies, University of Puerto Rico, 1970); Sybil Lewis and Thomas G. Mathews, eds., *Caribbean Integration* (Institute of Caribbean Studies, University of Puerto Rico, 1967); and Enid M. Baa, *Theses on Caribbean Topics, 1778-1968* (University of Puerto Rico, 1970). Another worthwhile account is Havelock Brewster and Clive Y. Thomas, *The Dynamics of West Indian Economic Integration* (Mona, Jamaica: Institute of Social and Economic Research, 1967). The newspapers *Correio da Manhã* (Rio de Janeiro), *Daily Gleaner* (Jamaica), *Trinidad Guardian*, *Excelsior* (Mexico), *Barbados Advocate*, *New York Times*, *Washington Post*, and *Times of the Americas* (Washington, D.C.) are useful for current events.

10/Larman C. Wilson

The Dominican Republic and Haiti

MAJOR POLICY PROBLEMS

The major foreign policy problems of the Dominican Republic and Haiti have been foreign intervention, economic dependency—which is related to intervention—and mutual distrust. These problems have been determined to a large extent by the violent history of the island of Hispaniola, which conditioned the racial attitudes and the reactions to foreign intervention of these two countries. Haiti developed a hatred of whites, which was both a cause and a result of its successful slave uprising (the only one to succeed in Latin America), independence in 1804 (the first in Latin America), and the creation of a black republic. Later, Haitian animosity was directed against a mulatto elite. Whereas Haiti won its independence from a European power, the Dominican Republic gained its independence in 1844 after twenty-two years of Haitian occupation. The rigors of the Haitian occupation and the resultant twelve-year effort of the Haitians to reunite the island—subsequently exaggerated and incorporated into Dominican folklore—produced in this mainly mulatto country a hatred of blacks and a fear of Haitian "Ethiopianization."

Both countries have been subjected to considerable foreign interference—first by Europe and then by the United States. Both were subjected to the U.S. Caribbean policy, including the corollaries of the Monroe Doctrine, with its goals of preventing foreign influence and maintaining political stability.[1] The United States set up customs receiverships in the Dominican Republic and Haiti early in the 1900s and later occupied them militarily—the former from 1916 to 1924 (troops landed again in 1965) and the latter from 1915 to 1934. During the military occupations the United States established constabularies, the *Garde d'Haiti* and the *Policía Nacional Dominicana*, to assure stability.[2] During World War II both countries cooperated with the United States. They permitted the use of their ports and territory and exported food stuffs and raw materials to the United States, and they received economic and

NOTE: I wish to express my appreciation to Patrick Bellegarde-Smith and Piero Gleijeses for their comments on an earlier draft of this chapter.
    1. For a fuller discussion of U.S. goals and means vis-à-vis Latin America, see the opening pages of chap. 3, above.
    2. For a critical article, see Carl Kelsey, "The American Intervention in Haiti and the Dominican Republic," *Annals of the American Academy of Political and Social Science* 100 (March 1922): 110-22.

military aid. In the cold war period, both countries—Rafael L. Trujillo in the Dominican Republic and François Duvalier and his predecessors in Haiti—played the "anti-Communist game" and maintained good relations with the United States. Relations rapidly deteriorated, however, with Trujillo in the late 1950s and with Duvalier in the early 1960s.

DOMESTIC FACTORS AFFECTING FOREIGN POLICY

The Dominican Republic

A comparison of certain Dominican and Haitian domestic factors indicates how they condition foreign policy. The Dominican Republic, which occupies the eastern two-thirds of the island of Hispaniola, has a population exceeding 4,000,000. Although there is a population movement from rural to urban areas, almost 70 percent of the people live in rural areas. The essentially rural-agricultural composition is reflected in the fact that only one city—Santo Domingo, the capital—has more than 600,000 inhabitants. There is a correlation both between racial composition and population distribution and between the ethnic makeup and place in the social pyramid. With a breakdown of about 20 percent black, 65 percent mulatto, and 15 percent white, the rural areas, where the greatest illiteracy and poverty are found, have a particularly large proportion of blacks and mulattoes. Throughout the nation the lower sector, which includes about two-thirds of the population—mainly the rural and urban workers—is primarily black and mulatto. The relatively small middle sector includes the descendants of Spanish and other European immigrants, including Jews, and recent immigrants from Spain and the Middle East. This sector is made up of farmers and merchants. At the apex of the social pyramid are the owners of the large estates—typically, white creole families.[3]

Rafael L. Trujillo was responsible for increasing the size of the middle sector and upgrading the mulattoes at the expense of the white social elite. This he did in large part by greatly expanding the armed services and the government bureaucracy. Trujillo rose to power through the U.S.-created constabulary, which he headed shortly after the U.S. withdrawal in 1924. He manipulated his election as president in 1930 and soon consolidated his position by strengthening the military as his power base. Trujillo developed the military, particularly the army, and the government bureaucracy as a spoils system personally dependent upon and loyal to him. The result of his approach, in addition to giving him control of all opposition, was that the military, especially the army, became a chan-

3. Howard J. Wiarda, *The Dominican Republic: Nation in Transition* (New York: Frederick A. Praeger, 1969), chaps. 6 and 7.

nel of upward social mobility for low- and lower middle-sector mulattoes and blacks.

A mulatto himself, Trujillo was very sensitive about color, partly because of his awareness of racial attitudes in the United States and partly because he wanted to develop a Dominican national identity distinct from that of Haiti. He claimed that he was "white," had pictures of himself and family members retouched, saw to it that only whites were pictured in tourist publications, claimed that the Dominican Republic was a "white nation," and reinforced popular Dominican fears of Haitian "Ethiopianization." Trujillo made efforts to "whiten" the Dominican population by immigration. In the 1930s, he encouraged, with great humanitarian fanfare, immigration from Europe of Catholic refugees from the Spanish Civil War and Jews from Hitler's Germany. (This also was designed to divert world opinion from the massacre of thousands of Haitians at his order in 1937.)[4]

Haiti

The western third of the island is occupied by Haiti, which has a population approaching 5,000,000. The overwhelming majority of the people are black, illiterate (about 90 percent) peasants, living in rural areas and engaged in subsistence farming. Port-au-Prince, the capital, with around 270,000 inhabitants, is the major urban area. There are three social classes: the mulattoes and the educated blacks, who together constitute 5 percent of the population and include the elite and the middle class; and the black masses, who make up the other 95 percent.[5] For many decades the educated mulattoes and blacks have controlled the country economically and politically and have been the chief beneficiaries of the educational system. They have been culturally and socially oriented toward France; they are French-speaking and Roman Catholic. The black masses have been influenced by the official religion (Roman Catholic) but have little knowledge of the official language (French). They believe in and practice a mixture of voodoo (*vodun*) and Catholicism, and they speak Creole, which is basically African but has a French vocabulary with a mélange of words from other languages. (Five percent also speak Spanish.)

After World War II, in the "Revolution of 1946," President Dumarsais Estimé initiated a number of reforms designed to downgrade the mulattoes in government and bring in more blacks. Although Estimé had little success, Dr. François Duvalier got his inspiration from him when he

4. Robert D. Crassweller, *Trujillo: The Life and Times of a Caribbean Dictator* (New York: Macmillan Co., 1966), p. 154.
5. Gérard R. Latortue, "Contemporary Political Developments in Haiti," in *Politics and Economics in the Caribbean*, ed. T. G. Mathews and F. M. Andic (Rio Piedras, P.R.: Institute of Caribbean Studies, University of Puerto Rico, 1971), p. 51.

became president in 1957, and Duvalier had much greater success. He expanded the government bureaucracy and moved blacks in at the expense of mulattoes, did the same in the army (particularly the officer corps), and created his own private military organizations made up of blacks. This enlarged the middle sector.

Duvalier came to power by a quite different route from Trujillo's. He graduated from the medical school of the University of Haiti and later gained worldwide acclaim and popularity in Haiti working as a physician to eradicate yaws. In 1957 he ran for president as a popular black candidate and was elected (he was the choice of both the United States and the Haitian military). As a student of Haitain politics, Duvalier had observed that the *Garde* (its name was changed later to the *Forces Armées d'Haiti*) was the final arbiter in politics, stepping in to overthrow governments that continued beyond their term, became oppressive, or threatened the *Garde's* interests. He decided, therefore, as a means of establishing his personal power, to emasculate the army and create his own personal military forces. Duvalier achieved both his objectives. The first—the "neutralization of the army," in Professor Gérard R. Latortue's words[6]—by removing the career officers, ending the training of army recruits, and taking away most of its weapons. At the same time he organized three groups personally responsible to him: a rural militia, a larger urban militia (the *Tonton-Macoutes*, or "bogey-men," in Creole), and a palace guard. These groups, particularly the *Tonton-Macoutes*, who went around Haiti shaking down businessmen and torturing and killing those suspected of being anti-Duvalier, constituted new and violent channels for black upward mobility. Accompanying these developments, Duvalier stressed black nationalism and *négritude*,[7] and he turned to Africa. (In 1964, to emphasize the color black, he had the Haitian flag changed from its horizontal blue and red rectangles to two vertical rectangles—one black and the other red.)

Duvalier's rule was unique in that he made voodoo a part of his system, thus challenging the Catholic church.[8] While working among the people during the yaws campaign, he had been impressed by voodoo, by the emotional effect it had on him and by its hold upon the people, and when he became president he combined it with black nationalism. Duvalier used voodoo as an instrument of government to legitimize his rule and maintain the support of the black masses. Since the church would not cooperate with him and was critical of voodoo, he attacked the church. He

6. Gérard R. Latortue, "The European Lands," in *The United States and the Caribbean*, ed. Tad Szulc (Englewood Cliffs, N.J.: Prentice-Hall, 1971), p. 177.
7. For an explanation of *négritude*, see Leopold Sédar Senghar, "Pourquoi une idéologie négro-africaine?" *Africaine Présence*, no. 82 (2d trimester 1972), pp. 11–38.
8. François Duvalier and Lorimer Denis, *L'Evolution Stadiale du Vodo* (Port-au-Prince: Imprimerie de l'Etat, 1944).

curtailed the activities of the Jesuits and foreign priests and expelled the archbishop. Subsequently, he carried out the "Haitianization of the Roman Catholic clergy."[9] Although the Vatican later approved this "Haitianization," its immediate response was to break its ties with the Haitian government and to excommunicate Duvalier. Relations with the Vatican were restored in 1966 after Duvalier made his peace with the church.

DOMINICAN-HAITIAN RELATIONS

The history of border disputes between the two countries of Hispaniola has had a racial dimension, the border having always been viewed as a barrier against a Haitian black invasion or a Dominican mulatto invasion. Although these disputes date from the 1800s, Duvalier renewed them in 1968 with the publication of his *Politique Etrangère et Politique Fronterale*. These disputes and racial feelings perhaps help explain why there has been little trade between the two countries, although considerable smuggling is carried on; the movement of persons across the border was severely restricted. (The Dominican Republic does permit the entry of Haitian workers during the sugar harvest, but they are required to leave thereafter.)

The border disputes, although recurrent, have never involved the entire length of the almost two hundred-mile border, only the southern half below the Massacre River. A provisional treaty of 1874 failed to establish the limits owing to a disagreement over the application of the legal principles of *jus postliminii* or *uti possidetis* (Haiti preferred the former and the Dominican Republic the latter); during 1929–1935, a time of friendly relations, there were a series of agreements between Trujillo and President Sténio Vincent of Haiti; in 1936 a treaty became effective providing for the cession of several thousand acres to Haiti.

Friendly relations were seriously strained in 1937 when Trujillo ordered his army to kill thousands of Haitians in the Dominican Republic.[10] Although the number killed (Haiti claimed 12,000; Trujillo later claimed 18,000) and Trujillo's exact reasons for the killings are unknown, the drastic action was easily rationalized in Dominican eyes. Not surprisingly, Trujillo received worldwide condemnation. President Vincent did not protest to the world but relied instead upon secret diplomacy, since good relations with Trujillo were more important than peasants' lives. Mounting Haitian pressure prompted him to invoke the Inter-American Gondra Treaty, and he appealed to Cuba, Mexico, and the United States for their good offices in this connection. The Mediation Commission

9. Latortue, "The European Lands," pp. 177–78.
10. Crassweller, *Trujillo*, p. 154.

finally forced Trujillo to agree to pay an indemnity of $750,000 ($250,000 was paid in cash, and the balance was later reduced to $250,000 in cash).[11]

Trujillo's regular strategy was to have a Haitian president fearful of him, dependent upon him, or obligated to him. A good example may be seen in the case of Élie Lescot. Trujillo had cultivated, bribed, and compromised Lescot when Lescot was ambassador to the Dominican Republic, and Trujillo had helped elect him president of Haiti in 1941. For a short time Trujillo had in Lescot a compliant counterpart, one who was also corrupt and increasingly oppressive. But in 1943 Lescot turned against him. Trujillo responded by organizing an assassination attempt, using some U.S. lend-lease arms and equipment. The assassination attempt failed, but Trujillo brought Lescot down by making public their personal correspondence—letters that indicated Lescot's dependence upon Trujillo—thus provoking the coup that toppled Lescot in 1946.[12]

President Dumarsais Estimé, elected in 1946, was no admirer of Trujillo and resisted his pressure tactics. He admitted the Dominican exiles and gave them funds. Trujillo plotted to have Estimé assassinated and then overthrown by conspiring with Haitian army officers. In 1949 Haiti appealed to the Organization of American States (OAS) for protection against this threat. The OAS considered the Haitian charges against Trujillo and referred them to the Inter-American Peace Committee. From this time on Trujillo bore the brunt of increasing criticism and was the target of the efforts of Dominican exiles to organize armed invasions. These attempts against Trujillo were aided by the governments of Costa Rica, Cuba, Guatemala, and Venezuela as well as Haiti.

Paul Magloire was elected president in 1950, and his rule witnessed a lull in the internal mulatto-black struggle. Although no friend of Trujillo (Trujillo had tried to have him assassinated when Magloire commanded the Palace Guard), Magloire was preoccupied with his own power and financial enrichment and got along well with Trujillo. He was finally forced out of office for ignoring the new constitution and resorting to dictatorial measures.

In September 1957, Dr. Duvalier (later nicknamed Papa Doc) was elected president over one opposition candidate, Louis Déjoie—the others had either withdrawn or gone into exile—by receiving the bulk of the votes of the black masses. The question of how "free" the election was is debatable. Almost from the start Duvalier and Trujillo became bitter rivals, using their radios to attack each other, urging each other's populace to revolt, and helping exiles to invade each other's country. They soon realized, however, that they were both regarded as dictators by the Caribbean Legion and also by the leaders of certain Central and South

11. Ibid., 156–59.
12. Ibid., pp. 160–63.

American countries. This prompted them to meet in 1958 and sign the
Agreement of Malpasse, an anti-Communist mutual assistance pact.
Their anticommunism soon put them on Castro's blacklist as well. The
continuing tensions in the Caribbean, attributable to the activities of the
Dominican and Haitian exiles and the countermeasures of the dictators
against them, resulted in the OAS Fifth Meeting of Consultation of
Foreign Ministers in August 1959. Collective action against dictators was
turned down, but resolutions were adopted condemning dictatorial
governments as being responsible for the tension.

In 1960, the Sixth Meeting of Consultation of Foreign Ministers met to
consider Venezuela's charges that the Dominican government had attempted to assassinate its president, Rómulo Betancourt. After establishing Trujillo's complicity in the plot, the foreign ministers voted diplomatic and economic sanctions against the Dominican Republic.
Although Haiti voted for sanctions, Duvalier had mixed feelings about
Trujillo's subsequent assassination in May 1961, for at least he and
Trujillo had come to tolerate each other.

Two years later a major crisis developed between the two neighbors—this time with President Bosch. After the OAS sanctions were lifted
in early 1962, the Dominican Republic had a political campaign and
prepared for elections. In the December 1962 OAS-observed elections,
Juan Bosch was elected president. Bosch, an exile for twenty-five years
and an arch foe of Trujillo, had participated in some of the attempted
exile invasions, using Haitian territory as a base and receiving aid from
an earlier Haitian government. He was violently opposed to Duvalier,
whom he claimed had planned to kill him,[13] and he had many commonly
held Dominican views of Haiti as a threat to the Dominican Republic,
even though in some of his late writings, such as *Composición Social
Dominicana, Historia e Interpretación*, he expressed warm and sympathetic views of the neighboring republic. But the persistent prejudice
against Haiti appears in his retrospective book about his short presidency,
in which he speaks of the "conflicts" with Haiti:

Today Cuba is the 'Pearl of the Antilles,' but the name originally belonged to
Hispaniola, . . . A political act, however, demeaned our island. . . . It became
divided into two separate countries, . . . And our isle ceased to be known as the
Pearl of the Antilles.
Haiti's presence on the western part of the island represents an amputation of
the Dominican future. . . . Thus, Dominicans cannot ignore that past in writing
their history, since in the last three centuries the whole course of the lives of our
people has been shaped by this factor: the existence of Haiti at our side. . . .

13. Juan Bosch, *The Unfinished Experiment: Democracy in the Dominican Republic*
(New York: Frederick A. Praeger, 1965), pp. 183–84.

. . . We Dominicans know that because Haiti is there, . . . we can never realize our full potential. We know that inevitably, because of the Haitian revolution, we will sooner or later be dragged down to our neighbor's level. . . .[14]

Bosch's crisis with Haiti developed in April 1963, first, over the presence in Haiti of members of the Trujillo family presumably lining up support to regain power and second—and more important—over the Haitian police breaking into and searching the Dominican embassy for refugees and political opponents of Duvalier. Bosch responded to the violation of extraterritorality by presenting a twenty-four-hour ultimatum demanding that Haiti stop harassing the Dominican embassy or else face the consequence of serious countermeasures; he called for an urgent meeting of the OAS Council. Bosch also moved tanks and troops to the Haitian border and ordered Dominican gunboats to wait off the Haitian coast. Duvalier responded by severing diplomatic relations with the Dominican Republic. At the request of the OAS, which had agreed to send an investigating committee to Haiti, the ultimatum deadline was extended. In the face of the Dominican war footing and Bosch's threats, and also the stationing of U.S. naval units offshore to evacuate U.S. nationals, Duvalier announced his compliance with Dominican demands.[15] But Duvalier failed to honor his pledge to issue safe-conduct passes to the refugees in the Dominican embassy, and so the crisis continued, causing the investigating committee to return to the island; by then Bosch had withdrawn his troops from the border. The committee's final report was critical of both governments, but it did not condemn either one, nor did it recommend sanctions. After a third visit, the committee issued a report calling upon both governments to resort to direct negotiations.[16] (In August 1963, the International Commission of Jurists in Geneva, which had tried to conduct an on-the-spot investigation but was refused entry by Duvalier, issued a very critical report on human rights violations in Haiti.)

Duvalier welcomed the news in late September 1963 that Bosch had been overthrown by the military. Although one of his major antagonists had been removed, his relations with the Dominican Republic did not improve much, for Haitian exiles were still permitted to use Dominican territory to organize invasions.

14. Ibid., pp. 179–80. (In a later book, *Composición Social Dominicana, Historia de Interpretación* [Santo Domingo: Arte y Cine, 1970], Bosch took a pro-Haitian and revisionist historian's position.)
15. Ibid., pp. 185–86. According to Bosch's own account, he never planned to invade, but only to bluff. He planned to have his Air Force drop leaflets upon the major cities, inciting the Haitians to rise up and overthrow Duvalier, thus ending the Duvalier regime.
16. Pan American Union, *Inter-American Treaty of Reciprocal Assistance Applications, 1960–1964*, (Washington, D.C., 1964), vol. 2, pp. 159–77.

When Donald Reid Cabral, the head of the subsequent Dominican government, was overthrown in April 1965, by an army faction with wide civilian support that demanded the recall of Bosch, Duvalier became concerned. The countercoup by the bulk of the military to forestall Bosch's return resulted in a civil war that at the outset appeared to be going in favor of the pro-Bosch side. Duvalier feared this outcome and the reports that the Dominican Republic would be a "second Cuba," for Castro was his avowed enemy and was aiding Haitian exiles. Therefore, he favored and supported the U.S. military intervention as the much lesser evil and bargained his vote in the OAS for U.S. aid. Haiti voted with the United States for the creation of the Inter-American Peace Force to be used in the Dominican Republic. Despite the civil war and the presence of the Peace Force in the Dominican Republic, Duvalier charged before an emergency session of the OAS in July 1965 that 2,000 Haitian exiles were massing in the Dominican Republic for an attack. (He implied that the United States might be behind it.) After the end of the civil war and the formation of a provisional Dominican government, elections were held, in June 1966. Joaquín Balaguer, the acting president at the time of Trujillo's death, was elected president over Bosch. Duvalier was overjoyed at Bosch's defeat and sent a cable of congratulations to President-elect Balaguer; he announced that he was resuming diplomatic relations.

RELATIONS WITH THE UNITED STATES
SINCE WORLD WAR II

Following World War II the United States continued to pursue its goals of preventing foreign influence and maintaining stability, but within the context of the cold war. A major means was to maintain relations with and provide aid to anti-Communist governments. Under the 1951 Mutual Security Act, the United States made military aid available to the Dominican Republic and Haiti and entered into bilateral military assistance agreements (in effect with the Dominican Republic in 1953 and with Haiti in 1955). As a result, both countries supported U.S. policies in the United Nations and the OAS. Trujillo was particularly vocal in stressing his anticommunism, his devotion to democracy, and his loyalty to the United States. He had two major expectations in return for his support: increasing the sugar quota and buying from the United States the quantities and types of arms he needed. He was fairly successful in achieving the former aim, partly attributable to a major lobbying campaign in the U.S. Congress, but not the latter. In the late 1940s, because of exile invasions, he engaged in an arms buildup and requested heavy equipment from the United States. When his requests were turned down because of legislative restrictions, he turned to European suppliers and also built his own arms factory.

Trujillo's international popularity started to decline in the mid-1950s as his acts of repression became known. A major act contributing to this process was his presumed order to kidnap a leading critic of his regime in the United States, Columbia University Professor Jesús de Galíndez, who disappeared in March 1956, having been flown to the Dominican Republic and presumably murdered.[17] The celebrated case was debated in the press, governmental circles, and on the floor of the U.S. Congress. However, after the rise of Castro, the United States found Trujillo to be a major liability, Batista's overthrow having suggested the inadequacy of the tactic of aiding dictators as long as they were anti-Communist. In 1960 the United States cut off all military aid to Trujillo. Total aid, both economic and military, to the Dominican Republic since World War II was relatively small, and most of it was for the Mutual Security Act period (fiscal 1953-1961): a total of $2.1 million in economic, $6.7 million in military, assistance.[18]

The major postwar presidents in Haiti—Estimé, Magloire, and Duvalier—also played the anti-Communist game; they supported the United States and in return gained an increase in their Haitian sugar quota and received some economic and military aid. In the spring of 1958, Duvalier requested a Marine Corps survey team as a prelude to a training mission for the army (there were already U.S. Air Force and Navy missions in Haiti) and sent a letter to President Eisenhower expressing regret for Vice-President Nixon's treatment in Peru and Venezuela during his Latin American trip. Besides his goal of securing a Marine Corps mission (a temporary one arrived in late 1958), which he could use to demonstrate U.S. support, he wanted to increase his internal power position vis-à-vis his opponents and obtain U.S. aid in building a jet airport. Duvalier got aid for the airport, imported a large quantity of heavy military equipment from Italy to improve his internal power position, and worked out a modus vivendi with Trujillo (the Agreement of Malpasse) so he could concentrate on domestic matters.

The overthrow of Batista at the end of 1958 was a shocking surprise to both island dictators, for Castro had triumphed over a well-armed military force, and Duvalier and Trujillo were now on his blacklist. Duvalier, however, immediately recognized Castro in January 1959 as a protective hedge. He lined up later with the United States when it broke relations with Castro in early 1961. He then capitalized on the Cuban

17. One of the best accounts is in Crassweller, *Trujillo*, chap. 21.
18. Agency for International Development, *U. S. Overseas Loans and Grants and Assistance from International Organizations, Obligations and Loan Authorizations, July 1, 1945-June 30, 1972* (Washington, D.C., 1973), p. 46.

scare to wipe out many of his opponents and distracted the United States by offering her a naval base. The rise of Castro accelerated an earlier major change in U.S. policy, which the Kennedy administration for a time attempted to make operational. Dictators were now opposed as a means of preventing foreign influence and maintaining stability, since their demise resulted in a political vacuum.

In early 1959, the Marine mission, headed by Colonel Robert D. Heinl, Jr., arrived in Haiti. Heinl assumed that its role was to train a professional army, whereas Duvalier intended to use its presence merely as a buttress to his own regime and as a means of obtaining U.S. aid. Not surprisingly, Duvalier's opponents viewed the Marine mission and Colonel Heinl as pro-Duvalier, which was untrue.

When the United States abolished the Cuban sugar quota and redistributed it, Haiti got 25 percent (Trujillo did not get his allocation on account of the OAS sanctions). A debate about U.S. aid to Duvalier developed in the United States over U.S. stress upon long-term aid designed to improve agricultural production and the standard of living and Duvalier's demand for short-term aid without any strings attached. A review of U.S. aid to Haiti by the U.S. embassy in 1960 revealed that $40.6 million had been granted since 1950, of which $21.4 million had been given to Duvalier's regime.[19] The total amount of aid to Haiti from fiscal 1953 to fiscal 1961 was considerably higher than that to the Dominican Republic. Economic assistance, for example, was $72 million (thirty-five times larger), whereas military assistance was $3.4 million (less than half).[20]

As a result of Trujillo's efforts to assassinate the Venezuelan president in 1960, the OAS had imposed diplomatic and economic sanctions upon the Dominican Republic. The OAS and the United States utilized the sanctions as a lever to bring about democratic reform and the scheduling of elections. The process was facilitated by Trujillo's assassination in May 1961.

While this bargaining with Dominican authorities continued, the United States was pursuing certain unilateral and multilateral goals against the Castro government. Unilateral action was best illustrated by the April 1961 Bay of Pigs fiasco, which resulted from President Kennedy's putting into operation a plan that he inherited from the Eisenhower Administration to sponsor an invasion of Cuba by Cuban exiles. Although the sponsored invasion provoked an outcry of "intervention" charges against the United States in Latin America, there was some definite unofficial support for it among Latin American leaders, for example, Duvalier. Prior to the multilateral approach (OAS) at the

19. Bernard Diederich and Al Burt, *Papa Doc: The Truth about Haiti Today* (New York: McGraw-Hill, 1969), pp. 140–41.
20. AID, *U.S. Overseas Loans and Grants*, p. 48.

Eighth Meeting of Consultation of Foreign Ministers (January 1962), the United States had been trying to use its aid to Haiti as a bargaining tool to curb Duvalier's corruption. In 1961, the United States threatened to cut off all aid as a result of Duvalier's arranging his own unconstitutional popular "re-election by acclamation" to another six-year term. However, at the OAS eighth meeting of consultation in 1962 the United States needed Haiti's vote to get the required two-thirds vote that would exclude Cuba from "participation" in the OAS. Haiti bargained her swing vote, assuring the OAS action against Cuba, and U.S. aid to Haiti was continued. A few months later the United States suspended almost all Haitian aid; the Agency for International Development (AID) and the Alliance for Progress announced that they were making major aid reductions. At the end of the year a limited program of aid was resumed, mainly for the construction of the airport. As the end of Duvalier's original six-year term approached in May 1963 (the month before he had requested the United States to withdraw its naval mission), the United States applied pressure, urging him to step down; economic aid was cut off, and diplomatic relations were suspended for a month in protest when the pressure was ignored. In June 1964 a rigged popular referendum made him "President for life."

In July 1962, Colonel Heinl sent a critical letter to the Haitian army chief of staff attacking Duvalier's militia, which had replaced the army, and recommending its abolition. Colonel Heinl pointed out how the president had been "using" the training mission. A few days later the United States announced the suspension of most aid to Haiti. Duvalier responded by rejecting all U.S. aid, claiming not to need it. Subsequent events, however, soon enabled him to bargain with the United States. In October 1962, President Kennedy announced the discovery of missile-launching sites and missiles in Cuba and announced the imposition of a "quarantine" upon "offensive weapons." The OAS, including Haiti and the Dominican Republic, gave its overwhelming support to the "quarantine." Duvalier gave wide publicity to his support and to the U.S. use of Haitian airfields and ports. Throughout 1963 Haitian–U.S. relations continued to worsen, mainly, however, because of Haitian abuse of the limited U.S. aid. Duvalier responded by changing from a policy of attack on the United States to one of indifference and by turning inward to emphasize *négritude*.

As already noted, Bosch won the Dominican elections held in December 1962, an outcome which pleased the United States, since he was considered to be a democratic reformer. Two months after Bosch had been inaugurated, the United States swung into action, for it believed that his government provided the opportunity for proving the efficacy of the Alliance for Progress, the new means for democratic reform and economic development to prevent Communist influence and to maintain democratic stability. A great spurt in U.S. economic and technical assistance resulted, and hundreds of officials and experts went to the Dominican Republic to hasten reform and development and to cancel out the Trujillo dictatorial legacy. The extent of U.S. influence—and even pressure—became considerable; it appeared at times that Ambassador John Bartlow Martin was Bosch's main advisor.[21] Surprisingly, during the Dominican-Haitian crisis of April 1963 (see above), when it appeared that Bosch might invade Haiti, Duvalier was able to convince some U.S. officials that he, Duvalier, was going to step down and leave the country. Despite U.S. efforts, Bosch was overthrown by the military after seven months for, among other things, "being soft on Communism." Kennedy pursued his antidictator and antimilitary policy by cutting off all aid and recalling all officials and personnel (except the Peace Corps). This action was designed to get the military to move aside and to schedule elections. The policy was unsuccessful, in this case, as it had recently proved to be in Argentina, Peru, Ecuador, and Honduras.

The assassination of President Kennedy in November 1963, came as a shock to Anglo- and Latin America, and he was widely mourned—but not in Haiti, where Duvalier publicly claimed credit for the death by means of a voodoo death curse (ouanga-à-mort).

During 1964 and 1965 Duvalier tried to get more U.S. aid by criticizing the United States, playing the anti-Communist game, trying to change his image by hiring public relations firms in the United States, and stressing tourism. On 22 January 1964, when he dedicated the opening of his pet project, the jet airport, he had his spokesman appeal to North American blacks in the hope of attracting their tourist dollars. "I think that perhaps because we are a Negro nation, the American Negro might be interested in coming," he said.[22]

Duvalier, as has already been noted, accepted the U.S. rationale for intervening in the Dominican civil war,[23] inasmuch as he certainly did not want the return of Bosch and a "second Cuba." Consequently, Haiti supported the United States in the OAS debates on the Dominican issue, particularly the efforts to obtain OAS endorsement of its action—and thus "collective legitimation"—and OAS involvement in the Dominican Republic. The instrument for these aims was the creation of an Inter-

---

21. See John Bartlow Martin, *Overtaken by Events: The Dominican Crisis from the Fall of Trujillo to the Civil War* (Garden City, N.Y.: Doubleday & Co., 1966).

22. Diederich and Burt, *Papa Doc*, p. 287.

23. For the first scholarly North American study of the civil war, see Jerome Slater, *Intervention and Negotiation: The United States and the Dominican Revolution* (New York: Harper & Row, 1970). Two subsequent scholarly studies are those by Abraham F. Lowenthal and Piero Gleijeses (see Bibliographical Note). For a legal study, see Larman C. Wilson, "La intervención de los Estados Unidos de América en el Caribe: la crisis de 1965 en la República Dominicana," *Revista de Política Internacional* (Madrid), no. 122 (July–August 1972), pp. 37–82.

American Peace Force. Despite considerable opposition, especially vocal on the part of such important states as Chile, Mexico, and Uruguay, the resolution creating the Peace Force was finally passed in late May with the bare two-thirds majority. Haiti voted for it (Haitian exiles opposed the resolution), as did the Dominican Republic. The Dominican vote was counted despite strong protest that the Dominican delegate represented an overthrown government, that of Donald Reid Cabral. The usual procedure in the OAS is for the state or states involved in a dispute to abstain from the deliberations. However, this time the Dominican vote was needed in order to achieve the required two-thirds majority, and the Council acquiesced.

The Peace Force, which amounted to a Latin American fig leaf for U.S. forces in the Dominican Republic, was headed by a Brazilian general (the commanding general of the U.S. forces became his deputy), and the Latin American contingents came mainly from countries with military governments—Brazil, Honduras, Nicaragua, and Paraguay. Haiti responded to the OAS secretary-general's request for Peace Force participation—as did six other countries, Mexico, Peru, Uruguay, Bolivia, Ecuador, and Panama—by stating that she would not participate. The Peace Force was used as a bargaining lever in the long negotiations between the two sides in the civil war in the Dominican Republic to get them to agree upon an interim provisional government. This was achieved in the late summer. The provisional government tried to stabilize the economic and political situation so that a national campaign and election could be held. In another OAS-supervised election, Dr. Joaquín Balaguer, of the Reformist party, who had been the titular president when Trujillo was shot, defeated Bosch, the PRD (Dominican Revolutionary party) candidate, on 1 June 1966. In late September, the last units of the Peace Force were withdrawn.

In 1966, Duvalier's regime bore the brunt of critical reports by the International Commission of Jurists and the Inter-American Press Association. He remained indifferent to the criticisms and announced that he would receive Haile Selassie, the emperor of Ethiopia, on his Caribbean tour. Duvalier gave Selassie a regal reception with extravagant pomp and elaborate cuisine. In 1966 the United States also slowly increased the amount of aid. Most of this aid had been cut off in 1962, all except the support for the UN malaria eradication program and the U.S. Food for Peace program. AID now provided $500,000 for community development, to be administered by CARE. By this time the Inter-American Development Bank had made three loans available to Haiti in the fields of agriculture, industry, potable water, and education, which totaled around $8 million.[24]

24. Diederich and Burt, *Papa Doc*, p. 339.

Dominican–U.S. relations have been close and good since Balaguer's election in 1966 and reelections in 1970 and 1974; the Dominican Republic has regularly supported the United States in the OAS and the United Nations. U.S. economic and military aid has continued and the amount of the former, which includes both AID and the Export-Import Bank, has steadily increased. Even though there has been impressive economic progress in terms of the annual growth rate, increasing first to 6.5 percent and then to 12.5 percent in the early 1970s, there has been little improvement in the distribution of this increased income over that achieved under Trujillo. Balaguer has remained in power, and wants to continue in power, by moving to the Right, relying upon the military. He has tolerated, if not encouraged, the Right's mounting attacks upon his leftist opponents, especially Bosch's former party, the PRD. Balaguer finally did act against the Right in September 1971, prompted by increasing internal and external criticism, when he ordered mass arrests of members of *La Banda*, a group of rightists and their hirelings apparently organized by the police. (Balaguer has had some trouble on the Right also, for in the preceding summer he claimed to have uncovered a rightest plot led by General Elías Wessín, who was subsequently deported to Spain.) In early 1973 Balaguer announced a guerrilla invasion of the island that was alleged to include Colonel Francisco Caamaño Deñó, the head of the constitutional group during the 1965 civil war. A state of emergency was declared, and the government reported the invaders' defeat and the death of Caamaño. The reported crisis was used to justify the arrest of hundreds of Balaguer's political opponents, and Bosch was accused of being behind it. Before he could be arrested, however, he escaped and went underground.

Duvalier's relations with the United States became difficult and his attitudes ambivalent, particularly from the mid-1960s until his death in April 1971. He usually supported the United States in the United Nations and the OAS and expected foreign assistance in return, frequently bargaining and trading his vote for more aid. (The last example of Duvalier's acting in the OAS came in early 1971 at the Third Special General Assembly, when a draft convention on terrorism was being discussed. Led by Brazil, the "hard line" states—Ecuador, Guatemala, Haiti, and Paraguay—walked out in protest over the limited scope and sanctions provided in the convention.) On the other hand, Duvalier attacked the United States, indicating his indifference to and lack of dependence upon her; he turned inward, stressing black nationalism, and he turned outward, to Africa. Thus, in 1969 Duvalier recognized Biafra during the Nigerian civil war. But he also tried to improve his image in the outside world and thereby attract foreign aid, private investment, and tourists.

Although Duvalier was successful in getting more U.S. aid and attracting more foreign business during the last few years of his rule, many foreign observers had dire apprehensions about what would happen in Haiti once Duvalier had died or been killed. Haitians and others speculated about the likelihood of U.S. or OAS intervention. Contrary to expectations, Duvalier's death from natural causes was quiet and caused no turmoil. His nineteen-year-old son, Jean-Claude Duvalier, became the titular head of the Council of State, a unique arrangement in Haitian history. With Jean-Claude as "President for life," the members of the Council of State were Duvalier's widow (Simone Ovide), Luckner Cambronne, minister of the interior and of national defense, and the two Raymond brothers, Claude and Adrien, the army chief of staff and the foreign minister, respectively. Until he was dismissed in November 1972, it was commonly believed that Cambronne, Papa Doc's leading hench-man, was the real power behind the throne. Cambronne's dismissal, however, and his subsequent exile in late 1972, reflect the developing role of Jean-Claude and his mother in Haitian affairs. Another contributing factor is Jean-Claude's interest in improving Haiti's image so that she can obtain aid from the United States and from international agencies and attract foreign investment and tourists.

Jean-Claude has been quite successful in achieving this goal, and the economic situation started improving in 1972, especially after a three-man Haitian mission visited Washington in March, making a strong case for the resumption and expansion of assistance by the U.S. and by international organizations. Later that year, following the visit of a U.S. military mission to Haiti, the United States placed Haiti back on the list of countries eligible to receive U.S. military sales and credit. In the spring of 1973, AID approved a $3.5 million loan for road maintenance in Haiti; and in 1974 AID joined a number of international organizations in making funds available to support Haiti's five-year development plan. These developments, contributed to by the favorable reports of the U.S. ambassador to Haiti, Clinton Knox (who was kidnapped by terrorists in early 1973 and successfully ransomed by the Haitian government), indicate both the new U.S. attitude and the end of Haiti's isolation.

A comparative look at total U.S. aid to the Dominican Republic and Haiti clearly indicates how much more the former has received, especially since Trujillo's regime. (This does not include the sugar quota, which provided under the 1971 U.S. Sugar Import Act a basic quota of 635,000 short tons for the Dominican Republic and 31,000 for Haiti.) From fiscal 1946 through fiscal 1972 (less repayments and interest), the Dominican Republic received $450.2 million in economic aid and $31.0 million in military aid, while for the same period Haiti received only $115.6 million and $4.2 million, respectively.[25] Despite these varying levels of aid, U.S. influence was still limited, even during the periods of greatest effort—in the Dominican Republic under Bosch and in Haiti under Duvalier *père*.

25. Agency for International Development, *U.S. Overseas Loans and Grants*, pp. 46, 51.

A comparison of the assistance provided to the two countries by international agencies and organizations from fiscal 1946 to fiscal 1972 also indicates the preferred position of the Dominican Republic. The total amount of aid from the World Bank, the International Development Agency, the Inter-American Development Bank, and the UN Development Program for the twenty-six-year period was $103.3 for the Dominican Republic and $31.2 for Haiti.[26] Since then additional loans demonstrate that the government of Duvalier *fils* is becoming much more attractive. For example, in 1973 and 1974 Haiti was awarded $22.2 million for highway construction and $23.5 million for her five-year plan. The Dominican Republic was awarded $24.8 million for agricultural production and $4.5 million for rural power projects in 1972; in 1973 she received $18.8 million for an irrigation project, $18.6 million for a water supply system, and $7.1 million for a cement plant.[27]

RELATIONS WITH OTHER COUNTRIES

While Trujillo sought economic and political ties with the United States and felt more comfortable dealing with dictatorial governments in Latin America and southern Europe, Bosch, while wanting to maintain relations with the United States, preferred relations with democratic governments in Latin America and Europe. His desire to reduce his economic reliance upon the United States prompted his early 1963 trip to Europe to attract European assistance. Since then, under Balaguer, the Dominican Republic has been broadening her economic ties, with the continuing exception of those with the Soviet bloc nations. Although she is still a major importer of manufactured products and has had only limited trade with her Latin American neighbors, Dominican trade with Venezuela, Mexico, and Brazil has been expanding. The Dominican Republic has been giving serious consideration to joining the Caribbean Free Trade Association (CARIFTA). In addition to an expansion of trade with England and southern Europe, her relations with Israel, which have included both economic and technical assistance, have increased substantially since the late 1960s. The main reason for these expanding contacts is that the Dominican Republic considers the Israeli model of development to be relevant. Close and extensive economic ties with Formosa continue, probably facilitated by the existence of a sizeable Chinese colony in the Dominican Republic. Finally, trade relations with Japan have been expanding.

Duvalier, more isolationist than Trujillo, avoided relations with his democratic neighbors as well as with the communist nations. In the mid-

26. Ibid., pp. 181–82.
27. *OAS Weekly Newsletter* 11 (1973) and 12 (1974).

1960s, he did make some gestures toward Africa, viz., recognizing Biafra and receiving Haile Selassie. The Haitian elite has always looked to French culture, but economic ties with France have been modest. This situation started to change in the early 1970s, however, when France began a concerted effort to expand her economic relations with Haiti. Japan is another country whose trade with Haiti has been expanding. In the late 1960s, Duvalier started to move in the direction of changing Haiti's image as a means of attracting foreign business and tourists. This program, followed by his son with increasing success, resulted in an influx of outside business; it also fostered the expansion of light manufacturing, particularly that of assembly and product transformation.

FORMULATION OF FOREIGN POLICY

During the regimes of Trujillo and Duvalier the entire machinery of government was dominated by them and all decisions were centralized in their hands. Foreign policy decision making was a one-man process, with little advice and consultation, since their legislatures were mere rubber stamps and the position of minister of foreign affairs in their cabinets was that of an assistant, usually engaged in a process of musical chairs.

Following the deaths of Trujillo in 1961 and Duvalier in 1971 the stature of the Dominican and Haitian ministers of foreign affairs changed markedly. In the Dominican Republic, Balaguer, as acting president, was very concerned about foreign policy, since at that time his country was the subject of OAS economic and diplomatic sanctions. He consulted widely with experienced Dominican diplomats, both within and outside of his cabinet, in order to make the decisions best able to convince the OAS to lift the sanctions. President Bosch, who was elected in December 1962 and assumed office in March 1973, also placed great stress upon the importance of foreign policy and was committed to a consensual process. He selected as his respective ministers of foreign relations the former ambassadors to England and the United States.

In Haiti, when Jean-Claude replaced his father, he adopted a more consensual system, employing experienced officials to help him make the decisions necessary to modify his country's image in order to attract outside financial assistance.

CONCLUSION

This chapter has maintained that the major foreign policy problems of the Dominican Republic and Haiti are to prevent or oppose foreign intervention and to reduce their economic dependency. Each country has had a fear and distrust of the other, which has a racial dimension.

Whereas Trujillo tried to "whiten" his predominantly mulatto country, Duvalier stressed *négritude* and black nationalism. Although U.S. influence has been considerable, militarily and economically, it has been limited. Both countries have played the anti-Communist game, bargained and traded their votes for U.S. aid, and turned to Europe for the arms the United States would not supply. Haiti at one point turned away from Anglo-America and looked to Africa, a change that was mainly symbolic and of short duration. During the last few years the Dominican Republic and Haiti have tried to obtain more U.S. aid, and also aid from the Inter-American Development Bank and the United Nations; they have also tried to attract foreign business, foreign capital investment, and tourists. The Balaguer Government has been especially successful in securing outside assistance, starting in the late 1960s, whereas the efforts of Jean-Claude Duvalier began to pay off in 1972 and have been increasingly successful ever since. These two governments are still strongly anti-Communist and support the U.S. Cuban policy. In an era of détente they have adopted a wait-and-see position, stressing their serious economic problems and preferring to rely upon the non-Communist nations for assistance.

BIBLIOGRAPHICAL NOTE

The paucity of works on the foreign policies of the Dominican Republic and Haiti, especially their relations with each other and also contemporary Haitian–U.S. relations—not to mention foreign policy formulation—is evident in recent bibliographies: Patrick Bellegarde-Smith, *A Select Bibliography on Haiti*, mimeographed (Washington, D. C.: Latin American Studies Program, The American University, 1969); Deborah S. Hitt and Larman C. Wilson, *A Selected Bibliography of the Dominican Republic* (Washington, D.C.: Center for Research in Social Systems, 1968); Sidney W. Mintz and Vern Carroll, "A Selective Social Science Bibliography of the Republic of Haiti," *Revista Interamericana de Ciencias Sociales* 2 (1963): 405–19; and Howard J. Wiarda, *Materials for the Study of Politics and Government in the Dominican Republic, 1930–1966* (Santiago, R.D.: Universidad Católica Madre y Maestra, 1968).

The major works on foreign policy, particularly Dominican-Haitian relations, by writers in these countries are: *Histoire du peuple haitien, 1492-1952* (Lausanne: Imprimerie Held, 1953), by Dantès Bellegarde, one of Haiti's leading intellectuals and diplomats; *Historia de la cuestión fronteriza dominicano-haitiana* (Cuidad Trujillo, R. D.: Editora L. Sánchez Andújar, 1946), by Manuel Peña Batlle, a leading critic of Trujillo, who later served him and who was violently anti-Haitian; and *La Republique d'Haiti et la Republique dominicaine; les aspects divers d'un problème d'histoire, de geographie et d'ethnologie* (Port-au-Prince: n.p., 1953; also in Spanish), by Jean Price-Mars, an anthropologist and sociologist and the best known Haitian writer. The leading book by a U.S. historian is Rayford W. Logan's *Haiti and the Dominican Republic* (New York:

Oxford University Press, 1968). For other works that stress domestic conditions but also include some foreign policy aspects, see various works by Bellegarde and Price-Mars, and Emilio Rodríguez Demorizi, the leading Dominican historian, especially his *Historia de la República Dominicana*, 3 vols. (Cuidad Trujillo, R. D.: n.p., 1944-1959); and Howard J. Wiarda, *The Dominican Republic: Nation in Transition* (New York: Frederick A. Praeger, 1969). For the leading biography of Trujillo, by a U.S. lawyer and specialist on the Caribbean, that includes aspects of Dominican-Haitian and Dominican-U.S. relations, see Robert D. Crassweller *Trujillo: The Life and Times of a Caribbean Dictator* (New York: Macmillan Co., 1966). Two other important works on Trujillo and Dominican society during his rule are: Jesús de Galíndez, *La Era de Trujillo: un estudio casuístico de dictadura hispano-americana* (Santiago: Editorial del Pacífico, 1956), Galíndez's dissertation at Columbia University; and *Dictatorship and Development: The Methods of Control in Trujillo's Dominican Republic* (Gainesville: University of Florida Press, 1968), by Howard J. Wiarda, a political scientist who has written extensively on the Dominican Republic.

Two useful works on Haitian-U.S. relations are Rayford W. Logan, *The Diplomatic Relations of the United States with Haiti, 1776-1891* (Chapel Hill: University of North Carolina Press, 1941) and Ludwell Lee Montague, *Haiti and the United States, 1714-1938* (New York: Russell & Russell, 1966); both are by historians.

There are a number of recent works on Dominican-U.S. relations and U.S. Dominican policy: G. Pope Atkins and Larman C. Wilson, *The United States and the Trujillo Regime* (New Brunswick, N.J.: Rutgers University Press, 1972), by two political scientists; and John Bartlow Martin, *Overtaken by Events: The Dominican Crisis from the Fall of Trujillo to the Civil War* (Garden City, N.Y.: Doubleday & Co., 1966). The major works on the Dominican civil war and U.S. intervention are: Theodore Draper, *The Dominican Revolt: A Case Study in American Policy* (New York: Commentary, 1968), by a well-known writer and researcher; Piero Gleijeses, *La Crise Dominicaine, 1965* (Milan: A. G. Battaia, 1973), by a European political scientist who is now a professor in the United States; Abraham F. Lowenthal, *The Dominican Intervention* (Cambridge: Harvard University Press, 1972), by a political scientist with the Ford Foundation who was working in the Dominican Republic during the civil war; and Jerome Slater, *Intervention and Negotiation: The United States and the Dominican Revolution* (New York: Harper & Row, 1970), by a political scientist.

Other useful works are: Juan Bosch, *Composición Social Dominicana, Historia de Interpretación* (Santo Domingo: Arte y Cine, 1970) and Bosch, *The Unfinished Experiment: Democracy in the Dominican Republic* (New York: Frederick A. Praeger, 1965); Emilio Cordero Michel, *La revolución Haitiana y Santo Domingo* (Santo Domingo: Editora Nacional, 1968), by one of a group of young Dominican revisionists who recommends Price-Mars' view and criticizes the racist views of Sumner Welles's classic *Naboth's Vineyard: The Dominican Republic, 1844-1924*, 2 vols. (New York: Payson & Clarke, 1928); Bernard Diederich and Al Burt, *Papa Doc: The Truth about Haiti Today* (New York: McGraw-Hill, 1969), by two journalists; John Edwin Fagg, *Cuba, Haiti, and the Dominican Republic* (Englewood Cliffs, N.J.: Prentice-Hall, 1965), by an historian; Leslie François Manigat, *Haiti of the 1960s: Object of International Concern*

(Washington, D.C.: Washington Center of Foreign Policy Research, Johns Hopkins School of Advanced International Studies, 1964), by an historian from Haiti, who is now in Paris; Thomas G. Mathews and F. M. Andic, *Politics and Economics in the Caribbean* (Rio Piedras, P.R.: Institute of Caribbean Studies, University of Puerto Rico, 1971), especially chapters by Latortue (a former economics professor at the University of Haiti, who now teaches in Puerto Rico) and Lowenthal; O. Ernest Moore, *Haiti, Its Stagnant Society and Shackled Economy* (New York: Exposition Press, 1972), by an economist; *Area Handbook for the Dominican Republic*, 2d ed. (Washington, D.C.: Foreign Area Studies, The American University, 1973), by a group of interdisciplinary researchers; Robert I. Rotberg (with Christopher K. Clague), *Haiti: The Politics of Squalor* (Boston: Houghton Mifflin, 1971), by an historian and political scientist (and economist); Richard P. Schaedel and Vera Rubin, eds., *Research and Resources in Haiti* (New York: Teachers College Press, 1973), by two anthropologists who edited this collection of conference papers; *Area Handbook for Haiti* (Washington, D.C.: Foreign Area Studies, The American University, 1973), by a group of interdisciplinary researchers; and Howard J. Wiarda *The Dominican Republic: Nation in Transition* (New York: Frederick A. Praeger, 1969).

The two major sources for all official acts are *La Gaceta Oficial* and *Le Moniteur*.

The major professional journal, which has a section on bibliography, is *Caribbean Studies*. Other sources of information on publications and conferences are the University of Puerto Rico's Institute of Caribbean Studies and the University of the West Indies Institute of International Relations.

IV

Brazil

II/Brady B. Tyson
Brazil

THE DRIVE FOR GREAT POWER STATUS:
NEW PROBLEMS FOR BRAZILIAN FOREIGN POLICY

In terms of her relations with the rest of the world, Brazil may probably be best understood today as striving for great power status and expanded influence in world economic and political systems. This aspiration is not new, but its achievement has only recently come to seem possible; for the first time in modern history Brazil has put together a dynamic (if badly biased in favor of the richest 30 percent of the population) economy and a strong, relatively efficient and decisive (if repressive and arbitrary) government. Thus, for the first time, Brazil's large population and land area and her great natural resources have begun to have an impact on other nations.

Given this new conjuncture of facts and dynamics, for the first time Brazil's Latin American neighbors have grounds for their fears of economic, political, or cultural domination by the finally awakening giant. Isolated frontiers between nations that have had little previous commercial contact are rapidly being breached as Brazil builds her tremendous new highway system and as Brazilian merchants, bankers, investors, aid missions, and tourists begin to pour into neighboring countries.

The picture is further complicated by two new, but overriding, factors of the world economic and political system: the détente among the three superpowers, the People's Republic of China, the USSR, and the United States, and the still-emerging new framework of the world economic system. At times it appears that the détente could be shattered by a succession crisis in one of the superpowers, leaving Brazil and many other nations largely at the mercy of events beyond their influence or control, and almost beyond prediction. The new rules and balance of economic power and influence occasioned by the sudden emergence of the oil-producing nations as major and autonomous actors in the world economic system are still evolving, and it will probably be some years before foreign policy makers can again rely upon some measure of predictability. The potential instability of the superpower détente and uncertainty about the price of petroleum and the kind of influence and power that the oil-producing nations will now exercise have created new uncertainties for the Brazilian government in its relations with the rest of the world.

Unless world events overtake her aspirations in a dramatic way (for example, a world depression), Brazil will likely continue to develop policies that have emerged in the past few years, policies designed to enhance her growing claim to great power status and a new, more confident national self-image. First, Brazilian diplomacy must try to open up new markets and keep the existing markets open for the export of Brazilian products, both raw and manufactured, in order to maintain the favorable balance of trade she has enjoyed for most of the past ten years. The growing edge of the Brazilian export trade is in manufactured goods, over half of which are sold to other Latin American nations. This growth in the export of manufactured goods is essential for the maintenance of the "economic miracle" on which the Brazilian government has relied so heavily for justification in recent years, because through it Brazil has earned the foreign exchange necessary to service her large foreign debt and finance (in part) the rapidly rising standard of living of her upper and middle classes. To assure the continuation of this process, which is necessary for domestic political as well as economic reasons, it is necessary that Brazil at the very least avoid the creation of an anti-Brazilian bloc among other Latin American nations and at the best use diplomacy to facilitate continued economic penetration.

The second policy that will probably be continued as Brazil strives for great power status is the maintenance of an attractive climate for continued foreign investment and a favorable financial rating with the international lending agencies. Both of these conditions are apparently necessary, at least in the short run, to maintain the pace of economic growth. Because the influence and the interests of the United States are so intertwined with those of the multinational corporations, the private banks, and the international lending agencies, it is also probably essential for Brazil to maintain a good working relationship with the U.S. government.

The third challenge to contemporary Brazilian foreign policy is new: the maintenance of access to vital raw products, specifically, petroleum from Bolivia, Venezuela, and the Middle East. Since Brazil is almost as vulnerable as Japan (importing about 80 percent of her petroleum), this may well continue to be a major (if publicly muted) concern of the Brazilian Foreign Ministry. The continued economic growth of the nation, and thus her continued political stability with the present configuration of alliances, is dependent at this time upon her ability to continue to obtain large amounts of petroleum from foreign sources. Since the oil crisis of the fall and winter of 1973–74, Brazilian policy abruptly moved from a "pro-Israeli neutrality" to an open "moderate pro-Arab" policy.

A comparison of these challenges to Brazilian foreign policy indicates two basic facts. First, the way to successfully meet them is beset with difficulties—there are conflicts or at least different emphases among them—and will demand all the skill of the Brazilian diplomatic corps in addition to a favorable unfolding of events. Second, all three challenges show to what extent foreign policy has become a conscious instrument of an increasingly conscious national development policy. Indeed, national development is the increasingly accepted way of defining the Brazilian national interest and has been for the past twenty years.

THE PROBLEM OF DEFINING BRAZILIAN "NATIONAL INTEREST"

The national motto of Brazil, inscribed on her flag, is Order and Progress, and was adopted at a high point of positivist thinking in the nation's history. The belief that it is possible to devise a rational, scientific plan persists in Brazil, especially in the army, which has been the ultimate source of authority and power in Brazilian politics since 1964. Since words and concepts are so consciously defined and developed and since such a serious effort is made to apply such rational formulas to policy and, furthermore, since the substance as well as this style of thought is relatively unknown in the United States and other nations, it is perhaps a useful exercise to look at Brazilian foreign policy in Brazilian terms and in the Brazilian language of discourse.

Brazil today is a nation whose military leaders are attempting to implement a general policy of "security and development," which can be seen as a modern translation of Order and Progress. The whole of these concepts and policies is referred to as the Brazilian model of development,[1] and it has had a profound impact not only on Brazilian foreign policy but also on many other poor nations aspiring for modernity who have evidently studied and adapted parts of this model. Under very self-conscious leadership, Brazil is seeking today to become a modern, dynamic, respected, influential, rich, autonomous, powerful nation and to create and project a more positive national self-image. Several national policies—all of them with importance for foreign policy—have emerged in the ten years of military rule, but all of them have their parallel policies in earlier, democratic regimes.

"Security," or order, has been one of the first goals of the military regime. It means the maintenance against all threats of the process of national direction in the hands of those who work in the name of the continuity of traditional Brazilian values and a traditional understanding of nationalism but use the most modern means of planning and adminis-

1. There is an extensive literature in Portuguese examining and debating various aspects of the Brazilian model of development. The best article readily available in English is probably Celso Furtado, "The Brazilian 'Model' of Development," in *The Political Economy of Development and Underdevelopment*, ed. Charles Wilber (New York: Random House, 1973), pp. 297-330. For an attempt to describe the impact on Brazilian society of the first nine years of this model, see Brady Tyson, "Brazil: Nine Years of Military Tutelage," *Worldview* 16, no. 7 (July 1973): 29-34.

tration.[2] "Security" meant the smashing of internal subversion as defined
by the military, and it became the first priority of the military government, just as it had provided the reason for seizing power in 1964. Only
very recently has the government felt secure enough to shift the focus to
"development," and this shift has been reflected in several ways in foreign
policy.

The meaning of the word "development" is much contested among
Brazilian and Latin American intellectuals. It is the word that the
Brazilian government uses to symbolize its aspirations for the nation. The
critics of the government, however, characterize the government as
seeking modernization rather than development or liberation. "Modernization" signifies the maximization of efficiency, production, and material
wealth through the adaptation of advanced technology ("hard" and
"soft") and especially the improvement by those means, of the existing
system. "Development" is used by some critics of the government way as a
positive alternative to modernization; that is, it signifies the growth
towards self-realization of the whole society, of the whole person, and of
all persons. It has a normative and humanistic overtone and encompasses
a desired set of political, cultural, and economic dynamics. Some leftist
critics, however, use "developmentalism" pejoratively as a reformist way
of frustrating the just desire for liberation and as a word to characterize
the welfare-oriented approach of the international lending agencies, the
U.S. government, and others that want to maintain control (cultural,
economic, and political) while modernizing. To the Brazilian government, the concept of development to which so much of its foreign policy
is geared implies the modernization of the national systems of production, consumption, administration, communication, transportation, and
education.

As one of the policies designed to move the nation towards development, the present government advocates a policy of "national integration." This means the assimilation of all regions of Brazil and all
Brazilians into a modernizing Brazil and the rational use of all national
resources, including human resources, in the national "development
project."

Another key, and contested, concept is "nationalism." In the context of
the term "development" (as used by both the government and its critics),
it means the realization of specifically Brazilian goals, aspirations, and

2. There is an extensive bibliography in Portuguese discussing the concept of security
as it is used in contemporary Brazil, though little has yet appeared in English beyond the
material in the books by Stepan and Schneider (see Bibliographical Note). For expositions
on the concept of security the student might consult Filho Luiz Ferreira Lima, "Desenvolvimento e Segurança Nacional," *Segurança e Desenvolvimento*, no. 134 (1969), pp. 31–39;
Augusto Estellita Lins, "Analise da Segurança Nacional," *Revista Brasileira de Estudos
Políticos*, no. 18 (January 1965), pp. 7–13; and Antonio Saturnino Braga, "Introdução ao
Estudo da Segurança Nacional," *Revista Brasileira de Estudos Políticos*, no. 21 (July 1966).

interests in order to free Brazil from "the structures of dependency."[3] The question of how to do this is, of course, one of the key issues in Brazilian politics, and the definition of and identification with nationalist policies is the focus of much intellectual and political struggle. But it is perhaps especially important to recognize that in Brazil, "nationalism" must also be understood as a dynamic intellectual and cultural process.[4]

To the degree that Brazil has become a more dynamic and powerful actor on the international scene in the last few years, her foreign policy has become a better instrument for attaining national goals—a function of national development policy—and relatively less responsive to external political events. These concepts of national goals and interest are, of course, historically conditioned. But they have also reflected the world-view of the particular interest group or elite that has dominated the political process at any given time. And in recent Brazilian history at least, these concepts have been in a steady process of modification or evolution, from generation to generation and even within generations. Brazilian foreign policy has been formed in the matrix of these often dynamic concepts and in response to the real pressures of interests and events.

Furthermore, the particular social, economic, and political background of the dominant class or elite that makes foreign policy may be a significant determinant of that group's perception of the national interest. This does not deny, of course, the evident fact that the dominant elite of the moment may quite honestly consider itself an objective and honest broker of the whole nation's interests. Since there have been several changes of dominant political elites in Brazil since 1930, such changes in perception have had an important impact on foreign policy.

THE FOUR PILLARS OF TRADITIONAL
BRAZILIAN FOREIGN POLICY

It is a commonplace to assert that the pace of history has accelerated dramatically during the past one hundred years. In the case of Brazil,

3. Dependency theory is a body of concepts developed by a group of social scientists (mostly Latin Americans). It seeks to explain how and why the nations of the Third World have failed to develop as rapidly as other nations and to describe the way in which the rich and powerful nations have profited from keeping other nations in a state of dependency. A good example of this literature by a leading exponent of this school is Oswalso Sunkel's "Big Business and 'Dependencia': A Latin American View," *Foreign Affairs* 50, no. 3 (April 1972): 517-32. For a survey of the approach see Frank Bonilla and Robert Girling, eds., *Structures of Dependency* (Stanford, Calif.: Institute of Political Studies, 1973), a collection of essays on dependency theory.
    4. For a suggestive attempt to relate the concepts of nationalism and development and to outline some useful categories, see Ronald H. Chilcote, "Development and Nationalism in Brazil and Portuguese Africa," *Comparative Political Studies* 1, no. 4 (January 1969):

one can discern four continuing threads in her foreign relations that only began to be substantially altered under the impact of industrialization, usually dated as beginning in 1930 in Brazil.

The Lusitanian heritage of the Brazilian nation helped determine that one focus of her early history would be the expansion and then the stabilization of her frontiers. The major orientation of the foreign policy of the empire (1829-89) and the Old Republic (1889-1930) was toward the frontier. The expansionist *bandeirantes* ("pioneers") began to push beyond the Tordesillas demarcation line well before the time of Brazilian independence from Portugal, in part because none of Brazil's South American neighbors were sufficiently integrated or powerful to compete in the race to occupy the South American heartland. It seems clear that the early Portuguese and Brazilian rulers and diplomats were instinctive geopoliticians, even as were the founders of the North American republic. The particular geopolitical vocabulary and rationalizations came much later, as will be noted below. But the colonial administrators, the imperial rulers, and even the patriarchs of the Old Republic clearly believed in some doctrine of Brazilian "Manifest Destiny," and there was at work a Brazilian version of the frontier as a national challenge-to-be-met,[5] though the pattern of settlement was basically different.[6]

To rationalize the possession of the interior by the *bandeirantes*, in the name of the nation, the Portuguese and Brazilian diplomats early became advocates of the doctrine of *uti possidetis*, opposing their Spanish neighbors on the continent who found it more in keeping with their interests to rely upon the concept of *pacta sunt servanda*. It might not be stretching cause and effect too much to suggest that this expansionist dynamic made it more convenient in later generations for Brazilian diplomats to advocate conciliation and arbitration as the most desirable methods for settling international disputes, since time and talk usually favor those who are in possession of the disputed territory or right.

501-24. The best survey of the evolution of the concept of Brazilian nationalism is E. Bradford Burns, *Nationalism in Brazil: A Historical Survey* (New York: Frederick A. Praeger, 1968). Professor Burns, who has written extensively on the history of Brazilian foreign policy, relates the changing understandings of nationalism to foreign policy. In a sense, this chapter seeks to update Burn's book.

5. For an exposition of this line of thought see Lewis Tambs, "Geopolitical Factors in Latin America," in *Latin America: Politics, Economics, and Hemispheric Security*, ed. Norman A. Bailey (New York: Published for the Center for Strategic Studies by Frederick A. Praeger, 1965), pp. 31-49. This prescient article, which draws upon historical analysis and geopolitcal concepts and clearly outlines the main currents of the long tradition of Brazilian geopolitcal thinking, is essential reading for the student of Brazilian foreign policy.

6. The different historical experiences and memories, which so often defy comparison, have been carefully analyzed and compared in Clodomir Vianna Moog's famous book, *Bandeirantes and Pioneers*, trans. L. L. Barrett (New York: G. Braziller, 1964). Any North American aspiring to understand Brazil would do well to start with this book.

If the expansion and consolidation of the territory of the nation was the first concern of traditional Brazilian foreign policy, Portuguese administrators and Brazilian rulers alike also saw the national interest as most vulnerable in the South, and in a sense, Uruguay, Paraguay,[7] and Bolivia can all be seen as buffer states, or neutral zones, that evolved to keep one or the other of the major South American powers (Brazil, Argentina, Peru, or Chile) from gaining a decisive advantage over the others by completely dominating the heartland.[8] Traditional Brazilian foreign policy sought to maintain a balance of power in the Rio de la Plata area, Argentina being seen (and seeing herself) as the natural rival of Brazil for dominance in the southern part of the continent. In a series of wars and interventions (1825-28, 1852, and 1864-70) the buffer belt evolved, and the Brazilian army became a larger, more modern force and therefore a more significant domestic political actor. This traditional concern with some threat from the South is still a part of the Brazilian mentality, conditioned, as is every nation's, by historical memory. And in 1972 and 1973 Brazilian newspapers gave extensive play to real and imagined conflicts and negotiations with Argentina, with Paraguay as a coy pawn between the two.

The third basic theme of traditional Brazilian foreign policy has been that of securing the recognition of Brazil as an important member of the community of nations. This coming of age occurred after the voyage of Dom Pedro II to the Centennial Exposition in Philadelphia in 1876, which awakened in literate Brazilians an interest in how the rest of the world perceived their nation that has remained very much alive ever since. The aspiration for great power status as the "land of tomorrow," pictured by Stefan Zweig in his famous book,[9] was initially expressed by cultivating and projecting an image of Brazil as a nation that was as European as the most European nation (meaning especially France), at least in the culture of its dominant but small elite. Further, the drive for recognition as at least a potentially great power led Brazil to an early advocacy of international arbitration. Brazilians also cultivated the image of having a very competent and cosmopolitan foreign service.

The fourth pillar of traditional Brazilian foreign policy has been friendship with the United States. Brazil has long harbored a desire to be the United States of South America and, thus, the equal of her Anglo-Saxon neighbor. Also, she has had some fears of isolation vis-à-vis a neighboring, united Hispanic bloc. Brazilians have written about the "three Americas"—Anglo-Saxon America, Hispanic America, and Luso-

7. It took the savage War of the Triple Alliance to reduce Paraguay to buffer status.
8. See Tambs, "Geopolitical Factors in Latin America." The whole article essentially deals with the South American heartland.
9. Stefan Zweig, *Brazil: Land of the Future* (New York: Viking Press, 1941).

America—and have seen their national role as that of a bridge nation between the United States and the Hispanic-American nations, interpreting the one to the others.

The traditional foreign policy was represented by and representative of the small, latifundia-based oligarchy that dominated Brazilian politics until 1930. It was the period of the *bacharel* (the graduate of the law school, noted for a broad and cosmopolitan culture), in which government was entrusted to the "notables" (outstanding representatives of the traditional virtues, chosen from the closed ranks of the oligarchy). The foreign policy that was derived from this base was one of "virtue" (profession of civilized values, advocacy of adherence to international law, etc.), but it was the virtue of a small club of literate, European-oriented, landholding Brazilians. In a vast country run by a small elite, without any tradition or need of trade with or dependency upon its immediate neighbors, Brazil's international situation was much like that described by Alexis de Tocqueville in the early days of the U.S. Republic:

. . . The United States is a nation without neighbors. Separated from the rest of the world by the ocean, and too weak as yet to aim at the dominion of the seas, it has no enemies and its interests rarely come into contact with those of any other nations of the globe.[10]

Thus was Brazil from its independence (1822) until about 1930. It was dependent upon the relatively benevolent protection of the British fleet, British merchants, and British banks.[11] Its economy remained to a large degree dependent upon—and was integrated into—the worldwide British commercial system, until the beginning of World War II. Although the oligarchs were unchallenged rulers in their own country, they recognized their economic dependency and happily adjusted their foreign policy to serve a system in which they, if not the great majority of their fellow countrymen, profited.

To summarize, traditional Brazilian foreign policy was largely a formal exercise, conducted on behalf of a nation that was nearly isolated from the rest of the world and conducted in a gentlemanly legal rhetoric by representatives of a cosmopolitan elite. Foreign policy tried to put the best face on, or extract the maximum advantage from, dynamics and events almost completely outside Brazilian governmental control—even the expansion of the *bandeirantes* must be viewed in this way. Where not isolated by ocean, jungle, mountains, or lack of roads and a merchant and

10. Quoted in Amaury de Riencourt, *The Coming Caesars* (New York: Capricorn Books, 1957), pp. 329–30.
11. See, for example, Alan K. Manchester, *British Preeminence in Brazil, Its Rise and Decline: A Study in European Expansion* (Chapel Hill: University of North Carolina Press, 1933); and Richard Graham, *Britain and the Onset of Modernization in Brazil: 1850–1914* (Cambridge: At the University Press, 1968).

naval fleet, Brazil was still economically a nation largely dependent upon the interests of the richer, more modern nations that consumed her tropical products and controlled the seas and access to markets.

THE IMPACT OF MODERNIZATION AND
INDUSTRIALIZATION ON BRAZIL

The modernizing effects of industrialization ensured that Brazil would not remain on the margin of international intercourse or continue to be dominated by a small caste of great landholders. European immigrants speeded up the processes of urbanization and industrialization and a new, industrially and commercially-based banking and managerial elite, a new modernizing middle class, and groups of urban factory workers appeared, affording other domestic political configurations than traditional rule by the representatives of the club of oligarchs. Finally, industrialization expanded the range of Brazilian foreign entanglements and the kinds of foreign policy postures that were necessary.

The seizure of power by Getulio Vargas in 1930 marked the dramatic end of the monopoly of power over the central government by the coffee, mining, and ranching oligarchs of the two giant states of São Paulo and Minas Gerais, though they continue to be significant political factors.

The advent of Vargas does not, however, mark the sudden emergence of a modern nation state called Brazil on the world scene. Rather, from 1930 until the present, Brazil can probably be best understood as a sometimes loose federation of several Brazils in various stages of development or stagnation. Because the country is so large and only superficially integrated on the administrative level in many sectors of government action, the central government (and foreign policy) has sometimes been subject to the ambiguities of a prolonged transition period from a government dominated by a landholding oligarchy to a modern, integrated nation state. Only in 1964 was a modernizing, integrated central government imposed (by the army), and it has, since that time, been attempting to evolve a foreign policy consistent with its own goals.

Vargas was a paternalistic caudillo with a keen sense of populist aspirations and an immense charismatic appeal. Uninterested for the most part in foreign policy, only rarely did he attempt to set guidelines for his diplomats. A flirtation with the Axis powers, probably because he found their form of government and official ideology compatible and appealing, ended under U.S. pressure and persuasion in the late 1930s and early 1940s, and Vargas displayed his political adroitness by using his bargaining leverage to extract from the United States the resources necessary to build Brazil's first major steel mill at Volta Redonda, begun in 1939. This was perhaps the first major use of foreign policy as a

conscious aid to national economic development, and the first time that
Brazilian nationalism and national development were identified in the
public mind with the foreign policy of their nation. Henceforth, foreign
policy, once the private reserve of a professional elite, would become
increasingly politicized and identified with one or another concept of
national development.

World War II marked the end of the dominance of the Brazilian
economy by British interests, but the influential, if not determinant, role
the British abdicated was taken up by U.S. corporations and the U.S.
government.

The dynamics of modernization in Brazil did not automatically
transform overnight either the domestic political structure or Brazil's
relations with other countries. "Developmentalism" really only came to
be generally accepted (at least as rhetoric) as the major national goal, both
domestically and internationally, during the period of Juscelino Kubitschek's presidency (1955–61). A group of intellectuals coalesced to elaborate and diffuse a new, popular, and dynamic concept of nationalism and
development that was designed to replace the status-oriented, legalistic
nationalism of the traditional oligarchy. The group was called the
Instituto Superior de Estudos Brazileiros (ISEB), and its members were
called *Isebianos*.[12]

It was Kubitschek who first proposed the broad outlines of the plan
that became the Alliance for Progress, calling it Operation Pan America.
He uncritically accepted the interdependence of which John Foster Dulles
spoke, and he sought to attract private foreign capital to Brazil to aid in
national development. Using the concepts of the Isebianos, politicians of
almost all persuasions began during Kubitschek's term to equate the
long-hoped-for great power status and national welfare and harmony
with national development.

An inevitable result of the politicization of great numbers of hitherto
passive and marginal Brazilians was the use of foreign policy for domestic
political purposes. The rhetoric of national developmental status and
security goals was often manipulated by politicians to gain the support of
one or another domestic political group. This in turn facilitated the even

12. The story of ISEB (sometimes called the *Grupo de Itatiaia*) is succinctly told by
Frank Bonilla in *Expectant Peoples: Nationalism and Development*, ed. Kalman Silvert
(New York: Random House, 1963), pp. 232–64. The standard work of the ISEB school is
Helio Jaguaribe, *O Nacionalismo na Atualidade Brasileira* (Rio de Janeiro: Instituto
Superior de Estudos Brasileiros, 1958). This dynamic group of intellectuals, the majority of
them from either Rio de Janeiro or São Paulo, furnished the driving ideas behind the
Kubitschek regime and the creation of a nationalist "developmentalist" mentality. The
group began to fragment during the Goulart regime and was declared illegal by the military
government. Another interesting work on the ISEB school is Candido Mendes's *Nacionalismo e Desenvolvimento* (Rio de Janeiro: Instituto Brasileiro de Estudos Afro-Asiáticos,
1963), which is concerned with foreign policy alternatives and the uses of foreign policy to
promote development. Many of the concepts of the Independent Foreign Policy evolved
from the thinking of the ISEB school.

more rapid breakdown of the gentlemen's consensus that had been the undergirding of traditional Brazilian foreign policy.

THE INDEPENDENT FOREIGN POLICY
OF QUADROS AND GOULART

There appeared to be a contradiction to many Brazilians between the twin concepts of nationalism and development as formulated and practiced in the Kubitschek years. Foreign financial interests seemed to be making the largest profits from the burgeoning development of Brazil, thus frustrating or limiting many nationalist aspirations. The traditional yearning for national prestige and autonomy had not been dissipated by popularizing it and marrying it to the concept of national development. In 1960 the successful reform governor of the state of São Paulo, Jânio Quadros, ran against the candidate of Kubitschek, who was forbidden by law to succeed himself. Quadros ran on a reform ticket, promising more development, more nationalism, an end to corruption, and efficient administration. Armed with a substantial victory at the polls, Quadros proceeded to launch his Independent Foreign Policy, reversing or modifying many of Brazil's traditional foreign policy postures. Politically, he sought to attract part of the new populist vote by the use of a nationalist, somewhat anti-U.S. (in the sense of no longer being blatantly pro-U.S.) foreign policy. Quadros sought to capture and channel some of the mushrooming desire for national identity and greatness. He spoke of a new posture of friendship with all nations, of an anticolonial foreign policy, and of the primacy of national development.[13]

Frustrated after only nine months in office by a Congress that would neither follow his lead nor give him what he considered to be sufficient power to act himself, Quadros dramatically resigned in August 1961, blaming what Vargas had called occult forces in his disputed suicide note. Quadros had by then proved himself unable or unwilling to translate his charisma and vision into practical cooperation with "the political class." He probably hoped by resigning to bring his electoral power into the streets, to force the political class that dominated the Congress to recall him and grant him the desired discretionary power to enact the reforms he advocated. He was, however, disappointed; the electoral majority did not, or could not, manifest itself effectively.

13. Quadros argues his foreign policy brilliantly in "Brazil's New Foreign Policy," *Foreign Affairs* 40, no. 1 (October 1961): 19–28. Further insight into the Independent Foreign Policy can be found in Victor Wallis, "Brazil's Experiment with an Independent Foreign Policy," in *Contemporary Inter-American Relations: A Reader in Theory and Issues*, ed. Yale H. Ferguson (Englewood Cliffs, N.J.: Prentice-Hall, 1972), pp. 35–50. The best and most extensive analysis of the Independent Foreign Policy is Larry Keith Storrs, *Brazil's Independent Foreign Policy, 1961–64: Background, Tenets, Linkages to Domestic Politics, and Aftermath,* mimeographed (Ithaca, N.Y.: Cornell University, Dissertation Series no. 44, January 1973).

The succession process became critical because the vice-president, who had been elected at the same time as Quadros but who had run on the other (Vargas) ticket, was considered by some key military men to be dangerously leftist. A compromise—installing a parliamentary system with a consequently weakened presidency—allowed João Goulart to succeed to the presidency, however. But, like his predecessor Quadros, Goulart was faced with a Congress that would unite only to block almost any presidential proposal. And, like Quadros, Goulart attempted to use foreign policy to help mobilize popular domestic support to overcome congressional opposition to his proposed basic reforms. Goulart continued the main outlines of Quadros's Independent Foreign Policy, criticizing the United States, but still seeking and relying upon aid from the U.S. government and remaining vulnerable to the pressures of U.S. banks and corporations operating in Brazil and the heavily U.S.-influenced international banks and lending agencies.

Like Quadros before him, Goulart understood national development and dignity to mean more independence from U.S. influence and control. Also like Quadros, he tried to project a foreign policy that would make Brazil a spokesman for and leader of the Third World nations. Goulart called his foreign policy one of "development, disarmament, and decolonization." In the words of Frank Bonilla, before 1961 Brazil had "always hewed docilely to United States leadership," but the Independent Foreign Policy of Quadros and Goulart was a "coherent and carefully thought-out effort to construct a determinedly independent Brazilian policy aimed at wresting the greatest political and economic advantage possible for Brazil from the present crisis in international relations within the hemisphere and the world at large."[14]

It would perhaps be an oversimplification to say that Vargas thought Brazil would become a great power if the workers could be protected by the government and certain basic industries could be built. Kubitschek, in such an oversimplification, saw national development as the attraction of foreign capital and government cooperation with and protection of all private enterprise. Quadros believed that national development could only occur if the centers of economic decision-making power in Brazil could be "Brazilianized." And Goulart added to this by wanting to break the power of the national industrialists and bankers and place the planning power in the hands of the people, through the government.

Another way of trying to capture the essence of the evolving sense of nationalism and development would be to list the impediments or obstacles as they were perceived at different times. Vargas saw the

14. Frank Bonilla, "Operational Neutralism: Brazil Challenges United States Leadership," *American Universities Field Staff Reports,* East Coast South America Series 9, no. 1 (1962), p. 1.

indifference to the common people of the traditional ruling class, along with the selfishness of foreign business, as the major obstacles. Kubitschek believed that lack of capital and know-how, often restricted by government red tape, was the chief obstacle. Quadros thought that bureaucratic inefficiency and foreign meddling were the major impediments. Goulart saw the influence of Brazilian and foreign privileged classes behind his inability to mobilize the requisite political base to make the development program a reality.

The Independent Foreign Policy was one manifestation of an attempted shift in political power toward a more inclusive political system by both Quadros and Goulart. Both presidents were essentially trying to organize the newly politicized sectors of society to offset the power of the entrenched, privileged classes. Both tried to do this electorally, constitutionally, and in final frustration, through mass (but peaceful) rallies. In addition, Goulart talked about strikes and the nationalization of some foreign industries, even some of the great latifundias. It is a matter of record (in hearings of the Brazilian Congress) how foreign and Brazilian industrialists and bankers spent large amounts of money in what can only be described as a largely successful attempt to subvert the Brazilian Congress and abort the rather clearly expressed popular mandate of Quadros and Goulart.[15]

THE ARMY ASSUMES CONTROL

The struggle to achieve the necessary political base created a good deal of social unrest and political tension in Brazil. The privileged classes talked about the "communization" or "Cubanization" of Brazil, which they attributed to Goulart. On the other hand, the shadow of U.S. imperialism was seen everywhere by Goulart's supporters.

A sufficient number of army officers were able to unite against the government and overcome their constitutionalist scruples only after they had become convinced that the authority structure of the army was threatened by the appeals of Goulart to a rebellious group of 3,000 sergeants and other noncommissioned officers. On 31 March–1 April 1964, in a nearly bloodless coup, Goulart was forced to flee the country, and the army (supported by the other armed forces and some governors of major states who thought that *they*, for a while, had made the revolution!) began an immediate purge from public life of leading supporters of the

15. Cf. Eloy Dutra, *IBAD: Sigla da Corrupção* (Rio de Janeiro: Editora Civilização Brasileira, 1963). An extensive Brazilian congressional report on IBAD (Instituto Brasileiro para Ação Democratica—Brazilian Institute for Democratic Action) was due to be published about the same week as the military coup in 1964 but was apparently suppressed. Dutra, in a sensationalist way, makes many of the charges and uses many of the documents that would have been a part of this report.

policies of Goulart and Quadros. These men, and later Kubitschek, too, were stripped of their political rights for ten years, as were hundreds of other elected public officials. These actions occurred without public hearings, communication to the accused of the charges against him, or right of appeal.

While the tanks were still rolling, and even before Goulart had had time to get to Uruguay, President Lyndon Johnson, acting upon the advice of U.S. Ambassador Lincoln Gordon, had cabled to the new government his congratulations and satisfaction that the change of government had been achieved in a "constitutional" way. The relief of the American (and Brazilian) business and banking communities was audible and visible, and the joy of Ambassador Gordon was scarcely contained. The attempts to extend the political process in Brazil and create a more equitable and democratic society were aborted when the fears of a mobilizing class of the poor became sufficiently real among generals, bankers, and businessmen to move them to action. The Quadros-Goulart efforts at political mobilization were characterized by their opponents as stimulants of "communism, chaos, and corruption."

THE FOREIGN POLICY OF CASTELO BRANCO

Nine days after deposing Goulart, the High Command of the army designated one of the chief conspirators, General Humberto Castelo Branco, to be the candidate of the revolution of 1964 (sometimes called the Revolution of 31 March) for the presidency. A purged and intimidated Congress, now dominated completely by anti-Goulart forces, happily went along.

Castelo Branco immediately sought to reverse the policies of his predecessors. Whereas they had been given to populist appeals, he remained aloof, closeting himself with his ideological advisor, General Golbery, and his master technocrat and strategist of development, Roberto Campos. Whereas Quadros and Goulart had openly baited the United States at times, Castelo Branco and his foreign minister, Vasco Leitão da Cunha, frankly proclaimed their admiration for the United States and acknowledged her role as the leader of the free world and the defender of Western Christian civilization, of which Brazil was a part. Whereas Quadros had decorated Ernesto "Che" Guevara, Castelo Branco broke relations with Cuba. At Punta del Este, in 1962, Brazil had voted against suspending Cuba from the OAS, but in 1965, with Castelo Branco as president, Brazil sent troops to aid the U.S. military in its occupation of the Dominican Republic, and a Brazilian general was made commander of the Inter-American Peace Force. Whereas Quadros and Goulart had tried to place some restrictions and controls on the remission of profits by foreign firms operating in Brazil, Castelo Branco made special concessions to some foreign firms to attract them to Brazil. On the other hand, when Goulart was president, U.S. AID managed to direct most of its loans to selected state governors (selected by the United States—the so-called islands of sanity policy of the U.S. government), thus interfering in Brazilian politics by dealing directly with state officials. Once Castelo Branco was in power, U.S. AID funds increased dramatically.[16]

The Independent Foreign Policy had talked about a Third World alliance; Castelo Branco asserted the loyalty of Brazil to the bloc headed by the United States. Goulart and Quadros had talked about nationalism; Castelo Branco and Golbery talked about the "ideological frontiers" that separated the free world from the Communist camp. Whereas Quadros and Goulart had tried to stimulate development through political means, Castelo Branco disdained politics and relied on a technocratic and autocratic approach.

Generals Castelo Branco and Golbery and Roberto Campos represented, however, only a relatively small (if markedly competent) minority of the group that had conspired to overthrow Goulart. The Americanophile policies can be traced in part to the respect and admiration for U.S. power and efficiency developed in certain Brazilian army officers (including Castelo Branco) by the experience in Italy with the Brazilian Expeditionary Force in World War II. Furthermore, an uncritical acceptance of the cold war doctrine of the Senator Joseph McCarthy period and a grounding in U.S. managerial attitudes contributed to a policy of complete identification with U.S. policies and philosophies of world politics and development.

For a while, the concept of national security was nearly identical in the minds of the military rulers of Brazil with the U.S.-inspired doctrine of hemispheric solidarity that designated the U.S. armed forces as the "shield of the hemisphere" against external threats and the Latin American armed forces as the guardians against internal subversion. But the concept of security was also invoked against agitation and anything that might denigrate the Brazilian Armed forces. In 1964 and 1965, security tended to mean stability. Since that time, it has also come to mean development.

The ideological conflict involved in defining these concepts and the national project can be partly understood as a conflict between the think

16. U.S., Congress, Senate, *Hearings before the Subcommittee on Western Hemisphere Affairs of the Committee on Foreign Relations, United States Senate, May 4, 5, and 11, 1971: United States Policies and Programs in Brazil.* (Washington, D.C.: Government Printing Office, 1971) In a table submitted to Senator Church's hearing the U.S. Agency for International Development showed that the total assistance from AID in fiscal years 1961, 1962, and 1963 (the period of the Independent Foreign Policy) was $177.8 million. The total for 1964, 1965, and 1966 (Castelo Branco's policy of Interdependence) was $450.6 million (p. 162). The reaction against the foreign policy of Quadros and Goulart by Castelo Branco is described by Burns, *Nationalism in Brazil*, pp. 120-23.

tanks ISEB and ESG. ISEB spoke about "nationalism and development," and ESG (Escola Superior de Guerra—the Brazilian National War College) speaks about "security and development," which can perhaps be better understood as "security and modernization," following the distinction made earlier in this chapter between "development" and "modernization."

The muted Brazilian Left managed to irritate Castelo Branco and the generals by repeated accusations of subservience to U.S. interests. Castelo Branco was accused of being an *entreguista* (literally, "one who delivers," i.e., a citizen of Brazil or another poor nation who sells his nation's interest or wealth to a rich nation for his personal gain; one who sells out the interest of his nation) for such acts as the concessions he granted the Hanna Mining Company. Some commentators made the mistake of assuming that the military government was permanently committed to pro-U.S. policies. In retrospect, one can see that Castelo Branco was primarily concerned with security and stability—meaning an end both of agitation (and indeed, of free political life) and inflation. In his reaction and in that of the *Grupo de Sorbonne* (as those identified with ESG were called) against the inflation of Kubitschek and the populism of Quadros and Goulart, Castelo Branco overcompensated from the viewpoint of the Brazilian army's concept of nationalism and left himself open to the criticisms—from within the Brazilian army as well as from the Left—of being a puppet of the U.S. government.

Thus, the period 1964-66 can now be seen as a period of uncritical acceptance of the doctrine of internal security, as propagated by the U.S. military. This approach encouraged the Latin American armed forces to involve themselves in social and economic programs "to aid the process of development and to act as a bulwark against revolution."[17] The military thus prepared themselves, under U.S. tutelage, for the task of nation building.

THE FOREIGN POLICY OF COSTA E SILVA

The transition of leadership from General Castelo Branco to General Costa e Silva in early 1967 gave the new foreign minister and the president an opportunity to reassert a more traditional nationalism and to modify somewhat the technocratic image projected by the Grupo de Sorbonne.[18]

17. Testimony by Alfred Stepan, U.S., Congress, House of Representatives, *Hearings before the Subcommittee on National Security Policy and Scientific Development of the Committee on Foreign Affairs of the House of Representatives of October 6, 7, 8, December 8 and 15, 1970: Military Assistance Training* (Washington, D.C.: Government Printing Office, 1970), p. 107.

18. The shift to a more nationalistic foreign policy, less aligned with the United States, as a result of the transition from Castelo Branco to Costa e Silva, has been described in some detail by Burns, *Nationalism in Brazil*, pp. 123-26.

The theme of the foreign policy of Costa e Silva was announced as the "diplomacy of prosperity," supposedly building on the necessary period of austerity and correction of the Castelo Branco period. The phrase "security and development" (the name of the official magazine of the Association of Graduates of the Escola Superior de Guerra) was much used to diffuse among the new elite the program of the revolution of 1964. On the other hand, the critics of the military government argued that, in the words of Otavio Ianni, the new regime replaced "an ideology of development with an ideology of modernization"[19]—that is, that the military government accepted the "structures of dependence" that seriously compromise Brazilian sovereignty by causing its continued reliance upon and integration into the U.S.-headed Western economic system and sets as its development priority the modernization of that sector of Brazil already in the money economy through a regulated but basically neocapitalist method. Like the criticisms of José Honorio Rodrígues of Castelo Branco,[20] the criticisms of Ianni have been more true of the Costa e Silva government than of the Médici period (1968-74).

The military intellectuals of Brazil had become concerned by the end of 1968 that the root of the continued agitation in the country was to be found not only in the activities of subversives (usually disaffected middle-class young adults protesting against repression) but also in the lack of social integration or the excessive gaps between various sections of the country and between various social classes in terms of wealth and social welfare. For these military planners the original plan of purging from the political life of Brazil the demagogic (populist) and corrupt politicians and of containing inflation through austerity measures was now seen to be only a step toward realizing the goals of the army. The army's goals expanded from an announced intention to cleanse public life of "chaos, communism, and corruption" and restrain the runaway economy by firm discipline to a total but still vague program of national development and integration. Only when this broader mission had been accomplished would the nation be ready to return to civilian and constitutional rule.

GENERAL MÉDICI BECOMES PRESIDENT

Foreign policy initiatives and declarations under Costa e Silva were largely limited to affirmations of the importance of national sovereignty, which was consistent with his rather unimaginative and noninnovative style. Emilio Garrastazu Médici, the third president-general of the revolution of 1964, assumed power upon the illness of Costa e Silva near the end of 1969. Médici was chosen by the High Command, who also set aside

19. Octavio Ianni, *Crisis in Brazil* (New York: Columbia University Press, 1970), p. 170.
20. José Honório Rodrigues, *Interesse Nacional e Política Externa* (Rio de Janeiro: Editora Civilização Brasileira, 1966). See esp. pp. 213-15.

arbitrarily the constitutional procedures and the civilian vice-president they themselves had named to serve with Costa e Silva. Médici was fully aware of the problems inherited from his predecessor, and he immediately set about to identify his administration with popular aspirations for national assertiveness and development. These included the continued refusal of Brazil to sign the Nuclear Non-Proliferation Treaty,[21] the much-publicized beginning of the trans-Amazonic highway, and the assertion of a Brazilian claim to a 200-mile maritime zone. In private conversations, Brazilian army officers have talked about the third phase of the work of the revolution; the first phase (Castelo Branco) was to establish "national order," wipe out subversion, and contain inflation; the second phase (Costa e Silva), to achieve a dynamic rate of economic growth; and the third (Médici) phase, to integrate into the nation the "marginal masses," so that they might participate in (and contribute to) national growth. In foreign policy, these phases could be identified as: (1) a period of "integration and interdependence" in the bloc headed by the United States during the time of Castelo Branco; (2) a slight pull-back from this position under Costa e Silva; and (3) a modest "national-ist" foreign policy and "open diplomacy" under Médici, to develop possible channels of cooperation with other Latin American republics.

The reaction against populist-developmentalism of the Quadros-Goulart type, which had so frightened the Brazilian establishment, led in the beginning to sporadic and later (1968 on) to systematic political repression. The traditional desire for international status, together with the myth of a nonviolent Brazil, were both threatened by the insistent reports of systematic torture of some political prisoners that began to circulate in 1969. Some countermeasures to protect the image of Brazil were undertaken, even though the Brazilian government has steadfastly refused to allow any international agency to investigate the alleged violations of human rights. And though the adverse publicity might restrict U.S. public aid in the future, all signs indicate a continued warm relationship between U.S. and Brazilian military leaders and a continued belief by U.S. investors that Brazil is a very desirable place to send capital. The impressive economic growth rates of 1969 and 1970 might have meant little to the majority of the Brazilian people (critics argued that the rates only corroborated the theory of modernizing an already developed Brazil); but, still affirming their faith in the "trickle down" theory of the industrial period, American investors and diplomats seemed little inter-ested in questions of human rights and political democracy.[22]

21. H. Jon Rosenbaum and Glenn Cooper, "Brazil and the Nuclear Non-Proliferation Treaty," *International Affairs* 46, no. 1 (January 1970): 74–90.
22. For example, see *"United States Policies and Programs in Brazil,* pp. 304–5; or "Statement of Stephen Low, Country Director for Brazil, Department of State," in U.S., Congress, House of Representatives, *Hearings Before the Subcommittee on International*

In January 1971 the Brazilian government launched a campaign of "active diplomacy," or "open diplomacy," designed to discover and test possible combinations of interests with other Latin American nations. Evidently, the relative neglect of foreign policy during the years of consolidation of the revolution and foreign criticism of political repression had left a sense of the dangers of diplomatic isolation. If, as appeared evident, Médici felt compelled to reduce even further the identification of his government with the United States, and if domestic tranquility and economic growth had awakened new visions of a leadership role for Brazil among the Latin American republics, these probes showed a pragmatic and flexible approach. Evidently, if other nations were not suspected of exporting subversion to Brazil, the military government was willing to ignore the military populism of the Peruvian government and the socialist populism of the Chilean government in its search for the role of catalyst of a Latin American bloc able to bargain effectively as a unit on the world scene, especially vis-à-vis the United States.

THE FOREIGN POLICY OF GENERAL GEISEL

General Ernesto Geisel was inaugurated as fourth president (and fourth general) of the Revolution of 1964 on 15 March 1974. Brazil was more stable, perhaps, than at any time since 1964, and only certain elements of the church and some judges and lawyers continued to protest the arbitrary, authoritarian-bureaucratic style of governance. The torture of political prisoners continued, and a struggle for power between the repressive apparatus of police and military men on the one hand, and the generals and their technocratic advisors on the other, began even before Geisel took office.

The economic policies of Roberto Campos and Delfim Neto (minister of finance under Médici) had indeed stimulated the growth of the Gross National Product, but the gap between the middle and upper classes (in which some of the professionals are now paid more than their U.S. counterparts) and the approximately 70 percent of the Brazilian people who still live in poverty or near poverty and whose lives had not been affected by the economic growth continued to grow. If Brazil was "stable" when General Geisel assumed command it was only because the poor majority had been effectively intimidated, denied free communication and uncensored news, and deprived of the right of organization, and because dissidents from among the literate classes had been imprisoned, exiled, or harrassed.

Organizations and Movements of the Committee on Foreign Affairs House of Representatives; International Protection of Human Rights (Washington, D.C.: Government Printing Office, 1974), pp. 201-2.

Domestic stability might endure for the length of his term, but General-President Geisel faced an uncertain international scene in which stability might not continue to offer Brazil the opportunities it had so exploited by export promotion since about 1967. The shifts in influence and power occasioned by the emergence of a coherent and coordinated Arab oil policy will take some years to appear and be evaluated. The détente among the three superpowers, so artfully nurtured by Henry Kissinger and so glowingly described by Richard Nixon as a "structure of peace," was already beginning to show signs of being an "alliance of the wolves against the sheep," i.e., the superpowers against the Third World to maintain the existing world balance of power or being subject to the vicissitudes of potential internal instability in first one, then another, of the superpowers themselves. A world recession or a succession crisis in one of the three superpowers promised to unsettle the balance so carefully constructed out of the remains of the cold war.

President Geisel had to write scenarios based upon these possibilities as he considered his foreign policy options. The possibility of a world recession that would severely diminish Brazil's exporting potential could substantially affect Brazil's economy and economic growth. A clear Democratic victory in the presidential election of 1976 in the United States might signal some changes in U.S. foreign policy that *could* affect Brazil. For instance, the promotion of human rights and democracy might once again become an important aspect of U.S. policy and aid. The United States might be less sympathetic to periodic "rollbacks" of the Brazilian foreign debt and to giving more aid to Brazil. And there might be a U.S. attempt to secure greater regulation of multinational corporations or even a resurgence of protectionism to conserve jobs against the threat of "cheap" labor ("cheap" because not permitted to organize or strike). Even the possibility of any one of these things occurring has to be a factor in the formulation of Brazilian foreign policy during the administration of General Geisel.

It is Geisel's task, according to the Brazilian military intellectuals, to build upon the work of his predecessors, especially the political stabilization of Castelo Branco and the economic growth of Médici, and to begin what is expected to be a long process: the "reinstitutionalization" of Brazilian politics and the phasing out of "the regime of exception." Unless strong and unexpected opposition developed, Geisel and his advisors planned a very slow liberalization of censorship and political repression—including the phasing out of torture as a tool of social control and intimidation. In part this was intended to improve the image of Brazil abroad and thus maintain ready credit, markets, and the continued flow of investment into Brazil; in part to improve the image of the army in Brazil herself. The Spinola Model of the spring of 1974, in which Portuguese officers overthrew an authoritarian regime, had a profound impact on certain sectors of the Brazilian military officer corps, who saw in the Portuguese experience a promise that the army could recapture its popularity with the mass of Brazilians—a popularity that had been eroding steadily since the army takeover in 1964. In other words, the young, idealistic officers could force a change in the rhetoric of the government and modify its more repressive practices in order to capture the imagination of the people, without really modifying the political base of the nation. Thus, a military-inspired populist, but paternalistic, rhetoric, based on the patriotism of the young military officers, would turn on the discredited "hard line" of the Médici years but would not really yield power to the civilians. Whether or not Geisel can preempt or coopt or dismantle such sentiments or whether he will be called upon to play Brazil's Spinola by young officers, the process will probably be slower and more behind-the-scenes in Brazil than it was in Portugal, and the occasion for a change will be an economic crisis rather than a question of African colonies or even political repression.

Geisel is reported by all sectors to be more of a nationalist (i.e., more distrustful of multinational corporations and banks and of the United States) than his predecessors, but also more of a pragmatist. As a nationalist he is probably eager to ransom the traditional good reputation of the Brazilian army from the accusations that it has sold the nation out to foreign investors and the majority of its people to the richest 30 percent. He is aware of the fallen prestige of the army and the fact that recruitment for the army officer corps is much more difficult today than it was ten years ago. But his options are, and will probably continue to be, severely limited, unless some unforeseen crisis occurs. As this chapter is being written, it is impossible to foresee the effects of the elections of 1974.

The new pragmatism of Brazilian foreign policy was evident in the difference between the attitudes of Mario Gibson Barboza (foreign minister under Médici) at the meeting of the foreign ministers at Tlateloco in Mexico, in February 1974, and those of Antonio Silveria (foreign minister for President Geisel) at the General Assembly of the OAS at Atlanta, in April 1974. Silveira succeeded in communicating that the Brazilian government had changed its earlier position and would now support Argentina's demand that national sovereignty over multinationals be recognized. Silveira also agreed that Panama should be granted her just demands for a new treaty recognizing her immediate sovereignty over the Canal Zone. Brazilian diplomats brightened noticeably with the advent of Geisel, commenting privately that the "primitivism" and "ideological hysteria" of the Costa e Silva and Médici days were past and that now Brazilian foreign policy would be much more flexible and subtle. More attention would be given to relations with the Hispanic-American nations, and the sensibilities of the Argentines would be considered. Foreign Minister Antonio Silveira seemed to be indicating that Brazil was abandoning its pretensions of leading, or even being an active member of, an anti-Communist bloc or a Latin American bloc.

The major foreign policy task of the Geisel administration remained: to use diplomacy to expand and sustain Brazil's export trade, especially her manufactured products. At best, Brazil can continue to earn sufficient foreign capital through a favorable balance of trade to subsidize her foreign debt maintenance and the expansion of her domestic industrial plant. At the worst, she must continue to increase her export trade to offset the increase in petroleum costs.

SOME KEY BRAZILIAN BILATERAL RELATIONS

Brazilian–U.S. Relations

Brazilian–U.S. relations continue to be the single most important component of Brazilian foreign policy and have been so considered by the Brazilian government since 1905 when Joaquim Nabuco, Brazil's leading diplomat at the time, was appointed ambassador to the United States.[23] In the late 1930s, with Great Britain beseiged by the Axis powers, U.S.-based corporations and U.S. government aid replaced British economic preponderance in Brazil.[24] The United States is more important to Brazil than any other single nation for a series of reasons: she is the single largest market for both Brazilian natural and manufactured products. U.S. corporations and banks are the single largest group of foreign investors in the Brazilian economy. The United States is Brazil's single largest source of imported technology, manufactured goods, and cultural products (films, books, etc.). Most Brazilian elitists have viewed, and continue to view, the United States with a mixture of envy, distrust, and admiration and tend to compete with or imitate the United States in certain areas of development. Also, the traditional "special relationship" that the United States assumes in relation to all the Latin American nations has given Brazil a special role in this relationship. Although both the style and substance of the U.S. policy towards the other nations of the Western Hemisphere has differed from time to time, the United States has almost always sought to have a veto power, if possible, over basic changes in institutions and policies. Brazil has been seen by the United States as the essential pillar of stability and continuity on the South American continent.

Since the rise to power of Fidel Castro, U.S. policy towards all of Latin America has been affected by certain cold war attitudes and policies. In part, the Alliance for Progress was designed to preempt the awakening movement for reform or revolution, and the United States attempted to

23. This very conscious evaluation of the primacy of relations with the United States is told in Carolina Nabuco, *The Life of Joaquim Nabuco*, ed. and trans. Ronald Hilton (Stanford, Calif.: Stanford University Press, 1950), chap. 25.
24. See n. 11, above.

send significant support to governments of the "democratic left." Both Presidents Kubitschek and Quadros benefited to a limited extent from this new attitude of the U.S. government. But early in 1964 there was a significant—for Brazil—policy change in Washington. The U.S. government decided either that the Alliance for Progress was destined to fail or that it tended to awaken more discontent than it could resolve and that henceforth the United States would not shy away from stability-oriented military regimes.[25] No doubt encouraged both by this shift in policy and by top U.S. diplomats and military personnel in Brazil at that time, the Brazilian army soon seized power.

Even if it cannot be demonstrated that U.S. influence was decisive in the turbulent sixties in Brazil, it is evident that there was an active AID, military, and diplomatic policy during this period. By the beginning of the 1970s a pattern was fixed. The U.S. and Brazilian governments were working closely with each other, each regarding the other as a staunch ally.[26]

The inauguration of President Geisel can be seen as the end of the period of consolidation of the military government and the beginning of a more self-confident and pragmatic foreign policy. It also marks the resurgence of some temporarily repressed nationalist feelings both within and outside of the army. Brazil remains committed to attracting foreign investment, but she is trying to diversify its source so that her dependence upon capital from any one nation is reduced. Prudent and selective attempts to increase national control over sectors of the economy deemed "sensitive to the national security" and attempts to promote the "Brazilianization" of the executive and technical forces in such key industries and commercial sectors as mass communications and strategic minerals do not appear to be affecting the relationship between the two governments.

Brazilian Policies towards Her South American Neighbors

In his first major address upon taking office, President Geisel declared: ". . . We will give emphasis to our relations with our neighboring sister-

25. If a specific turnaround date could be specified, perhaps 18 March 1964 would be as adequate as any. On that date Thomas Mann, undersecretary of state for Inter-American Affairs, reportedly addressed a meeting of U.S. ambassadors to Latin America, expressing the opinion that henceforth the United States would not actively oppose military takeovers in Latin America but would be more concerned with supporting anti-Communist groups, and obtaining security for U.S. investments. This Mann Doctrine certainly was not a negative signal to the Brazilian military, who seized power about two weeks later. This episode is recounted by Edwin Lieuwen, *Generals vs. Presidents: Neo-Militarism in Latin America* (New York: Frederick A. Praeger, 1964), p. 142.

26. See Peter Bell, "Brazilian-American Relations," in *Brazil in the Sixties*, ed. Riordan Roett (Nashville, Tenn.: Vanderbilt University Press, 1972), pp. 77–102, for the best available description and analysis of U.S.-Brazilian relations in this period.

nations, both on the continent and beyond the sea. We will encourage our diplomacy to be always alert to discover new opportunities and be of particular help to our foreign commerce, in order to guarantee an adequate supply of primary materials and essential products and access to the most modern technology that we do not yet have. . . ."[27] Thus, Brazilian diplomacy appears to be increasingly at the service of the dynamic Brazilian export trade, with its leading edge of manufactured products. The South American continent and the African nations of the "South Atlantic community" would appear to be the natural potential markets for a "Japanese-style" export trade, except that Brazil intends to find its expanding markets among poor nations rather than among the rich nations as do the Japanese.

There can be no doubt that the new Brazilian dynamism—the rapid growth of the Brazilian economy, especially the export trade; the redefinition of national goals, and the "national integration" programs—has raised the level of anxiety of Brazil's South American neighbors. Brazilian economic, cultural, and touristic penetration of its neighbors has increased rapidly, assisted by Brazilian diplomacy. The Trans-Amazonic and Peripheric highway systems are admittedly based on geopolitical concepts of a strong, integrated nation, and the Peruvians, Colombians, and Venezuelans must wonder what it will be like when the "collossus of the South" reaches full maturity as an economic power. For the first time in her history Brazil is expanding to occupy as an integrated national system the land up to her borders, and she is seeking greater interchange with her neighbors. Both the Bolivians and the Paraguayans are aware that they are becoming more and more integrated into a Brazil-centered economic system, and they find themselves in a much less favorable position via-à-vis Brazil than Mexico's position vis-à-vis the United States.

Argentina, Brazil's traditional rival for leadership of a nascent South American, or Latin American, bloc, now seems destined to fall steadily behind its northern neighbor. Brazil's land mass, natural resouces, population size and growth rate, and newly found economic dynamism and governmental efficiency and decisiveness need only be compared with Argentina's continuing political stalemate, relative lack of economic growth, and more stable rate of population growth. There have been open conflicts between the two nations, especially over the use of the water of the Paraná River, but the less obvious competition for economic paramountcy in Paraguay, and to a lesser degree in Uruguay, is probably more important. Buenos Aires has become a prime attraction for Brazil's *nouveaux riches*, thus making more obvious to all the growing disparity between the wealth and power of the two nations.

27. Untitled and undated mimeograph of President Orlando Geisel's address to the first meeting of his cabinet, p. 6; my translation.

Uruguay continues to occupy the role of a buffer state, but her internal instability would offer an open invitation to intervention and division.

The Chilean coup d'état of 11 September 1973 eliminated a potential concern of the Brazilian government, which saw in Salvador Allende a potential source of subversion and popular mobilization that could be contagious. In spite of the fact that General Pinochet, chief of the Chilean junta, was rebuffed at the inauguration of General Geisel in early 1974 by a Chilean proposal to form an anti-Communist alliance between Chile and Brazil, the traditional good relations between the two nations seemed firmly established. Brazil was the first government to recognize the new military government in Chile in 1973.

Bolivia has long been the object of covert expansionist desires by several of her neighbors, representing as she does a sort of geopolitical heartland of the South American continent. Her three more powerful neighbors, Chile, Peru, and Brazil, still occasionally try to use Bolivia in their competition. Chile and Brazil are both concerned with the apparent military populism of the Peruvian generals and tend to use their influence in Bolivia for anti-Peruvian purposes. Meanwhile, illegal but apparently spontaneous migration of Brazilian peasants into eastern Bolivia (long coveted by some Brazilian geopolitical thinkers) has apparently increased, as has Brazilian economic penetration of Bolivia. Also, Brazilian trade, cultural, and military missions are much in evidence in La Paz, and the Bolivian government seems willing to accept Brazilian protection and assistance.

Many Peruvian and Brazilian generals now apparently believe that the real contest for leadership and dominance in South America lies between the Brazilian and the Peruvian models.[28] The Peruvian vision of a restored Inca empire, embracing the Andean heartland and the dorsal spine of the continent, is not palatable to the Brazilian government, which has its own grand design that includes a strong Brazil bordered by a series of relatively weak and independent Hispanic-American nations.

Brazilian Policy towards Portugal

Portuguese-Brazilian relations represent a special case of cultural and historical bonds and affinity that is important to both nations and their respective self-images. Friendship with Portugal has traditionally been used by Brazilian politicians as a way of strengthening conservative domestic political support; opposition to Portugal and its traditional colonial policies has usually represented an attempt to mobilize new sectors into political activity in Brazil or to secure Third World UN votes

28. For an attempt to compare and analyze the different mentalities of the two army officer corps see Brady Tyson, "The Emerging Role of the Military as National Modernizers and Managers in Latin America: The Cases of Brazil and Peru," in *Latin American Prospects for the 1970s: What Kinds of Revolutions?*, ed. David H. Pollock and Arch R. M. Ritter (New York: Praeger Publishers, 1973), pp. 107–30.

or new African markets for Brazilian exports. The Independent Foreign
Policy had as one of its three main policies "decolonization," with
Angola and Mozambique specifically in mind. The tension thus created
with the Salazar government was speedily undone, and traditional close
ties were reestablished by Castelo Branco in 1964, with a consequent shift
in the Brazilian position in the United Nations. Brazil has wanted to be
a friend of her "little grandfather" Portugal (as that nation is often
affectionately but perhaps also a bit condescendingly called in Brazil) but
also to open up markets and friendships in black Africa. The coup d'état
in Lisbon in April 1974 created great excitement in Brazilian army circles,
because it apparently opened up the way to be both pro-Portugal and pro-
black Africa. It also cast the Portuguese army in the role of the protector
and Godfather of the poor and of democracy—a role that the Brazilian
army believes it has traditionally played and that some of its members
would like it to assume once again.

Brazilian Policies towards International and
Regional Organizations

Brazil has traditionally championed the development of international law
and arbitration and has found avenues to express her frustrated sense of
greatness in the forums of the League of Nations and international
conferences. Her diplomats still cherish the United Nations and play an
effective role in its activities, considering Brazil's relative political weakness in the United Nations, where only solid voting blocks and superpowers have real leverage. Brazilian diplomats, however, have begun to return
to another aspect of the much deprecated Independent Foreign Policy in
their UN activities: cultivating the friendship of the African nations with
an eye to obtaining new markets for Brazilian goods.

The rapid growth of the Gross National Product, the dramatic decrease
in the rate of inflation, and the political stability that are associated with
the first ten years of the military regime in Brazil have tended to make
Brazil an attractive model and partner not only for the private multinational corporations and banks but also for the international lending
agencies, such as the World Bank, the International Monetary Fund, and
the Inter-American Development Bank. The reservations about the
trends in income distribution in Brazil expressed by the president of the
World Bank, Robert McNamara, at the Third UN Conference on Trade
and Development (UNCTAD), in Santiago in September 1972, did not
seem to affect confidence in Brazil as an economy worthy of loans and
investment.

Historically, Brazilian diplomats have always remained a bit aloof
from the Organization of American States, even while participating fully
in its formal meetings and organization. Except for the period of the
Independent Foreign Policy, when Brazil aspired to be one of the leaders

of a Third World bloc, Brazilian governments have traditionally felt that if U.S.–Brazilian relations were good, the OAS would have little to offer Brazil. But the inauguration of President Geisel signifies a renewed interest in good relations with Brazil's Hispanic neighbors, for the reasons previously outlined. Without aspiring to a leadership role, the new pragmatism will nonetheless try to integrate Brazil into the Latin American majority—a majority that can speak on a parity with the United States without being compulsively defensive.

The Brazilian attitude towards the Latin American Free Trade Association (LAFTA) has been, at best, ambivalent. LAFTA is seen as especially cumbersome, because it requires coordination among several governments, private corporations, and banks, and it is seen as subject to sabotage through noncooperation by U.S. and other foreign-based multinational banks and corporations who do not want to be frozen out of lucrative markets and investment possibilities. Increasingly, as the economy grows and diversifies, Brazilians are coming to feel that LAFTA is unnecessary and that the natural process of Brazilian economic growth will integrate the area in a way more efficient and more in keeping with Brazilian interests than the regional grouping. It is no secret that both Brazilian government planners and some top Brazilian banking and industrial planners have studied the Japanese model of trading companies and also the kind of close cooperation between the leaders of the private industrial sector and the government that has characterized modern Japan. Certainly, the relative economic inferiority of her Hispanic neighbors offers little incentive to Brazil to accept the rules of "sovereign equality" among nation states as long as there are other channels in which her superior economic power can be exercised.

Brazilian Policy towards Africa

It was the advocates of the Independent Foreign Policy who first discovered Africa as a potential ally and market for Brazil. The years of the "hard line" that immediately followed the coup of 1964 reversed this emphasis, but it later reappeared. During the more ideological days there was some talk, especially among Brazilian naval officers, of an alliance with such stalwart anti-Communist nations as South Africa, Greece, and Indonesia. Today's pragmatic policy tends to be neither anticolonial nor obsessively anti-Communist (in international affairs, at least). Brazil seeks markets for both her raw products and her rapidly expanding line of manufactured items among African nations of whatever ideology, race, or political organization.

Brazilian Policy towards the Socialist Nations

One of the first acts of the military government in 1964 was to break off relations with Cuba. Time has not only given a new sense of power and security to the Brazilian military government, it has also diminished both the appearance and the reality of any Cuban-based continental subversive movement. Nonetheless, Brazil will probably not take the lead in reversing the decision to expell Cuba from the OAS but will await U.S. initiative or support for such a proposal from another quarter.

The military government never really stopped trying to expand its trade with the Soviet Union and in 1973 initiated serious but limited efforts to establish commercial links with the People's Republic of China. These latter efforts have had some domestic repercussions, since they are seen by some as "an opening to the Left"—although the government's reasons are probably much more economic than political.

Brazilian Policy towards Western Europe

Historically, strong commercial links with Great Britian—which continue to be significant—cultural ties with France and Germany, and a desire to identify with the anti-Communist free world have sustained Brazil's interest in Western Europe. European investment in Brazil has increased, as has trade. Inevitably, an integrated Europe would be a major competitor for the markets for manufactured goods that are so important to Brazil during the 1970s.

THE FORMULATION OF FOREIGN POLICY IN CONTEMPORARY BRAZIL

Brazil, like almost all other Latin American republics, invests in its president the power to formulate and administer foreign policy and conduct foreign relations. The Congress is limited to the approval of treaties, the confirmation of diplomatic appointments, and the appropriation of funds. Even this limited power of the legislative branch is more illusory than real in the present Brazilian political system, since the dominant political party is really controlled by the executive branch.[29] Thus, the key questions in the formulation of foreign policy in Brazil today are the following:

1. To what political restraints (domestic and international) is the president subject in the formulation of foreign policy? What is the basis of his political support, and to what pressure groups is he accessible?
2. What type of information and analysis does the president receive? Who are his advisers, and how are they chosen?
3. What are the president's concepts, or models, of international politics, his sense of national image and goals, and his perceptions of the roles of foreign policy?

29. For a description of the progressive debilitation of the Brazilian Congress, see Brady B. Tyson, "Brazil Congress a Rubber Stamp," *Washington Post* (Outlook Section), Sunday, 4 April 1971.

Since the army took power in 1964, the president of Brazil has in many ways been able to operate on a "Bonapartist" model, i.e., he is relatively free from domestic political pressures because his actions are subject to veto and significant influence only by the High Command of the army and because he owes his political position and the power of his administration to the fact that the army is effectively loyal to the High Command. The army regimes have, in practice, opted for an alliance with certain national and multinational corporations and banks and with large sectors of the middle and upper class in Brazil, including many professionals. These are the groups that have both created and profited the most from the process of rapid economic growth that has been the chief legitimizing claim of the army-backed regimes. In exchange for governmental policies that stimulated the kind of economic growth that Brazil has experienced since 1964, the classes favored by this process conceded the right to participate in the political process almost exclusively to the army. Nonetheless, it is probable that these tacit alliances must increasingly have a certain inhibiting effect on the president's freedom of action in foreign policy matters. In specific policies, however, the president and his foreign minister are still largely insulated from specific pressure groups.

To the degree that he demands information, the president of Brazil is no doubt well served, not only by Itamaraty (the common name for the Brazilian Foreign Ministry—taken from the old palace that was for many years its headquarters in Rio) but by the military intelligence services. There is probably a lingering distrust between these two groups of advisers, but Itamaraty is well aware where political power resides in contemporary Brazil and has a history of accomodating its long-range perspective of the national interest and goals to the political demands and rhetoric of the group in power.

The four army generals who have occupied the post of president since 1964 have all been loyal career officers, more easily understood as organization men and tough executive types than as ideologues. Anticommunism is a convenient way to denigrate antihierarchical (or rival hierarchical) movements. The driving concept behind each of these men has been that of a modernized, efficient, respected Brazil, assuming its rightful place in the sun. Foreign policy for them has been one of many instruments to be used pragmatically in promoting this vision of the national interest.

The Brazilian foreign service has a justified reputation as a highly professional corps of competent diplomats.[30] Until very recently, even many years after foreign policy issues had begun occasionally to be made domestic political issues, the men of Itamaraty usually managed to insulate themselves from domestic political pressures. Even the president

---

30. For a description and critical analysis of the Brazilian Foreign Service, see H. Jon Rosenbaum, "A Critique of the Brazilian Foreign Service," *The Journal of Developing Areas* 2, no. 3 (April 1968).

of the Republic, usually thinking of himself as a symbol of national unity and above politics, tended to play the role of the moderating power keeping order among the elites, as Dom Pedro I and Dom Pedro II and the presidents of the Old Republic had done. This meant that the president tended to act more as a cross between a chief of staff who delegated basic decisions to trusted senior lieutenants (such as the members of his cabinet) and a patriarchal "Godfather." In practice, foreign policy had been left almost entirely to the suave professionals of Itamaraty until the presidency of Juscelino Kubitschek; since that time it has been steadily integrated more and more into national development policy. The traditional insulation of the foreign policy process from domestic politics has sometimes extended to the point that even with a very weak government at home, Brazilian diplomats have been able to pursue an active and successful foreign policy, thus offering an exception to an old rule-of-thumb of diplomacy.[31]

The corps of diplomats that has earned such a distinguished reputation is not without its own concepts of national interest and development. Drawn until very recently from the sons of the highest and most sophisticated (i.e., most Europeanized) levels of the traditional Brazilian oligarchy, it has continued to pursue such traditional foreign policy goals as the achievement of international status, the advocacy of arbitration to settle international disputes, and friendship and equality with the United States—even after successive presidents, beginning with Kubitschek, began to direct foreign policy toward achieving national developmental goals and after nationalism came to be something more than a literary exercise for the sons and daughters of the elite. Except for a small group of diplomats, the populist rhetoric of an alliance with the Third World was alien to Itamaraty's traditional style and attitudes. Only Santiago Dantas, Antonio Houaiss, Josué de Castro and a few others were able to sound as if they fully accepted the postulates of the Independent Foreign Policy. On the other hand, with the subtle intelligence of the true professional, Itamaraty used the rhetoric of the Independent Foreign Policy, adapting it to traditional concepts and styles, assimilating many of the new concepts of the *Isebianos* into their own understanding of Brazilian national goals. The flexibility of the professional Brazilian diplomat can be well illustrated by the fact that the last foreign minister of João Goulart, João de Araujo Castro, who had articulated the foreign policy of the "Three D's" (disarmament, decolonization, and development) for Goulart, not only survived the purges that followed the military coup of 1 April 1964 but became the ambassador to the United States in 1971.

31. A case in point would be the way in which the Brazilian delegation headed by the brilliant Santiago Dantas defied John Foster Dulles at Punta del Este in 1962 on the question of sanctions against Cuba. At that moment Brazil's domestic politics was a shambles and its president a political basketcase. This ought to illustrate that diplomatic skill can occasionally negate the old truism, "strong government, strong foreign policy."

The *Isebianos* had begun the task of integrating foreign policy into a national policy of development. In spite of the apparent divergences, the military-managerial approach of the military governments since 1964 has reenforced the tendency to replace the traditional diplomacy with one more geared to a broader (though economist) concept of a total national policy of security and development. The military governments, however, have interfered little in the day-by-day administration and execution of foreign policy, preferring to integrate foreign policy into their national policy by direction through the foreign minister. Thus, many of the traditional attitudes persist, although at the service of a somewhat more demanding central government and with a set of national goals that has been derived from both the traditional nationalism of the period before the Independent Foreign Policy and from the concepts of the *Isebianos* of the Quadros-Goulart years as well. Though the military modernizers who rule Brazil today are not to be identified with the old oligarchy, nor with the populist politicians they overthrew in 1964, there is a basic compatibility between the traditional elitism of Itamaraty and the modernizing managerialism of the army officers that affords a basis for a harmonious relationship. But the sophistication of the Brazilian diplomat affords him little doubt as to who really wields power in contemporary Brazil; thus, in any conflict between Itamaraty and the army or the presidency, the diplomat will tend to anticipate and prevent the conflict by accomodating the dominant domestic political force.

In many ways, the modernizing, military-managerial mentality, with its particular type of flexibility, its sense of both tactics and strategy (and the relation between the two), its geopolitical understanding of world politics, its acceptance of hierarchically- and functionally-defined spheres of decision making, its acceptance of the role of the expert, and its healthy respect for the capabilities and uses of technocrats, is ideally suited for leading a national process of modernization (as differentiated from development) and integrating foreign policy into that process. Even while ISEB was developing its concepts of a national project of development, the Higher War College (ESG) was simultaneously but separately arriving at many of the same ideas, though clothed in different language and embodying some radically different social values. The ESG approach sees foreign policy, for instance, as consciously integrated in an overall national policy that is derived from the explicit "permanent national objectives" and made concrete in annually revised "immediate national objectives."[32] The ESG is the think tank to which leading Brazilian

32. "Permanent National Objectives"—"Objetivos Nacionais Permanentes" (usually abbreviated in the ESG literature as ONP) and "Immediate National Objectives"—"Objetivos Nacionais Atuais" (abbreviated ONA). These two terms are only part of a complex and very important special language that has been developed by the ESG in its role as official national think tank. For an excellent survey of this special language and these concepts, see Thomas G. Sanders, "Development and Security are Linked by a Relationship of Mutual Causality," *American Universities Field Staff Reports,* East Coast South

diplomats come each year to lecture and to which selected diplomats are invited for a year of study. From these lectures, discussions, and reports a continuously evolving national project is made available, complete with alternate scenarios, to the decision makers and national planners of the various ministries of the central government. In this way, foreign policy is projected as an integrated part of a national development plan. This almost praxiological method perhaps allows for even more flexibility and experimentation than the traditional styles of foreign policy formulation and application. Certainly, the diplomats of Itamaraty are much more involved than ever before in the process of the definition of national goals and programs (with the few exceptions, previously noted, of those who supported the Independent Foreign Policy).

But the authoritarian, centralized, and technocratic nature of the post-1964 government does not mean that foreign policy has never been used by a military government for purposes of domestic political mobilization, as it was often used by recent civilian and constitutional governments. During the Costa e Silva and Médici regimes a more nationalistic foreign policy, less closely identified with the United States, was at least partially a concession to some elements in the army officer corps and the Brazilian banking and industrial community. President Médici, with a touch of the flair of the authoritarian-populist leader, used foreign policy on occasion to increase the popularity of his regime and to identify it with Brazilian patriotic themes and nationalist aspirations. President Geisel's rhetoric of liberalization and a pragmatic approach (as opposed to an ideological approach) is also partially designed to gain support among certain other groups—in this case to placate certain banking and industrial elements allied with multinational firms. In both cases it is interesting to note that the president used the appearance of a foreign policy that moderated his approach to placate his critics. It is an old tradition in Brazilian foreign policy. Quadros used a leftist foreign policy to placate the critics of what were really rather conservative domestic programs. Médici used the appearance of a nationalist foreign policy to compensate for continued cooperation with multinational corporations and banks. Geisel, always considered more of a nationalist, has made moves in conformity with an internationalist and pragmatic foreign policy. Thus, even in an authoritarian regime such as Brazil's, foreign policy is used not only to im-

America Series 15, no. 3 (1971). The title of the article is a quote from an address by the first military president, Humberto Castelo Branco. Sanders has captured the flavor of this language in addition to describing its content. When he wrote this article the emphasis was still heavily on security, whereas with the advent of President Geisel the emphasis has moved towards development. See also *Segurança e Desenvolvimento*, no. 138 (1970), especially the article by Francisco de Souza Brasil, "Objetivos Nacionais Permanentes," pp. 107–19. Also, cf. General A. de Lyra Tavares, *Segurança Nacional: Antagonismos e Vulnerabilidades* (Rio de Janeiro: Biblioteca do Exército, Editora, 1965).

plement the national development plan but to reenforce the government's selfimage and domestic propaganda, to broaden its political base, or to undercut its critics. This domestic propaganda, in turn, must be seen as part of the system of social control (as differentiated from mobilization) and the continuous quest for legitimacy.

CONCLUSIONS AND PROSPECTS

Brazil appears to be emerging from a long period in which most of her energies were necessarily absorbed in domestic struggles into a time in which she must necessarily devote a good deal of attention to foreign affairs. What is remarkable is that this transformation has occurred without any basic modification of the traditional paternalistic and authoritarian style of governance and that Brazil still retains a prerevolutionary political and social system. The continuity of the traditional Brazilian political system—usually called the system in Brazil[33]—has successfully withstood the assault of the *Estado Novo* of Vargas and the populist interlude of Quadros and Goulart and has even incorporated some elements of these into itself. The essence of the system is not, as *O Estado de Sao Paulo* continues to affirm,[34] rule by a gentlemanly club of oligarchs, which characterized pre-1930 Brazil. The essence of the system is continuity of paternalistic-authoritarianism and containment of all attempts at initiative from below. The system insists that continuity of rule by the elite, in the name of traditional Brazilian values, must be maintained, even if this means some change in the dominant elites. One way to interpret recent Brazilian history would be to claim that the laissez-faire ideology of the entrepeneurs of Brazilian commerce and industry was no longer able to maintain a stable government, and a military elite was needed to contain the rising tide of expectations.

Developmentalism has become very much a part of the ideology of the competing elites in Brazil, and indeed a part of the popular consciousness, associated by all with nationalism. These new goals for the nation

33. The concept of the system—very old in Brazilian political reflection but very often used with the carelessness with which North Americans talk of the establishment—was brilliantly developed by a conservative critic, Oliveiros S. Farreira, in a series of essays in *O Estado de São Paulo* (see n. 34, below) in 1964 and 1965. Ferreira, who is professor of political science at the University of São Paulo and an editor of *O Estado*, was appealing for a genuine corporatism as opposed to rule by a corporatist elite without any sense of organic solidarity with the nonelite members of their respective syndicates or corporations. For a summary and definition of "the system" in English, three excellent essays by James Rowe are very useful: "The 'Revolution' and the 'System': Notes on Brazilian Politics," *American Universities Field Staff Reports*, East Coast South American Series, vol. 12, no. 3 (1966) (part 1); vol. 12, no. 4 (1966) (part 2); vol. 12, no. 5 (1966) (part 3).

34. *O Estado de São Paulo* is one of the two or three most influential Brazilian daily newspapers, generally thought of as representing a very conservative (but pro–U.S.) business and banking community in the city of São Paulo.

were initially developed by ISEB and the ESG independently, using different language and with some significant difference in their models. Even when the army intervened in 1964 to maintain the essence of the system, the evolution of a doctrine of national development was not permanently interrupted. The concept of development was significantly narrowed to exclude many of its political and social connotations, as developed by ISEB. Since then foreign policy has been used to protect the security and stability of Brazil, and more recently to promote development.

The main use of Brazilian foreign policy as a tool of national development policy will be to protect and promote Brazil's export trade, in order to sustain the economic growth that is the justification and support of the military regime. This means that, at the very least, an alliance of the Hispanic-American states against Brazil must be avoided, and Brazil must be seen as a helpful and friendly member (not an aspirant for hegemony or leadership of a bloc) of the Latin American community of nations. Furthermore, Brazilian diplomats must aid Brazilian exporters to open new markets, wherever they may be. President Geisel began his term by focusing on Brazil's South American neighbors and the nations of the west coast of Africa, but the whole world is obviously under constant survey for potential markets. To protect Brazil's import trade, its favorable balance of trade and favorable credit ratings, and her attractiveness to foreign investors, Brazilian diplomats must promote abroad the image of a stable, happy, growing Brazil. The government of the United States and the international and regional organizations and lending agencies must continue to believe in the Brazilian model. Brazilian diplomats must be active; Brazil cannot afford to be isolated or overidentified with any bloc. For instance, Brazilian diplomats, like the Japanese, must assiduously cultivate contacts with oil-producing nations, given Brazil's vulnerability in this field.

The Brazilian model of development—much like the Japanese model —is based on promoting exports by concentrating capital and exploiting both cheap labor and the aggresivity and skill of Brazilian traders. Thus, the tendency at home is for the leaders of the Brazilian government, the export manufacturers, and the national bankers to form alliances, although Brazil still needs investments from the multinational corporations and international lending agencies. The deescalation of ideological commitments presages a growing "Mexicanization" of Brazilian policy. That is, Brazil will avoid any attempt to lead Third World or Latin American nations for fear of jeopardizing her export trade with other nations and groups. At the same time, to maintain the domestic image—and the self-image—of the army, some largely symbolic acts of national defiance will be undertaken that are not likely to threaten seriously Brazil's ties with any important nation or group. An example would be the assertion of the 200-mile maritime zone by Brazil, an issue that was given great publicity with strong nationalist overtones at home but which, for the present at least, is not a serious challenge or affront to any other power. The U.S. government (as in the case of Mexico) has shown a certain forbearance for this kind of "Yankee-baiting," apparently believing that as long as it is largely symbolic, it should be overlooked as a domestic political necessity for the nations that occasionally indulge in it.

Foreign policy has continued to be integrated into a more and more conscious national development policy during the first ten years of military rule. Explicitly geopolitical and developmental-economic concepts have continued to supplant traditional legal and political concepts as major components of the thought of Brazilian foreign policy planners. The new pragmatism of Geisel replaced the ideological foreign policy of his military predecessors as a consequence of the struggle to maintain the rapid rate of economic growth, and the practical disappearance of significant domestic political opposition. Economic growth, which is necessary to the army to maintain both its self-image as a benefactor of Brazil and its legitimacy with that part of the population that supports it, and the new governmental decisiveness and efficiency have given new impetus to the old Brazilian hunger for recognition as a great power. To become a great power is the current manifestation of the traditional nationalism of the army officers. Foreign policy is being used as a tool in this quest, but not in the old style of seeking attention through erudite displays at international forums. Rather, the current rulers of Brazil tend to link status as a great power to economic power and national unity of purpose.

The first decade of military rule for modern Brazil ended at almost the same time as the fourth general-president was inaugurated. During the first ten years the military searched for security and stability and stimulated rapid economic growth. The military found no way satisfactory to them to return the political system to civilian control, and it must be assumed that the military will maintain control for the forseeable future. New efficiency and clarity of purpose has been achieved through authoritarian and repressive means, and Brazil is well on its way to becoming an integrated, modern nation, even if over half of its population is apparently being contained in pauperism and the whole civilian population is denied any significant political participation. The turning point marked by the transfer of power from Médici to Geisel shifted the emphasis to development (as understood by the military), once it had become clear that security and stability were no longer major concerns.

Present trends in Brazil point to the continuation of an authoritarian (but not a personalist) and technocratic regime that has as its power base the Brazilian army but which will continue to be allied with both the

national upper and middle class and with the multinational corporations
and banks. Its rhetoric will continue to be anti-Communist, antipopulist,
and antiliberal, and this will have a limited influence on foreign policy.
The uncertain future of the international economic system in the last half
of the 1970s makes it difficult to predict the particular directions foreign
policy will take in Brazil, since it depends so heavily upon Brazil's
need to continue to promote exports. Even though present indications
show no significant move towards either relaxation of political repression or the adoption of economic policies designed to distribute more
equally among the population the fruits of Brazil's economic growth,
there does not appear to be any significant domestic dynamic that will
force an alteration of either of these facts—unless there is a schism in the
army officer corps. If such liberalization and redistributive policies are
to be adopted, they will probably come as the result of external pressures, most probably from a world economic crisis. But such a world
depression would more than likely produce an even more repressive,
Salazar-type regime, not a liberalization. It is the tragedy of modern
Brazil that as she is moving to become, for the first time, a significant
world-actor, the majority of her people appear to be condemned, for the
foreseeable future, to continuing poverty and political repression.[35]

BIBLIOGRAPHICAL NOTE

The best available survey of Brazilian foreign policy in English is E. Bradford
Burns, *Nationalism in Brazil: A Historical Survey* (New York: Frederick A.
Praeger, 1968), though it was not written with that specific purpose in mind. A
good, general history of Brazilian foreign policy in Portuguese is Delgado de
Carvalho, *História Diplomática do Brasil* (São Paulo: Companhia Editora
Nacional, 1959). The best and broadest analysis of continuing themes in Brazilian
foreign policy is José Honório Rodrigues, *Interesse Nacional e Política Externa*
(Rio de Janeiro: Editora Civilização Brasileira, 1966), which, however, suffers
from a certain inability to put the events of 1964 and 1965 in historical perspective
because of proximity to those events and the author's strong reaction against the
military.
   Other useful articles and books on various aspects of Brazilian foreign policy
include the following:

"Brazil's International Role in the Seventies: A Conference Report," *Orbis* 16,
   no. 2 (Summer 1972): 545-60.
Burns, E. Bradford. "Tradition and Variation in Brazilian Foreign Policy,"
   Journal of Inter-American Studies 9 (April 1967): 195-212.

35. In his book on Brazil, *Brazil: Awakening Giant* (Washington, D.C.: Public Affairs
Press, 1974), former U.S. diplomat Philip Raine entitles his last chapter "Prospect: Great
Power or Tropical Slum?" Unfortunately, *or* might be replaced by *and*.

DePaiva, Leite C. "Constantes et Variables de la Politique Etrangère du Bresil," *Politique Etrangère* 34, no. 1 (1969): 33-55.

Gordon, Lincoln. "Brazil's Future World Role," *Orbis* 16, no. 3 (Fall 1972): 621-31.

Lafer, Celso. "Una Interpretación del sistema de las relaciones internacionales del Brasil," *Foro Internacional* 9, no. 3 (January-March 1969): 298-318.

Meira Penna, J. O. de. *Política Externa: Segurança e Desenvolvimento* (Rio de Janeiro: Livraria Agir Editora, 1967) is an attempt by a career diplomat to integrate the traditional style and thought of Itamaraty with the technocratic style and substance of the ESG.

Reisky de Dubnic, Vladimir. "Brazil's New Foreign Policy: From Nonalignment to Solidarity with the West," in *Latin American International Politics: Ambitions, Capabilities, and the National Interest of Mexico, Brazil and Argentina*, pp. 274-86. Edited by Carlos A. Astiz, Notre Dame, Ind.: University of Notre Dame Press, 1969. This article assumed that the foreign policy of the Castelo Branco period would be the permanent stance of the military government.

Rodrigues, José Honório. "The Foundations of Brazil's Foreign Policy," *International Affairs* 38, no. 3 (July 1962): 324-38; also reprinted in the Astiz volume and in Irving Louis Horowitz, *Revolution in Brazil* (New York: E. P. Dutton & Co., 1964).

Rosenbaum, H. Jon. "Brazil Among the Nations," *International Journal* 24, no. 3 (Summer 1969): 529-44.

———. "Brazil's Foreign Policy: Developmentalism and Beyond," *Orbis* no. 1 (Spring 1972): 58-84.

Sousa Sampaio, Nelso de. "The Foreign Policy of Brazil," in *Foreign Policies in a World of Change*, pp. 617-41. Edited by Joseph E. Black and Kenneth W. Thompson. (New York: Harper & Row, 1963.)

For a survey of the style and substance of Brazilian geopolitical thinking, the student should first look at Lewis Tambs's article (see n. 5, above). Basic material not available in English includes Everardo Backheuser, *Curso de Geopolítica Geral e do Brasil* (Rio de Janeiro: Biblioteca do Exército, 1952-), vols. 178-79. The most recent and influential work in this area is certainly General Golbery do Couto e Silva, *Geopolítica do Brasil*, 2d ed. (Rio de Janeiro: Livraria José Olympio Editora, 1967). General Golbery was a very high official and a confidant of Castelo Branco, and he occupies the same position with president Geisel. Golbery continues to be one of the most influential thinkers in the evolution of the ESG. An interesting criticism of his thought is Oliveiros S. Ferreira, "La Geopolítica y el ejército brasileño," *Aportes*, no. 12 (April 1969), pp. 111-32.

Among the most interesting interpretations of Brazil's "Manifest Destiny" are two books by Raymundo Pimentel Gomes: *O Brasil Entre as Cinco Maiores Potências* (Rio de Janeiro: Editora Leitura, S.A., 1969); and *Porque Não Somos Uma Grande Potencia?* (Rio de Janeiro: Editora Civilização Brasileira, 1965).

A recent literature, largely in Spanish and largely polemical or sensational, has analyzed potential Brazilian "subimperialism." A calm survey of Brazil's aspirations for great power status, as directed by the military government, is found in Norman A. Bailey and Ronald Schneider, "Brazil's Foreign Policy: A Case Study in Upward Mobility," *Inter-American Economic Affairs* 27, no. 4 (Spring 1974): 3–25.

In addition to the items cited in n. 13, above, more information and interpretation about the Independent Foreign Policy may be found in the several books and articles of José Honório Rodrigues. See also Francisco Clementino de San Tiago Dantas, *Política Externa Independente* (Rio de Janeiro: Editora Civilização Brasileira, 1962), and the three numbers (May 1965, August 1965, and January 1966) of the journal *Política Externa Independente* (Rio de Janeiro: Editora Civilização Brasileira) that were published before its suppression.

Two journals published in Brazil are important sources for students of Brazilian foreign policy: *Revista Brasileira de Política Internacional* (Rio de Janeiro) and *Boletim da Sociedade Brasileira de Direito Internacional* (Rio de Janeiro). Both are quasi-official journals, closely linked to official sources. Both publish treaties and documents in addition to academic studies. In addition, the embassy of Brazil in Washington publishes a weekly bulletin, *Boletim Especial,* that often contains summaries of important statements by Brazilian officials on foreign policy. The *Jornal do Brasil* (Rio) and *O Estado de São Paulo* (São Paulo) probably give more and better coverage to foreign policy than most other newspapers in Brazil. Essential (but very difficult to find) to understanding the assumptions behind the present foreign policy is the journal of the Association of Graduates of the Higher War College (ADESG—Associação dos Diplomados da Escola Superior de Guerra), *Segurança e Desenvolvimento,* published three times a year.

V

Plate River Area: Argentina, Uruguay, and Paraguay

12/John J. Finan

Argentina

The magnitude and variety of political, social, and economic change in Argentina during the past half century cause one to approach any monistic analysis of Argentine foreign policy with great hesitation. However, in the historical experience of Argentina in foreign relations one can discern several policy constants, or continuities in policy. These historical continuities are the principal theme of this chapter.

MAJOR INTERNATIONAL PROBLEMS

Before discussing the continuities of Argentine foreign policy, let us enumerate the major international problems confronting Argentina. First, there is the structural problem of her international trade. Argentina continues to export most of her products to Europe, although a significant portion of her imports comes from the United States. Second, there is the great power imbalance in South America owing to the extraordinary economic growth and internal development of Brazil during the past decade. What will or can Argentina do to redress this imbalance? Third, there is the continuing problem of border definition with Chile, especially in the Straits of Magellan. Fourth, there is the important matter of Argentine relations with the small states on her borders: Bolivia, Paraguay, and Uruguay. A fifth problem relates to foreign investment. The foreign capital that Argentina has sought for economic growth during the past decade has been forthcoming only in a limited way, largely because of domestic political instability. To what extent can the forces of nationalism, often finding expression in moves for expropriation of foreign-owned enterprises, be reconciled with the need and desire for foreign investment? A final problem is the very profound one of international identity. Having played a leading role in Latin America many times in the past, Argentina has been almost invisible on the international scene more recently because of her severe internal political disunity. This international identity crisis raises questions for Argentina concerning her role in Latin America and the Inter-American system and also her relations with the United States and other great powers.

HISTORICAL ANTECEDENTS

A number of historical factors must be taken into account in an analysis of Argentina's foreign policies. Lacking both important resources in precious metals or gems and a large productive Indian population, the viceroyalty of La Plata did not have an important place in Spanish imperial concerns until the last quarter of the eighteenth century. Then, in response to a Portuguese expansionist threat southward from Brazil and the growth of commerce in the area, Spain began to give more serious attention to the colony. Until Buenos Aires became the capital of a viceroyalty in 1776, it was an insignificant port village, unlike the great viceregal centers at Lima and Mexico City. Therefore, in the long view of the historian, the colonial tradition, so important in the Mexican and Peruvian experience, is much less important as a formative factor in Argentine policy.

Just as the Plate region came late to a position of colonial worth, after independence Argentine development as a nation was also retarded. Largely because of severe disagreements among the provinces of the country, no national constitution was brought into being until 1853; even then serious secessionist moves prevented effective union until the early 1860s. During most of this unorganized period after independence the country had no central government, and the nation's foreign relations were conducted by her most important province, Buenos Aires. Because of the autonomy that the province enjoyed at this time it would not have been surprising if several of them, including Buenos Aires, had either become independent national states or joined in a larger federation with Uruguay or Paraguay.[1]

CONTINUITIES IN ARGENTINE POLICY

What are the continuities in Argentine foreign policy? First, Argentina has always been interested in defining and securing the boundaries with her most powerful neighboring state, Chile. This concern, real but latent during much of the nineteenth century, became significant after the Argentine campaign of 1879–80 against the Indians, who had controlled the Pampas since colonial times. The opening of these rich western and southern lands brought the question of the boundary with Chile to national attention. In subsequent negotiations it was agreed that the boundary line was to be the Andes crest—in other words, as it was then believed, the continental divide; the Island of Tierra del Fuego was to be divided and the Strait of Magellan neutralized. When it became clear that the Andean crest and the watershed were not identical, both Chile and Argentina sought the territory presented by the differential. The question was ultimately decided in 1902, just short of war, by arbitration of the British Crown.[2] With improved mapping of the watershed, several

    1. This is pointed out persuasively by H. S. Ferns, *Britain and Argentina in the Nineteenth Century* (Oxford: Clarendon Press, 1960), p. 292.
    2. C. H. Haring, *South American Progress* (Cambridge: Harvard University Press, 1934), pp. 139–40.

controversies have since arisen, but they have all been settled amicably. In 1971, Argentine President Alejandro Lanusse, in two meetings with Chilean President Salvador Allende, settled a controvery over the Beagle Channel, which had been the most serious impediment in Argentine-Chilean relations.[3]

Another continuity in Argentine foreign policy is a concern for preventing foreign domination or control of the neighboring countries of the former viceroyalty: Bolivia, Paraguay, and Uruguay. During the movements for independence, Argentina tried unsuccessfully to maintain these states as part of a united independent republic. Subsequently, it was the policy of the regime of Juan Manuel de Rosas (1835-52) not to recognize the independence of Paraguay, to seek to impose pro-Argentine governments in Uruguay, and to prevent by force the union of Bolivia with Peru (1839). These policies changed after Rosas's fall, when Paraguay was recognized (1852) and active meddling in Uruguayan domestic politics ended.

Since the War of the Triple Alliance (1865-70), Argentina has been especially concerned with Brazilian influence on Paraguay. Argentina assumed an active role in attempting to achieve peace in the Chaco War in the 1930s, as a means of asserting her interest in Paraguay and successfully frustrating, for a time, the peacemaking actions of an Inter-American Committee of Neutrals, comprising the United States, Colombia, Cuba, Mexico, and Uruguay. It is significant that the armistice ending the war in 1935 was signed in Buenos Aires, with the Argentine foreign minister presiding.[4] One of the first actions of the military government that came to power in Argentina in 1943 was the signing of a commercial treaty with Paraguay to reduce Brazilian influence there.[5] In 1953, on a visit to Paraguay (during which he returned, as a goodwill gesture, several trophies from the War of the Triple Alliance), President Juan Perón signed an economic agreement with Paraguay with a view towards creating a customs union.[6] More recently, in 1971, the Argentine government, aware of Brazilian economic assistance to Paraguay, signed an agreement granting credits, subsidies, and promises of support for Paraguayan development plans.[7]

With reference to Bolivia, Argentina has also maintained a close interest. On the occasion of Bolivia's conflict with Chile in the War of the Pacific (1879-81), Argentine participation on Bolivia's side—a prospect that was imminent and real—was avoided only by Chile's initiatives

3. Luis Guagnini, "La política exterior de Lanusse," *La Opinión* (Buenos Aires), 8 Jan. 1972, p. 11.

4. Alberto Conil Paz and Gustavo Ferrari, *Política exterior argentina, 1930-1962* (Buenos Aires: Editorial Huemel, 1964), p. 40 (also in English, *Argentina's Foreign Policy*, trans. John J. Kennedy [Notre Dame, Ind.: Notre Dame University Press, 1966]).

5. Ibid., p. 135.

6. Ibid., p. 206.

7. Guagnini, "La política exterior de Lanusse."

toward settlement of Chilean-Argentine boundary questions.[8] Argentina's attempts to mediate in the Chaco War owed as much to her interest in Bolivia as in Paraguay. In 1943, the Argentine military government of General Pedro Ramírez, through its military attaché in La Paz, is believed to have assisted in the overthrow of the anti-Axis government of General Peñaranda, apparently as part of an overall plan to assure friendly governments on the borders of neutral Argentina.[9] In 1954 President Perón, in anticipation of economic union with Bolivia, signed an agreement similar to the one he had signed a year earlier with Paraguay.[10] In 1971, the Argentine president, General Lanusse, met with the Bolivian president, Colonel Hugo Banzer Suárez, and signed an agreement for the improvement of bilateral relations; in this agreement Argentina offered financial help, trade benefits, and transport facilities.[11]

The extraordinary stability of Uruguay in the twentieth century has in general prevented Argentina and Brazil from meddling directly in Uruguay's internal affairs (with a view toward influencing Uruguayan foreign relations), as they had done during the nineteenth century. Uruguay was especially concerned during World War II with regard to possible subversion from Argentina, especially after the Bolivian coup of 1943 in which Argentina was implicated.[12] Uruguay became a haven for Argentine political refugees during the first presidential tenure of Perón, when relations between the two countries were severely strained. Yet relations between the two countries are necessarily close. Thus, Uruguayan President Jorge Pacheco Areco made a state visit to Argentina in 1971 to discuss with President Lanusse problems of trade and means of fighting the subversion both countries were experiencing.[13]

A third continuity of Argentine foreign policy is a concern for maintaining a power balance with Brazil. Rivalry with Brazil is ancient, preceding Argentina's attainment of independence. The area we know today as Uruguay had been disputed by Spain and Portugal for two-hundred years, until it was clearly ceded to Spain in 1777. After Argentine indepdence the dispute was revived, with both Brazil and Argentina desiring to control the territory. Uruguay was reconquered and annexed by Brazil in 1821. However, in a three-year war (1825–28) Argentina supported the successful Uruguayan uprising led by the so-called Immortal Thirty-Three. Through British mediation, Uruguay became an independent (buffer) state. But direct intervention in Uruguayan affairs by

8. Haring, *South American Progress*, pp. 166–67.
9. Harold F. Peterson, *Argentina and the United States, 1810–1960* (Albany: State University of New York Press, 1964), p. 434; Conil Paz and Ferrari, *Política exterior argentina*, p. 135.
10. Conil Paz and Ferrari, *Política exterior argentina*, p. 206.
11. Guagnini, "La política exterior de Lanusse."
12. Robert A. Potash, *The Army and Politics in Argentina, 1928–1945* (Stanford, Calif.: Stanford University Press, 1969), p. 231.
13. Guagnini, "La política exterior de Lanusse."

Argentina and Brazil occurred frequently, until the end of the War of the Triple Alliance in 1870.[14]

The rivalry between Argentina and Brazil, largely confined in the nineteenth century to the River Plate area, was intensified in the twentieth century when the Baron de Rio Branco assumed control of Brazilian foreign affairs in 1902. Rio Branco enunciated policies designed to enhance Brazilian international prestige and assert Brazilian leadership in South America.[15] He succeeded in having the Brazilian primate named a cardinal three decades before any other Latin American country was so honored. Through a policy of close association with the United States, he arranged to have the Brazilian legation in Washington raised to the status of an embassy, the first of any South American country.[16] These moves were not ignored in Buenos Aires. Brazilian opposition to the (Argentine) Drago doctrine (discussed below) and her support for U.S. interventions in the Caribbean further exacerbated tensions between the two countries.[17]

Argentine jealousy of Brazil was expressed explosively in the famous "Telegram Number Nine" incident. In 1908, the Argentine foreign ministry intercepted and decoded a message from Rio Branco to his legation in Chile and charged, falsely as it turned out, that Brazil was plotting with the United States and Chile against Agrentina.[18] Later, after World War I, as plans for a League of Nations got underway, Argentina, which had been neutral during the war, resented the precedence given to Brazil, who had entered the war on the side of the Allies.[19] A decade later, U.S. Secretary of State Cordell Hull noted the Argentine-Brazilian rivalry at the Inter-American Conference at Montevideo (1933) when Brazilians complained to him that he had given too much time to the Argentines at the meeting.[20] During World War II, neutral Argentina expressed concern to the United States about the massive military and economic aid being given to Brazil, an active participant in the war; the Argentines asked fruitlessly for similar assistance, "to restore Argentina," in Foreign Minister Segundo Storni's words, "to the position of equilibrium to which Argentina is entitled" in relation to Brazil.[21] Since the war, this rivalry between Argentina and Brazil has been expressed most noticeably in arms competition; both countries maintain what are by far the largest military establishments in South America.

14. Haring, *South American Progress*, p. 111.
15. E. Bradford Burns, *The Unwritten Alliance* (New York: Columbia University Press, 1965), pp. 37–38.
16. Ibid., pp. 168, 181.
17. Ibid., p. 121.
18. Ibid., p. 185.
19. Conil Paz and Ferrari, *Política exterior argentina*, pp. 37–38.
20. Ibid., p. 48.
21. Ray Josephs, *Argentine Diary* (New York: Random House, 1944), pp. 149–51.

Just as there are continuities in Argentine relations within South
America, so are there consistencies in Argentine policies with reference to
the great powers. First and most important of these is Argentina's
pioneering espousal of the principle of absolute sovereignty and juridical
equality of nation states. This *principista*, or natural law, position has
been expressed several times. Emphasizing that recognition of sovereignty
means the acceptance of a sovereign state's laws and the competence of its
judicial system, Foreign Minister Carlos Tejedor, as early as 1872,
condemned appeals by British immigrants to their government for
protection against Indian attack on the insecure Indian frontier. He
argued, rather, that foreigners have no right to seek within a country a
protection that nationals do not enjoy.[22] While the Tejedor doctrine is
now recognized as a Latin American contribution to developing international law, insufficient emphasis has been placed on it as a distinct
foreign policy of Argentina in relation to large powers. The Tejedor
principle was extended to foreign corporations by Foreign Minister
Bernardo Irigoyen in 1876 when, in the face of a British gunboat, he
affirmed that foreign companies have no more rights than domestic ones
and that the dispute of the Bank of London and the River Plate with local
authorities should be addressed to the Argentine judicial system.[23]

On the issue of debt collection Argentina may likewise be credited with
pioneering assertions of sovereignty. Carlos Calvo's contention that
foreigners may not seek diplomatic or military support from their home
governments for the collection of private debts has, since the middle of
the nineteenth century, been so influential that the "Calvo Clause," inserted into contracts or concessions relating to foreign investments, is
all but synonymous with a doctrine of absolute sovereignty.[24] Argentine
Foreign Minister Luis Drago asserted a comparable position concerning
public debts in 1902. The Drago doctrine has come to be viewed as one
of the most important assertions of the principle of absolute sovereignty
and has served as a doctrinal counterpoise to the interventionism explicit
in the Roosevelt Corollary of the Monroe Doctrine. Eventually it found
expression in somewhat broader form in the Montevideo Treaty on the
Rights and Duties of States (1933).

Argentina's assertion of juridical equality was strong, too, in deliberations concerning the organization of the League of Nations. Argentina's
firm position was that no distinction should be made between large and
small states in the organization and that the League Council should be

22. José Julio Santa Pinter, "The Foreign Policy of Argentina," in *Foreign Policies
in a World of Change* (New York: Harpers, 1963.)
23. Ferns, *Britain and Argentina in the Nineteenth Century*, pp. 381–86.
24. For example, see this interpretation in J. Lloyd Mecham's *The United States and
Inter-American Security, 1889–1960* (1961; reprint ed., Austin: University of Texas Press,
1963), p. 54.

democratically elected. Failing to secure acceptance of this principle, Argentina withdrew her delegation in 1920, although she reentered the League later.[25] Similarly, Argentina opposed in principle the great power veto in the United Nations as an offense against the juridical equality of states.[26] In further defense of the principle of absolute sovereignty, Argentina sought to require in the Charter of the Organization of American States (OAS) unanimous (rather than two-thirds) acquiescence of members in decisions of the organization.[27]

Another continuity in Argentina's foreign policy is her resistance to hemispheric multilateralism under U.S. hegemony. The long and consistent Argentine reluctance to support Pan Americanism as it developed in the twentieth century is associated with Argentina's complex relations with the United States and also her historic ties with Europe. During much of the nineteenth century, Argentine–U.S. relations were friendly and commercially important. For many years the United States stood second only to France as Argentina's best wool market. But after 1890, when the McKinley tariff raised the duty on wool, trade declined, and U.S.–Argentine relations in general cooled.[28]

Argentina, as has been pointed out, used the Drago principle to oppose U.S. interventions in the Caribbean and, as a counterpoise to the threat of U.S. expansionism, espoused first a Latin America multilaterality independent of the United States and then a universalism aimed at turning Latin America from a hemispheric outlook to a broader one involving the League of Nations (of which the U.S. was not a member). The first position was enunciated by the government of President Hipólito Yrigoyen in reaction to a peace pact that President Woodrow Wilson was espousing for the hemisphere in the years before the United States entered the war. During the war, Yrigoyen called unsuccessfully for a congress of Latin American states.[29]

The universalistic position of Argentina was enunciated by Argentine Foreign Minister Carlos Saavedra Lamas in 1933, when Argentina returned, after four years of absence, to the League of Nations. Just as the United States was proclaiming the Good Neighbor Policy, with a view to hemispheric solidarity, Saavedra Lamas drafted an Anti-War Treaty of Non-Aggression and Conciliation, obtained for it the signatures of the ABC powers (Argentina, Brazil, and Chile) and Mexico, in addition to Paraguay and Uruguay, and called upon other countries in the world at large to sign the document.[30] In the tug-of-war between U.S. advocacy of

25. Conil Paz and Ferrari, *Política exterior argentina*, p. 38.
26. Peterson, *Argentina and the United States*, p. 471.
27. Conil Paz and Ferrari, *Política exterior argentina*, pp. 195–98.
28. Ferns, *Britain and Argentina in the Nineteenth Century*, pp. 433–34.
29. Peterson, *Argentina and the United States*, p. 322.
30. Mecham, *The United States and Inter-American Security*, p. 118.

hemispheric solidarity and Argentine universalism, the United States, under the leadership of President Franklin D. Roosevelt and Secretary of State Hull, shrewdly agreed to a compromise by placing the antiwar treaty on the agenda of the Seventh Pan American Conference meeting in Montevideo in December 1933.

In another universalistic move, Saavedra Lamas proposed to refer to the League of Nations the question of the Chaco War, thereby removing it from the purview of the Committee of Neutrals, which had been created at the Special Inter-American Arbitration Conference of 1928–29. It is also significant that in an opening address at the Inter-American Conference for the Maintenance of Peace (Buenos Aires, 1936) proposed by President Roosevelt to affirm hemispheric unity, Argentine President Agustín P. Justo called for support of the League of Nations in the evolving European crisis; the Argentine delegation at the conference opposed the U.S. proposal for the creation of a Permanent Inter-American Consultative Committee to address threats to hemispheric peace.[31] Argentina's opposition to hemispheric solidarity was further affirmed by Foreign Minister José M. Cantilo in his address to the Eighth International Conference of American States in Lima in 1938. He decried regional pacts, asking that there be raised not a hemispheric standard but one "for all men—that of liberty and justice." Cantilo spelled out Argentina's close cultural, intellectual, and economic ties with Europe in affirming Argentina's "ecumenical spirit."[32]

Argentina's continued resistance to hemispheric multilateralism was manifested after World War II when she delayed for four years her ratification of the Rio Pact of 1947 and for eight years her ratification of the Charter of the OAS—the last of the original signers to do so. While cooperation with the Inter-American system was more forthcoming during the military governments from 1966–73, it is significant that the civilian regime that came to power in 1973 indicated a desire to join the Community of Non-Aligned Nations.

A final continuity to be considered is Argentina's defiant assertion of independence in foreign policy in relation to the rivalries and conflicts of the great powers. From her rejection of alliance with either Britain or France in their rivalries in Latin America, especially in the first half of the nineteenth century, to her positions of neutrality during World War I and most of World War II, to her "third position" during much of the cold war, Argentina has maintained a consistent stance of independence, asserting noninvolvement.

The defiance of the Rosas regime toward pressures and blockades by Britain and France in the 1830s and 1840s was unparalleled in the Latin American experience. Also, Argentina's long assertion of a claim of

31. Conil Paz and Ferrari, *Política exterior argentina*, p. 50.
32. Ibid., pp. 58–60.

sovereignty over the Falkland (Malvinas) Islands and Dependencies has been as much an expression of defiance of British power as a manifestation of the importance of the strategic location of the islands in relation to the Straits of Magellan and Antarctica.

The neutral position of Argentina during World War I was not, as was widely believed in the United States at the time, an expression of pro-German feeling; it was merely "pro-Argentine."[33] The U.S. ambassador in Buenos Aires at the time understood this, interpreting Argentine neutralism as the expression of a desire to establish a stronger and more independent bargaining position between British and German interests.[34]

The sources of Argentine neutrality in World War II are complex and have not been systematically analyzed. German influence on the Argentine army, motives of economic gain, a desire to assume a world leadership role of mediation, uncertainty until very late about the outcome of the war, and a widespread belief that the Axis powers would be victorious —these and other causes have been put forward. But none has been entirely validated, and it would be inappropriate to attempt to decide the issue here. The fact remains that, alone among the Latin American countries, Argentina defiantly maintained relations with both sides during the war until early 1944 and then ruptured relations with the Axis only formally. The price paid for her neutrality was enormously high in diplomatic isolation during the war, in an egregious military imbalance favoring U.S.-aided Brazil, and in loss of international bargaining power at the end of the war. Thus an unreasoning assertion of independence as an element in her neutral stance must be considered at least plausible.

The first important action taken by Argentina in asserting her independent foreign policy in the cold war was to reestablish relations in 1946, after almost three decades of rupture, with the Soviet Union. At the Inter-American Conference at Caracas in 1954, Argentina abstained from supporting the U.S.-sponsored Declaration of Solidarity for the Preservation of the Political Integrity of the American States against International Communist Intervention. As another example of independence, Argentina also abstained from supporting the resolution, passed at the Punta del Este Conference of January 1962, expelling Cuba from the Organization of American States.[35]

In summary, what are the distinctive continuities of Argentina foreign policy, viewed in historical perspective? Apart from her desire to affirm her boundaries with Chile and assure the friendliness of the small buffer states on her borders, Argentina's overriding concern has been to maintain a balance of power with Brazil. Especially distinctive has been Argentina's role in relation to the great powers. Argentina took the lead

33. Haring, *South American Progress*, p. 52.
34. Peterson, *Argentina and the United States*, p. 314.
35. Conil Paz and Ferrari, *Política exterior argentina*, pp. 208, 254.

in asserting doctrines of sovereignty, juridical equality, and nonintervention on behalf of the Latin American states. Also, whether in assertion of
her own continental leadership or in an attempt to reduce the hemispheric influence of the United States, she has on the whole resisted the
development since the 1930s of Pan Americanism under U.S. hegemony.
Finally, Argentina has demonstrated extraordinary and often defiant
steadfastness in detaching herself from involvement in the conflicts of the
great powers, in World War I, World War II, and the cold war.

FACTORS AFFECTING FOREIGN POLICY

What are the several factors bearing on Argentine foreign policy making
and foreign relations behavior? The geographic conditions are of fundamental importance. First among these is the location of Argentina in the
South Atlantic. Situated thus, the country has a great sense of distance
and isolation from Europe, her principal export market. In this South
Atlantic position, Argentina also has a strong feeling of identification
with the Antarctic, the Falkland Islands and Dependencies, and the
Straits of Magellan and a sensitivity to their strategic importance. Within
Latin America, Argentine relations with Chile have been affected by the
Andes chain that borders them and gives each a barrier against intrusion.
Small buffer states to the east, north, and northwest—Uruguay, Para-
guay, and Bolivia—provide a security zone separating Argentina from
her great rival in South America, Brazil.

Among the economic background factors that bear on Argentine
foreign relations, perhaps the most important is that Europe continues
to be the biggest market for Argentine exports. Whereas Great Britain
was once the largest buyer of Argentine goods, in recent years Italy has
assumed this position. Sales to the United States have always taken a
lower place than sales to Europe, largely because Argentine exports
compete with rather than complement U.S. primary products. As a
result, the Argentine–U.S. trade relationship is severely unbalanced,
and a triangular structure—sales to Europe and purchases from the
United States—is a distinctive characteristic of Argentine international
commerce.[36]

Ethnically, the fact that Argentina, unlike most of the Spanish-
American countries, has a relatively small Indian population has meant,
from a foreign policy point of view, that the country has not had to
address the inward-looking task of integrating the Indian into national
life. Many of the nomadic and hostile Indians who controlled the Pampa
until 1880 were killed or forced to migrate to isolated areas in the south

36. On Argentine economic relations, see especially Carlos Díaz Alejandro, *Essays on the Economic History of the Argentine Republic* (New Haven: Yale University Press, 1970) and Aldo Ferrer, *The Argentine Economy* (Berkeley: University of California Press, 1967).

and the west. Consequently, while "Indo-Argentines" (persons of Indian and Mestizo antecedence) do exist, all but a small part of the population is of European background. Spanish and Italian ancestral strains predominate. The myth that there is a large German population in Argentina, propagated perhaps by Argentine neutrality in World War I and most of World War II, dies hard; in fact, the German component is only about 2 percent of the country's entire population.

As one assesses the cultural influences on Argentine foreign relations, it is important to keep in mind the high cultural level of the Argentine people themselves. Having perhaps the highest literacy rate in Latin America, they have a distinguished educational system that reaches almost everyone in the society. There is no country in Latin America where a larger percentage of the population is aware of foreign policy issues. Newspaper coverage of foreign news is probably more comprehensive in Argentina than anywhere else in the region, especially in Buenos Aires with its two internationally renowned newspapers, *La Prensa* and *La Nación*.

The responsible spokesman for foreign policy in Argentina is the foreign minister, who, constitutionally, is appointed by the president with the approval of the Senate. Ambassadors are also appointed with Senate confirmation. A permanent, career foreign service has an important role in the conduct of foreign relations.

As this chapter is being completed in late 1974, it is difficult to discern with assurance any new trends in Argentine foreign policy, because the country is having to give primary attention to the problem of domestic unrest. However, in the formulation of Argentine policy during the next decade, many of the continuities discussed above will be manifest in one form or another. Argentine relations with neighboring Chile, for example, will continue to be dominated by a concern for border security. Relations with Bolivia and Paraguay will be directed toward preventing undue foreign influence there. Argentine policy toward Brazil will continue to seek a power balance in South America. Argentina's lukewarm position toward hemispheric multilateralism and the Inter-American system will continue as long as the U.S. role is hegemonic. Argentine relations with Europe will continue to be close, not only because of historic economic ties but also because Argentina sees in Europe a means of offsetting U.S. influence in Latin America. In the emerging period of détente, Argentina's traditional noninvolvement in great power struggles will be less dramatic and attention-getting; but a close alliance with either the United States or the Soviet Union is unlikely.

One of the glories of Argentine diplomacy, expressed intermittently but unambiguously during the past century, has been her espousal of the cause of small states in their relations with larger powers. How will this commitment find expression in future policy? It could well be in a role of leadership of the states of Spanish South America. But it could be a leadership role in the broader Third World arena. In the past, Argentina has taken the lead in asserting the political rights of small states in the hemisphere. But it is not inconceivable, given her power potential, that Argentina will in the future asert in comparable fashion the economic rights of all small states in their relations with the great industrial powers.

BIBLIOGRAPHICAL NOTE

Works devoted totally to Argentine foreign policy are few. Alberto Conil Paz and Gustavo Ferrari's *Política exterior argentina, 1930-1962* (Buenos Aires: Editorial Huemel, 1964) is almost unique in its cogent, succinct analysis of issues during the period indicated. A brief but legalistic summary is José Julio Santa Pinter's "The Foreign Policy of Argentina," in *Foreign Policies in a World of Change,* ed. Joseph E. Black and Kenneth W. Thompson (New York: Harpers, 1963). Sergio Bagú, *Argentina en el mundo* (Mexico: Fondo de Cultura Económica, 1961) examines some of the main underpinnings of Argentine foreign policy. Belying its broad title, Carlos A. Florit's *Política exterior nacional* (Buenos Aires: Ediciones Anayú, 1960) is a series of very limited and unrelated essays on narrow themes. On Argentine foreign policy during World War II see Enrique Ruíz-Guiñazú, *La Política argentina y el futuro de América* (Buenos Aires: Librería Huemel, 1944), to be read in conjunction with the more detached analysis in Robert Potash, *The Army and Politics in Argentina, 1928-1945* (Stanford, Calif.: Standford University Press, 1969). A perceptive beginning analysis of Peron's "third position" is in Gonzalo H. Cárdenas et al, *El Peronismo* (Buenos Aires: C. Pérez, 1969).

A very detailed survey of Argentine relations with the United States, drawing heavily on documentation in this country, is Harold P. Peterson, *Argentina and the United States, 1810-1960* (Albany: State University of New York Press, 1964). On early foreign interventions see John Cady, *Foreign Interventions in the Rio de la Plata, 1838-1850* (Philadelphia: University of Pennsylvania Press, 1929). For nineteenth-century developments see Vicente G. Quesada, *Historia diplomática hispanoamericana,* 2 vols. (Buenos Aires: "La Cultura Argentina," 1918-20). Thomas F. McGann examines early Argentine-U.S. rivalry in *Argentina, the United States, and the Inter-American System* (Cambridge: Harvard University Press, 1957). H. S. Ferns, *Britain and Argentina in the Nineteenth Century* (Oxford: Clarendon Press, 1960) is magisterial. Isidro Ruíz Moreno's *Historia de las relaciones exteriores argentinas 1810-1955* (Buenos Aires: Editorial Perrot, 1961) is useful for its broad historical framework. C. H. Haring's *South American Progress* (Cambridge: Harvard University Press, 1934) is still valuable for its succinct background summaries of issues in international relations.

The international economic relations of Argentina are treated in Carlos Díaz Alejandro, *Essays on the Economic History of the Argentine Republic* (New Haven: Yale University Press, 1970) and in Aldo Ferrer, *The Argentine Economy* (Berkeley: University of California Press, 1967).

13/G. Pope Atkins

Uruguay

Uruguay has played a significant and constructive role in inter-American relations, despite its small-state status in the international system, and it has maintained a relatively independent position in both hemispheric and world affairs. Uruguay has consistently supported the concepts of nonintervention and inter-American solidarity against aggression. In the past, as the most egalitarian society in Latin America, Uruguay has pursued a foreign policy that strongly defended the Pan American principles of representative democracy and the protection of human rights. Although her political stability and democratic government have deteriorated in recent years because of severe internal problems, these changes do not seem to have significantly affected Uruguay's traditional foreign policy.

This chapter will consider three broad questions about the foreign policy of Uruguay. First, what are the most important factors that shape Uruguayan foreign policy? Second, in terms of these factors, what means have been selected and what ends pursued in foreign affairs? Finally, what major specific policies and relations, past and present, have developed as Uruguay has functioned in the international political system?

MAJOR FACTORS INFLUENCING POLICY

The realities of Uruguay's capability (power) and the nature of her nationalism, which constitute the sources of her strengths and weaknesses and her perception of national destiny, are the most important factors bearing on the choice of foreign policy ends and means.

Power Position

As a small state, Uruguay operates from a position of relative weakness in international politics. She ranks low in the order of world and regional power stratification, primarily because of her limited physical resources. With a land area slightly in excess of 72,000 square miles (about the size of Washington State), Uruguay is the smallest territorial state on the South American continent. As of 1973, the population was about three million (ranking fifteenth among the Hispanic-American states). In recent years,

Note: The author acknowledges with appreciation the information and suggestions provided by Robert K. Goldman from the perspective of his special knowledge of contemporary Uruguay.

population growth has been about 1.3 percent per year, among the lowest in Latin America.

Elements of strength are also evident. In inter-American relations and to some extent in world politics, Uruguay has developed influence based on the factor of prestige stemming from her social and political democratic achievements. Her high educational level (literacy is estimated at 91 percent), high standard of living, and various concerns for the health and welfare of her citizens have distinguished Uruguay from most of the other Latin American nations. Uruguay has also attained a high level of national integration in terms of social homogeneity. From the early twentieth century until recently, few deeply divisive forces have existed in Uruguayan life, but severe economic problems in the 1960s and 70s, and the concomitant decline in national morale, have led to at least a temporary interruption of her democratic system and a loss of vitality and international prestige.

Uruguay's major source of weakness is her economy, which has steadily declined since the mid-1950s. In prior years, beginning near the turn of the present century, political stability allowed Uruguay to develop economically. She grew prosperous on cattle and sheep ranching and other agricultural and pastoral enterprises. As of the early 1970s, about 70 percent of the land was devoted to livestock raising, accounting for two-thirds of the total agricultural production. An advanced welfare state and an extensive system of government-controlled service industries were built on the agrarian affluence. Some of the many state monopolies were profitable, but many were not, resulting in net losses for government enterprises. Thus, industrial imports, the welfare system, and many government operations depended on exports of beef, wool, and hides.

This unbalanced economic system worked successfully as long as traditional products could be exported profitably. While structural economic weaknesses were apparent during the world depression in the 1930s, stagnation was averted by the full market demands for Uruguay's products during World War II and the Korean conflict. Since about 1955, however, the economy has steadily deteriorated, as export products have competed in a shrinking world market characterized by declining prices. The result has been large-scale deficit financing, high inflation, progressive currency devaluation, and default on international loan payments. While a government-imposed austerity program in 1966 and an economic stabilization program in 1968 (involving such measures as currency devaluation and wage-price freezes) have mitigated some of the problems, as of 1974 they remained severe. Serious labor and student unrest, political violence, and other social dislocations grew out of the economic crisis.[1]

---

1. Recent treatments of these problems are Eric N. Baklanoff, "The Decline of South America's First Welfare State: Uruguay's Economic Problems in Historical Perspective,"

A capability analysis of Uruguay must pay special attention to geography. One must emphasize Uruguay's strikingly unique geopolitical situation in the "southern cone" of the Western Hemisphere. Uruguay's foreign policy has been profoundly conditioned by her location on the southeastern (South Atlantic) coast of the South American continent. The nation's proper name, *La República Oriental del Uruguay*, is derived from its position on the eastern shore of the Uruguay River. This area has remained isolated from world politics and beyond the immediate (Caribbean) sphere of U.S. influence, but it has been intimately caught up in the local rivalry between Argentina and Brazil. Uruguay's location between these immensely larger and more powerful adjoining states led to the birth of the Uruguayan nation in 1830 as a buffer state and has greatly influenced her domestic and foreign politics ever since.

Both Argentina and Brazil affected the course of events in Uruguay throughout most of the nineteenth century. One of the most important of all Latin American international wars was fought in the 1860s as a result of Argentine and Brazilian resistance to Paraguayan imperial designs on Uruguay. Argentina continued its efforts to coerce Uruguay to its will as late as the years of the Perón regime (1945–55). An important contemporary problem has been to accommodate these states while remaining independent of them, to remain aloof of great power rivalries in the world at large and to be unfettered by the United States in inter-American relations. The specific policies examined later in this chapter demonstrate more than anything else the consequences of Uruguay's geographic position and the balance of power between Argentina and Brazil.

Nationalism

In addition to its capability, Uruguay's foreign policy is largely determined by its nationalism. Modern Uruguayan nationalism and unity, which date essentially from the beginning of the twentieth century, are rooted in values associated with the process of political, social, and economic modernization and with the high level of development that has been achieved. Until recently, Uruguay ranked as the most democratic and progressive of Latin American states. Its political system has been characterized by effective representative democracy and the protection of civil rights, substantive social egalitarianism, popular political sovereignty, respect for individual freedom, faithfulness to constitutional forms and practices, an extensive social welfare system, and widespread government control of the economy. Since the early part of the twentieth century Uruguay has lived an intense political life, sacrificing its demo-

Revista Brasileira de Economía 24 (1970): 166–82; and Arturo C. Porzecanski, "Uruguay's Continuing Dilemma," *Current History* 66 (January 1974): 28–30.

cratic traditions only briefly. The constitutional system was suspended for short periods during the Great Depression and the early years of World War II. Government since 1968 has been characterized by increased strong-arm rule in the wake of political crisis, culminating in military intervention in the government in early 1973 and the establishment of a military-controlled executive in June of that year. Thus, in the mid-1970s, Uruguay's democratic future is uncertain.

Communications in Uruguay are good, and its ethnically and culturally homogeneous population is highly urbanized. At least 90 percent of all Uruguayans are European immigrants or their descendents, largely of Spanish and Italian extraction. The remaining 10 percent are mostly mestizo, with a few Negroes and almost no Indians. By 1973 about 80 percent of the population was considered urbanized, with about half living in the Montevideo area. The immigrants have created a middle-class society of professional and commercial people and tradesmen with vocational specialization. Class and economic differences persist, and illiteracy and poverty are still found. But the sharpness of class differences has been attenuated. All of these elements together add up to a unique Uruguayan sense of national identity, unity, and integration.

Modern Uruguay has been profoundly influenced by the work and thought of José Batlle y Ordóñez, who more than anyone else stimulated popular nationalism based on economic and social change.[2] Batlle was twice president of Uruguay (1903–7 and 1911–15), dominating the political scene until his death in 1929; his legacy has remained a powerful influence. Through the reformed Colorado party he succeeded in ending endemic partisan military conflict; he designed a welfare state with a form of state socialism, introduced the idea of a plural executive as a protection against dictatorship, and absorbed a large immigrant population into national life.[3] But since 1955 Uruguay has been a troubled land. The opposition Blanco party, representing conservative interests, has argued that the Batlle system has been responsible for Uruguay's economic crisis and political problems.[4] Democratic tradition was carried on with orderly transfers of executive power after elections in 1958 and 1966, but both parties had become more fragmented than ever before by the time of the military intervention in 1973.

2. The leading political biography is by Milton I. Vanger, *José Batlle y Ordóñez of Uruguay: The Creator of His Times, 1902–1907* (Cambridge: Harvard University Press, 1963).

3. The story of pre–World War II economic development and the government's role is told by Simon G. Hanson, *Utopia in Uruguay: Chapters on the Economic History of Uruguay* (New York: Oxford University Press, 1938).

4. Arthur P. Whitaker and David C. Jordan, *Nationalism in Contemporary Latin America* (New York: Free Press, 1966), pp. 127–28. The treatment of Uruguay on pages 121–29 is reflected in the present discussion.

During the 1960s the radical Left all but abandoned the traditional Uruguayan social values, including peaceful constitutional political processes. Government attempts to solve the economic situation led to prolonged, often violent, political crises, including mass labor union and civil servant strikes, widespread student rebelliousness, and terrorist activities by the *Frente de Liberación Nacional* (National Liberation Front), popularly called the Tupamaros. The government met these activities with suspension of constitutional guarantees, decrees of martial law, press censorship, and curtailment of union activities. For workers the major issue was wage control, but many students claimed to have lost faith in Uruguayan democracy.[5] The Tupamaros charged the government with imposing an unnecessary austerity program and suppressing labor unions, the press, and student organizations in order to support a "phony bourgeois democracy."[6]

Special mention should be made of the Tupamaros, who developed for a time the most effective urban terrorist group in Latin America. Organized in 1963 as a rural guerrilla band, they soon turned to urban activities and became centered in Montevideo, the capital and only important city. Operations were increased after 1966 and the organization strengthened, as the Tupamaros engaged in numerous and often spectacular activities —casino and bank robberies, armory raids, radio station bombings, mass distributions of printed propaganda, gun battles with police and army units, and kidnappings and assassinations of police officers, high-ranking government officials, and foreign diplomatic personnel. The most notable international incidents were the murder of a U.S. Agency for International Development police adviser and the holding of the British ambassador for nearly nine months in 1971, after which he was released.

The Tupamaros seemed to enjoy substantial popular support, especially from students and Montevideo's white-collar middle class. Apparently the rebels accurately expressed the frustration these groups felt over Uruguay's national problems. Although the Tupamaros expressed Marxist convictions and spoke of "taking power for the Socialist revolution," their ideology was vague and not clearly identifiable. They were nationalist and strongly anti-U.S.; they were against the established order and advocated radical change, including an end to what they considered to be economic dependency on the United States. Their tactics were aimed at discrediting the government and gaining resources and public support for their movement. The government consistently refused to negotiate with the terrorists. After six years of considerable success, the Tupamaros were

5. News report by John Goshko, *Washington Post,* 16 Aug. 1970.
6. Articles by James Nelson Goodsell in the *Christian Science Monitor,* 5 Aug. and 25 Sept. 1968.

finally brought under control by the army in 1972. In April of that year constitutional guarantees were again suspended and the army was given special powers to facilitate their crackdown against the Tupamaros. Nine months later, after making some thirteen hundred arrests, the army could accurately claim that its campaign had been a success. But then, inspired by this success, the armed forces decided to impose their will in broad areas of "national corruption." This effort led them to play a direct political role after the Tupamaros had been brought under control. Thus, democratic traditions have been assaulted both by revolutionaries and by the armed forces that stopped their efforts.[7]

Uruguay's nationalism has been based not only on its own cultural values but on opposition to those of others, especially the United States. During the first third of the twentieth century, Latin Americans were outraged by U.S. military and economic intervention into their affairs. The most influential literary expression of this *antiyanquismo* at the time was the writing of the Uruguayan philosopher and nationalist José Enrique Rodó. His most important and widely read work, *Ariel*,[8] reflected his view that no matter how essential material things might be, intellectual and spiritual values were immensely more important. On this basis Rodó was disillusioned with the course the U.S. democratic experiment had taken.

In more recent years Uruguayans have had an ambivalent attitude toward the United States. The extensiveness of North American intervention has been greatly reduced, and Uruguay has not suffered any real coercion. However, the United States continues to be sharply criticized. University students are especially prone to anti-Americanism, no matter what their political persuasion might otherwise be. Uruguay's government has cooperated with the United States in a number of areas of international relations but has also insisted upon independent action.

THE MEANS AND ENDS OF POLICY

The combination of the realities of Uruguay's capability and the nature of her nationalism largely shape her foreign policy goals and determine the techniques selected to achieve these ends. Uruguay's primary interests have been (1) to maintain her independence from all stronger powers, especially Argentina, Brazil and the United States (in that order); (2) to continue her own stable, democratic welfare system of government, promote representative democracy, and protect human rights in the other

7. For a useful bibliography and commentary regarding the Tupamaros, see Charles A. Russell, James A. Miller, and Robert E. Hildner, "The Urban Guerrilla in Latin America: A Select Bibliography," *Latin American Research Review* 9 (Spring 1974): 70–74.
8. José Enrique Rodó, *Ariel* (Cambridge: At the University Press, 1967).

American states; and (3) to strengthen her economy by expanding traditional exports. The range of techniques available to Uruguay has been limited because she must rely on other than physical power, either military or economic. She tends to use the same means chosen by most small states, such as (1) playing active roles in international organizations; (2) promoting international law and supporting such principles and procedures as nonintervention and peaceful settlement of disputes; and (3) exploiting the rivalries of greater powers while remaining as noncommital as possible herself. Uruguay's relative weakness goes far to explain the means she has adopted—and rejected—to achieve her ends. She has not, for example, used military techniques in any important way, nor has she attempted to build up significantly her military strength. As William S. Stokes has pointed out, since defense against either Brazil or Argentina is realistically impossible, Uruguay has not spent large sums on defense.[9]

Independent Role

The desire for and general achievement of an independent role in international politics has been a reflection of both Uruguay's national consciousness and her political stability. In some important areas, however, Uruguay must depend on outside assistance. She has felt that she must rely upon the United States for protection against possible European incursions in the La Plata region. Uruguay participated in hemispheric defense measures in both world wars and has accepted U.S. assistance in order to maintain her minimum military requirements. The greatest dependence on others, especially the United States, has been in economic and financial areas, where Uruguay is most vulnerable. Her need for aid and loans, both public and private, has somewhat circumscribed her independence. Furthermore, being highly dependent on her traditional exports for her well-being, she must maintain friendly relations with her best customers, especially the United States and Europe. Expansion of her exports must be sought as much as possible. To this end, Uruguay has recently developed more trade contacts with Communist countries.

Uruguay has attempted to play the greater powers against each other, especially Argentina against Brazil. In recent years, Uruguay seems to have become more suspicious of Argentina than of Brazil and to have worked more closely with her northern neighbor. Any lessening of the Brazilian-Argentine rivalry, which has occurred from time to time, works to Uruguay's benefit, as she then has less to fear from encroachments from either power. In world-wide terms, Uruguay has been able to maintain a

9. William S. Stokes, *Latin American Politics* (New York: Thomas Y. Crowell Co., 1959), p. 219.

relatively noncommital position in the cold war, refusing to submit as a client to either the United States or the Soviet Union. She can afford to do this largely because of her geographic remoteness from North America, Europe, and cold-war concerns. Because Uruguay is the client of no other state and because she has assumed trade contacts with Communist countries, one should not assume that she has adopted or will adopt a position ideologically opposed both to that of the United States and that of the USSR and identified with that of the Third World of Africa and Asia.[10] Rather, these facts reflect a basically isolationist posture, except in economic matters, on the part of Uruguay (a posture characteristic of most of the rest of Latin America), but one oriented toward the United States in times of world crisis.

On the inter-American scene, Uruguay has actively sought to extend her democratic political and social values through proposals to the other members of the inter-American regional system (discussed below). Other than this extension of her ideology and value system, however, Uruguay has not seemed interested in furthering her prestige or power. Despite her relatively high level of development, but in conformity with her lack of international political power, Uruguay accepts her isolated position in world and inter-American affairs and her unquestionably small-state status. Uruguayans are proud of their country, as Russell Fitzgibbon has noted, but they realize that they cannot compete with the great powers of the world.[11]

International Organization and Law

Uruguay turns largely to international organization and law to implement her foreign policy. She was an active participant in the Second Hague Peace Conference and in the League of Nations, and today she plays an energetic role in the United Nations and the Organization of American States (OAS). Such institutions are viewed as counterpoises to stronger states because they tend to limit the actions of the great powers more than those of the small and because they offer the latter a permanent framework within which to ally with one another and pool their persuasive resources in an effort to achieve the common goals of remaining politically independent while deriving economic and financial benefits. Thus, through both the United Nations and the OAS, Uruguay, along with other "developing" nations, has worked for international economic cooperation and for development funds. International organization also provides machinery for the peaceful settlement of disputes, compatible

10. For an investigation of the sentiment that has existed, see Aldo E. Solari, *El tercerismo en el Uruguay. Ensayo* (Montevideo: Editorial Alfa, 1965).

11. Russell H. Fitzgibbon, *Uruguay: Portrait of a Democracy* (New Brunswick, N.J.: Rutgers University Press, 1954), p. viii.

with the interests of small states—especially one such as Uruguay, which functions as a buffer state between considerably stronger powers.[12] In addition, it has been through the forum of inter-American organization that Uruguay has presented concrete proposals for the promotion of democracy and the protection of human rights in the Americas.

Reliance upon international law, based upon the concept of "sovereign equality," also serves Uruguayan interests as a small state. Inter-American law stresses the corollary of nonintervention, which legally limits stronger states and protects weaker ones. As will be demonstrated later, Uruguay has not adopted an "absolutist" position toward nonintervention. On the one hand, she adheres to inter-American treaties and the Charter of the OAS, which outlaws unilateral intervention of any kind, and she is unwilling to allow collective military intervention by a multilateral inter-American force, either ad hoc or permanent. On the other hand, she has been willing to condone a form of multilateral political intervention in another Latin American state when she felt her own security was threatened. Uruguay proposed such intervention in Argentina at the end of World War II, and she has espoused collective intervention to promote representative democracy and to protect human rights.[13]

DEVELOPMENT OF MAJOR FOREIGN POLICIES

A brief examination of Uruguay's major foreign policies as they have developed over the years substantively illustrates the nationalism, capability factors, ends of policy, and policy techniques discussed above.

The Nineteenth Century

Uruguay's national beginnings grew out of the rivalry between Argentina and Brazil for control of Uruguay, then called *La Banda Oriental*. During the Spanish-American struggle for independence, Uruguayan patriots achieved liberation from Spain and seceded from Buenos Aires, which considered Uruguay an Argentine province. But in 1822 Uruguay was annexed as the Cisplatine province of the independent Brazilian empire.[14]

12. Ibid., p. 254.
13. Almost no research has been done concerning Uruguayan foreign policy formulation, so one must depend largely upon impressions and logical deduction regarding the roles of political parties and pressure groups, the bureaucracy, public opinion, and the armed forces in the decision-making process. See the bibliographic note at the end of this chapter for some general sources from which some information may be gleaned.
14. John Street, *Artigas and the Independence of Uruguay* (Cambridge: At the University Press, 1959). On the Argentine-Brazilian colonial rivalry in Uruguay, see Carlos Carbajal, *La penetración luso-brasileña en el Uruguay* (Montevideo: Talleres Gráficos Prometeo, 1948). Spain did not recognize Uruguay until 1882.

In 1825, Uruguay declared her independence from Brazil, and Argentina entered the dispute on the side of the rebels, fighting an indecisive three-year war with Brazil. Britain, its commercial interests in the area disrupted, used its influence to pressure Argentina and Brazil into signing the Treaty of Montevideo (1828), in which they agreed to recognize Uruguayan independence. With the promulgation of a constitution in 1830, Uruguay began its sovereign existence as a buffer state between the two South American giants.

Uruguayans soon divided into rival political parties, the Colorados and the Blancos, and carried on intermittent civil war for the rest of the century. This unstable, polarized political system invited intervention from Uruguay's neighbors, despite the agreement in the 1828 treaty. Associated with this strife were boundary disputes with Argentina and Brazil. One of the more important developments growing out of this complex milieu was what Uruguayans call the Great War, which began in 1836. An alliance between Argentine dictator Juan Manuel de Rosas and the Blancos conducted a siege of Montevideo from 1841 to 1851 against the Colorados and the anti-Rosas Argentines. From 1845 to 1850 the French and British navies blockaded Buenos Aires and simultaneously supported the Montevideans;[15] after their withdrawal, Brazil joined the anti-Rosas alignment and Rosas and the Blancos were soon defeated. Brazil had aligned with the Colorado party in part because she had been assured of a favorable settlement of her Uruguayan boundary. In 1851 Brazil forced upon Uruguay a treaty in which she renounced an earlier claim to almost half of her national territory along the northern frontier.[16]

From 1865 to 1870 the Colorados united with Argentina and Brazil to resist the expansionist moves of Paraguayan dictator Francisco Solano López. This union produced the Paraguayan War, known in Paraguay as the War of the Triple Alliance. A Blanco government, having poor relations with both Argentina and Brazil, responded to Paraguayan overtures for a common policy in 1862 when López held out "vague promises of military support."[17] López had in mind a Paraguay-led empire of central South American states, including Uruguay. In 1864, Argentina and Brazil supported a Colorado uprising that unseated the Blancos, and López responded by invading both states near their Uru-

---

15. John Frank Cady, *Foreign Intervention in the Rio de la Plata, 1838–50* (Philadelphia: University of Pennsylvania Press, 1929), and Dexter Perkins, *The Monroe Doctrine, 1826–1867* (Baltimore: Johns Hopkins Press, 1933), pp. 127–37.

16. Gordon Ireland, *Boundaries, Possessions, and Conflicts in South America* (Cambridge: Harvard University Press, 1938), treats Uruguay's boundary disputes with Argentina and Brazil and describes her treaty relations with several South American states. Also useful is José Aguiar, *Nuestra frontera con el Brasil, su evolución histórico-geográfica* (Montevideo: Imprenta Militar, 1937).

17. Harold Eugene Davis, *History of Latin America* (New York: Ronald Press, 1968), p. 413. The subject is treated fully by Pelham H. Box, *Origins of the Paraguayan War* (Urbana: University of Illinois Press, 1930).

guayan borders. In May 1865 a triple alliance of Brazil, Argentina, and Uruguay was formed against Paraguay; the resulting war dragged on for five years until March 1870, ending with Paraguay's complete defeat.

Early Twentieth Century

As Uruguay became more politically stable in the twentieth century, her foreign policy expanded beyond her parochial nineteenth century interests and she became active in world and hemispheric affairs. Uruguay was represented at the Second Hague Peace Conference in 1907, where she proposed a form of treaty for obligatory arbitration.[18] During World War I, the Uruguayan government supported the principle of American solidarity, and the Uruguayan president proposed an inter-American conference to give it expression.[19] But because this solidarity was lacking, Uruguay never declared war, although she severed diplomatic relations with Germany on 7 October 1917. Uruguay took part in the Versailles conference and ratified the treaty, thereby becoming one of ten Latin American charter members of the League of Nations. Unlike several others, Uruguay never seceded from the league. As a member, she promoted both international arbitration and international humanitarian activities.[20]

One of the best known Uruguayan international proposals was made on 21 April 1920, by President Baltasar Brum. He proposed that the Monroe Doctrine be multilateralized and an American League of Nations be established, based upon this expanded doctrine. Dr. Brum was only mildly critical of the existing Monroe Doctrine and even defended its basic purpose of safeguarding the Americas from European territorial ambitions. However, he recognized that Latin Americans objected to the doctrine because it had been used to convert Latin America into a kind of North American protectorate. But Brum believed that these objections could be overcome, Latin America could be placed on a level of juridical equality with the United States, and inter-American solidarity could be strengthened if each state would make a similar declaration, agreeing to intervene on behalf of another American state and defend the rights of all against extracontinental encroachments.[21]

Three years later, the Brum proposal was submitted by the Uruguayan delegation to the Fifth International Conference of American States (Santiago de Chile, 1923). But neither the other Latin American govern-

18. Marvin Alisky, *Uruguay: A Contemporary Survey* (New York: Frederick A. Praeger, 1969), p. 147.
19. Samuel Flagg Bemis, *The Latin American Policy of the United States* (New York: Harcourt, Brace & Co., 1943), p. 290.
20. Alisky, *Uruguay*, pp. 142–43.
21. Baltasar Brum, *American Solidarity: Conference by the President of the Republic of Uruguay, Dr. Baltasar Brum, at the University of Montevideo, on the 21st of April, 1920* (Montevideo: Imprenta Nacional, 1920); Brum, "A Defensive Alliance for the Americas," in *The Monroe Doctrine*, ed. Donald M. Dozer (New York: Alfred A. Knopf, 1965), pp. 83–86.

ments nor the United States offered encouragement. The Latin American delegations were intent on attacking the interventionist policies of the United States, which were being justified in the name of the Monroe Doctrine. The United States was no more interested in developing a regional league than a universal one, nor did she wish to pledge protection of the territorial integrity of the Americas from her own intervention. The Brum proposal was sent to the Governing Board of the Pan American Union "for further study," a diplomatic way of abandoning the idea.[22] Nevertheless, Brum's ideas, although initially frustrated, were eventually adopted by the inter-American system, beginning at the Montevideo conference in 1933, and most importantly in the 1947 Inter-American Treaty of Reciprocal Assistance, which pledged the mutual defense of the Americas.

World War II

Uruguay continued its cooperative but independent policy toward the United States during World War II, although at the beginning of the hostilities her government was neutral toward Germany. In December 1939, in violation of Western Hemispheric neutrality, the German "pocket battleship" *Graf Spee* engaged in a South Atlantic battle with three British cruisers. Badly damaged, the German ship put into Montevideo for repairs but was soon ordered by Uruguay to leave. After the crew sank the ship in Uruguayan territorial waters, Uruguay merely lodged a formal complaint with the German government.[23] In the meantime, an Uruguayan journalist and professor, Hugo Fernández Artucio, made sensational charges that the German embassy in Montevideo was the center for clandestine activities in South America and was plotting to help overthrow the Uruguayan government.[24] An investigation by the National Congress in 1940 confirmed the charges, and the government took steps to stop such activities.

After the fall of France in 1940, the United States moved to develop closer military ties with Latin America. According to J. Lloyd Mecham, the conversations and agreement with Uruguay concerning military bases there resolved a number of issues and provided a model for agreements

22. J. Lloyd Mecham, *A Survey of United States–Latin American Relations* (Boston: Houghton Mifflin Co., 1965), p. 105; see also p. 76.

23. For an account of Uruguayan policy by the minister of national defense at the time, see Alfredo R. Campos, *Un episodio de la Segunda Guerra Mundial en aguas territoriales de la República Oriental del Uruguay* (Montevideo: Centro Militar, 1952). An official documentary collection is contained in Uruguay, Ministerio de Relaciones Exteriores, *Antecedentes relativo al hundimiento del acorazado "Admiral Graf Spee" y la internación del barco mercante "Tacoma"* (Montevideo: Ministerio de Relaciones Exteriores, 1940). For a British view of Uruguayan policy, see Eugene Millington Drake, comp., *The Drama of Graf Spee and the Battle of the Plate: A Documentary Anthology, 1914–1964* (London: Peter Davies, 1965), part 7.

24. An abridgement of the official text in English is *The Nazi Underground in South America* (New York: Farrar & Rinehart, 1942).

with other Latin American states.[25] The major issue was the U.S. request for full jurisdiction over bases for a long term. An agreement concluded in November 1940 provided that Uruguay, with U.S. assistance and for the purposes of hemispheric defense, would construct a naval and air station on the Plata River, to remain under Uruguayan sovereignty and to be manned by Uruguayans, with technical help from the United States. Shortly thereafter, the Uruguayan government reiterated its past support for continental solidarity, urging that all Latin American governments agree to the Uruguayan position during World War I, that no American state fighting for its rights against a non-American power would be considered a belligerent.

In January 1942, shortly after the United States had entered the war, Uruguay broke off diplomatic relations with the Axis powers. A few days earlier Uruguay had signed a lend-lease agreement with the United States to receive $17 million worth of armaments and munitions, thus concluding negotiations that had begun in 1940. In February, President Alfredo Baldomir dissolved Congress because of the obstructionist tactics of the pro-Axis-dominated Nationalist (Blanco) party, which had bitterly opposed the agreement with the United States. Uruguayan airports were made available to the air forces of all American nations, and the free use of ports for the purpose of defense was extended to the navies of the American belligerents. Uruguay joined in the South Atlantic submarine patrol.[26]

During the war Uruguay was an important member of the Emergency Advisory Committee for Political Defense (CPD), authorized by the Third Meeting of Ministers of Foreign Affairs in Rio de Janeiro in 1942. Headquartered in Montevideo, the CPD was chaired by Uruguayan Foreign Minister Alberto Guani. Consisting of representatives from seven governments, the CPD sought to combat Axis activities in South America. In December 1943, after a coup in Bolivia, the CPD proposed that the American governments collectively refuse to recognize governments that had come to power through force during the war, a policy known as the Guani doctrine. But the major concern of the CPD was with Argentina after the 1943 coup by an ultranationalist army faction of which Juan Perón was a part. As Arthur P. Whitaker has said, "Actually, any threat of war in the River Plate area came from the military dictatorship at Buenos Aires itself, and the most likely target was Uruguay, where Argentine refugees were carrying on a vigorous campaign against the [Argentine government]."[27] At the Bogotá conference in 1948 Uruguay attempted to have the CPD continued as an inter-American agency aimed at the

25. Mecham, *A Survey of United States–Latin American Relations*, pp. 136–38.
26. J. Lloyd Mecham, *The United States and Inter-American Security, 1889–1960* (Austin: University of Texas Press, 1961), pp. 196–97, 216.
27. Arthur P. Whitaker, *The United States and Argentina* (Cambridge: Harvard University Press, 1954), p. 127.

promotion of democracy and human rights, but the CPD was not included in the Charter.

An important Uruguayan proposal approving collective (multilateral) intervention to oppose dictators and promote democracy in the Americas was offered to the inter-American system by Uruguay's foreign minister, Eduardo Rodríguez Larreta, in late 1945. The Rodríguez Larreta proposal (often erroneously referred to in English as the Larreta proposal) was consistent with Uruguay's own democratic ideals, but it was also directed against Axis-inclined Argentina (although Argentina was not mentioned by name). Dr. Rodríguez argued that "peace is safe only where democratic principles of government prevail," and he urged that in a case of the violation of the basic rights of man in any American republic, "the community of nations should take collective multilateral action to restore full democracy there." He anticipated that the greatest objection to his proposal would revolve around Latin American insistence on absolute nonintervention. He said that the principle of nonintervention should not be invoked "in order to violate all other principles with immunity," and he pointed out that multilateral action was not prohibited by the inter-American community.[28] The diplomatic response to the Uruguayan note reflected the tension between the two hallowed principles of Pan Americanism—nonintervention and the promotion of democracy—with most Latin American states deciding in favor of the former. Some governments responded favorably to the Rodríguez Larreta proposal, but the majority either rejected it or so qualified their acceptance as to make it tantamount to rejection.[29] The United States, simultaneously pursuing a diligent unilateral anti-Perón policy, fully endorsed the proposal. The opposition was unwilling to permit any modification of the nonintervention principle.

Post-War Policies

Uruguay, a charter member of the United Nations, has been an active member of world organization. She supported UN intervention in Korea in 1950, donating the equivalent of $2 million in aid and supplying blankets and other woolen goods. Uruguay has been especially active in the United Nations Educational, Scientific, and Cultural Organization (UNESCO).[30] She has received economic assistance from international

28. For the text, see (U.S.) *Department of State Bulletin* 13 (25 Nov. 1945): 864–66. The Spanish text and a number of related documents are in Uruguay, Ministerio de Relaciones Exteriores, *Paralelismo entre la democracia y la paz . . .* (Montevideo: Sección Prensa, Informaciones y Publicaciones, 1946).
29. The text of the U.S. endorsement is in (U.S.) *Department of State Bulletin* 13 (2 Dec. 1945): 892. The best reference collection is Pan American Union, "Consulta del gobierno del Uruguay y contestaciones de los gobiernos . . .," mimeographed (Washington, D.C., 1946).
30. Uruguayan Institute of International Law and Carnegie Endowment for International Peace, *Uruguay and the United Nations* (New York: Manhattan Publishing Co., 1958).

organizations associated with the UN system (see table 13.1). Uruguay has favored regional (OAS) settlement of such inter-American disputes as those involving Guatemala, Cuba, and the Dominican Republic in 1960, however, rather than allowing UN jurisdiction. But she so opposed U.S. intervention in the Dominican Republic in 1965 that she declared in favor of UN involvement in this inter-American dispute.

The United States has been Uruguay's major supplier of economic and military assistance. From the U.S. point of view, all aid has been in keeping with the needs of mutual security. The security aspect is obvious in the case of military cooperation, but the U.S. policy also assumes that economic development furthers political stability, which lessens the threat of internal subversion and redounds to the security of the United States. Table 13.2 indicates the net obligations and loan authorizations of U.S. economic (including technical) assistance to Uruguay since World War II, and also multilateral programs of the OAS, to which the United States is the largest contributor. Both President Truman and President Eisenhower emphasized private capital and international agencies as sources for development funds. As a result, Uruguay received relatively small sums of direct U.S. aid, along with the rest of Latin America, although aid increased substantially during the Mutual Security Act period. Important technical assistance projects were undertaken and foodstuffs were purchased under the Agricultural Trade Development and Assistance Act of 1954 (PL 480). Since the advent of the Alliance for Progress, aid to Uruguay has been augmented significantly in all areas of assistance.

Uruguay has not been inclined toward cold-war concerns nor anxious to increase her standing military forces. However, her strategic location on the Plata River and the tenuous relationship between the United States and Argentina after World War II made a military agreement desirable

Table 13.1 Economic Assistance to Uruguay from UN—associated
International Organizations

(in millions of $U.S.)

Organization	Fiscal Years	Amount
International Bank for Reconstruction & Development (IBRD)	1951–72	141.7
UN Development Program: Special Fund	1962–72	8.6
UN Development Program: Technical Assistance	1953–72	3.4
Other	1959–72	0.9
Total		154.6

Source: Agency for International Development, *U.S. Overseas Loans and Grants and Assistance from International Organizations, Obligations and Loan Authorizations, July 1, 1945–June 30, 1972* (Washington, D.C., May 1973).

Table 13.2 U.S. Economic Assistance to Uruguay

(in millions of $U.S. by fiscal year)

	Aid Programs			
Organization	Post-War Relief 1946-48	Marshall Plan 1949-52	Mutual Security Act 1953-61	Foreign Assistance Act 1962-72
AID & predecessor agencies	–	0.4	10.7	65.3
PL 480 (Food for Peace)	–	–	23.4	35.8
Peace Corps	–	–	–	2.3
Inter-American Development Bank	–	–	–	88.2
Export-Import Bank	–	2.6	–	6.6
Other	2.0	0.4	–	10.4
Total	2.0	3.4	34.1	208.6

Source: Agency for International Development, *U.S. Overseas Loans and Grants and Assistance from International Organizations, Obligations and Loan Authorizations, July 1, 1945–June 30, 1972* ([Washington, D.C.,] May 1973).

from the U.S. point of view. In later years, as U.S. policy shifted from hemispheric defense to combatting internal subversion, it has been concerned with terrorism in Uruguay. A bilateral military assistance treaty between the two states was signed on 30 June 1952, but it did not come into force until 11 June 1953. Although the negotiations were friendly, Uruguayan ratification was delayed for a year in the face of congressional opposition not only from nationalists and Yankeephobes but also from liberals who opposed such arrangements.[31] Under the treaty, Uruguay has received grant assistance from the United States for the performance of some military services in support of hemispheric defense plans and the Rio Treaty of 1947.[32] From 1953 through 1972, the value of U.S. military deliveries, including equipment, training, and related support, totaled $58.7 million.[33] Uruguayan officers and men have been trained in the United States and the Canal Zone, and military missions have been sent to Uruguay.

Uruguay has opposed the creation of an Inter-American Peace Force. While she approved the activities of the Inter-American Defense Board during World War II and voted in 1945 to make it a permanent organization charged with planning hemispheric defense, Uruguay has since been unwilling to approve either an ad hoc or a permanent military force. Uruguay voted against a resolution passed at the May 1965 Meeting of

31. Whitaker, *The United States and Argentina,* pp. 242–43.
32. U.S., Department of State, *Treaties and Other International Acts,* ser. 2778, pubn. 5176, *Mutual Defense Assistance, Agreement Between the United States of America and Uruguay, signed at Montevideo June 30, 1952.*
33. Agency for International Development, *U.S. Overseas Loans and Grants and Assistance from International Organizations, Obligations and Loan Authorizations, July 1, 1945-June 30, 1972* ([Washington, D.C.], May 1973).

Ministers of Foreign Affairs authorizing a peace force to be sent to the Dominican Republic, and she was one of the leading critics in both the OAS and the United Nations of the Dominican intervention by the United States (although she supplied medical support for the OAS Police Force in 1965). Uruguay cast one of the eleven negative votes against an unsuccessful Argentine effort in February 1967 to amend the OAS Charter so as to establish a permanent consultative defense committee to prepare for "collective defense against aggression." This proposal, made at the Third Special Inter-American Conference in Buenos Aires, which extensively amended the charter, raised the question of a permanent force, even though it was not part of the amendment. Nevertheless, in the debate Uruguay expressed her opposition on the grounds that the amendment implied such a force.[34]

Fidelismo has been dealt with in Uruguay in accordance with her tradition of tolerance, but strong action has been taken in specific cases of Communist activities within her borders. Uruguay was the first Latin American nation to recognize the Soviet Union in 1926, and soon thereafter Montevideo was serving as Latin American headquarters for the Comintern and the dissemination point for its propaganda.[35] In 1935, however, Uruguay severed relations with the USSR when Soviet diplomats in Montevideo helped organize subversive activities in Brazil; in 1939 Uruguay supported the expulsion of the Soviet Union from the League of Nations. Relations were reestablished during World War II when the Soviet Union joined the Allies and have been maintained since that time. Nevertheless, Uruguay has disapproved of Soviet activities; in 1961 she expelled the Soviet first secretary, along with the Cuban ambassador, for engaging in subversive activities, and in 1968 three Soviet diplomats were ejected for their activities during strikes in Uruguay.[36] In January 1962 Uruguay was one of six Latin American states to oppose the denial of further participation in the OAS by the Castro government, and one of four who continued to maintain ties with Cuba. However, when the OAS further condemned Cuba in 1964 for intervention in Venezuela, Uruguay complied and supported her fellow democratic government in Caracas in favoring the OAS sanctions against Cuba.[37]

One of Uruguay's most important international endeavors is her foreign trade (see table 13.3). Uruguay's best customers and largest suppliers have been the United States, Great Britain, and Western Europe, although trade with other Latin American states has increased over the

34. James R. Jose, *An Inter-American Peace Force within the Framework of the Organization of American States: Advantages, Impediments, and Implications* (Metuchen, N.J.: Scarecrow Press, 1970).
35. Alisky, *Uruguay*, p. 151.
36. *New York Times*, 13 Jan. 1961 and 25 Sept. 1968.
37. John N. Plank, ed., *Cuba and the United States* (Washington, D.C.: Brookings Institution, 1967), pp. 83–84.

Table 13.3 Foreign Trade of Uruguay, 1953–72

(in millions of $U.S. by calendar year)

Trading Partner	1953 E	1953 I	1954 E	1954 I	1955 E	1955 I	1956 E	1956 I	1957 E	1957 I
United States	57.8	25.1	34.2	45.7	16.2	40.0	27.8	36.5	19.7	53.0
United Kingdom	86.1	23.3	48.4	38.2	30.2	21.9	33.2	14.7	30.0	22.3
Soviet Union and E. European bloc	1.0	0.3	24.8	1.2	11.6	1.3	17.1	5.4	23.1	1.3
LAFTA countries	19.0	51.7	42.2	57.7	36.5	52.8	33.9	51.3	13.3	55.2
All others	134.1	76.0	89.8	92.0	80.2	78.9	113.1	73.2	87.5	77.5
Total	298.0	176.4	239.4	234.8	174.7	194.9	225.1	181.1	173.6	209.3

Trading Partner	1958 E	1958 I	1959 E	1959 I	1960 E	1960 I	1961 E	1961 I	1962 E	1962 I
United States	9.6	28.0	20.2	36.3	24.0	63.2	25.1	49.7	26.5	45.5
United Kingdom	23.7	8.1	16.9	9.7	34.6	17.9	44.4	23.8	30.6	20.3
Soviet Union and E. European bloc	31.3	7.7	27.1	10.4	6.5	12.3	8.6	1.9	11.7	2.6
LAFTA countries	16.2	44.4	3.3	44.6	4.1	55.9	6.6	36.8	10.7	38.0
All others	62.6	54.9	63.7	55.4	65.1	65.4	83.9	84.3	71.1	101.8
Total	143.4	143.1	131.2	156.4	134.3	214.7	168.6	196.5	150.6	208.2

Trading Partner	1963		1964		1965		1966		1967	
	E	I	E	I	E	I	E	I	E	I
United States	26.8	31.5	14.6	36.9	40.0	20.3	33.6	24.9	14.5	21.6
United Kingdom	49.8	18.9	40.3	15.4	36.2	13.5	35.5	8.8	38.1	9.5
Soviet Union and E. European bloc	8.0	1.6	14.4	3.0	10.9	2.0	17.8	2.6	12.4	4.8
LAFTA countries	19.0	39.4	18.2	63.4	25.9	41.9	33.5	49.8	17.4	41.4
All others	79.9	78.6	109.2	74.1	104.9	49.2	119.3	67.5	92.3	56.6
Total	183.5	170.0	196.7	192.8	217.9	126.9	239.7	153.6	174.7	133.9

	1968		1969		1970		1971		1972	
	E	I	E	I	E	I	E	I	E	I
United States	24.2	38.4	16.6	30.9	21.1	40.6	12.2	31.9	9.4	37.3
United Kingdom	42.0	8.1	31.5	11.6	20.5	15.4	16.0	18.3	15.6	11.4
Soviet Union and E. European bloc	9.4	1.9	11.6	6.1	31.3	7.7	7.6	3.1	17.5	2.5
LAFTA countries	24.3	50.7	30.4	54.9	32.7	85.1	49.5	74.3	26.8	63.5
All others	93.1	62.1	115.7	85.3	111.5	91.4	141.5	94.0	153.2	69.9
Total	193.0	161.2	205.8	188.8	217.1	240.2	226.8	221.6	222.5	184.6

E   Exports from Uruguay
I   Imports into Uruguay
Source: EXPOIMPO Computer Program by John A. Hutchins, Department of Political Science, U.S. Naval Academy, Annapolis, Md.

decade of the 1960s, the increase continuing into the 1970s. The Uruguayan economy is vulnerable to changing world prices and other market conditions affecting its primary exports of wool and beef. For example, when Britain devalued the pound and barred imports of South American beef in 1967 to help control hoof-and-mouth disease, Uruguay suffered a financial blow; but the following year, when the ban was partially lifted, Uruguay was able to reduce her beef surplus significantly. Also, in 1967 Uruguay began negotiations with the Soviet Union and other Communist states to increase trade with them. While this relationship now represents a small portion of Uruguay's total trade, the Soviet bloc began at this time to provide oil for Uruguay, her greatest import need, and was willing to accept an unfavorable balance of trade with Uruguay in order to maintain the relationship.[38]

Uruguay is a charter member of the Latin American Free Trade Association (LAFTA), created by the 1960 Treaty of Montevideo and headquartered in the Uruguayan capital city. The goals of LAFTA are "to establish, gradually and progressively, a Latin American common market," and to achieve economic integration "on the basis of an effective reciprocity of benefits." Despite its hopeful economic potential for increased trade—the initial attraction for Uruguay—the fear of the smaller countries in LAFTA has been that new industries stimulated by the expanded regional markets will move to the already more developed nations of Brazil, Mexico, and Argentina. As a result, tariff cutting has proceeded at a considerably slower pace than was originally anticipated.[39] Uruguayan disillusionment with LAFTA was summed up by a government official in August 1970 when he said: "We had nothing to bargain with when the tariffs were being lowered. The necessities that we imported were already coming in without tariffs. We were left to the new imperialists, the big countries of the zone. . . ."

On 23 April 1969, Uruguay joined Argentina, Bolivia, Brazil, and Paraguay, all of whom border on the Rio de la Plata or its tributaries, in signing a treaty for the development of the river basin, especially its hydroelectric potential.

SUMMARY

Uruguay's foreign policy problems and opportunities result from a number of factors, the most important being her status as a small state but

38. For the ups and downs of Uruguayan trade relations with Communist states, see Alisky, *Uruguay*, pp. 153–54.
39. Sidney S. Dell, *A Latin American Common Market?* (London: Oxford University Press, 1966); Miguel S. Wionczek, ed., *Latin American Economic Integration* (New York: Frederick A. Praeger, 1966); and Joseph Grunwald, *Latin American Economic Integration and U.S. Policy* (Washington, D.C.: Brookings Institution, 1972).

one with a highly integrated society; her location in the "southern cone," which places her in the vortex of the great rivalry for power between Argentina and Brazil but distant from world power struggles; and the nature of her economy, which is dependent on the export of wool and meat. Uruguay has been able to assume independent positions in a number of areas, but she is limited by her dependence on world markets for her products and on foreign economic aid. These factors, coupled with Uruguay's own highly developed democracy—in considerable difficulty since 1968—have been reflected in her policy positions. Various doctrines named for Uruguayan statesmen who proposed them—Brum, Guani, Rodríguez Larreta—have expressed traditional Uruguayan concerns with international cooperation, juridical equality of states, promotion of democracy, and suspicion of Argentina. The most difficult continuing international problem for Uruguay is her foreign trade, the kingpin of her economy.

BIBLIOGRAPHICAL NOTE

Little has been written concerning the foreign policy of Uruguay and no study deals with the broad aspects of the subject at any length. The reader interested in pursuing the subject must glean information from general works on Uruguay and on the international relations of Latin America, news reports, and official publications of Uruguay, the United States, and the Organization of American States. The following general introductions to Uruguay have chapters on foreign policy and related information throughout: Marvin Alisky, *Uruguay: A Contemporary Survey* (New York: Frederick A. Praeger, 1969); Russell Fitzgibbon, *Uruguay: Portrait of a Democracy* (New Brunswick, N.J.: Rutgers University Press, 1954); George Pendle, *Uruguay*, 3d ed. (London: Royal Institute of International Affairs, 1963); and the *Area Handbook for Uruguay* (Washington, D.C.: Foreign Area Studies, The American University, 1971). For sources on specific topics, the reader is directed to the corresponding notes to the same treatments in this study. Uruguay publishes a treaty series and an annual *Memoria* by the Ministry of Foreign Affairs.

14/Hans J. Hoyer

Paraguay

In the conduct of foreign relations during the 1970s, Paraguay's major problems concern (1) critical economic and political ties, primarily with Brazil, Argentina, and the United States; (2) trade expansion through the Latin American Free Trade Association (LAFTA); (3) the necessity for a strong posture of defense against subversive elements; and (4) expansion of transportation and communications networks through cooperation in multinational projects.

THE PROBLEMS OF FOREIGN RELATIONS

With respect to Argentina and Brazil, it is of vital interest to Paraguay to maintain cordial relations, since these nations control Paraguay's outlets to the Atlantic Ocean. Moreover, good relations with these powers are also essential because Paraguay's independence has been maintained, in part, through her ability to profit from the rivalry between Argentina and Brazil. Therefore, Paraguay has sought the support of international law and institutions in her relations with these countries. A case in point occurred during the 1960s and 1970s, when the Ministry of Foreign Affairs devoted considerable attention to Argentina's interference with river traffic in Paraguay and to alleged Brazilian encroachment on Paraguayan territory in the Guirá Rapids area of the Alto Paraná River. There has also been cooperation, for example, in the joint development of the River Plate Basin.[1]

In the area of trade, Paraguay's landlocked location creates economic disadvantages, since she must compete in the world market, and her export economy can be described as depending almost entirely upon the economic health of the Argentine construction industry. Shipping goods from Asunción to Buenos Aires for shipment to final destinations is expensive. This has been the chief factor limiting a more rapid growth of exports, and until 1972 it contributed to Paraguay's unfavorable trade balance. Paraguayan exports, which consisted predominantly of agricultural products, amounted to $266.5 million between 1966 and 1970; but imports, which consist principally of vehicles, machinery, and to a lesser degree wheat and fuel oil, totalled $306.5 million during that same period. By 1972, however, the unfavorable trade balance was reversed temporarily. In 1972, Paraguay's exports amounted to $86.2 million while

1. *Area Handbook for Paraguay* (Washington, D.C.: Foreign Area Studies, The American University, 1972), pp. 164–65; *Latin America* (London), 15 Dec. 1972; interview with Dr. Luis Guzmán, Inter-American Foundation, March 1973.

imports totalled $69.8 million. The picture improved even more during the first eight months in 1973 when exports came up to $96.7 million and imports fell to $65.5 million. During the period in 1973 meat became the most important export item. West Germany was the best customer, taking nearly 20 percent of the total, followed by Argentina with over 13 percent and the United States with almost 13 percent.[2] By November 1974, however, considering the drastic fall in soya bean prices, the drop in the value of meat, exports, and the increased cost of oil and other imports, Paraguay experienced a balance of trade deficit. There was even talk of a threat to the exchange rate of the guarani, which has been fixed at 126 to the dollar for the past fifteen years.

Although Paraguay does not depend on one or two items for export, as do many of the other Latin American countries, more than half of Paraguayan exports between 1960 and 1969 went to Argentina and the United States. Exports to Argentina were principally wood and wood products. Paraguay's export and import economy is, in fact, tied to that of Argentina and the United States and to an increasing extent also to Brazil and West Germany, with nations such as Great Britain, the Netherlands, Uruguay, and France playing a secondary role in what amounts to economic dependency for Paraguay.[3]

Paraguay's foreign policy has included efforts to realize results from the tariff concessions gained through the LAFTA. The concessions granted by Argentina, Brazil, Mexico, and Uruguay called for duty-free entry of Paraguayan products into these countries. Considering Paraguay's transportation difficulties and a number of clauses in the agreements, many of the so-called concessions proved meaningless and have led to increasing Paraguayan bitterness vis-à-vis the cooperating nations.[4]

Paraguay's defensive posture against outside subversive elements has been an especially important factor in foreign policy since the beginning of the authoritarian regime of General Alfredo Stroessner. In efforts to preclude elements deemed undesirable to national security, Paraguay has worked closely with the United States, the Organization of American States (OAS), and neighboring countries. In 1947 Paraguay ratified the Inter-American Treaty of Reciprocal Assistance, which was designed to

2. U.S., Department of Commerce, Bureau of International Commerce, "Basic Data on the Economy of Paraguay," *Overseas Business Reports* (OBR 68-57) (Washington, D.C.: Government Printing Office, July 1970); Tomás Sepúlveda Whittle, *Transporte y Comercio Exterior del Paraguay* (Buenos Aires: Banco Interamericano de Desarrollo, 1967); *Yearbook of International Tables* (New York: United Nations, 1970); and International Monetary Fund, *Direction of Trade* (Washington, D.C.: November 1973), p. 47.

3. Joseph Pincus, *The Economy of Paraguay* (New York: Frederick A. Praeger, 1968); Republic of Paraguay, Banco Central del Paraguay, *Boletín Estadístico Mensual* (Asunción) (June 1970): 27-48.

4. Edward G. Cale, *Latin American Free Trade Association: Progress, Problems, Prospects* (Washington, D.C.: Government Printing Office, 1969).

provide for collective defense in the event of aggression against its signatory members. In her capacity as a charter member of the OAS, she has, with others, consistently supported strong measures to curb any type of subversive activity.

In fact, Paraguay has been one of the most consistent defenders of the United States in the OAS and the United Nations when questions have arisen about hemispheric security and related matters. Paraguay severed relations with Fidel Castro as early as 1961, supported Cuba's expulsion from the OAS, agreed to collective armed action during the Cuban missile crisis in 1962, voted for OAS authorization to investigate subversive elements in the Americas, supported U.S. intervention in the Dominican Republic in 1965 (contributing a task force of 200 men), and participated in a protest in which several nations, including Brazil, Argentina, Haiti, Ecuador, and Guatemala, demanded that the right of asylum for persons accused of acts of political sabotage in the Americas be revoked.[5]

Paraguay has outlawed the Communist party, and as of 1974 she is the only South American nation that has not established diplomatic relations with the Soviet Union.

HISTORICAL ANTECEDENTS

Paraguay's foreign policy in the nineteenth century was predominantly the achievement of three men: Dr. José Gaspar Rodríguez de Francia, Carlos Antonio López, and Francisco Solano López. Its most important goal, from Francia's time, was the complete independence of Paraguay and her freedom in external affairs. Everything else was subordinate —trade, culture, external contacts, the army, and administration. Francia knew that Paraguay could not sustain the fratricidal warfare that was destroying neighboring countries. He rejected all attempts by the caudillos to form pacts—Artigas against Buenos Aires, Ramírez against Artigas, Brazil against Buenos Aires, or Buenos Aires against the Spaniards. The principle of nonintervention constituted Francia's most important policy in the protection of Paraguay's sovereignty and independence. This, plus autarchy and relative isolation, was to give Paraguay additional protection against both external foes and the anarchy proliferating throughout Latin America.[6]

Carlos Antonio López rejected Francia's policy of isolation, however, particularly in his relation with his immediate neighbors, in favor of a

5. Lyman B. Kirkpatrick, "Cold War Operations: The Politics of Communist Confrontation, IV: Communism in Latin America," *Naval War College Review* 20, no. 11 (June 1968): 3–10; James R. Jose, *An Inter-American Peace Force Within the Framework of the Organization of American States* (Metuchen, N.J.: Scarecrow Press, 1970); J. Lloyd Mecham, *The United States and Inter-American Security: 1889–1960* (Austin: University of Texas Press, 1961).

6. Philip Raine, *Paraguay* (Metuchen, N.J.: Scarecrow Press, 1956), pp. 114–44.

more open policy. López's international goals were (1) to gain general recognition of Paraguayan independence; (2) to settle pending boundary disputes with Brazil and the United Provinces of Argentina; and (3) to open the country to foreign trade. Paraguay had declared her independence in 1811, and Francia had maintained that independence for about thirty years; but during that time the country had taken almost no part in world trade, and no nation had recognized Paraguayan independence. The López government marked the international recognition of a new nation. Brazil, for a beginning, not only recognized the independence of Paraguay in 1844 but also worked actively on behalf of that independence. As for other European and American nations, although they did not formally recognize Paraguay's independence until after the fall of Juan Manuel de Rosas in 1852, nonetheless many, including England and France, were determined to maintain Paraguay's national integrity, notwithstanding the efforts of Argentina to incorporate "the province."[7]

Carlos Antonio López's son, Francisco Solano López, inherited with the presidency a complicated international situation that was to plunge Paraguay into one of Latin America's most disastrous wars. It is difficult to deny that López's aggressive policy vis-à-vis Argentina, Brazil, and Uruguay helped bring about the War of the Triple Alliance (1865–70). But there were other factors, such as border disputes and the politically unstable interrelationships of Argentina, Uruguay, and Brazil. The war is alleged to have proved fatal to 90 percent of Paraguay's fighting men, and 55,000 square miles of territory were lost; moreover, perhaps as much as half of the arable land of Paraguay came into the hands of Argentine absentee landowners.[8]

After the War of the Triple Alliance, during the last two decades of the nineteenth century and the first two decades of the twentieth, foreign affairs had a low priority among Paraguay's political leaders. By the 1920s, however, impending territorial disputes with Bolivia over the Chaco resulted in another disastrous war (1932–35); this time Paraguay emerged as the victor, but at a tremendous cost in human lives and national resources. Paraguay, however, revindicated her sense of nationalism and renewed her pride and faith in herself as a nation. The eruption of this longstanding border dispute between Paraguay and Bolivia should also be seen in the light of increased colonization efforts in the Chaco (chiefly by Mennonites) and the discovery of allegedly important petroleum resources in the Chaco. Despite efforts by the League of Nations to mediate the unresolved differences, a full-scale war broke out in which Paraguay defeated the German-trained Bolivian armed forces, thereby gaining three-quarters of the disputed area in the Chaco.

7. Brazil, Ministerio das Relacões Exteriores, Comissão de Estudos de Textos de Historia do Brazil, *A Missão Pimenta Bueno (1843–47): Documentos*, by Pedro Freire Ribero (Río de Janeiro: Divisão de Documentacão, 1966), pp. 2–15.
8. Hubert Herring, *A History of Latin America* (New York: Alfred A. Knopf, 1968).

During World War II, Paraguay conducted her foreign policy in a way that enabled her to obtain loans and technical assistance from the United States and other nations, while at the same time maintaining friendly relations with pro-Axis leaders in Argentina and retaining flexibility in respect to the "German problem." Paraguay did not declare war on the Axis until 1945, just shortly before the meeting of the United Nations in San Francisco.[9]

FORMULATION OF FOREIGN POLICY

Most current decisions on foreign policy seem to be made by President Alfredo Stroessner. The Paraguayan citizenry at large and the press appear to have little influence on the foreign policy process. Although it seems clear that Stroessner could not maintain his position in government without their support, the military seems not to enter directly into foreign policy decision making.

Indications are that President Stroessner is permitting his elder son Gustavo Adolfo to play an increasing role in the formulation of domestic and foreign policy. Trained in Brazil and a regular participant in Stroessner's cabinet, Gustavo already enjoys the political allegiance of a wide sector of the younger army officers and Colorado Party members. He has also acted as the personal representative of his father on visits to the United States, Japan, and West Germany. Although the diplomatic receptions in those countries were less than glamorous, perhaps even cool, they have given Gustavo an opportunity to see the country's foreign policy problems in perspective.[10]

FOREIGN POLICY PROBLEMS TODAY

It is important to the Paraguayan government to maintain the cordial relations enjoyed with the United States since World War II. The basis for these relations stems from a mutual concern over hemispheric security and a concomitant desire to keep out "foreign" ideologies that may threaten the interests of both nations as those interests are defined by their respective governments rather than their peoples. Paraguay's perceived fear of physical invasion by exiled Paraguayans (it has been estimated that about one-third of the Paraguayan population was living outside the country in 1956) and the possibility of ideological invasion by leftist revolutionary groups has made her a most consistent supporter of U.S. security policies in the Americas. One is led to wonder what role the

9. Harris Gaylord Warren, *Paraguay: An Informal History* (Norman: Oklahoma University Press, 1949).
10. *Latin America* (London), 16 June 1972, pp. 188–89.

United States has played in discouraging any meaningful opposition to Stroessner's authoritarian regime.[11]

Paraguay's interest in the continuation of developmental assistance provided by the United States is reciprocated by active private U.S. interest in trade and investment in Paraguay. Moreover, in order to translate U.S. security interests in Paraguay into reality, from 1951 until the 1970s the United States provided over $10 million in the form of military training and military assistance program grants, naval vessels, and excess stocks. Argentina, Brazil, and Chile have also played an important role in training some of Paraguay's air force officers.[12]

In 1972 and 1973 the normally cordial relations between Paraguay and the United States were strained by President Stroessner's inability or unwillingness to crack down on drug smugglers who have coordinated the flow of heroin from Marseilles through Asunción and on to the United States. The United States, among other things, pressured the Paraguayan government to extradite to the United States the French-born Argentine international drug smuggler Auguste-Joseph Ricord, who was alleged to be a key figure in the drug traffic. When Stroessner did not or could not comply with U.S. demands, the United States retaliated by cutting off Paraguay's sugar quota and by passing a congressional resolution to end economic aid to any nation that failed to cooperate in solving the drug problem.[13]

In terms of development, since 1946 the United States has contributed over $130 million to Paraguay. A large share of these funds have been channeled into Paraguay through the activities of the Agency for International Development (AID). Transportation-related projects and agricultural projects have enjoyed the greater part of AID support. Since the mid-1960s, AID has lent technical assistance in the fields of tax and fiscal administration, in the development of local private enterprise, and in investment promotion. The twenty-five major U.S. companies that have invested in the Paraguayan economy have centered their activities in banking, meat packing, and oil refining. Although a 1968 U.S. Department of Commerce report on business firms in Paraguay failed to give accurate figures concerning the extent of foreign investment in Paraguay, private U.S. investments may have been between $10 million and $20 million in 1970. The total foreign investments have been estimated to be as much as $100 million.[14]

11. Paul H. Lewis, *The Politics of Exile: Paraguay's Febrista Party* (Chapel Hill: University of North Carolina Press, 1968); U.S., Congress, House of Representatives, Committee on Foreign Affairs, *Report of the Special Study Mission to the Dominican Republic, Guyana, Brazil, and Paraguay*, 90th Cong., 1st sess., 1966.

12. Richard Bourne, *Political Leaders of Latin America* (New York: Alfred A. Knopf, 1970), pp. 125-27; *Area Handbook for Paraguay*, pp. 278-79.

13. *Latin America*, 15 Oct. 1971, pp. 329-30; 26 May 1972, pp. 161-62; and 25 Aug. 1972, pp. 269-70.

14. U.S., Department of Commerce, Bureau of International Commerce, *Business Firms: Paraguay, 1968* (Washington, D.C.: Government Printing Office, 1968); ibid., "Market

Because of her disastrous history of conflict with her neighbors, Paraguay is determined to maintain friendly relations with them. This determination has been translated into recent joint efforts by Argentina, Bolivia, Brazil, Uruguay, and Paraguay to develop the economic potential of the River Plate Basin. By 1974, Paraguay was well on the way toward developing her potential in hydroelectric power, thereby providing a source of energy needed by her industrial neighbors Brazil and Argentina. Paraguay and Argentina are jointly producing electric power on the Acaray River in Eastern Paraguay, and Paraguay has signed an agreement with Brazil to tap the hydroelectric potential of the Guairá Falls in the Alto Paraná River (Itaipú project). Although Brazil is providing almost 90 percent of the capital required for this undertaking, Paraguay will obtain 50 percent of the electric energy produced. Unable at this time to absorb the power resources obtained from the Acaray River and the Guairá Falls, Paraguay is presently in a position to export surplus electric energy to both Brazil and Argentina.[15]

Increased Brazilean economic penetration into the country in the 1970s has brought about considerable alarm in Paraguay and in Argentina, Brazil's arch rival, about the possibility of Paraguay becoming an economic satellite of Brazil. Although in 1974 Brazil agreed to modify the terms of the treaty covering the building of the Itaipú hydroelectric project, under which Brazil had the right to take "security and political" measures on its own or Paraguayan territory, the Brazilian government gained an advantage over Argentina in Paraguay by granting credits of over $100 million in 1974 at the current international rates. Under the Treaty of Itaipú, the work was to be shared equally between the two countries as far as possible. But considering the relatively elementary Paraguayan industrial and technological know-how, most of the work was being done by Brazil. Therefore, it was agreed that Paraguay would obtain most of the contracts for timber, sand, and cement. In late 1974, however, it appeared that many Paraguayan businessmen were complaining that they were receiving only a few of the agreed-upon contracts. Moreover, Paraguayans have consistently complained that immigration into Paraguay by Brazilian peasants has increased (by an estimated 25,000 to 30,000 over the past four years) and that Brazilians are buying up too much land, often with the questionable assistance of the Instituto de Bienestar Rural. Furthermore, more Brazilian capital is taking over Paraguayan firms; Brazilian food, goods, radio propaganda, and even music are replacing Paraguayan products.[16]

Indicators for Latin America," *Overseas Business Reports* (OBR 67–74) (Washington, D.C.: Government Printing Office, November 1967).

15. Pincus, *The Economy of Paraguay.*
16. *Latin America*, 1 Feb. 1974, p. 40; 15 Nov. 1974, p. 359.

Paraguay's geographical isolation and the problems that are a direct consequence of this isolation continue to have an important impact on foreign policy. The main international transportation outlet is the Paraguay-Alto Paraná River system, which runs through Argentine territory until it reaches the port of Buenos Aires; 90 percent of Paraguay's exports pass through Argentine ports for a distance of eight hundred miles. Because of passage through Argentine territory, freight costs downstream have been extremely high and have prevented Paraguay from competing in world markets, except with products that can be produced by cheap labor. Added to the transportation costs have been the high duties (70 percent) imposed by Argentina, the principal customer for Paraguay's semimanufactured products. Unless Paraguay finds alternate routes for transporting her goods, she will continue to be economically dependent on Argentina. In addition, a large portion of Paraguay's land is owned by Argentine absentee owners.[17]

There may be significance in recent efforts to export goods to the Brazilian port of Paranaguá and in Chile's offer to provide free port facilities at Antofagasta after the proposed road across the Andes has been completed. In fact, in 1969 Brazil completed the construction of a paved road from the Atlantic coast port of Paranaguá to Iguaçú Falls, where it is connected by the Alfredo Stroessner bridge to the Paraguayan road system. These efforts have helped to strengthen further the economic ties between the two countries.[18]

An examination of trade statistics involving Paraguay and Argentina further shows an economic interrelationship which affects foreign policy. Between 1955 and 1968, Argentina was the principal supplier of Paraguay, i.e., Argentina provided 26 percent of Paraguay's imports and took 27 percent of her exports. To bring pressure to bear on Argentina, Paraguay obtained the cooperation of Bolivia in joint resistance to discriminatory economic practices on the part of their neighbor. Furthermore, in the 1970s both governments conducted numerous conversations about the development of the Mutún iron ore reserves and their export via the river Paraguay.[19]

Militarily, current foreign relations of Paraguay with Argentina and Brazil have shown improvement, especially during the presidencies of Juan Carlos Onganía and Juan D. Perón of Argentina and Brazil's

17. Bourne, *Political Leaders of Latin America*, pp. 123–24; interview with Dr. Guzmán.
18. Republic of Paraguay, Ministerio de Industria y Comercio, *Paraguay, Censos Económicos: 1963* (Asunción, 1966); Pincus, *The Economy of Paraguay*; George Pendle, *Paraguay: A Riverside Nation*, 3d ed. (London: Oxford University Press, 1967); and Daniel Fretes Ventre, "Paraguay desde adentro. Algunas consideraciones sobre la estructura económica," *Aportes* (Paris), no. 12, April 1969, pp. 6–23.
19. Republic of Paraguay, Banco Central del Paraguay, Departamento de Estudios Económicos, *Boletín Estadístico Mensual, June 1970* (Asunción: Banco Central, 1970); *Area Handbook for Paraguay*, pp. 227–31.

military strongman Humberto Castello Branco and his successors. Both
Argentina and Brazil have regularly coordinated military intelligence
plans and activities with the armed forces of President Stroessner.[20]

RELATIONS WITH WESTERN EUROPE

Paraguay's relations with the Western European nations continue to play
an important part in overall foreign policy. (Except for Yugoslavia,
Paraguay still does not maintain diplomatic relations with the Eastern
European nations and the Soviet Union. As of 1974, there is little
indication that Paraguayan policy vis-à-vis the Communist nations will
change, even if Stroessner's son Gustavo takes over the government).
Relations with West Germany, France, Great Britain, Spain, the Netherlands, Italy, Sweden, and Belgium have focused on trade, technical
assistance, and cultural exchanges and programs. After Argentina and the
United States, Great Britain and West Germany are Paraguay's third
largest importers of goods, followed by the Netherlands, France (tobacco),
Spain (tannin), Belgium, Sweden, and Italy. In 1973 and 1974 Paraguay
imported more goods from West Germany than from any other European
nation. These imports consisted mainly of trucks and buses. Paraguay
also imported goods from Italy, Great Britain, and the other European
nations. Although the French claimed to be Paraguay's supplier of oil, in
fact, the oil originates in Algeria but is drilled by a French company.[21]

At the turn of the century and until about 1939, the German and
Paraguayan governments published a substantial body of literature
encouraging prospective German settlers to move to Paraguay. Although
the actual numbers of Germans migrating to Paraguay never fulfilled the
expectations of either nation, Germans have undoubtedly been the most
important non-Spanish-speaking European immigrant group in Paraguay. Their importance has been measured in terms of actual numbers of
families residing in Paraguay and in terms of business enterprises and
agricultural colonies.[22]

RELATIONS WITH ASIA AND AFRICA

Paraguay's contacts with countries other than the United States, Western
Europe, and Latin America are minimal but increasing. For example,

20. Bourne, *Political Leaders of Latin America*, pp. 124–25.
21. U.S., Department of Agriculture, Economic Research Service, *Agriculture and Trade of Paraguay*, by Gordon Patty (ERS–Foreign 6) (Washington, D.C.: Government Printing Office, 1961).
22. U.S., Department of Commerce, Bureau of International Commerce, "Foreign Trade of Paraguay," *Overseas Business Reports* (Washington, D.C.: Government Printing Office, December 1969); Hans J. Hoyer, *Germans in Paraguay: A Study of Social and Cultural Isolation* (Ph.D. diss., The American University, 1973).

diplomatic relations, especially with Japan, are becoming increasingly important. Before World War II, Paraguay invited Japan to send over agricultural workers; with generous land concessions, thousands of Japanese have entered Paraguay since the 1930s, and the number of Japanese are expected to surpass German immigrants by many thousands. Increased Japanese-Paraguayan contacts are anticipated, and several Japanese firms have recently opened offices in Paraguay. On his trip to Japan in 1972, President Stroessner asked Japan for a $36 million credit for the development of telecommunications, railways, and water supplies. He also sought a $20 million loan to finance the import of Japanese capital goods and the export of Paraguayan products to Japan, in addition to Japanese technical aid and industrial investment.[23]

Although Paraguay already maintains diplomatic relations with South Korea and the Republic of China (Formosa), the potential for closer economic relations is being explored. Diplomatic relations with the Communist nations, except for Yugoslavia, are not maintained. Nor has Paraguay established any type of relations, either formal or informal, with the People's Republic of China, with most of the Asian nations (except for South Korea, the Republic of China, and India), or with the African nations. However, relations are maintained with Egypt and Israel.

PARAGUAY IN INTERNATIONAL ORGANIZATIONS

The internationalization of the foreign policy of Paraguay has been evident in the Organization of American States. She participates in most of the specialized agencies of the OAS, and she ratified the Protocol of Buenos Aires (1967), which, in effect, strengthened the economic, social, and cultural functions of the OAS and weakened the functions of the Permanent Council. Paraguay is also a member of LAFTA, a participant in the Inter-American Development Bank, and a member of the Alliance for Progress, through which she is receiving economic aid and technical assistance from the United States. In LAFTA, Paraguay's status as a lesser developed country has obtained for her special concessions; but, because of transportation difficulties and "opt-out" clauses, these concessions have not proved as favorable as expected. Paraguay is also a member of the Rio de la Plata group, a subregional unit within LAFTA designed to foster the economic integration of Argentina, Bolivia, Brazil, Uruguay, and Paraguay.[24]

23. Norman R. Stewart, *Japanese Colonization in Eastern Paraguay*, pubn. 1,490 (Washington, D.C.: National Academy of Sciences, National Research Council, 1967); Joseph Winfield Fretz, *Immigrant Group Settlements in Paraguay* (Newton, Kans.: Bethel College, 1962).
24. Cale, *Latin American Free Trade Association; Area Handbook for Paraguay*, pp. 231-32.

Capping her international commitments, Paraguay is a charter member of the United Nations. She has participated actively in the specialized UN agencies and served as a nonpermanent member of the Security Council between 1968 and 1972. Outside the UN, Paraguay has participated in a number of international trade conferences involving sugar and rice. She also signed the Treaty on the Non-Proliferation of Nuclear Weapons in 1968 and the Latin American Nuclear Free Zone Treaty in 1967, which she ratified the following year.[25]

BIBLIOGRAPHICAL NOTE

Literature on the formulation of Paraguay's contemporary foreign policy is almost nonexistent. While several fine historical studies have been written by Paraguayans and other authors concerning the conduct of wars, etc., in the nineteenth and twentieth centuries and the diplomatic problems surrounding these wars, it is difficult to obtain current data on Paraguay. Probably the best available source in the United States, although recognizably scanty, is the British weekly political and economic report *Latin America*. The relatively "closed" nature of Paraguayan society makes it difficult to find information about the formulation of foreign policy and the impact of domestic forces on foreign policy. An interview with Dr. Luis Guzmán of the Inter-American Foundation gave some useful perspectives.

Area Handbook for Paraguay. Washington, D.C.: Foreign Area Studies, The American University, 1972.

Bourne, Richard. "Alfred Stroessner." In *Political Leaders in Latin America*, pp. 98–130. New York: Alfred A. Knopf, 1970.

Brazil. Ministerio das Relacões Exteriores. Comissão de Estudos de Textos de Historia do Brazil. *A Missão Pimenta Bueno (1843–47). Documentos*, by Pedro Freire Ribero. Rio de Janeiro: Divisão de Documentacão, 1966.

Cale, Edward G. *Latin American Free Trade Association: Progress, Problems, Prospects*. Washington, D.C.: Government Printing Office, 1969.

Fretes Ventre, Daniel. "Paraguay desde adentro. Algunas consideraciones sobre la estructura económica." *Aportes* (Paris), no. 12 (April 1969).

Fretz, Joseph Winfield. *Immigrant Group Settlements in Paraguay*. Newton, Kans.: Bethel College, 1962.

Hoyer, Hans J. *Germans in Paraguay, 1881–1945; A Study of Cultural and Social Isolation*. Ph.D. diss., The American University, 1973.

Kirkpatrick, Lyman B. "Cold War Operations: The Politics of Communist Confrontation, IV: Communism in Latin America." *Naval War College Review* 20, no. 11 (June 1968).

25. Norman A. Bailey, *Latin America in World Politics* (New York: Walker & Company, 1967); M. Margaret Ball, *The OAS in Transition* (Durham, N.C.: Duke University Press, 1969).

Latin America (London). 15 Oct. 1971; 26 May, 25 Aug., 16 June, 15 Dec. 1972; 1 Feb., 15 Nov. 1974.

Lewis, Paul H. *The Politics of Exile: Paraguay's Febrista Party.* Chapel Hill: University of North Carolina Press, 1968.

Mecham, J. Lloyd. *The United States and Inter-American Security: 1889-1960.* Austin: University of Texas Press, 1961.

Pincus, Joseph. *The Economy of Paraguay.* New York: Frederick A. Praeger, 1968.

Raine, Philip. *Paraguay.* Metuchen, N.J.: Scarecrow Press, 1956.

Republic of Paraguay. Banco Central del Paraguay, Departamento de Estudios Económicos. *Boletín Estadístico Mensual.* Asunción, June 1970.

————. Ministerio de Industria y Comercio. *Paraguay Censos Económicos: 1963.* Asunción, 1966.

Stewart, Norman R. *Japanese Colonization in Eastern Paraguay.* Washington, D.C.: National Academy of Sciences, 1967.

U.S. Congress. House of Representatives. Committee on Foreign Affairs. *Report of the Special Study Mission to the Dominican Republic, Guyana, Brazil and Paraguay.* 90th Cong., 1st sess., 1966.

U.S. Department of Agriculture. Economic Research Service. *Agriculture and Trade of Paraguay* (ERS-Foreign 6). Washington, D.C.: Government Printing Office, 1961.

U.S. Department of Commerce. "Foreign Trade of Paraguay." *Overseas Business Reports* (OBR 67-74). Washington, D.C.: Government Printing Office, December 1969.

———— Bureau of International Commerce. "Basic Data on the Economy of Paraguay." *Overseas Business Reports* (OBR 68-57). Washington, D.C.: Government Printing Office, July 1970.

————. ————. *Business Firms: Paraguay, 1968.* Washington, D.C.: Government Printing Office, 1968.

————. ————. "Market Indicators for Latin America," *Overseas Business Reports* (OBR 67-74). Washington, D.C.: Government Printing Office, November 1967.

Warren, Harris Gaylord. *Paraguay: An Informal History.* Norman: Oklahoma University Press, 1949.

Whittle, Tomás Sepúlveda. *Transporte y Comercio Exterior del Paraguay.* Buenos Aires: Banco Interamericano de Desarrollo, 1967.

VI

Andean Countries, South: Chile, Bolivia, and Peru

15/Orville G. Cope

Chile

Political scientists have begun to analyze foreign policy as a response to domestic and international influences. In emphasizing the interrelationship between internal and external variables that condition a nation's foreign policy process, the political scientist has proceeded to develop a conceptual framework known as "linkages" whereby recurring sequences of behavior originate in one system and are reacted to in another.[1] In such a perspective, the formation of foreign policy is seen as a response to a variety of internal and external sequences.

Although this study discusses the historical antecedents or orientations of Chilean foreign policy, it concentrates on certain internal economic and political variables as they relate to Chile's present-day foreign policy problem. The fact that Chile's contemporary internal economic development is primarily dependent upon the exportation of copper as a means to earn foreign exchange is an example of domestic and international "linkage." Furthermore, until 1971 much of Chile's copper industry was owned by private foreign interests, a situation that subjected the nation's political system to foreign penetration and influence. Even with the total nationalization of the copper industry, Chile remains dependent upon the vagaries of the price of copper in the world market and upon her ability to ·negotiate needed credit and assistance from international agencies and a number of nations in the Western Hemisphere, Europe, and Asia. In view of the complexity of the effect of the internal economic and political variables on recent foreign policy, this study also traces the degree of continuity and change in the formation and conduct of modern Chilean foreign policy by comparing the policies of the Christian Democratic administration of Eduardo Frei (1964-70) with those of the Socialist administration of Salvador Allende (1970-73) and those of a conservative military junta that installed itself in power in 1973.

HISTORICAL ORIENTATIONS

Decisions relating to foreign policy are influenced by the values and perceptions of political and diplomatic leaders, by internal social and economic interests, and by the "agents" of the international political system, namely nation states, individuals, and international organiza-

1. Consult James N. Rosenau, "Toward the Study of National-International Linkages," in Rosenau, ed., *Linkage Politics* (New York: Free Press, 1969), pp. 44-63. In the same volume see also Douglas A. Chalmers, "Developing on the Periphery: External Factors in Latin American Politics," pp. 67-93.

tions. The principal task of foreign policy makers is to adjust the changing internal values and interests of a nation to the changing conditions prevailing in the international system in order to achieve specific objectives. Since the early 1870s, a series of cumulative decisions has established a varied pattern of conduct that led Chile to become more actively involved in international affairs. Foreign policy makers, responding to the domestic and international environments, committed the nation to a fundamental orientation or strategy to accomplish certain external objectives.[2]

Historically, Chilean foreign policies promoted territorial expansion, regional internationalism, and extracontinental internationalism. The outcome of the War of the Pacific (1879-83), in which Chile gained control of the northern nitrates of Antofagasta from Bolivia and of Tarapacá from Peru, was a consequence of an expansionist policy determined by internal commercial interests that sought to exploit the nitrate and silver potential of the region.[3] In an effort to protect the geographic and economic resources won in the conflict, Chile opted for an "armed peace," expanded her military and naval power, and refused to accept compulsory arbitration and conciliation of the Tacna-Arica border dispute with Peru, thereby preventing a legal settlement of the conflict for forty-five years.

Chilean involvement in international affairs during the first three decades of the twentieth century was limited. Despite a civil war in 1891-92 that fragmented internal political power among various political party elites, Chile's foreign policy orientation evolved from a subregional policy of creating a strong Bolivia as an ally against Argentina and Peru to a continental orientation, which was reinforced by a policy of nonalignment during World War I. However, continued opposition to compulsory arbitration of the Tacna-Arica border dispute by Chilean foreign policy makers placed Chile in a less than effective bargaining position in relation to other Latin American nations and the United States. It was not until the first administration of Arturo Alessandri (1920-24) that Chile abandoned her opposition to compulsory arbitration in order to consider whether a plebescite should be held as called for by the Treaty of Ancón, which had marked the end of the War of the Pacific in 1883. Eventually, in 1929, the Tacna-Arica controversy was resolved with the signing of the Washington Protocol, thus allowing Chile greater flexibility in the conduct of her foreign policy.

2. On the subject of "orientations," or historical patterns of state behavior in international politics as variables in foreign policy analysis, see R. J. Holsti, *International Politics* (Englewood Cliffs, N.J.: Prentice-Hall, 1972), pp. 102-3.
3. William J. Dennis, *Tacna-Arica* (New Haven: Yale University Press, 1931), pp. 66-100.

Gradually, Chile reoriented her objectives toward greater international involvement. Prompted by the military and economic intervention of the United States in Latin American affairs, Chile and other Latin American nations recognized the need to apply unified diplomatic pressure on the United States to make her accept the equal rights and sovereignty of the Latin American nations and the principle of nonintervention. Although for many years Chilean international jurists and diplomats had viewed the regional international system as a legal order, it only became a reality with the acceptance by the United States of the precepts of American international law at the Seventh Inter-American Conference in Montevideo in 1933.[4]

In the succeeding three decades, Chilean foreign policy makers sought to achieve closer diplomatic and commercial ties with other nations within the Western Hemisphere, particularly the United States. Although Chile played a minor supportive role in the defense of the Western Hemisphere during World War II, she and other Latin American nations were confronted by a revised international system at the conclusion of the war. The United States, in its effort to thwart possible Soviet penetration of Western Europe, initiated and administered the economic revival of Europe while providing only residual treatment for Latin America, which suffered serious economic problems after a new industrial base had been developed during the war.

In the post-World War II period, the international system has developed to the point that the number of international actors and the level of interaction among them has greatly increased. Not only do nations compete for advantage through alliances and coalitions, but universal and regional organizations, international financing agencies, and regional economic alliances have also emerged as a consequence of increased internal demands of nations to share economic and technical resources. Chilean political leaders and diplomats have begun to take advantage of the new institutional flexibility of the international system to establish a variety of favorable aid and trade arrangements, and also to promote regional and subregional economic integration.

The orientation of Chilean foreign policy during the 1960s and early 1970s became extracontinental as Chile increased her frequency of contact with Western and Eastern Europe, the Soviet Union, the African nations

4. Respective appraisals of Chile's international role in the nineteenth century, the domestic and international problems confronting resolution of the Tacna-Arica dispute, and the subsequent acceptance of international law as a means of control by Chile and the United States may be found in the following: Robert N. Burr, *By Reason or Force: Chile and the Balancing of Power in South America, 1830–1905* (Berkeley: University of California Press, 1965); Frederick B. Pike, *Chile and the United States, 1880–1962* (Notre Dame, Ind.: University of Notre Dame Press, 1963), pp. 214–35; and Gordon Connell-Smith, *The Inter-American System* (London and New York: Oxford University Press, 1966), pp. 83–91.

of Zambia and Zaire, Australia, and such Asian nations as Japan and Communist China. Although Chile was greatly dependent upon the United States for public and private economic aid and technical assistance, particularly during the early years of the Frei administration, the election of a Marxist administration in 1970 initiated a foreign policy orientation increasingly independent of the United States yet increasingly dependent on other nations and international agencies as sources of credit and assistance. However, the violent *golpe* of September 1973, which brought the Chilean armed forces to power, initiated a revision of Chilean foreign policy. Chilean extracontinentalism was modified as diplomatic relations were broken between Chile and a number of Communist nations, including the Soviet Union and Cuba, and the military junta sought to improve relations with the United States. In essence, Chile's progression toward greater involvement in international affairs during this century has been determined by political leaders and diplomats who are conditioned by their own domestic economic and political situations and by international perspectives and objectives.

CAPABILITIES: THE INTERNAL VARIABLES

The prime objective of Chile's foreign policy is to influence the structure of the international system to assist her own economic development. The act of influencing depends, in part, on power capabilities, that is, the available resources or means that when mobilized by Chilean leaders may induce other nations and international political and financial organizations to respond to Chile's principal external objective.[5]

Chile's influence in contemporary inter-American and international politics depends less on the quantity of power capabilities and more on the willingness and ability of Chilean foreign policy makers to mobilize available national and international capabilities to effect foreign policy objectives at a given time. Resources within the economic system can be mobilized at times, but they are scarce, and international military capacity is limited. From 1932 to 1973 the Chilean political system was composed of competing political party elites who utilized the representative institutions of a participant political culture to organize and mobilize internal political power for domestic and foreign policy objectives.[6] During the 1960s, Chilean foreign policy was effective in acquiring specific interna-

5. On the subject of capabilities consult Holsti, *International Politics*, pp. 154-71, or David O. Wilkenson, *Comparative Foreign Relations: Framework for Analysis* (Belmont, Calif.: Dickenson Publishing Co., 1969), pp. 32-71.
6. The concept of political culture refers to the character and distribution of attitudes toward the political system as held by individuals and the attitudes regarding one's role within the political system. See Gabriel Almond and Sidney Verba, *The Civic Culture* (Princeton: Princeton University Press, 1963).

tional objectives that would assist internal economic development, suggesting, perhaps, that such a democratic political system and its resultant
political and diplomatic leaders served as prime capabilities to enable
Chile to maintain as much influence as she did in international politics.
On the other hand, the military *golpe* of 1973 came at a time when the
traditional political system and its leaders could not reconcile the political conflicts of an increasingly polarized society. In addition, Chilean
foreign policy had become less effective because of the internal political
crises, the deterioration of the nation's economic capability, and the
negative reactions of certain nations and international financial agencies
in the international political system. How a military junta will effectively
use the nation's economic and political capabilities to construct a viable
foreign policy for short-range and long-range economic development is a
critical question.

Economic Capabilities

The resources and the structural problems of Chile's domestic economy
play a decisive role in the development of her foreign policy. In her effort
to secure external economic and technical assistance through the extension of trade, Chile is confronted by her limited economic capabilities. As
a consequence of these limitations, Chile's importance in the world
market is based on her capacity to produce copper, copper products,
nitrates, iron ore, and fishmeal. Although possessing the world's largest
copper reserves, Chile ranks third, behind the United States and the Soviet
Union, in copper production. Her copper exports represent one-third of
all the copper exported in the world and attract considerable foreign
exchange, which determines Chile's capacity to import goods and to meet
international payments. Hence, copper alone is capable of accounting for
approximately 75 percent of export earnings annually and of aiding in
financing public expenditures.[7] Copper exports as a capability, however,
are limited; the use of copper to earn foreign exchange depends not
only on increased production but also on the demand from importing
countries. Chile's share of the world's copper production has decreased
slowly since 1940, and the annual rate of growth in production during the
1960s was only 2.8 percent.[8] Furthermore, the fluctuations in the demand
and price of copper that occur periodically place Chile in a position

7. Despite the importance of copper and nitrates in the world market, the mining
industry was not the most productive sector; it accounted for only 6 percent of Gross
Domestic Product and roughly the same proportion of employment. Manufacturing was the
most rapidly changing and dynamic economic sector during the 1960s, with an annual
growth rate of 9 percent (Inter-American Development Bank, Social Progress Trust Fund,
Socio-Economic Progress in Latin America, Annual Report, 1967 [Washington, D.C.,
1967]).
8. United Nations Economic Commission for Latin America, *Economic Survey of Latin
America, 1969* (New York, 1970), pp. 141–44.

where it can no longer expect high per capita income nations to trade consistently; thus, it must find new markets.

The extent to which foreign exchange contributes to Chile's economic development is limited by various domestic economic problems that ultimately affect Chile's world trade position. In 1964 the Frei administration inherited a deficit in the nation's balance of payments resulting from a loss of foreign exchange because exports had not increased sufficiently to counter new import demands. However, with the increase in demand for copper by the United States, a rise in the price of copper on the world market, and an increased capacity to export, Chile began to create yearly balance of payment surpluses. But by 1967, foreign exchange reserves began to decline as imports of capital goods and consumer products increased and the rate of commodity exports other than copper fell. In the first two years of the Allende administration, export earnings decreased, inducing approximately a $400 million reduction in foreign reserves. This critical situation was attributed not only to the low price of copper on the world market but also to the increased costs of importing food-stuffs and to a level of copper production that fell below Chile's world commitments.[9] The decline in copper production was a result of a serious transitional stage in the nationalization of the copper industry, a stage characterized by petty conflicts between state managers, Socialists, Communists, and the miner's union, in addition to the loss of trained technicians and the lack of spare parts.[10]

The importance of copper to Chile's world commercial position and internal economic development is apparent. Prompted by the uncertainties of the world market, the Frei administration's economic development policies reflected a concern to protect and expand the capability of earning greater foreign exchange so that increased imports, services, loans, and investments that produced capital for economic development could be paid for. The creation of "mixed corporations"—private copper firms in which the government held an interest—permitted the government to participate in decisions relating to the refining of copper and the diversification of products and markets for the sake of earning greater foreign exchange.[11] During the first year of the Allende administration

9. *Quarterly Economic Review: Chile*, no. 3 (London) (30 Sept. 1972), p. 10.

10. See Norman Gall, "Copper Is the Wage of Chile," *American Universities Field Staff Reports*, West Coast South America Series 19 (April 1972): 4–11.

11. In 1966 the Chilean government purchased 51 percent of the Braden Copper Company's El Teniente mine and 25 percent of each of two new mining companies formed by Anaconda and Cerro de Pasco. Under this scheme, the "mixed corporations" invested more profits in Chile, received some lower tax rates, and contributed to capital expansion of industry. In June 1969, the Chilean government had agreed with Anaconda to purchase 51 percent of two additional mining properties (El Chuquicamata and El Salvador) with an option to purchase the remaining 49 percent no sooner than January 1973 and no later than 30 December 1981.

the Chilean Congress, composed of political parties of the Left and the
Right, voted unanimously to nationalize the large copper producers,
principally the Anaconda, Kennecott, and Cerro mining facilities.[12]
However, the declines in the production of copper and the price of copper
on the world market and the persistent low productivity of Chilean
agriculture and industry by 1972 placed a considerable drain on foreign
exchange reserves and undermined the nation's international credit. Even
the subsequent rise in copper prices because of the high cost of food
importation did little to increase foreign exchange.

Traditionally, Chile has borrowed from other nations and international financial agencies to cover the balance of payments deficits on
current account. However, some of these sources of credit—the International Monetary Fund (IMF) and the Export-Import Bank (EXIMBANK),
an agency of the U.S. government—became constrained as Allende
restructured the economy along Socialist lines and refused to compensate
some of the privately owned U.S. companies for the nationalized
property. EXIMBANK, responding to the compensation issue, deferred
its loans and demanded demonstration of "credit worthiness." The
IMF, however, provided compensatory loans to help offset the copper
price declines of 1971-72. But, responding to U.S. pressure, it refused to
provide a "standby agreement" for additional foreign exchange funds.

Other international financial agencies, such as the International Bank
for Reconstruction and Development (IBRD) and the Inter-American
Development Bank (IADB), which provide loans for specific development
projects, were less concerned about the nationalization and compensation
issues than about the Allende administration's internal economic
strategy. The IBRD and the IADB provided previously negotiated loans
during 1970-72 and, in the case of IADB, Chile payed considerable sums
on interest and amortization on past loans.[13] Nonetheless, in pursuit of
full employment and the redistribution of income to lower income
groups, the Allende administration adopted policies that provided substantial wage increases and froze prices, anticipating that the resulting
increase in demand for consumer goods would induce investment and
spur productivity to higher levels. Such policies were not congruent with
the rather strict monetarist views of the IBRD and the IADB. For a short
time, the economic strategy was successful; unemployment declined and
production increased. But when needed investment was not forthcoming,
supply did not match demand, and public expenditures for social services

12. The nationalization of the major copper companies passed the Joint Session of the
Chilean Congress, 158-0.
13. For an interesting assessment of the interaction of the Allende administration, the
international financial agencies, and the United States, see Paul E. Sigmund, "The
'Invisible Blockade' and the Overthrow of Allende," *Foreign Affairs* 52 (January 1974):
322-48.

increased, inflation occurred, and foreign reserves diminished. Chile's ability to service foreign debts was questioned. In an effort to maintain some international credit, Chile renegotiated some of her foreign debts with the Paris Group (Canada, Japan, the United States, and several Western European nations) and with Eastern European Socialist nations, including the Soviet Union. Renegotiation permitted Chile to postpone from 1972 until 1975 about seventy percent of her debt service payments to the Paris Group nations. It also permitted a relief of some $200 to $300 million in her balance of payments. Chile's 1973 foreign debt payments were in the process of renegotiation at the time of the military *golpe*.

The varying policy experiences of past administrations indicate that Chile's ability to produce copper to aid economic development is both an asset and a liability. The nation's capability to earn greater foreign exchange through the exportation of copper has limits, as we have seen. The mixed corporation idea was an attempt by the Frei administration to control copper production and refining; it enabled the nation to obtain some private capital investment, foreign exchange, and credit from traditional sources. Although hard pressed by a decline in the price of copper, by the political and technical problems incurred by nationalization, and by the deterioration of the domestic economy, the Allende regime was successful in renegotiating some of its foreign debts and in finding a few new markets for copper. Subsequently, the military junta, led by General Augusto Pinochet, initiated some drastic domestic economic policy changes by returning to the original private owners a number of Chilean and foreign companies that the Allende administration had nationalized without compensation. Yet some policy continuity in regard to domestic and international economics is evident. In order to control the nation's primary source of foreign exchange, the military government maintains and operates the major copper mines nationalized by the Allende government, although compensation, previously denied to the former foreign owners, is in the process of negotiation at this writing. Furthermore, in an effort to sustain some internal economic growth, the new government will negotiate periodically Chile's debt payments to some of her creditors.

Political Capabilities: Political Institutions and Processes

Before the *golpe* of September 1973, which established the first military regime in forty-one years, Chile was a constitutional and democratic republic. Formal authority for foreign policy decisions was diffused between the executive and legislative branches of government. Much of the power to generate and execute foreign policy resided in the president and in the Ministry of Foreign Relations, but the Senate and the Senate Committee for Foreign and Defense Affairs served as critics with some veto power. Within Chilean political culture, periodic and competitive elections at the presidential, congressional, and municipal levels were regarded as the legitimate means to maintain and transfer political power. Those responsible for foreign policy sought to mobilize electoral power and consent for various foreign policy objectives within a politically divisive multiparty system composed of a variety of political parties and personalities. Although domestic issues were of greater concern during the electoral campaigns of the 1960s and early 1970s, such foreign policy issues as Chile's commercial and diplomatic position toward Cuba, the United States, the Soviet Union, Western and Eastern Europe, and the other nations of Latin America were articulated within the context of partisan electoral politics. In 1964 Eduardo Frei, a Christian Democrat advocating changes in both domestic and foreign policies, was elected by a large majority of voters. The Frei administration initiated new foreign policies that were extended and accelerated by the Socialist government of President Allende.

The Chilean political system from 1932 to 1973 was subject to an amount of political divisiveness that made agreement on many public issues difficult. The multiparty system, based on proportional representation, created a variety of competing political parties advocating conflicting ideologies and policy options at the congressional and presidential electoral levels that often reflected the interests and attitudes of various sectors of a socially fragmented society. In addition, the system of separation of power often placed the Chilean Congress in an intense conflict with the president—at times a president who had been elected by a plurality rather than a majority of the popular vote.[14] Yet the system permitted the resolution of conflicts upon some, although not all, issues. As in most multiparty systems, coalitions were formed at various levels, providing politicians with the means to mobilize and pursue policy goals. Coalition situations existed at the presidential and legislative levels that permitted political party elites to agree to form party coalitions for the expressed purpose of gaining electoral power and developing policies. Therefore, the confrontation among social, economic, and political interests in Chile was confined to the electoral and legislative institutions where political parties competed and coalesced, thus lending stability to the political system and enhancing continuity and incremental change of various policies, including foreign policy. Furthermore, Chilean political

14. President Allende, for example, did not receive a majority of the popular vote in the three-way presidential election in 1970. Consequently, a Joint Session of the Chilean Congress, as authorized by the Constitution, selected a president from the two candiates who had led in the balloting. After considerable bargaining between the Christian Democrats and Allende, the full Congress selected Allende, who had received the greater number of popular votes. See Orville G. Cope, *Coalition Formation, Christian Democracy, and the 1970 Presidential Election in Chile*, Institute of Government Research, Research Series no. 11 (Tucson: University of Arizona, February 1972), pp. 15–16.

attitudes, despite the divisiveness of competing ideologies as articulated by leaders of the Christian Democratic, Communist, National, Socialist, and Radical parties, possessed a "constitutional ethic," that is, a common belief held by political leaders and followers that the constitutional system was to be complied with in the transfer and maintaining of political power.[15]

Political coalitions and conciliatory political attitudes could no longer hold the Chilean political system together by September 1973. The Allende administration's political methods of implementing many of its economic and social policies failed to anticipate the resistance of Chile's urban and politically sophisticated upper and middle sectors of society,[16] including the *petit bourgeoise* and the traditionally neutral officer corps of the Chilean armed forces. Increased polarization between Marxists and anti-Marxists rendered coalitions inoperable as attitudes became rigid and interests became uncompromising. President Allende could not hold together the government coalition composed of conservative Communists, revolutionary Socialists, and various ideological factions, some of whom sought to build cadres of rural peasants and armed urban workers. Polarization became more evident as violence in the form of street riots and even assassination pitted leftist revolutionaries against an armed Fascist organization, *patria y libertad*. The largest single political party, the reformist Christian Democratic party, became a vehement critic of the regime and aligned itself with members of the National party, with whom it agreed only in opposing a Marxist government. The polarization of attitudes and interests may have been a direct result of the process of increased participation and mass mobilization advocated by the Marxist parties and the Christian Democrats during the 1960s. The political ideologies raised expectations, and party organizations were extended into many aspects of public life in an effort to mobilize electoral support. Political party conflict became increasingly intense as party ideologues articulated demands and as larger numbers of people without previous political experiences became party *militantes*.[17]

In an atmosphere of economic deterioration, political polarization, and increased violence, the existing institutions of government lost their legitimacy. The only viable institution remaining was the traditionally

15. A most comprehensive treatment of the pre-*golpe* Chilean political process can be found in Federico G. Gil, *The Political System of Chile* (Boston: Houghton Mifflin Co., 1966).

16. In rural areas, the Allende administration tolerated forced seizure of landholdings by restless peasants and Mapuche Indians led by the revolutionary *Miristas*. The administration expropriated numerous factories through a questionable law instituted by the short-lived "Socialist Republic" in 1932 that permitted the government to intervene if a factory failed to maintain a certain level of production. Interventions became permanent.

17. This thesis has been advanced by Lawrence Whitehead in the very perceptive and articulate article "Why Allende Fell," *World Today* 29 (November 1973): 465.

neutral Chilean armed forces which, in less than a year, underwent a rapid politicalization process induced by the immediate circumstance of politics. The politicalization of the military was initiated with the integration of several high military officials into an Allende cabinet in November 1972 and again in July 1973. In each case, the appointments were designed to ease crisis situations that had resulted from a reaction by the urban middle sectors to Allende's economic policies or the recurrence of violence. Eventually, it seemed evident to the military within the cabinet that they were being used by Socialists and some Communists in the civil bureaucracies to support a false image of stability for a government that the military could not identify with in terms of policies and personnel. When the ideological political Left attempted to create political cell organizations within the lower ranks of the Chilean navy in an effort to urge sailors to disobey their superiors, it was viewed by the middle echelon officer corps as subversive to discipline and as a breach of military neutrality in politics. Once the middle echelon of the officer corps of all the armed forces became convinced that its middle-sector interests might not be preserved by the Allende administration, the *golpe* became imminent.[18]

What form of government will emerge ultimately from military rule in Chile is a matter of conjecture. The outlawing of political parties, the disbanding of Congress, the suppression of civil liberties, the banning of the free press, and the exile and execution of former leaders does not bode well for the return to the old liberal democratic republic, with its plethora of political parties and personalities. A corporatist state may emerge, with an indirectly elected head of state having fewer powers of decree and a legislature composed of interest groups, including the military. However, Chile is a politically sophisticated nation with economic problems that the military may not be equipped to deal with. In such circumstances, at least the Christian Democrats and the conservative Nationals will compete to control the policies and personnel of government.

The Foreign Policy Elite

At present, as prior to the 1973 *golpe*, Chilean foreign policy is decided upon by a small, university-educated, multilingual, and mobile elite that has been recruited from the upper echelons of Chile's social structure. As a subsystem of the national community, this elite represents a linkage system with a variety of formal and informal contacts in the international system and the national political system. The foreign policy elite, unlike the general population, has access to decision-making positions for reasons of advanced education, cultural attitudes, social position, wealth, and experience in national and international political life.

18. Ibid., pp. 472–73.

Two methods of recruiting for the diplomatic service occur within the Chilean political system. First, ministers of foreign relations, many ambassadors, and delegates to specialized meetings of international organizations generally owe their positions to a political patronage system operating through the military junta or, as in the past, through the office of the president and the minister of foreign affairs. Before the *golpe*, patronage within the government party and across political party lines aided in building consensus on policy within a political system that relied on coalition formation. At present, the military junta has selected persons who are closely associated with conservative civilian elements of Chilean society, some of whom served in the Foreign Ministry during the Conservative Jorge Alessandri government (1958–64) or in the cabinet of Christian Democrat Eduardo Frei (1964–70). In addition to those appointed through political patronage, careerists who compose the bureaucracy of the diplomatic service are recruited by the Foreign Ministry after a suitable university education.

The career patterns of the bureaucrat and the politician show a number of similarities in social background, in educational and professional experience, and in physical mobility.[19] Some variation exists, however, in regard to educational and professional experience. Generally, both possess formal education in law or the humanities or, more recently, in economic development (which represents a national aspiration). But the professional careerists do not stray far from the international field as they change from staff positions in the ministry or various embassies and consulates to temporary or permanent positions in such international organizations as the United Nations or the OAS.[20] The career structure of the politician, on the other hand, indicates a past involvement in domestic political party conflict, multiple job holding in various occupations, and an association with public and private activities not essentially related to foreign policy. High-level political appointees, such as ambassadors, have been involved in party politics, and some have held positions as elected party functionaries, deputies, and senators or as appointed cabinet or subcabinet ministers.[21] Furthermore, they are not without

19. Generalizations contrasting the career structures of career diplomats and political appointees of the Chilean diplomatic service are based on data gathered principally from *Diccionario biográfico de Chile*, 13th ed. (Santiago: Editorial Empresa Periodística de Chile, 1965–67).

20. Before his appointment by President Allende as ambassador to the United States, Orlando Letelier spent ten years with the IADB and the United Nations. Before the 1973 *golpe*, he served as foreign minister and as defense minister.

21. The late Pablo Neruda, who had been involved in Chilean Communist party political activities and had once served as a Communist Senator, served as ambassador to France during the first two years of the Allende administration. During the Christian Democratic regime, Radamiro Tomic, one of the founders of the party, served as a Senator from Aconcagua and Valparaíso provinces until his appointment as ambassador to the United States in 1968; Miguel Goray, one of the PDC's earliest adherents and a member of the party's National Junta, was appointed ambassador to the United Arab Republic.

significant international consultation and negotiation experience prior to their appointments. Many have served as temporary delegates to special meetings of some international organization or special consultative meetings between Chile and another nation. Despite some differences in career structure, careerists and politicians complement one another on a functional basis, and some careerists have obtained ambassadorial portfolios.[22]

The attitudes of Chile's foreign policy elite may express an important capability in the conduct of the nation's foreign policy. Whether serving during the democratic regime with its political party conflict or during the subsequent military regime with its problems of the domestic economy, the foreign policy elite is somewhat removed from internal situations, although the previous experiences of ministers of foreign relations, ambassadors, and special emissaries indicate some association with party politics and the articulation of restrictive ideologies. It is difficult to estimate the cultural and psychological biases of Chile's foreign policy elite, but during the Frei and the Allende administrations it seems that the careerist and the politician were realistically cognizant of the empirical basis of an international system composed of competing nations, international political and economic organizations, and economic blocs and alliances. Although some critical revisions have occurred in Chilean foreign policy since the 1973 *golpe*, a no less realistic attitude toward international politics may emerge in time.

By and large it appears that restrictive ideologies have not served as the principal standards for the Chilean foreign policy elite to perceive international politics. The Frei administration's foreign policy priorities were based on the very practical and modern model of "induced development," using European and North American economic growth as a goal. Given the need for economic and technological resources in a nation where leadership attitudes respond to developmental expectations of a diverse polity, the strategy of the Frei foreign policy demanded flexibility and skill to respond to an international system composed of new forms of cooperation and conflict. The Allende administration, advocating greater government involvement and less U.S. penetration of the development process, initiated a foreign policy which, as Claudio Véliz argued, utilized "the general outline of the previous administration, but with a significant difference of intent."[23] For example, Chilean–U.S. relations had been

22. For example, two ambassadors appointed during the Frei administration emerged through the bureaucratic structure of the diplomatic service: Horacio Suárez, ambassador to Guatemala, entered the Ministry of Foreign Relations in 1928 and served in embassy posts in Rio, Buenos Aires, Washington, and London, in addition to being a delegate to the UN General Assembly and the OAS; Fausto Soto, ambassador to Canada, served in embassy posts in Madrid, London, and Washington and also in various UN and OAS organs.
23. Claudio Véliz, "The Chilean Experiment," *Foreign Affairs* 49, no. 3 (April 1971): 442–53.

carried on in a climate of amicable consultation in the past, but in attempting to achieve a more favorable balance of trade with other nations it became necessary for Allende to accelerate diplomatic consultation and commercial contact with an increasing number of nations in Western and Eastern Europe, Latin America, Africa, and Asia. Such a trend of seeking wider markets and credits was initiated as a tactical solution by the previous administration in 1965 and supported by a decrease of U.S. aid beginning in 1967.

During the initial and bloody aftermath of the 1973 *golpe*, the military junta permitted a number of internal incidents to occur that ultimately affected Chile's relations with other nations. The Chilean diplomatic service had at that time little or no influence on foreign policy decisions, which reflected the attitudes and perspectives of a few high-ranking military officers. While announcing its intentions to maintain diplomatic relations with all nations (except Communist Cuba and North Korea), the junta allowed various military officials to abuse the embassy personnel and property of various nations, some of which had enjoyed very good relations with the Allende government. International criticism over the new regime's harsh treatment of officials and followers of the Allende administration, of foreign newsmen, foreign political refugees in Chile, and foreign embassies became widespread in Western and Eastern Europe and within the United Nations. A number of Socialist governments eventually severed diplomatic relations with Chile. Confronted with international criticism and severe economic problems, the junta sought relief by embarking on a foreign policy which reemphasized Chile's relations with capitalist nations, particularly the United States and the international financial agencies.

Military Capabilities

Chile's involvement in international politics has not been determined by a military capability. Although the War of the Pacific demonstrated Chile's willingness and ability to carry out military actions, the logistical problems imposed by geographic isolation and the acceptance by Chile and other Latin American nations of present boundaries based on early Spanish administrative divisions have prohibited any subsequent large-scale military operations. Occasionally, border disputes have erupted with Argentina, but with no major military implications. However, the present military government of Chile views its relations with its northern neighbor, Peru, with some apprehension. The acquisition of Soviet tanks by Peru, the effectiveness of the "preemptive strike" by such tanks in the Middle East conflict between Israel and Egypt, and the prevailing nationalism of both Chile and Peru, the antecedents of which may be found in Chile's conquests in the War of the Pacific, have raised questions about the durability of relations between the two nations.

Before the military's rise to power, Chile had been governed by eight successive and elected civilian administrations. During the liberal democratic republic, the military was a prestigious interest group, capable of lobbying effectively for its budgetary interests and defending itself against any antagonistic civilian action.

What small international role the Chilean military assumes is owing to the nation's continual commitment to the defense of the Western Hemisphere through the Military Assistance Pact with the United States. Much of the equipment of the armed forces has been purchased from the United States, Great Britain, and Sweden. The Allende administration acceded to the wishes of the Chilean military and allowed the armed forces to buy equipment according to "continuing needs and performances," thus maintaining traditional ties with the U.S. military. As adherents of "national recuperation," the present military regime's capability is internal, for it is obligated to maintain order and to govern a society, which includes formulating and administering public policies.

FOREIGN POLICY OUTPUT

The implementation of foreign policy is an adaptive function of a nation, one that anticipates a particular response from other nations and international agencies. The success of adaptation to international environment is dependent upon the skillful use of particular capabilities by foreign policy makers. In an era of international power politics, Chile has not been a formidable contender. However, despite scarce economic resources, a small population, and geographic isolation, Chile has played an expanding role in inter-American and international affairs. The strategic nature of mineral deposits has enhanced Chile's bargaining position in the world market at times, but prior to the military intervention, the most important capability permitting Chile to be influential in international affairs was the degree to which internal political institutions and processes allowed her foreign policy elite to view rationally the realities of the international system and link the nation's international objectives to capabilities in order to achieve effective response. Although the military chiefs may not be overly experienced in diplomacy or, for that matter, governance, they are apparently aware of the needs of Chile's economy and may prove to be effective in the area of foreign policy, particularly if they rely upon those civilians who have had international negotiating experience.

When the Christian Democratic party gained control of the executive administration of the nation in 1964, new policies designed to expand formal and informal diplomatic and commercial contact with other nations and international agencies were initiated to build a broad external support system for internal economic development. The Allende administration continued many of the innovative policies of the Frei administration, but diplomatic and commercial interaction with the Socialist nations of Eastern Europe increased because of a need to find new markets and a more favorable balance of trade. Since 1973 the military junta, however, has been more restrictive in its conduct of foreign policy. It is less concerned with the reactions and economic trade potential of the Socialist nations than with reemphasizing Chile's traditional diplomatic and commercial relations, particularly with the United States.

Diplomatic and Commercial Relations
with Europe and the USSR

The Frei administration implemented a policy of expanded diplomatic and commercial relations with Western and Eastern European nations, including the Soviet Union. Aware that European economic assistance could only complement U.S. aid, confronted by an external debt, and apprehensive of U.S. commitments in Southeast Asia, the Frei administration sought long-term and short-term development loans at low interest rates from European nations. Long-term loans and the reduction of tariffs by the EEC nations for exported semimanufactured and manufactured goods from Latin America, however, did not materialize. Chile had to settle for short-term credit to purchase machinery and materials and had to rely on small-scale technological assistance programs from several European nations. Sweden, Denmark, Finland, France, Britain, West Germany, and Italy extended credit and technical assistance.

One of the most dramatic innovations of the Frei administration was the resumption of diplomatic and consular relations with the Soviet Union, Czechoslovakia, Poland, Romania, Bulgaria, and Hungary. After seventeen years, the reestablishment of diplomatic relations between Chile and these nations led to the exchange of numerous trade missions. The Soviet Union agreed in 1968 to expand the sale of machine tools through credit extension and to loan $42 million for industrial development in Chile. During the Allende administration, Chile formally requested cooperation with the Council of Mutual Economic Assistance (COMECON) of the East European bloc, and an increasing amount of copper was sent to Eastern Europe and the Soviet Union. Moscow agreed to purchase 130,000 tons of copper over a three-year period until 1975. The Soviets also offered substantial credit for the purchase of mining and copper refining equipment. Although the Soviet Union became more influential in Chile during the Allende administration, she was reluctant to commit herself on a large scale to underwrite the Chilean Socialist regime. In turn, Chilean nationalism and the configuration of party politics in Chile prohibited any policy that would permit penetration of

Chile by yet another large foreign power. As a consequence of the violent overthrow of President Allende by the Chilean armed forces, the Soviet Union and several East European nations denounced the *golpe* and shortly thereafter severed diplomatic relations. Since Chile's closest economic tie is to the dollar economy of the United States, it is unlikely that Chile will quickly resurrect diplomatic and commercial ties with the Soviet Union or Eastern Europe.

Diplomatic and Commercial Relations with Asia and Africa

Traditionally, Chile's diplomatic and commercial contact has been confined to the nations of the Atlantic community and Latin America. However, in an effort to gain a better balance of trade, the Frei administration sought to extend its diplomatic and commercial relations with several Asian *and* African nations. By 1968, Chile had become the second most important supplier of iron ore to Japan, and both nations established several credit programs for joint exploration and development of Chile's copper-mining industry. Although the Frei administration did not establish diplomatic relations with Communist China (possibly because at the time Chile was dependent on U.S. public and private capital for economic development and aware of U.S. opposition to diplomatic recognition of China), it nonetheless entered into a trade agreement with China to sell electrolytic copper in 1966.

Since three-fourths of the net copper exports in the world emanate from Chile, Peru, Zambia, and Zaire, the leaders of these nations sought to exert greater control over the production and marketing of the mineral. Concerned about the extent to which copper exports could be more beneficial to each nation's economic development, the Frei administration and the other nations established the Inter-Governmental Council of Copper Exporting Countries (CIPEC) to coordinate new policies for marketing copper in anticipation of changing world conditions and markets. The Allende administration participated in CIPEC in the hope of finding methods to protect the sales of copper when price decreases threatened. Despite the prospect of controlling the marketing of copper, CIPEC was unsuccessful in coordinating prices and production. In addition, the future of CIPEC is seriously open to question, since Zambia withdrew diplomatic relations from Chile as a result of the *golpe*. Chile and Zambia together produce one-half of the world's copper for export.

The Allende administration departed somewhat from its predecessor's Asian policies by establishing diplomatic relations with Communist China in January 1971. It also supported China's entry into the United Nations and severed diplomatic relations with Nationalist China. China granted a long-term, interest-free loan of $68 million to Chile in 1972. As an assertion of independence in international politics and a desire to expand trade, Chile established trade missions and diplomatic relations with North Korea and North Vietnam by 1972. Although North Korean diplomats were evicted and the relations between Chile and North Korea were severed at the outset of the military regime, the foreign policy of the Chilean junta seeks to maintain relations with a number of Asian countries. Since Mainland China has not intervened in the political affairs of Chile, diplomatic relations between the two nations probably will be maintained.

The Andean Common Market

Chilean support of and participation in attempts to create regional economic integration serve as examples of both change and continuity in foreign policy. The administration of President Jorge Alessandri (1958–64) committed Chile to regional economic integration through the formation of the Latin American Free Trade Association (LAFTA) in 1961. However, the numerous problems inherent in facilitating economic integration based on tariff reduction and the exchange of goods induced the Frei administration to seek alternatives in its integration policies.

Compared to the economic integration efforts of the Central American Common Market nations, intraregional trade in the southern half of Latin America declined as a proportion of its total income in the last decade. Consequently, Chile and several Latin American nations sought the creation of a subregional economic integration system. In August 1966, Chile, Colombia, and Venezuela agreed to create a new structure, *Corporación Andina Fomento* (CORFO-ANDINA), which was designed as a multinational development corporation, owned by the signatory governments and their private economic sectors, to encourage national development planning and rapid achievement of objectives.[24] With the signing of the Cartagena Agreement in 1969, Bolivia, Chile, Colombia, Ecuador, and Peru agreed to establish a functional common market system, the Andean Economic Union. Although Venezuela withdrew from the negotiations on economic union because of internal political pressure exerted by industrialists in the Caldera administration, she became a member in February 1973.

The Allende government regarded the Andean integration experiment as crucial to its relations with its neighbors as well as to Chile's economic development. During Allende's 1971 goodwill tour of Ecuador, Colombia, and Peru, the president repeated Chile's desire to participate in the

---

24. CORFO-ANDINA operates as a financial institution by providing loans to facilitate integration. It seeks credit from the World Bank, the IADB, and other credit agencies in Western Europe. ANDINA relies on public capital, and participating governments and their semiautonomous development institutions may subscribe by purchasing shares. See *Ercilla* (Santiago), 15 Aug. 1967, pp. 20–21, and ibid., 6 Sept. 1967, p. 11.

Andean scheme, and Chilean policymakers agreed with other members to establish a common policy regarding foreign investments in their economies. Since the mixed corporation idea transcends Chilean ideologies, it is quite likely that the military junta in Chile will continue to support CORFO-ANDINO and the common market mechanism.

Diplomatic and Commercial Relations with Cuba

Just prior to the election of President Frei in 1964, Chile severed diplomatic and consular relations with Cuba, presumably in compliance with the sanction resolution passed by the OAS foreign ministers' conference in July 1964, which called upon member nations to break diplomatic and commercial relations with the Castro regime as a result of the charge of aggression brought to the OAS by Venezuela. Little effort had been made to restore diplomatic relations between Chile and Cuba until mid-1969, when both nations initiated discussions on the subject that culminated in the negotiation of a $15 million agricultural trade agreement and a cultural exchange program. Shortly after President Allende's inauguration, full diplomatic relations with Cuba were established. In an effort to assert Chile's leadership within the Latin American community, particularly the Andean bloc, Allende sought and achieved, during his 1971 trip to Ecuador, a joint declaration recognizing the right of Latin American nations to reestablish diplomatic reactions with Cuba. By mid-1972, however, only seven nations within the OAS were ready to vote to lift the sanctions of the 1964 resolution and thus permit members to resume diplomatic relations with Cuba without violating the OAS Charter. The motion to rescind the resolution failed since the votes of sixteen of the twenty-three OAS members are necessary. Although the Frei administration initiated rapprochement with Cuba, the election of a Socialist as Chile's chief executive provided the impetus for the restoration of diplomatic relations with Cuba. One of the first foreign policy decisions of the military junta shortly after the 1973 *golpe* was the expulsion of the Cuban diplomatic corps from Chile and the severence of diplomatic relations with Cuba. The Allende administration had permitted an influx of Cuban advisors and technicians, many of whom served in Chilean ministries and nationalized industries.

Chilean–U.S. Relations

Traditionally, Chile and the United States have enjoyed mutually effective diplomatic, commercial, and cultural relations. Chile has depended on U.S. private and public capital and technical assistance and, in turn, the United States has depended on Chile's copper and nitrates. However, on a number of occasions during the Frei years, strains in the relations between the two nations were evident. First, Chile, committed to the

principles of nonintervention and self-determination, criticized the unilateral military action of the United States in the Dominican Republic in
1965. Second, President Frei mildly criticized the Alliance for Progress as
an ineffective political instrument for promoting economic and political
development, and he suggested that the OAS Council be revamped to
clarify priorities and centralize foreign assistance in one agency.[25] Finally,
a basic disagreement between Chile and the United States emerged at the
Presidents' conference in Montevideo in 1967 regarding Chile's advocacy
of permitting borrower nations greater freedom to choose economic
projects when using U.S. credits.

Despite the strains in Chilean–U.S. relations on a variety of international political issues, both nations attempted to maintain policies of
interdependence during the Frei administration. Chile successfully lob-
bied for much needed credit to aid economic development, while the
United States served as a market for Chilean copper. Beginning in 1967,
however, internal politics and economics in each nation induced revision
of some existing policies. The United States, disillusioned by the Vietnam
experience and the results of its foreign aid program, reduced U.S. Agency
for International Development (AID) operations to Chile in anticipation
of increased political demands in Chile for total nationalization of U.S.
private interests. In turn, Chile intensified her search for new sources of
external support for economic development at the multilateral level,
principally the IMF, the IBRD, and the IADB. By using such international finance agencies, a donor nation such as the United States could
contribute to the economic development of the less wealthy borrower
nations without being charged with direct political involvement in the
borrower's affairs of state and could also provide a greater amount of
long-range policy continuity.

The Nixon administration's response to the election of an avowed
Marxist to the Chilean presidency in 1970 was cool to the extent that
traditional protocol may have been initially violated. An atmosphere of
potential retaliation by each nation indicated that Chilean–U.S. relations
would enter a new stage of development. President Nixon did not send the
customary written congratulations to the new Chilean president, but
through Assistant Secretary of State Charles Meyer, he presented a verbal
message to President Allende at his inauguration. In his State of the
World address in 1971, President Nixon accepted the legitimacy of
President Allende's election; but the nationalization by Chile of industries
owned or partially owned by private U.S. interests represented the
principal corrosive element in Chilean–U.S. relations from 1971 to 1973.
During the first year of the Allende administration, Chile nationalized the

25. Eduardo Frei Montalva, "The Alliance that Lost its Way," *Foreign Affairs* 46 (April
1967): 437–48.

steel, coal, cement, nitrate, and textile industries and also the large copper mines partially owned and operated by the Anaconda, Kennecott, and Cerro corporations. In addition, a number of foreign-owned banking firms, such as the Bank of America, the Bank of London, and the First National City Bank of New York, were purchased by the Chilean government. Nationalization of banking is not a serious departure in Chile, because the *Banco de Estado* has controlled approximately half the nation's banking for many years.

Most of the foreign-owned industries negotiated mutually satisfactory terms for the Chilean government to purchase their operations. However, the situation of the Anaconda and Kennecott mining operations appeared to be another matter that increased the diplomatic tension between Chile and the United States. Although the nationalization bill that emerged from the Chilean Congress allowed for payment, President Allende declared that both companies accumulated "excess profits" and damaged the mines to the extent that indemnification would not be forthcoming.[26] In addition, the Chilean government decided that payment on the sale of interest in the mining properties during President Frei's "Chileanization" program would also be nullified by the charge of "excess profits" and damages.

Prior to the Allende administration's decision not to compensate Anaconda and Kennecott, the United States exerted some pressure on Chile to make compensation for expropriation. EXIMBANK, a U.S. agency designed to provide credit for nations with balance-of-payment problems, labeled Chile a "high credit risk," and the Inter-American Committee for the Alliance for Progress refused to allow a Chilean delegation to talk with senior U.S. officials about a program report on Chile's economy. When the Allende administration announced that "excess profits" would eliminate compensation, U.S. Secretary of State William P. Rogers is said to have declared that such action was contrary to international law; but he did not indicate that retaliatory measures would be taken. Consequently, the State Department's initial "soft line" on the compensation issue was predicated on three important factors: (1) economic or political retaliation would focus great attention on the United States in Chile as a cause of Chile's deepening economic crises under President Allende; (2) the Chilean treatment of Anaconda and Kennecott did not mean that all U.S. private interests would be prevented from obtaining compensation for their nationalized properties; and (3) there was little the United States could do in the wake of increasing nationalization of foreign-owned properties in Chile and in other Latin

26. The controller general of the Chilean government determined the book value (net value) of the companies' investments. Excess profits were then deducted from these figures to determine any compensation (*Wall Street Journal*, 24 Sept. 1971).

American nations in which nationalism has a tendency to unite internal power contenders within political systems.

The strains in Chilean-U.S. relations intensified in 1972 when Chile sought to renegotiate with the Paris Group of the IMF debt repayments owed to the United States and certain European nations. The declines in the price and the exportation of copper forced Chile to suspend payments on her external debt, thus prompting the Allende administration to request rescheduling of payment on a portion of its debts due from 1971 to 1974. The United States took a much harder line on the noncompensation issue when President Nixon announced that the United States would take "punitive measures" against those nations that expropriate private U.S. property without compensation. Whether President Nixon's warning was intended to force Chile to pay for the Kennecott and Anaconda properties or to strengthen the U.S. position at the Paris meetings, forcing Chile to establish more effective monetary policies in order to settle her external debt, was not clear. During the Allende administration, Kennecott and Anaconda failed ultimately in their attempts to gain compensation, but Chile eventually agreed to permit the IMF to review periodically her monetary credit and trade performance as part of the agreement to obtain refinancing of the debt.

By the beginning of 1973 the noncompensation and debt renegotiation issues had been overshadowed by another critical issue—the role of the multinational corporation in domestic *and* international politics—which contributed to the deterioration of relations between Chile and the United States. Washington news columnist Jack Anderson had revealed in March 1972 that the International Telephone and Telegraph Corporation (ITT) had "plotted" with the Central Intelligence Agency (CIA) to induce the Chilean military to prevent President-Elect Allende from taking office after he had won a plurality vote in the 1970 presidential election. Anderson's revelations prompted an investigation by the U.S. Senate Foreign Relations Committee to study the influence of multinational corporations on American foreign policy. The transnational role of large private corporations came under further scrutiny by European and Latin American nations when, after a Chilean court ruled on an appeal by the Kennecott company that nationalization was legal and that no further compensation was due, Kennecott sought an embargo on the sale of Chilean copper to France by seeking injunctions in the courts of the Netherlands, Sweden, and France. However, a Paris court lifted the embargo and allowed the French purchasers to pay the government-owned Chilean Copper Corporation (CODELCO). The ITT and the attempted embargo incidents presented a significant international opportunity to President Allende when he visited the United Nations in December 1972. Speaking before the General Assembly, he asserted that a severe conflict had emerged between large multinational corporations and sovereign nations and warned the smaller developing nations to be wary of powerful U.S. firms.

It would appear that such issues would lead to a severe reversal in Chilean–U.S. relations during the Allende regime. Relations were certainly less cordial since mutual consultation on specific economic issues was no longer undertaken. However, in less publicized areas the two nations maintained fairly effective relations. Most importantly, smaller privately owned U.S. industries, including the Cerro mining company and a number of banking firms, negotiated compensation after their properties had been nationalized. In addition, the U.S. Peace Corps continued to provide some technical assistance, and the United States continued to grant credit to Chile for the purchase of military equipment. During the months preceding the *golpe*, the United States, possibly influenced by its policy of détente with the Soviet Union and China, began to rethink its relations with Chile.[27] The United States was conciliatory toward Chile's desire to renegotiate her foreign debt, and the IMF, within which the United States possesses considerable influence, allowed Chile to use Special Drawing Rights up to $39.5 million to aid her foreign exchange problem.

At the time of the military *golpe*, it was asserted in some Latin American and European newspapers that the United States aided either directly or indirectly the downfall of the Allende government. The withdrawal of U.S. assistance programs, begun during the Frei administration, and the lobbying by the United States within the international financial agencies to defer *new* loans no doubt had some impact on the Chilean economy. In an effort to obtain compensation for the nationalized companies, EXIMBANK deferred all new loans to Chile, and the U.S. Congress passed the Gonzales Amendment, which instructed U.S. representatives in the international financial agencies to vote against nations that expropriated private U.S. interests without compensation. However, the United States did not object to the providing of "pipeline" credits and aid to Chile by the multilateral finance agencies. From December 1970 to December 1972 the IADB disbursed $54 million authorized from earlier loans. Although apprehensive about Chile's "credit worthiness," the IBRD disbursed from July 1970 to June 1973 over $46 million in loans that had been approved earlier. The United States, as a member of the International Monetary Fund, did not object to the IMF providing compensatory loans in December 1972. Furthermore, as a member of the Paris Group the United States was willing to agree on the renegotiation of Chile's foreign debt. Although U.S. policy indicated a use of what leverage it possessed in the international financial agencies to aid the

27. Federico G. Gil, "Socialist Chile and the United States," *Inter-American Economic Affairs* 27 (Autumn 1973): 29–47.

noncompensation issue, the international agencies were not engaged in
political subversion but, given their rather strict monetarist views, were
concerned about the prospects of the Allende administration's seemingly
unorthodox internal economic strategy. The basic causes that led to the
golpe, as already indicated, were strictly internal.[28]

Aware of the international criticism of the Chilean military during and
after the *golpe*, the United States initially assumed a cautious attitude
toward the new regime. After the junta had announced its intentions of
encouraging ties with the United States and England, traditional diplomatic partners, the U.S. government recognized the new government, and
several Latin American nations immediately followed suit. The military
leaders embarked on a series of foreign policy announcements designed to
influence the United States and the international financial agencies to
assist Chile in dealing with its critical economic problems. In its efforts to
gain favorable disposition on lending, the junta announced that it would
institute a free market system, honor its foreign debt, return to some
Chilean and foreign owners that property expropriated without compensation, and begin negotiations on compensation to the private copper
companies whose mining interests had been nationalized by the previous
Chilean administration.

It is obvious that Chilean–U.S. relations have shifted direction as a
result of the *golpe* and the renunciation by the Chilean military of many
of the economic policies of the Allende government. The United States
has become favorably disposed to the junta and has aided in influencing
the IADB and the IMF to extend needed credit to Chile. In addition, the
Chilean junta requested that some private U.S. industries reenter the
economic structure of the nation. Since the late 1960s it has been a matter
of U.S. foreign aid policy to place greater emphasis on channeling credits
and grants to the developing nations through multilateral international
financial agencies rather than through the bilateral level of AID. The
United States will continue to utilize the multilateral approach in the
ensuing years in view of its own internal and external economic problems
and the serious apprehension of its policy makers about the effectiveness
of past bilateral aid programs. Although the military governors in Chile
emphasize the important role that government institutions must play in
national economic development, particularly in the areas of copper

28. According to Tad Szulc of the *Washington Post*, the secret testimony of CIA Director
William E. Colby before the House Subcommittee on Inter-American Affairs on 11 October
1973 was equivocal in regard to CIA activities in Chile between 1970 and the *golpe*. See Tad
Szulc, "The View From Langley," *Washington Post*, 21 Oct. 1973. For a fairly balanced
debate on the question see Elizabeth Farnsworth, "More Than Was Admitted," *Foreign
Policy*, no. 16 (Fall 1974), pp. 127–41, and Paul Sigmund, "Less Than Charged," *Foreign
Policy*, no. 16 (Fall 1974), pp. 142–50. Despite CIA efforts to finance opposition to Allende in
1970 and later, such external factors were minor, for the internal ones were decisive in
initiating the military *golpe*.

mining, banking, and agrarian reform, they can anticipate more active support from the U.S. government and from private interests in international affairs, and quite possibly, in internal economic affairs.

CONCLUSION

Historically, certain economic and political capabilities have enabled Chile to make numerous claims upon the international political system. These capabilities represent the manipulative internal variables of national power which, when mobilized by Chile's foreign policy elite, influence the actions of other entities of the international political system to assist in Chile's economic development. The Chilean economic system suffers from periodic and often intense inflation, a variety of infrastructural problems, and a lack of indigenous capital investment. At times, the production and exportation of copper can enhance the nation's economic capability in international trade. Hence, the Frei administration initiated a program designed to control part of the production, processing, and marketing of copper in order to pay for loans that produce capital for economic development. The Allende administration embarked on a total nationalization program of mining interests, but the instability of world copper prices and the decline in the production of copper contributed to a rapid dwindling of foreign earnings for a nation that acquires two-thirds of its foreign exchange from copper sales. Under the military junta and whatever form of government may follow, the control of the production, refining, and marketing of Chilean copper will remain a matter of governmental decision making.

Whether a democratic and republican form of government or a military junta exists in Chile, the most important political capability is the foreign policy elite. Chile's career diplomats and political appointees serve to link the foreign policy objective of assisting internal economic development to the various components of the international system. Most Chilean foreign ministers have held realistic views of the international system as composed of other nations, formal international political and economic organizations and associations, and various blocs, or alliances of nations, in which negotiations must be conducted to achieve Chile's objective. In most cases, Chilean foreign policy makers have transmitted to various actors of the international system an attitude designed to encourage bilateral or multilateral negotiations to provide mutual services and support for Chile's economic development.

The foreign policy agenda of the Frei administration emphasized the extension and the maintenance of commercial and diplomatic contact on a continental and extracontinental scale. In an effort to take advantage of the shifting trends of trade and the allocation of credit and capital, Chile

maintained commercial exchange and received aid from her traditional
ally, the United States, while developing a broader base of diplomatic
exchange, credit, and trade with Western and Eastern European nations,
the USSR, Zaire, Zambia, Japan, and to a very small extent, the People's
Republic of China. The Frei administration found it difficult to realize
economic integrationist goals through LAFTA and thus contributed to
the creation of a subregional integration mechanism, the Andean Economic Union.

Foreign policy under Allende diverged somewhat from that of the Frei
administration in that it did not rely as extensively on the credit and the
technical assistance of the United States. However, much of the Frei
foreign policy remained intact and was further extended. The Allende
administration, dependent upon Chile's limited economic but talented
political capabilities, sought to link the nation's need for economic
development to the willingness of Western Europe, the Socialist nations
of Eastern Europe and Asia, Japan, and the Andean Economic Union to
provide trade, credit, and technical assistance. It also sought successfully
to renegotiate its foreign debt repayments with various international
financial agencies and with several Western and Eastern European nations.

The military junta that came to power as a result of the deteriorating
internal economic and political situation found itself in a somewhat
restrictive foreign policy situation. No longer committed diplomatically
to the Socialist nations of Eastern Europe, the Soviet Union, Cuba, and
North Korea and harshly criticized internationally for the violent methods by which it had established itself in power, the military government
sought to reemphasize Chile's traditional diplomatic and commercial ties
to the United States, Britain, and Brazil. Furthermore, it set out to
reestablish its "credit worthiness" with the United States by offering to
negotiate compensation for the nationalized copper industries. As the
production and world market price of copper increased, thus making
more foreign exchange available to Chile, the nation's leaders sought to
renegotiate her foreign debt payments with the international financial
agencies and with other nations in the hope of supporting some kind of
economic growth and diversity in the 1970s.

BIBLIOGRAPHICAL NOTE

Chilean historians and international jurists have contributed a wide variety of
scholarly works in recounting and analyzing the conduct of Chilean foreign
policy. Much of the work, however, has been devoted to appraisals of a specific
inter-American or international incident involving Chile and other nations or
international organizations. Among the more prominent works on nineteenth

century Chilean diplomacy and foreign policy are: Augustín Boanchi Barros, *Bosque histórico de las relaciones chileno-norteamericanas durante la indepedencia* (Santiago: n.p., 1946); Gonzalo Bulnes, *Guerra del Pacífico*, 2d ed., 3 vols. (Santiago: Editiorial del Pacífico, 1955); Ricardo Montaner, *Historia diplomática de la independencia de Chile* (Santiago: Universidad de Chile, 1941); Francisco Antonio Encina, *Historia de Chile desde la prehistoria hasta 1891*, 20 vols. (Santiago: Editorial Nacimento, 1949-52); and Carlos Walker Martínez, *Política internacional de la administración Errázuriz en 1898* (Santiago: Imprenta Moderna, 1902).

Some scholarly efforts pertaining to Chile's twentieth-century diplomatic situation are Alejandro Alvarez, *Chile ante la segunda conferencia de la Haya* (Santiago: n.p., 1907); Ernesto Barros Jarpa, *La 'segunda' independencia* (Santiago: Zig Zag, 1956) and Jarpa, *Hacia la solución* (Santiago: Imprenta Universitaria, 1921); Augustín Edwards, *La américa latina y la liga de las naciones* (Santiago: Editorial Universitaria, 1937); and Aquiles Vergara Vicuña, *Bolivia y Chile: Lecciones del pasado, advertencias para el porvenir* (La Paz: Intendencia General de Guerra, 1936). Luis Galdames's *A History of Chile*, trans. Isaac J. Cox (Chapel Hill: University of North Carolina Press, 1941) is an historical account of Chile's internal political development *and* international politics from the time of the Spanish Conquest to 1936.

Outstanding works by North American historians who appraise Chile's international role in the nineteenth and twentieth centuries are: Robert N. Burr, *By Reason or Force: Chile and the Balancing of Power in South America, 1830-1905* (Berkeley: University of California Press, 1965); and Frederick B. Pike, *Chile and the United States, 1880-1962* (Notre Dame, Ind.: University of Notre Dame Press, 1963), esp. chaps. 1, 3, 5, and 7.

Important statements dealing with the foreign policies of the Frei administration (1964-70) and the Allende administration (1970-73) are Eduardo Frei Montalva, "The Alliance That Lost Its Way," *Foreign Affairs* 46 (April 1967): 437-48; Claudio Veliz, "The Chilean Experiment," *Foreign Affairs* 49, no. 3 (April 1971): 442-53; and Federico G. Gil, "Socialist Chile and the United States," *Inter-American Economic Affairs* 27 (Autumn 1973): 29-47.

In view of the political uses of statistical surveys regarding the economy and society by various Chilean administrations and political party leaders and by the North American press, it is sometimes difficult to assess accurately economic conditions in Chile. Furthermore, the "monetarist" versus "structuralist" debate has been a continuing issue with Chilean policy makers and within international organizations for close to two decades. During the first two years of the Allende administration, a variety of conflicting reports on annual growth rates and productivity emerged from the administration itself, from ODEPLAN (the government's economic planning office), from the Institute of Economic Sciences at the University of Chile, and from various political parties in opposition. However, several reliable sources exist. Two of the most important are the *Quarterly Economic Review*, published by the Economic Intelligence Unit, Ltd., of London, which provides economic studies of individual nations on a quarterly basis, and the *Economic Survey of Latin America*, published by the Economic Commission for Latin America (ECLA) of the United Nations. Additional sources for economic data are the *Annual Report* of the Inter-American Development Bank in Washington, D.C. and *The Statistical Compendium of the Americas*, published by the Pan American Union in Washington, D.C.

Valuable sources on the past role of the Chilean military include Liisa North, *Civil-Military Relations in Argentina, Chile, and Peru* (Berkeley: University of California Press, 1966); and Frederick M. Nunn, *Chilean Politics, 1920-1931: The Honorable Mission of the Armed Forces* (Albuquerque: University of New Mexico Press, 1970). Statistical data on Chilean military capability is available in *The Statesman's Yearbook, 1972-73*, ed. John Paxton (New York: St. Martin's Press, 1972), pp. 807-8; and *Survey of the Alliance for Progress: The Latin American Military* (Washington, D.C.: Government Printing Office, 1967; published for the U.S. Senate Committee on Foreign Relations), pp. 33-34.

Some of the most important traditional works on Chilean politics in Spanish include Ricardo Cruz-Coke, *Geografía electoral de Chile* (Santiago: Editorial del Pacífico, 1952); Alberto Edwards Vives and Eduardo Frei Montalva, *Historia de los partidos políticos chilenos* (Santiago: Editorial del Pacífico, 1950); and Sergio Guilisasti Tagle, *Partidos políticos chilenos* (Santiago: Editorial Nacimento, 1964). A very important analysis of Chilean politics is Maurice Zeitlin's "Determinantes sociales de la democracia política en Chile," *Revista Latinoamericana de Sociología* 2 (July 1966): 223-76.

More systematic efforts, however, have emanated from North American political scientists, many of whom gained considerable research experience in Chile during the 1960s. Among the most important books are Alan Angell, *Politics and the Labour Movement in Chile* (New York: Oxford University Press, 1972); Ben G. Burnett, *Political Groups in Chile* (Austin: University of Texas Press, 1970); Federico G. Gil, *The Political System of Chile* (Boston: Houghton Mifflin Co., 1966); Ernst Halperin, *Nationalism and Communism in Chile* (Cambridge, Mass.: MIT Press, 1965); Robert K. Kaufman, *The Politics of Land Reform in Chile, 1950-1970* (Cambridge: Harvard University Press, 1972); and James Petras, *Politics and Social Forces in Chilean Development* (Berkeley: University of California Press, 1969).

Additional functional analyses of certain aspects of the Chilean political system appear in several academic journals and special studies: Weston H. Agor, "The Senate in the Chilean Political System," in *Legislatures in Developmental Perspectives*, ed. Allan Kornberg and Lloyd A. Musolf (Durham, N.C.: Duke University Press, 1970); Robert L. Ayres, "Economic Stagnation and the Emergence of Political Ideology of Chilean Underdevelopment," *World Politics* 5 (October 1972): 34-61; Orville G. Cope, *Coalition Formation, Christian Democracy, and the 1970 Presidential Election in Chile*, Institute of Government Research, Research Series no. 11, (Tucson: University of Arizona, February 1972); R. H. McDonald, "Apportionment and Party Politics in Santiago, Chile," *Midwest Journal of Political Science* 9 (August 1967): 455-70; Sandra Powell, "Political Change in the Chilean Elecorate, 1952-1964," *Western Political Quarterly* 25 (June 1970): 364-83; Arpad von Lazar and Luis Quiros Varela, "Chilean Christian Democracy: Lessons in the Politics of Reform Management," *Inter-American Economic Affairs* 21 (Spring 1968): 51-72; and Arturo Valenzuela, "The Scope of the Chilean Party System," *Comparative Politics* 4 (January 1972): 179-200.

More recent essays on the nature and causes of the military *golpe* of 11 September 1973, are Alan Angell, "Counterrevolution in Chile," *Current History* 66 (January 1974): 6-9; Thomas G. Sanders, "The Process of Partisanship in Chile," *American Universities Field Staff Reports,* West Coast South America Series 20 (October 1973): 1-14; Paul E. Sigmund, "The 'Invisible Blockade' and the Overthrow of Allende," *Foreign Affairs* 52 (January 1974): 322-48; and Lawrence Whitehead, "Why Allende Fell," *World Today* 29 (November 1973): 461-74.

16/E. James Holland

Bolivia

Landlocked in the center of South America is the large (slightly smaller than the combined areas of Texas and California) but poor and sparsely populated Republic of Bolivia. Although Bolivia's size and location might suggest to the uninformed that she plays a strategically crucial role in Latin American relations, Bolivia has never achieved a place of leadership in inter-American affairs. Nevertheless, though not a major Latin American power in traditional terms (gross national product, military capability, population, etc.), this Andean nation's record of foreign relations is a graphic example of the inseparable relationship between domestic affairs and foreign relations. First, unresolved problems of governance, economics, and social structures have prevented Bolivia from developing a capability for defending the national domain she claimed at the time of independence in 1825; by 1938 over half of Bolivia's original territory had been incorporated by the bordering states of Chile, Peru, Brazil, Argentina, and Paraguay. Second, general agreement exists among scholars that Bolivia was the second Latin American country in the twentieth century to have experienced an authentic social revolution, beginning in 1952.[1] Bolivian foreign relations since that time exemplify the crucial role of external factors in the complex processes of national development and social change. Bolivian foreign policy also serves to illustrate a number of the methods utilized by government leaders in modernizing countries to fulfill their responsibilities of directing the national development process.

MAJOR PROBLEMS IN BOLIVIAN FOREIGN RELATIONS

Three broad categories of problems in the foreign relations of Bolivia can be identified, relating to (1) foreign trade, (2) foreign development assistance, and (3) national security.

Foreign Trade

Bolivia's foreign trade plays a crucial role in the economic and political life of the country and in the process of national development. Since

---

1. Paul E. Sigmund, ed., *Models of Political Change in Latin America* (New York: Praeger Publishers, 1970), p. 3. The Mexican Revolution of 1910 is viewed generally by Latin Americanists as the first great social revolution in the twentieth century among Latin American countries.

Bolivia's agricultural and manufacturing productivity has been unable to meet national needs, exports provide the foreign exchange earnings required to buy essential imports, including materials needed in development projects. Export industries, especially mining and more recently petroleum, also provide the Bolivian government with tax revenues that are needed to finance public services and development programs.

Bolivia's historical dependence on mineral exports, especially tin in the twentieth century, continues into the 1970s.[2] One of the perennial concerns of the Bolivian government is to maintain and expand markets for the nation's exports with prices that will obtain maximum foreign exchange earnings. Fluctuating mineral prices on the world market have a resounding impact on the Bolivian economy. For example, on the basis of tin production figures in 1966, a price drop of one cent per pound would reduce the gross value of Bolivian tin exports by nearly $600,000.[3] Since the revolution of 1952, Bolivia has made significant efforts to reduce its dependence on tin and other mineral exports through the development of a petroleum and gas industry with export capabilities.

Bolivia's interest in increasing exports and adopting a foreign trade policy that supports national development has led her to a cautious posture with respect to such Latin American movements toward economic integration as the Latin American Free Trade Association (LAFTA) and the subregional Andean Group. Bolivian officials have given much attention to defining the appropriate policy for a poorly developed country in its economic relations with other Latin American countries with more highly industrialized economies.

The problems of providing adequate facilities for transporting Bolivia's products to foreign markets and acquiring and safeguarding free transit guarantees as a landlocked country are also perennial concerns for government leaders in La Paz.

Foreign Development Assistance

Since the end of the Chaco War with Paraguay in 1935, the Bolivian government for the most part has been dedicated to the task of promoting national economic and social development. While acknowledging the fact that such development requires sweeping domestic reforms, even

2. Inter-American Development Bank, Social Progress Trust Fund, *Socio-Economic Progress in Latin America, Annual Report, 1971* (Washington, D.C., 1971), pp. 127–29. According to data provided by the Inter-American Development Bank, 1970 tin exports of $101 million accounted for half of the total value of Bolivian exports. Tin and other minerals, such as antimony, silver, lead, copper, tungsten, and zinc, represented nearly 80 percent of Bolivia's total export value in 1971.

3. Bolivian tin production in 1966 according to provisional data contained in the *United Nations Statistical Yearbook, 1967*, was 25,932 metric tons (a metric ton equals about 2204 pounds).

Bolivia's most vocal nationalists have recognized the need for foreign technical and economic assistance. With a per capita income among the lowest in Latin America ($201) and an annual gross national product of approximately $1,000 million ($900 million in 1970), Bolivia's capacity for providing adequate investment capital is severely limited.[4]

Since the early years of World War II and especially since the 1952 revolution Bolivian leaders have aggressively sought development assistance from the United States, a number of other countries, and a variety of international agencies. In the 1970s, Bolivia still seeks substantial foreign development assistance. The problem is complicated, however, by at least three factors: (1) recent Republican administrations have encouraged the expansion of private investment abroad, deemphasizing somewhat the public foreign assistance programs of the 1960s; (2) Bolivia's service on its foreign debt requires substantial and continuous foreign assistance inflow; and (3) nationalist sentiment has created an uncertain climate for foreign private investment. Thus, the challenge of obtaining crucial foreign assistance is a formidable one for the Bolivian government.

National Security

Matters relating to national security are sensitive concerns to Bolivians. In a nation that has suffered humiliating diplomatic and military defeats, policy makers are ever alert to new threats to national honor and security and also to opportunities to ameliorate certain adverse situations stemming from the past. Foremost among such concerns is Bolivia's well-known objective of escaping from her landlocked condition, which resulted from the loss of her seacoast to Chile in the War of the Pacific (1879–83). This most important issue has prevented friendly relations with Santiago in the twentieth century. In the early 1960's, Bolivian relations with Chile were complicated further when Chile initiated irrigation and hydroelectric projects on the Lauca River, which flows from Chile into Bolivia. The disagreement over water rights led to a break in diplomatic relations between the two countries that has continued into the 1970s.

National security has also been involved in the Bolivian government's successful campaign against the leftist guerrilla group known as the

4. U.S., Department of State, *World Data Handbook*, Issues in United States Foreign Policy, Pubn. 8665 (Washington, D.C.: Government Printing Office, 1972), p. 5. Recent comparative per capita income figures (1970) show Bolivia's low ranking among Latin American countries. Venezuela's per capita income that year was $974. Only Haiti's per capita income of $91 (1968 figures) was less than that of Bolivia. Domestic savings in the Bolivian economy for 1970 have been estimated at a relatively low 8.8 percent of Gross Domestic Product, and in the 1967–70 period, 39 percent of investment in Bolivia was derived from foreign sources. See Inter-American Development Bank, *Socio-Economic Progress in Latin America*, p. 65.

Ejército de Liberación Nacional (ELN). First organized in 1966 under the leadership of the Argentine revolutionary Ernesto "Che" Guevara, the ELN struggled for survival after Guevara's death in 1967.[5] By 1970, most of the remaining guerrilla force had been captured or killed by the Bolivian army and the survivors exiled to Chile.[6] The government of Colonel Hugo Banzer Suárez has waged a relentless drive against remaining ELN members and sympathizers since coming to power in August 1971, resulting in significant reductions in the strength of leftist groups in Bolivia. The persistent fear of a renewal of revolutionary activities, however, may well encourage government leaders to pursue a policy of closer relations with the United States and the military government of Brazil in the years ahead.

THE BOLIVIAN EXPERIENCE IN FOREIGN RELATIONS

Bolivia's present foreign policy can be better understood with some knowledge of her unfortunate history in international affairs. Bolivia's experience in foreign relations may be viewed in terms of three major quests: (1) for territorial integrity and security; (2) for export markets and favorable trade arrangements; and (3) for development assistance, both public and private.

Territorial Integrity and National Security

Bolivia's quest for territorial integrity began with her creation as an independent state in 1825. Attempts to establish a confederation between Peru and Bolivia, first by Bolivian and then by Peruvian leaders, were finally thwarted in 1842 with the military defeat of the Peruvian caudillo Agustín Gamarra. Because of Chile's role in this defeat, relations with Chile became the foremost concern in Bolivian foreign relations.

The problem with Chile related to the control over and exploitation of a narrow strip of territory along the Pacific coast (about 240 miles from north to south), which was claimed by Bolivia at the time of independence. Guano and later nitrate deposits in the Atacama desert made the region attractive to Chilean investors, and in 1842 the Chilean government laid claim to much of the disputed territory. Following decades of negotiations, inept Bolivian political leadership and strong Chilean expansionist sentiment led to the War of the Pacific in 1879, in which

5. Robert F. Lamberg, "Che in Bolivia: The 'Revolution' That Failed," *Problems of Communism* 19 (July–August 1970).
6. *New York Times*, 17 Nov. 1970. The Torres government authorized the voluntary exile to Chile of about seventy members of the Army of National Liberation, including Bolivians, Chileans, and Peruvians.

Chile decisively defeated both Peru and Bolivia, occupied Bolivia's coastal region, and conquered extensive regions of southern Peru. The Treaty of Ancón ended the war between Chile and Peru in 1883, but Bolivia, hoping that Chile later might agree to cede her an outlet on the Pacific, delayed until 1904 before agreeing to the Treaty of Peace and Friendship.[7] For most of the period since 1904, Bolivian foreign policy has included as one of its objectives the acquisition of some type of sovereign outlet on the Pacific.

The dispute with Chile, however, is only one of the territorial disputes in which Bolivia has been involved. The Treaty of Petropolis, signed between Bolivia and Brazil in November 1903, permitted the great Amazonian state to incorporate the rubber-rich Acre region, claimed by Bolivia under terms of an earlier boundary treaty. Bolivia's early relations with Argentina also were troubled by territorial questions, and boundary disputes with Peru and Argentina persisted long after basic territorial issues had been settled. Portions of the Bolivian-Brazilian frontier have still not been precisely defined.[8]

Bolivia's most recent territorial loss came as the result of the disastrous Chaco War with Paraguay (1932-35). Oblivious to warnings of unpreparedness from high military leaders, Bolivia's President Daniel Salamanca adopted a nationalistic policy that led the nation to war with Paraguay in 1932, resulting in the loss of thousands of lives, extensive territory, and the capability of Bolivia's traditional political parties to govern.[9]

Bolivian foreign policy since the Chaco War has been characterized by persistent efforts to guarantee national security. At the Buenos Aires Peace Conference following the close of hostilities in the Chaco (1935) and later at the Eighth International Conference of American States in Lima (1938), Bolivian diplomats championed the doctrine of nonrecognition of territory acquired by force, a principle contained in an inter-American declaration of 3 August 1932.[10] Bolivia ultimately entered into a series of agreements with Peru, Argentina, and Brazil that contained nonaggression or territorial guarantee provisions.

An even more distinctive Bolivian foreign policy position, properly understood within the context of the nation's experience of territorial

7. Miguel Mercado Moreira, *Historia Internacional de Bolivia*, 2d ed. (La Paz: Imprenta "Atenea," 1930), pp. 408-526. In the Treaty of Peace and Friendship between the two countries, Bolivia ceded its coastal territory to Chile in return for a railroad linking La Paz with the Chilean port of Arica, free commercial transit rights through Chilean territory, and $300,000 sterling.

8. Harold Osborne, *Bolivia: A Land Divided*, 3d ed. (London: Oxford University Press, 1964), pp. 49-64.

9. See Herbert S. Klein, *Parties and Political Change in Bolivia, 1880-1952* (London: Cambridge University Press, 1969) for an excellent historical treatment of the period immediately preceding the Chaco War.

10. Alberto Ostria Gutiérrez, *La doctrina del no-reconocimiento de la conquista en América* (Rio de Janeiro: Borsoi & Cia., 1938).

dismemberment, was the early and persistent support given by La Paz to a regional and, later, an international system of collective security.[11] Following the Chaco War, Bolivia had also hoped to help defend her national territory by establishing new practical commercial contacts with neighboring states. In seeking to implement this strategy, other basic foreign relations problems of trade and aid became prominent.

Export Markets and Foreign Trade

As mentioned previously, Bolivia's economy has long been dependent on tax revenue and foreign earnings obtained through mineral exports. Since the early 1930s, Bolivian trade policy has actively supported international commodity stability agreements for tin. When world prices for tin fell in 1929, Bolivia's tin king, Simón Patiño, assumed the leadership role in organizing an international cartel to control tin production.[12] The International Tin Agreement of 1931, supported by the Bolivian government, remained in effect until World War II. Following the war, Bolivian officials were active in efforts to revive the international agreement, participating in the UN tin conference at Geneva in 1953 and signing the international tin agreement that resulted from that conference. Since 1953, Bolivian leaders have given strong support to three subsequent international tin agreements (1960, 1965, 1970) and have given leadership to UN efforts to improve market conditions for other mineral exports, such as tungsten and antimony.[13]

Markets for Bolivia's petroleum industry have been of considerable concern since March 1937, when the Bolivian government gained control of the oil industry through the nationalization of the properties of the Standard Oil Company of New Jersey.[14] It was easy to find markets for

11. The Bolivian delegation to the Second Meeting of Consultation of Ministers of Foreign Affairs in Havana, Cuba (July 1940), supported the concept of a regional security system to cope with all threats to the peace, regardless of source. At the Inter-American Conference on Problems of War and Peace at Mexico City (February–March 1945), Bolivian representatives continued the policy in favor of an effective regional security system. Later the same year, La Paz strongly backed the creation of a general collective security system at the UN Conference on International Organization in San Francisco (April–June 1945). Details of Bolivia's foreign policy objectives at these international conferences are contained in Emmett James Holland, "A Historical Study of Bolivian Foreign Relations, 1935-1946" (Ph.D. diss., The American University, 1967).

12. Klein, *Parties and Political Change in Bolivia*, pp. 118-20.

13. Bolivia took an active role in the UN tin conferences of 1960, 1965, and 1970, which continued the basic provisions of the international tin agreement of 1953 (*New York Times*, 25 June 1960; 15 Apr. 1965; and 16 May 1970). Bolivia strongly supported the creation of UN committees on tungsten and antimony, according to former President Alfredo Ovando Candia. See his statement in "Política Internacional de la H. Junta Militar de Gobierno," *Revista Diplomática e Internacional* 1, no. 1 (1 Sept. 1966): 20.

14. Klein, *Parties and Political Change in Bolivia*, pp. 260-63; see also Bryce Wood's "The Principle of Discrimination: Bolivia," in Wood, *The Making of the Good Neighbor Policy* (New York: Columbia University Press, 1961).

Bolivian petroleum in Argentina and Brazil, but not until the 1950s was the National Petroleum Agency of Bolivia able to produce significant exportable surpluses, most of which went to Argentina. Between 1965 and 1969, petroleum exports increased from $700,000 to $23 million, with substantial quantities going to the United States. The nationalization of the Bolivian Gulf Oil Company in 1969 resulted in a substantial reduction in 1970 oil exports and delayed construction of a gas pipeline from the Santa Cruz region to Yacuiba on the Argentine border until 1972.[15] However, the value of petroleum exports increased to $24 million in 1971, and prospects are good for increased hydrocarbon exports at substantially higher prices to Argentina, Brazil, Peru, and Chile by the mid-1970s.[16]

Since the War of the Pacific, Bolivia has sought consistently to obtain bilateral and multilateral guarantees of unlimited, free transit rights through the bordering states. Dissatisfied with the delays incurred in the transit of essential war materials through Chilean ports during the Chaco War, Bolivian diplomats gained additional guarantees for "free transit" which "comprehends all classes of cargo and at all times without exception" in a convention on transit signed with Chile in 1937.[17] Transit rights for transporting oil by pipeline across Chilean territory were also obtained in the 1950s and 1960s, but not without prolonged negotiations. In international councils, Bolivia champions the doctrine that international law should consider unrestricted transit an inherent right of landlocked countries.[18]

Since the Chaco War, Bolivia has entered into numerous trade agreements with her neighboring states, other Latin American countries, and an increasing number of European and Asian states. Trade relations with other Latin American countries have remained relatively less important for this Andean nation owing to the nature of Bolivia's export and import requirements. However, the relative importance of these relations has increased significantly in recent years.[19] Bolivia's major trade partners in

15. Inter-American Development Bank, *Socio-Economic Progress in Latin America*, p. 129. For information about the Bolivian Gulf Oil Company's concession from the Bolivian government, see Robert J. Alexander, *The Bolivian National Revolution* (New Brunswick, N.J.: Rutgers University Press, 1958), pp. 164–70. The Bolivian government in 1970 negotiated a twenty-year compensation agreement with Bolivian Gulf Oil Company (*New York Times*, 12 Sept. 1970).

16. U.S., Department of the Interior, Bureau of Mines, "The Mineral Industry of Bolivia," by V. Anthony Cammarota, Jr., in *Minerals Yearbook, 1971*, vol. 3, *Area Reports: International* (Washington, D.C.: Government Printing Office, 1973), p. 149. A very favorable forecast for the Bolivian petroleum industry also is contained in U.S., Department of Commerce, "Bolivia," in *Foreign Economic Trends and Their Implications for the United States*, ET 73–139 (Washington, D.C.: Government Printing Office, November 1973).

17. Luis de Iturralde Chinel, *Colección de tratados vigentes de la república de Bolivia*, 6 vols. (La Paz: Editorial "Universo," 1940) 4: 399.

18. Ovando Candia, "Política Internacional de la H. Junta Militar de Gobierno," p. 21.

19. Mukhtar Hamour and Kenneth Ruddle, eds., *Statistical Abstract of Latin America, 1970* (Los Angeles: Latin America Center, University of California, 1971), pp. 332–36. Between 1965 and 1970, the value of Bolivia's exports to the member countries of LAFTA

recent decades have been the United States, Great Britain, the Federal Republic of Germany, and Japan. Japan, Great Britain and the United States purchased about 74 percent of Bolivia's exports in 1970. The United States provided approximately 33 percent of 1970 Bolivian imports; the Federal Republic of Germany, 12.7 percent; and Japan, 11.5 percent.[20] Successive Bolivian governments in the 1960s and early 1970s also entered into trade agreements with Eastern European countries (Czechoslovakia and Poland) and most recently with the Soviet Union—actions that indicate Bolivia's desire to expand trade relations into new geographical areas and strengthen her bargaining position with traditional trade partners.[21]

Foreign Development Assistance

Foreign capital and technical assistance have been essential in the development of Bolivia's economy. Most Bolivian governments since World War I have recognized the necessity of attracting foreign investment capital and obtaining loans, exchange credits, technical assistance, and grants from abroad to support national development. In the 1920s this assistance came in the form of private foreign loans from New York banking houses and was used for the completion of railroad projects and for re-funding previous internal and foreign debts.[22] In 1938 and 1941, agreements with Brazil and Argentina provided loans and technical assistance for the construction of railroads linking Bolivia's eastern region (the *oriente*) with these bordering states and for the development of the nation's petroleum industry. Beginning early in World War II, economic cooperation programs were developed with the United States, which gave attention to highway construction, monetary stabilization, airline development, and public health. Following the 1952 revolution, a multifaceted U.S. aid program was initiated in Bolivia, which by 1969 had provided assistance amounting to about $500 million.[23] Foreign development assistance from other countries has helped Bolivia in recent years. West Germany participated with the United States and the Inter-American Development Bank in the Triangular Operation initiated in

---

increased from less than 3 percent (1965) of total Bolivian exports to approximately 8.2 percent (1970). Imports from these same countries also increased from less than 12 percent of total imports (1965) to approximately 18 percent (1970).

20. Ibid.

21. *Alliance for Progress Weekly Newsletter*, 26 Oct. 1970, p. 3. In 1970, agreements to expand trade relations and exchange trade missions were signed in Moscow by Bolivian Ambassador Julio Garret Aillon and Soviet Minister of Foreign Trade Nikolai Patolichev.

22. Klein, *Parties and Political Change in Bolivia*, p. 79.

23. Cornelius H. Zondag, *The Bolivian Economy, 1952-65: The Revolution and Its Aftermath* (New York: Frederick A. Praeger Publishers, 1966), pp. 190-200; see also Agency for International Development, *The Foreign Assistance Program: Annual Report to the Congress for Fiscal Year 1968* (Washington, D.C.: Government Printing Office, 1969) and ibid., *Annual Report to the Congress for Fiscal Year 1969* (Washington, D.C.: Government Printing Office, 1970).

1961 to rehabilitate the Bolivian Mining Corporation (COMIBOL). France, Great Britain, and most recently Brazil have extended loans for development projects, but in much smaller amounts than those provided by the United States. However, Bolivia has begun to turn more to Argentina and Brazil for development assistance, as U.S. assistance programs are curtailed.

Bolivia has received substantial economic and technical assistance from various international agencies, most prominently the World Bank and the Inter-American Development Bank. Credits have been received also from such diverse sources as the UN Development Program and the Inter-American Institute of Agricultural Sciences.[24]

With respect to public development assistance on both a bilateral and multilateral basis, Bolivia's policy has been to support the basic principles adopted at the first UN Conference on Trade and Development held at Geneva in 1964. These include recommendations that each economically advanced country make available financial resources to the developing countries of a minimum net amount as near as possible to 1 percent of its national income and that loans be provided to developing countries at interest rates not exceeding 3 percent.[25]

Although Bolivia's governments have approved assistance from foreign governmental agencies, some question might be raised about Bolivia's position vis-à-vis foreign private investment capital, since the nationalization of foreign-owned petroleum and mining properties has played a prominent role in the post-Chaco War history of Bolivia.[26] While official pronouncements make it clear that Bolivian leaders prefer public assistance from abroad, government leaders insist that foreign private investments are needed and will be protected as long as such investments serve Bolivia's national needs.

THE DOMESTIC FACTORS IN BOLIVIAN FOREIGN RELATIONS

To appreciate the relevance of domestic factors in Bolivian foreign relations, one needs to be aware of certain facts of life with which Bolivian

24. See *Alliance for Progress Weekly Newsletter*, 25 Aug. 1969 and 24 Nov. 1969. An Inter-American Development Bank news release, NR–1/73, dated 15 Jan. 1973, indicated that in 1972 Bolivia received a higher loan volume from IADB than in any previous year, an amount in excess of $54 million.

25. See the *Yearbook of the United Nations*, 1964, pp. 195–206. Also, Ovando Candia, "Política Internacional de la H. Junta Militar de Gobierno", p. 20.

26. The Toro government nationalized the properties of Standard Oil of New Jersey in March 1937; the *Movimiento Nacionalista Revolucionario* government led by Víctor Paz Estenssoro nationalized the "Big Three" mining firms of Simón I. Patiño, the Aramayo Company, and Mauricio Hochschild in October 1952; Bolivian Gulf Oil Company was nationalized in October 1969 by the military government headed by Alfredo Ovando Candia.

leaders have had to contend. Although large in land area (424,179 square miles), Bolivia has a population of only 4,930,000 (midyear estimate, 1970), concentrated to a large extent in the bleak highlands region, the *altiplano*, located in western Bolivia between parallel ranges of the Andes. Included in this population is a high percentage of Indians (about 62 percent), divided largely between two large language groupings, the Aymaras of the northern altiplano, and the Quechuas of the central and southern highlands, neither of which has been assimilated effectively into the political and economic life of the nation. Until the revolution of 1952, most of Bolivia's Indians were subject to virtual serfdom on the great landed estates of Bolivia's Spanish-speaking elite, working the land and performing menial household and personal services in return for the privilege of cultivating their own small plots of land.

Bolivia's economy remains primarily agricultural, with two-thirds of the nation's labor force still employed in this sector.[27] Since mining has been the country's most productive economic activity, Bolivia's railroad development has been oriented toward the transportation of the nation's mineral wealth to foreign markets, primarily via Chilean ports. Consequently, Bolivia's internal rail and road transportation system has been sadly underdeveloped until recent years, a situation that reflected the small size of the domestic market and contributed to its slow growth, fostering strong regionalist loyalties within the country.

Political instability has been another prominent characteristic of Bolivian life. Not until the last decades of the nineteenth century were Bolivians able to establish anything resembling a civilian political party system.[28] The revolution of 1952, which saw the *Movimiento Nacionalista Revolucionario* (MNR) come to power, was recorded as the 179th such violent overthrow of power in Bolivia's 127-year history up until that time.

The revolution of 1952, however, was not just another revolution. The MNR, a nationalistic middle-class party that had gained significant labor support during the 1940s, capitalized on the anger, disillusionment, and dissatisfaction resulting from Bolivia's disastrous adventure in the Chaco War. Under the leadership of Víctor Paz Estenssoro, the MNR initiated numerous major reforms in the 1950s, which fundamentally altered Bolivia's traditional economic, social, and political system.[29]

27. Inter-American Development Bank, *Socio-Economic Progress in Latin America*, p. 128.
28. Klein, in *Parties and Political Change in Bolivia*, chap. 1, argues that the "great political development of the last quarter century in Bolivian history was the creation of a viable civilian political party system . . ." (pp. 23–30).
29. Extensive literature analyzing the Bolivian revolution exists. Prominent studies include Alexander's *Bolivian National Revolution*, various writings by Richard Patch in the *American Universities Field Staff Reports*, and the recent works by James M. Malloy. The four most significant achievements of the revolution were: (1) the Agrarian Reform Law of 1953,

In the early years of the revolution, the MNR also dismantled the
Bolivian army, the traditional arbiter of national politics, and organized
civilian militias of laborers and peasants. By 1964, however, the ruling
MNR had lost its capacity to govern. Factionalism within the party, the
reemergence of the armed forces, and a sad record of political repression
all led to the overthrow of the Paz Estenssoro regime in 1964. In its place
emerged a military junta led by Air Force General René Barrientos Otuño
and Army General Alfredo Ovando Candia, ostensibly dedicated to
restoring the revolution to its original course. After an uneasy interim
period of junta governance, General Barrientos was elected constitutional
president in July 1966.

When President Barrientos was killed in a helicopter accident in April
1969, Bolivia entered a period of pronounced instability, characterized by
numerous changes in government. Barrientos' successor, the constitutional vice-president, Adolfo Siles Salinas, was ousted in September 1969
by an army coup led by General Ovando Candia, who assumed the
presidency. In October of the following year President Ovando Candia
resigned, to be replaced by General Juan José Torres, a self-styled
"revolutionary nationalist."[30] The Torres government, supported by
socialist-oriented unions, militant leftist students, Marxist politicians,
and portions of the military, soon alienated important segments of the
Bolivian middle class, including leaders of the business community,
professionals, and churchmen. A conservative coalition consisting of
older MNR leaders—including former President Víctor Paz Estenssoro—
the Bolivian Socialist Falange party, and key units of the military supported the overthrow of the Torres government in August 1971. Colonel
Hugo Banzer Suárez, one of the leaders of the coup, became president.[31]

The military is the most prominent group in Bolivian politics in the
1970s. Operating within a fragmented political spectrum including more
than a dozen political parties, none of which commands the loyalty of a

which expropriated unproductive estates and provided for distribution of land to the Indians;
(2) the nationalization of the three largest mining complexes in 1952; (3) the universal suffrage
decree of 21 July 1952, which extended the right to vote to all Bolivians over the age of twenty-
one, including the Indian population which for the most part had been excluded prior to the
decree; and (4) the decree on educational reform of 1956 designed to provide educational
opportunities for all Bolivian children for the first time in the nation's history.

30. *New York Times*, 7, 8, and 10 Oct. 1970. President Alfredo Ovando Candia resigned
on 6 October 1970, under pressure stemming from a growing division within the military
between those who favored a more vigorous nationalist and socialist policy and the more
conservative military leaders. On 7 October 1970, General Juan José Torres assumed
presidential power and pledged to give Bolivia "a popular nationalist government" resting
on four pillars—the peasants, workers, university students, and the military.

31. *New York Times*, 20, 22, 23, 24, 25, 28, and 29 Aug. 1971. Colonel Hugh Banzer Suárez
described his government as "nationalistic, revolutionary and loyal to the fatherland." Suárez
had studied at Fort Hood in Texas and was considered pro-American at the time he assumed
power in August 1971.

majority of Bolivians, the military since 1964 has assumed political leadership. For the most part, the Bolivian military has been sympathetic to the nationalist and reformist orientation of the 1952 revolution. Nevertheless, the military remains staunchly anti-Communist, as evidenced in its effective actions against the Guevara guerrillas in 1967, its vigorous harassment of the National Liberation Army, and its support for the coup that ousted President Torres after he had opened the country to increased Soviet influence and moved toward recognition of Castro's regime in Cuba.[32]

Other powerful groups continue to wield important political influence. The Bolivian *campesinos*, or peasants, chief beneficiaries of the agrarian reform law, gave strong support to the Barrientos government, and they remain alert to any signs of a reversal of the MNR's land reform decree. The loyalty of this sector of the population was a key factor in the government's successful fight against guerrillas in 1967 and has implications for the future defense capabilities of the nation.[33]

Bolivian labor, especially the mine workers, continues to be a most significant interest group. Basic differences between the mine workers and the military in recent years, caused by government efforts to make the national mining industry more efficient and by the devaluation of the Bolivian peso (1972) without concurrent wage increases, continue to threaten the stability of the army-dominated government.[34] The labor unions exerted strong influence in the Torres government and were instrumental in the adoption of policies hostile to the United States. However, the urban middle class, merchants, industrialists, private mine owners, professionals, and dominant factions within the armed forces constitute an important conservative political force, supporting a policy of closer cooperation with Washington.

As one might suspect, foreign policy is an important instrument of domestic politics for Bolivian governments lacking broad public support and under continuous attack from opposing forces within a fragmented political milieu. Since the Chaco War, strongly nationalistic foreign policies, frequently anti-American, at least in tone, have been politically popular. The three normative nationalization decrees (see n. 26) have all been motivated in part by the government's quest for popular political support.

The Chilean port issue is another problem in which national aspiration and domestic political necessity are combined. Bolivia's desire for a sovereign outlet on the Pacific coast is a quest for economic independence

32. Lamberg, "Che in Bolivia," pp. 32–34. Colonel Hugh Banzer Suárez, after the August 1971 coup, reminded Bolivians of the Guevara threat and stated that his government would not favor readmitting Cuba to the OAS (*New York Times*, 25 Aug. 1971).

33. Robert F. Lamberg, "Che in Bolivia," pp. 26, 33–36.

34. *Times of the Americas*, 8 Nov. 1972, p. 1.

and restored national dignity. At the same time, as an immensely popular cause, the frequent reopening of the Chilean issue is an indication that Bolivian governments are aware of the political value of such a campaign.

BOLIVIA'S POSTURE IN INTERNATIONAL RELATIONS

Relations with the United States

Relations with Washington continue to be extremely important for Bolivia. U.S. assistance programs, private investment, and support for international lending agencies all play a crucial role in Bolivian development plans. Although links with Washington have improved under the Banzer Suárez government, these relations are troubled by two factors. One is the strong nationalist and socialist sentiment in Bolivia, shared by labor, student, and some political groups, that supports policies of nationalization of foreign investments and of diminished relations with the United States.[35] The second is the deep concern of Bolivian leaders about the direction of U.S. foreign policy.

Important differences exist between La Paz and Washington with respect to what the United States should be doing in support of national development in Latin America. Among the most important items on which Bolivian leaders take issue with U.S. policy are the following:

1. The role of foreign private investment capital. Bolivian leaders, while not opposed to foreign private investment, want increased, not decreased, public assistance programs and are displeased with the trend in U.S. policy that places greater emphasis on the role of foreign private investment in national development processes. Nevertheless, the Banzer government, by promulgation of a new investment law and hydrocarbons law, is seeking to attract substantial private foreign capital into the country.[36]
2. Commodity price stability. Bolivian leaders have objected strenuously since 1962 to the U.S. policy of selling surplus tin stocks on the world market. This policy is interpreted as "economic aggression" in La Paz since it has the effect of lowering tin prices so critically important for Bolivia.
3. Low priority for Latin America. Bolivian officials feel that the United States is once again assigning Latin America a subordinate rank in its hierarchy of foreign policy concerns.
4. Emphasis on military assistance. Bolivian leaders fear that on the strength of recommendations in the report to the president by Governor Nelson Rocker-

---

35. Under the Torres regime (1970-71), for example, additional mining and metal processing properties owned by U.S. companies were nationalized, and Peace Corps activities in Bolivia were terminated. See U.S., Department of State, *Republic of Bolivia: Background Notes* (Washington, D.C.: Government Printing Office, 1972).

36. U.S., Department of Commerce, "Bolivia," in *Foreign Economic Trends and Their Implications for the United States* (Washington, D.C.: Government Printing Office, 22 Sept. 1972), p. 5.

feller in 1969, increased emphasis will be given to military assistance programs by the United States when it is believed that increased attention should be given to economic and social programs.[37]

The Banzer government, in contrast to its immediate predecessors, has followed a policy of strengthening friendly relations with the United States. The government's stand against readmitting Cuba to the Organization of American States, its expulsion of many Soviet embassy staff members in March 1972,[38] its favorable posture toward private foreign investment, and its general antileftist orientation have all contributed to closer ties with Washington. The United States has reciprocated with increased assistance in the form of loans for economic infrastructure development and for support of private sector growth in agriculture and industry.[39]

Bolivia's relationship with the United States will continue to be crucial for her economically and politically in the 1970s. While La Paz will persist in its support of efforts to formulate a common Latin American front vis-à-vis the United States, national leaders will continue to seek favorable assistance agreements and trade policy modifications in its bilateral relations with Washington.[40] In view of the chronic unstable political situation, however, the Bolivian policy on private foreign investment will be modified in accordance with the shifting political climate.

Relations with Latin American Nations

Bolivian government leaders are seeking to forge important new relationships and to strengthen traditional ties with other Latin American states. However, a number of the problems that have troubled these relationships in the past remain. Many of the difficulties stem from the fact that Bolivia's level of economic development is considerably lower than that of her four neighboring states. Bolivia produces relatively few export items of interest to these countries, except for gas and petroleum products. The small size of her domestic market and the understandable desire to

37. Richard W. Patch, "The Manifest Ethos of North and South: Nixon Speaks, Bolivia Replies," *American Universities Field Staff Reports*, West Coast South America Series 17, no. 1 (1970).

38. *New York Times*, 30 Mar. 1972, 6 Apr. 1972. Bolivian leaders implied that Soviet Embassy staff members were financing antigovernment leftist rebels. *New York Times* writer Juan de Onis reported that Bolivian military intelligence believed that the National Liberation Army had been receiving aid from the Soviet Embassy.

39. "Republic of Bolivia," p. 5; H. J. Maidenberg reported in the *New York Times*, 12 Dec. 1971, that after the coup that brought Banzer Suárez to power, the U.S. aid tap had been turned on again, at least partially.

40. Patch, "The Manifest Ethos of North and South," p. 4. Bolivian leaders have given strong support to the Latin American Consensus of Viña del Mar, a document defining the position of the Latin American countries with respect to the changes needed in the international order to promote development in the poorer countries. The statement was formulated at a meeting of the Special Latin American Coordinating Committee, held at Viña del Mar, Chile, in May 1969.

protect nascent national industry from competitive imports also discourage growth in trade with other Latin American countries. Her cooperation within the OAS has also been strained at times by the organization's reluctance to intervene in her old controversy with Chile.

Since the loss of the Pacific coastal region in 1879, Bolivia has maintained significant relations with Argentina politically and economically. Numerous loan and trade agreements have been concluded with Buenos Aires since the Chaco War that have greatly facilitated the development of important highway, railroad, and pipeline links between the two countries. When Bolivian Gulf Oil was nationalized in October 1969, financing for a gas pipeline linking major Bolivian gas fields with the Argentine market was jeopardized. The Argentine government promptly gave assurances to the World Bank that it would provide guarantees for the loan needed to complete the crucial pipeline.[41]

Bolivian-Brazilian relations have grown closer in recent years, especially under the Banzer government. In April 1972, President Banzer Suárez and Brazilian President Emílio G. Médici signed several agreements providing for Brazilian financial and technical assistance, the extension of Bolivian railroad construction debt repayments to Brazil, and the purchase of Bolivian crude oil. Although negotiations for these agreements were initiated during the presidency of General Torres, stronger ties between La Paz and Rio de Janeiro are emerging under the present regime.[42]

Although significant political differences with Peru have troubled relations for decades, recent governments in Bolivia have expressed strong support for the government of President Juan Velasco Alvarado in Lima. Although the foreign policy of the Banzer government may not be as compatible as those of his predecessors with the strong nationalist policy followed in Lima, especially with respect to the United States, trade between these two member countries of the Andean Group continues to expand.[43]

Though the port issue continues to hinder La Paz's relations with Chile, Bolivian leaders in the late 1960s and early 1970s responded favorably to Chilean support of the nationalization of Bolivian Gulf Oil Company and to Chileanization of U.S. owned copper industries. During this period, traditional Chilean-Bolivian differences were mitigated by a trend favoring the formation of a common Latin American front in relations with the United States and also by the pronounced nationalist and socialist orientations of the governments in both countries. Relations deteriorated appreciably when President Torres was ousted in August 1971.[44] Bolivian

41. *New York Times*, 14 Dec. 1969.
42. *New York Times*, 5 and 9 Apr. 1972.
43. *Peruvian Foreign Trade News*, no. 2 (October 1972), pp. 10–11. Although trade between Bolivia and Peru is small, the value of Bolivia's exports (oil and livestock) to Peru increased from $700,000 in 1970 to $5.1 million in 1971. The value of imports from Peru remained steady at about $2 million.
44. *New York Times*, 29 Aug. 1971.

foreign policy directions under the Banzer government, especially in regard to relations with Washington and Cuba, were inconsistent with those of Chilean policy during the Allende regime. Periodic Bolivian charges that antigovernment revolutionaries exiled in Chile were organizing to overturn the Banzer government strained relations further.[45] In spite of political differences that have precluded official diplomatic relations between these two countries since 1962, Bolivia and Chile maintain large consular missions in Santiago and La Paz and are members of the six-nation Andean Group.

Bolivia is cooperating also in regional ventures with Brazil, Paraguay, Uruguay, and Argentina. In addition to common membership with these countries in LAFTA, Bolivia signed a treaty in April 1969 that provides for joint development of the River Plate Basin, an area covering 1.2 million square miles in Brazil, Bolivia, Paraguay, Uruguay, and Argentina.[46]

Bolivia's relations with bordering states and other Latin American countries have involved extensive negotiations with respect to regional economic integration. In February 1967, Bolivia became the eleventh member of the Latin American Free Trade Association on the basis of her acceptance by other member governments as a "relatively underdeveloped" country. This designation entitles Bolivia to certain special tariff concessions from the more developed states.[47]

After almost three years of negotiation, Bolivia joined Chile, Colombia, Ecuador, and Peru in signing the Andean Subregional Pact, or Cartagena Agreement, of May 1969, which formally established an association designed to develop into an Andean common market by 1980.[48] LAFTA later approved the pact as compatible with the Treaty of Montevideo. Countries of the Andean Group have made progress in removing barriers to reciprocal trade, establishing a common external tariff, and adopting arrangements for joint planning of regional development. Bolivia and Ecuador, the two least developed member countries economically, have received preferential treatment allowing them to protect national industries in early stages of development and follow extended timetables for implementing Andean Group agreements.[49]

Ties with Western Europe

Bolivia has maintained important trade relations with Great Britain and other Western European countries throughout most of the twentieth century. Large quantities of Bolivia's tin concentrates are shipped to

45. *New York Times*, 9 Feb. 1972.
46. *Américas* 21, no. 8 (August 1969): 45; *Facts on File*, 22-28 May 1969, p. 327.
47. *New York Times*, 9 Dec. 1966; 9 Feb. 1967.
48. *New York Times*, 28 May 1969. Early in 1973 Venezuela became the sixth member country of the Andean Group.
49. For examples of the special concessions granted Bolivia and Ecuador, see *Alliance for Progress Weekly Newsletter*, 25 May 1970 and 1 Feb. 1971.

smelters in Great Britain, and exports to the island kingdom represented about 38 percent of total 1970 Bolivian exports.[50] Bolivia in return imports substantial quantities of finished manufactured goods from Western Europe, especially from the German Federal Republic and Great Britain. As mentioned earlier, Bolivia also looks to Western European countries for development assistance and has obtained important loans and technical support from Great Britain and West Germany.[51]

Relations with the USSR and the Eastern European Countries

During the 1960s and early 1970s Bolivian leaders continued the cautious development of a more "independent" foreign policy based on a desire to establish friendly relations with all nations. President Ovando Candia, upon accession to power in September 1969, stated his intentions of establishing better relations with the Eastern European Communist countries, declaring, "We hope to have friendly relations with all countries, and we are not closing the door to any provided they respect our sovereignty."[52] Early in 1970, Bolivia and Poland reestablished diplomatic relations for the first time since 1939, and the governments of Bolivia and Hungary agreed to raise their diplomatic representatives to ambassadorial rank.

Although Bolivia had recognized the government of the Soviet Union since 1945, and Soviet offers of technical and economic assistance have been made at least since 1960, not until September 1969 did the two countries agree to exchange ambassadors. This development led in mid-1970 to trade, technical, and scientific exchange agreements between the two countries, including the sale of large quantities of Bolivian tin ores and concentrates to the Soviet Union.[53]

Bolivia's nationalist orientation in foreign affairs and her preoccupation with national development help to account for the willingness of La Paz to seek closer ties with the Soviet Union and the countries of Eastern Europe. If prospects for obtaining important development assistance from

50. Hamour and Ruddle, *Statistical Abstracts of Latin America*, pp. 332–36.

51. British loans of modest amounts were extended to the Bolivian public mining corporation and for the rehabilitation of Bolivian railroad lines early in the 1960s. The West German government contributed substantially to the Triangular Plan for rehabilitation of Bolivia's public mining sector over a three-year period, beginning in 1962. A total investment of $38 million from the West German government, the Inter-American Development Bank, and the U.S. government was included in the project. See *Area Handbook for Bolivia* (Washington, D.C.: Special Operations Research Office, The American University, 1963), pp. 501, 576, and 601.

52. *New York Times*, 30 Sept. 1969.

53. Brief factual reports of Bolivian-Soviet relations in the early 1960s are contained in *Area Handbook for Bolivia*; see also *Alliance for Progress Weekly Newsletter*, 27 July 1970, p. 3; 26 July 1971, p. 3; and *New York Times*, 28 Dec. 1969.

these countries appear promising, Bolivian leaders may seek even closer relations, at the same time making efforts to maintain friendly relations with the United States. As mentioned earlier, however, tensions emerged during 1972 in relations between the anti-Communist Bolivian government of Banzer Suárez and the Soviet Union. Although formal diplomatic relations continue between the two countries, the growth of closer relations appears problematical.

Relations with Asian and African States

Bolivian leaders have identified the Andean state closely with the causes and policies of the nonaligned and economically underdeveloped states of Asia and Africa. At the same time, important commercial relations have developed between the industrialized leader of Asia—Japan—and Bolivia. While Japanese development assistance has been slight, that nation's share of Bolivia's imports has been steadily increasing. Japan provided over one-sixth of Bolivia's 1969 imports, much of which was electronic equipment.

In 1961 and 1964, Bolivia sent observer delegations to the conferences of nonaligned countries held in Belgrade and Cairo. Observers from Bolivia also were among the representatives participating in the fourth conference of nonaligned nations held in Algiers, Algeria in 1973.[54] Once again Bolivia's policy should be understood in terms of the Andean nation's concern with the problems of economic development and trade, problems shared with many of the newly independent states of Asia and Africa. Policy confluence with these nations goes beyond the sphere of economic development, however. The Bolivian government shares policy positions with these states with respect to racial discrimination, anticolonialism, the peaceful settlement of disputes, and restraints on nuclear armament.[55]

Bolivia's Role in International Organizations

In the last three decades Bolivia has assumed an active role in international organizations such as the Organization of American States and the United Nations. Since the creation of the League of Nations, most Bolivian leaders have recognized the possibilities that international organizations provide for maximizing and supplementing Bolivia's scanty military, economic, and political resources. In addition to the routine political benefits (prestige, communication, etc.) gained from participation in these organizations, Bolivian diplomats for more than two decades have been active in supporting a policy designed to strengthen national security, obtain development assistance, foster better conditions of world trade

54. *New York Times*, 10 Sept. 1973.
55. Ovando Candia, "Política Internacional de la H. Junta Militar de Gobierno," p. 20. On 14 February 1967, Bolivia joined with thirteen other Latin American nations in signing a treaty banning nuclear weapons in Latin America (*New York Times*, 15 Feb. 1967).

for Andean products, and support the national cause of free access to the Pacific Ocean.

Bolivia is a charter member of the United Nations and has held several prestigious positions in important councils of that organization, including membership on the Security Council (1964–65), the Economic and Social Council (1974–74) and the Trusteeship Council (1961–62). The Andean nation is a member of numerous UN affiliated agencies, including the Food and Agriculture Organization, the International Labor Organization, the International Civil Aviation Organization, UNESCO, and the World Health Organization. Bolivia also holds memberships in the International Bank for Reconstruction and Development, the International Monetary Fund, the International Development Association, and the International Finance Corporation. Membership in the United Nations and in UN-related organizations has benefited the Andean nation significantly in terms of numerous awards of technical and financial assistance.[56]

In General Assembly and Security Council debates, Bolivian spokesmen have repeatedly championed several themes that reflect the nation's basic foreign policy principles and preoccupations. These themes include (1) the desirability of obtaining pacific settlement of disputes through the United Nations on the basis of such principles of international law as the inviolability of territorial integrity, guarantees of political independence, and the nonrecognition of territorial rights gained through conquest;[57] (2) the necessity of establishing effective arms control arrangements and agreements establishing nuclear free zones in order to strengthen peace and to reallocate resources toward peaceful purposes; (3) support for international efforts to further the decolonization process and condemn racial discrimination policies; (4) the primacy of increasing international cooperation in support of the economic and social development of poor countries through trade promotion and stabilization arrangements and development assistance programs; and (5) the Andean nation's perennial aspiration for sovereign access to the Pacific.

Bolivia has been an active member of the Organization of American States, acting in a manner consistent with her obligations under the UN Charter. She is a signatory to the major treaties that structure the Western Hemispheric regional organization, and in February 1970 she deposited in

56. In addition to the reports pertaining to development assistance to Bolivia from various UN funds and affiliated agencies contained in the *Yearbooks of the United Nations*, from 1947 to 1967, and in the *UN Monthly Chronicle*, from 1961 to 1970, see Alexander's chapter on earlier UN projects in Bolivia in *The Bolivian National Revolution*, pp. 242–54.

57. Speaking to the UN General Assembly on 11 October 1968, Bolivian Foreign Minister Samuel Alcoreza Meneses said that "small states must rest their hopes of conserving and preserving integrity on the maintenance of an international legal order which will be binding on all states equally" (*UN Monthly Chronicle* 5, no. 10 [November 1968]: 121).

Washington her instrument of ratification of the Protocol of Amendment to the OAS Charter.

La Paz, however, when domestic political requirements have necessitated such a posture, has demonstrated definite signs of a policy of independence from the dominant hemispheric position. In 1962, at the Eighth Meeting of Consultation of Ministers of Foreign Affairs in Punta del Este, Uruguay, Bolivia abstained from voting on the resolution excluding the government of Cuba from participation in the Inter-American system, which obtained the necessary two-thirds majority vote from the member states of the OAS.[58] Also in 1962, Bolivia withdrew from participation in the political and administrative activities of the OAS in protest over the Council's unwillingness to take decisive action to resolve the Bolivian-Chilean dispute over the use of the waters of the Lauca River. The Bolivian walkout ended in December 1964.[59] In April 1967, Bolivian President René Barrientos refused to attend the meeting of American chiefs of state held in Punta del Este, Uruguay, because the agenda for the conference did not include the problem of Bolivia's landlocked geographical position. Despite these expressions of dissatisfaction with the regional organization, and perhaps because of the conviction widely held by Bolivian leaders that the inter-American system needed to be modified and strengthened, La Paz participated actively in the efforts to revise the Charter of the OAS in the latter half of the 1960s.

Bolivia's major concerns with respect to participation in the OAS are readily defined. First, La Paz is intent on securing the support of the regional organization for national security matters in order to augment Bolivia's limited defense capability. This objective was apparent when the Bolivian foreign minister dramatically presented evidence of "Che" Guevara's leadership of guerrilla operations in Bolivia to the Twelfth Meeting of Consultation of Ministers of Foreign Affairs (Washington, September 1967) and asked for new regional measures to combat subversive intervention fostered and supported by Cuba.[60] At the same time, however, Bolivia has consistently opposed the organization of an inter-American defense force, apparently viewing it as a channel of increased U.S. influence in the hemisphere. Second, Bolivian leaders have persistently sought to gain political and moral support within the OAS for their nation's claim to a sovereign Pacific outlet. In discussions regarding amendments to the Charter of the OAS, Bolivia strongly favored granting new peacemaking powers to the OAS Council, which would authorize that

58. *New York Times,* 24 Jan. 1962; and 28 Jan. 1962. Important groups within Bolivia, especially the trade unions and university students, were sympathetic toward the values and objectives of the Cuban revolution and critical of Washington's anti-Castro policy.

59. *New York Times,* 4 Sept. 1962; 13 Dec. 1964; and 30 Dec. 1964.

60. *New York Times,* 23 Sept. 1967; 24 Sept. 1967; and 25 Sept. 1967.

body to initiate peacemaking activities without the consent of all the parties involved in a dispute. Such provisions would give La Paz new leverage in the perennial coastal dispute with Chile.[61] Third, and perhaps most importantly, Bolivia has given strong backing to Latin American efforts to place greater emphasis in the regional organization's charter, structure, and activities on supporting economic and social development within the hemisphere.

CONCLUSION

Bolivian foreign policy should be understood as the pursuit of vital national objectives through relations and agreements with other countries and international agencies. Because of limited capabilities for promoting national development and assuring national security, this Andean nation has attempted consistently to obtain from external sources the necessary financial and technical assistance for socioeconomic development and also satisfactory legal and political guarantees of her national security. A prominent aspect of this policy has been the continuing preoccupation with acquiring and maintaining foreign markets for Bolivia's exports, since foreign exchange earnings are essential for economic development.

In the 1960s and the early 1970s Bolivia has had considerable success in obtaining substantial amounts of foreign public assistance and in gradually expanding and diversifying foreign trade. More substantial progress has been hindered, however, by continuing domestic political instability that has prevented the implementation of consistent policies toward private foreign investment and ties with Washington. Because Bolivia's foreign policy is rooted so deeply in the realities of her political, socioeconomic, and physical existence, the major thrusts of that policy, as identified in this chapter, are likely to continue in the 1970s and beyond.

BIBLIOGRAPHICAL NOTE

Alexander, Robert J. *The Bolivian National Revolution*. New Brunswick, N.J.: Rutgers University Press, 1958. A sympathetic and useful description of the major features of the Bolivian revolution between 1952 and 1957.

Area Handbook for Bolivia. Washington, D.C.: Special Operations Research Office, The American University, August 1963. An extensive collection of background information pertaining to numerous aspects of Bolivia's social, economic, and political life.

Klein, Herbert S. *Parties and Political Change in Bolivia, 1880-1952*. London: Cambridge University Press, 1969. An excellent, comprehensive historical

61. *New York Times*, 13 Mar. 1966.

study that focuses on political change. Expecially valuable in its treatment of the years immediately preceding and following the Chaco War. A brief postscript extends Klein's study to the presidency of René Barrientos (1966).

Malloy, James M. *Bolivia: The Uncompleted Revolution.* Pittsburgh: University of Pittsburgh Press, 1970. A detailed analysis of the Bolivian experience in the years shortly before and after 1952 as a case study in revolutionary social change. Careful attention is given to the social, economic, and political dimensions of the revolution. A major section is devoted to the rise and fall of the *Movimiento Nacionalista Revolucionario* (MNR).

Malloy, James M., and Thorn, Richard S., eds. *Beyond the Revolution: Bolivia since 1952.* Pittsburgh: University of Pittsburgh Press, 1971. A useful collection of essays on the revolutionary process in Bolivia set in motion in 1952. Chapters on revolutionary politics, economic development, land reform, literature, and U.S.-Bolivian relations and numerous tables of relevant data are included.

Osborne, Harold. *Bolivia: A Land Divided.* 3d ed. London: Oxford University Press, 1964. A brief general treatment of Bolivian geography, society, economy, and political history.

Patch, Richard W. "The Manifest Ethos of North and South: Nixon Speaks, Bolivia Replies." In *American Universities Field Staff Reports,* West Coast South America Series 17, no. 1 (1970). Useful field reports on selected topics pertaining usually to social, economic, and political reform and developments in Bolivia.

Revista Diplomática e Internacional. La Paz, Bolivia. A monthly periodical devoted to articles and news relating to Bolivia's foreign policy and international relations. Contains the texts of selected official statements and some book reviews in the foreign policy field.

Sigmund, Paul E., ed. *Models of Political Change in Latin America.* New York: Praeger Publishers, 1970. Contains selected basic source materials and articles relating to the Bolivian revolution and political process.

Vidaurre, Juan José. *Diez Años de Política Internacional Boliviana.* La Paz: Ministerio de Relaciones Exteriores y Culto, 1964. A brief but helpful discussion of the major principles of Bolivian foreign policy and the basic problems in Bolivia's foreign relations primarily for the period 1952-64 by a Bolivian Foreign Ministry career officer.

Zondag, Cornelius. *The Bolivian Economy, 1952-1965: The Revolution and Its Aftermath.* New York: Frederick A. Praeger, 1966. A more specialized analysis of the effects of the 1952 revolution on the Bolivian economy. Useful sections deal with Bolivia's foreign trade and with foreign assistance programs in the Andean country.

17/Thomas J. Dodd

Peru

FOREIGN POLICY: DIRECTIONS, PROBLEMS, AND CHOICES

Peruvian foreign policy objectives in the modern world reflect a continuous search for acceptance of Peru's political and territorial independence. Peru's present goal in the international arena is to make certain that the community of states accepts her government's role in modernizing a society and directing the development of national resources in a manner independent of external pressures and domestic privilege. Specifically, the nation's political leaders and chief foreign policy spokesmen hope to maintain the government's powers of decision in matters relating to such recent domestic actions as operating a state-owned petroleum corporation and implementing agrarian and industrial reform laws. Structural changes affecting the economy and society at large have been institutionalized by organizing peasant and industrial workers, and even large segments of the middle class, into federations with the prime object of creating a consensus at home. At the same time, Peru must also select the approaches that are best suited to help her widen income distribution, increase exports, and negotiate international trade agreements.

The development of a multilateral approach in foreign affairs has included participation in the frequent conferences on maritime fishing and mineral resources held, since 1952, with Ecuador and Chile. On these occasions Peru has decreed her sovereignty and that of her neighbors over seas two hundred miles from the coastline. Moreover, her membership in the Latin American Free Trade Association (LAFTA) and the subregional Andean Pact also reflects the requirement that Peru find new markets for her products as she reduces her economic dependence on the United States. Her membership in economic blocs points out the need to increase her intraregional trade in the Americas by establishing with other nations common tariffs and foreign investment policies. In order to maintain her independence from wealthier nations, Peru must look for financial and technical assistance from private investment sources and agencies of the United Nations and the Organization of American States (OAS). She has also demonstrated her independence by expropriating and nationalizing the U.S.-owned International Petroleum Company (IPC), the sugar plantations and chemical plants of W. R. Grace, and the vast mining properties of Cerro de Pasco. These actions give further indication that the country must cooperate with other nations that want to end economic and political recrimination from states whose interests have also been affected by domestic reforms.

In the last few years there has been a decline in the economic and political presence of the United States in Latin America. This has been due in part to the lessening possibility of a global confrontation between the superpowers and in part to the increasing presence on the international scene of European nations and Japan. This trend has in turn drawn more attention to local-regional foreign policy problems in Central and South America. There is a possibility that Peru can expect to be drawn into a number of important international conflicts with her closest neighbors. For example, Ecuador, Bolivia, and Brazil have expanded their economic interests in the eastern regions of the Amazon Basin, searching for new resources, especially petroleum. Boundary problems are therefore likely to erupt, as they have before, between these countries, as each state vies for regional leadership, economic markets, and control of unsettled border domains. Peru's chief foreign policy objective will be to select the best means to end what has been called the "traditional assistance-intervention cycle,"[1] either by unilateral action or in cooperation with other nations. A cautious and wise choice of either of these approaches, or both, may establish for Peru a truly independent role in the community of nations and an influential voice for her government at home.

NINETEENTH-CENTURY POLICIES

When Simón Bolívar began his campaign for the liberation of northern South America and General José de San Martín declared the independence of Argentina and Chile, each hoped to liberate Peru, Spain's richest fortress in South America. Ultimately, the country's freedom was to be negotiated and proclaimed by leaders and forces outside her borders. This unfortunate aspect of Peruvian development took place in large part because Peruvians were deeply divided on the issue of independence. Some wished to join the movement for separation, others wanted to remain a part of Spain; these domestic political divisions prevented Peru from exercising a single effective voice in the councils of Latin America's wars for independence. Thus, her entrance into the family of new states was limited and precarious. Bolívar fully appreciated the need for some kind of confederation of nations in the hemisphere to protect countries like Peru from attack by the European powers of the Holy Alliance. Hence, from Lima, he proposed a "Plan for Unity," to be achieved in a conference to be held in Panama.

Peru's participation in the Panama Conference of 1826 and ten years later in the formation of the Peru-Bolivian Confederation of 1836 reflected the country's earliest foreign policy goal, namely, the establishment of a

1. See Luigi Einaudi, *Beyond Cuba: Latin America Takes Charge of Its Future* (New York: Crane Russak & Co., 1974), pp. 195, 226.

continental and subregional defense system for preserving political independence and guaranteed peace in boundary disputes with Ecuador, Bolivia, and Brazil. Both efforts failed, partly because the domestic policies of the various Latin American states were plagued by feuding military caudillos in what has been called an age of heroes and rogues, but also because of the rivalry of Mexico, Colombia, and Argentina for hemispheric leadership.

A collective security goal was beyond Peru's reach until 1845, when President Ramón Castilla took an active interest in the formation of a continental defense system. By mid-century a considerable degree of domestic peace had been achieved; Castilla then reorganized the diplomatic service and established numerous legations in other parts of Latin America and Europe. At this point Peru abandoned the continental isolation that internal quarrels had previously imposed upon her.[2]

The fundamental goal of Peru's foreign policy in the period from 1845 to 1862 was to merge her national interests with those of other Spanish-American republics. Castilla was fully aware of his country's economic dependence on Great Britain for foreign credit and a market for exports of guano, but he thought it imperative to protect the hemisphere from extracontinental political-military encroachments. Thus, in 1847–48, when he thought that the ousted and exiled Ecuadorian President, Juan José Flores, intended to place a European prince at the head of Ecuador's government, Castilla convened an American conference in Lima (December 1847–March 1848). His objective was to have Peru's neighbors adopt a Treaty of Confederation and agree to work in concert to prevent any attempt at conquest or subversion that might emerge in the face of this crisis or that of the Mexican War with the United States. Peru therefore played a major role in a developing pattern for discussion and deliberation in continental diplomacy. Ramón Castilla's often expressed goal for creating a permanent hemispheric defense system continued to be his country's principal foreign policy objective in the mid-nineteenth century.

Peru's representatives were active spokesmen in a meeting of Ecuadoran, Peruvian, and Chilean diplomats in Santiago, Chile, in 1856, in the aftermath of the Mexican War of 1848 and the filibustering expedition of William Walker in Nicaragua.[3] This time a treaty similar to the one concluded at the previous Lima Conference in 1847–48 was drawn up. It included various provisions for mutual aid and assistance among the signatories in the event that one Latin American state threatened the sovereignty of another; but neither this agreement nor the earlier one came into effect.

2. See Robert Marett's *Peru* (London: Ernest Benn, 1969), chap. 9, for foreign policy objectives of Ramón Castilla.
3. The Tennessee-born Yankee led a group of some three hundred U.S. citizens to Nicaragua and ultimately became that nation's president, from 1856 to 1857.

Later, a direct threat to Peru's independence occurred between 1862 and 1866 when Spain seized and held her guano-rich Chincha Islands and bombarded both her port of Callao and Chile's coast city of Valparaiso. Once again Peru called a meeting of her sister republics in Lima. No concrete proposals for organizing the west coast states into an effective security system emerged from this meeting, as the treaty concluding the war was made only between Chile and Spain. The end of further armed intervention by Europe seemed apparent when Maximilian, France's puppet-monarch in Mexico, was executed in 1867. Consequently, the urgency and top-priority aspects of Peru's mid-century foreign policy objectives for collective security became less important.[4]

THE EMERGENCE OF BILATERALISM AND TERRITORIAL CLAIMS

By the early 1870s, Chile's energetic and expanding economy had invaded the nitrate deposits in Bolivia's Antofagasta region and Peru's Tarapacá Desert. When the Chilean Nitrate Company increased its mining concessions in Bolivia, Peru, anxious to develop a nationalized nitrate industry, searched for allies in an attempt to isolate Chile diplomatically. She concluded a secret alliance with Bolivia to protect herself against hostile action by Chile.

The humiliating defeat of Bolivia and Peru in the subsequent War of the Pacific (1879–83) further removed them from exercising major roles in hemispheric affairs. Peru's hitherto prominent voice urging some form of continental cooperation for security was muted by her defeat in this conflict. Unfortunately, this occurred just as the United States, with Mexican support, was urging the creation of a Pan American Union. Peru failed to take the initiative at this time, largely because she was preoccupied with national security problems involving bitter territorial conflicts.

After the War of the Pacific, in an effort to restore her lost "international prestige" during the last quarter of the nineteenth century, Peru concentrated on settlement of her boundary problems in accordance with the principle of *uti possidetis* as of 1810. According to this doctrine, a Spanish-American state claimed title to all territory formerly under the jurisdiction of the Spanish colonial administration (in 1810) out of which a new nation was formed. As a viceregal capital in Spain's New World empire, Peru's interests in this doctrine were obviously extensive. From the end of the nineteenth century to the outbreak of World War II, she frequently clashed, on the basis of this principle, with her neighbors, particularly Ecuador, over disputed territory in the upper Amazon Basin.

4. See *Area Handbook for Peru* (Washington, D.C.: Foreign Area Studies, The American University, 1965), chap. 14.

The basis of the Ecuadoran-Peruvian claim to this region goes back to the Treaty of Guayaquil in 1829 when the Republic of Colombia and Peru agreed to the frontier boundaries established by the viceroyalty of New Granada in 1739. Peru also accepted the Marañón-Amazon River as her northern boundary. When Ecuador withdrew from the Republic of Colombia in 1830, Peru did not accept the newly independent Ecuador's claim to the region. Only through the mediation efforts of Argentina, Brazil, and the United States was conflict avoided in 1910. The territorial dispute between the two states continued to smolder until 1941 when Peru launched an armed attack against Ecuador and occupied some seventy thousand square miles of the disputed territory. Lima's action was motivated by her past foreign policy setbacks and her national economic interests. Ecuador in turn did not wish to be confined to the Andean mountains, separated from the Amazon port of Iquitos, which gave her access to the Atlantic Ocean. Peru was fortunate in that most of the major states were interested in a settlement. The American republics, particularly the United States, wanted to maintain peace in the hemisphere as World War II began. Ecuador, under considerable diplomatic pressure and forced by Peruvian military occupation of the disputed territory, agreed to sign the Rio de Janeiro Protocol of 1942, thereby losing approximately one half to two thirds of what she considered to be her national patrimony in the Upper Amazon Basin.

From 1911 to 1932, Peru and Colombia feuded over possession of the strategic Amazon port city of Leticia. Economic interests, particularly the search for raw materials and international prestige in the aftermath of the War of the Pacific, were the chief motivating forces behind Peru's claim to the city. In 1922, both states concluded a treaty under the auspices of the United States whereby a considerable amount of territory was given to Colombia, including the left bank of the Putumayo River and a corridor to the port city of Leticia. The settlement was very unpopular in Peru, but succeeding governments failed to obtain a more favorable agreement. So, later in the fall of 1932, Peruvians seized Leticia. When Oscar Benavides succeeded the assassinated Sánchez Cerro in April of 1933, efforts were made by the new Peruvian chief executive to end hostilities with Colombia. Peru finally accepted a cease-fire proposal by the League of Nations and agreed to abide by the 1922 treaty whereby Colombia had acquired Leticia.

PATTERNS IN DOMESTIC AND
FOREIGN POLICY DIRECTIVES

The face of Túpac Amaru II, the eighteenth-century revolutionary Indian leader, has recently appeared on the Peruvian fifty sol note, on flags, and on public buildings. This effort to resurrect the past and recall a popular folk hero, as a symbol of independence from both foreign and domestic oppression, symbolizes the direction Peru is taking in her foreign relations today. She claims to be building a program of modernization in the tradition of the grandeur of a bygone era, when the pre-Columbian Inca capital, Cuzco, controlled a large portion of western South America. Accompanying this symbolic resurrection of a glorious Incaic past, the country's revolutionary military leaders who seized power in October 1968 have demonstrated a wish to give the nation greater influence in the Western Hemisphere and in world affairs. To accomplish this objective they are seeking to reduce the dominant influence, the "presence" of the foreign interests that have owned or controlled the economy. Ironically, the country's greatest riches, her soil and minerals, have in the past prevented her from pursuing a truly independent foreign policy. During the colonial period, her resources were exploited in the interest of Spain's European policies. Since independence, economic dependence, first on Great Britain and then on the United States, has precluded the pursuit of her true national interests.

When a military coup removed President Fernando Belaunde Terry in the early morning hours of 3 October 1968, a "new departure" in domestic policy aimed at national development was announced by a self-proclaimed "revolutionary government."[5] One of the leading philosophers of the revolution, General José Graham Hurtado, declared that Peru would begin a series of social and economic reforms in an effort to create what he called a "new Peruvian man." The traditional obstacles to this achievement, he confidently proclaimed, would be destroyed, namely, underdevelopment, imperialism, and concentration of power. New objectives and guidelines for the country's foreign affairs and domestic programs were announced in late 1968 when the revolutionary military government, headed by General Juan Velasco Alvarado, released a document entitled *The Strategy for Peru's Long Range National Development.*[6]

Since 1969, numerous sections of this plan have been implemented, a plan designed essentially to give the government a dominant role in the economy. The Agrarian Reform Law of 1969, which provides for the expropriation of a large number of landed estates, began the transforma-

5. The best and most recent sources on the Peruvian military are S. L. Rozman, "The Evolution of the Political Role of the Peruvian Military," *Journal of Inter-American Studies* 12 (October 1970): 539-64; Marcel Niedergang, "Revolutionary Nationalism In Peru," *Foreign Affairs* 49, no. 3 (April 1971): 454-63; José Yglesias, "Report from Peru: Reformers in Brass Hats," *New York Times Magazine*, 14 Dec. 1969; George W. Grayson, Jr., "Peru's Military Populism," *Current History* 60 (February 1971): 71-77; and Grayson, "Peru's Military Government," *Current History* 58 (February 1970): 65-72, 114.

6. The National Planning Institute, *Strategy for Peru's Long-Range National Development* (Lima, 1968).

tion of a rural, predominantly Indian peasantry into a market economy. The Industrial Reform Law of 1970 "Peruvianized" private enterprise by promoting profit sharing in and joint ownership of the nation's basic industries. An industrial code stipulated that eventually all essential produc'ions were to be state controlled. This law radically changed the influence private industry would play in the country. In 1826, Simón Bolívar had permitted the state to sell "abandoned mines" to private entrepreneurs in order to pay the government's debts. This decision established the precedent whereby the nation's resources were inextricably linked with her debt obligations to foreign powers and private businesses. This situation was now to be changed.

Since the late 1960s Peru has excluded altogether, or controlled the operations of, foreign firms and domestic monopolies whose behavior she felt has violated the political rules and economic guidelines established to foster industrial development. A number of local industrial plants and foreign-owned estates have been expropriated or nationalized since 1968. They include the IPC, a subsidiary of Standard Oil of New Jersey, the sugar plantations and chemical and paper products plants of W. R. Grace, and the U.S.-owned Cerro de Pasco Corporation, with its huge reserves of copper, lead, gold, and silver. Yet Peru has granted oil concessions to such foreign private concerns as Amoco-Shell, Atlantic Richfield, and Getty for the exploration and development of her oil-rich northeastern jungle region. Lima has also accepted different forms of foreign assistance for her domestic development, but with the view that only the state will benefit, not the special interest groups, as before.

Since the mid-1960s Peru has maintained diplomatic relations with Communist countries around the world, regardless of ideological differences. This policy has made her a leading advocate of Cuba's return to active membership in the OAS. The expansion of diplomatic ties—a kind of political pluralism—has been seen as an important way to gain new markets for her export economy. Greater attention has also been given to international organizations that can provide financial assistance and thereby help protect and guarantee the enlarged role the state has chosen to play in economic development and social integration. In the last few years, Peruvian leaders have called upon the OAS to represent the interests of the Latin American states exclusively, as they try to reschedule their foreign debts and prevent large capital flows out of the Western Hemisphere.[7] These broad shifts in government policy in both foreign and domestic matters have reflected a profound change in the nation's social structure. Domestic pressure groups, such as the labor

7. President Velasco Alvarado, "Opening Address" to the 12th Annual Meeting of the Governors of the Inter-American Development Bank, Lima, 10 May 1971, published in *Latin American Documentation*, ser. 2 (Washington, D.C.: Division for Latin America, U.S. Catholic Welfare Conference, September 1971).

force, the Roman Catholic Church, and the professions, have exerted an influence on government policy, contributing to the formation of a national leadership in the last few years that is nationalistic, populist, and pragmatic in the pursuit of its goals at home and abroad.

THE FORMATION OF POLICY

Political Parties

Peru has had various types of political parties, ranging from the traditional ideological organizations to the highly personalistic ones. But for most Peruvians politics is a means of acquiring assistance from the government, and political parties have traditionally reflected racial and class goals. Consequently, interest groups, whose aims have been for the most part limited, have generally identified themselves with the social structure.[8] In the past, however, various methods used by pressure groups to exert influence on the government have been largely ineffective, because the major decision-making powers have been exercised by the president.

Since independence, the chief executive has dominated the formulation of internal and foreign policy objectives. He has been held accountable for the successes and failures in domestic as well as international ventures.[9] As a result, his role as a major policy maker has eclipsed that of other branches of the government, such as the legislature, which has never been an independent body and therefore has had little impact on public opinion. Yet, the group of military officers who formed the government headed by General Juan Velasco Alvarado after President Fernando Belaunde Terry had been ousted in 1968 has been directed by a form of collective executive leadership. The country's chief magistrate today does not wield the all-encompassing power of his predecessors but must share the decision-making role with his fellow officers. By and large, however, the president's authority and influence today, as over the years, has neutralized competing interest groups, thereby inhibiting the growth of truly influential parties as foreign policy makers.

A notable exception to the limited effectiveness of political parties was the emergence of the American Popular Revolutionary Alliance (APRA), founded by Víctor Raúl Haya de la Torre in 1924. For some time, APRA was a major domestic force demanding economic and social reform. The

8. For a detailed analysis of political parties and their role in policy formulation, see Carlos A. Astiz's *Pressure Groups and Power Elites in Peruvian Politics* (Ithaca, N.Y.: Cornell University Press, 1969), chap. 6.

9. Rosendo A. Gómez, "Peru: The Politics of Military Guardianship," in *Political Systems of Latin America*, ed. Martin Needler (New York: Van Nostrand Co., 1964), pp. 310–12.

force of its original call for a hemispheric-wide movement of the Latin American states against the industrial might of the Anglo-Saxon world lost force, however, as the world crisis of the late 1930s deepened. In the post-World War II period, the party also lost much of its reformist fervor as it moved to the Right. The left wing of the party split with the main organization in the late 1950s, prompting the emergence of the Revolutionary Movement of the Left (MIR). Although some of APRA's members have found common cause with the "reform minded" military government since 1968, the party remains largely intact.

National Planning Agencies

After World War II the Peruvian government began to play a more active role in national development. It has dealt with such matters as industrialization and the acquistion of new external financial resources to supplement domestic capital development and to increase exports. During the same period, numerous specialized agencies of the United Nations and the OAS offered the country opportunities for acquiring needed technical assistance and capital. Consequently, through such government organizations and ministries as the National Planning Institute, which deals with economic integration and development, international agencies have indirectly exerted an influence on foreign policy formulation within the state, particularly in matters relating to domestic and foreign economic conditions. The multiplicity of these numerous governmental agencies and their activities has reduced the role of the President and the foreign ministry as spokesmen for Peru in world affairs. Their increase has also enlarged the public bureaucracies, thereby opening new jobs for the middle sector and giving it a greater voice in policy making on socioeconomic matters at home and abroad.

The Oligarchy

Traditionally, the principal force maintaining Peru's reliance on the industrialized nations has been the upper-class oligarchy, functioning as a socioeconomic group. Its members have been the landlords of the sierra, the sugar growers, the bankers, and the industrialists of the coast. For the most part their interests have led them to maintain cordial ties with foreign investors, who in turn assured them that their products would be exported and reach world markets. Since World War II organizations representing such "upper-class" economic interests as the National Agrarian Society of the Coast and the Industrial Society have successfully promoted the economic interests of this group alone.

The power of this long-entrenched oligarchy has been significantly reduced by interests that have emerged from new population settlement patterns. For example, since the turn of the century Peru's population has increased from roughly five to twelve million people. The literacy rate has risen from 42 percent in 1940 to 67 percent in 1973. A sizeable internal migration from the rural areas to the city has occurred, changing considerably the living pattern of millions of people. As a result, urban growth has preceded industrial development by a sizeable margin. These changes in Peruvian society have produced a potentially viable unionized labor force and a strengthened middle class, both of whose economic and political demands the current Peruvian government has taken into consideration in the formulation of its domestic and foreign policy decisions. In recent years the oligarchy has been decimated by the state, losing its sugar and cotton plantations and its financial control in a number of industries. Since the late 1960s the economic interests of the elites have been subjected to much greater government control and regulation. As elements from the middle and lower classes have acquired more power because of their developing class consciousness and political and economic goals, the dependency relationship with foreign governments, supported by the oligarchy, has changed significantly.[10]

The Middle Class

Although Peru has had an important middle sector since the 1940s, it has never exerted much political pressure toward acquiring class benefits or forcing other groups and institutions to assist it. Generally the middle class has had to depend on the state for employment. Its members have come from the military, the government bureaucracy, the teaching professions, private offices, and retail stores. Their interests are narrow and their economic and social goals limited, self-serving, and opportunistic.[11] They seek good salaries and opportunities for jobs. As a group, they compose about 18 to 20 percent of the population. Since 1968 greater employment opportunities have accrued to them from the nationalization of domestic and foreign industries. The government has had to find ways to respond to demands from this middle sector. As a consequence, the profitable relationship between foreign industry and the oligarchy has been largely disrupted by this economically aggressive middle class, this new "constituency" for the state to consider when dealing with foreign interests on such matters as employment, salaries, and related working benefits.[12]

The army has been an important voice speaking for the interests of this sector in recent years. It is one of the few—perhaps the only—professions in which a man from the middle or lower class, especially a provincial, may achieve social respectability and position. The establishment of

10. Astiz, *Pressure Groups and Power Elites*, chap. 4.
11. Ibid., chap. 9.
12. See ibid. for a detailed analysis of the goals sought by the middle class.

military schools at the turn of the century began a process by which a sense of professionalism emerged within this group. In 1956 the Center for Higher Military Studies (CAEM) was founded through the efforts of General José del Carmen Marín. One of this school's objectives was "to provide the military with a positive philosophical base to replace the sterile and negative opposition to the APRA (American Popular Revolutionary Alliance) that had dominated the Peruvian army for decades."[13] One of the most important goals of the center has been the education of military officers as domestic and foreign policy makers in the nation's development. The school's curriculum has emphasized ways in which Peru may modernize its human and national resources, thereby strengthening the nation's position in world affairs.

A group of army officers, many of whom were graduates of CAEM, seized power in October 1968, in the name of nationalism, responding to what it considered to be critical economic and social demands. These "soldier-revolutionaries" wanted to increase their influence by exercising their skills in finance and technology, in order to regulate the economy and impose the state's will on the national and foreign corporations and individuals in Peru.[14] Thus, the Agrarian Reform Law of July 1968 expropriated eight of the country's largest sugar plantations. The Industrial Community Law of 1970 ordered managers in industries, mining, and telecommunications to allocate a percentage of gross earnings each year to "labor communities" composed of workers in a firm. Under this law, employees can elect voting members on a company's board of directors.[15]

The enactment of numerous national planning projects, accompanied by the nationalization and expropriation of the U.S.-owned International Petroleum Company, the Cerro de Pasco Corporation, and the W. R. Grace interests, has also placed in Peruvian hands the power to direct the nation's economy independent of concentrated domestic wealth and foreign business interests. The overall economic structure of the country is to be divided into four sectors—"public," including the basic industries, which will be reserved exclusively for the state; "reformed private," encompassing those industries affected by the Industrial Community Law; "social property," which will involve worker ownership of whole industries rather than individual factories; and "nonreformed private," which will include small enterprises. Understandably, these actions

13. APRA was one of the first radical non-Communist parties of the Left to emerge in Latin America after the Mexican Revolution of 1910. See Harry Kantor, *The Ideology and Progress of the Peruvian Aprista Movement* (Berkeley: University of California Press, 1953).

14. Astiz, *Pressure Groups and Power Elites.*

15. Article 21 of the *Ley General de Industrias*, Decreto-Ley 18350, articles 22–29, deals with "Communidades Industriales." See also Marvin Alisky, *Peruvian Political Perspective* (Tempe: Center for Latin American Studies, University of Arizona, 1972), p. 24.

initiated by the military have challenged the political and economic interests of foreign nations, especially those of the United States.

As the Peruvian "military reformers" expanded their role dramatically in the domestic economy from 1968 on, more civil servants, presumably from the middle class, were needed to administer the widening national bureaucracy. For example, the National System for Support of Popular Mobilization (SINAMOS), a social mobilization agency, was established in the early 1970s to rally people behind such new government run institutions as the cooperatives and industrial communities. As an interest group, the middle sector then began to pressure the government for a more independent role in foreign affairs. Like that of other middle-class groups the military's ideology is secular, intensely nationalistic, and pragmatic. It typifies the middle-class temperament along with its economic and political goals.[16]

The Labor Force

The bulk of the Peruvian labor force has included urban workers, marginal inhabitants of rural areas, plantation hands, and the Indian peasants of the sierra. In many respects, this sector of the population has sought benefits for itself, never advocating fundamental revolutionary changes.[17] Labor's political activity has been diversified, in that both APRA and the Communist party have absorbed its civic interests. The General Confederation of Peruvian Workers, the nation's largest labor organization, alone never exerted much influence in the formulation of domestic or foreign policy. Yet riding on the wave of nationalization after 1968, when foreign and domestic industries passed to government control, labor has successfully demanded wider employment opportunities and better pay from the new manager, the state. The nation's rulers, in turn, have tried to dissolve various political trade unions, thereby enlarging their influence through the establishment of a single government-controlled labor organization known as the Confederation of Revolutionary Workers (CRT) in 1972. In the last few years the Communists have

16. See Edwin Lieuwen's *Generals vs. Presidents: Neo-Militarism in Latin America* (New York: Frederick A. Praeger, 1964) for an analysis of the Nasserist military regimes, specifically those that are concerned with modernization and reform. See also Richard Lee Clinton, "The Modernizing Military: The Case of Peru," *Inter-American Economic Affairs* 24 (Spring 1971), for a study of the military's role as an instrument of the middle class; and José Nun, "The Middle Class Military Coup," in *The Politics of Conformity in Latin America*, ed. Claudio Veliz (London: Oxford University Press, 1967); James Petras and Nelson Rimensnyder, "The Military and the Modernization of Peru," in *Politics and Social Structure in Latin America*, ed. James Petras (New York and London: Monthly Review Press, 1970), pp. 130–58.

17. An exception to this nonrevolutionary trend appears in the political leadership of Víctor Raúl Haya de la Torre and in the American Popular Revolutionary Alliance, founded in the 1920s (see n. 13 above). APRA's influence as a militant agrarian labor force diminished noticeably in the early 1950s.

gained control, with government backing, of the older General Confederation of Peruvian Workers (CGTP).

The labor movement has frequently resisted the efforts of the state to manage its affairs and enforce a plan for creating a nationally organized labor movement. When the government tried in 1973 to implement a pension law that substituted retirement at age sixty for termination of employment after twenty-five years of work, labor objected strongly. Yet the Industrial Community legislation enacted in the last five years expects to give workers as much as 50 percent control of factories. Consequently, labor's attitude toward a state-supervised economy will depend on the form of governance ultimately worked out between the "worker-managers" and the national administration.

The Catholic Church

Traditionally, the Roman Catholic church has supported the politics of the status quo, and her interests have been associated with the oligarchy. However, since World War II, Pope John XXIII's encyclicals *Mater et Magistra* (1961) and *Pacem in Terris* (1963) and Pope Paul VI's *Popolorum Progreso*, together with Vatican II, have urged the hierarchy to take a more active interest in social issues and economic development. In the summer of 1968 the Latin American Bishop's Council (CELAM) called upon church leaders to speak out on behalf of developing nations endeavoring to escape their economic dependence on the industrialized world.

In many respects the Peruvian Catholic church has responded to this call by identifying itself with local issues and popular causes. Thus, in the late 1960s, the hierarchy frequently applauded the government's decisions to nationalize foreign industries.[18] The cardinal archbishop of Lima, a relative of President Velasco Alvarado, endorsed the controversial Industrial Reform Law of 1970, which for all practical purposes enabled the government to regulate the entire economy.

A few priests in Peru have proclaimed violent revolution as a cure for the country's ills. But more have endorsed the more moderate and peaceful effort to fuse religion with social revolution. By approving actions that have dislodged the predominant foreign economic interests in the nation, particularly since 1968, the church has become identified with a government that has been concentrating on a radical restructuring of the entire society. Equally important, it has given the state a powerful and sympathetic "constituent" in its drive to build a broad base of popular support on as many interest groups as possible.

Thus, the once fragmented and isolated interests of the various social classes have recently been welded together under the banner and ideology

18. *La Prensa* (Lima), 19 May 1970, p. 6; and *Espreso* (Lima), 21 July 1970, p. 13.

of nationalism. The middle class, labor groups, even the oligarchy—all have found some specific goal in the government's effort to reduce the predominant influence of the foreigner. Ironically, all interest groups in this process have in one way or other found some common cause to unite them. As the government works to broaden its base of popular support, relations with other nations will be influenced more by the extent to which each interest group exerts its special kind of pressure on the state than by the simpler, less complicated structure of a single chief executive's independent direction of foreign policy, as in a past age.

PERU'S FOREIGN RELATIONS IN THE MODERN WORLD

The Western Hemisphere

Since 1968 Peru's steps for removing its economic dependence on the United States have opened up new possibilities for expanding and diversifying her foreign trade. Yet, this objective of "multilateralizing" her economic contacts has also been fraught with danger. Peru ranks fourth in size and fifth in population among the Latin American nations. Although her per capita income is not so small as that of Bolivia and Ecuador, it is nowhere near as high as that of Argentina or Venezuela. Peru occupies a dangerous middle position in the world. Her hopes for joining the community of the developed nations have rested largely on her ability to persuade other Latin American states to join her in a mutually beneficial economic bloc system.

Out of necessity Peru's foreign policy goals in the last few years have sought a common basis with those of her neighbors. This has been done to protect her economy, which has suffered directly from the punitive actions of expropriated or nationalized foreign and domestic interests that have influenced major international lending agencies against granting loans to Peru. In many respects this effort to attain an independent position in world affairs represents a return to the mid-nineteenth century interest in collective action. Essentially, an old doctrine has been resurrected, with economic goals as well as political interests, to solve a domestic social integration problem and to reassert the nation's independence. Since 1968, for example, agencies in the Inter-American system, such as the Latin American Coordination Commission and the Inter-American Development Bank, together with the United Nations Economic Commission for Latin America (ECLA), have been invited to meet in Lima to consider development problems. Peru's political leaders have frequently urged these international institutions to become exclusive instruments for the Latin American states in order to help them escape their economic dependency on the industrialized world.

When Peru joined the Latin American Free Trade Association in the late 1950s, she found that the more industrialized states of Argentina, Brazil, and Mexico threatened her economy and that of Ecuador and Bolivia. Like her neighbors, Peru was in a deficit position in finished and semifinished goods. In 1966, formal discussions among the west coast states—Ecuador, Chile, Bolivia, Columbia, and Peru—began for the establishment of a subregional group. The first result of the conferences was the creation of the Andean Development Corporation, organized as a multinational entity, capitalized at $100 million, and directed by the signatory states, which together would plan the basic economic integration and development of the area. The second outcome, the Cartagena Agreement, concluded in 1969, proposed to end all tariff restrictions and establish common rules for foreign investment. Thereafter, in December 1970 a subregional code for new investment was adopted. It specified that within fifteen to twenty years all foreign-owned concerns were to become mixed enterprises, 51 percent or more to be nationally owned.

Since the establishment of this Andean Pact, tariffs on numerous products have been significantly reduced and plans have been made to cooperate in the creation of an airline and marine fleets to facilitate trade among the member states. These joint ventures have undoubtedly downgraded the traditional rivalries among the nations. Peru, in the light of her growing economic nationalism and because of the resulting tensions in her situations with the United States, has come to regard neighboring Ecuador and Bolivia as new allies. Discussions have taken place, for example, with the Quito government on measures to develop the economic resources of their connecting frontiers. In the last few years, Peru and Bolivia have agreed to the joint construction of an Andean highway that is expected to facilitate intraregional trade among all the Andean Pact members. Moreover, both countries have discussed plans to utilize Lake Titicaca, which borders each country, for increasing trade between the two states.

Peru's relations with Chile are still clouded in many respects by her humiliating defeat in the War of the Pacific. Lima's irredenta, the Atacama Desert, acquired by Chile in 1883 and approved in the final settlement of 1929 giving Tacna to Chile and Arica to Peru, has precluded chances for a truly close relationship between these two nations. Yet, Chile and Peru have found a basis for cooperation on a number of issues. For example, with Ecuador, they issued the Declaration of Santiago in 1952, wherein all three states claimed a 200-mile jurisdiction over territorial waters adjacent to their coasts.[19] The economic resources of

19. Six other Latin American nations—Argentina, Brazil, El Salvador, Nicaragua, Panama, and Uruguay—have joined this effort, in the Declaration of Basic Principles on Maritime Rights, drawn up in Montevideo, Uruguay, 4–8 May 1970. See also Peru's position on maritime rights in Ministerio de Relaciones Exteriores del Perú, *Soberanía Marítima:*

these three nations, particularly their fishmeal and tuna industries, have at one time or other been threatened by U.S. maritime interests.

The United Front of Latin American States, organized in the spring of 1969 in Viña del Mar, Chile, and actively promoted by Peru did not, as some believe, create a solid bloc of nations that wanted the United States to reduce interest rates and cut tariff barriers. Moreover, in the same year, the meeting of the Latin American Coordinating Commission (CECLA), established to implement the Viña del Mar proposals, was postponed at the suggestion of nations that did not wish to be associated with Lima's strong anti-U.S. position—particularly at a time when she was announcing her expropriation and nationalization measures.

Peru's efforts to promote this coalition of Latin American interests reflected in part a growing suspicion of Brazil's foreign economic objectives among the Andean states. These nations noted, for example, that Brazil had developed large areas in the Amazon Basin and that a thirty-four hundred mile trans-Amazonian highway had almost been completed up to Peru's borders. This project for westward expansion to exploit such resources as oil may well complicate Brazilian relations with Lima in the future. Since the Andean states have planned to create an Andean Highway of their own from Colombia to La Paz, Bolivia, it is conceivable that Peru and her west coast neighbors might encounter conflicting economic interests with Brazil. Lima, for example, has signed eight service contracts with thirteen private companies for oil exploration in the Amazon since 1970. Yet she has attempted to establish a unified "oil policy" as it concerns her investment policies with Ecuador, hoping to forestall a direct conflict with Brazil.

A notable consequence of Peru's nationalization decrees and agrarian reform laws, as noted earlier, has been a weakening in her traditionally close ties with the United States. Conversely, this change has resulted in improved relations with Cuba, a by-product of her more pluralistic view of the political ideology of nations. Fidel Castro has frequently endorsed Lima's new independence and publically approved "all that is revolutionary in Peru." Speaking before members of the Cuban armed forces in the late fall of 1969, the Cuban leader pointed to the significant role the Peruvian military was playing as a revolutionary vehicle for change.[20] Having established diplomatic relations with Havana in 1971, Lima has since then tried to have the OAS reverse its 1964 decision to impose economic and political sanctions on the Caribbean nation. Essentially, Peru wants an organization of American states comprising members that

Fundamentos de la Posición (Lima, 11 May 1970) and "Foundations of the Maritime Sovereignty of Peru," a lecture delivered by the director of sovereignty and frontiers, Ministry for Foreign Affairs, Lima, 9 Apr. 1970 (Lima: Empresa Editorial del Diario Oficial "El Peruano," 1970).
20. *Washington Post*, 17 Dec. 1969, p. 20.

17 / THOMAS J. DODD

do not follow the traditional anti-Communist or anticapitalist policy. Since a basic feature of Cuban foreign policy has been an effort to establish the maximum number of formal relations among nationalist-minded governments, Peru's less cordial ties with Washington and her adoption of "revolutionary policies" at home have brought Havana and Lima closer together. Actually, the renewel of diplomatic relations with Cuba was only one aspect of wider changes in Lima's international relations with states in the Western Hemisphere and the world at large, as we shall see.

Ties with Europe, the Third World, and the United Nations

Peru has always maintained close cultural ties with Europe, never really severing links that bound her to the continent through three hundred years of Spanish colonial rule. Quite logically, then, as her associations with the United States have declined, she has again turned to Europe, particularly since World War II, in the rearrangement of her economic and political relationships. Thus, the Prado doctrine, announced by Peru's President Manuel Prado in 1957, called for the union of all Latin peoples in the New World and the Old in order to forge what was vaguely called a new Spanish force in international affairs. The Prado policy also reflected practical considerations such as diversifying the nation's export economy and enlarging the volume of trade in the European Common Market (EEC).

In the mid-1950s Peru opened additional diplomatic missions and concluded new commercial agreements with European states. Succeeding administrations continued the country's interest in this commercial and financial diversification. From 1964 to 1966, Presidents Heinrich Luebke of Germany and Charles de Gaulle of France and England's foreign minister, Michael Stewart, all made highly publicized visits to Lima, demonstrating their nations' growing interest in this Andean state as a source for raw materials and a market for industrial goods. Lima's diplomatic and economic ties with Western Europe were extended to the iron curtain countries in the late 1960s—to Czechoslovakia and Romania.

In respect to development, Peru lies somewhere between the developing states of Asia or Africa and the highly industrialized nations. Although Lima has expressed a shared concern with other less developed states, she has experienced considerable export competition with them in agricultural and mineral products. For example, the African states of Zaire and Zambia export a number of commodities similar to those of Peru and both have been given special trade preferences by their former colonial rulers, now members of the European Common Market.

As a result of the competition with other developing nations, Lima has had to approach her foreign policy goals by dealing with them in a very pragmatic way. Not wishing to be identified as a developing nation, and still very much aware of her dependence on an export economy, Peru has undertaken successfully to make mutually beneficial agreements with as many states as possible, both in the developing and the industrialized regions of the globe. For example, her leaders have taken special note of the fact that she is a "Pacific state," not simply an American nation. Therefore, diplomatic and commercial relationships have been established in a mutually profitable way with nations in the Far East since 1968. Japan has been willing to extend "unlimited credit" for the development of Peru's agricultural products and to assist her in building an oil pipeline to bring crude oil from the northeastern Selva fields to supply refineries on the east coast, particularly those in the Sechura Desert, whose products, mostly gasoline, will be exported. Lima also established diplomatic relations with mainland China in 1971 and since then has carried on discussions with Peking that have resulted in major sales of fishmeal, copper, lead, and zinc to that country.

Peru was one of the founding members of the United Nations after World War II and has always considered the United Nations an important forum in which developing nations can merge their political and economic interests. For example, in the UN Assembly, Lima has supported Argentina in her efforts to regain the Falkland Islands and Guatemala in her claim against British Honduras. The UN agencies have also been a source from which Peru has drawn financial and technical assistance in her development. The International Monetary Fund and the World Bank have provided approximately $22 million for investment projects in Peru from 1959 to 1971.[21] In the spring of 1971 Lima was chosen as the meeting place for the "Group of 77"—Third World states that are members of the United Nations—for the Third UN Conference on Trade and Development (UNCTAD). In that conference, Peru's chief executive and foreign minister took special note of the fact that, as a group, less developed nations could exert enough influence in the United Nations to resist effectively the economic and political influence of the industrialized world.

In many respects Peru views her role in the United Nations as that of a middle power like Canada, Sweden, or Poland, rather than as a poor state condemned to economic dependence, struggling to enter the community of developed nations. She has therefore led efforts to organize the Latin American states as a bloc within the United Nations in order to avoid cold war conflicts between the United States and Russia. Viewing the global struggle between the United States and the Soviet Union as a "confrontation of giants," she has developed a pragmatic foreign policy that deals

21. A figure of $22 million is given in United Nations Development Program Office, *DP-SF Report*, ser. A#72 (Washington, D.C., December 1972); see also Velasco, "Opening Address," pp. 1-6.

with both sides in the cold war. Peru therefore rejects capitalism and communism as "brand names" for her economic development at home.[22] This view coincides with a fundamental objective in a foreign policy that avoids alliances with any ideological bloc. Peru now works to develop economic and political ties with those nations in the world that serve her interests first and best. As her government liquidates the oligarchy's control of the economy, distributes hacienda lands to those who work them, and begins what has been described as "the inculcation in the public of at least a degree of social consciousness," Peru will have to participate in the international arena with a greater pragmatism and national self-interest.[23]

BIBLIOGRAPHICAL NOTE

The diplomatic history of Peru is an almost totally neglected field. Resource material in English and Spanish that deals exclusively with the subject is extremely rare; thus, the researcher is compelled to extract sections and chapters from numerous general works on inter-American problems and Peruvian history.

There are three useful guides that will introduce the student to some significant periods and major developments in Peru's international activities since independence. *The Handbook of Latin American Studies*, published annually since 1936 (volumes 1–14 by the Harvard University Press, Cambridge; subsequent volumes by the University of Florida Press, Gainesville), is organized by fields (art, history, literature, etc.), not subjects, and is then subdivided by regions. Irene Zimmerman, *A Guide to Current Latin American Periodicals: Humanities and Social Sciences* (Gainesville, Fla.: Kallman Publishing Co., 1961), is divided by states and subjects; international relations is included. *Latin American Newspapers in the United States* (Austin: University of Texas Press, 1960), Steven Charno, ed., includes various papers published in Peru beginning in 1820.

For an informative general account in the study of foreign policies of developing nations, Gustavo Lagos, *International Stratification of Underdeveloped Countries* (Chapel Hill: University of North Carolina Press, 1963), offers insights into the major obstacles a country like Peru faces in her search for economic and political independence. More directly related to Latin America, yet still a general treatise, is J. Fred Rippy, *Latin America: A Modern History* (Ann Arbor: University of Michigan Press, 1968). Chaps. 11, 20, 24, and 25 deal with the formative years in foreign policy of the Spanish-American states in the nineteenth century. Rippy's *Globe and Hemisphere* (Chicago: Henry Regnery, 1958) examines twentieth century issues and problems of these "Latin" states outside the

22. In a speech before the Inter-American Committee for the Alliance for Progress in Washington, D.C., on 26 May 1970, General Guillermo Marco del Pont, minister of the National Planning Institute, spoke on "Peru's Independent Course," rejecting both capitalism and communism as models for his nation's development in the formulation of foreign policy.
23. Clinton, "The Modernizing Military," pp. 65–66.

American continent. Norman Bailey, in chap. 3 of *Latin America in World Politics* (New York: Walker & Co., 1967), gives an interesting account of the basic competitive forces in the international relations of the states in the southern continent.

General works on Peruvian history include brief yet useful material on her foreign affairs activities since independence. Chaps. 2, 5, and 6 in Frederick B. Pike, *The Modern History of Peru* (New York: Frederick A. Praeger, 1967) and chap. 9 in Sir Hugh K. Marett, *Peru* (New York: Frederick A. Praeger, 1969), examine the country's nineteenth-century international relations.

One of the best sources that deals with intra–Latin American conflicts, including Peru's numerous bilateral difficulties, is Gordon Ireland's exhaustive, detailed, and still useful study, *Boundaries, Possessions, and Conflicts in South America* (Cambridge: Harvard University Press, 1938). James Carey's *Peru and the United States, 1900–1962* (Notre Dame, Ind.: University of Notre Dame Press, 1964) delves into all aspects, "official, unofficial, public and private," in the relationship between these two countries when Peru shifted from her dependence on Great Britain to dependence on the United States in the late nineteenth century.

Shifting away from strictly bilateral studies in Peru's foreign policy interests, the researcher will find John A. Houston, *Latin America in the United Nations* (New York: Carnegie Endowment for International Peace, 1956) and Thomas Hovert, Jr., *Bloc Politics in the United Nations* (Cambridge: Harvard University Press, 1960), chap. 3, two very useful sources that examine major trends in attitudes and objectives of the Spanish-American states in the world organization and its specialized agencies.

In the very difficult area of studying pressure groups and political parties as they have influenced the formulation of Peru's foreign policy, Francois Bourricaud, *Power and Society in Contemporary Peru*, trans. Paul Stevenson (New York: Praeger Publishers, 1970); Carlos A. Astiz, *Pressure Groups and Power Elites in Peruvian Politics* (Ithaca, N.Y.: Cornell University Press, 1969); and James L. Payne, *Labor and Politics in Peru: The System of Political Bargaining* (New Haven: Yale University Press, 1965) all explore in considerable depth how the various segments in the country's society affect the government's attitude when dealing with public and private foreign interests. An especially timely source for the study of Peru's military as it reforms and modernizes Peru's economy is Luigi R. Einaudi, *Peruvian Military Relations with the United States* (Santa Monica, Calif.: Rand Corporation, June 1970) and his "Professionalization and the Political Role of the Military in Peru," in *Models of Political Change in Latin America*, ed. Paul E. Sigmund (New York: Praeger Publishers, 1970).

General works on Peruvian diplomatic history in Spanish are considerably more numerous and also cover a wider range of issues and subjects than the English sources. Perhaps the best general guide for primary research on diplomatic issues is the *Anuario Bibliográfico Peruano* (Biblioteca Nacional de Lima), which includes the Ministry of Foreign Relations publications. Since the early 1960s this guide has published treaties, conventions, and numerous loan agreements. The *Revista Peruana de Derecho Internacional* has for sometime included major articles on significant aspects of Peruvian foreign relations over the years, especially important is volume 7 (1947), which reflects the country's growing interest in regional economic cooperation since 1940.

Very good sources for a nineteenth-century diplomatic history of Peru are
Arturo García Salazar, *Historia diplomática del Perú* (Lima: A. J. Rivas Berrio,
1930) and Pedro Ugarteche, *El Perú en la vida internacional Americana* (Lima:
n.p., 1927). Probably the best diplomatic history of the twentieth century to date is
Alberto Wagner de Reyna's *Historia diplomática del Perú, 1900-1945* (Lima:
Ediciones Peruanas, 1964). A Ph.D. dissertation by Ronald Bruce St. John,
"Peruvian Foreign Policy, 1919-1935: The Delimitation of Frontiers" (University
of Denver, 1970), is useful on the boundary questions.

Significant documents for study on current issues and trends in Peruvian
domestic politics and foreign policy interests appear in the publication of the
Oficina Nacional de Información. They include recent speeches by incumbent
President Juan Velasco Alvarado and his ministers of foreign affairs, mines, and
industry since 1968 and such important decrees as "Ley general de Industrias
Decreto Ley" and the "Texto de Ley Reforma Agraria Decreto Ley," no. 17716
(Empresa Editorial del Diario oficial, "El Peruano," 1970). Scholarly sources in
English include Richard Lee Clinton, "The Modernizing Military: The Case of
Peru," *Journal of Inter-American Economic Affairs* 24 (Spring 1971) and Stephen
T. Rozman, "The Evolution of the Political Role of the Peruvian Military,"
Journal of Interamerican Studies and World Affairs 12, no. 4 (October 1970).

VII

Andean Countries, North: Ecuador, Colombia, and Venezuela

18/Mary Jeanne Reid Martz
Ecuador

The key to Ecuadoran foreign policy has traditionally been the defense of her territorial sovereignty and political integrity against external aggression. While this foundation stone remains the same, the ramifications are much more far-reaching than they were even twenty years ago. Basically, there have been three critical issues of foreign policy that have faced Ecuadoran governments. First, for well over one hundred years Ecuador's paramount consideration has been to vindicate her claims to an outlet on the Amazon; during her entire republican existence, Ecuador has unsuccessfully fought the demands made by Peru to vast portions of the eastern jungle (Oriente) area. Second, in recent years Ecuador has attempted to extend her territorial rights to include sole sovereignty and jurisdiction over the natural resources and territorial sea within two hundred miles of the coastline. Finally, since World War II especially, Ecuador has sought to preserve her independence from foreign dominance. Originally concerned primarily with the potency of U.S. government influence, Ecuador is now attempting to hold the line on the economic ascendancy of U.S. oil interests.

As recently as 1941 Ludwig Bemelmans could still write in one of his colorful and now nostalgic books, *The Donkey Inside*, of an Ecuador that had been left sleeping through the first half of the twentieth century.[1] But World War II served to increase Ecuador's international contacts. Spurred by the founding of the United Nations and the Organization of American States (OAS), Ecuador has steadily broadened her horizons in a search for new markets and international aid. Now the discovery of vast petroleum reserves in the Oriente region seems about to catapult Ecuador into an increasing dependence on international—and especially North American—economic interests. As in other parts of Latin America, the current upsurge of Ecuadoran nationalism has merely exacerbated the controversy surrounding foreign policy goals.

CONTEMPORARY MOTIFS IN HISTORICAL PERSPECTIVE

Border Dispute with Peru

The basis for Ecuador's claim to a means of access to the Amazon River dates back to 1542. In that year Francisco de Orellano discovered the

---

1. Ludwig Bemelmans, *The Donkey Inside* (New York: Viking Press, 1941).

Amazon after having set out from Quito. Since Spanish colonial days, Ecuador has utilized every possible means to regain what is considered to be her national patrimony. The Ecuador-Peru boundary controversy is surrounded by an almost impenetrable array of colonial decrees, republican treaties, and more recent arbitrations and protocols. Spain had never been concerned with the exactitude of her colonies' artificial boundaries. The establishment of Ecuador's independence in 1822 merely compounded the difficulties. Simón Bolívar formed the Republic of Gran Colombia and proceeded to redraw frontiers. Following a brief war—fought in part over boundary issues—Gran Colombia and Peru signed the Treaty of Guayaquil in 1829. The treaty specified that the frontiers would correspond to those of the old viceroyalties of 1739; the exact demarcation of the border, however, was to be established by a boundary commission. Nevertheless, in the Pedemonte-Mosquera Protocol of 1830 Peru indicated acceptance of the Marañón-Amazon River line as her northern frontier. After Quito withdrew from the Gran Colombian federation later in 1830, Ecuador maintained the effectiveness of the protocol. But Peru denied that Ecuador had become the successor to Gran Colombian territory; Peru has further disputed the authenticity of the protocol.[2]

For many years the controversy was relatively quiescent. Then, in the late nineteenth century, traders and rubber workers—especially from Peru—began arriving in the area. Geographical barriers made communications more logical with Peruvian towns than with Ecuadoran. An agreement in 1887 to have the king of Spain arbitrate the dispute was not implemented. Instead, the García-Herrera Treaty of 1890 divided the territory between the two. Reluctantly, the Ecuadoran Congress ratified the treaty. Peru's Congress, however, gave its ratification subject to reservations. Enraged, the government in Quito broke diplomatic relations with Peru and prepared to fight. Mediation efforts by Colombia forestalled a war, but the Ecuadoran Congress withdrew its ratification of the García-Herrera Treaty in 1894. In desperation the disputants turned to the king of Spain in 1895. The arbitral proceedings finally established in 1910 that, on the one hand, many of Peru's claims were valid. On the other hand, the Spaniards noted that the region to be awarded Peru was not as extensive as previously thought. In fact, the Ecuadorans were to receive more territory in the west than under the García-Herrera Treaty, in addition to right of access to the Amazon. Ecuador expressly rejected the award in 1910. To avert a possible war, the king of Spain withdrew as arbiter. Only the mediation of the United States, Argentina, and Brazil prevented a full-scale war.

2. Georg Maier, "The Boundary Dispute Between Ecuador and Peru," *American Journal of International Law* 63 (January 1969): 28–46, argues that while Ecuador maintains an effective de jure title to the territory in question, Peru has an excellent de facto claim.

Between 1910 and 1941 Peru extended effective control over the disputed area. The government in Quito rendered protests, and frontier incidents continued to occur. A 1924 protocol provided for discussions in Washington, with the president of the United States to act as arbiter if no agreement could be reached. Nothing came of the meetings, and they were terminated in 1938. In 1941 Peru refused an offer of mediation by Argentina, Brazil, and the United States. Instead, in July the Peruvian government sent its army and air force to invade Ecuadoran territory. Outmanned and outclassed, Ecuadoran forces quickly capitulated, leaving several thousand square miles of the Oriente and all of El Oro Province to Peru. The three powers that had previously proferred mediation services arranged a ceasefire and sent six military observers into the area. From its militarily triumphant position, the government in Lima demanded that Ecuador agree to a treaty acceptable to the Peruvians; otherwise, Peru would seek a solution by force.

Both domestically and internationally Quito was in no position to argue with the Peruvians. Most of Ecuador's ill-equipped armed forces had been in the nation's cities engaged in propping up the shaky regime of President Carlos Arroyo del Río. On the world front the United States and its allies were concerned primarily with presenting a united hemispheric facade to the Axis powers. Moreover, the war had hampered the United States in its efforts to acquire the right to establish military bases on Ecuador's Galàpagos Islands. In consequence, Ecuador acquiesced in a Protocol of Peace, Friendship, and Boundaries (Rio Protocol), drawn up by the Third Meeting of Consultation of Foreign Ministers gathered in Rio de Janeiro in January 1942. Later ratified by the Congress of Ecuador, the protocol reduced Ecuador's Oriente by two-thirds.

Providing for a mixed Ecuadoran-Peruvian Boundary Commission, the agreement stipulated that any questions dealing with the interpretation, execution, or enforcement of the protocol were to be referred to a group of guarantor powers consisting of Argentina, Brazil, Chile, and the United States. A final border settlement was made in 1945. Pandora's box was opened in 1947, however, after a U.S. air force aerial survey discovered that the Cenepa River watershed was much more extensive than had been suspected. Since the Cenepa flows into the Marañón, Ecuadorans were enabled once more to see visions of their treasured Marañón-Amazon outlet.[3]

In August 1951, Ecuadoran President Galo Plaza Lasso declared that Ecuador could not accept a boundary settlement in the Cenepa area unless her right to an outlet on the Amazon through the Marañón were recognized. José María Velasco Ibarra focused attention on the festering

3. The foregoing historical account is based on information found in works cited in the Bibliographical Note.

border problem during his 1952 presidential campaign; soon after his inauguration he broke diplomatic relations with Peru. On 8 September 1955, Ecuador requested that a Meeting of Consultation of Foreign Ministers of the OAS be called to consider an excessive arms and troop buildup by Peru on Ecuador's border and coast. The Council, however, declined to invoke the Inter-American Treaty of Reciprocal Assistance, since Ecuador had already submitted the matter to the quartet of Rio Protocol guarantor states. An investigating committee composed of military representatives of the Rio Protocol guarantors initiated aerial and land reconnaissance missions but failed to observe "anything abnormal."[4]

The controversy was only briefly out of the limelight. By 1960 Ecuador's supreme *político*, Velasco Ibarra, had returned to the campaign trail seeking a fourth nonsuccessive term. Once again the boundary dispute became a cause célèbre. The guarantors announced their belief in the validity of the protocol, maintaining that under international law a unilateral act on the part of one party is not sufficient to invalidate a boundary treaty. Supported by both chambers of Congress and the Supreme Court of Justice, President Velasco declared the absolute nullity of the Rio Protocol almost immediately upon assuming office.[5] During the next few months, he kept up a steady barrage of inflammatory harangues that frequently incited demonstrations; such episodes reached their peak in December 1960, when both North American and Peruvian installations in Ecuador were attacked.

While explosive rhetoric and violent incidents never again reached the level of late 1960, the border dispute remained in the forefront of Ecuador's foreign policy concerns until the close of the 1960s. Consistently maintaining the thesis of the nullity of the Rio Protocol, governments in Quito have protested that the agreement was signed under extreme duress by a government that did not represent the will of the people. By 1969, however, the issue had receded into the background; it was replaced by the "tuna war" with the United States and by the question of oil exploitation by U.S. petroleum interests. On both of these topics, Ecuador found herself in common cause with her traditional antagonist, Peru. However, the possibility of oil in the two provinces taken by Peru in 1941 presents a potentially explosive situation.

Tuna War

The Tuna War is an extremely complex hemispheric issue grounded in economic self-interest, the ecological and conservation dilemma, interna-

4. Pan American Union, Department of Legal Affairs, *Inter-American Treaty of Reciprocal Assistance: Applications, 1948-1964*, 2 vols. (Washington, D.C., 1964), 1: 237.
5. *El Comercio* (Quito), 18 Aug. 1960; 18 Sept. 1960.

tional law issues, nationalistic pride, and currently popular anti–U.S. sentiment. Ecuador's controversy with the United States is actually a microcosm of the feelings shared by a majority of the other Latin American republics claiming a 200-mile limit. They allege that the authority for their claim is the 1945 unilateral Truman Proclamations on the Continental Shelf and Fisheries. Feeling threatened by great power policies seen as inimical to their national fishing interests, Ecuador, Chile, and Peru in 1952 joined in the Santiago Declaration on the Maritime Zone. The trio claimed that each nation had "sole sovereignty and jurisdiction over the area of sea adjacent to the coast of its own country and extending not less than 200 nautical miles from the said coast."[6] This constituted a maritime zone.

Prior to the 1960s the U.S. tuna fleet had found it necessary to acquire licenses from Latin American countries in order to enter the three-mile limit to obtain bait for tuna fishing. With the development of purse seine fishing, utilizing sonar, power blocks, and very large, powerful nets, bait was no longer necessary. As a result, U.S. fishermen refused to secure licenses to enter an area where their government did not recognize coastal fishery jurisdiction. Moreover, Washington officials feared that the purchase of such licenses would be equivalent to de facto recognition of the 200-mile claim. In September 1951, Ecuador captured her first U.S. fishing vessel. By 1963 such seizures had reached alarming proportions. Within this context, in 1963 the U.S. negotiated a secret *modus vivendi* on territorial waters with the ruling military junta. The arrangement, in force from September 1963 until early 1966 allowed North American fishing vessels to ply their trade at any point outside of a 12-mile limit.[7] Popular and official sentiment was outraged in 1966 by the discovery of what was branded as a traitorous act. Peru and Chile likewise took a dim view of the provisional military government's action as a violation of the Declaration of Santiago. Moreover, it is possible that the furor over the agreement actually led to Ecuador's later claim, in November 1966, to an unequivocal 200-mile territorial sea, as opposed to the previously established maritime zone.[8]

The inauguration of Velasco Ibarra for his fifth term as president of Ecuador in 1968 opened the way for the intensification of the tuna war. In that same year the seizure by Ecuador of six U.S. fishing boats had resulted in the temporary suspension of U.S. military aid. Following the

6. Secretaría General, *Conferencia sobre explotación y conservación de las riquezas marítimas del Pacífico Sur: Convenios y otros documentos, 1952-1969*, 3d ed. (Lima: Editorial Universo S.A., 1970), p. 31.

7. *El Comercio*, 30 and 31 Dec. 1966; *El Telégrafo* (Guayaquil), 20 Dec. 1966. Apparently there were also discrepancies between the Spanish and English texts of the modus vivendi.

8. The problem was further compounded in 1966 when U.S. President Lyndon Johnson signed a unilateral act establishing a twelve-mile fishery zone in seas adjacent to the U.S. coasts.

capture of ten California vessels in January 1971, the United States announced that it would invoke the Pelly Amendment and suspend all arms sales to Ecuador for one year.[9] This action served only to increase the anger and intransigence of the Ecuadorans. At Ecuador's request, the Permanent Council of the OAS unanimously (the United States abstaining) convoked the Fourteenth Meeting of Consultation of Foreign Ministers. Ecuador charged that the U.S. cessation of military assistance was a "coercive measure."[10] The meeting merely passed a resolution urging the two to negotiate their differences; Ecuador, however, claimed a moral victory. Subsequently, in retaliation for U.S. action, the government in Quito terminated the U.S. military assistance mission in Ecuador. During 1971 alone Ecuador seized fifty-one U.S. fishing boats and assessed some $2,478,252 in fines and fees.[11] The fact that other nations do not fish extensively in the area has turned the issue into a primarily U.S.-Ecuadoran dispute. Japanese fishing interests buy licenses "under protest."

Although the economic and legal ramifications of the fisheries controversy are felt in earnest by the participants, the situation has both ironic and comic aspects. First, many of the Ecuadoran naval vessels that have engaged in the seizures have actually been either sold, given, or placed on loan to Ecuador by the U.S. government. Second, the fines are actually paid by the U.S. government through reimbursements under the Fisherman's Protective Acts of 1954 and 1967. U.S. law then permits the government to recover the cost of reimbursement by deducting the amount from foreign aid intended for the country involved.[12] It is presently cheaper in the long run for North American fishermen to be captured and fined than it is for them to pay for licenses. Naturally, the Ecuadorans find that making arrests is much more lucrative than selling licenses. The Ecuadoran navy especially enjoys the chase, since it receives 70 percent of all fines paid.[13] In the third place, the majority of the Ecuadoran-owned fishing fleet and tuna processing plants are controlled by U.S. capital.[14]

9. *Latin America* (London), 22 Jan. 1971, p. 32.

10. Organization of American States, Fourteenth Meeting of Consultation of Foreign Ministers, *Documentos*, 30 Jan. 1971 (OEA/Ser.F/II.14/Doc. 6); and ibid., 31 Jan. 1971 (Doc. 11).

11. U.S., Congress, House of Representatives, Committee on Foreign Affairs, Subcommittee on Inter-American Affairs, Hearings, *Fishing Rights and United States–Latin American Relations*, 92nd Cong., 2d sess., 3 Feb. 1972, p. 9.

12. As of November 1972, the U.S. government had paid claims valued at approximately $4 million to the owners of seized vessels. U.S., Comptroller General, *Report to Congress: What Should U.S. Policy Be for Development Assistance to Ecuador?* (Washington, D.C.: General Accounting Office, 1973), p. 19.

13. *Registro oficial*, no. 132, 10 Mar. 1969, no. 110-CL, "Ley de pesca y fomento pesquero," tít. IX, art. 71.

14. House, *Fishing Rights and United States–Latin American Relations*, pp. 25, 30.

The rich coastal waters possess tremendous potential for Ecuadoran growth in the area of the export of fish products. Large-scale fishing is a relatively new industry for Ecuador, and lack of capital for the expansion and modernization of her fishing fleet has thus far restricted the rapid progress desired. Mid-century technological improvements in equipment and techniques for high-yield fishing have yet to reach Ecuador. The tuna is a migratory fish that appears each year between January and April off the coast of Ecuador and Peru. It was estimated that the value of the 1971 catch might go as high as $10 million, while the factory value might reach even $50 million.[15] At that time her fishing fleet—without refrigeration—could sail only as far as twenty-five miles off the coast.

Ecuador's claim to tuna farther off the coast is based partially on economic grounds; the purpose is to safeguard future interest in marine resources. It is also contended that the tuna may later swim in toward shore and be caught by Ecuadorans. In mid-1971 the Ecuadoran ambassador to the United States, Carlos Mantilla Ortega, extensively explained some of the basic issues.[16] The official Ecuadoran argument turns primarily on the ecological problems involved in the preservation of undersea resources. One of Ecuador's objections concerns the destructive fishing methods used by the U.S. vessels concerned. By "purse seining" with enormous nets U.S. fishermen indiscriminately capture massive amounts of all types of sea life. Only the tuna are kept, and most of the rest that are thrown back are dead. Another argument utilized by the Ecuadorans and other Latin Americans is that the 200-mile limit circumscribes the "biological boundary" of the Humboldt Current. The maritime zone is considered to be a distinct ecological unit; within this ecosystem the tuna and other marine life are linked by the food chain to the coast of Ecuador.

Technical level conferences (the Quadripartite Fisheries Conferences) on conservation of fisheries and ocean resources have been held intermittently between Chile, Ecuador, Peru, and the United States since late 1969. The Latin Americans would especially like the United States to lower or completely terminate its tariff on imports of canned fish products and give up its insistence that bonito not be called tuna. Basically, however, these are technical issues. The main distinction between the U.S. and Ecuadoran positions is that Washington views the situation in legal terms, whereas Quito's stand is based on economic and ecological grounds. The Third United Nations Law of the Sea Conference in 1974, although unsuccessful in producing an acceptable treaty, did result in a consensus, to be finalized at a later conference, for a 12-mile territorial sea limit and a 200-mile economic zone.

15. *Times of the Americas,* 7 Apr. 1971, p. 8.
16. Ibid., 12 May 1971, p. 5.

Oil

While oil in Ecuador has been exploited by foreign interests since 1917, until recently the known deposits were of very low productivity. Prior to 1967 the only proven petroleum deposits were in the Santa Elena Peninsula, west of Guayaquil. In that year, a U.S. oil consortium, Texaco-Gulf, brought in its first producing well on a concession in the Oriente, near the Colombian border. The consortium had signed a five-year exploration contract with the governing military junta in March 1964. Since 1967 glowing reports of tremendous petroleum reserves have served to titillate Ecuador's developmental aspirations and nationalistic sentiments. Increasingly, Ecuadoran governments have restricted the maneuvering of the foreign-owned companies almost to the point of nationalization. Nevertheless, by 1972 twenty-five oil companies were exploring in Ecuador.

When the renewal option on the Texaco-Gulf agreement came up for renegotiation, Velasco Ibarra had regained the presidency. In mid-1969, after comprehensive negotiations, the consortium found itself denuded of two-thirds of its original concession; undertakings by the company called for increased royalties and improvements in Ecuador's infrastructure.[17] The complexity of the situation was illustrated by the fact that the government in Quito refused to utilize a feeder line connecting the Ecuadoran oil fields to a trans-Andean pipeline laid in Colombia. National pride dictated that a wholly Ecuadoran line be constructed. In consequence, a 318-mile-long pipeline to Esmeraldas was completed in 1972 at a cost of $130 million. A new petroleum code decreed by the Velasco regime in late 1971 took careful note of the circumstances in other oil-exporting nations. It emphasized joint ventures with the state-owned oil enterprise, Corporación Estatal de Petróleo Ecuatoriano (CEPE). Concessions were replaced by "association" contracts with CEPE; these were to give the national concern an equal share of profits.[18]

One of the most important actions taken by the military regime during 1972 was to annul existing oil contracts as being of dubious legality. The principal effect of a June 1972 oil decree was to limit concessions to 160,000 hectares. In effect, this meant that the various oil concerns had to return 1.8 million hectares; pressure was considerably reduced, however, by the fact that the companies were given up to two years to decide which 160,000 hectares they would keep and which they would return.[19] The Ecuadoran government also canceled almost two million acres of oil

17. For details see Cyrano Tama Paz, *Petróleo: drama ecuatoriana* (Guayaquil: Artes Gráficos Senefelder, 1970).
18. *Times of the Americas*, 3 May 1972, p. 5.
19. See *Latin America*, 14 July 1972, p. 223; 10 Nov. 1972, p. 357.

concessions in the Gulf of Guayaquil. A group of North American companies had already spent some $20 million and proved the existence of a large gas field offshore. The government claimed serious irregularities in the issuance of the original leases to several Ecuadorans. The president, General Guillermo Rodríguez Lara, also moved to nullify several international oil related transactions that had been undertaken by the Velasco government. A contract with a Japanese firm for the construction of a $50 million state-owned oil refinery was canceled because it had been negotiated with "a lack of due consideration."[20]

In mid-1973 Ecuador renegotiated a twenty-year contract with Texaco-Gulf. The latter agreed to give Ecuador almost 80 percent of the gross profits of the consortium's petroleum exports. Until 1977 CEPE was to have the option of purchasing a 25 percent participation in the operation; in early 1974 the government decided to exercise this option. CEPE was also assigned the right to buy up to 51 percent of the companies' total oil production. Royalty fees were to be 16 percent, payable in kind. Half of this amount would go to the armed forces—a boon, with world oil prices soaring. Furthermore, Texaco-Gulf has agreed to transfer the trans-Andean pipeline to Ecuador once construction costs have been met.[21] By the close of 1973 Petrobras of Brazil and a number of U.S. oil interests were gingerly retreating from investments in Ecuadoran oil. The vacuum, however, was readily filled by the Japanese. One firm agreed to a joint venture with the Ecuadoran navy to finance an oil tanker fleet to carry over 50 percent of all oil shipped. Another Japanese firm offered to purchase 16 percent of CEPE's portion of crude oil.

There is some question as to the exact amount of Ecuador's proven oil reserves. In mid-1972 the extraordinary number of eight out of ten wells drilled in Ecuador had proven out. Modest estimates suggested a reserve of some 5,000.6 million barrels in the eastern jungle area. Some experts compared the reserves to those of Venezuela's Lake Maracaibo. Data from U.S. government sources suggest that the supply is substantial and that production may equal 2 percent of the world's crude oil.[22] Not all companies have met with success, however. At the close of 1972 Amoco suspended drilling activity due to dry holes; Anglo-Ecuadoran has also been disappointed. In fact, only the Texaco-Gulf consortium has really been fortunate in its explorations.

In 1973 the average rate of crude oil exports was more than 191,000 barrels per day. It has been estimated that if the pipeline capacity of 250,000 barrels a day is attained, Ecuador could reach a level of value of

20. *Times of the Americas,* 20 Dec. 1972, p. 8; 3 May 1972, p. 5.
21. *Times of the Americas,* 22 Aug. 1973, p. 2; *Latin America,* 24 Aug. 1973, p. 267; 19 Oct. 1973, pp. 335–36.
22. Comptroller General, *Report to Congress,* p. 36.

approximately $1,000 million of petroleum exports a year.[23] Hence, although the search for petroleum in the Ecuadoran jungle is both costly and hazardous, it does appear at the least to be competitive with oil from other Latin American countries.

As a consequence, U.S. oil concerns have a serious stake in Ecuador's petroleum future and will withstand a great deal more governmental pressure before they voluntarily surrender exploration rights. Since it has invested the greatest amount, Texaco-Gulf is the most vulnerable. By 1973 foreign oil interests had already invested more than $350 million in Ecuadoran explorations; much of this amount had been spent on fixed assets such as buildings, pipelines, and roads. It represented 90 percent of the total direct private foreign investment in Ecuador. Also, as of 1973, oil-producing countries were in a much stronger position vis-à-vis the importing countries than they had been a few years before. All over the world agreements were being revised in the producer's favor. Ecuador, however, cannot afford to alienate international oil interests completely. A poor country, Ecuador cannot develop her "liquid gold" resources without the assistance of foreign investment capital and technical aid. Moreover, cash is needed to finance past and present budget deficits. Governments previous to the 1972 military regime systematically overspent their budgets by an estimated 20 percent a year in anticipation of the oil wealth; some of this amount was covered by advance payments of oil taxes by Texaco-Gulf.[24]

Successive *quiteño* administrations have tightened their control over the blossoming oil industry, as already noted. President Rodríguez Lara took an especially hard line with foreign oil companies when he and the army assumed control in February 1972. There are several politically pragmatic reasons for this stance. It was a military junta that first negotiated liberal concessions with the North American petroleum groups. Further, that same junta was convicted in the eyes of the Ecuadoran populace of having literally given away its ocean resources to the United States in 1963. It is also widely believed that Velasco's civilian administration, riddled with corruption, had sold concessions to the highest bribers. On assuming the presidency in 1972, Rodríguez Lara declared that his government would encourage "autonomous economic development" and "do everything possible to end the country's dependence on the world's great centers of decision-making."[25] The question for the future (indeed, for the future of Ecuador's economic development)

23. Statement by Dr. Pedro Aguayo, chairman of the National Economic Planning and Coordination Board of Ecuador to the Subcommittee of the Inter-American Committee on the Alliance for Progress (*Times of the Americas*, 6 Feb. 1974, p. 9).
24. Ibid., 6 Sept. 1972, p. 8. There has been some speculation that the military takeover in 1972 was prompted by fear that oil money would be squandered by corrupt politicans.
25. *Latin America*, 11 March 1972, p. 88.

is whether the political climate in Ecuador will continue to provide investors with satisfactory prospects and a realistic return on their investment.

STRUCTURE AND PROCESS OF POLICY FORMATION

In recent years there has been considerable interplay between domestic politics and Ecuadoran foreign policy. The relationship has been both positive and negative. Affirmatively, foreign policy formation has been utilized to assist in Ecuador's search for socioeconomic development. Ecuadoran governments have pursued claims to territorial waters and negotiations for stricter control over oil exploration with a view to furthering Ecuador's national interests and gaining international prestige. The other side of the coin is that various politicians have made opportunistic use of Ecuador's positions on external matters in order to increase their popular political support. Velasco Ibarra has been especially adept at employing foreign policy issues to redirect popular attention away from the economically disastrous effects of his various inefficient administrations. Fiercely nationalistic, he has adroitly focused the public eye on such topics as the border dispute, the fisheries controversy, and U.S. economic imperialism. The instability of Ecuadoran governments since 1960 has enhanced this trend. There is every reason to believe that the latest military regime will continue to seek the maximum political profit from a staunchly nationalistic, and therefore popular, policy in the realm of foreign affairs.

Political parties in Ecuador have had only brief and transient influence on the course of foreign policy. Party organization has traditionally been weak, and programmatic bases are frequently modified in order to accommodate divergent views. Moreover, Ecuadoran parties bear the strong imprint of personalism. At various times—and especially with the advent of the 1970s—various parties have unfurled the banner of nationalism in the service of various causes. But generally, except for such issues as the boundary dispute and the Tuna War on which all parties are united, foreign affairs play a scant role in political campaigns.

Labor unions in Ecuador have also exercised little if any leverage on Ecuadoran foreign policy as a whole. There are three "national" confederations. Each of these is often criticized for connections with such foreign interests as communism, North American policy, or international Christian Democracy of the West German stamp. Since Eloy Alfaro restricted the power of the Catholic church at the turn of this century, it has had only limited impact on the political life of Ecuador, including her foreign relations. While student groups can be a disruptive force in society, they actually have minimal influence on policy decisions.

Only the military and the coastal commercial elite can be said to influence foreign policy to any significant degree. Frequently throughout Ecuadoran history the army has intervened in the normal functioning of government. This involvement has increased in recent years. Economic interests in Guayaquil have always tended to be more internationally oriented than other sectors of the country. Of course, this is consistent with their dependence on commerce and trade; the coastal area has provided most of Ecuador's exports, and Guayaquil is Ecuador's financial center. Guayaquil businessmen have been particularly concerned that oil discoveries in the Oriente might disperse their power. In 1972 there were rumors that the coastal oligarchy had joined with the strongly nationalistic navy to oppose the rule of the army from Quito. The army-dominated government could hardly allow itself to appear less nationalistic in its dealings with the petroleum companies. On the other hand, President Rodríguez needed the support of the oil concerns in his struggle to secure political power. The Ecuadoran navy has experienced a toughening of its nationalistic cast as a result of its involvement in the fishing dispute with the United States.

Ecuadoran foreign policy is officially conducted through the Ministry of Foreign Relations. Congress, of course, has a constitutional role in the formulation of foreign policy. However, even when the legislative branch is functioning, the president is the final arbiter in this field. Strong chief executives, such as José María Velasco Ibarra and Otto Arosemena Gómez, have largely directed their own foreign relations. Velasco especially dictated Ecuador's international policy on the five occasions that he was in office. Even with a military regime in power—as opposed to a one-man government—foreign policy is clearly an executive function in Ecuador.

OVERVIEW OF WORLD RELATIONS

Relations with the United States

Following World War II hostile feelings towards the United States emerged in Ecuador. In part this was due to increased economic dependence on her North American ally. When Washington procrastinated in vacating the military bases leased on the Galápagos Islands during the war, leftist Ecuadoran elements mobilized anti–U.S. opinion. The election of American-born and educated Galo Plaza Lasso to the presidency in 1948 brought an era of cordiality to U.S.–Ecuadoran relations. In 1952 the two signed a Mutual Military Assistance Pact. But the return of Velasco Ibarra to executive office in 1952 signaled a reversion to strongly nationalistic sentiment. From 1956 to 1960 President Camilo Ponce Enríquez maintained friendly rapport with Washington. Moreover, in 1960 Velasco returned to the presidency with a campaign that emphasized the pro–North American attitudes of his opponent, Galo Plaza.

Since 1960, however, Ecuador's relations with the United States have grown increasingly antagonistic. Played out against a backdrop of steadily ripening nationalism, the course of events has been rocky. The U.S. role as a guarantor of the Rio Protocol heightened tensions and led to belligerent demonstrations in 1960. This dissatisfaction was furthered by a short-lived popular pro-*fidelista* atmosphere, which prompted criticisms of U.S. policy toward the Castro regime. The military junta maintained cordial contacts with the United States from 1963 to 1966.[26] But, supported by his fellow Ecuadorans (and by much popular approval throughout Latin America), provisional President Otto Arosemena Gómez in 1967 indicated his impatience with U.S. diplomacy by refusing to sign the final declaration of the Meeting of American Chiefs of State at Punta del Este. Later that same year Arosemena ordered the departure of the U.S. ambassador who had protested the Ecuadoran president's caustic critique of the Alliance for Progress.

U.S. assistance, a perennial source of irritation to the Latin American republics, has, in the case of Ecuador, included loans, grants, and technical assistance. During the 1940s and 1950s, the magnitude of aid provided by the United States was small. In the 1960s, however, the amount became relatively significant. Together with international lending agencies, the United States has contributed most of Ecuador's foreign aid. From 1962 through 1972 direct and indirect assistance commitments from the United States to Ecuador totaled about $360 million. This amount represented about 78 percent of Ecuador's outside assistance.[27]

Of $148.8 million in private foreign investment in Ecuador by 1968, U.S. citizens or corporations invested approximately 70 percent. Almost 60 percent of U.S. investment was in the petroleum industry.[28] In 1972 the United States continued to be not only Ecuador's best customer but also her chief supplier. But the U.S. trading position has declined from its immediate post–World War II high. Ecuadorans complain that they pay high prices for U.S. imports, while the United States pays low prices for Ecuadoran products (usually raw materials). Ecuador will persevere in seeking tariff preferences for her commodities. Nevertheless, prospects are

26. Supporters of the 1963 military coup maintain that its action was necessary in order to prevent a deterioration in U.S.-Ecuadoran relations. See Martin C. Needler, *Anatomy of a Coup d'Etat: Ecuador, 1963*, Institute for the Comparative Study of Political Systems, Special Article Series no. 1 (Washington, D.C., 1964), p. 30.

27. Comptroller General, *Report to Congress*, p. 11.

28. Charles R. Gibson, *Foreign Trade in the Economic Development of Small Nations: The Case of Ecuador* (New York: Praeger Publishers, 1971), p. 261.

that the United States will continue to be Ecuador's principal trading partner for some time.

Entering the 1970s, the U.S. government sustained a lower profile in Ecuador. While some U.S. aid programs were restored after the 1972 overthrow of Velasco, the U.S. military mission in Ecuador has been greatly reduced from the sizeable contingent of the 1960s. However, for purposes of socioeconomic progress in Ecuador, it is important that the United States remain a significant trade ally and aid benefactor. Capital formation in Ecuador is still extremely modest, while oil represents the only mineral resource found in more than negligible quantities. Thus, Ecuador may have to look to U.S. government and private investment groups as major financing agents for the immediate future.

Relations With Latin America

As tensions between the United States and Ecuador have waxed, Ecuador's dealings with her Latin American neighbors have warmed. To a degree this is derived from a common anti-Yankee outlook. But it can be seen in great measure as a result of the initiation of the Andean Pact. The Latin American Free Trade Association (LAFTA), which Ecuador had joined in 1961, had proved itself a disappointment to all concerned. Although gaining certain preferential treatment, Ecuadorans felt strongly that they had given more important concessions than they had received. The Andean Subregional Group (ASG), or Andean Pact, was created in 1969 by Colombia, Ecuador, Peru, Bolivia, and Chile in an effort to provide a solution to benefit distribution problems among countries with great disparities in development levels. In its initial stages the group has focused on trade liberalization and foreign investment policy. Growing economic nationalism in Latin America is manifested in the ASG's Foreign Investment Code. It requires that foreign-owned industries in Ecuador divest themselves of majority control within twenty years; a loophole provides that the government may make exceptions for certain sectors. Both Bolivia and Ecuador, considered as less developed members, receive preferred treatment in their trade relations with their colleagues. For Ecuador the greatest export marketing potential in Latin America lies with the nearby large population centers of Colombia, Peru, and to a lesser extent, Chile.

Ecuador's relations with Colombia have been cordial in recent years. In part their common interest lies in the oil industry. Ecuador could prove to be a useful source of petroleum at a time when Colombian reserves are running low. Currently the two neighbors are discussing the industrial and infrastructure possibilities of integrating their frontier zone.[29] The

29. See *El Comercio*, 14 and 16 Oct. 1972.

cooperative spirit of the Andean Pact has fostered Ecuador's friendly collaboration, not only with neighboring Colombia but also with Peru, her historical enemy. Thus, in a unique act, Ecuador and Peru in 1971 jointly applied to the Inter-American Development Bank for technical assistance to study the development of their common frontier regions.[30] Ecuador emerged in 1972 as Peru's best customer within the Andean Group for industrial products. While members of Ecuador's military regime had not clearly demonstrated their political and economic allegiance by early 1974, it was apparent that they were studying the developmental aspects of the *peruanista* experiment with great interest. Likewise, little in the way of anti-Peruvian sentiment was heard. The development of their respective oil industries has produced conversations between Ecuador and Petroperu, Peru's state-operated petroleum organ. Further, the 200-mile limit controversy with the United States has made the two nations almost blood brothers. The only thorny issue that could easily strain Ecuador's relations with Peru would be the certain discovery of oil in the disputed frontier area.

This era of good will can be viewed as a move in the direction of what some have described as the "antiimperialist wing" of the Andean Pact. This grouping, generally composed of Peru and Chile, together with Ecuador, is wary not only of U.S. designs but also of those of Brazil. A number of Latin American republics are increasingly concerned about the aggressive political and economic nature of Brazilian foreign policy. Brazil's economic power and resource potential is tremendous, and the projected trans-Amazonian highway may not be far from completion. Brazilian businessmen have become active in various parts of Latin America; much to the annoyance of the Peruvian government, Petrobras of Brazil for awhile energetically sought oil concessions in Ecuador. Brazil is still, however, a somewhat intangible foe, while U.S. oil interests stand as a ready target. As a consequence, Ecuador, Colombia, and Peru want to encourage exploration by U.S. monied interests while maintaining a reasonably consistent set of petroleum policies in order to keep the oil concerns from playing off one country against another. On this point close collaboration among the three is likely to continue.

Extrahemispheric Relations

Ecuador has viewed her relations outside the Western Hemisphere primarily in economic terms. West Germany is her second largest consumer of exports. Demand for Ecuadoran bananas has been increasing in Europe. In Asia, Ecuador deals largely with Japan, her third best customer. Increasingly, Japanese interests are looking toward Ecuador as

30. *Times of the Americas*, 6 Oct. 1971, p. 5.

a potential arena for industrial development and investment as well as trade.[31] In 1973 Ecuador joined the Organization of Petroleum Exporting Companies (OPEC).

In recent years, except when a Conservative party government has been in power, Ecuador has viewed her position toward the Communist bloc in a pragmatic manner. An interest in Marxism and the activities of Communist countries became noticeable in Ecuador following World War II. It was, of course, coupled with a rise in anti–U.S. attitudes. Slightly Left-leaning when he attained the presidency in 1960, Velasco Ibarra demonstrated his interest in and sympathy for Castro's revolution. Nevertheless, he apparently accepted no assistance from foreign Communist elements. Moreover, in the latter half of 1961, he rejected proleftist pressures. He was ousted, however, by his vice-president, Carlos Julio Arosemena Monroy, who pressed for closer ties with the Soviet bloc and Cuba. Ecuador then voted against excluding Cuba from the inter-American system in January 1962. The impact of *fidelismo* eventually subsided, and moderates and conservatives were able to force Arosemena to break diplomatic relations with Cuba in April 1962.

In 1970 President Velasco established diplomatic relations with the Soviet Union. Actually, little trade has been conducted with Communist bloc countries. But even though diplomatic relations with mainland China had not been established by the opening of 1974, an agreement had been made with Peking for the sale of 20,000 tons of bananas to the Peoples' Republic of China.[32] Unless the present military regime takes an extreme right-wing turn, it is likely that—given the continuation of the worldwide thaw in East-West relations—Ecuador will continue to develop more economic ties with Communist countries.

Relations with International Organizations

Admitted to the United Nations in December 1945, Ecuador has remained a steadfast supporter. The small Latin American republic has contributed to and benefited from a number of UN agencies and activities, including the UN Development Programs, UNESCO, the International Monetary Fund, and the World Health Organization, among others. International lending agencies such as the World Bank and Inter-American Development Bank have contributed materially to Ecuador's development. While Ecuador has in the past been an active and loyal participant in the activities of the OAS, the relationship has suffered some strains. The vagaries of the previously discussed border controversy between Peru and Ecuador was an important element in the permanent postponement of the abortive Eleventh Inter-American Conference. In the early 1960s

31. A Japanese firm has agreed to assist Ecuador in the marketing of bananas in Japan in exchange for an investment agreement (ibid., 31 Oct. 1973, p. 5).
32. Ibid., 14 Mar. 1973, p. 8.

relations between the two neighbors were severely strained, anti-Peruvian and antiguarantor demonstrations were common in Ecuador, and Ecuadoran officials insisted that the conference should deal with the dispute. Such a highly unstable situation, in concert with broader inter-American problems, sounded the death knell to efforts to hold the eleventh conference.

The omnipresent issue of the Ecuador-Peru boundary dispute has served as the linchpin of continuing Ecuadoran endeavors to influence proposals for the peaceful settlement of inter-American controversies. When the Protocol of Buenos Aires (later to become the amended OAS Charter) was signed in 1967, Ecuador expressed keen dissatisfaction with the new settlement procedures; thus, Ecuador indicated her understanding that there would be no limitation in the nature or subject of disputes to be brought before the organization.[33] Doubtless, Ecuador will continue to support the OAS, but without the same commitment as in the past. Like many other Latin American countries, she sees her most important immediate problem to be economic development. With this end in view, the Andean Pact has presently become of greater significance to Ecuador than either the OAS or the United Nations.

CONCLUSION

As Ecuador enters the mid-1970s she is confronted by the pressure of an increasing need and desire for socioeconomic development. External attention to her fisheries and petroleum resources will perforce continue to dictate Ecuador's response to foreign policy questions. And it is these two issues, together with the importance of the Andean Pact, that will at least temporarily assist in the downplay of the boundary dispute with Peru. The 1971 military regime has avowed itself to be nationalistic, and extensive economic penetration by foreign interests is likely to serve as a catalyst to such sentiment. Increasingly, the interface to foreign policy formulation will be pervasive nationalism in the service of the exigencies of developmental goals.

BIBLIOGRAPHICAL NOTE

As is the case with most of Latin America, little has been written on the foreign relations of Ecuador. General historical works on Ecuador in Spanish usually touch only peripherally on twentieth-century affairs. In English, Lilo Linke, *Ecuador: Country of Contrasts*, 2d ed. (London: Royal Institute of International Affairs, 1955), gives minor attention to foreign affairs but is now dated. The same

33. Organization of American States, *Protocol of Amendment to the Charter of the Organization of American States: Protocol of Buenos Aires* (OEA/Ser.A/2, Add. 2; 1967), p. 57.

is true of the *Area Handbook for Ecuador* (Washington, D.C.: Foreign Area Studies, The American University, 1966). The most recent analysis of current foreign policy problems is contained in the general political work by John D. Martz, *Ecuador: Conflicting Political Culture and the Quest for Progress* (Boston: Allyn & Bacon, 1972).

The number of secondary works in Spanish on the Ecuador-Peru boundary dispute is overwhelming. Perhaps the most helpful are Jorge Pérez Concha, *Ensayo histórico-crítico de las relaciones diplomáticos del Ecuador con los estados limítrofes*, 2 vols. (Quito: Editorial Casa de la Cultura Ecuatoriana, 1961 and 1964), which discusses the problem up until 1940, and Rafael Euclides Silva, *Derecho territorial ecuatoriana* (Guayaquil: Universidad de Guayaquil, 1967), which contains an extensive bibliography. In English, both David H. Zook, Jr., *Zarumilla-Marañón: The Ecuador-Peru Dispute* (New York: Bookman Associates, 1964) and Georg Maier, "The Boundary Dispute Between Ecuador and Peru," *American Journal of International Law* 63 (January 1969): 28–46, offer good accounts. Mary Jean Reid Martz, "Ecuador and the Eleventh Inter-American Conference," *Journal of Inter-American Studies* 10 (April 1968): 306–27, covers the border controversy as it relates to the postponement of the conference.

On Ecuador's territorial waters position see in particular Teodoro Alvarado Garaicoa, *El dominio del mar* (Guayaquil: Universidad de Guayaquil, 1968), which deals generally with the question; Neftali Ponce Miranda, in *Dominio marítimo* (Quito: Inds. Gráfs. "CYMA," 1971), explains Ecuador's viewpoint while defending his own role in negotiating the secret *modus vivendi* with the United States.

For Ecuador's stance on foreign oil exploration, one can consult the monthly publications *Petroleum Press Service* (London) and *World Petroleum* (New York). Cyrano Tama Paz, in *Petróleo: drama ecuatoriano* (Guayaquil: Artes Gráficos Senefelder, 1970), discusses the technical and political aspects of the 1969 oil contract renegotiations. A best-selling if polemical anti-U.S. source is Jaime Galarza, *El festín del petróleo* (Cuenca: Ediciones Solitierra, 1972). *Foreign Trade in the Economic Development of Small Nations: The Case of Ecuador* (New York: Praeger Publishers, 1971) by Charles R. Gibson blames internal problems, rather than external constraints, for Ecuador's failure to achieve the maximum economic growth from its foreign trade. An important guide to Ecuador's role in Latin American economic integration efforts is Germánico Salgado, *Ecuador y la integración económica de América Latina* (Buenos Aires: Instituto Para la Integración de América Latina, Banco Interamericano de Desarrollo, 1970).

Significant primary sources for Ecuador's foreign policy include the annual *Memoria*, put out by the Ministry of Foreign Relations, and the government's *Registro Oficial*, which records laws such as those relating to fishing licenses and oil exploration. Also published in Ecuador are collections of speeches by presidents Velasco Ibarra, Galo Plaza, Camilo Ponce, and the 1963 military junta. Vela H. Wilson, *Política internacional del Ecuador, 1960–1961* (Quito: Ministerio de Relaciones Exteriores, 1961?), is also helpful.

El Comercio (Quito) and *El Universo* (Guayaquil) are newspapers that reflect the views of the elites in their respective cities. *Vistazo* (Guayaquil) is Ecuador's primary general news magazine published monthly. The most useful news sources in English are *Latin America*, the excellent weekly published in London, and the *Times of the Americas*, a weekly utilizing wire service dispatches.

19/David Bushnell

Colombia

Traditionally, the Republic has never been divided over international problems, and I refuse to admit that there are now differences of opinion on the kind of relations that we should maintain with the United States. The only possible division is the one posed by the Honorable Representative García: that we should ask them for more or should ask them for less.
Foreign Minister Julio César Turbay Ayala, in a speech of April 1959.

At the Panama Congress of 1826 Colombia played host to the first gathering of American states, the personal brainchild of the Colombian president, Simón Bolívar. Today Colombia is no longer the acknowledged leader among Spanish-American republics, but she has been one of the strongest supporters of the modern inter-American system that rests on permanent institutional arrangements. On the broader world scene, especially in terms of government policy, she has been a loyal though not quite unconditional ally of the United States as against the Communist bloc (or blocs); while at the subregional level she was, with Chile, one of the two prime movers in creating the Andean Group. At the same time it cannot be said that diplomatic relations per se are a primary concern of Colombian officials or public opinion. The one aspect of foreign relations that arouses persistent and lively interest is the economic, precisely because it impinges so directly on prospects for internal development and on the very structure of the Colombian economy and society. The central problem as Colombians tend to see it is to improve their terms of trade and enhance their own control over external participation in the national economy without either sacrificing traditional markets or choking off the flow of imported capital and technology. In a word, Colombians work to lessen their dependence on the industrial nations, in particular the United States, but not through measures that could truly be labeled revolutionary. This is not to say that other concerns are absent or unimportant, but they are almost always subsidiary except when, as in the border dispute with Venezuela, they relate directly to economic interests.

CURRENT ISSUES AND PROBLEMS

In the economic sphere, in fact, the distinction between domestic problems and foreign relations is often blurred. The well-being of the coffee industry, to cite what is perhaps the most obvious example, is equally the concern of domestic officials and Colombian agents abroad, since it is an immediate source of livelihood for a significant part of the population in almost every section of the country and provides roughly half the nation's

401

earnings of foreign exchange. It is coffee more than any other single factor that makes possible both infrastructural development and continued industrial expansion; and any significant fluctuation in its world price is bound to have a major impact on political and social as well as strictly economic conditions within Colombia. Colombia was therefore an active participant in the negotiations leading to the International Coffee Agreement (ICA) of 1962, by which the producing and consuming nations pledged to cooperate in controlling the volume of international coffee sales and thereby stabilize the price. The ICA did in fact help stem a disastrous decline in the price of coffee that had been underway since the mid-1950s. When unfavorable crop conditions in Brazil in 1972 brought a sharp price rise, consuming nations called upon the same ICA mechanism to moderate the increase by expanding export quotas; and as no agreement could be reached, the established quota system broke down. It was scarcely missed. Better yet, coffee went on to share in the more general upward trend of world commodity prices. But Colombia remains committed to the principle of joint action with other coffee-producing nations, especially Brazil, in defense of common interests. She would presumably be ready to limit exports again if need arose.[1]

The intermingling of domestic and foreign considerations in Colombian fiscal, monetary, and development policy is more complex than in the case of coffee but no less important. With a per capita gross national product of less than $400 and a long-term structural foreign exchange shortage, Colombia has eagerly accepted outside assistance not only for the financing of social and economic development programs but, in practice, to overcome current budgetary and balance-of-payments deficits. External financing has been granted to the Colombian government through both multilateral and bilateral channels, although the United States has provided the largest share, amounting to roughly $100 million yearly since the early 1960s.[2] Such foreign funds have sometimes been

1. Simon G. Hansen, "The Experience with the International Coffee Agreement," *Inter-American Economic Affairs* 19, no. 3 (Winter 1965): 38–44, 50–54; "Convenio internacional del cafe," *Revista del Banco de la República* 539 (September 1972): 1570–73, and also the section "El mercado mundial del cafe," which appears monthly in the same journal.

2. Published "aid" totals vary widely, as they necessarily depend on a prior definition of aid, and on this point reasonable men (to say nothing of unreasonable) may differ. Fairly typical, however, is the total of almost $1,000 million for the period 1961–70 that emerges from a table published by the *Andean Times* (Bogotá), 1 July 1971, p. 5. This lumps in Export-Import Bank loans as aid—an officially sanctioned though highly questionable practice—but does not include U.S. funds channeled through multilateral programs. For subsequent years, see "External Financing Plays Key Role in Colombia's Development," *Colombia Today* 7, no. 11 (1972), and "Over $1 Billion in Development Financing Proposed for 1973 and 1974," *Colombia Today* 8, no. 6 (1973). None of these sources refers to military aid, although quantitatively it would not make much difference. For fiscal years 1962–70, for example, it was stated as "$71.3 million worth of military training and equipment" (U.S., Department of State, *Republic of Colombia: Background Notes* [Washington, D.C.: Government Printing Office, November 1970], p. 7).

used unwisely,[3] but they have provided a needed margin of support for a number of development programs that were well conceived and relatively effective, especially during the administration of President Carlos Lleras Restrepo (1966-70). Certainly few Colombians would have wished to dispense altogether with this outside funding, even though it was often decried as inadequate in relation both to Colombia's needs and to the losses allegedly suffered by Colombia through the excessive profits gained by multinational corporations of the industrial nations, their manipulation of the terms of trade, and other methods of foreign economic exploitation. Further controversy has centered on the explicit or merely implied conditions attached to the granting of aid. The pressure of international lending agencies for abrupt devaluations of the Colombian peso was for some years a frequent source of irritation, culminating in a spectacular confrontation in November 1966 between President Lleras Restrepo and the International Monetary Fund. The outcome at that time was that Colombia adopted a gradually depreciating exchange rate—a policy that was chosen independently but nevertheless satisfied the international financial community and that also gave strong impetus to the growth of new export industries to lessen Colombian dependence on coffee.[4]

Despite the 1966 exchange rate crisis, the seriousness of which was exaggerated for domestic political purposes, Colombian negotiations with U.S. or other foreign development and financial sources have on the whole been uneventful. They have not been complicated at any rate by the appearance of major confrontations over foreign direct investment, of which the U.S. share, roughly $800 million,[5] is easily the most important. There is criticism of foreign capital in Colombia, as elsewhere, but the fact that the nation's leading industry, coffee, is almost wholly in native hands tends to lessen the impact of the issue. In recent years, most of the agitation concerning foreign capital has been directed at international petroleum companies engaged in exploration or exploitation of the Colombian subsoil, but the regulation of their status is so complex that

3. See, for example, U.S., Senate, Committee on Foreign Relations, Subcommittee on American Republics Affairs, *Colombia: A Case History of U.S. Aid* (Washington, D.C.: Government Printing Office, 1969), which amounts to a rather formidable indictment of the Colombian program. It should be noted, however, that it refers primarily to events prior to the administration of Carlos Lleras Restrepo, which saw a distinct improvement in the effectiveness of Colombian development policies.

4. Richard L. Maullin, *The Colombia-IMF Disagreement of November–December 1966: An Interpretation of Its Place in Colombian Politics*, Memorardum RM-5314-RC (Santa Monica, Calif.: Rand Corporation, 1967), which can be also found in *Contemporary Inter-American Relations: A Reader in Theory and Issues*, ed. Yale H. Ferguson (Englewood Cliffs, N.J.: Prentice-Hall, 1972), pp. 51-60.

5. Here again estimates vary widely, for the same kind of reasons that apply to "aid" totals. The figure given here is from a U.S. Embassy paper, *Colombia and the United States: A Briefing Paper*, mimeographed (Bogotá, April 1970), which notes that the figure arrived at in a Commerce Department survey was lower.

few Colombians (or foreigners) really understand it; nor does any one company so dominate the field as to provide a single convenient target.[6] The government, for its part, insists that it is duly protecting national interests, and it is fair to say that the question has not truly caught the public imagination. For the rest, new private investments in Colombia are subject to official approval, while profit or other remittances are likewise controlled.[7] Both in regard to oil and in the handling of foreign capital generally, discussion has mainly centered on whether controls are strict enough, not whether such investments should be eliminated entirely.

The Colombian commitment to Latin American integration is also firmly grounded on both economic and political and sentimental considerations, if only because expansion of intraregional trade has been chosen as the primary focus for integrationist activities. However, Colombia grew somewhat disillusioned with the slow progress of the Latin American Free Trade Association (LAFTA), of which she was a cofounder. During the latter part of the 1960s, therefore, Colombian officials devoted their main efforts to launching the Andean Group as a subregional association pledged to the elimination of trade barriers at a faster pace than LAFTA as a whole could achieve. The Andean Group became operational in April 1970, when its first free list went into effect. Since then more periodic reductions in duties and other restrictions on intraregional trade have taken place, while specific member nations have been assigned preferential status for the development of new industries within the bloc. The most troublesome aspect of the integration process, at least for Colombia, proved to be the adoption of a uniform Andean code on foreign investments, designed to encourage their conversion into mixed enterprises and further tighten profit and other controls. The instrument that was drawn up aroused strong opposition from members of the Colombian private sector on the ground that it would unduly restrict capital flow, and partly to by-pass such opposition the administration chose to adopt the investment code in Colombia by executive action instead of presenting it to Congress for approval. The maneuver failed, for the Supreme Court proceeded to rule the method of adoption uncon-

6. Herman J. Mohr, *Economía colombiana: una estructura en crisis* (Bogotá: Tercer Mundo, 1972), pp. 103-37. The chief source of current concern is not the role of foreign capital as such but the failure of production to keep pace with the growth of internal consumption, which raises the prospect that Colombia may become a net petroleum importer. Critics allege, however, that international corporations have been permitted by existing regulations to leave much of the Colombian subsoil as a speculative reserve rather than develop production in line with the nation's needs.

7. Mauricio Solaún and Fernando Cepeda, "Political and Legal Challenges to Foreign Direct Private Investment in Colombia," *Journal of Interamerican Studies and World Affairs* 15, no. 1 (February 1973): 84-89; "Colombia in the Andean Group," *Colombia Today* 8, no. 2 (1973).

stitutional in December 1971. But subsequently the Congress did approve enabling legislation.[8]

Initial efforts by Colombia and her associates to bring Venezuela into the Andean Group ended in disappointment,[9] essentially because of the disparity between Venezuela's high price and wage levels and those of the other members. Venezuela eventually joined the group in February 1973, and many, though by no means all, Colombian entrepreneurs look to a particularly fruitful expansion of trade with their neighbor to the east. However, the negotiations over Venezuelan entry created some incidental irritation on both sides while they lasted. In addition, the same relative affluence that delayed Venezuela's entry into the Andean Group has lured an ever growing number of Colombians to cross the Venezuelan border in search of economic opportunity; the fact that many do so without legal permission creates a problem similar to that of the Mexican "wetback" in the southwestern United States. While Venezuelans complain of unfair competition offered by "undocumented" Colombians in the labor market and tend to assume that the migrants include an excessive number of petty thieves and prostitutes, Colombians in turn decry the abusive treatment to which their compatriots are often subjected in Venezuela by employers and petty officials.[10]

Illegal border crossing is not practiced only by Colombian laborers. Large-scale smuggling in both directions is a traditional industry in the frontier zone and at the same time another international irritant, which the progress of Andean integration will only gradually remove. In addition, the offshore portion of the frontier itself is in dispute. The dispute revolves chiefly about the respective shares of the two countries in the continental shelf underlying the Gulf of Venezuela, which is bordered in part by the Colombian sector of the Guajira Peninsula. The petroleum potential of the area naturally increases the stakes involved. This dispute over the continental shelf is one of various reasons why Colombia has so far refrained (as has Venezuela) from joining the other Latin American countries that flatly claim some sort of 200-mile offshore jurisdiction.

8. Gail Richardson Sherman, "Colombian Political Bases of the Andean Pact Statute on Foreign Capital: National Influences on International Regulation of Foreign Investment," *Journal of Interamerican Studies and World Affairs* 15, no. 1 (February 1973): 102-21; "Colombia: Fully Committed," *Latin America* (London), 6 April 1973; and *Revista del Banco de la República*, 547 (May 1973): 863-80.

9. It is instructive to note that Venezuela had seen fit to resign from the jointly owned Flota Mercante Grancolombiana not long after it was formed in 1946, leaving just Colombia and Ecuador as members; Panama—which is also technically Gran Colombian—never joined (*Colombia Today* 1, no. 9 [October 1966]). This is not to suggest that Venezuela will also prove a transient member of the Andean Group but rather that there are precedents for the difficulties of integrating these neighboring economies.

10. The problem is well discussed in "Revelaciones sobre los indocumentados colombianos: abogado venezolano plantea soluciones al conflicto," *El Espectador* (Bogotá), 12 July 1970.

There is much support for such a position in Colombia. But as the two neighbors cannot even agree on a demarcation of inshore waters (the continental shelf), the Colombian government has feared that any unilateral move to claim control to a greater distance would, among other things, complicate a border settlement with Venezuela, since the eastern border of Colombia's claim would depend upon this settlement. Colombia recognizes that the 200-mile limit is a question of more importance to Venezuela than to Colombia and does not wish to upset Venezuela by acting out of unison with her. Hence, the Colombian position, as at the Third UN Conference on the Law of the Seas (Caracas, 1974), has been to favor an eventual compromise on the 200-mile limit, one in which all nations, including the United States, could join.[11]

The one other American nation whose relations with Colombia present a special problem is Cuba. Colombia suspended formal relations with the Castro regime in 1961, and while insisting on the desirability, in principle, of bringing Cuba back into the American system, the Colombian authorities have shown no real haste to reestablish ties. Such hesitation may well reflect official deference to the views of Washington, but without question it also reflects the fact that Colombia has suffered Cuban intervention in the form of training and subsidizing guerrillas operating in Colombia. Nevertheless, the chances for an eventual rapprochement were improved in 1974 by the election for president of the Liberal party candidate Alfonso López Michelsen, who in the course of his campaign emphasized that he had an open mind to the issue.[12]

HISTORICAL ANTECEDENTS

The recent lack of critical international problems—for even with Venezuela and Cuba there has been no true crisis—is a continuation of what has been more often the rule than the exception in Colombian history. During the period of the wars for independence, Colombia, together with Venezuela, Ecuador, and Panama, formed a single republic (Gran Colombia) and under the Liberator Simón Bolívar assumed a disproportionate share of the continental struggle against Spain. But with the separation of Venezuela and Ecuador in 1829-30, what was left of the union quickly lapsed into a state of international obscurity and isolation that was relieved only by the increasing importance, after the mid-19th century, of

11. Alfredo Vázquez Carrizosa, Colombia y los problemas del mar (Bogotá: Imprenta Nacional, 1971), pp. 154-70, 243-56 et passim.
12. The Liberal candidate, Alfonso López Michelsen, had emphasized during the campaign that he was prepared to take a fresh look at the Cuban question; cf. El Periódico (Bogotá), 1 Feb. 1974.

the Panamanian transit route.[13] Moreover, the isthmus was never a fully integrated portion—politically, economically, or culturally—of Colombian national territory, and in 1903 it was lost for good.

Because of the support given by the United States to Panama's bid for independence in that year, the Panamanian revolt had the further effect of introducing a pronounced chill in relations between Colombia and the leading hemispheric power.[14] But it could not prevent a major narrowing of U.S.-Colombian economic relations over the next few decades, in which Colombia became for the first time a world leader in the export of coffee, with the United States as her principal customer. U.S. private capital also began to enter Colombia in significant amounts through investment in banana production, petroleum, and (notably in the 1920s) the purchase of government bonds.[15] Concurrent with the expansion of economic ties was a gradual thaw in political and diplomatic relations, which had its best known exponent in President Marco Fidel Suárez (1918-21). Suárez proclaimed the "doctrine of the Polar Star," by which he meant that Colombia should look northward, to her powerful English-speaking neighbor, both as an example of social and political democracy and as a partner with whose destinies Colombia was inevitably linked by geographic proximity and economic complementarity.[16] Suárez did not wholly succeed in effecting a rapprochement with the United States, for his efforts in this direction contributed to the domestic political crisis that resulted in his own resignation from office. But the wounds left by the Panama affair were finally healed, at least on the official level, during the following administration, with the ratification of the Thomson-Urrutia Treaty (1922), which awarded Colombia an indemnity of $25 million.[17]

The growth of foreign investment naturally brought new problems of a different sort: bitter wrangling over concession rights claimed by international petroleum companies and resentment in the banana zone over the overwhelming presence of the Boston-based United Fruit Company, which was the object of a bitter and bloody strike in late 1928.[18] Nevertheless, the guiding principle of Colombian foreign relations

13. E. Taylor Parks, *Colombia and the United States, 1765-1934* (Durham, N.C.: Duke University Press, 1935), pp. 219-61, 272-391, et passim; Dwight C. Miner, *The Fight for the Panama Route: The Story of the Spooner Act and the Hay-Herrán Treaty* (New York: Colombia University Press, 1940).

14. Parks, *Colombia and the United States*, pp. 425-39.

15. J. Fred Rippy, *The Capitalists and Colombia* (New York: Alfred A. Knopf, 1931), pp. 123-98; William P. McGreevey, *An Economic History of Colombia, 1845-1930* (Cambridge: At the University Press, 1971), pp. 201-7.

16. Manuel Barrera Parra, ed., *El derecho internacional en los "Sueños de Luciano Pulgar"* (Bogotá: Ministerio de Relaciones Exteriores, 1955), p. 10 ff.

17. Parks, *Colombia and the United States*, pp. 440-57.

18. Miguel Urrutia Montoya, *Historia del sindicalismo en Colombia* (Bogotá: Ediciones Universidad de los Andes, 1969), pp. 128-33.

continued in practice to be something very much like Suárez's concept of the Polar Star, whether or not the same terminology was used, and it was duly reinforced by a warm Colombian response to the Good Neighbor Policy of Franklin D. Roosevelt. In World War II, Colombia's official position was unabashedly pro-U.S. Indeed, the immediate prewar and early wartime years saw the beginning of formal, institutionalized arrangements of military, financial, and technical cooperation with the United States that in their essentials have lasted to the present day.[19]

Relations with the United States were mildly strained in the early postwar period by official hostility in Colombia toward Protestants, including U.S. Protestant missionaries.[20] Yet this was, in considerable part, a mere side effect of the undeclared civil war then raging between a Conservative administration and Colombian Liberals, who happened to include virtually all the nation's Protestants in their ranks. During the same years, moreover, Colombia became the only Latin American state to contribute forces to the UN action in Korea,[21] and she continued to welcome U.S. investment, which for the first time obtained a major foothold in Colombian manufacturing.[22] When the overthrow of the dictatorship of Gustavo Rojas Pinilla in 1957 was followed by the series of Liberal-Conservative coalition governments known as the National Front, a greater cordiality than ever came to characterize official U.S.-Colombian relations. The ruling coalition, for its part, not only received the second contingent of Peace Corps volunteers sent to any foreign country but happily undertook, with mixed success, the task of converting Colombia into a "showcase" of the Alliance for Progress.[23]

The special relationship with the United States that has evolved in the present century has necessarily overshadowed Colombia's relations with Western Europe, which in economic terms had once been far more important. Colombia's relations with the other nations of Latin America, after the days of Simón Bolívar, long amounted to little more than a sentimental solidarity. The main exceptions naturally concerned Colombia's immediate neighbors, with whom there were borders to adjust, other occasional disputes to settle, and in some cases, actual hostilities. The best

19. David Bushnell, *Eduardo Santos and the Good Neighbor, 1938-1942* (Gainesville: University of Florida Press, 1967).

20. For two opposing accounts see Eduardo Ospina, *Las sectas protestantes en Colombia: breve reseña histórica con un estudio especial de la llamada "Persecución religiosa"* (Bogotá: Imprenta Nacional, 1954) and James E. Goff, *The Persecution of Protestant Christians in Colombia, 1948-1958* (Cuernavaca: Centro Intercultural de Documentación, 1968).

21. Russell W. Ramsey, "The Colombian Batallion in Korea and Suez," *Journal of Interamerican Studies and World Affairs* 9, no. 4 (October 1967): 546-50.

22. Alvaro Camacho Guizado, *Capital extranjero: subdesarrollo colombiano* (Bogotá: Punta de Lanza, 1972), pp. 42-43 (tables).

23. Pat M. Holt, *Colombia Today-and Tomorrow* (New York: Frederick A. Praeger, 1964), pp. 132; Robert H. Dix, *Colombia: The Political Dimensions of Change* (New Haven: Yale University Press, 1967), pp. 409-11.

known example is the Leticia conflict of 1932–33, in which a Peruvian irregular force seized but was later forced to evacuate Colombia's narrow foothold on the Amazon River.[24] That was also the last such outbreak. Colombia herself has shown a consistent preference for negotiation and arbitration in resolving difficulties with neighboring countries, and on the whole, peaceful means of settlement have been used.

Colombia likewise emerged sufficiently from her longstanding semi-isolation to take an active part in the organized inter-American system that had begun to function in the late nineteenth century, and after World War I she joined the League of Nations, whose participation in settling the Leticia dispute she subsequently welcomed. Under the leadership of Alberto Lleras Camargo, Colombia was one of the more prominent Latin American participants in the San Francisco conference that created the United Nations. She stood forth both as a last-ditch opponent of the big-power veto, on the ground that world collective security would be better served by greater juridical equality of states, and as one of the nations that insisted most strongly on including specific recognition of the role of regional organizations in the UN Charter.[25] In taking the latter position, of course, Colombia was seeking to safeguard the autonomy of the existing inter-American system, to which she felt an even stronger attachment at this time. It was thus wholly appropriate that the Charter of the present Organization of American States (OAS) was drawn up at the Bogotá conference of 1948 and that the OAS had as its first Secretary General the Colombian Alberto Lleras Camargo. But Colombia has also played a significant role in UN affairs, despite reservations about certain aspects of UN procedure. As already noted, she became the only Latin American nation to contribute to UN forces in Korea. A few years later, she again provided a contingent for the Suez peace-keeping operation.[26]

DOMESTIC INFLUENCES ON FOREIGN POLICY

The outstanding development of the last quarter-century on the Colombian domestic scene is, without question, the phenomenon known simply

24. Bryce Wood, *The United States and Latin American Wars, 1932–1942* (New York: Columbia University Press, 1966), pp. 169–251.

25. John A. Houston, *Latin America in the United Nations* (New York: Carnegie Endowment for International Peace, 1956), pp. 36, 49.

26. Ramsey, "The Colombian Battallion," pp. 549–50. Ramsey properly emphasizes the logical compatibility between participation in both Korea and Suez and Colombia's consistent support of international organizations. Yet Korean participation in particular also reflected Colombia's close relationship with the United States and a much-debated complex of domestic factors, ranging from the desire of the armed forces to modernize their training and equipment to (conceivably) the hope of creating a diversion to the civil strife then raging at home. Nor has Colombia taken part in any more such exercises.

as *la violencia*, which began in the late 1940s as a virtual civil war between
the Liberal and Conservative parties and was largely ended by the early
1960s, despite lingering enclaves of social banditry and leftist guerrilla
activity. Most of the time for at least a large part of the population, life
went on with a remarkable degree of normalcy, but *la violencia* itself,
with its antecedents and aftereffects, strongly colored both the conduct of
national affairs and the content of political debate. It directly affected
foreign affairs, as when Colombia broke relations with the Soviet Union
in 1948, implicitly rebuking the Russians for involvement in domestic
political unrest,[27] or when the National Front regime embraced the
Alliance for Progress with particular enthusiasm because of its hope that
massive external assistance would speed the essential work of national
rehabilitation. At the same time, *la violencia* and its multiple legacy of
problems also tended, over the years, to downgrade the *relative* importance for Colombians of their country's foreign relations.

There are no important pressure groups in Colombia that are significantly concerned with the influencing of foreign policy, except in
the economic sense. Economic trade associations are naturally eager to
make sure that governmental decisions, including those on import/ex-
port regulations and the like, are favorable to their interests; thus, while
generally supporting recent efforts at Andean integration, organizations
of Colombian producers have fought for exceptions in areas where they
feel their competitive position to be weak. These activities, however, form
just one part of normal business lobbying and consultation. A special
case, to be sure, is the *Federación Nacional de Cafeteros*, which is not
merely a growers' association but a semipublic corporation that takes part
in devising and administering official coffee policy. Its spokesmen are
inevitably assigned to the Colombian delegation at the international
coffee conferences, and the federation has its own permanent representatives abroad to promote the Colombian product.[28]

Except for the (Moscow-line) Colombian Communist party, whose
hard-core strength is around 1 percent of the electorate, none of the
political parties or major factions displays an intensive or consistent
interest in international affairs. As institutional entities, they are typically
more concerned with partisan strategy and distribution of spoils than
with the formulation of policy decisions—least of all foreign policy
decisions.[29] However, the dominant leadership of the two traditional

27. Ministerio de Relaciones Exteriores, *Memoria . . . presentada al Congreso Nacional
1948* (Bogotá, 1948), pp. 137–38. No specific charges were made in the note breaking
relations, but it was dated not quite a month after the Bogotá rioting of 9 April 1948, for
which official commentators took pains to blame the Communists. Cf. *Revista Javeriana*
(Bogotá) no. 145 (June 1948), pp. 216–20.
28. Holt, *Colombia Today–and Tomorrow*, pp. 113–19.
29. James L. Payne, *Patterns of Conflict in Colombia* (New Haven: Yale University
Press, 1968), pp. 248–52 et passim.

parties, Liberal and Conservative, has demonstrated a tacit consensus in support of the broadly pro–U.S., pro-Western, and (of late) Latin American integrationist positions adhered to by successive Colombian administrations. Under the National Front system this consensus has hardly been surprising, but it would be necessary to go back to the period of World War II, when Conservatives under the leadership of Laureano Gómez espoused an isolationism with strong anti–U.S. overtones, to find clearcut Liberal-Conservative differences on foreign policy.[30] Gómez's move was, in part, a mere tactic to embarrass the Liberal administration then in power. Certainly, when the Conservatives returned to power in 1946, the policies they pursued in foreign relations were quite in line with those of their Liberal predecessors; and it was Gómez himself, president from 1950 to 53, who ordered Colombian troops to Korea.

A standard complaint of the wartime Conservative opposition, and admittedly of some Liberals as well,[31] was that Colombia failed to receive a fair share of benefits from her cooperation in hemispheric affairs with the United States. The same charge has been made since then on numerous occasions, especially, but by no means exclusively, by political dissidents, with or without listing specific grievances. It forms one current theme of the opposition *Alianza Nacional Popular* (ANAPO), the followers of ex-dictator Rojas Pinilla, which has evolved into a third party of generally populist bent. ANAPO fought the elections of 1974 under a slogan of Colombian-style socialism (*socialismo a la colombiana*). Yet it has failed to offer truly coherent alternatives to existing foreign policy; much less has it gone on record against continued close association with the United States. ANAPO spokesmen merely call for a more "independent" and "nationalistic" approach to that relationship, while waging their struggles primarily along domestic lines.[32] Only the Communists and certain other leftist and revolutionary elements, some operating largely or wholly outside the present system, have demanded a sharp, Cuban-style (or Allende-style) reorientation of Colombian foreign policy.[33]

There is, then, a current of dissatisfaction but little systematic debate on foreign policy issues; under these circumstances a high degree of continuity, at least in the essentials of policy, is easily maintained.

30. Bushnell, *Eduardo Santos*, pp. 24–40, 44–49 et passim.
31. Ibid., pp. 40–43.
32. ANAPO policy positions are generally ignored by the Colombian daily press and also by foreign scholars; but see *Flash* (Bogotá), July 1971, which gives an account of ANAPO's becoming a separate party.
33. Several of these groups, including the Communist party, joined forces as the Union Nacional de Oposición (UNO) to support Hernando Echeverría Mejía for president in 1974. UNO's rhetoric was generally *allendista*, but its disappointing performance cast doubt on its potential to develop into a significant opposition party of the Left. Clearly there is potential support in Colombia for such a party, but whether UNO will develop into one remains unclear.

Detailed implementation is entrusted, in principle, to the Ministry of
Foreign Relations—which ranks higher in prestige than in budgetary
priority—and to a foreign service that constitutes a professional diplomatic and consular corps on paper but is less than fully professional in
practice. In particular, the theoretical admission standards and procedures have often been by-passed in obtaining entry to the corps. Because
of the pervasive economic content of Colombian foreign policy, actual
responsibility is shared to a significant extent with the Ministries of
Finance and Development and with a number of semiautonomous
economic agencies, all of which have increasingly attracted their own
corps of able young technocrats. At the same time, however, the Foreign
Ministry itself has an important subsidiary role in the field of church-state
relations, which are traditionally close in Colombia and are governed by a
formal concordat with the Vatican. The post of ambassador to the Holy
See is thus a key assignment in the Colombian diplomatic service, and in
recent years the preparation of a revised concordat—finally presented to
Congress in 1973—figured prominently among the Foreign Ministry's
concerns.[34]

COLOMBIAN PERSPECTIVES ON THE
OUTSIDE WORLD

The fundamental consistency of Colombian foreign policy over the last
half-century derives in large part from its being firmly based on the views
and interests of the interlocking elite groups that have dominated the
country's political and economic life. Scholars may disagree as to the
precise extent of structural openness and mobility within Colombian
society, but the actual conduct of affairs has remained in the hands of a
relatively small though expanding minority. And, with the inevitable
exceptions, that ruling sector has willingly accepted a Colombian role on
the world scene that in one way or another meets the central requirement
defined years ago by Marco Fidel Suárez, as the need to look always
toward the North.

   To Colombian leaders the necessity of looking northward to the
United States has been virtually self-evident, whether the necessity is faced
with enthusiasm, resignation, or more likely, a mixture of both. Strategically, these leaders have commonly assumed that the United States would
look with extreme displeasure, or worse, on any overtly hostile regime
facing the southern flank of the Panama Canal. Economically, they have
taken to heart the fact that the United States is the leading customer for
their leading export and, while always on the alert for new markets, they

34. A group of articles on and the text of the new concordat can be found in *Revista
Javeriana*, no. 398 (September 1973), pp. 218-48, 271-78.

have been unable to conceive of any wholly practical alternative to that primary dependence. (For one thing, Russians drink tea.) In import trade, dependence on the United States has been less pronounced, but the United States is still the leading supplier and one that is familiar, conveniently near at hand, and clearly more reliable in any eventual world crisis than extrahemispheric powers.[35]

Capital investment constitutes another material linkage between the Colombian establishment and the United States. Although foreign firms are often an irritant, an influential circle of Colombians (some also active in politics) has a personal stake in the well-being of wholly or partially U.S.–owned businesses, in the roles of local partners, managerial employees, legal representatives, suppliers, and the like. The Colombian government, for its part, looks upon U.S. private enterprise as an auxiliary source of funding for national economic development. It counts even more heavily, of course, on U.S. public funds, whether channeled directly or through multilateral agencies; this source of financing is particularly welcome to well-to-do Colombians, since it relieves some of the pressure to raise internal taxes. But the web of interests and associations tying upper- and middle-class Colombians to the United States goes farther than this. New York and Miami are regular destinations for vacation and shopping trips, and sons and daughters going abroad for an education more often go to the United States than to Europe. Some never return, or come home only for visits, thus contributing to one of Latin America's worst cases of brain drain. Nor is it just trained professionals who emigrate. Thousands of servant girls, technicians, and petty bureaucrats also dream of the opportunities to be had in the affluent United States, and thousands do get there.

Finally, it can be said that a majority of upper- and middle-class Colombians, certainly including the leaders of government, still look in some sense to the United States as the appointed leader of the free world. They may not like everything about the United States, but they like Marxism less, and as the "haves" of a still underdeveloped society they know they have much to lose. To what extent the lower-class majority shares this attitude is difficult to assess, though purely uncritical admiration for the United States is no doubt more common at the lower than the upper levels of society; but the lower class does not decide Colombian foreign policy.

In any case, frank acceptance of U.S. leadership, together with the feeling of historic and cultural solidarity toward other Latin Americans, readily accounts for Colombia's firm support of the organized inter-American system. To be sure, from the Colombian standpoint the greatest

35. J. Kamal Dow, *Colombia's Foreign Trade and Economic Integration in Latin America* (Gainesville: University of Florida Press, 1971), p. 55 ff.

current value of that system is to be found in the role of the OAS and its component or related institutions as administrative and disbursing agents for technical aid and development programs ultimately dependent on U.S. support. As a regional mechanism for the settlement of disputes, the OAS lost prestige in Colombia as elsewhere by its ineffectiveness vis-à-vis the Cuban problem, although Colombia is not prepared to write off the OAS altogether in that capacity. In the Dominican crisis of 1965, while Colombia formally condemned the initial U.S. intervention, she then gave approval, with sincere relief, to the multilateral OAS effort that followed.[36] (In private, official opinion was even less critical of the U.S. action than public statements suggested; but nonofficial opinion was no doubt harsher to the United States than official public statements.) And more recently, in 1973, Colombia greeted Peruvian and other proposals for radical restructuring of the OAS, or even creation of a purely Latin American hemispheric organization, with conspicuous lack of enthusiasm.

Within the Latin American bloc as such, contemporary Colombia has not claimed a position of active leadership, although she has at times exercised leadership on an ad hoc basis. In pre-*violencia* days, when Colombia was widely and sometimes inaccurately admired as one of Latin America's model democracies, there were Colombians who liked to think of their nation as a moral power, setting an example in Latin America of respect for both domestic and international law.[37] *La violencia*, naturally, was rather hard on this kind of self-image. Yet, traces of it remain or have been revived—for example, the Colombian feeling of superiority toward Latin American military dictatorships, which is conventional and widespread even if not quite unanimous.

While Colombian identification with Latin America as a whole is above all sentimental and theoretical, particularly in view of the slow progress of LAFTA, it becomes more intense where the Andean Group is concerned, for there it is reinforced by expectations of economic benefit and by conscious official policy. A still higher level of identification exists with other members of the Gran Colombian bloc, which includes those states carved out of what had been Bolívar's great republic. With respect to Venezuela, however, there are also countercurrents. Venezuela's slowness in joining the Andean Group has already been noted, as have other specific sources of tension. Clearly, too, Venezuela's affluence inspires envy, often thinly masked by an affectation of disdain for Venezuelan *nouveaux riches*. But these and other problems do not basically alter Colombia's desire to live in peace and friendship with her wealthy

36. Ministerio de Relaciones Exteriores, *Memoria . . . julio de 1964 a junio de 1965* (Bogotá, 1966), pp. 16–17, 126–42.
37. Cf. German Arciniégas, *The State of Latin America* (New York: Alfred A. Knopf, 1952), p. 154.

neighbor, paying common obeisance to the memory of the Liberator Simón Bolívar and gladly accepting whatever portion of Venezuelan prosperity trickles onto Colombian soil.

Colombian attitudes toward the nations of Western Europe are fundamentally similar in kind, if not intensity, to the attitudes that prevail toward the United States, just as the underlying relationships of trade and aid, investment, travel, and study are also comparable. One added feature, of course, is the special cultural affinity felt by many Colombians for the former mother country, Spain, and to a lesser extent for the other Latin nations of Europe. For the rest, since relations with Europe are quantitatively less significant than those with the United States and since the European presence in Colombia is not so pervasive, less thought is given to the European nations from day to day. As a result, while in principle a Colombian may complain about the treatment that developed industrial nations generally accord to developing nations such as his own, the one industrial nation that always comes to mind is the United States, which consequently must bear the guilt of Western Europe as well as her own. This is so despite the existence of some specific grievances against European trade practices, such as high tariffs charged on Colombian coffee (as against duty-free entry into the United States) and the outright preference demanded by France for the coffee and other products of her ex-colonies.[38]

Consciously or unconsciously, Colombia welcomes economic and other ties with Western Europe, not only for their own sake but as a means of lessening her relative dependence on the United States. Most, though not quite all, Colombians have come to welcome ties with Eastern Europe, including the Soviet Union, for a rather similar combination of reasons. Formal reestablishment of diplomatic or consular relations with Soviet Russia and the nations of the Soviet bloc dates only from the Lleras Restrepo administration. The prospect of reopening a Soviet embassy in Bogotá was then greeted with strong misgivings on the part of influential Conservatives, including former President Mariano Ospina Pérez, who had taken the step of breaking with Moscow in 1948.[39] Critics feared that regular relations with the Soviets would promote domestic subversion, and they cast doubt on the commercial advantages that were widely advertised in justification of the move. As things turned out, a definite increase in trade with the Soviet bloc did occur, much of it involving the exchange of coffee for industrial goods that Colombians would normally

38. Cf. Enrique Caballero, *Historia económica de Colombia*, 2d ed. (Bogotá: n.p., 1971), pp. 245–46.

39. *El País* (Cali), 20 Jan. 1968, pp. 1, 20; 23 Jan. 1968, p. 17. With Czechoslovakia, at least, consular relations had existed even earlier. The *Memoria* of the Ministry of Foreign Relations records year by year the renewal of formal relations with other Soviet bloc countries.

have preferred to buy in the West.[40] But administration spokesmen were careful not to justify their opening to the East purely in economic terms. They emphasized that no nation could presume to be an independent and self-respecting member of the world community without having representation in major capitals such as Moscow, both to observe developments directly and to make sure that its own views were heard.[41] It was even hinted that precisely by establishing diplomatic relations Colombia would be better able to induce the Soviets to restrain Fidel Castro and the pro-Communist guerrillas on Colombian soil.

Although the reasons given for diplomatic initiatives in Eastern Europe might well have justified overtures to Peking, the political uncertainties in that direction were even greater and prospective coffee sales much less, to say nothing of the complication posed by a preexisting relationship with Taiwan. Over the years, Colombia generally followed the lead of the United States on the question of Chinese membership in the United Nations, though in the end she abstained on the definitive vote for seating Peking and expelling Nationalist China.[42] Even before that outcome, a Colombian team had accompanied U.S. sportsmen to China in the memorable inauguration of "ping-pong diplomacy" in April 1971,[43] but Colombia soon fell behind the pace set by the United States in wooing mainland China. Nor has the China question been at any time a truly live issue, if only because Asia as such does not loom large in the Colombian view of the world. Self-styled Maoists wield remarkable and disproportionate influence at the level of university student politics, but the number of Colombians who seriously view the Chinese revolution as either a model or a menace is exceedingly small. Only Japan constitutes a significant Asian trade partner—but one that sells substantially more than she buys. (The Japanese, unfortunately, also drink tea.) Even the protracted struggle in Vietnam aroused little genuine interest. It was mainly regarded as one more example of U.S. shortcomings to be gently chided among friends or loudly denounced in student demonstrations.

Neither does Africa loom large to Bogotá or Bucaramanga or even Cartagena. She provides an occasional crisis headline in the daily press but otherwise is mainly important as a rival producer of coffee, whose long-term competitive threat was not entirely overcome by common adherence to the International Coffee Agreement. Although a substantial minority of the Colombian population is of pure or mixed African descent, concentrated largely in the coastal regions, that minority has not yet developed either a self-assertive cult of *négritude* or a special sense of identification with the new states of the African homeland.

    40. "Colombian Foreign Trade, 1960–1970," *Colombia Today* 7, no. 1 (1972).
    41. Ministerio de Relaciones Exteriores, *Memoria . . . agosto 1967-julio 1968* (Bogotá, 1968), pp. ix–xi.
    42. *El Espectador*, 27 Oct. 1971.
    43. Ibid., 24 April 1971.

The Afro-Asian problems that form so large a part of the workload of the United Nations naturally call for decisions to be made and votes cast in the name of Colombia, but more often than not she takes the same basic position as the United States, a position that does not exclude the possibility of occasional differences in both emphasis and detail. Cynics at home and abroad would attribute this policy to Colombia's status as a mere Yankee satellite, and there can be no doubt that a decent regard for the opinions of the U.S. State Department does play some part. But neither is there reason to doubt that Colombians, or more specifically those entrusted with Colombian foreign policy, actually share with the United States an ultimate preference for the goals and values of bourgeois democracy and a world order compatible with the same. In any case, Colombia has been at all times a strong supporter of the concept of peace through collective security as embodied in the United Nations itself. Colombian spokesmen would merely add, quite frankly, that their primary interest in the United Nations today is based on its potential for assisting the economic development of the Third World. This wholly realistic approach obviously parallels the current attitude toward the OAS and is fully in line with the central mission of Colombian foreign policy, which is not to engage in political diplomacy of the traditional sort but to deal, all too often from a position of relative weakness, with those external factors that can either hamper or promote domestic economic growth and social stability.

BIBLIOGRAPHICAL NOTE

The two standard surveys of Colombian foreign relations are Germán Cavelier, *La política internacional de Colombia*, 2d ed., 4 vols. (Bogotá: Editorial Iqueima, 1959) and Raimundo Rivas, *Historia diplomática de Colombia (1810-1934)* (Bogotá: Imprenta Nacional, 1961). Unfortunately, Cavelier gives only fragmentary coverage of the period since 1934, and Rivas does not cover it at all; the study by E. Taylor Parks, *Colombia and the United States* (Durham, N.C.: Duke University Press, 1934), has similar chronological limitations. On the late 1930s and early 1940s one can consult David Bushnell, *Eduardo Santos and the Good Neighbor, 1938-1942* (Gainesville: University of Florida Press, 1967); and for economic relations there is not only Seymour W. Wurfel, *Foreign Enterprise in Colombia: Laws and Policies* (Chapel Hill: University of North Carolina Press, 1965), and J. Kamal Dow, *Colombia's Foreign Trade and Economic Integration in Latin America* (Gainesville: University of Florida Press, 1971), but also the general economic literature, which is much more copious than that dealing with foreign affairs specifically. See, for example, International Bank for Reconstruction and Development, *Economic Growth of Colombia: Problems and Prospects* (Baltimore: Johns Hopkins University Press, 1972). See also, for a collection of Colombian indictments and analyses of "external dependency," Rodrigo Parra Sandoval, ed., *La dependencia externa y el desarrollo político de Colombia* (Bogotá: Imprenta Nacional, 1970).

In view of the almost complete lack of larger works by either Colombian or foreign scholars dealing with Colombian foreign policy over the past forty years, one should further consult the scattered professional articles and special reports that have appeared on limited topics, of which a sampling of titles will be found in the footnotes; the newspaper and periodical press; and of course the Colombian official publications. Basic among the latter, for both summary of events and publication of key documents, is the annual *Memoria* of the Ministry of Foreign Relations. Of special interest for economic relations is the monthly review *Colombia Today*, published in New York by the Colombia Information Service. And a good source on maritime problems, including the entire question of offshore jurisdiction and the dispute with Venezuela over the continental shelf, is the volume of text and documents published by Foreign Minister Alfredo Vázquez Carrizosa, *Colombia y los problemas del mar* (Bogotá: Imprenta Nacional, 1971).

20/Sheldon B. Liss
Venezuela

When Alonso de Ojeda reached Lake Maracaibo in 1499 the houses he sighted built on posts over the water reputedly caused his shipmate Amerigo Vespucci to call the area Venezuela, or "little Venice." Hardly could they have envisioned that this bucolic region (with a 1,750 mile Atlantic and Caribbean coastline) by the 1970s would be an ethnically mixed nation with a population exceeding ten million. From the sixteenth century onward foreigners continued to be intrigued by the region, particularly by its enormous natural resources. Today foreign capital dominates the economy of oil-rich Venezuela, poverty afflicts 40 percent of her people, and the government pursues a foreign policy ostensibly predicated upon the need to maintain sovereignty, sell oil abroad, and keep the peace at home.[1]

MAJOR FOREIGN POLICY
PROBLEMS AND OBJECTIVES

Since Venezuelan independence was declared in 1810 the country has experienced only limited democracy. Government has been exercised by an oligarchy dominated by a president, sometimes self-proclaimed, who has usually made decisions concerning foreign policy. Domestic issues have been the primary governmental concern, yet national income has depended on customs revenues and exports and thus on economic relations with other countries and their citizens. Funds from abroad, largely from European investors, financed nineteenth-century economic development. A strategic position vis-à-vis the Caribbean and the Panama Canal, plus the growth of the petroleum industry after World War I, brought Venezuela into the modern world. Today petroleum and iron ore exports account for approximately 90 percent of foreign exchange earnings. This export economy is primarily linked to and dependent upon relations with Canada, Great Britain, the Netherlands, the United States, and West Germany.

Venezuelan governments have shown the desire to further both national interest and international accord through membership in the United

1. This chapter is a microcosm of a study based upon extensive research by the author. It is a synthesis of many secondary works and interviews conducted with persons knowledgeable in areas where written records are inadequate or do not exist. It includes statements reflecting points of view substantiated by evidence precluded from inclusion here by space restrictions, but which should appear in the author's forthcoming book on the international relations of Venezuela.

Nations, the Organization of American States (OAS), the Inter-American Development Bank (IADB), the International Monetary Fund (IMF), the International Bank for Reconstruction and Development (IBRD), and the Organization of Petroleum Exporting Countries (OPEC).

Both within and outside these organizations Venezuela is confronted by foreign relations problems essentially economic in nature. She seeks favor with foreign powers in order to attract investment capital, to increase markets for her products, and to add to her foreign exchange reserves; while simultaneously trying not to create the impression, internally or internationally, of having "sold out" to alien interests by permitting foreign control of her territory and subsoil resources. In the petroleum industry, where she is the world's third ranking exporter and producer, Venezuela must combat such difficulties as U.S. restrictions on foreign imports. At the same time, her government has to devise ways of exercising greater control over the pricing and marketing of petroleum by foreign (mainly British, Dutch, and U.S.) producers. Since Venezuela's output of petroleum is not keeping pace with that of the rest of the world,[2] foreign investors are permitted to help build other sectors of her economy. The government wishes to decrease dependence upon outsiders and accomplish diversification by joint investment with foreign capital in companies outside the petroleum industries. It hopes these actions will reduce internal antiforeign sentiment.

Venezuela has also been enmeshed in a struggle to curtail scattered Castro-inspired insurgency and ideological subversion, which the government feels impedes its ability to foster institutions and conditions for rapid economic and social development. The government also handles persistent problems along the Colombia and Guyana borders,[3] and encounters constant pressure from increasingly vocal groups, identified on subsequent pages, for their own greater participation in the formulation of foreign policy. In the broader context, Venezuela expresses concern for more hemispheric and regional accord, for maintaining sovereignty through building a recognized corpus of international law, and for increasing the jurisdiction and enhancing the efficacy of the International Court of Justice in order to resolve conflicts such as the long-standing one regarding the extension of territorial waters. Yet in reality she is sometimes reluctant to appear to cede sovereignty to international arbitral authorities, as evidenced by her current refusal to accept Colombia's proposal to submit the dispute over the potentially oil-rich territorial waters in the Gulf of Venezuela to the International Court of Justice.

2. Venezuela's share of world production dropped from 15 percent in 1957 to 10 percent in 1967 when she was still the world's leading petroleum exporter. During the same period her share of world exports dropped from 37 to 18 percent.

3 Formerly British Guiana, known as Guyana since independence from Great Britain on 26 May 1966.

NINETEENTH-CENTURY BACKGROUND

Venezuelan diplomacy began when Francisco de Miranda sought funds in Europe to finance an independence movement. Simón Bolívar, pleading the case of all Spanish America, followed him to London, to become known as the "Ambassador of America." Beset by internecine warfare during the first century of independence, Venezuela largely neglected foreign political affairs. To handle international crises President José Antonio Páez in 1830 created an Office of Foreign Relations in the Ministry of Finance. One of its primary functions was to encourage trade by establishing diplomatic ties with other nations. Early Venezuelan diplomatic practices generally included recognition of newly created republican governments, granting of diplomatic asylum and immunity, respect of neutral rights, and protection of the life and property of aliens. Under the Conservative oligarchy (1830–48) the country was confronted with few diplomatic conundrums, foreign businessmen were protected, and international obligations were honored.

The first U.S. chargé d'affaires arrived in Venezuela in 1835. Claims registered by U.S. citizens against private and public interests in Venezuela plagued relations between the two republics for the next half century, causing an American diplomat in Caracas to remark in 1844: "I greatly fear that these claims never can be fairly and equitably adjusted without a resort to coercive measures on the part of the United States."[4] That prophecy proved valid.

Beginning with the Liberal regime of 1848, for over half a century Venezuela refused to settle any claims arising out of property damages suffered during frequent civil strife. When the fundless government declared a moratorium on payments due a British bank in 1848, England dispatched warships to La Guaira to force remittance, a procedure subsequently followed by other creditor nations. Thereafter, fearing such intervention, Venezuela sought Latin American agreement not to recognize a foreign nation's right to forcefully extract debt payments. Throughout the 1850s and 1860s conflicts with France, Holland, and Spain led to futile attempts by Venezuela to get the other Latin American nations to agree to a treaty against this kind of European intrusion. Meanwhile, Great Britain replaced Spain as the dominant economic power in Venezuela.

THE TWENTIETH CENTURY

Subsequently, under the despotic Cipriano Castro (1899–1908), Venezuela ran afoul of Belgium, France, Great Britain, Italy, Mexico, the Nether-

---

4. Allen A. Hall, chargé d'affaires, to John C. Calhoun, 27 June 1844, Record Group 59, "Diplomatic Dispatches, Venezuela," vol. 2, no. 36, National Archives, Washington, D.C.

lands, Spain, Sweden, Norway, and the United States, all of whom pressed claims on behalf of those of their nationals who had suffered personal and property damage during Venezuela's frequent periods of internal disorder. Foreign governments found it difficult to deal with Castro. To hasten claims payments, Germany, Britain, and Italy in late 1902 and early 1903 established a formal blockade of the Venezuelan coast. President Theodore Roosevelt, fearing that such international action would seriously breach the Monroe Doctrine, convinced Venezuela to submit the claims to arbitration, which succeeded because of substantial U.S. assistance. Washington was satisfied, as Secretary of State Elihu Root observed, that "the Monroe Doctrine was stronger than ever, and the United States stood better than ever before with the South American Republics."[5] Yet, throughout Latin America at the turn of the twentieth century, statements were made indicating increased fear of U.S. involvement in internal and external politics.

In both Latin America and the United States a general consensus held that Castro would continue to find in the Monroe Doctrine a refuge from European attempts to use force to collect debts. But Castro's policy of dependence on U.S. protection foundered when Washington broke relations in 1908 over claims disregarded by Caracas. Cipriano Castro was not ignorant of the principles of international relations. He simply preferred to overlook them, relying instead on Venezuela's image as a weak nation. His only statement of foreign policy, known as *la Doctrina Castro*, never proved to be anything more than a bombastic assertion advocating the reunification of Gran Colombia under a single leader—himself.

Assuming the presidency in late 1908, Juan Vicente Gómez immediately stated an intention to settle outstanding claims. Gómez feared such armed intervention as was occurring in neighboring Caribbean nations with debt problems, and he quickly restored relations with the United States, trying until his death in 1935 to avoid international incidents. He greatly raised Venezuelan prestige internationally by seeking advice from able ministers and by advocating hemispheric peace. The opening of the Panama Canal in 1914 increased Venezuelan trade by giving Venezuela access to the Pacific coast. At the same time, the growth of her world trade led to the expansion of her diplomatic and consular corps and to the establishment of permanent legations in Caracas by other Latin American nations.

Soon after the arrival of a German military mission in 1912 Venezuelan troops were goose-stepping through the streets of Caracas in Prussian-style uniforms and spiked helmets. Gómez, who had previously dressed like Teddy Roosevelt on safari, now adopted a uniform like that of the Kaiser. Prior to and during World War I, Germany desired a foothold in America.

5. Statement made to Herbert W. Bowen, U.S. Minister to Venezuela, who was instrumental in solving the claims problems (Herbert W. Bowen, *Recollections Diplomatic and Undiplomatic* [New York: Grafton Press, 1926], p. 275).

Yet despite Gómez's obvious predilection and Venezuelan indebtedness to Germany, Venezuela remained neutral during that conflict. Neutrality primarily benefited the Allies who utilized Venezuelan resources. After the war the dictatorship continued under Gómez, and the petroleum industry developed. Foreign policy was based on a primary concern with increasing domestic production of crude oil for export. Venezuela's economic dependence began to shift from Great Britain to the United States, and the Ministry of Foreign Relations functioned largely as a commercial liaison office. The years between the two world wars were marked by few foreign entanglements other than occasional border clashes and agitation induced by disenchanted anti-Gómez exiles. From Colombia, Venezuelan exiles fomented revolution, frequently straining relations between the two neighbors. In postrevolutionary Mexico Venezuelan exiles also plotted and won, as a prime mover to their cause, the noted educator José Vasconcelos, among others. So vitriolic became the rhetoric emanating from Mexico that relations between the two countries were suspended for a decade (1923–33). Simultaneously, Venezuelan exiles in New York tried and failed to gain anti-Gómez support from the U.S. government.

Undoubtedly, the greatest achievement of Gómez, in accord with his desire to be known as the "founder of peace," was the growth of international esteem for Venezuela. In this pursuit, as early as 1928, the Venezuelan government expressed a desire to see certain differences between Bolivia and Paraguay settled; later it used considerable diplomatic persuasion to try to terminate the Chaco War between those two nations. Venezuela also signed both the Kellogg-Briand Pact of 1928 and the (Saavedra Lamas) Anti-War Treaty of Non-Aggression and Conciliation of 1933.

When international tension mounted in the 1930s Venezuela was determined not to become directly involved in a global conflict. In 1937 she established an Office of Inter-American Relations in order to maintain peace, retain existing markets, and locate new ones. The government also supported continental security plans and voiced disapproval of any potential aggression against nearby European possessions in the Guianas and Caribbean islands. Throughout most of World War II she remained technically neutral but did not maintain diplomatic relations with the Axis. Her greatest fear, sabotage of the oil fields, never materialized; but Nazi submarines sank a few Venezuelan tankers. The war strengthened Venezuelan ties with Colombia, as frontier cooperation led to the settlement of the century-old boundary disputes discussed in the next section. U.S. military missions provided technical advice, and American vessels patrolled the Venezuelan coast. As the conflict neared its climax Venezuela declared war on Germany and Japan, in February 1945, and nationalized the property of their citizens. In the final analysis, Venezuela's principal wartime contribution was to supply petroleum to the Allies, a trade from which the government profited immensely.

By 1945 Venezuela had certain firmly established foreign policies. The government usually opposed the idea of a standing hemispheric peace-keeping force, considering diplomatic dialogue superior to military might. To avoid antagonizing foreign governments, it generally practiced a policy of recognizing de facto regimes. The Monroe Doctrine was accepted by Caracas when advantageous to national interests, but it was also resented as an usurpation of Venezuelan sovereignty when invoked unilaterally by the United States. Foreigners were prohibited from participating in politics but otherwise enjoyed equal rights with nationals. The country supported the Calvo and Drago Doctrines,[6] both of which in principle opposed intervention in the affairs of other nations.

More recently, President Rómulo Betancourt (1959–64) has contended that intervention might be necessary to impose democracy and that nonintervention was designed to protect legitimate and popular governments, not dictatorships. Venezuela, in an extension of the Tobar Doctrine,[7] urged OAS intervention under the Inter-American Treaty of Reciprocal Assistance against any regime maintained by force, averring that it was nonsensical to condemn European and Asiatic totalitarianism and permit it in the Americas. In accordance with this Betancourt doctrine Venezuela withheld or withdrew recognition from Argentina, Bolivia, Brazil, Cuba, the Dominican Republic, Ecuador, Guatemala, Honduras, Panama, and Peru. The most noteworthy application of the Betancourt doctrine followed the 1960 assassination attempt on President Betancourt's life by agents of Dominican strongman Rafael Trujillo, who had waged a personal vendetta against the Venezuelan president. Although Venezuela was successful in gaining OAS sanctions against the Dominican Republic, she did not get the OAS to adopt the Betancourt doctrine in the full sense of active intervention to overthrow an authoritarian regime. Leftists and rightists in Latin America still regarded the Betancourt doctrine as a dangerous interventionist policy that exceeded the provisions of the Rio Treaty. President Rafael Caldera (COPEI party) (1969–74) subsequently renounced the doctrine in 1969, announcing a return to the principle of recognition of all de facto regimes, regardless of origin or ideology.

6. In 1868 Argentine jurist Carlos Calvo stated that sovereignty is inviolable and that resident aliens do not have the right to have their own governments intervene on their behalf. In 1902 Argentina's foreign minister, Luis M. Drago, almost restated Calvo's ideas, declaring that public debt cannot occasion armed intervention or occupation of American territory. This concept was written into the Hague Conventions in 1907 in the form of the Porter Resolutions, which afforded it the weight of international law. Now the "Calvo Clause" is inserted for self-protection in all Venezuelan contracts with foreigners.

7. Named for Ecuadorian diplomat Carlos R. Tobar, who in 1907 wrote that new governments established by revolutions should not be recognized until sanctioned by free elections.

As of late 1974 a new controversy had developed over nationalization of the petroleum holdings—an action that was to occur under previous arrangements when the concessions (98 percent foreign owned) expired in 1983 and 1984. A Hydrocarbons Reversion Law, designed to prevent the oil companies from removing their capital and equipment and from phasing out their dependence on Venezuelan oil as their control over their Venezuelan properties became attenuated, was announced in 1971. Foreign firms, expecting ultimately to lose their concessions, were not shocked by the legislation; but they resented having to maintain their facilities and keep up production until the actual reversions took place. By this law the Caldera administration cleverly warned foreign companies well in advance to negotiate settlements acceptable to both parties. However, by 1972 the oil companies were already complaining about decreasing profits attributable to petroleum from the Middle East underselling their product and to unilateral price setting by the Venezuelan government, which was receiving seventy-seven cents on every dollar of oil company profit in the form of taxes or royalties. Caracas was still talking about "selective participation" while firms like the Creole Petroleum Corporation, a subsidiary of Standard Oil of New Jersey, protested and simultaneously hoped for some partnership arrangement in the 1980s when the Hydrocarbons Law is effected. In early 1974 newly elected President Carlos Andrés Pérez announced that oil holdings would revert to the nation within two years. Despite foreign protests the nationalization decision appeared to be irreversible.

BOUNDARY AND BORDER PROBLEMS: OLD AND NEW

Simón Bolívar's dream of a United States of Spanish America was only partially and briefly fulfilled by the unification from 1822 to 1830 of the present nations of Colombia,[8] Ecuador, and Venezuela as Gran Colombia. Its breakup left Venezuela with imprecise limits, so boundary problems with bordering Colombia, Brazil, and British Guiana rapidly became an important part of Venezuelan diplomacy. Although involved in boundary conflicts and clashes over the years, Venezuela is the only South American country never to have gone to war with a neighbor. After Gran Colombia was dissolved, the problem arose of demarcating limits with Colombia. In addition, a peace treaty with Spain in 1845 that recognized Venezuela's sovereignty over what formerly had been the captaincy-general of Caracas unfortunately did not define boundaries, leaving multiple disputes to future generations.

8. Panama was then part of Colombia.

Although during President Antonio Guzmán Blanco's several terms of office (between 1870 and 1888) pursuing foreign affairs was secondary to furthering national identity and internal integration, continuing border disputes strained relations with Colombia. The nations agreed in 1881 to let the king of Spain arbitrate their boundary differences. In 1894 they reached accord over the disputed territory and established a joint commission to work out future points of disagreement—most of which were settled by the 1940s.

The problem of the boundary with British Guiana, which originated in the colonial era, became significant in the 1890s. The disputed region, formerly owned by the Netherlands, had been acquired by Great Britain in 1814. After independence, Venezuela claimed the Essequibo River as her eastern boundary. Seeking to validate a border considerably west of that waterway, Britain commissioned the German geographer Robert Schomburgk, in 1841, to ascertain that line. He included considerable territory claimed by Venezuela in establishing this line at a point at the mouth of the Orinoco River. After years of squabbling over this stretch of jungle, Venezuela in 1887 broke relations with Great Britain. In 1895 the United States, responding to a Venezuelan appeal, announced that British incursions in the Orinoco area violated the Monroe Doctrine. Great Britain contended that the Monroe Doctrine was irrelevant in a controversy involving the frontier of a British possession, one which had belonged to England before Venezuela became a republic, and implied that the doctrine had little validity in international law.

Regarding the conflict, historian Dexter Perkings wrote, "Never perhaps, was the United States less actuated by economic gain or territorial ambition, or even by a sense of danger to its security, than in the Venezuela controversy."[9] However, historian Walter La Feber has refuted Perkins, arguing convincingly that the policy of Grover Cleveland was a direct response to British economic encroachment in an area that had become more vital to the United States since the severe depression of 1893. La Feber has demonstrated that Yankee businessmen wanted to keep British competition out of the Orinoco, which they considered essential to the expansion of trade into South America's interior.[10] Nevertheless, the British agreed to arbitation, leading some observers to perceive the growing acceptance of the Monroe Doctrine and the "paramount interest" of the United States in the area. However, Venezuela was not content with the arbitral award of 1899 and the dispute continued into the twentieth century.

9. Dexter Perkins, *A History of the Monroe Doctrine* (Boston: Little, Brown & Co., 1963), p. 190.
10. Walter La Feber, "The Background of Cleveland's Venezuelan Policy: A Reinterpretation," *American Historical Review* 66, no. 4 (July 1961): 947. In 1896 President Cleveland stated to a friend that the Venezuelan situation was not a foreign problem, but a domestic matter (ibid., p. 966).

Considerable tension has emanated from the protracted boundary controversy with Guyana that followed. The Guyanese contend that Caracas emphasized the dispute to stimulate nationalism and keep the military occupied and out of politics. In 1965 Venezuela, British Guiana, and Great Britain agreed to seek a solution. Accord was reached in the Port-of-Spain Protocol of June 1970 when Venezuela and Guyana consented to accept the status quo for at least twelve years. Whether viewed as a moratorium or a return to the status quo, the agreement made Venezuela appear magnanimous and somewhat eased the minds of the Guyanese, who had feared they might lose over two thirds of their territory.

Currently a perplexing smuggling problem exists along the Colombian-Venezuelan border. Considerable contraband from Colombia, primarily cattle and coffee, enters Venezuela. The illegal flow of Colombians into Venezuela is also a cause for concern, since the *indocumentados* compete with Venezuelans for jobs. Venezuela claims that these people are encouraged to emigrate by the Colombian government to redue unemployment, a charge denied by Bogotá. Nevertheless, by the 1970s an estimated half-million Colombians resided illegally in Venezuela and sent home large amounts of money, helping offset their nation's unfavorable balance of trade with Venezuela. While invective and mutual recriminations continue between the nations, especially at the provincial level, the governments in Caracas and Bogotá are striving to settle the conflict amicably. From time to time they also attempt to conclude the aforementioned dispute over the continental shelf of the Gulf of Venezuela.

Venezuela's border relations with her largest neighbor, Brazil, whom she sometimes views as a potentially dangerous "collosus of the South," have been and are excellent; a boundary commission composed of Venezuelans and Brazilians has been set up to handle any difficulties that may arise. The Office of Frontiers in Venezuela's Ministry of Foreign Relations works constantly to define boundaries and eliminate friction with Colombia, Brazil, and Guyana.

RECENT RELATIONS WITH THE UNITED STATES

The twentieth century saw a shift in commerce and cultural influence away from Europe and to the United States, which has traditionally assumed a paternalistic attitude towards Venezuela. Despite nationalist denials, Yankee influence is vast, and New York fashions, aggressive business methods, and *beisbol* ("baseball") are part of the life style. In foreign relations, too, the U.S. lead has frequently been followed.

Since 1945 Venezuelan–U.S. relations have been extremely cordial. During the corrupt Marcos Pérez Jiménez era (1952–58) the two nations enjoyed close economic ties, and the United States supported the tyrant. The Eisenhower administration saw fit to award Pérez Jiménez the Legion of Merit. As host to the Tenth Inter-American Conference in Caracas in 1954, Venezuela supported U.S. Secretary of State John Foster Dulles in his call for hemispheric action against the leftist government of Guatemala, which he termed dangerous to the security of the Americas. But Venezuelans from all sectors of society voiced displeasure at their government's ties to the Eisenhower administration by demonstrating against Vice-President Richard Nixon during his visit in 1958. Nixon dismissed the dissidents as "Communists," failing to comprehend that the majority of the protestors were frustrated nationalists who argued that Venezuelans rather than Wall Street should reap the benefits of close relations between the two countries.

Anti–U.S. sentiment was again visible in the protests that marred President John F. Kennedy's visit to Caracas in 1961. To enhance relations between the nations, Secretary of State Dean Rusk broke precedent by granting a 1963 Venezuelan request for extradition from Miami of former strongman Pérez Jiménez. In the same period the Alliance for Progress had begun to operate, unspectacularly. Venezuela was receptive to the Alliance as a means of fostering social justice and as a deterrent to Cuban aggression, but she was generally excluded from receiving loans because of her great dollar earnings in oil. Many Venezuelans regarded the *Alianza* as a farce, especially in respect to carrying out needed land reform. Few benefits were realized for the poor, and in general the Alliance suffered from mismanagement, leading Venezuelan critics to label it an "Alliance for Politics."

Further criticism of Washington's policies appeared in 1965 when the United States landed marines in the Dominican Republic. Although the Caracas government felt some kind of action was necessary, it called the unilateral decision to land troops "gunboat diplomacy." Venezuela requested a foreign ministers conference to discuss the "grave" situation as a possible violation of the OAS Charter. Caracas was officially less critical when the U.S. peace-keeping force in the Dominican Republic was incorporated into a unified OAS command headed by a Brazilian general who was "guided" by his subcommander, a U.S. officer. In general this 1965 incident reinforced the belief of many Venezuelans that unilateral intervention under the Monroe Doctrine was still a vital part of Washington's Latin American policy and that it had not been supplanted by the multilateral approach to hemispheric problems espoused by the Latin American states.

Although such criticisms of U.S. policy arise in Venezuela, the country remains primarily dependent upon Washington for military equipment and technical assistance. For example, between 1958 and 1969, $93.3 million worth of military equipment was sold to Venezuela on credit. The

Caracas government has more credit ($15 million in 1973 alone) than any other Latin American country towards the purchase of arms from Washington. Technical assistance and military training, which began in 1961, was valued at $7.7 million by 1969 and was continuing at the rate of about $1 million per year.[11] In addition, the nation has been receiving hundreds of thousands of dollars a year from private U.S. foundations. Thus, even though some Venezuelans, including some leaders in the Congress and the national bureaucracy, are critical of U.S. policies, their government believes it necessary to maintain friendly relations. To illustrate the point, U.S. involvement in Southeast Asia was unpopular in Venezuela, but Caracas officially remained quiet, even though many Venezuelans frequently criticized the U.S. role as world policeman. In fact, in the spring of 1970, President Caldera ordered a crackdown on youthful members of his Social Christian party who condemned the U.S. intrusion into Cambodia. Venezuela has apparently chosen, perhaps in the best interests of good diplomacy, not to comment upon aspects of U.S. policy repugnant to a number of her citizens.

RECENT RELATIONS WITH THE
THIRD WORLD AND EUROPE

Venezuela maintains relations with all the American nations (with Cuba since December 1974). Treaties with most states for the peaceful resolution of controversies reflect her efforts to build an image as the Caribbean counterpart of Mexico. This objective is emphasized by her leadership in the Conference of Caribbean Foreign Ministers and by her attempts to develop close ties with Puerto Rico. These are moves displeasing to the Andean states, who would prefer to see Venezuela primarily oriented towards them. Caracas enjoys excellent rapport with Mexico, watches Mexican foreign policy closely, and tries to emulate it by conducting her relations with similar tact. She adheres in part to the Estrada Doctrine,[12] stressing the necessity of communications and preferring negotiation to the severing of relations. Venezuela tenders her "good offices" to Latin American nations in need and in times of national disaster has been among the first to aid sister republics.

Although Venezuela is primarily concerned with relations with American and European nations, her policies extend to other regions as well. She exchanges ambassadors with India, Indonesia, and Japan in the

11. U.S., Department of State, *Background Notes: Venezuela*, rev. (Washington, D.C.: Government Printing Office, June 1974).

12. Also known as *la Doctrina Mexicana*. It was enunciated in 1930 by Mexican Foreign Minister Genaro Estrada and refined in 1964. It emphasizes the importance of open channels of communication by stipulating that diplomatic relations with another government do not imply approval or disapproval.

Far East and is represented by a minister in Formosa. Until 1972 she preferred to exclude China from the United Nations on the grounds that China aided aggression in Korea, Vietnam, Laos, and Tibet in violation of the UN Charter. However, when China was admitted to the United Nations, Venezuela voted with the majority, after initially supporting the U.S. plan for dual admission of China and Taiwan. Venezuela, as the founder of OPEC, has good relations with other oil-producing countries and is represented in principal Middle Eastern nations. Relations also exist with the emerging Asian and African states.

In 1974 Venezuala enjoys normal diplomatic relations with most nations of Western Europe, with Poland, the Soviet Union, and Yugoslavia. At times she has had ideological differences with Portugal and Spain, and occasionally her policies have been at variance with those of the Vatican. Thus, for example, in 1961 Pope John XXIII appeared to be meddling in Venezuelan internal affairs when he suggested that Catholics refrain from sending their children to the Caracas Central University because Communist sentiment there had caused students to drop plans to study for the priesthood. However, in 1964 Venezuela and the Vatican signed a convention regulating their relations, supplanting the *modus vivendi* in effect since 1824.

COMMUNISM AND CASTRO'S CUBA

Communism and other Marxist movements have had considerable impact on Venezuelan foreign policy. In official pronouncements Venezuela claims that the dignity of man supersedes politics and that she can flourish by accepting or rejecting select aspects of both socialism and capitalism. She maintains that ideological intervention is as odious as the imposition of military force. At the same time, Venezuelan political parties are the main targets of Communist propaganda—which is oriented primarily towards foreign policy, questions existing alliances, and induces dissidents to foster economic, political, and social change. The basic goals of the nationalistic Venezuelan Communist party (PCV) are (1) close diplomatic relations with the USSR and its bloc nations; (2) elimination of military influence upon the government; (3) broad agrarian reform; (4) curtailment of the U.S. petroleum monopoly; (5) nationalization of basic resources; and (6) the establishment of a coalition council, including Communists, to select political candidates. By the 1960s a struggle had emerged between the Communist factions oriented toward Moscow, Peking, and Havana. Each group appeared less concerned with the success of the struggle in Venezuela than with making certain no other faction gained the upper hand.

This discussion of the ideological struggle leads naturally to the question of Venezuelan-Cuban relations. After the fall of Fulgencio Batista, Venezuela promptly recognized the government of Fidel Castro. It soon became apparent, however, that Cuba desired to export her revolution to all Latin American countries and to Venezuela in particular. The Betancourt regime refused to sell oil to Castro on credit and presented to the OAS evidence of Cuban sabotage in the Maracaibo oil fields. The subsequent ouster of Cuba from the OAS was a Betancourt victory. Venezuela's Communists and *fidelistas*, orignally committed to urban action, found that mass support was not forthcoming and switched to rural guerrilla tactics. During the missile crisis of 1962, Venezuela was the first Latin American nation to mobilize and send warships, planes, and her only submarine to participate in the blockade of Cuba.

In 1963 the OAS investigated charges of Cuban aggression against Venezuela brought by President Betancourt; the next year it condemned the Cuban government for its hostile acts and voted diplomatic and economic sanctions against Havana. Censure by the OAS led Castro to urge more violence in Venezuela. The terrorism had abated considerably by 1966–67, and President Rafael Caldera offered the guerrillas amnesty in 1969, indicating that resumption of relations with Cuba was not impossible. By December 1970 a contingent of dedicated Communists who had opposed the government since the days of Pérez Jiménez left the Communist party of Venezuela and formed the *Movimiento al Socialismo* (MAS) with the intent of pursuing classic Leninism in a more professional way, basing their action on the belief that the guerrilla tactics of the 1960s had not been successful. On the other hand, the PCV, opposed to guerrilla struggles since 1966, claimed it had sustained its guerrilla warfare longer than Castro had and against the greater odds of a Venezuelan government strongly buttressed by the United States. When *Acción Democrática*'s anti-Communist and pro-U.S. Carlos Andrés Pérez was elected to the presidency in 1974, he declared Cuba an "aggressor" nation and stated his opposition to unilateral recognition of the Castro government—a policy that, as noted, he reversed at the end of 1974.

TIES TO INTERNATIONAL ORGANIZATIONS

Attaining prestige through membership in international organizations has been an integral part of Venezuelan foreign policy. The nation has participated fully in all the Pan American Conferences since 1889, except in 1906. It was Venezuela that in 1915 recommended to the Pan American Union the establishment of a federation of neutrals to protect common interests in times of international conflict. After World War I she joined the League of Nations and as a member supported compulsory arbitration and cultural cooperation. She also adhered to the concept of Hispanic-American solidarity within the League, in an attempt to counteract the power of the larger nations through concerted action by the smaller ones. Later, she shared the general loss of faith in the League's ability to curtail international aggression and protect small states. In 1938, after the League had failed to act to halt Japanese expansion in Manchuria and England and France had recognized Italy's conquest of Ethiopia, a discouraged Venezuela withdrew from the organization in 1938.

Disappointment with the League did not reduce Venezuela's desire for hemispheric cooperation. At the 1938 Lima Conference she initiated the inter-American movement for the defense of continental peace. She participated in the Chapultepec Conference of 1945 and actively supported the Inter-American Treaty of Reciprocal Assistance (Rio Treaty) in 1947. Venezuelans point with pride to the fact that many of the ideas of Bolívar's seminal 1826 Panama Congress were subsequently incorporated into the OAS Charter. Venezuela was honored when her outstanding novelist, and former president, Rómulo Gallegos, became chairman of the Inter-American Commission to draw up the OAS document on human rights and by his service as chairman of the OAS Commission on Human Rights. Despite their country's role in the OAS, Venezuelans continued to debate whether or not a subregional organization could be superior to the present OAS, which at times functions more in an aura of idealism than realism. Venezuela showed interest in the subregional alignment by participating in the negotiations leading to the creation of the Andean Subregional Group in 1969 (Agreement of Cartagena), although she did not join it until 1973, when her businessmen were convinced that their industries would be protected. Also, through the years the nation has cooperated with various congresses of the Bolivarian countries that have dealt with common economic, legal, and social problems. However, Venezuela maintains that the OAS should take preference over these subregional organizations and over the United Nations as the primary instrument to resist hemispheric aggression.

Venezuela uses the United Nations as a means of enhancing her primarily economic international role. She stresses the importance of the Latin American bloc in the United Nations and strives to have that body protect the role of the OAS and corroborate its decisions. Venezuela contends that free debate in the United Nations can come only if the principle of juridical equality is accepted; thus, she agitates for the abolition or modification of the veto afforded the great power Security Council members. She favors admission into the organization for all states, regardless of their ideology, and displays a special interest in underdeveloped nations.

When the United Nations is involved in a crisis, Venezuela supports solutions based on international cooperation. She has, for example, supported the maintenance of United Nations peace-keeping forces in the Middle East and Korea. During the Korean "police action" Venezuela did not send a military contingent to the battle zone, but she backed the UN resolution prohibiting the exportation of strategic materials to North Korea and the People's Republic of China. Throughout the Korean conflict the Venezuelan delegation favored the concept of a UN commission to search for solutions to problems involved in the possible reunification of Korea. She has also looked to the United Nations to settle disputes involving American states and nonhemispheric nations, such as the Argentine-British controversy over the Falkland Islands.

In UN councils, Venezuela encourages disarmament talks, the prohibition of nuclear arms in Latin America, the restriction of atomic power to peaceful purposes, and the use of space for scientific rather than military purposes. She prefers that nuclear testing, if it must take place, be carried out under UN supervision. Her delegation inveighs against all forms of discrimination and continuously backs international cultural and economic cooperation.

FOREIGN POLICY FORMULATION

Under Venezuela's constitution the president is responsible for the conduct of foreign affairs. He is empowered to negotiate international treaties, subject to congressional approval prior to ratification, and he is entrusted with national defense. Traditionally, all policy decisions have been made at the presidential level, since bureaucratic initiative has been nonexistent; the minister of foreign relations, unsupported by an effective middle echelon of international relations specialists, has had little to say in determining policy. Under President Caldera, however, more authority in the increasingly complex area of foreign policy formulation was delegated to the Ministry of Foreign Relations, which the Social Christian party (COPEI) government sought to strengthen as the nation's global commitments widened.

The Congress is authorized to designate chiefs of diplomatic missions, conduct ministerial interrogations, consent to treaties, and appropriate funds for Foreign Ministry expenses. But these powers are insufficient to give control over foreign policy. Both the Senate and the Chamber of Deputies have foreign policy committees, but they are poorly staffed, inadequately funded, and relatively powerless. Yet, various governmental branches desire added voice in the formulation of policy, and recently the president has consulted more frequently with them and with representatives of commerce, organized labor, the military, and political parties.

International affairs are eclipsed by domestic issues and, other than in a simple ideological sense, foreign policies appear to concern few individual voters. But groups of businessmen, politicians, students, and workers take an interest in Venezuela's foreign relations and have begun to question the president's ability to handle the diversity of international problems. Through the attitudes and activities of such groups one can see the interaction of domestic and foreign policy. Domestic policies, especially those established by the major political groups in power since 1959 (the Democratic Action Party [AD] and COPEI) have had a great bearing on this increasing interest in foreign policy. Both of these leading parties oppose internal and external totalitarianism of either the Right or the Left. They advocate national democracy and economic and political independence; they also seek Latin American solidarity to achieve these objectives. Both also favor collaboration with the United States. They feel that outside investment should be encouraged but regret that it has usually benefited foreigners more than nationals. They believe that government participation in, and regulation of, agriculture, industry, and land reform is essential to ensure to the nation (at least to some nationals) a fair share of future profits.

Foreigners are permitted to own property and do business in Venezuela, but they are subject to such domestic governmental controls as licensing and taxation. Venezuela's business community, with many links to the United States, avoids obvious pressures or improprieties designed to alter governmental regulation. Nevertheless, it influences the formulation of domestic and foreign policy. The internal business sectors, under the control of nationals, foreigners, or both, are often asked to assist in the negotiation of commercial pacts; but generally they remain subordinate to the president. For example, for seven years Venezuela's businessmen opposed affiliation with the Latin American Free Trade Association (LAFTA); but subsequently they acquiesced in a presidential decision to join it.

Large labor unions are the most influential of the pressure groups. They transmit ideas and opinions through the major political parties. On the other hand, Venezuela's military, maintained to prevent internal disorder rather than to engage in external war, rarely counsels the government on the formulation of foreign policy. Although the armed forces dominated the nation until 1959 and have subsequently possessed great political power, the *Alto Mando Militar* ("joint chiefs of staff") are only consulted—at least overtly—on specific matters relating to the defense of the nation, border disputes, or OAS police actions.[13]

13. On the formulation of Venezuelan policy see Thomas M. Cook, "The Dynamics of Foreign Policy Decision Making in Venezuela" (Ph.D. diss., The American University, 1968).

Venezuela's international conduct is theoretically based on (1) respect for human rights; (2) the right of all peoples to self-determination; (3) nonintervention in the internal affairs of other nations; (4) the juridical equality of states; (5) the inclusion of all classes in the political process; (6) the peaceful settlement of disputes between nations, preferably by arbitration or mediation; (7) the right of all peoples to peace and security; (8) respect for obligations and treaties; (9) the elimination of colonialism; (10) solidarity with democratic governments and on moral opposition to regimes that do not recognize the dignity of man; (11) the defense of independence and national interests; (12) development of agriculture and industry to improve life everywhere; (13) international economic cooperation; and (14) defense of the export price of primary products.

These principles are not always operational and sometimes they deteriorate to the level of mere "lip service," as already noted with reference to the nation's refusal to submit the dispute over the Gulf of Venezuela to arbitration. Another example of deviation is Venezuela's treatment of Cuba during the 1960s and 1970s, including economic ostracism, opposition on moral grounds, and an unwillingness to settle outstanding conflicts by peaceful means. Nevertheless, Venezuela's inability to live up to her principles vis-à-vis Cuba is understandable, given the various degrees of ill-will generated by the ideological differences between the two countries and U.S. pressure to undermine the Castro regime. Also, Venezuela, having reached a mature stage of neocolonialism with regard to the outside world, is simultaneously a practitioner of internal colonialism. Finally, despite liberal rhetoric about "democratic nationalism" as the criterion for decision making, Venezuelan foreign policy is not doctrinaire, but pragmatic and open to change subject to the dictates of national and international bureaucratic, corporate, institutional, political, and social elites under which national integration deteriorates.

In conclusion, it should be noted that Venezuelan diplomats are instructed to remain aloof from international and regional power struggles. Relations are not maintained with governments in exile, although Venezuelan embassies generally accord safe-conducts to political refugees. Until a 1974 reversal of policy, Venezuela also avoided a number of problems or conflicts of interest by neither requesting nor granting large sums of foreign aid.

FINAL OBSERVATIONS

In recent years Venezuela has officially sought to pursue a more independent economic policy in relation to the oil industry. The Hydrocarbons

Reversion Law indicates governmental cognizance of the need to control foreign involvement within the country and to lessen a dependency that in the past has often had too great an effect on foreign policy. Over-reliance upon a petroleum industry dominated by foreign companies, which have drawn inordinate amounts of capital out of Venezuela, has led to legislation designed to keep oil profits at home. But a question of utmost importance concerns whom such laws are designed to benefit. One wonders if foreign entrepreneurs are simply being supplanted in this vital industry by those from national elites. The socialistic party platforms of AD and COPEI have had little influence on the conduct of their foreign policy, which has been carried on under the influence of traditional, sometimes liberal, economic capitalism. Only select elements in the country have benefited, and Venezuelan prosperity has not reached the masses. While the government has recently permitted more right- and left-wing participation in the decision making process affecting the whole of Venezuelan society, this participation has only been to the extent neces-sary to placate some of the groups mentioned above. Increased entrée to government seems also to have enriched some of the leaders of the new groups, simultaneously diminishing their fervor for social change.

While the government moves to nationalize oil, it invites foreign participation in the development of other sectors of the economy, a policy which for the time being reinforces dependency. The Venezuelan scholar José Silva Michelena predicts that Yankee dominance will increase in his nation during the 1970s[14] and that with it will come a growth in anti–U.S. resentment, possibly turning more Venezuelans to the revolutionary Left unless a change occurs in the outmoded attitude of the United States towards Venezuela. But such a turnabout is unlikely, since Washington realizes that the Venezuelan government adheres to the balance-of-power concept of ensuring its own national security through a system of international principles subscribed to by a major world power. Going on the premise that all nations cannot reach accord on ideology and foreign policy, Venezuela has, despite protests to the contrary, aligned herself militarily and ideologically with the United States. Her past and present political stances, as outlined above, are hardly conducive to the achieve-ment of more genuinely independent international and diplomatic pos-tures.

BIBLIOGRAPHICAL NOTE

The primary sources consulted for this chapter are mostly archival materials but some published works are included. Significant are the *Libro Amarillo*, issued

14. José A. Silva Michelena, *The Illusion of Democracy in Dependent Nations*, vol. 3 of *The Politics of Change in Venezuela* (Cambridge, Mass.: M.I.T. Press, 1971), p. 274.

annually by Venezuela's Ministry of Foreign Relations, and the *Boletín del Ministerio de Relaciones Exteriores*; both contain selected diplomatic correspondence, speeches, and treaties. Secondary literature, in English or Spanish, dealing specifically or in part with Venezuelan foreign policy and international diplomacy, is sparse. The *Area Handbook for Venezuela* (Washington, D.C.: Foreign Area Studies, The American University, 1964), contains sections on various aspects of foreign relations. Such doctoral dissertations as Clyde Hewitt's "Venezuela and the Great Powers, 1902-1909: A Study in International Investment and Diplomacy" (University of Chicago, 1948), which focuses on major claims problems, add to the literature in the field. "The Organization for the Conduct of Foreign Relations in Venezuela, 1909-1935" (Ph.D. diss., University of North Carolina, 1951) by Douglas H. Carlisle, analyzes the Gómez era and is reinforced by Embert J. Hendrickson's "The New Venezuelan Controversy: The Relations of The United States and Venezuela, 1904 to 1914" (Ph.D. diss., University of Minnesota, 1963). Exceptionally useful are *La Contribución de Venezuela al Panamericanismo durante el Período, 1939-1943* (Caracas: Central University of Venezuela, 1945) by Eduardo Plaza A., and for foreign policy formulation, "The Dynamics of Foreign Policy Decision Making in Venezuela" (Ph.D. diss., The American University, 1968) by Thomas M. Cooke. *Rio Grande: Misunderstandings in the American Continent* (Caracas: Editorial Sucre, 1965), a bilingual nationalistic work by Rodolfo Luzardo, emphasizes hemispheric relations, the United States, Cuba, and imperialism. Castroism and political ideology are treated in *Six Years of Aggression*, published by the Central Information Office of Venezuela (Caracas, 1963) and in Robert J. Alexander's *The Communist Party of Venezuela* (Stanford, Calif.: Stanford University, Hoover Institution Press, 1969). Invaluable reading for the social scientist is the three-volume series *The Politics of Change in Venezuela*, published at Cambridge by the M.I.T. Press: vol. 1, *A Strategy for Research on Social Policy* (1967), was edited by Frank Bonilla and José A. Silva Michelena; vol. 2, *The Failure of Elites* (1970), was written by Bonilla; vol. 3, *The Illusion of Democracy in Dependent Nations* (1971), by Silva Michelena.

VIII
Conclusion

21/Harold Eugene Davis
and Larman C. Wilson

Some Conclusions

If the purposes of the authors have been fulfilled, the reader will have become aware of the distinctive character of the foreign policies, problems, and positions of the various nations treated in the preceding chapters. These are differences of substance as well as political style. They arise, as we have seen, from geographic factors; from the relations between neighboring countries concerning borders, trade, immigration, and political intervention; from economic factors; and from domestic political forces. The differing comments of the authors on dependence and independence of policy should at least have dispelled any simplistic view of this dependence-independence syndrome.

ARGENTINA

Argentina has a record of policy orientation toward Europe, especially Great Britain, deriving from her export trade to that country and from the historical influence of British capital and British immigrants. Later, this European orientation was maintained by immigration from southern Europe. Argentina has cultivated an aggressive stand opposing the predominance of the United States in Latin America, aiming to make herself a leader of the Spanish-American states. Her assertions of predominance in the Plata region have led her to an inveterate power rivalry with Brazil, including an arms race, but has also produced at times an uneasy, informal alliance with her larger neighbor, most recently in the Latin American Free Trade Association. Argentina's traditional policy of neutrality was maintained against great pressure until the end of World War II. Her Calvo and Drago doctrines have now become the policy of all the American states, at least formally.

BRAZIL

Brazil, by far the largest nation of the area, possessing a cultural and historical background different from the others, has been the nation best able to pursue an independent foreign policy. Originally tied more closely to British policy, she has sought closer relations with the United States in the twentieth century, and she dreams of achieving the status of a world power. In inter-American relations Brazil has often tried to play the role of mediator between the United States and Spanish America. She was expansionist under the monarchy, annexing Uruguay for a time and participating in the War of the Triple Alliance against Paraguay. But since the establishment of the Republic in 1889 she has consistently striven to arbitrate her boundary controversies with neighboring Spanish-American states and the Guianas. Her present-day expansionism takes the form of extending her national highways and railroads across the continent to unite with those of her neighbors. Her traditional links with Portugal, though not of great immediate influence, have helped to direct her attention to the problems of the Portuguese colonies in Africa. Brazil has also tended to incorporate foreign policy positions in her development policy.

CHILE

Chile has also been interested in an independent foreign policy. A power rivalry with Peru, stemming from the War of the Pacific, has resulted in her regular pursuit of balance-of-power politics, including an arms race. During World War I and until 1944 during World War II, she followed a policy of neutrality. In the twentieth century she has had a history of friendly relations with the United States, except under the government of the late Salvador Allende. Another aspect of her efforts to achieve an independent position in her foreign relations has involved the copper industry, her major source of foreign exchange and, until the 1960s, owned by U.S. corporations. The major means employed to rectify the situation was nationalization, the "Chileanization of copper." A gradual process at first, immediate national ownership was effected under Allende, adversely affecting relations with the United States. One other notable feature of Chilean foreign policy is its support of the principles of international law and organization. One of Chile's most famous jurists, Alejandro Alvarez, made a persuasive case for a regional school of American International Law distinct from general international law—a body of international law that grew out of the Pan-American movement. But this interest had earlier roots as well, reaching back to the days of Andrés Bello, a counselor of the ministry and author of the first Latin American textbook on international law. As a result, Chile has been a major supporter of legal principles and an active participant in both the League of Nations and United Nations and in the Organization of American States.

BUFFER STATES

Because of the past and current power rivalries of the South American states, some of the smaller states, such as Uruguay, Paraguay, Bolivia, and

Guyana, have been or have become political buffers (or, perhaps, economic satellites). This buffer status has been an important reality conditioning the foreign policies of these states. Bolivia, for example, has responded to the situation and to one consequence of the War of the Pacific, viz., the loss of her seacoast, by championing the principle, in American International Law and in general international law, that a landlocked state has a right to access to the sea.

CUBA

Until 1934, Cuba acted under the foreign policy restrictions of the Platt Amendment and under the special marketing agreements for Cuban sugar that tied her closely to the policies of the United States. Resentment against these restrictions gave an intense anti-Yankee direction to her domestic politics, coupled with demands for abrogation of the Platt Amendment provisions. After the abrogation of the amendment, her foreign policy, too, assumed an anti–U.S. direction. Following Castro's successful rise to power in 1959, Cuba broke her historical political and economic policy ties with the United States and sought support from the Soviet Union, which provided a market for her sugar and supplied her with capital goods, technology, and armaments. Yet, as we have seen, Cuba has at times asserted a kind of policy independence from Soviet influence, particularly in supporting guerrilla revolutionary movements elsewhere in Latin America. In fact, it appears in the early 1970s that Castro wants to reduce the influence of the Soviet Union over Cuban affairs; he is even interested, perhaps by capitalizing upon détente, in improving economic relations with the United States as a part of normalizing Cuban relations with all the American nations.

PANAMA

Panama has not received the attention it deserves, perhaps because it is linked with Central America. This is surprising, because control of the canal by the United States has made Panama historically the most economically dependent Latin American state and involves what would appear to be one of the most important issues in inter-American relations. Despite the issue of Panama's sovereignty, one wonders why her neighbors, particularly Colombia and Venezuela, which would appear to have a stake in the question, have not been more interested in the issue. Whereas earlier a major goal of the *Aprista* party in Peru had been to end U.S. control of the canal, the idea seems to have been discarded—it was revived momentarily following President Gamal Abdel Nasser's nationalization of the Suez Canal in 1956—and relegated to the level of rhetoric. Interestingly, given her economic dependency, Panama has gained over the years, starting in the 1950s, a limited degree of independence in her bargaining with the United States. By embarassing and pressuring the United States, Panama obtained a number of minor concessions from the Eisenhower and Johnson administrations. Mounting pressure convinced the latter that certain major changes in the treaty relationship were necessary, and the Nixon administration evinced the same conviction. As a result, the executive branch, with strong support from the U.S. Department of State, is involved in trying to work out a new agreement that will permit the original amended treaty to expire at a specified date in the future. The U.S. Congress is opposed to such an outcome as we approach the mid-1970s, but its position may change in time.

MEXICO

Mexico is another Latin American country that stands out for the independence of her foreign policy. Before World War II this attitude was less surprising; Mexico was continuously at odds with the United States and certain other countries during the years from 1910 to 1941. Since the war, she has strengthened her ties with the United States, especially in the economic realm, but at the same time she has maintained her independent stance, even to the point of refusing to join the OAS boycott of Cuba. Mexico's voice has been outstanding in opposition to all types of foreign (outside) intervention in national politics. Her most distinctive position, as a part of her consistent adherence to the principle of nonintervention, is expressed in the Estrada Doctrine, which denies the right of any nation to withhold diplomatic recognition from another nation. Her policy positions are generally stated in a low key, partly to avoid bringing international questions into domestic politics. Policy formulation seems to be tightly controlled within the government.

MILITARY INFLUENCE AND POLICY

We have seen in some nations how the military establishment has exercised a decisive influence in major foreign policy decisions. One example is the intervention of the Argentine military to force President Arturo Frondizi to alter his nation's stand on the "expulsion" of Cuba from the OAS. Another case is the Brazilian military's removal of President João Goulart and its subsequent participation as the principal Latin American collaborator in the Inter-American Peace Force sent into the Dominican Republic. In Peru the military overturned the government of President Fernando Belaunde Terry, partly, at least, to force the nationalization of the privately owned (U.S.) International Petroleum Company.

Serious discussion of international military policy, especially as it relates to hemispheric defense, has received less attention than it deserves by the authors of most of the chapters. Most nations, with the possible exception of Brazil, seem content to rely upon small military establishments with little capacity beyond their borders. Opinion is sharply divided on the creation of a multinational force within the OAS and over the need for revision of the Inter-American Treaty of Reciprocal Assistance, as mentioned below. No nation has embarked on the development of a nuclear capability, and most have ratified the treaty for the denuclearization of the hemisphere. All, except Cuba, rely upon the nuclear umbrella of the United States as a basic policy.

COMMON POLICIES

On the whole, the most striking fact emerging from this brief survey of the foreign policies of the Latin American republics is that they share many policy objectives and that on many major questions their policies have been virtually identical. It is inaccurate to speak of a Latin American bloc; but on a surprisingly large number of issues the Latin American states (excepting Cuba in recent years) have arrived by consultation at similar positions on matters before the United Nations and the OAS.

All are committed by treaty to the prohibition of intervention, especially by force, of one nation in the affairs of another—an example of the international Drago principle, which became the nonintervention cornerstone of the inter-American system. They also follow the Calvo principle, in accordance with which foreign enterprises agree to be treated legally as nationals and to exhaust all the remedies of local courts before appealing to their home governments for protection.

All the Latin American nations subscribe, by treaty, to the arbitration and peaceful settlement of international disputes and have done so in most cases, despite frequent difficulties in agreeing upon the bases for arbitration or mediation. The Spanish-American states have generally settled (or argued over) their boundaries upon the basis of the principle of *uti possidetis* of 1810. Brazil, while espousing a similar principle, has given it a meaning more or less equivalent to the Anglo-American legal principle of adverse possession.

Furthermore, all Latin American nations have followed the practice of granting asylum to political refugees who come to their borders, although individual countries have employed varying criteria for approving diplomatic asylum, especially when dealing with suspected subversives. The Latin American nations generally follow the practice of diplomatic asylum, as we have seen, but differ over the distinction between refugees fleeing prosecution for ordinary crimes and those fleeing danger to their lives on account of political actions. This problem, which occasioned an International Court of Justice opinion in the famous case of Víctor Raúl Haya de la Torre in Peru, arose in Chile on a large scale after the Chilean *golpe* in 1973.

All members of the OAS (except Cuba, which has denounced the Treaty of Reciprocal Assistance, and Barbados and Jamaica, which have not ratified it) are bound to support a policy of hemispheric defense under the provisions of this 1947 inter-American treaty (Rio Pact). This treaty requires consultation in the event of a threat to the peace of the hemisphere, whether arising from within or without the continent. Members of the OAS consult on the strategy for defense, nominally through the Inter-American Defense Board, although retaining complete freedom to join or refrain from any measures involving the employment of force. As we have seen, there have been debates among OAS members about the appropriate treaty to invoke for certain types of inter-American disputes—whether they should be considered under the Rio Pact, the OAS Charter, or the treaties for mediation and conciliation. And in recent years, certain Latin American nations have argued for a new security treaty on the ground that the Rio Pact has become "obsolete." In general, all states oppose foreign military bases, and the U.S. bases in Panama and Cuba, authorized under old treaties, are no exception. There is a lack of agreement upon—in fact, there is strong Latin American opposition to—the establishment and employment of joint inter-American military forces in the hemisphere.

Another common policy, reflecting the traditional interest in international law as reinforced in recent times by the needs of the developing countries, is the claim to a 200-mile offshore limit. First advanced in the early 1950s by a few Latin American states and strongly opposed by the United States and other developed nations since that time as contrary to the traditional territorial sea limit, the 200-mile claim has come to be the Latin American position, with the exception of the Caribbean insular nations. The Inter-American Juridical Committee has studied and been interested, and the United Nations is committed to the preparation of new treaties as a part of international law to resolve this and related problems by the end of 1975. To this end, the Third United Nations Law of the Sea Conference held its first substantive session at Caracas, Venezuela, during the summer of 1974; the final session to draft and approve the treaties will be held at Geneva in 1975. There emerged from the Caracas session the essence of the future agreement between the developed nations and the Latin American (and other developing nations):the establishment of a 12-mile territorial sea limit and the acceptance of a 200-mile economic zone.

Finally, a developing trend from the 1960s that is continuing in the 1970s—probably an early catalyst, for it was the work of the Economic Commission for Latin America—is increasing pragmatism and decreasing ideological concern in matters of foreign policy. Part of the concern with the national interest is in reaction to the United States and also to the pragmatic pressures exerted by the Agency for International Development, the Inter-American Committee for the Alliance for Progress, the Inter-American Development Bank, and the World Bank. The Latin American nations have demonstrated an increasing willingness to bargain with the United States—both in the OAS and the inter-American system—and with the developed countries—in the United Nations, especially in its Conference on Trade and Development. The above generalizations appear to apply to both authoritarian and nonauthoritarian governments in Latin America and are a reflection of mounting foreign policy independence, displayed, for example, in the Tlatelolco conference (1973), attributable in part to the expanding activities in Latin America of the European nations, the Soviet bloc, and certain Asian countries. This fact supports the proposition that the strengthening of the domestic political systems has had the effect of strengthening foreign policy independence and reducing economic dependency.

THE INTER-AMERICAN SYSTEM

Most of the foregoing principles have found expression in the treaty basis of the inter-American system, which is built around the OAS. To a surprising degree, a codification of the basic principles of the public law of the Americas has been incorporated into these treaties. The degree to which the inter-American system, including subregional structures such as the Central American Common Market and the Andean Pact, has been made a reality in the foreign policies of the member states shows that the concept of representation has found a real place in Latin American foreign policy. It is reflected even in the continuing efforts of the Latin American nations to restructure the OAS, which indicates their frustration with certain U.S. policies and their efforts to make the OAS a more effective economic instrument within the inter-American system.

ECONOMIC POLICY

In the realm of economic policy, it has been indicated that there is considerably less agreement on basic policies, despite the common goal of economic development and modernization. On paper the policy picture gives a strong impression of agreement. The Alliance for Progress, LAFTA, CACM, the Andean Group, the Caribbean Free Trade Association, various agreements of the presidents (e.g., that of 1966 for the achievement of a Latin American Common Market by 1985), commodity agreements, and the Consensus of Viña del Mar are encouraging aspirations, but little has been done to implement them in national foreign policies. Some evidence of the gap between commitment and effective policy is provided by the increasing concern over the "economic dependency" of certain Latin American nations whose single-export situation the above agreements were designed to alleviate.

FORMULATION OF FOREIGN POLICY

Most of the foregoing chapters have described to some extent how foreign policy is made in the individual Latin American countries. But this treatment of policy formulation is one of the least satisfactory aspects of our book. It is a defect largely because foreign policy formulation has been a neglected area of research. The literature on the subject is scanty and, with few notable exceptions, poor. Too often, the question tends to be dismissed with one or the other of two easy oversimplifications. Either we are told that the nation has no foreign policy, merely following the dictates of the United States, or we are told that foreign policy is merely what the president says at any given time. It is true, of course, that under the presidential system of government—and most of the nations have this system—the president directs foreign policy in its most basic aspects, leaving secondary matters to the minister for foreign relations and his staff. This is true whether we are speaking of France, Argentina, the United States, Mexico, Costa Rica, or Brazil. But it is also true in every nation that some kind of consultative process goes on. Even under the most authoritarian regime, the president must carry along with him the power structure through which he governs. Nor is the other generalization completely true, even for the weakest of the states—that they merely follow the dictates of the United States. This superficial conclusion often appears to be based on a few dramatic cases, overlooking the many less publicized decisions in which the strong feelings of nationalism impel the adoption of an adversary position. It is to be hoped that the reader will see in this shortcoming of our book an incentive or invitation to conduct research on this aspect of Latin American foreign policy.

FUTURE TRENDS

As this book goes to press, new trends in Latin America portend some basic changes in foreign policies. The lull in the cold war, represented in the détente between the United States and the Soviet Union, and the accompanying political changes not only in Southeast Asia and the Middle East but in many other parts of the world as well are taking the form in Latin America of an expansion of economic and political relations with the Communist nations, and the Third World countries (see Appendix). The nations are now reexamining their relations with Cuba, suggesting with increasing firmness that the time has come to end the sanctions imposed against that nation a decade ago. This was the proposition (defeated) before the Meeting of Consultation of Ministers of Foreign Affairs held at Quito, Ecuador, in November 1974. One also hears increasingly of the acceptance of political pluralism within the OAS, a change that may necessitate an amendment to the Charter.

Disillusionment with the arrangements and policy agreements of the Alliance for Progress has likewise begun to occasion thinking about some fundamental economic policy rearrangements, tying economic policies and agreements more closely to the needs of the export trade of the Latin American nations and to the need for increasing their trade with one another. Already we have seen some rather thoroughgoing inquiries into the need for redefining international economic policy with increasing emphasis upon commodity agreements and nation-to-nation trade arrangements, and we may well expect further activity along this line. One example of such activity was Venezuela's decision in November 1974 to support financially the Latin American coffee producers in the manner of OPEC as a means of maintaining the price level.

Finally, some serious rethinking of the arrangements within the OAS is going on with mounting insistence upon more control by the Latin American nations and less U.S. influence upon decisions within the institutions of the inter-American system. One should not, of course, expect any sudden resolution of the ambivalence that accounts for and dominates the life of the system. Latin America and the United States not only antagonize each other; they are attracted to each other because of a mutual sense of need. This ambivalence may explain the numerous cases in which small Latin American states seemingly depend upon the United States for economic aid and military defense but still take strong stands against the United States on certain foreign policy issues both within and outside the OAS. But even if Latin America—or a part of it, such as Brazil—should, by strengthening its ties, become another great world power—as could well occur—this attraction to the United States would doubtless continue; in such an eventuality, it might even increase.

Appendix
Relations with Communist States

We are in a period of increasing and expanding relations, both diplomatic and economic, between Latin America and the Communist nations, which is attributable to changing Cuban–Latin American relations and the détente between the United States and China and the Soviet Union. Although trade is expanding, Latin American trade with the Communist states is still relatively small (see table A.1). For example, trade with Communist countries constituted only 2 percent of Latin American trade in 1972 ($669 million in Latin American exports and $312 million in Latin American imports). Brazil was in first place with $312 million in exports and $91 million in imports.

It is interesting to note those Latin American states that received both U.S. economic or technical assistance *and* Communist country credits in fiscal 1974: Argentina, Bolivia, Brazil, Chile, Colombia, Guyana, and Peru.

A look at the contemporary experience of three Latin American countries indicates the expanding trend and the impact of changes in governments upon relations with communist countries.

In Argentina, the government of Héctor J. Cámpora established relations with Cuba, Albania, the German Democratic Republic, and North Korea in May and June of 1973. The successor government of Juan Perón recognized North Vietnam, and in 1973 Bulgaria, the People's Republic of China, Cuba, and Romania opened trade offices in Argentina. The same year Bulgaria, Czechoslovakia, Hungary, Poland, Romania, and the Soviet Union opened consulates in Argentina; and Argentina was the first Latin American country to extend a medium-term trade credit to Cuba, which provided for the furnishing of $200 million worth of equipment on an annual basis for a period up to six years.

In Chile, during the tenure of the late Salvador Allende (September 1970–September 1973) there was an increase in diplomatic and economic relations with the Communist countries, starting with Cuba, which included Albania, Bulgaria, East Germany, North Vietnam, Mongolia, and the People's Republic of China. Following President Allende's overthrow and death, the military government immediately broke relations with Cuba, and the Communist nations (except China and Romania) broke or suspended relations en masse.

In Peru, in the five months following the coming to power of Juan Velsco in October 1968, relations were renewed or reestablished with seven Communist states. The basis, however, for expanding ties had been laid over the previous two years by the government of Fernando Belaunde

Latin American Country	Albania	Bulgaria	People's Republic of China	Cuba	Czecho-slovakia	East Ger-many	Hungary	Mon-golia	North Korea	North Viet-nam	Poland	Romania	USSR
Argentina	NRA	E, T, C	E, T	E, T	E, T, C	E	E, T	NRA	E	R	E, T, C	E, T, C	E, T, C
Barbados				NRA									
Bolivia	NRM	NRA			E(NRA)	NRA	E(NRA)				E(NRA)	NRA	E, T
Brazil		E, 2T			E, 2C, 2T	E, 2T	E, 2T				E, 3C	E, 2T	E, 2T
Chile			E, T									E, T	
Colombia		E, T, C			E, T, C	E, T, C	E(NRA), T, C				E(NRA) C, T	E, T, C	E, T, C
Costa Rica	R	T, R			E(NRA), T, C	R	NRA	NRA			NRA	E, T	E, T, C
Ecuador		E(NRA), C			E, T	E	NRA				E(NRA), T, C	E(NRA), T, C	E, C, T
Guyana			E, T	R		R					R	NRA	NRA
Haiti											L		
Honduras											NRA	NRA	
Jamaica			E	E, C									
Mexico			E	E, 3C	E, T	E, T	T, R				E, T	R	E, T
Nicaragua											NRA		
Panama		R			NRA	R					E(NRA), T	R	
Peru	R	E, T	E, T	E	E, T	E, T	E, T		T		E, T	E, T	E, T, C
Trinidad & Tobago				NRA									
Uruguay		E			E, T	E(NRA), T	E(NRA), T				E(NRA), T	NRA	E, T
Venezuela					E, T	T	E				E	E(NRA)	E, T

E   Embassy
L   Legation
R   Relations, but no representatives exchanged

C   Consulate
T   Trade Office

E(NRA)   Nonresident ambassador, resident chargé
NRA   Nonresident ambassador
NRM   Nonresident minister

Source: This chart was drawn from the last edition of an annual research study of the Bureau of Intelligence and Research, *Communist Diplomatic, Consular, and Trade Representation in Latin America* (Washington, D.C.: Department of State, 1973) and has been updated by Larman C. Wilson upon the basis of State Department sources. The term *embassy* generally includes consular and commercial sections and only consulates in other cities are specially listed. Similarly, the term *trade office* generally indicates a commercial representation separate from an embassy (though in most cases in the same city), which in many cases was opened prior to the establishment of the diplomatic mission.

Note: Yugoslavia is not included among the Communist countries because she has many relations with most Latin American nations. The Bahamas, the Dominican Republic, El Salvador, Guatemala, and Paraguay are not included among the Latin American nations because they had no relations in 1973 with any Communist country.

Terry. A fourteen-year-old decree forbidding imports from Communist countries was annulled in 1967, and trade offices were established in Lima by some of these nations during 1968. In mid-1968 Peru announced the opening of consulates in three East European countries and began the upgrading of Communist trade offices in Lima to consulates and then to embassies.

Index

This book was composed in Baskerville text and Lydian display type by Jones Composition Company, Inc., from a design by Patrick Turner. It was printed on 60-lb. Warren 1854 paper and bound in Holliston Roxite cloth by Universal Lithographers, Inc.

Library of Congress Cataloging in Publication Data

Davis, Harold Eugene, 1902-
    Latin American foreign policies.

    Includes bibliographical references and index.
    1. Latin America—Foreign relations. I. Wilson,
Larman Curtis, joint author. II. Title.
F1415.D34   327'.098   74-24386
ISBN 0-8018-1694-7
ISBN 0-8018-1695-5 pbk.